INDEX TO
POETRY
for CHILDREN *and*
YOUNG PEOPLE
1976–1981

VOLUMES IN THIS SERIES

INDEX TO
POETRY
for CHILDREN *and*
YOUNG PEOPLE
1976–1981

A TITLE, SUBJECT, AUTHOR, AND FIRST LINE INDEX

TO POETRY IN COLLECTIONS

FOR CHILDREN AND YOUNG PEOPLE

Compiled by
John E. Brewton
and
G. Meredith Blackburn III
and
Lorraine A. Blackburn

THE H. W. WILSON COMPANY • NEW YORK 1984

International Standard Book Number 0-8242-0681-9

Printed in the United States of America

Library of Congress Cataloging in Publication Data

Brewton, John Edmund, 1898-1982.
    Index to poetry for children and young people,
1976-1981.

    1. Children's poetry—Indexes.   I. Blackburn,
G. Meredith. II. Blackburn, Lorraine A. III. Title.
PN1023.B723 1984   016.821'008'09282   83-10459
ISBN 0-8242-0681-9

CONTENTS

INTRODUCTION

The *Index to Poetry for Children and Young People: 1976–1981* is a dictionary index—with title, subject, author, and first line entries—to 110 collections of poetry for children and young people. Most of the collections were published between 1976 and 1981, inclusive; a few were issued at an earlier date but omitted from earlier editions of the *Index*. In this edition, more than 7,000 poems by approximately 2,000 authors and translators are classified under more than 2,000 subjects.

One of a series, this volume is the second supplement to the *Index to Poetry for Children and Young People: 1964–1969*. The series was initiated in 1942 with the publication of the *Index to Children's Poetry*, compiled by John E. and Sara W. Brewton. Additional volumes are listed on page ii.

Scope. The carefully-selected books of poetry that are indexed here include collections for the very young child (e.g., books such as those classified as "Easy Books" in *Children's Catalog*, Mother Goose rhymes, etc.); collections for the elementary school grades (e.g., the range of collections in class 811 in *Children's Catalog*); and collections suitable for junior and senior high school students (e.g., such collections as are found in class 821.08 in *Junior High School Library Catalog* and in *Senior High School Library Catalog*). In addition to anthologies or collections of poetry by more than one poet, volumes by individual poets (e.g., books by David McCord, Eve Merriam) and selections from the works of a single author (e.g., *Custard and Company; Poems by Ogden Nash*, selected by Quentin Blake and *I Greet the Dawn; Poems by Paul Laurence Dunbar*, selected by Ashley Bryan) are also included. Books partly in prose and partly in verse (e.g., *Bee Tree and Other Stuff*, by Robert Peck) are indexed, as well as collections of poems on a single subject (e.g., *The Poetry of Horses*, compiled by William Cole). The inclusion of comprehensive collections (e.g., *Celebrations; A New Anthology of Black American Poetry*, compiled by Arnold Adoff and *O Frabjous Day; Poetry for Holidays and Special Occasions*, compiled by Myra Cohn Livingston) gives the index a wide range.

Selection of Collections Included. Selection of the 110 collections indexed here is based on a list of titles voted on by consulting librarians and teachers in various parts of the United States. A comprehensive list of anthologies and volumes of poetry by individual authors was sent to the consultants, their advice secured, and the final selections made. A list of consultants follows this Introduction.

Entries. Entries are of four types: title, subject, author, and reference from first line to title. The addition of collection symbols to title, subject, and author entries makes these complete within themselves, thus obviating the necessity for cross references.

1. TITLE ENTRY. The fullest information is given in this entry. Although the symbols designating the books in which the poems are to be found are also given in the author and subject entries, the title entry is the only one which gives the full name of the

author, when known, and the full name of the translator. References to the title entry have been made (a) from variant titles (e.g., **Cure** for a pussy cat. See That little black cat); (b) from titles of selections to the source title (e.g., **Ring** out wild bells. See In memoriam); and (c) from first lines (e.g., "**Newborn,** on the naked sand." See Song for the newborn).

The title entry includes:

(a) Title, followed by first line in parentheses when needed to distinguish between poems with the same title. If a poem is untitled, the first line is treated as the title.

(b) Variant titles, indented under the main title. When the same poem appears in different books with different titles, one title, generally the one most frequently used, has been chosen as the title entry and all variations have been listed under this title.

(c) Full name of author, when known.

(d) Full name of translator.

(e) Symbols for collections in which the poem is found.

In order to bring together selections from a single source, selections are listed under source titles. An example follows:

> **In** memoriam, sels. Alfred Tennyson
> "The time draws near the birth of Christ."—LiPch
> "Unwatch'd, the garden bough shall sway."—PaB

All entries subordinated under source titles are also entered in their alphabetical position and referred to the source entry. Examples follow:

> **Ariel's** dirge. See the tempest
> The **mock** turtle's song. See Alice's adventures
>   in wonderland

A group title (e.g., **A lot** of limericks) under which several poems appear has been treated as a source title. An example follows:

> A **lot** of limericks. X. J. Kennedy
>   A bright idea.—KeP

2. SUBJECT ENTRY. Entries are listed alphabetically by title under various subject headings. For example, under **Animals** are listed the poems about animals in general, while poems about specific animals are grouped under the names of types of animals, as **Horses**. A single poem is often classified under a number of subject headings (e.g., Puppy and I is listed under the subject headings **Conversations, Dogs,** and **Walking**).

Both *See* and *See also* references have been made freely to and from related subjects. These are filed at the beginning of the entries for the subject. Examples follow:

> **Carousels**. See Merry-go-rounds
> **Idleness**. See also Laziness

In order that individual poems or selections from longer poems which have been subordinated to source titles in the title entries may be classified according to subject and may also be readily identified as to sources, they have been entered under subject headings as follows:

> **Walruses**
>   The walrus and the carpenter. From Through
>   the looking glass. L. Carroll.—WiP

Variant titles are treated in the same way in the subject entry as they are in the title and author entries.

The subject entry gives under the subject heading:

(a) Title, followed by first line in parentheses when needed to distinguish between poems with the same title.

(b) Last name and initials of author.

(c) Symbols for collections in which the poem is to be found.

3. AUTHOR ENTRY. All titles are listed alphabetically under the name of the author. Variant titles and titles of selections subordinated under source titles are entered in their proper alphabetical place and referred to the main title or source title.

The author entry gives, under the full name of the author:

(a) Title, followed by first line in parentheses when needed to distinguish between poems with the same title.

(b) Symbols for collections in which the poem is to be found.

(c) Cross references from variant titles to main titles.

(d) Cross references from titles of selections to source titles.

4. FIRST LINE REFERENCES. The first line is always given in quotation marks, even when it is also the title. When the title differs from first line, reference is made from first line to title.

Arrangement. The arrangement is alphabetical. Articles are always retained at the beginning of title and first line, but the articles (except articles in dialect and foreign languages) are disregarded in alphabetizing. Such entries are alphabetized by the word following the article, and this word is printed in **boldface** (e.g., The **cat**, is filed under C). Articles in dialect and foreign articles are filed under the article (e.g., "**D** blues" is filed under D, and **La** belle dame sans merci, under L). Abbreviations are filed as if spelled in full (e.g., **St** is filed as Saint). Contractions are filed as one word (e.g., **I'd** is filed as Id). Hyphenated compounds are filed as separate words (e.g., **Bed-time** precedes **Bedtime**). To facilitate quick use, the entries beginning with **O** and **Oh** have been filed together under O. Likewise, names beginning **Mac** and **Mc** have been filed together as Mac. Punctuation within a title or first line has been disregarded in filing. Where the wording is the same, entries have been arranged in the following order: author, subject, title, first line used as title, first line.

Grades. The books have been graded, and the grades are given in parentheses in the Analysis of Books Indexed and in the Key to Symbols. The grading is only approximate and is given to indicate in general the grades for which each book is suitable. A book that is comprehensive in nature and is suitable for a wide range of grades up to and beyond the twelfth is designated (r), reference.

Uses. The *Index to Poetry for Children and Young People* should serve as a practical reference book for all who desire to locate poems for children and young people by subject, author, title, or first line. It should prove especially useful to librarians, teachers in elementary and secondary schools, teachers and students of literature for children and young people, radio and television artists, parents, young people, and children. The variety of subject classifications should be particularly helpful to anyone preparing programs for special occasions, to teachers planning activities around interests of children and young people, to parents who desire to share poetry, and to anyone searching for poems on a given topic. The Analysis of Books Indexed, which gives in detail the contents of each book, number of poems included, number of authors represented, and number of poems in each group or classification, should prove valuable in the selection of collections for purchase or use. The comprehensiveness of the books indexed insures the usefulness of the *Index* to those interested in poetry from the nursery level through the secondary school and beyond.

Acknowledgments. The compilers thank the consultants who cooperated in checking lists of titles to be included. Grateful recognition is given to John Edmund Brewton, who assisted in the early preparation of this Index and was the originator and compiler, along with Sara Westbrook Brewton, of all five previous editions. Thanks are also due the publishers, who generously supplied copies of the books that are included in the *Index* and Bruce Carrick and Norris Smith of The H. W. Wilson Company for their painstaking work.

GEORGE MEREDITH BLACKBURN III
LORRAINE A. BLACKBURN

CONSULTANTS

Elizabeth Breting
Director, Children's Services
Kansas City Public Library
Kansas City, Missouri

Laurie Dudley
Special Services Librarian
Abilene Public Library
Abilene, Texas

Beth Greggs
First Assistant, Children's Services
King's County Library Department
Seattle, Washington

Amy Kellman
Head, Children's Department
Carnegie Library of Pittsburgh
Pittsburgh, Pennsylvania

Margaret H. Miller
Supervisor, Library Services
Los Angeles Unified School District
Los Angeles, California

Priscilla L. Moulton
Former Director, School Library
   Services
Public Schools
Brookline, Massachusetts

Linda Perkins
Supervising Program Librarian
Young People's Services
Berkeley Public Library
Berkeley, California

Marylett L. Robertson
Librarian, West Hills Elementary School
Knoxville, Tennessee

Marian Schroether
Children's Librarian
Waukegan Public Library
Waukegan, Illinois

Dr. Henrietta M. Smith
Instructor, Children's Literature
College of Education
Florida Atlantic University
Boca Raton, Florida

Della Thomas
Former Director, Curriculum
   Materials Laboratory
Oklahoma State University
Stillwater, Oklahoma

Helen Tyler
Former Media Services Specialist
Eugene School District 4J
Eugene, Oregon

Caroljean Wagner
Central Youth Library
Milwaukee Public Library
Milwaukee, Wisconsin

Jane Walsh
Chairperson, Evaluation Committee
The Newton Public Schools
Newtonville, Massachusetts

ANALYSIS OF BOOKS OF POETRY
INDEXED

Grades are given in parentheses at the end of each entry: (k), kindergarten or preschool grades; (1), first grade; (2), second grade; etc. Comprehensive general collections are designated (r), reference.

Adoff, Arnold, ed. Celebrations; a new anthology of Black American poetry. Follett 1977 (r)

Contents. 240 poems by 85 Black American authors, grouped as follows: The idea of ancestry, 20; Lineage, 21; The Southern road, 16; Where is the Black community, 18; Young soul, 16; True love, 23; Myself when I am real, 30; Make music with your life, 22; For Malcolm who walks in the eyes of our children, 10; A poem for heroes, 28; Shade, 22; For each of you, 15. Also preface by the editor, introduction by Quincy Troupe, and autobiographical notes. Indexed by authors, first lines, and titles.

Adoff, Arnold. Eats poems; illustrated by Susan Russo. Lothrop 1979 (k–3)

Contents. 37 poems ungrouped. Illustrations on each page.

Aiken, Joan. The skin spinners; poems; illustrated by Ken Rinciari. Viking 1976 (5–up)

Contents. 56 poems grouped as follows: Simple things, 14; Mysterious things, 15; Legends, 12; People, 8; Ballads, 7; Table of contents. Indexed by first lines.

Angelou, Maya. Oh pray my wings are gonna fit me well. Random House 1975 (4–up)

Contents. 36 poems grouped as follows: Part one, 4; Part two, 11; Part three, 6; Part four, 3; Part five, 12. Table of contents.

Atwood, Ann. Haiku-vision in poetry and photography. Scribner 1977 (k–up)

Contents. 21 haiku ungrouped. Color photographs by the author illustrate each page. History of haiku and explanatory text accompany the poems.

Barth, Edna, comp. A Christmas feast; poems, sayings, greetings, and wishes; etchings by Ursula Arndt. Houghton 1979 (r)

Contents. 169 poems and 49 sayings grouped as follows: Christmas is coming, 11; Then light ye up your candles, 5; At Christmas time we deck the hall, 9; A thousand bells ring out, 7; Peace on earth, 7; Rise, shepherds, 8; We have seen His star, 9; A child is born, 18; The friendly beasts, 9; I heard a bird sing, 7; The three kings, 6; Flood with light

xiii

earth's darkest places, 14; I'll find me a spruce, 6; Our joyful'st feast, 12; Draw round the fire, 5; Welcome, dear St. Nicholas, Santa Claus, and Father Christmas, 9; Do not open until Christmas, 8; To wish you a merry Christmas, 16; Yule's come and Yule's gone, 3; Superstitions and sayings, 49. Indexed by authors, first lines, and titles. Also introduction.

Bennett, Jill, comp. Roger was a razor fish and other poems; illustrated by Maureen Roffey. Lothrop 1981 [c 1980] (k–3)
    Contents. 22 poems ungrouped. Illustrations on each page

Blake, Quentin, ed. Custard and company; poems by Ogden Nash; illustrated by the editor. Little 1980 (r)
    Contents. 84 poems ungrouped. Also table of contents.

Blegvad, Lenore, comp. Hark, hark, the dogs do bark; and other rhymes about dogs; illustrated by Erik Blegvad. Atheneum 1976 [c 1975] (k–3). A Margaret K. McElderry book.
    Contents. 21 nursery rhymes ungrouped.

Bodecker, N. M. Hurry, hurry, Mary dear! and other nonsense poems; illustrated by the author. Atheneum 1976 (2–5). A Margaret K. McElderry book.
    Contents. 43 poems ungrouped.

Bodecker, N. M. A person from Britain whose head was the shape of a mitten; and other limericks; illustrated by the author. Atheneum 1980 (3–up)
    Contents. 56 limericks ungrouped. Index to titles.

Brewton, John E.; Blackburn, George M.; and Blackburn, Lorraine A., comps. In the witch's kitchen; poems for Halloween; illustrated by Harriett Barton. Crowell 1980 (k–up)
    Contents. 46 poems by 27 authors, ungrouped. Indexed by authors, first lines, and titles.

Brewton, Sara W.; Brewton, John E.; and Blackburn, John Brewton, comps. Of quarks, quasars and other quirks; quizzical poems for the supersonic age; illustrated by Quentin Blake. Crowell 1977 (3–up)
    Contents. 103 poems grouped as follows: Introduction, 1; Blast off, 19; Relax, it's sonic boom, 14; Modern science makes its mark, 18; Where the neuter computer goes click, 9; Bless our modern castle, 18; I'm lost among a maze of cans, 7; Progress takes its toll, I'm told, 17. Indexed by authors, first lines, and titles.

Bryan, Ashley, ed. I greet the dawn, poems of Paul Laurence Dunbar; illustrated by the editor. Atheneum 1978 (6–up)
    Contents. 126 poems grouped as follows: Because you love me, 42; And that is life, 30; Beyond the years, 18; The majesty of God, 18; Give us

comfort, 6; I sing my song, 12. Also introduction by the editor. Indexed
by titles and first lines.

J 208.81 ar

Cole, **William**, comp. An arkful of animals; poems for the very young; illustrated
by Lynn Munsinger. Houghton 1978 (k–7)
Contents. 53 poems by 32 poets, ungrouped. Indexed by authors and
titles.

821 Di

Cole, **William**, comp. Dinosaurs and beasts of yore; illustrated by Susanna Natti.
Collins [distributed by Philomel] 1979 (k–3)
Contents. 39 poems by 22 authors, ungrouped. Table of contents.

J 821 COL

Cole, **William**, comp. Good dog poems; illustrated by Ruth Sanderson. Scribner
1981 (4–up)
Contents. 88 poems by 69 authors, grouped as follows: Puppies, 6;
Doggone funny dogs, 14; Rough dogs, tough dogs, 5; Hounds and hunters,
8; Their dogginess, 15; Dog tales, 10; Mutts, 5; Thoroughbreds, 10; Trib-
utes, 8; Old dogs, 6; Have I got dogs, 1. Indexed by authors, first lines,
and titles. Also introduction by the compiler.

J 811.08 Im

Cole, **William**, comp. I'm mad at you; illustrated by George MacClain. Collins
[distributed by Philomel] 1978 (k–4)
Contents. 49 poems by 32 authors, ungrouped.

Cole, **William**, comp. Poem stew; illustrated by Karen Ann Weinhaus. Lippincott 1981 (3–up)
Contents. 57 poems by 32 authors, ungrouped. Indexed by authors
and titles.

Cole, **William**, comp. The poetry of horses; illustrated by Ruth Sanderson.
Scribner 1979 (r)
Contents. 111 poems by 84 authors, grouped as follows: Foals and colts,
6; Beginners, 7; Horse tales, 11; Riders, 21; Stable, ring and track, 18;
Horse laughs, 13; Workers, wild horses, and war horses, 10; At pasture,
11; Certain special horses, 14. Indexed by authors, first lines, and titles.

De Regniers, **Beatrice Schenk**. A bunch of poems and verses; illustrated by
Mary Jane Dunton. Seabury [distributed by Houghton] 1977 (k–3)
Contents. 33 poems grouped as follows: Winter, spring, fall, and other
weather thoughts, 7; Days, weeks, months, years, 7; Holidays, 15; Night
thoughts, 3; Swell smells, 1. Also table of contents.

J 811.08 Dow

Downie, Mary Alice and Robertson, Barbara, comps. The wind has wings,
poems from Canada; illustrated by Elizabeth Cleaver. Oxford 1978 (5–
up)
Contents. 72 poems by 38 authors, ungrouped. Indexed by authors.

Dugan, Michael, comp. Stuff and nonsense; illustrated by Deborah Niland. Collins [distributed by Philomel] 1977 (k–3)
    Contents. 65 poems by 33 Australian authors, ungrouped. Indexed by authors, first lines, and titles.

Farber, Norma. Small wonders; poems; woodcuts by Kazue Mizumura. Coward 1979 (2–5)
    Contents. 26 poems ungrouped. Table of contents.

Fisher, Aileen. Out in the dark and daylight; illustrated by Gail Owens. Harper 1980 (3–5)
    Contents. 140 poems in seasonal order. Indexed by titles.

Fleming, Alice, comp. America is not all traffic lights; poems of the Midwest; illustrated with photographs. Little 1976 (5–up)
    Contents. 32 poems by 26 authors, ungrouped. Also notes about the authors.

Fox, Siv Cedering. The blue horse and other night poems; illustrated by Donald Carrick. Seabury [distributed by Houghton] 1979 (k–3)
    Contents. 14 poems ungrouped.

Gardner, John. A child's bestiary; with additional poems by Lucy Gardner and Eugene Rudzewicz; illustrated by Lucy, Joel, Joan, and John Gardner. Knopf 1977 (4–up)
    Contents. 68 poems arranged alphabetically by animal. Also short essay on the hog-nosed snake.

Giovanni, Nikki. Vacation time; poems for children; illustrated by Marisabina Russo. Morrow 1980 (3–5)
    Contents. 22 poems ungrouped.

Greenfield, Eloise. Honey, I love; and other love poems; illustrated by Diane and Leo Dillon. Crowell 1978 (2–4)
    Contents. 17 poems ungrouped.

Grimes, Nikki. Something on my mind; illustrated by Tom Feelings. Dial 1978 (3–5)
    Contents. 19 untitled poems.

Hearn, Michael Patrick, comp. Breakfast, books, and dreams; a day in verse; illustrated by Barbara Garrison. Warne 1981 (k–8)
    Contents. 20 poems ungrouped. Illustrations on each page.

Hill, Helen; Perkins, Agnes; and Helbig, Alethea, eds. Dusk to dawn; poems of night; illustrated by Anne Burgess. Crowell 1981 (5–up)
    Contents. 35 poems by 25 authors, ungrouped. Indexed by authors, first lines, and titles. Also table of contents.

Hill, Helen; Perkins, Agnes; and Helbig, Alethea, eds. Straight on till morning; poems of the imaginary world; illustrated by Ted Lewin. Crowell 1977 (4–up)

> *Contents.* 90 poems grouped as follows: In our own world, 11; Fetch me far and far away, 14; Funny and fabulous friends, 11; Out of this world, 12; Mysteries, 11; What's there in the dark, 9; Words overheard, 14; Once there was and was not, 8. Indexed by authors, first lines, and titles. Also biographies of poets, preface by the editors, and table of contents.

Hoberman, Mary Ann. Bugs; poems; illustrated by Victoria Chess. Viking 1976 (3–5)

> *Contents.* 31 poems ungrouped.

Hoberman, Mary Ann. Yellow butter purple jelly red jam black bread; illustrated by Chaya Burstein. Viking 1981 (k–5)

> *Contents.* 58 poems ungrouped. Indexed by first lines.

Holman, Felice. At the top of my voice and other poems; illustrated by Edward Gorey. Scribner 1970 (k–3)

> *Contents.* 28 poems ungrouped with illlustrations on each page. Also table of contents.

Hopkins, Lee Bennett, comp. By myself; illustrated by Glo Coalson. Crowell 1980 (k–5)

> *Contents.* 16 poems by 13 authors, ungrouped. Also table of contents.

Hopkins, Lee Bennett, comp. Moments; poems about the seasons; illustrated by Michael Hague. Harcourt 1980 (4–up)

> *Contents.* 50 poems by 35 authors, grouped as follows: Autumn, 13; Winter, 11; Spring, 14; Summer, 12. Indexed by authors, first lines, and titles. Also table of contents.

Hughes, Ted. Moon whales and other moon poems; illustrated by Leonard Baskin. Viking 1976 (5–up)

> *Contents.* 54 poems ungrouped. Indexed by first lines.

Hughes, Ted. Season songs; illustrated by Leonard Baskin. Viking 1975 (7–12)

> *Contents.* 24 poems grouped as follows: Spring, 6; Summer, 6; Autumn, 6; Winter, 6. Indexed by titles.

Janeczko, Paul B., comp. Postcard poems; a collection of poetry for sharing. Bradbury 1979 (5–up)

> *Contents.* 104 poems by 72 authors, ungrouped. Indexed by authors. Also introduction by compiler.

Kennedy, X. J. The phantom ice cream man; more nonsense verse; illustrated by David McPhail. Atheneum 1979 (3–6)

> *Contents.* 49 poems grouped as follows: Unheard of birds and couldn't

be beasts, 11; Nonsensical notions, 14; Magical menaces, 8; My far out
family, 11; Cheerful spirits, 5. Also table of contents.

Kherdian, David. Country cat, city cat; woodcuts by Nonny Hogrogian. Four
Winds 1978 (k–up)
    Contents. 21 poems ungrouped. Illustrations on each page.

Kherdian, David, ed. I sing the song of myself; an anthology of autobiographical
poems. Greenwillow 1978 (7–up)
    Contents. 58 poems by 57 authors, ungrouped. Indexed by authors,
first lines, and titles. Also preface by the editor and biographical notes
on the authors.

Kuskin, Karla. Dogs & dragons, trees & dreams; a collection of poems; illustrated by the author. Harper 1980 (2–5)
    Contents. 56 poems ungrouped with explanatory notes. Indexed by
titles.

Kuskin, Karla. Roar and more; illustrated by the author. Harper 1978 [c 1956]
(k–3)
    Contents. 11 poems ungrouped.

Lee, Dennis. Garbage delight; illustrated by Frank Newfeld. Houghton [c 1977]
1978 (3–6)
    Contents. 42 poems ungrouped. Illustrations on each page.

Lee, Dennis. Nicholas Knock and other people; illustrated by Frank Newfeld.
Houghton 1977 (3–7)
    Contents. 30 poems ungrouped. Illustrations on each page.

Livingston, Myra Cohn, comp. Callooh, callay, holiday poems for young readers;
illustrated by Janet Stevens. Atheneum 1978 (3–up). A Margaret K.
McElderry book.
    Contents. 83 poems by 41 authors, grouped as follows: New year's day,
6; St. Valentine's day, 8; Birthdays, 8; Lincoln's birthday, 3; Washington's
birthday, 2; Easter, 6; April fool's day, May day, the fair and the circus,
6; Mother's day, 4; Father's day, 4; The fourth of July, 9; Columbus day,
3; Halloween, 8; Thanksgiving, 4; Christmas, 12. Indexed by authors,
first lines, and titles. Also indexed by translators.

Livingston, Myra Cohn. 4–Way stop and other poems; illustrated by James J.
Spanfeller. Atheneum 1976 (5–up). A Margaret K. McElderry book.
    Contents. 38 poems ungrouped.

Livingston, Myra Cohn. A lollygag of limericks; illustrated by Joseph Low.
Atheneum 1978 (5–up)
    Contents. 32 limericks ungrouped.

Livingston, Myra Cohn, comp. O frabjous day; poetry for holidays and special occasions; jacket illustration by Anita Siegel. Atheneum 1977 (5–up). A Margaret K. McElderry book.

    Contents. 129 poems by 81 authors grouped as follows: I. To celebrate: The new year, 12; Birth, birthdays and christenings, 13; Valentine's day, 11; Allhallow's eve and Halloween, 6. II. To honor: Lincoln's birthday, 8; Washington's birthday, 8; Memorial, Veterans and Armistice day, 10; Fourth of July, 6; Columbus day, 6; Assassinations, 9. III. To remember: Easter, 11; Thanksgiving, 9; Christmas, 11; Other religious holidays, 9. Indexed by authors, first lines, titles, and translators with notes on some of the poems. Also table of contents.

Livingston, Myra Cohn, ed. Poems of Christmas. Atheneum 1980 (5–up)

    Contents. 105 poems by 68 authors, grouped as follows: Long, long ago, 27; A fair and marvelous thing, 14; None of this has changed, 15; What sweeter music can we bring, 15; In the week when Christmas comes, 11; Let Christmas celebrate greenly, 23. Indexed by authors, first lines, titles, and translators. Also table of contents.

Livingston, Myra Cohn. The way things are and other poems; illustrated by Jenni Oliver. Atheneum 1974 (5–up). A Margaret K. McElderry book.

    Contents. 38 poems ungrouped.

Lobel, Arnold, comp. Gregory Griggs and other nursery rhyme people; illustrated by the editor. Greenwillow 1978 (k–3)

    Contents. 34 nursery rhymes ungrouped. Also an afterword.

Lueders, Edward and St. John, Primus, comps. Zero makes me hungry; a collection of poems for today; art and design by John Reuter Pacyna. Lothrop 1976 (5–up)

    Contents. 114 poems grouped as follows: Progress, 11; For poets, 10; Days, 9; The artist, 9; What my uncle Tony told my sister, Angie, and me, 11; Love song for a jellyfish, 13; Through the window, 12; Worms and the wind, 15; Explanations of love, 12; Yei-ie's child, 12. Also an author and title index and a pronunciation glossary.

Maestro, Betsy. Fat polka dot cat and other haiku; illustrated by Giulio Maestro. Dutton 1976 (k–3)

    Contents. 15 haiku ungrouped. Illustrations on each page.

Mayer, Mercer, comp. A poison tree and other poems; illustrated by the editor. Scribner 1977 (5–up)

    Contents. 20 poems by 20 authors, ungrouped.

McCord, David. One at a time; his collected poems for the young; illustrated by Henry B. Kane. Little 1974 (k–5)

    Contents. 255 poems ungrouped. Indexed by subjects and first lines. Also table of contents.

McCord, David. Speak up; more rhymes of the never was and always is; illustrated by Marc Simont. Little 1980 (3–6)
Contents. 38 poems ungrouped. Also table of contents.

Merriam, Eve. The birthday cow; illustrated by Guy Michel. Knopf 1978 (k–3)
Contents. 15 poems ungrouped. Also table of contents.

Merriam, Eve. Rainbow writing. Atheneum 1976 (4–up)
Contents. 39 poems ungrouped. Also table of contents.

Merriam, Eve. A word or two with you; new rhymes for young readers; illustrated by John Nez. Atheneum 1981 (3–up)
Contents. 17 poems ungrouped. Also table of contents.

Mizmura, Kazue. Flower moon snow; a book of haiku; illustrated with woodcuts by the author. Crowell 1977 (2–6)
Contents. 30 haiku grouped as follows: Flower, 10; Moon, 10; Snow, 10. Also note about haiku.

Momaday, N. Scott. The gourd dancer; illustrated by the author. Harper 1976 (5–up)
Contents. 43 poems grouped as follows: Angle of geese, 20; The gourd dancer, 11; Anywhere is a street into the night, 12. Also table of contents.

Moore, Lilian, ed. Go with the poem. McGraw Hill 1979 (4–up)
Contents. 90 poems grouped as follows: I'm the driver and the wheel, 7; The tiger has swallowed a black sun, 10; What shall I do with the seed, 12; When a friend calls to me, 8; The secret knows, 10; The city, we call it home, 11; Put it together, the world's like that too, 7; Invisible messages, 8; A rhyme for w, 9; Our mother the earth, our father the sky, 8. Also indexed by authors and titles.

Moore, Lilian. Think of shadows; illustrated by Deborah Robinson. Atheneum 1980 (2–5)
Contents. 17 poems ungrouped. Also table of contents.

Morrison, Lillian. Overheard in a bubble chamber and other sciencepoems; illustrated by Eyre de Lanux. Lothrop 1981 (5–up)
Contents. 38 poems grouped as follows: Natural histories, 9; Mathematical measures, 7; Physical properties, 7; Heavenly bodies, 7; In search of verities, 8. Also glossary.

Morrison, Lillian. The sidewalk racer and other poems of sports and motion; illustrated with photographs. Lothrop 1977 (5–up)
Contents. 38 poems ungrouped. Also table of contents.

Morrison, Lillian. Who would marry a mineral; riddles, runes, and love tunes; illustrated by Rita Flodén Leydon. Lothrop 1978 (5–up)
Contents. 54 poems ungrouped. Also table of contents.

Moss, Elaine, comp. From morn to midnight; illustrated by Satomi Ichikawa. Crowell 1977 (k–5)
  Contents. 20 poems ungrouped. Illustrations on each page.

Moss, Howard. Tigers and other lilies; illustrated by Frederick Henry Belli. Atheneum 1977 (4–7)
  Contents. 28 poems ungrouped. Also table of contents.

Norris, Leslie. Merlin and the snake's egg; illustrated by Ted Lewin. Viking 1978 (3–up)
  Contents. 27 poems grouped as follows: Walking, 4; Woodspells, 6; Some dogs, 3; From darkness underground, 3; An oddity of ogres, 2; Christmas animals, 5; Good night, 3; Merlin and the snake's egg, 1. Indexed by first lines. Also table of contents.

Oliver, Robert, S. Cornucopia; illustrated by Frederick Henry Belli. Atheneum 1978 (3–6)
  Contents. 26 poems ungrouped. Also table of contents.

Orgel, Doris. Merry merry Fibruary; illustrated by Arnold Lobel. Parents 1977 (k–3)
  Contents. 29 poems ungrouped.

Pagliaro, Penny, ed. I like poems and poems like me; illustrated by Wendy Kim Chee. Press Pacifica 1977 (k–3)
  Contents. 72 poems grouped as follows: Poems and I have things to do, 20; I go to the beach with poems, 11; It's shopping day for poems and me, 19; Poems and I spend the day at home, 22. Indexed by authors and titles. Also table of contents.

Parker, Elinor, ed. Echoes of the sea; illustrated by Jean Vallario. Scribner 1977 (r)
  Contents. 110 poems by 78 authors, grouped as follows: The great deep, 17; Fish and other creatures, 11; Sea serpents, 6; Birds of the ocean and shore, 16; Shells, 13; Seaweed, anemones, and coral, 17; Sunken cities, 6; Mermaids and mermen, 9; Neptune and his court, 6; Swimmers, 9. Indexed by authors, first lines, and titles. Also contains a preface by the editor.

Parsons, Ian, ed. Bird, beast, and flower; illustrated by Marie Angel. Godine 1980 (5–up)
  Contents. 48 poems by 35 authors, ungrouped. Also table of contents.

Peck, Robert Newton. Bee tree and other stuff; illustrated by Laura Lydecker. Walker 1975 (5–up)
  Contents. 42 poems grouped as follows: School, 3; Chores, 3; Hay, 5; Winter, 5; Death, 8; Hard work, 5; Sun dance, 7; Critters, 5; Final stone, 1. Also table of contents.

Plotz, Helen, ed. The gift outright; America to her poets. Greenwillow 1977 (r)
> *Contents.* 120 poems by 88 authors grouped as follows: You, Genoese mariner, 6; Buffalo dusk, 18; The westwardness of everything, 20; I have fallen in love with American names, 25; The stepping stones to thee today and here, America, 32; Idea of America, 18. Indexed by authors, first lines, and titles. Also a preface by the editor.

Plotz, Helen, ed. Life hungers to abound; poems of the family. Greenwillow 1978 (r)
> *Contents.* 124 poems by 89 authors grouped as follows: Marriage, 30; Parent to child, 26; Brothers and sisters, 13; Ancestors and descendants, 27; Child to parent, 28. Indexed by authors, first lines, and titles. Also an introduction by the editor.

Pomerantz, Charlotte. The tamarindo puppy and other poems; illustrated by Byron Barton. Greenwillow 1980 (k–3)
> *Contents.* 13 poems ungrouped. Poems intermingle English and Spanish words in the same verses. Illustrations on each page. Also table of contents.

Prelutsky, Jack. The headless horseman rides tonight; more poems to trouble your sleep; illustrated by Arnold Lobel. Greenwillow 1980 (2–6)
> *Contents.* 12 poems ungrouped.

Prelutsky, Jack. It's Halloween; illustrated by Marylin Hafner. Greenwillow 1977 (k–3)
> *Contents.* 13 poems ungrouped.

Prelutsky, Jack. Nightmares; poems to trouble your sleep; illustrated by Arnold Lobel. Greenwillow 1976 (2–6)
> *Contents.* 12 poems ungrouped.

Prelutsky, Jack. The Queen of Eene; poems; illustrated by Victoria Chess. Greenwillow 1978 (k–up)
> *Contents.* 14 poems ungrouped. Also a table of contents.

Prelutsky, Jack. Rainy rainy Saturday; illustrated by Marylin Hafner. Greenwillow 1980 (k–3)
> *Contents.* 14 poems ungrouped. Also table of contents.

Prelutsky, Jack. Rolling Harvey down the hill; illustrated by Victoria Chess. Greenwillow 1980 (k–3)
> *Contents.* 15 poems ungrouped. Also table of contents.

Prelutsky, Jack. The snopp on the sidewalk and other poems; illustrated by Byron Barton. Greenwillow 1977 (k–5)
> *Contents.* 12 poems ungrouped.

Russo, Susan, ed. The moon's the north wind's cooky; illustrated by the editor. Lothrop 1979 (k–3)
    Contents. 14 poems by 13 authors, ungrouped. Also table of contents.

Saunders, Dennis, ed. Magic lights and streets of shining jet; photographs by Terry Williams. Greenwillow 1978 (4–up)
    Contents. 60 poems by 48 authors, grouped as follows: Creatures small, 15; Weathers and seasons, 15; Colours, 15; Sea and shore, 15. Indexed by authors and first lines. Color photographs on each page.

Silverstein, Shel. A light in the attic; illustrated by the author. Harper 1981 (3–up)
    Contents. 136 poems ungrouped. Indexed by titles.

Smith, William Jay. Laughing time; nonsense poems; illustrated by Fernando Krahn. Delacorte 1980 (k–3)
    Contents. 91 poems grouped as follows: The king of hearts, 1; Laughing time, 33; Puptents and pebbles, a nonsense abc, 1; Boy blue's beasts, 38; The ole man from Okefenokee, loony and lopsided limericks, 11; The floor and the ceiling, 6; The King of Spain, 1. Also table of contents.

Starbird, Kaye. The covered bridge house and other poems; illustrated by Jim Arnosky. Four Winds 1979 (3–8)
    Contents. 35 poems ungrouped.

Thurman, Judith. Flashlight and other poems; illustrated by Regina Rubel. Atheneum 1976 (2–5)
    Contents. 25 poems ungrouped.

Tripp, Wallace, comp. Granfa' Grig had a pig and other rhymes without reason from Mother Goose; illustrated by the editor. Little 1976 (k–3)
    Contents. 121 nursery rhymes ungrouped. Indexed by first lines. Illustrations on each page.

Wallace, Daisy, ed. Fairy poems; illustrated by Trina Schart Hyman. Holiday House 1980 (k–5)
    Contents. 17 poems by 15 authors, ungrouped. Also table of contents.

Wallace, Daisy, ed. Ghost poems; illustrated by Tomie de Paola. Holiday House 1979 (k–5)
    Contents. 17 poems by 13 authors, ungrouped. Also table of contents.

Wallace, Daisy, ed. Giant poems; illustrated by Margot Tomes. Holiday House 1978 (k–5)
    Contents. 17 poems by 14 authors, ungrouped. Also table of contents.

Wallace, Daisy, ed. Monster poems; illustrated by Kay Chorao. Holiday House 1976 (k–5)
    Contents. 17 poems by 12 authors, ungrouped. Also table of contents.

Wallace, Daisy, ed. Witch poems; illustrated by Trina Schart Hyman. Holiday House 1976 (k–5)

Contents. 17 poems by 15 authors, ungrouped. Also table of contents.

J
821.08
Wi

Watson, Nancy Dingman. Blueberries lavender; songs of the farmer's children; illustrated by Erik Blegvad. Addison-Wesley 1977 (3–5)

Contents. 28 poems ungrouped.

Willard, Nancy. A visit to William Blake's inn; poems for innocent and experienced travelers; illustrated by Alice and Martin Provensen. Harcourt 1981 (2–5)

Contents. 17 poems ungrouped. Also introduction by the author, table of contents, and quotation from Blake. 16 poems illustrated.

J
811
Wil

Wilner, Isabel, ed. The poetry troupe; an anthology of poems to read aloud; decorations by the editor. Scribner 1977 (r)

Contents. 225 poems by 72 authors, grouped as follows: Conversations, 64; Characterizations, 24; Observations, 36; Narrations, 24; Repetitions, variations, 20; Lingual gyrations, 15; Charms, chants, incantations, 10; Songs, dirges, lamentations, 10; Admonitions, exhortations, 12; Exclamations, 10. Indexed by authors, first lines, and titles. Also table of contents and an explanation by the editor.

J
808.81
Poe

Worth, Valerie. More small poems; illustrated by Natalie Babbitt. Farrar 1976 (k–5)

Contents. 25 poems ungrouped. Also table of contents.

Worth, Valerie. Still more small poems; illustrated by Natalie Babbitt. Farrar 1978 (k–5)

Contents. 25 poems ungrouped. Also table of contents.

Yaroslava [Yaroslava Surmach Mills], comp. I like you and other poems for Valentine's day; illustrated by the editor. Scribner 1976 (3–up)

Contents. 28 poems by 27 authors ungrouped. Also table of contents. Illustrations on each page.

J
808.81
I 1

Yolen, Jane. Dragon night and other lullabies; illustrated by Demi. Methuen 1981 (k–3)

Contents. 16 lullabies ungrouped.

Yolen, Jane. How beastly; a menagerie of nonsense poems; illustrated by James Marshall. Collins [distributed by Philomel] 1980 (k–6)

Contents. 22 poems ungrouped. Also table of contents.

KEY TO SYMBOLS FOR BOOKS INDEXED

Grades are given in parentheses at the end of each entry: (k), kindergarten or preschool grade; (1), first grade; (2), second grade, etc. Comprehensive general collections are designated (r), reference.

Space is left under each symbol so that the library call number may be inserted.

HeB   Hearne, M. P. Breakfast, books and dreams. Warne 1981 (k–8)

HiD   Hill, H.; Perkins, A.; and Helbig, A. eds. Dusk to dawn. Crowell 1981 (5–up)

HiS   Hill, H.; Perkins, A.; and Helbig, A. eds. Straight on till morning. Crowell 1977 (4–up)

HoA   Holman, F. At the top of my voice. Scribner 1970 (k–3)

HoBm   Hopkins, L. B. comp. By myself. Crowell 1980 (k–5)

HoBu   Hoberman, M. A. Bugs. Viking 1976 (3–5)

HoMp   Hopkins, L. B. comp. Moments. Harcourt 1980 (4–up)

HoY   Hoberman, M. A. Yellow butter purple jelly red jam black bread. Viking 1981 (k–5)

HuM   Hughes, T. Moon whales. Viking 1976 (5–up)

HuSs   Hughes, T. Season songs. Viking 1975 (7–12)

JaPp   Janeczko, P. B. comp. Postcard poems. Bradbury 1979 (5–up)

KeP   Kennedy, X. J. The phantom ice cream man. Atheneum 1979 (3–6)

KhC   Kherdian, D. Country cat, city cat. Four Winds 1978 (k–up)

KhI   Kherdian, D. ed. I sing the song of myself. Greenwillow 1978 (7–up)

KuD   Kuskin, K. Dogs & dragons, trees & dreams. Harper 1980 (2–5)

KuR   Kuskin, K. Roar and more. Harper 1978 [c 1956] (k–3)

LeG   Lee, D. Garbage delight. Houghton 1978 [c1977] (3–6)

LeN   Lee, D. Nicholas Knock. Houghton 1977 (3–7)

LiCc   Livingston, M. C. comp. Callooh, callay, Atheneum 1978 (3–up)

LiF   Livingston, M. C. 4–Way stop. Atheneum 1976 (5–up)

LiLl   Livingston, M. C. A lollygag of limericks. Atheneum 1978 (5–up)

LiO   Livingston. M. C. O frabjous day. Atheneum 1977 (5–up)

LiPh   Livingston, M. C. Poems of Christmas. Atheneum 1980 (5–up)

LiWt   Livingston, M. C. The way things are. Atheneum 1974 (5–up)

LoG   Lobel, A. comp. Gregory Griggs and other nursery rhyme people. Greenwillow 1978 (k–3)

LuZ   Lueders, E. and St. John, P. comps. Zero makes me hungry. Lothrop 1976 (5–up)

MaFp   Maestro, B. Fat polka dot cat. Dutton 1976 (k–3)

MaP   Mayer, M. comp. A poison tree. Scribner 1977 (5–up)

McO   McCord, D. One at a time. Little 1974 (k–5)

McSu   McCord, D. Speak up. Little 1980 (3–6)

MeB   Merriam, E. The birthday cow. Knopf 1978 (k–3)

MeR   Merriam, E. Rainbow writing. Atheneum 1976 (4–up)

MeW   Merriam, E. A word or two with you. Atheneum 1981 (3–up)

MiF   Mizumura, K. Flower moon snow. Crowell 1977 (2–6)

MoF   Moss, E. comp. From morn to midnight. Crowell 1977 (k–5)

MoGd   Momaday, N. S. The gourd dancer. Harper 1976 (5–up)

MoGp   Moore, L. ed. Go with the poem. McGraw Hill 1979 (4–up)

MoO   Morrison, L. Overheard in a bubble chamber. Lothrop 1981 (5–up)

MoSr   Morrison, L. The sidewalk racer. Lothrop 1977 (5–up)

MoTo   Moss, H. Tigers and other lilies. Atheneum 1977 (4–7)

MoTs   Moore, L. Think of shadows. Atheneum 1980 (2–5)

MoW   Morrison, L. Who would marry a mineral. Lothrop 1978 (5–up)

NoM   Norris, L. Merlin and the snake's egg. Viking 1977 (3–up)

OlC   Oliver, R. S. Cornucopia. Atheneum 1978 (3–6)

OrM Orgel, D. Merry merry Fibruary. Parents 1977 (k–3)

PaB Parsons, I. ed. Bird, beast, and flower. Godine 1980 (5–up)

PaE Parker, E. ed. Echoes of the sea. Scribner 1977 (r)

PaI Pagliaro, P. ed. I like poems and poems like me. Press Pacifica 1977 (k–3)

PeB Peck, R. N. Bee tree and other stuff. Walker 1975 (5–up)

PlG Plotz, H. ed. The gift outright. Greenwillow 1977 (r)

PlL Plotz, H. ed. Life hungers to abound. Greenwillow 1978 (r)

PoT Pomerantz, C. The tamarindo puppy. Greenwillow 1980 (k–3)

PrH Prelutsky, J. The headless horseman rides tonight. Greenwillow 1980 (2–6)

PrI Prelutsky, J. It's Halloween. Greenwillow 1977 (k–3)

PrN Prelutsky, J. Nightmares. Greenwillow 1976 (2–6)

PrQ Prelutsky, J. The Queen of Eene. Greenwillow 1978 (k–up)

PrR Prelutsky, J. Rainy rainy Saturday. Greenwillow 1980 (k–3)

PrRh Prelutsky, J. Rolling Harvey down the hill. Greenwillow 1980 (K–3)

PrS Prelutsky, J. The Snopp on the sidewalk. Greenwillow 1977 (k–5)

ReB De Regniers, B. S. A bunch of poems and verses. Seabury [Houghton] 1977 (k–3)

RuM Russo, S. ed. The moon's the north wind's cooky. Lothrop 1979 (k–3)

SaM Saunders, D. ed. Magic lights and streets of shining jet. Greenwillow (4–up)

SiL Silverstein, S. A light in the attic. Harper 1981 (3–up)

SmL Smith, W. J. Laughing time. Delacorte 1980 (k–3)

StC Starbird, K. The covered bridge house. Four Winds 1979 (3–8)

ThFo Thurman, J. Flashlight. Atheneum 1976 (2–5)

TrGg Tripp, W. comp. Granfa' Grig had a pig. Little 1976 (k–3)

WaB Watson, N. D. Blueberries lavender. Addison-Wesley 1977 (3–5)

WaFp Wallace, D. ed. Fairy poems. Holiday House 1980 (k–5)

WaG Wallace, D. ed. Giant poems. Holiday House 1978 (k–5)

WaGp Wallace, D. ed. Ghost poems. Holiday House 1979 (k–5)

WaM Wallace, D. ed. Monster poems. Holiday House 1976 (k–5)

WaW Wallace, D. ed. Witch poems. Holiday House 1976 (k–5)

WiP Wilner, I. ed. The poetry troupe. Scribner 1977 (r)

WiV Willard, N. A visit to William Blake's inn. Harcourt 1981 (2–5)

WoM Worth, V. More small poems. Farrar 1976 (k–5)

WoSm Worth, V. Still more small poems. Farrar 1978 (k–5)

YaI Yaroslava [Y. S. Mills] comp. I like you. Scribner 1976 (3–up)

YoD Yolen, J. Dragon night. Methuen 1981 (k–3)

YoH Yolen, J. How beastly. Collins [Philomel] 1980 (k–6)

KEY TO ABBREVIATIONS

ad. adapted
at. attributed
bk. book
comp. compiler, compiled
comps. compilers
ed. edition, editor
eds. editors
il. illustrated, illustrator
ils. illustrators
jt. auth. joint author
jt. auths. joint authors
k kindergarten or preschool grade

pseud. pseudonym
pseuds. pseudonyms
r reference
rev. revised
rev. ed. revised edition
sel. selection
sels. selections
tr. translator
tr. fr. translated from
trs. translators
wr. at. wrongly attributed

DIRECTIONS FOR USE

The Title Entry is the main entry and gives the fullest information, including title (with first line in parentheses when needed to distinguish between poems with the same title); variant titles; full name of author; translator; and symbols for collections in which the poem is to be found. Variant titles and titles with variant first lines are also listed in their alphabetical order, with *See* references to the main title. If a poem is untitled, the first line is treated as the title.

> The **three** kings ("I am Gaspar, I have brought frankincense") Rubén Dario, tr. by Lysander Kemp.—BaC—LiPch
> **Three** kings ("Three kings came out of Indian land") Unknown.—BaC

> **"For** wandering walks." See Joe's snow clothes
> **Joe's** snow clothes. Karla Kuskin.—Kud
> "For wandering walks."—WiP
> **"Just** when winter spreads out." Arnold Adoff.—AdE

Titles of poems are grouped according to subject, in alphabetical order under a subject heading. Each Subject Entry gives the title of poem; last name of author with initials; first line where needed for identification; source title for subordinate selections; and the symbols for the collections in which the poem is to be found.

> **Night**
> The night ("The night creeps in") M. C. Livingston.—RuM
> "Peddling from door to door." From Four glimpses of night. F. M. Davis.—RuM

The Author Entry gives the full name of the author; title of poem with its variants (first line in parentheses when needed for identification); and the symbols for the collections in which the poem is to be found. Included under the author entry are references from variant titles and from titles of selections to the source title.

> **Carroll, Lewis, pseud. (Charles Lutwidge Dodgson)**
> Alice's adventures in wonderland, sels.
>   Beautiful soup.—WiP
>   "You are old, Father William."—WiP
> Beautiful soup. See Alice's adventures in wonderland
> "You are old Father William." See Alice's adventures in wonderland

First Lines of poems, enclosed in quotation marks, are listed in their alphabetical order with references to the title entry where all the information may be found. First lines are enclosed in quotation marks even when used as titles.

"**And** now all nature seemed in love." See On a bank
as I sat fishing
"**Coins**, coins, coins." See Spendthrift
"**Lilies** are white." Unknown—PaB

When the source of a poem is more familiar than the title of the poem, or when only selections from a longer work are given, such titles are grouped under the source title. All titles subordinated to source titles also appear in their alphabetical order with references to the source title.

"**Again** at Christmas did we weave." See In memo-
riam
In memoriam, sels. Alfred Tennyson
"Again at Christmas did we weave."—LiPch
"The time draws near the birth of Christ."—LiPcH
"Unwatch'd, the garden bough shall sway."—PaB
"The **time** draws near the birth of Christ." See In
memoriam
"**Unwatch'd**, the garden bough shall sway." See In
memoriam

INDEX TO POETRY FOR CHILDREN AND YOUNG PEOPLE

Adam and Eve—*Continued*
Cain and Abel. From Genesis.—PlL
The python. J. Gardner.—GaCb
Adams, Franklin Pierce
Lines to three boys, 8, 6 1/2, and 2 years of age.—PlL
The **adaptable** mountain dugong. Ted Hughes.—HuM
Adaptation of a theme by Catullus. Allen Tate.—PlL
"**Add** one letter to widow." See More or less
Addict. Jack Montgomery.—BrO
Address to the refugees. John Malcolm Brinnin.—PlG
Address to the scholars of New England. John Crowe Ransom.—PlG
Adelaide. Jack Prelutsky.—PrQ
"**Adelaide** was quite dismayed." See Adelaide
Adoff, Arnold
"After covering the continent."—AdE
The apple.—AdE
At the end of summer.—AdE
"The baker wanted me to know."—AdE
Burger.—AdE
Chocolate chocolate.—AdE
The coach said.—AdE
Corn.—AdE
Cut out.—AdE
Deep into winter.—AdE
Dinner thought.—AdE
"Getting the sweet strawberries."—AdE
Good for the head.—AdE
Grandma Ida's cookie dough for apple pie crust.—AdE
"Hard soft."—AdE
I am learning.—AdE
I love to eat.—AdE
"Just when winter spreads out."—AdE
Love song.—AdE
Measuring and mixing.—AdE
"Momma cooks with a wok."—AdE
"My mouth stays shut."—AdE
The new pants.—AdE
"Not me but cows walk up and beg to."—AdE
"Only the onions."—AdE
Peanut butter batter bread.—AdE
Recipe for eats poems.—AdE
Sun flowers.—AdE
Sunday morning toast.—AdE
"Sunny side up."—AdE
Take one apple.—AdE
There is a place.—AdE
Turn the oven on.—AdE
"Under this autumn sky."—AdE
"**Adown** the west a golden glow." See At sunset time
Adventure and adventurers. See also Camping and hiking; Explorers and exploration; Frontier and pioneer life; Heroes and heroines; Seafaring life; Space and space travel
The adventures of Isabel. O. Nash.—BlC

Blake leads a walk on the Milky Way. N. Willard.—WiV
Custard the dragon and the wicked witch. O. Nash.—BlC
Epilogue. N. Willard.—WiV
Momotara. Unknown, tr. by R. Fyleman.—WaG—WiP
The purist. O. Nash.—WiP
The **adventure** of Chris. David McCord.—McO
An **adventure** story. Furnley Maurice.—DuSn
Adventures of a frisbee. Shel Silverstein.—SiL
The **adventures** of Isabel. Ogden Nash.—BlC
The **adventures** of Tom Bombadil, sel. J.R.R. Tolkien
Oliphaunt.—CoA
Advertising
Clarence. S. Silverstein.—SiL
Summer song, after a surfeit of irresistible ads. W. W. Watt.—BrO
Tube time. E. Merriam.—MeW
Advice
Advice ("If you're sleepy in the jungle") M. A. Hoberman.—HoY
Beware, do not read this poem. I. Reed.—AdC
For poets. A. Young.—AdC
Mother to son. L. Hughes.—HiS
Advice ("If you're sleepy in the jungle") Mary Ann Hoberman.—HoY
Advice from a visiting poet. Eve Merriam.—MeR
Aelourophile. Eve Merriam.—MeR
Aelourophobe. Eve Merriam.—MeR
Affection
Puppy. F. Lape.—CoG
"An **affectionate** fellow in Cheddar." Myra Cohn Livingston.—LiLl
Afreet. David McCord.—McO
"**Afreet** I am afraid of." See Afreet
Africa
Africa ("Home") L. Clifton.—AdC
Africa ("Thus she had lain") M. Angelou.—AnO
"Driving through New England." L. Clifton.—PlG
For us, who dare not dare. M. Angelou.—AnO
"We're an Africanpeople." From African poems. H. R. Madhubuti.—AdC
Africa ("Home") Lucille Clifton.—AdC
Africa ("Thus she had lain") Maya Angelou.—AnO
African poems, sel. Haki R. Madhubuti
"We're an Africanpeople."—AdC
The **African** wild dog. John Gardner.—GaCb
"**Africanus** meant." See Abundance
"**After** a bad night's sleeping." See Moon walkers
After a bath. Aileen Fisher.—PaI
After a freezing rain. Aileen Fisher.—FiO
After a rain. Aileen Fisher.—FiO
After all. Lillian Morrison.—MoW

"After bringing forth eighteen." See For a shetland pony brood mare who died in her barren year

After Christmas ("A friend sent me some seeds") Myra Cohn Livingston.—LiWt

After Christmas ("There were lots on the farm") David McCord.—McO

"After covering the continent." Arnold Adoff.—AdE

"After Eli Whitney's gin." See Southeast Arkanasia

After ever happily. Ian Serraillier.—HiS

"After good night." Siv Cedering Fox.—FoB

"After I ate my dinner then I ate." See Confession of a glutton

"After its lid." See Pumpkin

"After many long months on the market." See Sold

"After my bath." See After a bath

"After such years of dissension and strife." See Natural tears

After supper. Hugh McNamar.—LuZ

"After supper I would trail." See After supper

"After that tight." See Barefoot

"After the brown harvest of rains, express lights." See December river

"After the gusty, dusty wind." See The quiet shining sun

After the killing. Dudley Randall.—AdC

"After the laboring birth, the clean stripped hull." See My father's death

"After the murder." See The last quatrain of the ballad of Emmett Till

After the rain ("John's words were the words") Stanley Crouch.—AdC

After the rain ("Your smile") Paul B. Janeczko.—JaPp

After the storm. See Resolution and independence

Afternoon
　Abracadabra. D. Livesay.—DoWh
　Rest hour. G. Johnston.—DoWh
　Winter dark. L. Moore.—HoMp

Afternoon, Amagansett beach. John Hall Wheelock.—PaE

"Again and again." Kazue Mizumura.—MiF

"Again at Christmas did we weave." See In memoriam

"Against these turbid turquoise skies." See The balloons

Age. See also Birthdays; Old age; Youth; Youth and age
　Being five. D. Lee.—LeG
　"The newt." R. S. Oliver.—OlC
　Turning 30 poem. J. Brandi.—KhI

"The age." See A different image

"Age will come suddenly." See Burning the steaks in the rain, reflections on a 46th birthday

Agee, James
　Lyric.—PlG

Agnew, Edith
　Los pastores.—LiPch
　Progress.—LuZ

"Ah-choo." See Flamingos.—OlC

"Ah, Douglass, we have fall'n on evil days." See Douglass

"Ah, look." See The divers

"Ah, love, my love is like a cry in the night." See A love song

"Ah, not this marble, dead and cold." See Washington's monument, February 1885

Ah, sunflower. William Blake.—PaB

"Ah, sunflower, weary of time." See Ah, sunflower

"Ah, William, we're weary of weather." See Two sunflowers move into the yellow room

Aiken, Conrad
　Atlantis.—PaE
　Changing mind, sel.
　　"My father which art in earth."—PlL
　Frog.—CoA
　"My father which art in earth." See Changing mind
　The owl.—CoA

Aiken, Joan
　Air on an escalator.—AiS
　Algebra.—AiS
　Apollo and Daphne.—AiS
　As good as a feast.—AiS
　Bad dream.—AiS
　The ballad of Newington Green.—AiS
　The bog people.—AiS
　"The boy with a wolf's foot."—AiS
　Bridge.—AiS
　Cat.—AiS
　Change of wind.—AiS
　Charter flight.—AiS
　Cherrystones.—AiS
　Dangerous journey.—AiS
　Do it yourself.—AiS
　Down below.—AiS
　The driver.—AiS
　Eskimo legend.—AiS
　Fable.—AiS
　The fisherman writes a letter to the mermaid.—AiS
　Footprints.—AiS
　Fruit thought.—AiS
　Grandfather.—AiS
　Guide to London.—AiS
　Hand over.—AiS
　He'd just come from the churchyard.—AiS
　House on Cape Cod.—AiS
　I have.—AiS
　If.—AiS
　In the old house.—AiS
　John's song.—AiS—HiD
　"Look out for the platform."—AiS
　Man and owl.—AiS
　The man who stopped the birds.—AiS
　Mice.—AiS
　Motorway reflection.—AiS
　My brother's dream.—AiS
　"My father remembers."—AiS
　Nate's song.—AiS
　New York sewers.—AiS
　Night landscape.—AiS—HiD—RuM

"All has stilled, magician sleep having cast his spell." See Those last, late hours of Christmas eve

"All men are locked in their cells." See Fall down

"All mixed up in blue sky." See Sky skimmers

"All my life, I guess, I've loved the clouds." See The clouds

All nature seems at work. Samuel Taylor Coleridge.—PaB

"All nature seems at work, slugs leave their lair." See All nature seems at work

"All night I wore the phone, a dead scarf." See Hello, hello

"All night the tall young man." See Merlin & the snake's egg

"All over the fields there was ice today." See Suddenly

"All over the world." See Polyglot

"All peacefully gliding." See The rapid

"All people agree." See Xylophagous insects

All Saint's Day
  To a violet found on All Saint's Day. P. L. Dunbar.—BrI

"All that is gold does not glitter." J.R.R. Tolkien.—WiP

"All that is left." See The little trumpet

All that sky. Aileen Fisher.—FiO

"All the Fibruary babies." Doris Orgel.—OrM

All the little animals. Muriel Rukeyser.—PlL

"All the smoke." Eli Siegel.—MoGp

"All the things, the objects." See Cold term

"All through the long night." Kazue Mizumura.—MiF

"All winter in the tree buds." See Leaf buds

"All winter the cottage." See Out of season

"All winter your brute shoulders strained against collars." See Names of horses

"All you that to feasting and mirth are inclined." See Old Christmas returned

"All you violated ones with gentle hearts." See For Malcolm X

Allen, L. H.
  The reaper.—SaM

Allen, Marie Louise
  Sneezing.—PaI

Allen, Samuel (Paul Vesey)
  Nat Turner.—AdC

Alley cat. David McCord.—McO

The alligate. Jane Yolen.—YoH

The alligator ("The alligator chased his tail") Mary MacDonald.—DuSn

The alligator ("When the alligator opens his jaws") John Gardner.—GaCb

"The alligator chased his tail." See The alligator

"Alligator, hedgehog, anteater, bear." See The animal song

Alligator on the escalator. Eve Merriam.—HiS—WiP

Alligator pie. Dennis Lee.—WiP

"Alligator pie, alligator pie." See Alligator pie

Alligators
  The alligator ("The alligator chased his tail") M. MacDonald.—DuSn
  The alligator ("When the alligator opens his jaws") J. Gardner.—GaCb
  Alligator on the escalator. E. Merriam.—HiS—WiP
  Alligator pie. D. Lee.—WiP
  New York sewers. J. Aiken.—AiS
  The purist. O. Nash.—WiP

Allin, Michael
  Zoo.—LuZ

Allingham, William
  The elf singing.—PaI
  The fairies.—WaFp
  A memory.—PaB

"Allosaurus, stegosaurus." See The dinosaurs' dinner

Almost ("Peterboo and Prescott") Harry Behn.—WiP

Almost ("The woodpecker") David Kherdian.—KhC

Almost ninety. Ruth Whitman.—JaPp

Almost perfect. Shel Silverstein.—SiL

"Almost perfect, but not quite." See Almost perfect

Almost spring. Judith Thurman.—ThFo

Alone ("Lying, thinking") Maya Angelou.—AnO

"Along about then, the middle of May." See Elm seed blizzard

"Along the line of smoky hills." See Indian summer

"Along the sea-edge, like a gnome." See The sandpiper

"Along train tracks, with yawning jaws." See The locomotive sloth

Alphabet
  A is for alpaca. W. J. Smith.—SmL
  Alphabet eta z. D. McCord.—McO
  B is for bats. W. J. Smith.—SmL
  C is for cabbages. W. J. Smith.—SmL
  "The consonants laid low." L. Morrison.—MoW
  D is for dog. W. J. Smith.—SmL
  E is for egg. W. J. Smith.—SmL
  F is for frogboy. W. J. Smith.—SmL
  F's and g's dancing. L. Morrison.—MoW
  G is for goat. W. J. Smith.—SmL
  H is for hat. W. J. Smith.—SmL
  I is for inkspot. W. J. Smith.—SmL
  Importnt. S. Silverstein.—SiL
  J is for jack-in-the-box. W. J. Smith.—SmL
  J's. R. S. Oliver.—OlC
  K is for king. W. J. Smith.—SmL
  L is for laundry. W. J. Smith.—SmL
  The likes and looks of letters. D. McCord.—McO
  M is for mask. W. J. Smith.—SmL
  Merry Christmas. Unknown.—BaC
  More or less. D. McCord.—McO
  N is for needle. W. J. Smith.—SmL
  New notebook. J. Thurman.—ThFo
  O is for owl. W. J. Smith.—SmL
  The ocean of vowels. L. Morrison.—MoW

Alphabet—*Continued*

P is for pirate. W. J. Smith.—SmL

Q is for queen. W. J. Smith.—SmL

R is for reindeer. W. J. Smith.—SmL

S is for springs. W. J. Smith.—SmL

T is for tub. W. J. Smith.—SmL

Those double z's. D. McCord.—McSu

U is for up. W. J. Smith.—SmL

V is for volcano. W. J. Smith.—SmL

W. J. Reeves.—MoGp

W is for well. W. J. Smith.—SmL

X and Y. D. McCord.—McO

X is for x. W. J. Smith.—SmL

Y is for yarn. W. J. Smith.—SmL

Z. D. McCord.—McO

Z is for zebu. W. J. Smith.—SmL

Alphabet eta z. David McCord.—McO

Altaha, Marylita

"Have you ever hurt about baskets."—LuZ

"Altho' the lion seems to wink." See The lion

"Although affirmative goals I sought." See Un-negative

"Although I know." See Shadows

"Although I saw you." See I like you

"Although it's hard to understand." See The zebu

"Although I've been to Kankakee." See Schenectady

"Although my father's only child." See Cecilia

"Although the snow still lingers." See Last snow

"Always be kind to animals." John Gardner.—GaCb

"Always read a poem twice." See Advice from a visiting poet

Always sprinkle pepper. Shel Silverstein.—SiL

"Always sprinkle pepper in your hair." See Always sprinkle pepper

"Always there's some boy." See Coda

"Am I a stone and not a sheep." See Good Friday

Amanda is shod. Maxine Kumin.—CoPh

The **ambiguous** dog. Arthur Guiterman.—CoG

Ambition

The ambition bird. A. Sexton.—KhI

The **ambition** bird. Anne Sexton.—KhI

"**Amelia** mixed the mustard." Alfred Edward Housman.—WiP

America. See also names of countries, as United States

America ("Centre of equal daughters, equal sons") W. Whitman.—PlG

America ("The gold of her promise") M. Angelou.—AnO

America the beautiful. K. L. Bates.—PlG

American names. S. V. Benet.—PlG

American plan. J. M. Brinnin.—PlG

Benjamin Franklin Hazard. E. L. Masters.—PlG

Buffalo dusk. C. Sandburg.—PlG

The end of the Indian poems. S. Plumly.—PlG

Fare thee well. E. Siegel.—PlG

"From Paumanok starting I fly like a bird." W. Whitman.—PlG

I am waiting. L. Ferlinghetti.—PlG

I hear America griping. M. Bishop.—BrO

"I read your testimony and I thought." From To Alexander Meiklejohn. J. Beecher.—PlG

Independence day ("Between painting a roof yesterday and the hay") W. Berry.—LiO

Indian names. L. H. Sigourney.—PlG

It is mine, this country wide. Unknown.—PlG

Like ghosts of eagles. R. Francis.—PlG

"A long time it seems today." From A New Year letter. W. H. Auden.—PlG

"Long, too long America." W. Whitman.—PlG

Love in America. M. Moore.—PlG

Lyric ("From now on kill America out of your mind") J. Agee.—PlG

Meredith Phyfe. E. L. Masters.—PlG

Midwest town. R. De Long Peterson.—FlA

Minority report. J. Updike.—PlG

Monticello. M. Sarton.—PlG

"My country need not change her gown." E. Dickinson.—PlG

N. Y. to L. A. by jet plane. S. Dorman.—PlG

"Next to of course God America I." E. E. Cummings.—LiO

Night journey. T. Roethke.—PlG

"Now it's Uncle Sam sitting on top of the world." From Good morning America. C. Sandburg.—LiO

"Oh, dearer by far than the land of our birth." R. H. Wilde.—PlG

Ode ("God save the rights of man") P. Freneau.—PlG

Of being numerous #24. G. Oppen.—PlG

On being brought from Africa to America. P. Wheatley.—PlG

"On the lawn at the villa." L. Simpson.—PlG

Refugee in America. L. Hughes.—PlG

Shine, republic. R. Jeffers.—PlG

Take time out. M. Angelou.—AnO

Yonder. R. Eberhart.—PlG

America—Discovery and exploration. See also the names of explorers, as Columbus

And of Columbus. H. Gregory.—LiO

Arrival, New York harbor. R. Peters.—PlG

The California oaks. Y. Winters.—PlG

"Chains, my good lord, in your raised brows I read." From Columbus. A. Tennyson.—LiO

Columbus ("Once upon a time there was an Italian") O. Nash.—LiO

Columbus ("Steer on, courageous sailor, through mockery and jeering") F. von Schiller.—LiO

The discovery. J. C. Squire.—LiO

"From his wanderings far to eastward." From The song of Hiawatha. H. W. Longfellow.—PlG

"How busie are the sonnes of men." R. Williams.—PlG

Immigration ("No ship of all that under sail or steam") R. Frost.—PlG

May 1506, Christopher Columbus speaking. W. T. Scott.—PlG

The Mediterranean.—A. Tate.—PlG

To the western world. L. Simpson.—PlG

The trail beside the River Platte. W. Heyen.—PlG

Upon the first sight of New England, June 29, 1638. T. Tillam.—PlG

"With hearts revived in conceit, new land and trees they eye." From Good news from New England. E. Johnson.—PlG

"You, Genoese mariner." W. S. Merwin.—PlG

America—Settlement

Daniel Boone ("When Daniel Boone goes by, at night") S. V. Benet.—PlG

The gift outright. R. Frost.—PlG

Jamestown ("Let me look at what I was, before I die") R. Jarrell.—PlG

The men of Sudbury. C. Baker.—PlG

A New England sampler. J. M. Brinnin.—PlG

Our country. H. D. Thoreau.—PlG

The prophecy of King Tammany. P. Freneau.—PlG

Stanzas on the emigration to America, and peopling the western country. P. Freneau.—PlG

The trail into Kansas. W. S. Merwin.—PlG

America ("Centre of equal daughters, equal sons") Walt Whitman.—PlG

America ("The gold of her promise") Maya Angelou.—AnO

America the beautiful. Katherine Lee Bates.—PlG

"America will never forgive you." See H. Rap Brown

American Indians. See Indians of the Americas

American names. Stephen Vincent Benet.—PlG

American plan. John Malcolm Brinnin.—PlG

American revolution. See United States—History—Revolution

Amey, David

My uncle Jack.—PaI

The aminals. Dennis Lee.—LeG

Ammons, A. R.

Belief for JFK.—PlG

Father.—PlL

Mirrorment.—JaPp

Needs.—LuZ

Nelly Myers.—KhI

Poem.—MoGp

Sitting down, looking up.—JaPp

An amoeba named Sam. Unknown.—BrO

"An amoeba named Sam and his brother." See An amoeba named Sam

Amoebas

An amoeba named Sam. Unknown.—BrO

"Among the hills of St. Jerome." See At St. Jerome

Among the millet. Archibald Lampman.—DoWh

"Among these mountains, do you know." See For Allan

Analysis of baseball. May Swenson.—HoMp

Anatomy. See Body, Human; also names of parts of the body, as Hands

Ancestors ("The child enquires about his ancestors") Roy Fuller.—PlL

Ancestors ("On the wind-beaten plains") Grey Cohoe.—LuZ

Ancestors ("Why are our ancestors") Dudley Randall.—AdC

Ancestry. See also Heritage

Ancestors ("The child enquires about his ancestors") R. Fuller.—PlL

Ancestors ("On the wind-beaten plains") G. Cohoe.—LuZ

Ancestors ("Why are our ancestors") D. Randall.—AdC

"Children's children are the crown of old men." From Proverbs, Bible, Old Testament.—PlL

Generations. J. D. Simmons.—AdC

How I got ovah. C. M. Rodgers.—AdC

The idea of ancestry. E. Knight.—AdC

Lineage. M. Walker.—LuZ

"My dad he was a yankee." N. M. Bodecker.—BoHh

"My father's forebears were all Midland yeomen." From Letter to Lord Byron, sel. W. H. Auden.—PlL

Old Salt Kossabone. W. Whitman.—PlL

On buying a dog. E. Klauber.—CoG

"Plowdens, Fins." From Beginnings. R. Hayden.—AdC

Sire ("Here comes the shadow not looking where it is going") W. S. Merwin.—PlL

To a race horse at Ascot. J. M. Palen.—CoPh

Anchored. Shel Silverstein.—SiL

"&." See Postcards

"And Adam knew Eve his wife, and she conceived." See Genesis—Cain and Abel

And all the angels. Unknown.—BaC

"And all the angels in heaven shall sing." See And all the angels

"And David sat between the two gates, and the." See The second book of David and Absalom

"And God said, let the waters generate." See Paradise lost

"And God said, let us make man in our image." From Genesis.—PlL

"And he said, a certain man had two sons." See Gospel according to Luke—The parable of the prodigal son

"And I love to eat a lot." See I love to eat

"And I say nothing—no, not a word." See My sister Jane

"And I took the night train to the country where nothing lasts." See Dreaming

"And I'm thinking how to get out." See History

"And in a far country." See Every man heart lay down

"And in the cold bleak, winter time." See Moonlight

"And Joseph also went up from Galilee, out of the city." See Gospel according to Luke—The nativity

Anger

Anger ("I was angry and mad") Y. Lowe.—CoI

Crab ("The dead crab") V. Worth.—WoM

"I'm so mad I could scream." W. Cole.—CoI

A poison tree. W. Blake.—MaP

Anger ("I was angry and mad") Yvonne Lowe.—CoI

Angle of geese. N. Scott Momaday.—MoGd

Animal crackers. See From the kitchen—Animal crackers

"**Animal** crackers, I ate them years." See From the kitchen—Animal crackers

The **animal** song. Unknown.—CoA

The **animal** store. Rachel Field.—PaI

Animals. See also Circus; Fables; names of classes of the animal kingdom, as Birds; names of animals, as Elephants

Abundance. M. Moore.—PaB

"All animals like me." R. Souster.—DoWh

All the little animals. M. Rukeyser.—PlL

The animal song. Unknown.—CoA

Awake. D. McCord.—McSu

Bedtime. F. Holman.—HoA

The big tent under the roof. O. Nash.—BlC

Blake tells the tiger the tale of the tailor. N. Willard.—WiV

Buteo regalis. N. S. Momaday.—MoGd

Christmas eve legend. F. Frost.—BaC

Christmas in the country. A. Fisher.—FiO

A Christmas prayer. G. MacDonald.—LiPch

Civilization ("I've stood here lately, looking at the path") M. C. Livingston.—LiF

"The cow has a cud." From Five chants. D. McCord.—McO

Crocodile. W. J. Smith.—SmL

Daybreak. D. McCord.—McO

Elephant. W. J. Smith.—SmL

The end. J. Gardner.—GaCb

The fall. M. Spark.—LuZ

Familiar friends. J. S. Tippett.—CoA

Feet. R. N. Peck.—PeB

The forest greeting. P. L. Dunbar.—BrI

The friendly beasts. Unknown.—BaC—LiPch

The gibbon. E. W. Rudzewicz.—GaCb

The guppy ("Whales have calves") O. Nash.—BlC—MoGp

"Hey diddle, diddle." Mother Goose.—BlH

Hymn to joy. J. Cunningham.—LiPch

In the middle. D. McCord.—McO

In the snow or sun. A. Fisher.—FiO

Laughing time. W. J. Smith.—SmL

Lone dog. I. R. McLeod.—CoG

Lost ("I have a little turtle") D. McCord.—McO

"The lynx." J. Gardner.—GaCb

The marmalade man makes a dance to mend us. N. Willard.—WiV

Midnight in Bonnie's stall. S. J. Johnson.—LiPch

"The mite." E. W. Rudzewicz.—GaCb

Noah's ark ("The mice squeak") S. Silverstein.—CoA

Notice ("I have a dog") D. McCord.—McO

Old Noah's ark. Unknown.—CoA

The oxen ("Christmas Eve, and twelve of the clock") T. Hardy.—LiPch

Pad and pencil. D. McCord.—McO

Probability and birds. R. Atkins.—AdC

"Quack, said the billy goat." C. Causley.—BeR—CoA

Queer story of the fowse or fox. D. McCord.—McO

The small. T. Roethke.—HiS

Speak up. D. McCord.—McSu

The stable. G. Mistral.—BaC

The stable cat. L. Norris.—LiPch

Tails. M.C. Livingston.—CoA

That's not. D. McCord.—McO

"There's a fire in the forest." W.W.E. Ross.—DoWh

"They've put a brassiere on the camel." S. Silverstein.—SiL

A thought. M. A. Hoberman.—HoY

Up the hill. W. J. Smith.—SmL

The wapiti. O. Nash.—BlC

The warm and the cold. T. Hughes.—HuSs

When Christmas comes. A. Fisher.—BaC

Who is sad. E. Coatsworth.—WiP

Wild child's lament. J. Yolen.—YoD

The witnesses. X. J. Kennedy.—LiPch

"The wolf also shall dwell with the lamb." From Isaiah.—BaC

The wombat. O. Nash.—BlC

Wood's litany. E. Coatsworth.—BaC

Animals—Care

Albert. D. Abse.—MaP

"Always be kind to animals." J. Gardner.—GaCb

Birdfoot's grampa. J. Bruchac.—MoGp

Buying a puppy. L. Norris.—NoM

Cat bath. V. Worth.—WoSm

"A fairy went a-marketing." R. Fyleman.—PaI

Four little foxes. L. Sarett.—WiP

Horses graze. G. Brooks.—AdC

"Hurt no living thing." C. Rossetti.—SaM—WiP

"I had a little pony." Mother Goose.—WiP

The bad rider.—CoPh

Jack and his pony, Tom. H. Belloc.—CoPh

Kindness to animals. L.E. Richards.—CoA

Lions ("Bars, wire") V. Worth.—WoM

"Mrs. Malone." E. Farjeon.—WiP

The mole. R. Daniells.—DoWh

More to it than riding. J. A. Lindon.—CoPh

The needing. R. N. Peck.—PeB

Pourquoi. Unknown.—CoG

"Who's that ringing at the front door bell." Mother Goose.—WiP

Zoo manners. E. Mathias.—CoA

Animals—Prehistoric. See Dinosaurs and other prehistoric animals

"**Ann** Eleanor, a child of ten." See A small elegy

Anna. Joe Johnson.—AdC

Anna Banana. Dennis Lee.—CoPs

"Anna Banana, jump into the stew." See Anna
    Banana
Anne Rutledge ("Out of me, unworthy and
    unknown") Edgar Lee Masters.—LiO
Annunciation over the shepherds, sel. Rainer
    Maria Rilke, tr. by M. D. Herter Norton
    "Look up, you men, men there at the fire."—
    LiPch
Anonymous. Martin Steingesser.—WiP
An anonymous verse from a Puerto Rican
    Christmas card. Unknown, tr. fr. the
    Spanish by Langston Hughes.—BaC
"Another season centers on this place." See
    The gourd dancer
Another year come. W. S. Merwin.—JaPp—LiO
"Another year, I left NY, on west coast in." See
    Kaddish
The answer is no. E. B. White.—PaB
Answering your question. David McCord.—
    McO
Answers ("What weighs the littlest") Aileen
    Fisher.—FiO
The ant ("The ant has made himself
    illustrious") Ogden Nash.—BlC
"The ant has made himself illustrious." See The
    ant
The ant in the windmill. Kaye Starbird.—StC
Ant song. Mary Ann Hoberman.—HoBu
Antarctic regions. See Polar regions
Anteater ("The anteater makes a meal of ants")
    William Jay Smith.—SmL
Anteater ("A genuine anteater") Shel
    Silverstein.—SiL
"The anteater makes a meal of ants." See
    Anteater
Anteaters
    Anteater ("The anteater makes a meal of
        ants") W. J. Smith.—SmL
    Anteater ("A genuine anteater") S.
        Silverstein.—SiL
Antelope ("When he takes a bath, the
    antelope") William Jay Smith.—SmL
Antelopes
    Antelope ("When he takes a bath, the
        antelope") W. J. Smith.—SmL
    Gazelle. M. A. Hoberman.—HoY—WiP
Anthony, Edward
    The bloodhound.—CoG
    The collies.—CoG
    The dachshund.—CoG
Anthropoids. Mary Ann Hoberman.—HoY
"The antique Indian should be Henry James."
    See American plan
"Anton Leeuwenhoek was Dutch." See The
    microscope
Antoninus, Brother
    A canticle to the waterbirds, sel.
        "Clack your beaks you cormorants and
            kittiwakes."—PaE
    "Clack your beaks you cormorants and
        kittiwakes." See A canticle to the
        waterbirds

Ants
    The ant ("The ant has made himself
        illustrious") O. Nash.—BlC
    The ant in the windmill. K. Starbird.—StC
    Ant song. M. A. Hoberman.—HoBu
    Anteater ("The anteater makes a meal of
        ants") W. J. Smith.—SmL
    Ants ("Ants in a line playing follow the
        leader") M. A. Hoberman.—HoBu
    Ants ("I like to watch the ants at work") M.
        A. Hoberman.—HoY
    Ants ("This morning at five I awoke with a
        cough") R. S. Oliver.—OlC
    Ants and sailboats. D. McCord.—McO
    Carpenter ants. M. A. Hoberman.—HoBu
    A gard'ner whose plants. N. M. Bodecker.—
        BoP
    If an ant. M. A. Hoberman.—HoBu
    Penthouse. A. Fisher.—FiO
    Praise to the little. N. Farber.—FaS
    "There's an ant on the front windowsill."
        From Limericks. D. McCord.—McSu
    Under a stone. A. Fisher.—FiO
Ants ("Ants in a line playing follow the leader")
    Mary Ann Hoberman.—HoBu
Ants ("I like to watch the ants at work") Mary
    Ann Hoberman.—HoY
Ants ("This morning at five I awoke with a
    cough") Robert S. Oliver.—OlC
Ants and sailboats. David McCord.—McO
"Ants in a line playing follow the leader." See
    Ants
Any day now. David McCord.—BrO
"Any Fibruary morning." Doris Orgel.—OrM
"Any hound a porcupine nudges." See The
    porcupine
Anywhere is a street into the night. N. Scott
    Momaday.—MoGd
Apartments and apartment life. See also City
    life
    My four friends. J. Prelutsky.—PrRh
    The people upstairs. O. Nash.—BlC
    Zebra. J. Thurman.—MoGp
Apes. See Gorillas; Monkeys
Apollo and Daphne. Joan Aiken.—AiS
"The appetite." See Yom Kippur, fasting
The apple ("Is on the top") Arnold Adoff.—
    AdE
"An apple a day." See Fruit thought
"An apple a day." Mother Goose.—TrGg
Apple scoop. Emilie Glen.—MoGp
Apple trees
    The apple ("Is on top") A. Adoff.—AdE
    Grandma Ida's cookie dough for apple pie
        crust. A. Adoff.—AdE
    "So soon the apple blossoms." K.
        Mizumura.—MiF
    Take one apple. A. Adoff.—AdE
    "Through all the orchard's boughs." From
        Autumn nature notes. T. Hughes.—HuSs
    The tree and me. K. Kuskin.—KuD
    Visitor ("Old tree") M. C. Livingston.—LiF
Apples
    The apple ("Is on top") A. Adoff.—AdE

"An apple a day." Mother Goose.—TrGg
Apple scoop. E. Glen.—MoGp
Apples ("Some people say that apples are red") W. J. Smith.—SmL
At the end of summer. A. Adoff.—AdE
August weather. K. Tynan.—SaM
Bobbing for apples. J. Prelutsky.—PrI
Dividing. D. McCord.—McO
Eco right. W. Gavenda.—BrO
Fruit thought. J. Aiken.—AiS
Grandma Ida's cookie dough for apple pie crust. A. Adoff.—AdE
Man for Mars. D. McCord.—McO
A man in Northchapel. N. M. Bodecker.—BoP
"Three pale foxglove lamp mantles, in full flare." From Autumn nature notes. T. Hughes.—HuSs
Up the pointed ladder. D. McCord.—McO
Whipping apples. R. N. Peck.—PeB
Apples ("Some people say that apples are red") William Jay Smith.—SmL
"The **apples** falling from the tree." See Night magic
"**Apples** for the little ones." See Father Fox's pennyrhymes
Applesauce. Mary Ann Hoberman.—HoY
April
April ("The snowman's buttons are undone") A. Fisher.—FiO
April bird. A. Fisher.—FiO
April birthday. T. Hughes.—HuSs
April fool ("April started out to cry.") A. Fisher.—FiO
April inventory. W. D. Snodgrass.—KhI
April rain song. L. Hughes.—HoMp
April 68. S. Cornish.—AdC
Oh have you heard. S. Silverstein.—HoMp
"An oak tree on the first day of April." From Spring nature notes. T. Hughes.—HuSs
"The sun was warm but the wind was chill." From Two tramps in mud time. R. Frost.—HoMp
April ("The snowman's buttons are undone") Aileen Fisher.—FiO
April bird. Aileen Fisher.—FiO
April birthday. Ted Hughes.—HuSs
April fool ("April started out to cry") Aileen Fisher.—FiO
April Fool's day
Oh have you heard. S. Silverstein.—LiCc
"**April** has come to Vermont with a shout." See Manhood
April inventory. W. D. Snodgrass.—KhI
April rain song. Langston Hughes.—HoMp
April 68. Sam Cornish.—AdC
"**April** started out to cry." See April fool
"**April** sun awakes the sleeping land." See Flutter wheel
"**April** winter." David Kherdian.—KhC
"**April's** here, to cut for me." See Sumac whistle
Arabia
Arabian dance. O. Nash.—BlC

Arabian dance. Ogden Nash.—BlC
Araucanian Indians. See Indians of the Americas—Araucanian
"**Arbuckle** Jones." Peter Wesley-Smith.—CoPs—DuSn
Archery. See Bows and arrows
Arctic regions. See Polar regions
"**Are** all the dragons dead." See Concerning dragons
"**Are** like comets." See Some lives
"**Are** silver white." See Moon ravens
"**Are** the reindeer in the rain, dear." See Conversation between Mr. and Mrs. Santa Claus
"**Are** wild strawberries really wild." See Wild strawberries
"**Are** you the guy." Unknown.—WiP
"**Are** zebras black with broad white stripes." See Zebra
"**Aren't** you fearful you'll trip and fall." See Ice-creepers
Arguments
Bickering. N. M. Bodecker.—BoHh—CoI
"My little old man and I fell out." Mother Goose.—TrGg
"Tweedledum and tweedledee." Mother Goose.—TrGg
Ariel's dirge. See The tempest
Ariel's song. See The tempest
Arithmetic. See also Mathematics
Exit x. D. McCord.—McO
That's the way it is. L. Morrison.—MoO
Who hasn't played gazintas. D. McCord.—McO
Zimmer's head thudding against the blackboard. P. Zimmer.—JaPp
Arizona
Dickey in Tucson. R. P. Dickey.—KhI
"The **armadillo**." John Gardner.—GaCb
Armadillos
Advice. M. A. Hoberman.—HoY
"The armadillo." J. Gardner.—GaCb
The **armies** of the moon. Ted Hughes.—HuM
Armistice day. See Veterans' day
Armor. See Arms and armor
Armour, Richard
Deus ex machina, or, roughly translated, God only knows what comes out of the machine.—BrO
A man for all seasonings.—CoPs
Money.—WiP
Arms and armor
Hunting Civil War relics at Nimblewill Creek. J. Dickey.—PlG
Moon weapons. T. Hughes.—HuM
The war horse. From Job.—CoPh
War horses. W. Cole.—CoPh
Armstrong, Peter
Butterfly.—JaPp
Arnold, Matthew
The forsaken merman.—PaE
"So, some tempestuous morn in early June." See Thyrsis

Arnold, Matthew—*Continued*
  Thyrsis, sels.
    "So, some tempestuous morn in early
      June."—PaB
"**Around** a distant bend the wagon showed."
  See Dust
Around and around. Karla Kuskin.—KuD
"**Around** and around a dusty little room."
  Margaret Johnson.—WiP
Around my room. William Jay Smith.—SmL
Around Thanksgiving. Rolfe Humphries.—LiO
Arrival, New York harbor. Robert Peters.—PlG
Arrows. See Bows and arrows
Arrows ("I shot an arrow toward the sky") Shel
  Silverstein.—SiL
Arrowy dreams. Witter Bynner.—PlG
Art and artists. See also Paintings and pictures;
  Sculpture and sculpturing
  The artist ("Mr. T bareheaded in a soiled
    undershirt") W. C. Williams.—LuZ
  "An artist who set up his easel." From
    Limericks. D. McCord.—McSu
  The clean platter. O. Nash.—BlC
  Hands ("Inside a cave in a narrow canyon
    near Tassajara") R. Jeffers.—PlG
  How to paint the portrait of a bird. J.
    Prevert.—LuZ
  Mobile. D. McCord.—McO
  My coloring book. J. Prelutsky.—PrR
  My creature. J. Prelutsky.—PrR
  Poets and mathematicians. L. Morrison.—
    MoO
  Things men have made. D. H. Lawrence.—
    JaPp
  To Desi as Joe the smoky the lover of 115th
    street. A. Lorde.—AdC
"An **art** as meagre as a quilt." See The spare
  quilt
Artful pose. Maya Angelou.—AnO
Arthur, King
  "When good King Arthur ruled this land."
    Mother Goose.—TrGg
"**Arthur** O'Bower has broken his band." Mother
  Goose.—TrGg
Artichokes. Pyke Johnson.—CoPs
Artie. Kaye Starbird.—StC
The **artist** ("Mr. T bareheaded in a soiled
  undershirt") William Carlos Williams.—LuZ
"An **artist** who set up his easel." From
  Limericks. D. McCord.—McSu
"An **artistic** young person of Churt." Myra
  Cohn Livingston.—LiLl
Artists. See Art and artists
Arudra
  Poetic art.—JaPp
"**As** day sinks slowly past the trees." See Plenty
  of time
"**As** everyone knows." See The snail
"**As** far as statues go, so far there's not." See
  Trollope's journal
"**As** far as the eye can see." See Midwinter
"**As** fly the shadows o'er the grass." See The
  Irish wolf hound

"**As** gay for you to take your father's ax." See
  To a young wretch
As good as a feast. Joan Aiken.—AiS
"**As** he moves the mine detector." See Hunting
  Civil War relics at Nimblewill Creek
"**As** I was cruising through the galaxies." See
  Time zones
"**As** I was going out one day." Mother Goose.—
  LoG
"**As** I was going to Darby." Mother Goose.—
  TrGg
"**As** I went out a crow." See The last word of a
  bluebird as told to a child
"**As** I went over the water." Mother Goose.—
  TrGg
"**As** I went up October Street." See The wave
"**As** I went walking one fine Sunday." See
  Coati-mundi
"**As** if I carried a charm." See Her going
"**As** in some dim baronial hall restrained." See
  Behind the arras
"**As** Joseph was a-walking." See The cherry tree
  carol
"**As** life runs on, the road grows strange." See
  Sixty eighth birthday
"**As** May was opening the rosebuds." See Birth
  of the foal
"**As** Pluto ruled the underworld." See Neptune
"**As** some rapt gazer on the lowly earth." See
  Love's humility
"**As** soon as the stars are suburbs." Kaye
  Starbird.—StC
"**As** the moon glides through." See Opening
  the door on the 18th of January, late in the
  evening, to let the cat in
"**As** virtuous men pass mildly away." See A
  valediction: forbidding mourning
"**As** Wulfstan said on another occasion." See
  Speech for the repeal of the McCarran Act
Asheron, Sara
  Echo.—WaGp
"**Ashes** to ashes, dust unto dust." See Mortality
"**Ask** a squirrel when he's cracking a nut."
  From Limericks. D. McCord.—McSu
"**Ask** me no more where Jove bestows." See
  Song
"**Asked** for another name for Santa Claus." See
  A Christmas package
Asleep and awake. David McCord.—McO
"**Asleep** in the deep." See Hale's lullaby
Asquith, Herbert
  Birthday gifts.—LiO
  The hairy dog.—PaI—SaM
  The mare.—CoA—CoPh
Aspiration. See Ambition
The **assassin.** From Assassination poems. J.
  Ridland.—LiO
The **assassination** ("Do you not find something
  very strange about him") Robert Hillyer.—
  LiO
Assassination ("It was wild") Don L. Lee.—LiO
Assassination poems, sels. John Ridland.—LiO
  (Complete)
  The assassin

The friends
Knowing it
The nation
Not believing it
Not wanting to believe it

Assassinations
The assassin. From Assassination poems. J. Ridland.—LiO
The assassination ("Do you not find something very strange about him") R. Hillyer.—LiO
Assassination ("It was wild") D. L. Lee.—LiO
Belief for JFK. A. R. Ammons.—PlG
Booth killed Lincoln. Unknown.—LiO
Death of Dr. King. S. Cornish.—LiO
Down in Dallas. X. J. Kennedy.—LiO
"For King, for Robert Kennedy." From Words in the mourning time. R. Hayden.—AdC
For Malcolm, after Mecca. G. W. Barrax.—LiO
The friends. From Assassination poems. J. Ridland.—LiO
Knowing it. From Assassination poems. J. Ridland.—LiO
The nation. From Assassination poems. J. Ridland.—LiO
Not believing it. From Assassination poems. J. Ridland.—LiO
Not wanting to believe it. From Assassination poems. J. Ridland.—LiO

Asses. See Donkeys
Aster. Robert Newton Peck.—PeB

Astronauts
Astronaut's choice. M. M. Darcy.—BrO
Astronaut's choice. M. M. Darcy.—BrO

Astronomical note. Lillian Morrison.—MoO

Astronomy. See also Moon; Planets; Stars; Sun; Tides; World
Rhyme for astronomical baby. From Boston nursery rhymes. J. Cook.—BrO

"At Christmas, play and make good cheer." Thomas Tusser.—BaC
At Christmas time. Unknown.—BaC
"At Christmas time we deck the hall." See At Christmas time
At dawn. Michael Patrick Hearn.—HeB
"At dawn the virgin is born." Lope de Vega, tr. by W. S. Merwin.—LiPch
"At every stroke his brazen fins do take." See The whale
"At first I thought it was the moon." See Night game
At first sight. Lillian Morrison.—MoW
"At four p.m. small fingers moved the dial to one-six-O." See Riders
At grandmother's. John Haislip.—LuZ
At long last. Lindsay Patterson.—AdC
At low tide. David McCord.—McO
At milking. Robert Newton Peck.—PeB
"At Mount Rushmore I looked up into one." See Edgar's story
"At my grandmother's life I look." See A near pantoum for a birthday

At night ("In the dust are my father's beautiful hands") Richard Eberhart.—PlL
At night ("When night is dark") Aileen Fisher.—FiO
"At night the aminals go marching." See The aminals
"At night when the bats." See B is for bats
"At nineteen." See The bloody show
At quitting time. Robert Sund.—LuZ
At St. Jerome. Frances Harrison.—DoWh
"At sunset, only to his true love." See Bird of paradise
At sunset time. Paul Laurence Dunbar.—BrI
"At sunset, when the night dews fall." See The snail
At the beach. Lillian Morrison.—MoW
"At the blackboard I had missed." See Zimmer's head thudding against the blackboard
"At the circus I was watching." See Singing ghost
At the end of summer. Arnold Adoff.—AdE
"At the end of the train, in the big red caboose." See The goose
"At the foot of the stairs." See Hope
At the garden gate. David McCord.—McO
"At the golden gate of song." See Inspiration
"At the gym in Fibruary." Doris Orgel.—OrM
At the keyhole. Walter De La Mare.—WiP
"At the kiss of my heel." See The gentled beast
At the manger. See For the time being
At the ring of a bell. Norma Farber.—FaS
At the sandpile. Aileen Fisher.—FiO
At the top of my voice. Felice Holman.—HoA
"At thy nativity a glorious quire." See Paradise regained

Athletes and athletics. See also names of sports, as Baseball
The angels of motion. L. Morrison.—MoSr
"At the gym in Fibruary." D. Orgel.—OrM
I love all gravity defiers. L. Morrison.—MoSr
Kevin scores. L. Norris.—NoM
Love fifteen. L. Morrison.—MoSr
Pole vault. S. Murano.—LuZ
The spearthrower. L. Morrison.—MoSr

Ations. Shel Silverstein.—SiL

Atkins, Russell
Dangerous condition, sign on inner city house.—AdC
Inner city lullaby.—AdC
Probability and birds.—AdC

Atlanta, Georgia
An old woman remembers. S. A. Brown.—AdC

Atlantis
Atlantis ("There was an island in the sea") C. Aiken.—PaE
Cities drowned. H. Newbolt.—PaE
The city in the sea. E.A. Poe.—PaE
Fragments. J. Masefield.—PaE
Leviathan. P. Quennell.—PaE
Atlantis ("There was an island in the sea") Conrad Aiken.—PaE

"Out in the wilds of South Australia." M. Varday.—DuSn
Up from down under. D. McCord.—McO
Authors and authorship. See Writers and writing
Autobiographia literaria. Frank O'Hara.—KhI
Autograph album verses
"God made the French." Unknown.—CoI
"God made the rivers." Unknown.—CoI
Grow up. Unknown.—CoI
"Mind your own business." Unknown.—CoI
"Sticks and stones." Unknown.—CoI
The way to the zoo. Unknown.—CoI
"When you're dead." Unknown.—CoI
Automats
Two girls. C. Reznikoff.—JaPp
Automobiles
Blake's wonderful car delivers us wonderfully well. N. Willard.—WiV
Car wash. M. C. Livingston.—LiWt
A crusty mechanic. N. M. Bodecker.—BoP
Kit, six years old, standing by the dashboard keeping daddy awake on a trip home from the beach. W. Stafford.—LuZ
Longmobile. S. Silverstein.—SiL
Man on wheels. K. Shapiro.—JaPp
Parking lot full. E. Merriam.—MeR
"Pumberly Pott's unpredictable niece." J. Prelutsky.—PrQ
Solstice song. T. Hughes.—HuSs
"Through the automatic carwash." R. Vas Dias.—LuZ
The windshield wipers' song. D. McCord.—McSu
Autumn. See also September; October; November; also Seasons
Around Thanksgiving. R. Humphries.—LiO
At the end of summer. A. Adoff.—AdE
Autumn ("Now the summer is grown old") C. Zolotow.—HoMp
"Autumn already." A. Atwood.—AtH
Autumn concert. A. Fisher.—FiO
Autumn for me is. H. Mackay.—SaM
Autumn garden. A. Fisher.—FiO
Autumn ghost sounds. Unknown.—BrIt.
Autumn leaves. A. Fisher.—FiO
Back to school. A. Fisher.—FiO
Betsy Robin. W. J. Smith.—SmL
"The chestnut splits its padded cell." From Autumn nature notes. T. Hughes.—HuSs
Crabapples. C. Sandburg.—HoMp
The defenders. T. Hughes.—HuSs
Early supper. B. Howes.—HiD
Fall ("When I go walking in the fall") K. Kuskin.—KuD
Fall wind ("Everything is on the run") A. Fisher.—FiO
Fall wind ("I scarcely felt a breath of air") M. Hillert.—HoMp
Flight. G. Johnston.—DoWh
The harvest moon. T. Hughes.—HuSs
The huntress. G. Johnston.—DoWh
"I like winter, spring, summer, and fall." B. S. De Regniers.—BrIt

Indian summer. W. Campbell.—DoWh
Indoors. R. Burgunder.—HoMp
"The laburnum top is silent, quite still." From Autumn nature notes. T. Hughes.—HuSs
The last waltz. R. N. Peck.—PeB
The last word of a bluebird as told to a child. R. Frost.—HoMp
The last word of a bluebird.—HiS
The leaves ("When the leaves are young") D. McCord.—McO
Leaves ("Who's killed the leaves") T. Hughes.—HuSs
The leaves fall down. M. W. Brown.—WiP
"The leaves turn gold." B. S. De Regniers.—ReB
Little white birches. A. Fisher.—FiO
Long shadows at Dulce. N. S. Momaday.—MoGd
The mist and all. D. Willson.—PaI
Morgans in October. S. Brabant.—CoPh
"Oceanic windy dawn." From Autumn nature notes. T. Hughes.—HuSs
October ("Yours is the hair of a golden girl") M. C. Livingston.—LiF
"Over the leaf crisp ground." A. Atwood.—AtH
The phantom ice cream man. X. J. Kennedy.—KeP
September ("Fall is coming") M. C. Livingston.—HoMp
Sestina. E. Bishop.—PlL
The seven sorrows. T. Hughes.—HuSs
Solstice song. T. Hughes.—HuSs
"Something told the wild geese." R. Field.—HoMp
Song ("The feathers of the willow") R. W. Dixon.—PaB
Song ("A spirit haunts the year's last hours") A. Tennyson.—PaB
Squirrel ("The squirrel in the hickory tree's a") L. Moore.—HoMp
"The sun finally tolerable." From Autumn nature notes. T. Hughes.—HuSs
Sunflowers ("One frosty evening") N. B. Bodecker.—BoHh
Theme in yellow. C. Sandburg.—MoGp
There came a day. T. Hughes.—HoMp—HuSs—MoGp
"This leaf." B. S. De Regniers.—ReB
"Three pale foxglove lamp mantles, in full flare." From Autumn nature notes. T. Hughes.—HuSs
"Through all the orchard's boughs." From Autumn nature notes. T. Hughes.—HuSs
To autumn. J. Keats.—PaB
"Under this autumn sky." A. Adoff.—AdE
The wave. D. McCord.—McO
Weathers. T. Hardy.—PaB
"When the elm was full." From Autumn nature notes. T. Hughes.—HuSs
Wind circles. A. Fisher.—FiO
Winter news ("The new November wind") D. Kherdian.—KhC

My Mami takes me to the bakery. C.
Pomerantz.—PoT
Turn the oven on. A. Adoff.—AdE
"Under this autumn sky." A. Adoff.—AdE
Balaban, John
Faith and practice.—PlG
Baldwin, Faith
Christmas.—BaC
"The **baleful** banshee, pale and worn." See The
banshee
Ballad ("I know my love is true") Paul
Laurence Dunbar.—BrI
The **ballad** of Befana. Phyllis McGinley.—BaC
The **ballad** of Newington Green. Joan Aiken.—
AiS
Ballad of the goodly fere. Ezra Pound.—LiO
Ballad of the morning streets. Imamu Amiri
Baraka.—AdC
The **ballade.** David McCord.—McO
Ballade, an easy one. David McCord.—McO
Ballade of the old time engine. Eda H.
Vines.—BrO
"A **ballade** rhymes with odd, and it is odd, and
not." See The ballade
Ballades
The ballade. D. McCord.—McO
Ballade, an easy one. D. McCord.—McO
"A **balloon.**" See Balloons
The **balloon** man. Rose Fyleman.—PaI
Balloons
The balloon man. R. Fyleman.—PaI
The balloons ("Against these turbid turquoise
skies") O. Wilde.—SaM
Balloons ("A balloon") J. Thurman.—ThFo
Balloons ("Kate's on for two, Elise is three")
D. McCord.—McO
Eight balloons. S. Silverstein.—SiL
The prize in the sky. X. J. Kennedy.—KeP
"What's the news of the day." Mother
Goose.—TrGg
The **balloons** ("Against these turbid turquoise
skies") Oscar Wilde.—SaM
Balloons ("A balloon") Judith Thurman.—ThFo
Balloons ("Kate's on for two, Elise is three")
David McCord.—McO
Balls
"I'm banged and chopped and sliced." L.
Morrison.—MoW
"**Balls** of fire, cried chameleon Betty." See A
confused chameleon
The **ballyoons.** S. J. Graham.—DuSn
Bananas
"Bananas and cream." D. McCord.—McO
When monkeys eat bananas. D. McCord.—
McO
"**Bananas** and cream." David McCord.—McO
Banbury fair. Edith G. Millard.—WiP
"The **bandersnatch** is a strange affair." See
Wash day wonder
Bandit. A. M. Klein.—DoWh
Bandit bee. Norma Farber.—FaS
"A **bandy**-legged man named Ted." Wilbur G.
Howcroft.—DuSn

Bangs, John Kendrick
The little elf.—PaI
Banjo tune. William Jay Smith.—SmL
Banks and banking
The debt. P. L. Dunbar.—BrI
The **banshee.** Jack Prelutsky.—PrH
Bantista, Rudy
Looking north to Taos.—LuZ
Pony song.—LuZ
Baptisms. See Christenings
Baraka, Imamu Amiri (Leroi Jones)
Ballad of the morning streets.—AdC
Black people, this is our destiny.—AdC
Cold term.—AdC
Funeral poem.—AdC
Ka'ba.—AdC
Leadbelly gives an autograph.—AdC
SOS.—AdC
Tight rope.—AdC
Young soul.—AdC
"**Barber,** barber, come and get me." See I'll get
one tomorrow
"**Barber,** barber, shave a pig." Mother Goose.—
TrGg
Barbers and barbershops
"Barber, barber, shave a pig." Mother
Goose.—TrGg
I'll get one tomorrow. O. Nash.—BlC
Barefoot ("After that tight") Valerie Worth.—
WoSm
Barefoot ("Let's pick clovers") Aileen Fisher.—
FiO
Barefoot days. Rachel Field.—PaI
Barefoot in the clover. Aileen Fisher.—FiO
"**Barefoot** Monday." See Sally Lun Lundy
"**Barefoot** on the hard wet sand." See Seaside
The **barge** horse. Sean Jennett.—CoPh
Barlow, George
Mellowness and flight.—AdC
Sweet Diane.—AdC
Barn chores. Nancy Dingman Watson.—WaB
Barn fire. Nancy Dingman Watson.—WaB
"**Barnabus** Browning." See Fear
Barnes, Jim
These damned trees crouch.—KhI
Barnes, Kate
Hector the dog.—CoG
A mare.—CoPh
Barnham, Dorothy
Chook chook.—DuSn
Peas.—DuSn
"Poor old Mollie Haggarty."—DuSn
Barns and stables
Barn chores. N. D. Watson.—WaB
Barn fire. N. D. Watson.—WaB
I saw a stable. M. E. Coleridge.—LiPch
Lamplighter barn. M. C. Livingston.—BeR
Manger tale. R. N. Peck.—PeB
Midnight in Bonnie's stall. S. J. Johnson.—
LiPch
Old gray barn. R. N. Peck.—PeB
The palomino stallion. A. Nowlan.—CoPh
The riding stable in winter. J. Tagliabue.—
CoPh

Barns and stables—*Continued*
The stable ("On the threshold of the stable smelling") J. Hoffman.—CoPh
The stable ("When midnight came") G. Mistral.—BaC
The stable cat. L. Norris.—LiPch
"Up the hill." Mother Goose.—CoPh
White cat. R. Knister.—DoWh
"Barns grow slowly out of the dark." See Lenox Christmas eve '68
Barnstone, Aliki
Numbers.—LuZ
The barracuda. John Gardner.—GaCb
Barrax, Gerald William
Christmas 1959 et cetera.—LiO—LiPch
For Malcolm, after Mecca.—AdC—LiO
If she sang.—AdC
Your eyes have their silence.—AdC
"The Barrier Reef is a coral puzzle." Marguerite Varday.—DuSn
Barrington, Patric
I had a hippopotamus.—WiP
Barrows, Marjorie
The cricket.—PaI
"Bars, wire." See Lions
Barto, Agnia
My seashell.—SaM
Baruch, Dorothy W.
Merry-go-round.—PaI
Baseball
The abominable baseball bat. X. J. Kennedy.—KeP
Analysis of baseball. M. Swenson.—HoMp
Don Larsen's perfect game. P. Goodman.—LuZ
Fair or foul. L. Morrison.—MoSr
Little league. D. McCord.—McO
"Mama never understood." N. Grimes.—GrS
Mr. Mulligan's window. J. Prelutsky.—PrRh
The new kid. M. Makley.—MoGp
Night game. L. Morrison.—MoSr
Pitcher McDowell. N. M. Bodecker.—BoP
Play ball. S. Silverstein.—SiL
Rural recreation. L. Morrison.—MoSr
Witch baseball. S. Kroll.—WaW
Basketball
The coach said. A. Adoff.—AdE
Fernando. M. Ridlon.—MoGp
Forms of praise. L. Morrison.—MoSr
Foul shot. E. A. Hoey.—MoGp
Reggie. E. Greenfield.—GrH
"Basketball players." See Forms of praise
Bass, Madeline Tiger
Name and place.—KhI
The bat ("By day the bat is cousin to the mouse") Theodore Roethke.—BrIt—SaM
The bat ("Myself, I rather like the bat") Ogden Nash.—BlC
The bat and the scientist. J. S. Bigelow.—BrO
"Bat, bat, come under my hat." Mother Goose.—TrGg
"A bat of rather uncertain age." See The bat and the scientist

Bates, Katherine Lee
America the beautiful.—PlG
The bath ("Hang garlands on the bathroom door") R. C. Lehmann.—CoG
Bath song. Dennis Lee.—LeG
Bathing
After a bath. A. Fisher.—PaI
Antelope. W. J. Smith.—SmL
The bath ("Hang garlands on the bathroom door") R. C. Lehmann.—CoG
Bathtub. M. C. Livingston.—LiWt
Cat bath. V. Worth.—WoSm
Crowded tub. S. Silverstein.—SiL
The games of night. N. Willard.—WaGp
Getting ready. N. M. Bodecker.—BoHh
I only watch the bubbles. N. Giovanni.—GiV
"If I should take a bath in mud." E. Dare.—DuSn
Ivory. D. McCord.—McO
Pleasures of the bath. E. Merriam.—MeR
T is for tub. W. J. Smith.—SmL
"There was a young lady named Harris." O. Nash.—BlC
Two birds with one stone. J. A. Lindon.—CoPs
"Who are you." Mother Goose.—LoG
Bathtub. Myra Cohn Livingston.—LiWt
Bats
The abominable baseball bat. X. J. Kennedy.—KeP
B is for bats. W. J. Smith.—SmL
The bat ("By day the bat is cousin to the mouse") T. Roethke.—BrIt—SaM
The bat ("Myself, I rather like the bat") O. Nash.—BlC
The bat and the scientist. J. S. Bigelow.—BrO
"Bat, bat, come under my hat." Mother Goose.—TrGg
Batty. S. Silverstein.—SiL
Five little bats. D. McCord.—McO
"Let me weigh what to say of the bat." From Limericks. D. McCord.—McSu
Point of view. D. McCord.—LuZ
Vampires. R. S. Oliver.—OlC
Battle won is lost. Phil George.—LuZ
Battles. See also War; Warships
Cannon Park. M. St. Germain.—JaPp
Concord hymn. R. W. Emerson.—PlG
Hunting Civil War relics at Nimblewill Creek. J. Dickey.—PlG
Warren's address at Bunker Hill. J. Pierpont.—PlG
The warrior of winter. T. Hughes.—HuSs
Batty. Shel Silverstein.—SiL
Baum, L. Frank
Queen Zixi of Ix, sel.
Witches' spells.—WaW
Witches' spells. See Queen Zixi of Ix
Baylor, Byrd
Children of the desert, sel.
"This is no place."—MoGp
"This is no place." See Children of the desert
"Be careful what." See Zoo manners

"**Be** links no longer broken." Charles
    Mackay.—BaC
"**Be** me a Pharaoh." See For us, who dare not
    dare
"**Be** wary of the loathsome troll." See The troll
"**Be** who you are and will be." See For each of
    you
Beach ("Close in, near to the sand") Myra
    Cohn Livingston.—LiWt
Beaches. See also Seashore
    Eating peaches on the beaches. A.
      Kisvardai.—DuSn
    Work and play. T. Hughes.—HuSs
Beaches ("There are reaches of beaches") Karla
    Kuskin.—KuD
Beagles. W. R. Rodgers.—CoG
Beans
    Jumping bean. M. A. Hoberman.—HoBu
The **bear** ("If somebody offers you a bear, bow
    low") John Gardner.—GaCb
The **bear** ("What ruse of vision") N. Scott
    Momaday.—MoGd
Bear in there. Shel Silverstein.—SiL
The **bear** who came to dinner. Adrien
    Stoutenburg.—HiS
The **bear** with the golden hair. Karla Kuskin.—
    KuD
Beards
    Captain Blackbeard did what. S.
      Silverstein.—SiL
    "There was an old man named Michael
      Finnegan." Mother Goose.—LoG
Beardsley, Aubrey
    To his brother dead. tr.—PlL
Bears
    The adventures of Isabel. O. Nash.—BlC
    The bear ("If somebody offers you a bear,
      bow low") J. Gardner.—GaCb
    The bear ("What ruse of vision") N. S.
      Momaday.—MoGd
    Bear in there. S. Silverstein.—SiL
    The bear who came to dinner. A.
      Stoutenburg.—HiS
    The bear with the golden hair. K. Kuskin.—
      KuD
    Bears ("Bears") E. Coatsworth.—CoA
    Bee tree. R. N. Peck.—PeB
    Furry bear. A. A. Milne.—CoA
    Grandpa bear's lullaby. J. Yolen.—YoD
    The lady and the bear. T. Roethke.—HiS
    Part of the darkness. I. Gardner.—FlA
    Penguin. W. J. Smith.—SmL
    Polar bear ("I think it must be very nice") W.
      J. Smith.—SmL
    A rabbit reveals my room. N. Willard.—WiV
    Self-portrait, as a bear. D. Hall.—HiS
    "There was an old person of Ware." E.
      Lear.—WiP
Bears ("Bears") Elizabeth Coatsworth.—CoA
"**Bears.**" See Bears
The **beast.** Theodore Roethke.—HiS
"The **beast** that is invisible." See The invisible
    beast
"The **beast** that is most fully dressed." See Lion

Beasts. See Animals
"**Beat** me and bite me." Dennis Lee.—LeG
Beautiful Ben. Lillian Morrison.—MoSr
The **beautiful** lawn sprinkler. Howard
    Nemerov.—JaPp
"**Beautiful** O beautiful." See The moon bull
"**Beautiful** rain." See Rain
Beautiful soup. See Alice's adventures in
    wonderland
"**Beautiful** soup, so rich and green." See Alice's
    adventures in wonderland—Beautiful soup
Beauty
    Axiom. L. Morrison.—MoW
    "The delicate shells lay on the shore." From
      Each and all. R. W. Emerson.—PaE
    An epitaph. W. De La Mare.—WiP
    Hippopotamus. M. A. Hoberman.—HoY
    "I wandered lonely as a cloud." From
      Daffodils. W. Wordsworth.—PaB
    A lady comes to an inn. E. Coatsworth.—HiS
    The peacock and the great blue heron. J.
      Gardner.—GaCb
    Sea-change. W. Gibson.—PaE
    That woman and this woman. N. S.
      Momaday.—MoGd
    Yei-ie's child. C. C. Long.—LuZ
"**Beauty** is bait and biter." See Axiom
Beauty, personal
    The act. W. C. Williams.—LuZ
    Black magic. D. Randall.—AdC
    Me ("My nose is blue") K. Kuskin.—KuD—
      WiP
    Naturally. A. Lorde.—AdC
    Poem no. 21. D. Long.—AdC
    "Ugly babies." Mother Goose.—TrGg
    The way it is. G. Oden.—AdC
    When Sue wears red. L. Hughes.—AdC
    Wicked witch admires herself. X. J.
      Kennedy.—KeP
    The yawn. P. Blackburn.—MoGp
The **beaver** ("When the trees the beaver
    requires for his dam") John Gardner.—
    GaCb
Beavers
    The beaver ("When the trees the beaver
      requires for his dam") J. Gardner.—GaCb
"**Because** I had loved so deeply." See
    Compensation
"**Because** I waddle when I walk." See The
    dachshund
"**Because** it is short." See Haiku
"**Because** Miss Casper gets annoyed." See Miss
    Casper's cow
"**Because** there was a man somewhere in a
    candystripe silk shirt." See Homage to the
    empress of the blues
"**Because** there's a race." See The covered
    bridge house
"**Because** you love me I have much achieved."
    See Encouraged
Becker, John
    "Jill Withers had a farthingale."—WiP
"**Becoming.**" See The suspense of the coming
    word

Bed in summer. Robert Louis Stevenson.—PaI
Bed-time. See also Good-night poems; Lullabies
A is for alpaca. W. J. Smith.—SmL
"After good night." S. C. Fox.—FoB
Andrew's bedtime story. I. Serraillier.—HiD
"Are all the dragons dead." From
    Concerning dragons. H. Pepler.—MoF
Bed in summer. R. L. Stevenson.—PaI
The bedpost. R. Graves.—HiS
Bedtime ("Five minutes, five minutes more,
    please") E. Farjeon.—PaI
Bedtime ("Now the mouse goes to his hole")
    F. Holman.—HoA
Bedtime ("Shut, closet door") M. C.
    Livingston.—LiF
The bedtime concert. D. Lee.—LeG
The big blue frog and the dirty flannel dog.
    D. Lee.—LeG
The coming of teddy bears. D. Lee.—LeG
Conversation. D. McCord.—HiS—McO
Counting birds. F. Holman.—HoA
"Diddle, diddle, dumpling, my son John."
    Mother Goose.—TrGg
Falling asleep. I. Serraillier.—HiD
Going to bed. M. Chute.—PaI
Good night ("Father puts the paper down")
    A. Fisher.—FiO
Goodnight ("Goodnight Mommy") N.
    Giovanni.—GiV—RuM
Gumble. M. Dugan.—DuSn
The happy family. J. Ciardi.—HiD
The huntsmen. W. De La Mare.—CoPh
"If a bad dream comes." S. C. Fox.—FoB
In bed ("When I am in bed") C. Zolotow.—
    HeB
"In jumping and tumbling." Unknown.—MoF
"In the evening." S. C. Fox.—FoB
A little lullaby to be read a little bit out loud.
    C. Pomerantz.—PoT
"The llama who had no pajama." M. A.
    Hoberman.—HoY
Lullaby. F. Holman.—HoA
Magic jellybean. J. Prelutsky.—PrR
The middle of the night. K. Kuskin.—KuD
Moonstruck. A. Fisher.—FiO
My own room. N. D. Watson.—RuM—WaB
The night ("The night creeps in") M. C.
    Livingston.—RuM
Night landscape. J. Aiken.—AiS—HiD—RuM
Night magic. A. J. Burr.—PaI
Night sounds. F. Holman.—RuM
Onkerpled. M. Dugan.—DuSn
Plenty of time. A. Fisher.—FiO
A rabbit reveals my room. N. Willard.—WiV
The sand-man. P. L. Dunbar.—BrI
Shadows ("Although I know") S. C. Fox.—
    FoB
Skin stealer. S. Silverstein.—SiL
Skindiver. D. Lee.—LeG
Sleep song. S. Kroll.—WaFp
"Slug-a-bed." Mother Goose.—TrGg
Sweet dreams. O. Nash.—BlC
Things. W. J. Smith.—SmL

The tiger asks Blake for a bedtime story. N.
    Willard.—WiV
Tiger pajamas. S. C. Fox.—FoB
"To bed, to bed." Mother Goose.—WiP
Two in bed. A. B. Ross.—PaI
    "When my brother Tommy."—MoF
A variation on 'to say to go to sleep.' R.
    Jarrell.—YaI
When candy was chocolate. W. J. Smith.—
    SmL
You too lie down. D. Lee.—LeN
"You've no need to light a night light."
    Unknown.—RuM
Beddoes, Thomas Lovell
The old ghost.—WaGp
The bedpost. Robert Graves.—HiS
Beds
The blessing of the bed. E. Coatsworth.—PlL
Insomnia the gem of the ocean. J. Updike.—
    BrO
Like a giant in a towel. D. Lee.—WaG
Magic story for falling asleep. N. Willard.—
    WaG
A maid in Old Lyme. N. M. Bodecker.—BoP
My bed. E. M. Scott.—PaI
Rift tide. R. M. Walsh.—BrO
Bedtime. See Bed-time
Bedtime ("Five minutes, five minutes more,
    please") Eleanor Farjeon.—PaI
Bedtime ("Now the mouse goes to his hole")
    Felice Holman.—HoA
Bedtime ("Shut, closet door") Myra Cohn
    Livingston.—LiF
The bedtime concert. Dennis Lee.—LeG
Bee ("A bee thumps against the dusty
    window") Robert Sund.—MoGp
"Bee, I'm expecting you." Emily Dickinson.—
    HiS
"A bee put on a zephyr." See Bandit bee
"The bee thrives." See Rhyme
"A bee thumps against the dusty window." See
    Bee
Bee tree. Robert Newton Peck.—PeB
"The bee will choose to spend his hours." Karla
    Kuskin.—KuR
Beech. David McCord.—McO
Beech trees
Beech. D. McCord.—McO
Beecher, John
"I read your testimony and I thought." See
    To Alexander Meiklejohn
To Alexander Meiklejohn, sel.
    "I read your testimony and I thought."—
    PlG
The beefalo. John Gardner.—GaCb
"The beefalo is a bison and a cow." See The
    beefalo
The beefburger. Ogden Nash.—BlC
Beerbohm, Max
Brave Rover.—CoG
Bees
Ariel's song. From The tempest. W.
    Shakespeare.—PaB
B. M. A. Hoberman.—HoBu

Bandit bee. N. Farber.—FaS
Barefoot in the clover. A. Fisher.—FiO
Bee ("A bee thumps against the dusty
    window") R. Sund.—MoGp
"Bee, I'm expecting you." E. Dickinson.—HiS
Bee tree. R. N. Peck.—PeB
"The bee will choose to spend his hours." K.
    Kuskin.—KuR
Bees ("Every bee") J. Prelutsky.—WiP
Bees ("Stop, and be") R. S. Oliver.—OlC
Beware of me. Unknown.—MoGp
Bumblebee ("The bumblebee is bumbly") D.
    McCord.—McO
Bumblebee ("I sat as still") A. Fisher.—FiO
Clover field. A. Fisher.—FiO
Combinations. M. A. Hoberman.—HoBu
Early bee. A. Fisher.—FiO
Hammock. D. McCord.—McO
Honeycomb. V. Worth.—WoSm
Kisses ("Flowers for hours") N. Giovanni.—
    GiV
Looking around. A. Fisher.—FiO
The March bee. E. Blunden.—PaB
The old man and the bee. E. Lear.—WiP
Spelling bee. S. Silverstein.—SiL
"There is obviously a complete lack of
    understanding." O. Nash.—BlC
"There was life in the dead tree that fell."
    From Limericks. D. McCord.—McSu
To be a clover. A. Fisher.—FiO
Weather conditions. M. C. Livingston.—LiF
Wings ("Bees have four wings") A. Fisher.—
    FiO
Zizzy bee. N. D. Watson.—WaB
Bees ("Every bee") Jack Prelutsky.—WiP
Bees ("Stop, and be") Robert S. Oliver.—OlC
"**Bees**." See Looking around
"**Bees** have four wings." See Wings
Beetle thoughts. Aileen Fisher.—FiO
Beetles
    Beetle thoughts. A. Fisher.—FiO
    Clickbeetle. M. A. Hoberman.—HoBu
    "Down in the hollow." A. Fisher.—PaI
    For a ladybug. A. Fisher.—FiO
    I want you to meet. D. McCord.—McO—WiP
    "Ladybird, ladybird." I. O. Eastwick.—WiP
    Ladybug ("Ladybug red, when you fly away
        home") M. A. Hoberman.—HoBu
    Ladybug ("We say ladybug") D. McCord.—
        McSu
    Ladybug's Christmas. N. Farber.—LiPch
    "Little ladybug." B. Maestro.—MaFp
    Raindrops. A. Fisher.—FiO
"**Beetles** that blow in the breeze." See Things
    as they are
"**Befana** the housewife, scrubbing her pane."
    See The ballad of Befana
Before an old painting of the Crucifixion. N.
    Scott Momaday.—MoGd
Before Christmas. Aileen Fisher.—FiO
"**Before** I fed." See Through the vines
"**Before** Mrs. Williams died." See Keepsake
"**Before** the children say goodnight." See The
    happy family

"**Before** the January thaw." See Deep into
    winter
"**Before** the paling of the stars." See A
    Christmas carol
Beggars
    "Christmas is coming, the geese are getting
        fat." Unknown.—LiC—LiPch
        Christmas.—BaC
    "Hark, hark, the dogs do bark." Mother
        Goose.—BlH—LoG
Beginnings and endings. Phyllis
    Koestenbaum.—KhI
Beginnings, sel. Robert Hayden
    "Plowdens, Finns."—AdC
Behavior
    The African wild dog. J. Gardner.—GaCb
    The ambiguous dog. A. Guiterman.—CoG
    Artichokes. P. Johnson.—CoPs
    Bad boy's swan song. W. J. Smith.—CoI
    Brave Rover. M. Beerbohm.—CoG
    Brother. M. A. Hoberman.—HoY
    Brother and sister. L. Carroll.—WiP
    The dog. O. Nash.—CoG
    The family dinner party. Menander.—PlL
    Father and I in the woods. D. McCord.—
        McO
    For a good dog. A. Guiterman.—CoG
    Harvey never shares. J. Prelutsky.—PrRh
    Homework ("What is it about homework") J.
        Yolen.—HeB
    Hot line. L. Dunann.—BrO
    Hot line to the nursery. D. McCord.—McO
    A household. W. H. Auden.—PlL
    The howlery growlery room. L. E.
        Richards.—CoI
    "I remember." N. Grimes.—GrS
    "I woke up this morning." K. Kuskin.—KuD
    Jim, who ran away from his nurse, and was
        eaten by a lion. H. Belloc.—WiP
    Jonathan sitting in mud. N. Giovanni.—GiV
    Katawumpus. E. A. Parry.—CoI
    The King of Umpalazzo. M. A. Hoberman.—
        HoY
    Ladies first. S. Silverstein.—SiL
    "Lazy witch." M. C. Livingston.—WaW
    Leave me alone. F. Holman.—HoA
    Little Abigail and the beautiful pony. S.
        Silverstein.—SiL
    "Marty's party." D. McCord.—McO—WiP
    Montgomery, with acknowledgements to T.
        S. Eliot's Macavity. H.A.C. Evans.—CoG
    My mother said. Unknown.—WiP
    Nobody calls him Jim. J. Prelutsky.—PrRh
    Oilcan Harry. D. Lee.—LeN
    Old grey goose. H. Behn.—CoA
    Over the coffin. T. Hardy.—PlL
    Patsy Doolin. K. Starbird.—CoI
    The practical joke. J. Prelutsky.—PrRh
    Put something in. S. Silverstein.—SiL
    Rebecca, who slammed doors for fun and
        perished miserably. H. Belloc.—HiS
    Rolling Harvey down the hill. J. Prelutsky.—
        PrRh
    Rules. K. Kuskin.—KuD—WiP

Bennet, Peggy
Over the green sands.—PaE
Bennett, Lerone
And was not improved.—AdC
Bennett, Rowena
Conversation between Mr. and Mrs. Santa Claus.—BaC
Benson, Gerard
Horse.—CoPh
Berrigan, Ted
Resolution.—LiO
Berry, Wendell
Independence day.—LiO
Berryman, John
Loss.—PlL
Minnesota Thanksgiving.—PlG
"**Beside** the blaze of forty fires." See Grim
"**Beside** the road." See Roadside
Best of show. Barbara Howes.—CoG
"A **bestiary,** or book of beasts." John Gardner.—GaCb
Beth-Gelert. William Robert Spencer.—CoG
Bethlehem
Bethlehem ("A little child") Unknown.—BaC
"How far is it to Bethlehem." F. Chesterton.—LiPch
"In Bethlehem is born the holy child." From The messiah. C. Jennens.—BaC
Long, long ago. Unknown.—BaC—LiPch
The nativity. From Gospel according to Luke.—BaC
One glorious star. Unknown.—BaC
So come we running. Unknown.—BaC
Bethlehem ("A little child") Unknown.—BaC
Betjeman, John
Hunter trials.—CoPh
Betsy Robin. William Jay Smith.—SmL
"**Betsy** Robin packs her bag." See Betsy Robin
Better than a pussycat. William Cole.—CoDb
"**Better** than any cartoon or comedy." See The biggest laugh
"**Bettlebombs** make jelly jam." See Makers
Between birthdays. Ogden Nash.—BlC
"**Between** our house and Jack's next door." See The cellar hole
"**Between** painting a roof yesterday and the hay." See Independence day
"**Between** the microcosm." See Who, where
Between the porch and the altar, sel. Robert Lowell
"Meeting his mother makes him lose ten years."—PlL
Beware, do not read this poem. Ishmael Reed.—AdC
"**Beware,** my child." Shel Silverstein.—BrIt
"**Beware,** my love, lest you should see." See To his wife
Beware of me. Unknown, fr. the Cherokee Indian.—MoGp
"**Beware** the murdering turtle." See The turtle
"**Bewildered** in our buying throng." See Patrum propositum
"**Beyond** a whopping owse or ox." See Queer story of the fowse or fox

"**Beyond** the shadow of the ship." See The rime of the ancient mariner—Water-snakes
Beyond the years. Paul Laurence Dunbar.—BrI
"**Beyond** the years the answer lies." See Beyond the years
Bhagavatula Sankara Sastri. See Arudra
Bibbilbonty. Rose Fyleman.—WiP
Bible—New Testament
"And some of the Pharisees from among the multitude." See Gospel according to Luke
"And there were in the same country shepherds." See Gospel according to Luke
The angels. See Gospel according to Luke—"And there were in the same country shepherds"
"For we have seen his star in the east, and are come." See Gospel according to Matthew
The Magi. See Gospel according to Matthew
The nativity. See Gospel according to Luke
The parable of the prodigal son. See Gospel according to Luke
The shepherds. See Gospel according to Luke—"And there were in the same country shepherds"
"There is one glory of the sun, and another glory." See Corinthians
Bible—Old Testament
"And God said, let us make man in our image." See Genesis
Cain and Abel. See Genesis
"Children's children are the crown of old men." See Proverbs, sels.
David and Absalom. See The second book of Samuel
"A father of the fatherless, and a judge of the widows." See Psalms—Psalm 68
"Make a joyful noise unto the Lord, all ye lands." See Psalms—Psalm 100
Praise of a good woman. See Proverbs, sels.
Psalm 100. See Psalms
Psalm 68. See Psalms
The war horse. See Job
"The wolf also shall dwell with the lamb." See Isaiah
Bible characters. See names of Bible characters, as Daniel
Bickering. N. M. Bodecker.—BoHh—CoI
Bicycles and bicycling
"As soon as the stars are suburbs." K. Starbird.—StC
Bike ride. L. Moore.—MoTs
Bike twister. D. Lee.—LeG
Making work for father. X. J. Kennedy.—KeP
On our bikes. L. Morrison.—MoGp—MoSr
Big and little. William Jay Smith.—SmL
The **big** blue frog and the dirty flannel dog. Dennis Lee.—LeG
"**Big** boys do." See Big and little
"The **big** city is rude to snow." See Blizzard
"**Big** clocks go tick." See Tick tock talk
A **big** deal for the tooth fairy. X. J. Kennedy.—KeP
"**Big** dog." Philip Booth.—CoG

A widow bird sate mourning. P. B. Shelley.—
    PaB
Wingtip. C. Sandburg.—JaPp
The woods at night. M. Swenson.—HiD
Birds—Eggs and nests
Baby birds. A. Fisher.—AiO
Egg ("Somehow the hen") V. Worth.—WoSm
Nest. R. N. Peck.—PeB
"One egg in the nest of that crow." From
    Limericks. D. McCord.—McSu
The secret. M.C. Livingston.—LiF
Birds ("The fierce musical cries of a couple of
    sparrow hawks") Robinson Jeffers.—PaE
The **birds** ("From out of a wood did a cuckoo
    fly") Unknown.—LiPch
The **birds** ("I wonder how birds, going back
    and forth") Kaye Starbird.—StC
Birds ("Mouths of birds are very strange")
    Aileen Fisher.—FiO
"**Birds** are flowers flying." See Mirrorment
"The **birds,** are they worth remembering." See
    Wingtip
"**Birds** circling at dusk." Ann Atwood.—AtH
"**Birds** fly in the broken windows." See Two
    beers in Argyle, Wisconsin
Birds in the garden. Unknown.—CoA
Birds in the rain. David McCord.—McO
Birmingham, Alabama
Birmingham 1963. R. R. Patterson.—AdC
Birmingham 1963. Raymond R. Patterson.—
    AdC
Birney, Earle
Quebec May.—DoWh
Birth
All the little animals. M. Rukeyser.—PlL
Birth ("The rain is over") A. Gilboa.—LiO
Birth of the foal. F. Juhasz.—CoPh
The blessing of the bed. E. Coatsworth.—PlL
The bloody show. J. Murray.—KhI
The donkey. Unknown.—CoA
The guppy. O. Nash.—BlC—MoGp
Infant sorrow. W. Blake.—PlL
A leave taking. Y. Winters.—PlL
Mississippi born. P. C. Lomax.—AdC
My stars. A. Ibn Ezra.—LiO
"Oh, dearer by far than the land of our
    birth." R. H. Wilde.—PlG
On the naming day. J. M. Kunjufu.—AdC
Sarah's wondrous thing. R. N. Peck.—PeB
Saturday's child. C. Cullen.—LiO
"Taffy was born." Mother Goose.—TrGg
Twice born. A. Fisher.—FiO
Winter calf. R. N. Peck.—PeB
Birth ("The rain is over") Amir Gilboa, tr. fr.
    the Israeli by Robert Mezey and Shula
    Starkman.—LiO
Birth of the foal. Ferenc Juhasz, tr. fr. the
    Hungarian by David Wevill.—CoPh
Birthday ("My heart is like a singing bird")
    Christina Georgina Rossetti.—PaB
The **birthday** bus. Mary Ann Hoberman.—HoY
The **birthday** cow. Eve Merriam.—MeB
Birthday gifts. Herbert Asquith.—LiO

A **birthday** memorial to Seventh Street. Audre
    Lorde.—AdC
"**Birthday** of but a single pang." Emily
    Dickinson.—LiO
Birthday present. Aileen Fisher.—FiO
Birthdays
Almost perfect. S. Silverstein.—SiL
April birthday. T. Hughes.—HuSs
Between birthdays. O. Nash.—BlC
Birthday ("My heart is like a singing bird")
    C. G. Rossetti.—PaB
The birthday bus. M. A. Hoberman.—HoY
The birthday cow. E. Merriam.—MeB
Birthday gifts. H. Asquith.—LiO
"Birthday of but a single pang." E.
    Dickinson.—LiO
Birthday present. A. Fisher.—FiO
Birthdays ("If birthdays happened once a
    week") M. A. Hoberman.—HoY
Burning the steaks in the rain, reflections on
    a 46th birthday. R. Dana.—KhI
Conversation with Washington. M. C.
    Livingston.—LiO
"Crawl, laugh." Issa.—LiO
Dog's day. S. Silverstein.—SiL
Felicitations. L. Morrison.—MoO
First day of spring. B. S. De Regniers.—ReB
"Happy birthday, silly goose." From Father
    Fox's pennyrhymes. C. Watson.—LiCc
Happy birthday to me. E. Merriam.—LiCc
"How old will you be on your birthday." B.
    S. De Regniers.—ReB
"Late April and you are three, today." From
    Heart's needle. W. D. Snodgrass.—PlL
"Monday's child is fair of face." Unknown.—
    LiCc
The monster's birthday. L. Moore.—WaM
A monstrous mouse. X. J. Kennedy.—LiCc
My name. L. B. Hopkins.—LiCc
A near pantoum for a birthday. B. Howes.—
    PlL
On reaching forty. M. Angelou.—AnO
Sixty eighth birthday. J. R. Lowell.—JaPp
Strokes. W. Stafford.—JaPp
Tim. D. McCord.—McO
To my brothers. J. Keats.—PlL
Trala trala trala la-le-la. W. C. Williams.—LiO
Turning 30 poem. J. Brandi.—KhI
What someone said when he was spanked on
    the day before his birthday. J. Ciardi.—BeR
"Who wants a birthday." D. McCord.—McO
Writ on the eve of my 32nd birthday. G.
    Corso.—KhI
"Your birthday comes to tell me this." E. E.
    Cummings.—LiCc
Birthdays ("If birthdays happened once a
    week") Mary Ann Hoberman.—HoY
The **birthplace.** Robert Frost.—LiO
"A **biscuit,** a basket, a bath in a hat." See Bath
    song
Bishop, Elizabeth
"As far as statues go, so far there's not." See
    Trollope's journal
Manners for a child of 1918.—PlL

Bishop, Elizabeth—*Continued*
  Sestina.—PlL
  Trollope's journal, sel.
    "As far as statues go, so far there's
      not."—PlG
Bishop, John Peale
  Southern pines.—PlG
  The spare quilt.—PlG
Bishop, Morris
  An Englishman with an atlas or America the
    unpronounceable.—PlG
  I hear America griping.—BrO
  The perforated spirit.—BrO
  Song of the pop bottlers.—CoPs
  "There's a lady in Washington Heights."—
    BrO
The bishop of Atlanta, Ray Charles. Julian
  Bond.—AdC
"The bishop seduces the world with his voice."
  See The bishop of Atlanta, Ray Charles
Bison. See Buffaloes
"Bitter batter boop." See The last cry of the
  damp fly
Black (color)
  Black ("Black the angry colour") J. Chester.—
    SaM
  Black ("Black the angry colour") Jane
    Chester.—SaM
"Black and white kitten." Betsy Maestro.—
  MaFp
Black cat ("A cat as black") Jack Prelutsky.—
  PrI
"The black cat yawns." See Cat
The black fern. Leslie Norris.—NoM
"Black folks have got to be superhuman." See
  A poem about beauty, blackness, poetry,
  and how to be all three
"Black girl black girl." See Black magic
"The black haired girl." See The yawn
Black heritage. See Heritage—Black
"Black hill black hall." See Haunted
"Black is the first nail I ever stepped on." See
  Negritude
Black, Isaac J.
  Roll call, a land of old folk and children.—
    AdC
  Talking to the townsfolk in Ideal, Georgia.—
    AdC
"The black kitten." See Kitten
Black magic. Dudley Randall.—AdC
"A black man." Sam Cornish.—AdC
"Black men bleeding to death inside
  themselves." See Eulogy for Alvin Frost
A black-nosed kitten. Mary Mapes Dodge.—
  CoA
"A black-nosed kitten will slumber all the day."
  See A black-nosed kitten
The black pebble. James Reeves.—MaP—WiP
Black people, this is our destiny. Imamu Amiri
  Baraka.—AdC
"Black poets should live, not leap." See For
  black poets who think of suicide
Black star line. Henry Dumas.—AdC

"A black steel carcass in a field of sheep." See
  Scrap iron
"Black the angry colour." See Black
"Black was the color of the peddler's wagon."
  See Needles and pins
A black wedding song. Gwendolyn Brooks.—
  AdC
Blackberries
  Picking berries. A. Fisher.—FiO
Blackbirds
  "As I went over the water." Mother Goose.—
    TrGg
  "Sing a song of sixpence." Mother Goose.—
    TrGg
Blackburn, Paul
  Good morning, love.—KhI
  The yawn.—MoGp
"Blackie is a mother." See Mother cat
Blackmen, who make morning. Angela
  Jackson.—AdC
Blacks. See also Dialect—American—Black;
    Heritage—Black; Race relations; Slavery
  Big momma. H. R. Madhubuti.—AdC
  Birmingham 1963. R. R. Patterson.—AdC
  Black magic. D. Randall.—AdC
  "A black man." S. Cornish.—AdC
  Booker T. Washington. P. L. Dunbar.—BrI
  Boys, black. G. Brooks.—AdC
  Carol of the brown king. L. Hughes.—BaC
  Child dead in old seas. M. Angelou.—AnO
  Coal ("Is the total black, being spoken") A.
    Lorde.—AdC
  Cold term. I. A. Baraka.—AdC
  Death of Dr. King. S. Cornish.—LiO
  Determination. J. H. Clarke.—AdC
  A different image. D. Randall.—AdC
  "Do not think." C. Freeman.—AdC
  "Don't wanna be." S. Sanchez.—AdC
  Douglass. P. L. Dunbar.—BrI
  Effendi. M. S. Harper.—AdC
  El-Hajj Malik El-Shabazz, Malcolm X. R.
    Hayden.—AdC
  Elegy for Harriet Tubman and Frederick
    Douglass. M. Angelou.—AnO
  Eulogy for Alvin Frost. A. Lorde.—AdC
  "For all things black and beautiful." C. K.
    Rivers.—AdC
  For black poets who think of suicide. E.
    Knight.—AdC
  For deLawd. L. Clifton.—AdC
  For Edwin R. Embree. O. Dodson.—AdC
  For Malcolm, after Mecca. G. W. Barrax.—
    AdC
  For Malcolm X ("All you violated ones with
    gentle hearts") M. Walker.—AdC
  For Mattie and eternity. S. D. Plumpp.—AdC
  For muh' dear. C. M. Rodgers.—AdC
  For my people. M. Walker.—AdC
  Frederick Douglass ("When it is finally ours,
    this freedom, this liberty, this beautiful") R.
    E. Hayden.—PlG
  Generations. J. D. Simmons.—AdC
  Give me five. W. J. Harris.—AdC
  Good times and no bread. R. Lockett.—AdC

Harriet Tubman. E. Greenfield.—GrH
Here where Coltrane is. M. S. Harper.—AdC
High on the hog. J. Fields.—AdC
"I am a black woman." M. Evans.—AdC
"I remember how she sang." R. Penny.—
    AdC
Identities. A. Young.—KhI
If we cannot live as people. C. Lynch.—AdC
It happened in Montgomery. P. W. Petrie.—
    MoGp
"It's comforting." J. D. Simmons.—AdC
Ka'ba. I. A. Baraka.—AdC
Malcolm ("Nobody mentioned war") L.
    Clifton.—AdC
Malcolm, a thousandth poem. C. K. Rivers.—
    AdC
Naturally. A. Lorde.—AdC
Negritude. J. A. Emanuel.—AdC
A negro love song. P. L. Dunbar.—BrI
Now poem for us. S. Sanchez.—AdC
Of Dewitt Williams on his way to Lincoln
    cemetery. G. Brooks.—FlA
On being brought from Africa to America. P.
    Wheatley.—PlG
On the naming day. J. M. Kunjufu.—AdC
"Our blackness did not come to us whole."
    L. B. Bragg.—AdC
Patience of a people. F. J. Bryant.—AdC
Paul Robeson. G. Brooks.—AdC
A poem about beauty, blackness, poetry, and
    how to be all three. L. B. Bragg.—AdC
Poem at thirty. S. Sanchez.—AdC
Present. S. Sanchez.—AdC
The pusher. M. Angelou.—AnO
Refugee in America. L. Hughes.—LiCc—PlG
Shade. C. Lynch.—AdC
Song for the old ones. M. Angelou.—AnO
SOS. I. A. Baraka.—AdC
"Standing at the gate." N. Grimes.—GrS
Strange legacies. S. A. Brown.—AdC
Sun song. L. Hughes.—AdC
"Those boys that ran together." L. Clifton.—
    AdC
"Tomorrow the heroes." A. B. Spellman.—
    AdC
Trellie. L. Jeffers.—AdC
The way it is. G. Oden.—AdC
"We're an Africanpeople." From African
    poems. H. R. Madhubuti.—AdC
"When black people are." A. B. Spellman.—
    AdC
When the wine was gone. A. Aubert.—AdC
"Where is the black community." J. C.
    Thomas.—AdC
Who can be born black. M. Evans.—AdC
Blacksmiths and blacksmithing
    Amanda is shod. M. Kumin.—CoPh
"The **blacksmith's** boy went out with a rifle."
    See Legend
Blake leads a walk on the Milky Way. Nancy
    Willard.—WiV
Blake tells the tiger the tale of the tailor. N.
    Willard.—WiV

Blake, William
    Ah, sunflower.—PaB
    Dream.—PaB
    "He whose face gives no light." See Proverbs
        of hell
    Holy Thursday.—LiO
    Infant joy.—PlL
    Infant sorrow.—PlL
    Night.—MoF
    Nurse's song.—MoF
    A poison tree.—MaP
    Proverbs of hell, sel.
        "He whose face gives no light."—WiV
    Spring song.—SaM (at.)
    The tiger.—PaB
Blake, William (about)
    Blake leads a walk on the Milky Way. N.
        Willard.—WiV
    The tiger asks Blake for a bedtime story. N.
        Willard.—WiV
    William Blake's inn for innocent and
        experienced travelers. N. Willard.—WiV
Blakely, Henry
    H. Rap Brown.—AdC
    Morning song.—AdC
Blake's wonderful car delivers us wonderfully
    well. Nancy Willard.—WiV
The **blame**. Shel Silverstein.—CoA—SiL
Blasing, Randy
    Horse.—CoPh
"The **blatt**, though flat, was also fat." See Splatt
A **blessing**. James Wright.—FlA
The **blessing** of the bed. Elizabeth
    Coatsworth.—PlL
Blind
    Ernesto Maestas instructs Ynocencia Saavedra
        in the art of acting. N. S. Momaday.—
        MoGd
    Riding a one eyed horse. H. Taylor.—CoPh
Bliss. Eleanor Farjeon.—YaI
Bliss, Paul Southworth
    Lucas Park, St. Louis.—FlA
Bliven, Bruce
    Not lost in the stars.—BrO
Blizzard ("The big city is rude to snow") Judith
    Thurman.—ThFo
The **blizzard** ("I can't forget the second night
    of the snow") Kaye Starbird.—StC
Blizzards
    Blizzard ("The big city is rude to snow") J.
        Thurman.—ThFo
    The blizzard ("I can't forget the second night
        of the snow") K. Starbird.—StC
Block, Allan
    In those times.—KhI
Blocks. See Toys
Blok, Alexander
    Little catkins.—LiCc—LiO
Blood
    National security. A. MacLeish.—Plg
    The **blood** horse. Bryan W. Procter.—CoPh
"**Blood** will not serve." See A poem for heroes
The **bloodhound**. Edward Anthony.—CoG
Bloody Bill. Dennis Lee.—LeG

The **bloody** show. Joan Murray.—KhI
"**Blow** a curve." Lillian Morrison.—MoO
Blow, wind. Norma Farber.—FaS
"**Blow,** wind, blow today." See The wind
Blue alert. Eve Merriam.—MeR
Blue Bell. Unknown.—BlH
"A **blue-bell** springs upon the ledge." See
     Spring song
"A **blue** day." See March
The **blue** horse. Siv Cedering Fox.—FoB
"**Blue,** I'm not David's girl anymore." Nikki
     Grimes.—GrS
Blue jay ("So bandit eyed, so undovelike a
     bird") Robert Francis.—JaPp
Blue jays. See Jays
"The **blue** train for the south—but the green
     train for us." See The green train
"**Blueberries.**" See Indian pipe
Blueberries
     Blueberries lavender. N. D. Watson.—WaB
     "Blueberry eyes." N. D. Watson.—WaB
     Indian pipe. M. A. Hoberman.—HoY
     Yellow jacket. D. McCord.—McO
Blueberries lavender. Nancy Dingman
     Watson.—WaB
"**Blueberries** lavender, blueberries blue." See
     Blueberries lavender
"**Blueberry** eyes." Nancy Dingman Watson.—
     WaB
Bluebirds
     The last word of a bluebird. R. Frost.—HiS—
     HoMp
Blues (music)
     Blues note. B. Kaufman.—AdC
     Chromo. S. W. Fabio.—AdC
     Homage to the empress of the blues. R.
          Hayden.—AdC
     "I remember how she sang." R. Penny.—
          AdC
     The music ("Your archival voice") E.
          Hoagland.—AdC
     Poem for Otis Redding. J. C. Thomas.—AdC
     "South African bloodstone." Q. Troupe.—
          AdC
     Transformation. Q. Troupe.—AdC
Blues note. Bob Kaufman.—AdC
"**Bluff** King Hal was full of beans." See Henry
     VIII
The **bluffalo.** Jane Yolen.—YoH
Blunden, Edmund
     The dog from Malta. tr.—CoG
     The March bee.—PaB
Blunderbore. Roy Fuller.—WaG
Bly, Robert
     "The lamb was bleating softly." tr.—LiPch
     Love poem.—JaPp
     Three kinds of pleasures.—FlA
"**Bo-talee** rode easily among his enemies, once,
     twice." See The fear of Bo-talee
"A **boa** constrictor from Goa." See A boa from
     Goa
Boa constrictors
     A boa from Goa. N. M. Bodecker.—BoP
A **boa** from Goa. N. M. Bodecker.—BoP

The **boar** and the dromedar. Henry Beissel.—
     DoWh
Boats and boating. See also Canoes and
     canoeing; Ferries; Ships
     Anchored. S. Silverstein.—SiL
     Ants and sailboats. D. McCord.—McO
     The big blue frog and the dirty flannel dog.
          D. Lee.—LeG
     "The boats on the sea."—AtH
     Butterfish Bay. M. A. Hoberman.—HoY
     "Called a boatman at Charing Cross Pier."
          M. C. Livingston.—LiLl
     The cellar hole. D. McCord.—McO
     Christmas goes to sea. R. Field.—BaC
     "A flock of little boats." S. Menashe.—SaM
     In our tethered boats. L. Morrison.—MoW
     "Little Tee Wee." Mother Goose.—LoG
     Lullaby ("The long canoe") R. Hillyer.—HiD
     Midsummer. D. McCord.—McSu
     My boat. J. Prelutsky.—PrR
     Out in the boat. L. Morrison.—MoSr
     The rapid ("All peacefully gliding") C.
          Sangster.—DoWh
     The refusal to be wrecked. L. Morrison.—
          MoW
     Rowing in Lincoln Park. J. M. Brinnin.—PlL
     Sailing, sailing. L. Morrison.—MoSr
     Sailor John. D. McCord.—McO
     The ships of Yule. B. Carman.—DoWh
     To the statue. M. Swenson.—PlG
"The **boats** on the sea." Ann Atwood.—AtH
Boaz, Frank
     "When I am a man." tr.—LiCc
"**Bob** bought a hundred dollar suit." See
     Outside or underneath
Bobbing for apples. Jack Prelutsky.—PrI
Bodecker, N. M.
     A baker in France.—BoP
     Bickering.—BoHh—CoI
     A boa from Goa.—BoP
     A bride of North Conway.—BoP
     A cook whose dishes.—BoP
     A crusty mechanic.—BoP
     Day moon.—BoHh
     "Dear Sybil."—BoHh
     "The doves stay in their cotes."—BoHh
     A driver from Deering.—BoP
     An explorer named Bliss.—BoP
     A farmer of Cwm.—BoP
     Five little piggies. tr.—CoI
     "For neatness and comfort."—BoHh
     A fountain pen poem.—BoHh
     Garden calendar.—BoHh
     A gardener's roses.—BoP
     A gard'ner whose plants.—BoP
     Geronomo Hacket.—BoP
     Getting ready.—BoHh
     "Good-by my winter suit."—BoHh
     A guard at Fort Knox.—BoP
     The hat, the gown and the ring.—BoHh
     A hound of Cohasset.—BoP
     House flies.—BoHh
     "Hurry, hurry, Mary dear."—BoHh
     "I am a constant walker."—BoHh

"I'm sad today."—BoHh
Ink hats.—BoHh
John.—BeR
King Johan of Bavonia.—BoP
"The king whose crown was upside down."—
    BoHh
A kirgize in a yurt.—BoP
"The lady in gold."—BoHh
A lady in Madrid.—BoP
A lady in Plummer.—BoP
"The lady in white."—BoHh
"The lady in yellow."—BoHh
A lady of Venice.—BoP
A lass from Milwaukee.—BoP
A lass on Ben Nevis.—BoP
"A little bit of this, sir."—BoHh
Long johns.—BoHh
A maid in New York.—BoP
A maid in Old Lyme.—BoP
A maid of Great Baddow.—BoP
A man in a suit.—BoP
A man in a tree.—BoP
A man in Guam.—BoP
A man in Karachi.—BoP
A man in Northchapel.—BoP
A man of Cologne.—BoP
A maid of Great Baddow.—BoP
A man of Pennang.—BoP
A man of the dunes.—BoP
"Mice are nice."—BoHh
Midwinter.—BoHh
Milton Trimmer.—BoHh
Morning fog.—BoHh
Murdoch of Mugg.—BoP
"My dad he was a yankee."—BoHh
"My father he was a cranky old man."—
    BoHh
"Never, ever let them know."—BoHh
"Never mind the rain."—BoHh
"Night crawler."—BoHh
Occupations.—BoHh
One year.—BoHh
Owning up.—BoHh
Penny song.—BoHh
A person from Britain.—BoP
A person in Aruba.—BoP
A person in Corning.—BoP
A person in Rome.—BoP
A person in Skye.—BoP
A person in Spain.—BoP
A person in Stirling.—BoP
A person named Briggs.—BoP
A person of Deeping.—BoP
A person of Ealing.—BoP
A person of Florence.—BoP
A person of Haxey.—BoP
A person of Keene.—BoP
A person of Nigg.—BoP
A person of Pinsk.—BoP
A person of Rame.—BoP
Pitcher McDowell.—BoP
A poor man whose pajamas.—BoP
"Poundcake from Ealing."—BoHh
The rain in Maine.—BoHh

"Row, row, row."—WiP
A sheik from Riff.—BoP
"Sing me a song of teapots and trumpets."—
    BoHh
Sunflowers.—BoHh
A talented duckling.—BoP
"This is Elmer Johnson."—BoHh
"Three little guinea pigs." tr.—CoA—WiP
A traveler for Dakota.—BoP
Travelers lugging valises.—BoP
"Two cats were sitting in a tree."—WiP
"Under my hat is my hair."—BoHh
A viper named Sam.—BoP
When all the world is full of snow.—BoHh
When kings wore crowns.—BoHh
"When you stand on the tip of your nose."—
    BoHh
A woman of Ware.—BoP
Body, Human. See also names of parts of the
    body, as Hands
  Beautiful Ben. L. Morrison.—MoSr
  Here's to adhering. M. Angelou.—AnO
  "In a cottage in Fife." Mother Goose.—LoG
  Me ("My nose is blue") K. Kuskin.—KuD—
    WiP
  My body. W. J. Smith.—SmL
  Poem no. 21. D. Long.—AdC
  Stop thief. S. Silverstein.—SiL
  Unscratchable itch. S. Silverstein.—SiL
  What verve. L. Morrison.—MoO
  The wound. N. S. Momaday.—MoGd
  The young ones, flip side. J. A. Emanuel.—
    JaPp
The bog people. Joan Aiken.—AiS
Bogan, Louise
  Packet of letters.—JaPp
  To my brother.—PlL
The bogeyman. Jack Prelutsky.—PrN
The bohemian. Paul Laurence Dunbar.—BrI
Boll weevils
  The weevil ("Alfalfa, rice, and especially boll,
    the") R. S. Oliver.—OlC
Bombers and bombing
  Early warning. S. Marks.—BrO
  "Flight Sergeant Foster flattened
    Gloucester." From A leaden treasury of
    English verse, sels. P. Dehn.—BrO
  "If all the thermo-nuclear warheads." K.
    Burke.—BrO
Bond, Harold
  Foibles.—KhI
Bond, Julian
  The bishop of Atlanta, Ray Charles.—AdC
Bones
  Skeleton parade. J. Prelutsky.—PrI
  What verve. L. Morrison.—MoO
"The bones of our fathers." See Talking to the
    townsfolk in Ideal, Georgia
Bontemps, Arna
  Southern mansion.—AdC
Boo moo. David McCord.—McO
The book ("You, hiding there in your words")
    Adrienne Rich.—PlL

Boxers and boxing
  The boxer. L. Morrison.—MoSr
  Boxer pup. G. MacBeth.—MoGp
  Girl child. L. Morrison.—MoSr
  Kangaroo. W. J. Smith.—SmL
  The knockout. L. Morrison.—MoSr
Boxes
  Bundles. J. Farrar.—BaC
  "The **boxes** break." See Christmas ornaments
Boxing. See Boxers and boxing
Boy at the window. Richard Wilbur.—MaP
The **boy** fishing. E. J. Scovell.—MaP
"The **boy** in the foam." Ann Atwood.—AtH
"The **boy** in the stone." Leslie Norris.—NoM
Boy on the bus. Lee Bennett Hopkins.—HoBm
"The **boy** wasn't ready for a hat." See The
  trouble was simply that
The **boy** who laughed at Santa Claus. Ogden
  Nash.—BlC
Boy with a hammer. Russell Hoban.—JaPp
"The **boy** with a wolf's foot." Joan Aiken.—AiS
Boyden, Polly Chase
  Mud.—PaI
Boyer, Jill Witherspoon
  Detroit city.—AdC
  Dream farmer.—AdC
  King lives.—AdC
  "When brothers forget."—AdC
Boys and boyhood. See also Babies; Childhood
  recollections; Children and childhood
  Aunt Nerissa's muffin. W. Irwin.—CoPs
  Big and little. W. J. Smith.—SmL
  Boys, black. G. Brooks.—AdC
  For my father, P. Whalen.—KhI
  Fresh meat. R. Koertge.—KhI
  Here I am. M. C. Livingston.—CoI
  Knock on wood. H. Dumas.—AdC
  "Lumpy chases pigeons." J. Prelutsky.—PrRh
  Lumpy is my friend. J. Prelutsky.—PrRh
  Messy room. S. Silverstein.—SiL
  Mr. Mulligan's window. J. Prelutsky.—PrRh
  My four friends. J. Prelutsky.—PrRh
  The new pants. A. Adoff.—AdE
  No girls allowed. J. Prelutsky.—PrRh
  Nobody calls him Jim. J. Prelutsky.—PrRh
  The practical joke. J. Prelutsky.—PrRh
  The race ("Harvey think's he's something") J.
    Prelutsky.—PrRh
  Rolling Harvey down the hill. J. Prelutsky.—
    PrRh
  Smoking in the cellar. J. Prelutsky.—PrRh
  Snowflakes ("Little boys are like") N.
    Giovanni.—GiV
  "Those boys that ran together." L. Clifton.—
    AdC
  Timothy Toppin. M. A. Hoberman.—HoY
  Tony and the quarter. J. Prelutsky.—PrRh
  Willie ate a worm. J. Prelutsky.—PrRh
  Young soul. I. A. Baraka.—AdC
Boys, black. Gwendolyn Brooks.—AdC
"**Boys**, black, black boys." See Boys, black
Brabant, Suzanne
  Morgans in October.—CoPh
  Two at showtime.—CoPh

Brachiosaurus. Mary Ann Hoberman.—CoDb—
  HoY
Bradstreet, Anne
  In memory of my dear grandchild Elizabeth
    Bradstreet, who deceased August, 1665,
    being a year and half old.—PlL
  To my dear and loving husband.—PlL
Brady, June
  Far trek.—BrO
Bragg, Linda Brown
  "Our blackness did not come to us whole."—
    AdC
  A poem about beauty, blackness, poetry, and
    how to be all three.—AdC
Brains
  "Blow a curve." L. Morrison.—MoO
  The maze. L. Morrison.—MoO
  Plate tectonics on waking. L. Morrison.—
    MoO
  Problems. L. Morrison.—MoO
Brandi, John
  Turning 30 poem.—KhI
Brasier, Virginia
  Time of the mad atom.—BrO
"The **brasses** jangle and the hausers tighten."
  See The barge horse
The **bratty** brother, sister. Dennis Lee.—LeG
Braude, Michael
  "The mastodon."—CoDb
  The tyrannosaur.—CoDb
Brautigan, Richard
  The chinese checker players.—MoGp
  In a cafe.—JaPp
  Late starting dawn.—JaPp
Brave new world. Archibald MacLeish.—LiO
Brave Rover. Max Beerbohm.—CoG
Braxton, Jodi
  Sometimes I think of Maryland.—AdC
Bread
  "Fe, fi, fo, fum." Unknown.—WaG
  My Mami takes me to the bakery. C.
    Pomerantz.—PoT
  Peanut butter batter bread. A. Adoff.—AdE
  The toaster. W. J. Smith.—SmL
  Turn the oven on. A. Adoff.—AdE
  "Under this autumn sky." A. Adoff.—AdE
Breakfast
  Breakfast ("Morning, morning will produce")
    D. McCord.—McO
  Good for the head. A. Adoff.—AdE
  "Here lies a greedy girl, Jane Bevan."
    Unknown.—CoPs
  Measuring and mixing. A. Adoff.—AdE
  "Only the onions." A. Adoff.—AdE
  Sunday morning toast. A. Adoff.—AdE
Breakfast ("Morning, morning will produce")
  David McCord.—McO
Breaking through. Judith Thurman.—ThFo
Breaklight. Lucille Clifton.—LuZ
Breath and breathing
  The frost pane. D. McCord.—McO
Breath in my nostrils. Lance Jeffers.—AdC
"**Breath** in my nostrils this breasty spring day."
  See Breath in my nostrils

"A **breeze** wipes creases off my forehead." See
   Poem in June
Brews, Margery
   Unto my valentine.—LiO
Bridal song. John Fletcher.—PaB
A **bride** of North Conway. N. M. Bodecker.—
   BoP
Brides and bridegrooms
   Bridal song ("Roses, their sharp spines being
     gone") J. Fletcher.—PaB
   A bride of North Conway. N. M. Bodecker.—
     BoP
   A wedding toast. R. Wilbur.—PlL
Bridge ("Here on the river's verge he stood")
   Joan Aiken.—AiS
Bridges
   Bridge ("Here on the river's verge he stood")
     J. Aiken.—AiS
   The covered bridge house. K. Starbird.—StC
   Terrible troll's trollbridge. X. J. Kennedy.—
     KeP
   This bridge. S. Silverstein.—SiL
"**Bridges** are for going over water." See Over
   and under
Bridges, Robert
   The cliff-top, sel.
     "The cliff-top has a carpet."—MoF
   "The snow lies sprinkled on the beach."—
     PaE
   "Spring goeth all in white."—SaM
Brierley, Ronald Oliver
   "Oodnadatta."—DuSn
   Un-natural history.—DuSn
"**Bright** as a fallen fragment of the sky." See
   The rock pool
"**Bright** clasp of her whole hand around my
   finger." See To my daughter
A **bright** idea. From A lot of limericks. X. J.
   Kennedy.—KeP
"A **bright** mountaintop." See V is for volcano
"**Bring** an old towel, said Pa." See Buying a
   puppy
"**Bring** me the livery of no other man." See
   The bohemian
"**Bring** the comb and play upon it." Robert
   Louis Stevenson.—MoF
Bring your pipes. Unknown.—BaC
"**Bring** your pipes and bring your drum." See
   Bring your pipes
Brinnin, John Malcolm
   Address to the refugees.—PlG
   American plan.—PlG
   A New England sampler.—PlG
   Rowing in Lincoln Park.—PlL
"The **brittle** grass." See After a freezing rain
"**Broad** August burns in milky skies." See Day
   dreams
"The **broad** beach." See Afternoon, Amagansett
   beach
"A **broken** saucer of the sea." See At low tide
Broken sky. Carl Sandburg.—JaPp
The **broncho** that would not be broken. Vachel
   Lindsay.—CoPh

Bronco busting, event #1. May Swenson.—
   CoPh
The **brontosaurus**. H.A.C. Evans.—CoDb
"The **brontosaurus** ranged the earth." See The
   brontosaurus
The **brook** in February. Charles G. D.
   Roberts.—DoWh
"The **brook** moves slowly." Ann Atwood.—AtH
Brooks. See Streams
Brooks, Gwendolyn
   A black wedding song.—AdC
   Boys, black.—AdC
   Five men against the theme, my name is red
     hot, yo name ain' doodley squat.—AdC
   Friend.—AdC
   Horses graze.—AdC
   The last quatrain of the ballad of Emmett
     Till.—AdC
   Malcolm X.—AdC—LiO
   Martin Luther King Jr.—AdC
   Of Dewitt Williams on his way to Lincoln
     cemetery.—FlA
   Otto.—LiCc—LiPch
   Paul Robeson.—AdC
   A penitent considers another coming of
     Mary.—LiPch
Brooks, Phillips
   A Christmas carol, sel.
     "Look, the earth is aflame with
       delight."—BaC
   "The dark night wakes, the glory breaks."
     See O little town of Bethlehem
   "Look, the earth is aflame with delight. See
     A Christmas carol
   O little town of Bethlehem, sel.
     "The dark night wakes, the glory
       breaks."—BaC
Brooms
   "Around and around a dusty little room." M.
     Johnson.—WiP
   Witch's broom. D. McCord.—McSu
Brooms ("On stormy days") Dorothy Aldis.—
   PaI
The **broomstick** train, sel. Oliver Wendell
   Homes
   "Look out, look out, boys, clear the track."—
     BrIt
Brother ("I had a little brother") Mary Ann
   Hoberman.—CoI—HoY
Brother and sister. Lewis Carroll.—WiP
Brotherhood
   To my brothers. J. Keats.—PlL
   "When black people are." A. B. Spellman.—
     AdC
   "When brothers forget." J. W. Boyer.—AdC
Brothers. See also Brothers and sisters
   Adaptation of a theme by Catullus. A. Tate.—
     PlL
   The bratty brother, sister. D. Lee.—LeG
   Brother ("I had a little brother") M. A.
     Hoberman.—CoI—HoY
   The brothers ("Last night I watched my
     brothers play") E. Muir.—PlL

Brothers ("That handsome little chimpanzee") W. Cole.—CoA
Cain. L. Clifton.—PlL
Cain and Abel. From Genesis.—PlL
Carl. M. Van Doren.—PlL
"Father says." M. Rosen.—CoI
The four brothers. C. Pomerantz.—PoT
In the tree house at night. J. Dickey.—PlL
It isn't. E. Merriam.—MeW
A meditation. H. Melville.—PlG
The parable of the prodigal son. From Gospel according to Luke.—PlL
The prodigal son. T. Spencer.—PlL
To his brother dead. G. V. Catullus.—PlL
To his brother Hsing-Chien. Po Chu-i.—PlL
To my brother. L. Bogan.—PlL
Tom McGreevy, in America, thinks of himself as a boy. From Our stars come from Ireland. W. Stevens.—PlG
Two in bed. A. B. Ross.—PaI
   "When my brother Tommy."—MoF
The brothers ("Last night I watched my brothers play") Edwin Muir.—PlL
Brothers ("That handsome little chimpanzee") William Cole.—CoA
Brothers and sisters
Bad boy's swan song. W. J. Smith.—CoI
Brother and sister. L. Carroll.—WiP
"Feeling special." N. Grimes.—GrS
"For thou art with me here upon the banks." From Lines composed a few miles above Tintern Abbey. W. Wordsworth.—PlL
Impetuous Samuel. H. Graham.—CoI
Let her have it. W. Cole.—HeB
Little. D. Aldis.—PaI
   "I am the sister of him."—MoF
"Little sister." N. Grimes.—GrS
"Mama never understood." N. Grimes.—GrS
Measuring and mixing. A. Adoff.—AdE
My own room. N. D. Watson.—RuM
My sister Jane. T. Hughes.—HiS
Reggie. E. Greenfield.—GrH
Rhinos purple, hippos green. M. P. Hearn.—HeB
A sister's grave. R. N. Peck.—PeB
Spoiled sister song. M. C. Livingston.—LiF
To his brother Hsing-Chien. Po Chu-i.—PlL
Winter verse for his sister. W. Meredith.—PlL
Brown (color)
Chocolate chocolate. A. Adoff.—AdE
"**Brown** and furry." See The caterpillar
Brown, Audrey Alexandra
The strangers.—DoWh
The **brown** birds. Eleanor Farjeon.—BaC
Brown eyes are watching. Norma Farber.—FaS
"**Brown** furry rabbit." Betsy Maestro.—MaFp
Brown, H. Rap (about)
H. Rap Brown. H. Blakely.—AdC
Brown, Margaret Wise
The leaves fall down.—WiP
Old snake has gone to sleep.—WiP
The sad sliced onion.—WiP
The secret song.—WiP

Brown, Palmer
"The spangled pandemonium."—WaM
Brown, Sterling A.
An old woman remembers.—AdC
Strange legacies.—AdC
Strong men.—AdC
Brown, T. E.
Scarlett rocks.—PaE
Browne, Michael Dennis
Iowa.—FlA
Brownies. See Fairies
Browning, Elizabeth Barrett
Sonnets from the Portuguese, sel.
   "Unlike are we, unlike, O princely heart."—PlL
"Unlike are we, unlike, O princely heart." See Sonnets from the Portuguese
Browning, Robert
Home thoughts, from abroad.—PaB
Pippa passes, sel.
   "The year's at the spring."—MoF
   Pippa's song.—PaB
Pippa's song. See Pippa passes
To E.B.B., sel.
   "What were seen, none knows, none ever shall know."—PlL
"What were seen, none knows, none ever shall know." See To E.B.B.
"The year's at the spring." See Pippa passes
Brownjohn, Alan
Chameleon.—SaM
To see the rabbit.—WiP
Bruchac, Joseph
Birdfoot's grampa.—MoGp
Bryant, F. J.
Patience of a people.—AdC
Bubble gum. Myra Cohn Livingston.—LiF
Bubbles
Bubble gum. M. C. Livingston.—LiF
Forever blowing. N. Farber.—FaS
I only watch the bubbles. N. Giovanni.—GiV
Soap bubble. V. Worth.—WoM
"**Bucephalus** is neighing me a love song." See Hossolalia
Buck, Chief John
Memorial ode.—PlG
Buckin' bronco. Shel Silverstein.—SiL
Budbill, David
New York in the spring.—MoGp
Buddha
"Person after person." From Oraga Haru. Issa.—LiO
Buff. Mother Goose.—BlH
Buffalo dusk. Carl Sandburg.—PlG
Buffaloes
The beefalo. J. Gardner.—GaCb
Buffalo dusk. C. Sandburg.—PlG
"I rise, I rise." Unknown.—FlA
Plainview: 4. N. S. Momaday.—MoGd
The trail beside the River Platte. W. Heyen.—PlG
Unreal the buffalo is standing. Unknown.—PlG
The water buffalo. J. Gardner.—GaCb

Butterfly ("Metamorphosis") M. A. Hoberman.—HoBu
Butterfly ("Of living creatures most I prize") W. J. Smith.—SmL
Butterfly ("Said he didn't know") D. McCord.—McSu
Caterpillar's lullaby. J. Yolen.—YoD
Cocoon ("I found a little sleeping bag") A. Fisher.—FiO
Flying crooked. R. Graves.—JaPp—LuZ
In payment. A. Fisher.—FiO
Mari Rosa and the butterfly. C. Pomerantz.—PoT
"The sun finally tolerable." From Autumn nature notes. T. Hughes.—HuSs
To a tiger swallowtail butterfly. M. A. Hoberman.—HoBu
Twice born. A. Fisher.—FiO
White butterfly. Tai Wang-Shu.—LuZ
"**Butterflies** roost." David Kherdian.—KhC
Butterfly ("The butterfly it's") Peter Armstrong.—JaPp
Butterfly ("Metamorphosis") Mary Ann Hoberman.—HoBu
Butterfly ("Of living creatures most I prize") William Jay Smith.—SmL
Butterfly ("Said he didn't know") David McCord.—McSu
"The **butterfly**, a cabbage white." See Flying crooked
"The **butterfly** it's." See Butterfly
"**Butterfly** trembles when the wind blows." See Notes
"A **buttery**, sugary, syrupy waffle." See The groaning board
Buttons of gold. Aileen Fisher.—FiO
"**Buy** our little magazine." See Do it yourself
Buying a puppy. Leslie Norris.—NoM
Buying and selling. See Markets and marketing; Peddlers and venders; Shops and shopkeepers
The **buzzard.** John Gardner.—GaCb
"**By** day the bat is cousin to the mouse." See The bat
"**By** end of March, the cold will ease." See September creek
"**By** flat tink." See Bell
By Frazier Creek Falls. Gary Snyder.—PlG
"**By** mid-Fibruary moonlight." Doris Orgel.—OrM
By myself. Eloise Greenfield.—GrH
"**By** rocket, to visit the moon." See Interplanetary limericks
By rugged ways. Paul Laurence Dunbar.—BrI
"**By** rugged ways and thro' the night." See By rugged ways
"**By** that withering oak." See Daybreak
"**By** the pool that I see in my dreams, dear love." See The pool
"**By** the rude bridge that arched the flood." See Concord hymn
By the saltings. Ted Walker.—PaE
By the sea ("Morning") Eve Merriam.—MeR

By the sea ("Why does the sea moan evermore") Christina Rossetti.—PaE
"**By** the shores of Lake Michigan." See The Great Lakes suite—Lake Michigan
By the shores of Pago Pago. Eve Merriam.—MeR
By the stream. Paul Laurence Dunbar.—BrI
"**By** the stream I dream in calm delight, and watch as in a glass." See By the stream
"**By** the stream, squatting." See Assassination poems—Knowing it
"**By** the wave rising, by the wave breaking." See The crow
"**By** ways remote and distant waters sped." See To his brother dead
"**Bye** baby Bunting." See Boston nursery rhymes — Rhyme for astronomical baby
Bye baby walnut. Norma Farber.—FaS
Bynner, Witter
Arrowy dreams.—PlG
On New Year's eve. tr.—LiO
The sandpiper.—PaE
Spring thoughts. tr.—LiO
Byron, George Gordon (Noel), Lord
Epigram on my wedding day.—PlL
Epitaph to a dog.—CoG
The ocean.—PaE

C

C is for cabbages. William Jay Smith.—SmL
Cabbages
C is for cabbages. W. J. Smith.—SmL
Moon cabbage. T. Hughes.—HuM
Nocturn cabbage. C. Sandburg.—HiD
"**Cabbages** catch at the moon." See Nocturn cabbage
"**Cabbages** on the moon are not cabbages." See Moon cabbage
Cachita. Charlotte Pomerantz.—PoT
"**Cachita** is a little dog." See Cachita
Cactus sickness. Ted Hughes.—HuM
Cain. Lucille Clifton.—PlL
Cain
Cain. L. Clifton.—PlL
Cain and Abel. From Genesis.—PlL
Cain and Abel. See Genesis
Cake. See From the kitchen—Cake
"A **cake** of soap, a toothpick mast." See Ivory
Cakes and cookies
Catherine. K. Kuskin.—KuD
"Duckle, duckle, daisy." L. F. Jackson.—BaC
"Handy-spandy." Mother Goose.—LoG
"The moon's the north wind's cooky." V. Lindsay.—RuM
"**Caleb** likes a good sad clown." See Circus
Calico ball. Nancy Dingman Watson.—WaB
California
The California oaks. Y. Winters.—PlG
The **California** oaks. Yvor Winters.—PlG
"**Call** for the robin red breast and the wren." See The white devil—Cornelia's song

"**Called** a boatman at Charing Cross Pier."
Myra Cohn Livingston.—LiLl
"**Calling** black people." See SOS
Calvary. Edwin Arlington Robinson.—LiO
Calves
A March calf. T. Hughes.—HuSs
Camel ("The camel has a heavy bump") Mary
Ann Hoberman.—HoY
The **camel** ("The camel has a single hump")
Ogden Nash.—BlC
Camel ("The camel is a long-legged
humpbacked beast") William Jay Smith.—
SmL
The **camel** ("God and the Son and Muhammad
the Prince") John Gardner.—GaCb
"The **camel** has a heavy bump." See Camel
"The **camel** has a single hump." See The camel
"The **camel** is a long-legged humpbacked
beast." See Camel
Camels
Camel ("The camel has a heavy bump") M.
A. Hoberman.—HoY
The camel ("The camel has a single hump")
O. Nash.—BlC
Camel ("The camel is a long-legged
humpbacked beast") W. J. Smith.—SmL
The camel ("God and the Son and
Muhammad the Prince") J. Gardner.—
GaCb
The camels, the Kings' camels. L. Norris.—
LiPch—NoM
"In dromedary Fibruary." D. Orgel.—OrM
A sheik from Riff. N. M. Bodecker.—BoP
"They've put a brassiere on the camel." S.
Silverstein.—SiL
Twelfth night. E. Coatsworth.—BaC
The **camels**, the Kings' camels. Leslie Norris.—
LiPch—NoM
"The **camels**, the Kings' camels, haie-aie." See
The camels, the Kings' camels
"**Camera** one, take." See Highway one, movie
camera
"**Cammie** takes the fly swatter." See Spotter
and swatter
Campbell, Joan
A sealess world.—PaE
Campbell, Joseph
Harvest song.—LiCc—LiO
"I will go with my father a-ploughing."—LiO
"I will go with my father a-reaping."—
LiCc (sel.)
"I will go with my father a-reaping." See "I
will go with my father a-ploughing"
Campbell, Wilfrid
Indian summer.—DoWh
Campfire. Judith Thurman.—ThFo
Camping and hiking
Campfire. J. Thurman.—ThFo
Eat it all Elaine. K. Starbird.—CoPs—WiP
The hiker. E. Merriam.—MeR
The pole bean tent. K. Starbird.—StC
Slim Slater. K. Starbird.—StC
Watch out. K. Starbird.—StC

Campion, Thomas
In praise of Neptune.—PaE
"**Can** a mere human brain stand the stress and
the strain." See Capsule philosophy
"**Can** anybody tell me, please." See Help
Can I get you a glass of water, or please close
the glottis after you. Ogden Nash.—BlC
"**Can** the single cup of wine." See To his
brother Hsing-Chien
"**Can** you ride the buckin' bronco." See Buckin'
bronco
Canada
At St. Jerome. F. Harrison.—DoWh
Canada—History
1838. D. Lee.—LeN
The **canal** bank. James Stephens.—YaI
Canaries
The canary ("The song of canaries") O.
Nash.—BlC
"In Fibruary, my canary." D. Orgel.—OrM
The **canary** ("The song of canaries") Ogden
Nash.—BlC
"**Candle**, candle, burning bright." See
Christmas chant
Candles
Christmas candle. R. Field.—BaC
Christmas candles. A. Fisher.—BaC
Green candles. H. Wolfe.—WiP
"Jack be nimble." Mother Goose.—TrGg
Candy
"After covering the continent." A. Adoff.—
AdE
Chocolate chocolate. A. Adoff.—AdE
Conversation hearts. N. Payne.—LiCc
The cupboard. W. De La Mare.—PaI
"Huckleberry, gooseberry, raspberry pie."
From Father fox's pennyrhymes. C.
Watson.—LiCc
Jujubes. D. McCord.—McSu
"The reason I like chocolate." N. Giovanni.—
GiV
"Rock candy: hard sweet crystals on a
string." From A Christmas package. D.
McCord.—McO
Sweets. V. Worth.—WoSm
When candy was chocolate. W. J. Smith.—
SmL
Canine amenities. Unknown.—CoG
Cannibals
"A thousand hairy savages." S. Milligan.—
CoPs
Cannon arrested. Michael S. Harper.—AdC
Cannon park. Mark St. Germain.—JaPp
Canoes and canoeing
The rapid ("All peacefully gliding") C.
Sangster.—DoWh
"**Canst** thou draw out leviathan with an hook,
or his." See Job—Leviathan
The **canterpillar.** Jane Yolen.—YoH
"The **canterpillar** comes and goes." See The
canterpillar

A **canticle** to the waterbirds, sel. Brother
     Antoninus
   "Clack your beaks you cormorants and
     kittiwakes."—PaE
Canton, William
   Day dreams.—PaB
"**Capital** letters prompting every line." See
     Poem, a reminder
Capsule philosophy. Felicia Lamport.—BrO
Captain Blackbeard did what. Shel
     Silverstein.—SiL
"**Car.**" See Car wash
Car wash. Myra Cohn Livingston.—LiWt
The **carcajou** and the kincajou. Ogden Nash.—
     BlC
Cardigan bay. John Masefield.—PaE
Cardinals (birds). See Red birds
"**Careen.**" See Irish tune
"**Careless** and still." See The rabbit hunter
Carew, Thomas
   Song.—PaB
Carey, N.
   The wind.—SaM
Carl. Mark Van Doren.—PlL
Carman, Bliss
   The ships of Yule.—DoWh
Carol ("I saw a sweet, a seemly sight")
     Unknown.—BaC
Carol ("Villagers all, this frosty tide") From
     The wind in the willows. Kenneth
     Grahame.—BaC
   "Villagers all, this frosty tide."—LiPch
Carol for a New Zealand child. Dorothy Neal
     White.—BaC
Carol of the birds ("A star rose in the sky")
     Unknown, fr. the Spanish.—BaC
Carol of the birds ("Whence comes this rush of
     wings afar") Unknown, fr. the French.—
     BaC
Carol of the brown king. Langston Hughes.—
     BaC—LiCc—LiPch
Carol of the three kings. W. S. Merwin.—LiPch
Carousel brunch. Norma Farber.—FaS
Carousels. See Merry-go-rounds
Carpenter ants. Mary Ann Hoberman.—HoBu
Carpenters and carpentry
   Trades. A. Lowell.—PaI
Carr, Mary Jane
   Halloween.—BrIt
"**Carree** my cousin's." See Cousin Carree's
     cubic cuisine
Carriages and carts
   Going to town. F. Lape.—CoPh
   How we drove the trotter. W. T. Goodge.—
     CoPh
   "Up at Piccadilly, oh." Mother Goose.—TrGg
Carriers of the dream wheel. N. Scott
     Momaday.—MoGd
**Carroll, Lewis, pseud. (Charles Lutwidge
     Dodgson)**
   Alice's adventures in wonderland, sel.
     Beautiful soup.—WiP
     The mock turtle's song.—WiP

   "You are old, Father William, the young
     man said."—WiP
Beautiful soup. See Alice's adventures in
     wonderland
Brother and sister.—WiP
The mock turtle's song. See Alice's
     adventures in wonderland
Through the looking-glass, sel.
     The walrus and the carpenter.—WiP
The walrus and the carpenter. See Through
     the looking-glass
"You are old, Father William, the young man
     said." See Alice's adventures in wonderland
Carruth, Hayden
   My father's face.—PlL
"**Carrying** my world." See Father
"**Cars** are wicked, poets think." See Man on
     wheels
Castillo, Ana
   Mi maestro.—LuZ
"A **castle** has." See Having
Castor oil. David McCord.—McO
Cat ("The black cat yawns") Mary Britton
     Miller.—CoA
Cat ("Cats are not at all like people") William
     Jay Smith.—SmL
Cat ("Missak on his") David Kherdian.—KhC
Cat ("Old Mog comes in and sits on the
     newspaper") Joan Aiken.—AiS
The **cat** ("One gets a wife, one gets a house")
     Ogden Nash.—BlC
The **cat** ("While you read") William
     Matthews.—LuZ
The **cat** ("Within that porch, across the way")
     W. H. Davies.—SaM
Cat ("The yellow bedspread") David
     Kherdian.—KhC
Cat and mouse. Robert Newton Peck.—PeB
The **cat** and the dog. John Gardner.—GaCb
The **cat** and the wizard. Dennis Lee.—LeN
"A **cat** as black." See Black cat
Cat bath. Valerie Worth.—WoSm
The **cat** heard the cat-bird. John Ciardi.—HiS
The **cat** lady. Kaye Starbird.—StC
Cat of cats. William Brighty Rands.—CoA
"The **cat** was once a weaver." See What the
     gray cat sings
The **cat** who aspired to higher things. X. J.
     Kennedy.—KeP
"**Cat,** who hast pass'd thy grand climacteric."
     See Sonnet to a cat
The **cataclysm.** Edward Shanks.—PaE
"The **Catalina** mountains romp, saddled with
     snow." See Dickey in Tucson
"**Catapulted** by charm." See Volare
A **catch.** Mary Ann Hoberman.—HoY
"**Catch** a smile." See How to be serious
A **catch** by the hearth. Unknown.—BaC
"**Catch** the blues song." See Transformation
Catching. Shel Silverstein.—SiL
Catching a horse. Barbara Winder.—CoPh
Catching-song a play rhyme. Eleanor
     Farjeon.—WiP

True. L. Moore.—WiP
"Two cats were sitting in a tree." N. M. Bodecker.—WiP
"The two gray kits." Mother Goose.—TrGg
Victims 3 cat 0. D. Kherdian.—KhC
What the gray cat sings. A. Guiterman.—WiP
White cat. R. Knister.—DoWh
"Who's that ringing at the front door bell." Mother Goose.—WiP
The witch's cat. I. Serraillier.—HiS
Y is for yarn. W. J. Smith.—SmL
"A young man from old Terre Haute." W. J. Smith.—SmL
"Cats and owls." See Boo moo
"Cats are not at all like people." See Cat
Cats sleep fat. Rosalie Moore.—MoGp
"Cats sleep fat and walk thin." See Cats sleep fat
Cattle. See also Calves; Cows
"Cows are coming home in Maine." R.P.T. Coffin.—HiD
The moon bull. T. Hughes.—HuM
The musk ox. J. Gardner.—GaCb
The oxen. T. Hardy.—BaC—LiPch
"The quiet eyed cattle." L. Norris.—LiPch—NoM
Catullus Gaius Valerius
To his brother dead.—PlL
Causley, Charles
"Quack, said the billy goat."—BeR—CoA
Riley.—HiS
"Tell me, tell me, Sarah Jane."—WiP
A caution to everybody. Ogden Nash.—BlC
"Consider the auk."—BrO
Cavalry
Tallyho-hum. O. Nash.—CoPh
The war horse. From Job.—CoPh
War horses. W. Cole.—CoPh
"The caved in cardboard box." See Words, like spiders
Cavendish, Margaret, Duchess of Newcastle
Song by Lady Happy, as a sea-goddess.—PaE
Caves
Grim and gloomy. J. Reeves.—SaM
"Caw, caw, caw." See Many crows, any owl
"Ceaselessly he watched TV." See Addict
Cecilia. Unknown, tr. fr. the French by William McLennan.—DoWh
Celery. Ogden Nash.—BlC—CoPs
"Celery, raw." See Celery
"Celestial choir, enthroned in realms of light." See To his excellency George Washington
A cellar and an attic. Donald Finkel.—MoGp
"A cellar and an attic are friends." See A cellar and an attic
The cellar hole. David McCord.—McO
Cellars
A cellar and an attic. D. Finkel.—MoGp
The cellar hole. D. McCord.—McO
Smoking in the cellar. J. Prelutsky.—PrRh
Cemeteries. See also Epitaphs; Tombs
Horse graveyard. F. Lape.—CoPh
Rainy mountain cemetery. N. S. Momaday.—MoGd

Voices of heroes overheard in a churchyard dedicated to the memory of 1776. H. Gregory.—LiO
Waldheim cemetery. R. Sward.—FlA
"The cemetery stone New England autumn." See Voices of heroes, overheard in a churchyard dedicated to the memory of 1776
The centaur. May Swenson.—CoPh—HiS
Centaurs
The centaur. M. Swenson.—CoPh—HiS
The centerpede. Jane Yolen.—YoH
"The centerpede on one flat foot." See The centerpede
Centipede ("A dollar is a hundred cents") Mary Ann Hoberman.—HoBu
The centipede ("I objurgate the centipede") Ogden Nash.—BlC
Centipede ("This centipede has fifty legs") David McCord.—McO
Centipedes
Centipede ("A dollar is a hundred cents") M. A. Hoberman.—HoBu
The centipede ("I objurgate the centipede") O. Nash.—BlC
Centipede ("This centipede has fifty legs") D. McCord.—McO
Sticky situation. From A lot of limericks. X. J. Kennedy.—KeP
Central Park West. Stanley Moss.—JaPp
"Centre of equal daughters, equal sons." See America
"Century Farms." See Once upon a nag
The ceremonial band. James Reeves.—WiP
Ceremonies for Christmas, sel. Robert Herrick
"Wassail the trees, that they may bear."—LiPch
"A certain old widow of Chipping." Myra Cohn Livingston.—LiLl
A certain peace. Nikki Giovanni.—AdC
A certain sandpiper. X. J. Kennedy.—KeP
"A certain young person of Ealing." See A person of Ealing
"Chaff is in my eye." See Preoccupation
Chaffin, Lillie D.
Haiku, for Cinnamon.—CoPh
Chaikin, Miriam
I hate Harry.—CoI
"Chains, my good lord, in your raised brows I read." See Columbus
Chamber music, sel. James Joyce
"All day I hear the noise of waters."—SaM
The chambered nautilus. Oliver Wendell Holmes.—PaE
Chameleon. Alan Brownjohn.—SaM
The chameleon. John Gardner.—GaCb
Chameleons. See Lizards
"Chang McTang McQuarter cat." John Ciardi.—WiP
Change
Arrowy dreams. W. Bynner.—PlG
Brave new world. A. MacLeish.—LiO
Breaking through. J. Thurman.—ThFo
Bulldozers. F. Dec.—JaPp

Hen ("The little red hen does not write with a pen") W. J. Smith.—SmL

The hens. E. M. Roberts.—PaI

"Higgleby, piggleby, my black hen." Mother Goose.—TrGg

"I had a little hen." Mother Goose.—WiP

"In a roostery somewhere near Fen." M. C. Livingston.—LiLl

Opening the door and entering the barnyard, etc. D. Kherdian.—KhC

Papa bantam's goodnight. J. Yolen.—YoD

Plymouth Rocks, of course. D. McCord.—McO

Polyglot. E. Merriam.—MeR

"Probable-Possible, my black hen." From The space child's Mother Goose. F. Winsor.—BrO

The riddle ("Why does the chicken cross the road") K. Starbird.—StC

Rooster rue. N. D. Watson.—WaB

Roosters. E. Coatsworth.—HiS—WiP

Chico. Lillian Morrison.—MoSr

"Chief of our aunts, not only I." See To auntie

Child. See Song of the banner at daybreak

Child dead in old seas. Maya Angelou.—AnO

"The child enquires about his ancestors." See Ancestors

A child is born. Mary Ann Hamburger.—BaC

"The child is father to the man." Gerard Manley Hopkins.—PlL

"The child is on my shoulder." See Laughing child

"Child of my winter, born." See Heart's needle

"The child that came a stranger from." See Lyric for the father of a girl

"A child went out one day." See I eat kids yum yum

The child who cried. Felice Holman.—HoBm

Childhood. See Childhood recollections; Children and childhood

Childhood recollections

After supper. H. McNamar.—LuZ

"And in the cold, bleak winter time." From Moonlight. W.G. Vincent.—FlA

Apple scoop. E. Glen.—MoGp

Autobiographia literaria. F. O'Hara.—KhI

The Bagley Iowa poem. A. Darr.—KhI

Beginnings and endings. P. Koestenbaum.—KhI

"The boy in the foam." A. Atwood.—AtH

The chinese checker players. R. Brautigan.—MoGp

Class of 19—. F. Dec.—JaPp

Conversation about Christmas, the useful presents. From A child's Christmas in Wales. D. Thomas.—LiPch

Conversation about Christmas, the useless presents. From A child's Christmas in Wales. D. Thomas.—LiPch

The cultivation of Christmas trees. T. S. Eliot.—LiO

December fragments. R. Lattimore.—LiPch

Elegy. T. Roethke.—PlL

Emma. Yvonne.—AdC

Father's voice. W. Stafford.—PlL

The first poem I ever wrote. N. Shihab.—KhI

For the sisters of the Hotel Dieu. A. M. Klein.—DoWh

In those times. A. Block.—KhI

Jesus drum. P. C. Lomax.—AdC

Love necessitates. E. Redmond.—AdC

Mothers ("The last time I was home") N. Giovanni.—AdC

"My father played the melodeon." From A Christmas childhood. P. Kavanagh.—LiPch

"My father remembers." J. Aiken.—AiS

"My father's forebears were all Midland yeomen." From Letter to Lord Byron. W. H. Auden.—PlL

My mother's sister. C. D. Lewis.—PlL

My nurse. S. Shu Ning Liu.—KhI

My papa's waltz. T. Roethke.—MaP

Nowata. D. Ray.—KhI

Ode: Intimations of immortality from recollections of early childhood, sels. W. Wordsworth.—PlL

Of kings and things. L. Morrison.—MoSr

Once upon a great holiday. A. Wilkinson.—DoWh

Orange ("Once the long season had us in its reach") V. Gale.—KhI

Otto. T. Roethke.—PlL

Piano lessons. C. Clayton.—LuZ

Poem at thirty. S. Sanchez.—AdC

Prospectus. J. Nieto.—LuZ

The rain reminds me. J. Moore.—MoGp

"Remembering Grandma filling up this porch." N. Grimes.—GrS

Rowing in Lincoln Park. J. M. Brinnin.—PlL

Scrapbooks. N. Giovanni.—AdC

A snapshot of the Auxiliary. R. Hugo.—KhI

So will I. C. Zolotow.—HoBm

Sometimes I think of Maryland. J. Braxton.—AdC

The song turning back into itself. A. Young.—AdC

Thanksgiving ("In childhood you think") J. N. Morris.—LiO

"They're tearing down a town." J. Strunk.—BrO

Those winter Sundays. R. Hayden.—AdC—MaP—PlL

Visitor ("Old tree") M. C. Livingston.—LiF

The walnut tree. D. McCord.—McO

The way it is. G. Oden.—AdC

The winter of the separation. P. Booth.—PlL

Wood box ("Behind the old black kitchen stove.") R. N. Peck.—PeB

Zimmer in grade school. P. Zimmer.—KhI

"Children." See Children and other creatures

"The children." See Recess

Children and childhood

Alarm ("Mother come quick") X. J. Kennedy.—KeP

Albert. D. Abse.—MaP

Andrew's bedtime story. I. Serraillier.—HiD

Any day now. D. McCord.—BrO

Around my room. W. J. Smith.—SmL

"Our birth is but a sleep and a forgetting."
From Ode: Intimations of immortality from recollections of early childhood. W. Wordsworth.—PlL
The outlaw. F. Holman.—CoI
"Outside, I want to play." N. Grimes.—GrS
Palace cook's tale. J. Aiken.—AiS
The park at evening. L. Norris.—HiD
Party in winter. K. Shapiro.—JaPp
A pavane for the nursery. W. J. Smith.—HiD
Put something in. S. Silverstein.—SiL
Rain ("What a day, does it rain, is it rainy") D. McCord.—McSu
Request. M. Angelou.—AnO
Rest hour. G. Johnston.—DoWh
The right place. M. C. Livingston.—LiWt
Rites of passage. A. Lorde.—AdC
Rock 'n' roll band. S. Silverstein.—SiL
Rough. S. Spender.—MaP
The sad child's song. M. Van Doren.—HiS
"Sally over the water." Unknown.—WiP
A sandpile town. A. Fisher.—FiO
Saturday's child. C. Cullen.—LiO
Science for the young. W. Irwin.—BrO
Sea-change. W. Gibson.—PaE
"She sent me out to play again." N. Grimes.—GrS
A small elegy. R. Snyder.—JaPp
"The snow lies sprinkled on the beach." R. Bridges.—PaE
Some cook. J. Ciardi.—CoPs
Spoiled sister song. M. C. Livingston.—LiF
Suddenly. A. Fisher.—HoMp
Supermarket. F. Holman.—BrO
Sweet Diane. G. Barlow.—AdC
Tableau at twilight. O. Nash.—BlC—CoPs
"Tell me, tell me, Sarah Jane." C. Causley.—WiP
"There was a child went forth every day." From Leaves of grass. W. Whitman.—PaB
Thesis, antithesis, and nostalgia. A. Dugan.—JaPp
Those last, late hours of Christmas eve. L. A. Welte.—LiPch
Ticklish Tom. S. Silverstein.—SiL
Tiptoe ("On tiptoe") F. Holman.—HoA
Tiptoe ("Yesterday I skipped all day") K. Kuskin.—KuD
To a child running with outstretched arms in Canyon de Chelly. N. S. Momaday.—MoGd
To a small boy standing on my shoes while I am wearing them. O. Nash.—BlC
To auntie. R. L. Stevenson.—PlL
Tommy's mommy. N. Giovanni.—GiV
The twins ("Likeness has made them animal and shy") K. Shapiro.—PlL
Two people. E. Merriam.—MeW
Union for children's rights. S. Silverstein.—SiL
Unrealized. T. Hardy.—PlL
Up in the pine. N. D. Watson.—WaB
Venus in the tropics. L. Simpson.—KhI
"Waiting for someone to play with." N. Grimes.—GrS

Watch out. K. Starbird.—StC
The waves of the sea. E. Farjeon.—SaM
What someone said when he was spanked on the day before his birthday. J. Ciardi.—BeR
When candy was chocolate. W. J. Smith.—SmL
Where. K. Patchen.—LuZ
Whipping apples. R. N. Peck.—PeB
"William and Mary, George and Anne." Mother Goose.—TrGg
William's toys. K. Kuskin.—KuD
The wind has wings. Unknown.—DoWh
The worst. S. Silverstein.—CoI
"Yea, there thou makest me sad and makest me sin." From King Henry IV. W. Shakespeare.—PlL
A year later. M. A. Hoberman.—HoY
You and me. N. D. Watson.—WaB
Children and other creatures. Felice Holman.—HoA
"**Children** are as good as gold." See Good and bad
"**Children** aren't happy with nothing to ignore." See The parent
"**Children** born of fairy stock." See I'd love to be a fairy's child
"**Children**, if you dare to think." See Warning to children
"**Children** of mine, not mine but lent." See Godchildren
Children of the desert, sel. Byrd Baylor
"This is no place."—MoGp
"**Children** we have not borne." See To my daughter the junkie on a train
The **children's** carol. Eleanor Farjeon.—LiPch
"**Children's** children are the crown of old men." See Proverbs, sels. Bible—Old Testament
A **child's** Christmas in Wales, sels. Dylan Thomas
Conversation about Christmas, the useful presents.—LiPch
Conversation about Christmas, the useless presents.—LiPch
Child's game. Judson Jerome.—HiD
A **child's** song. Dennis Lee.—LeN
"**Chill** December brings the sleet." See The garden year
Chimes. See Bells
Chinaware. See Tableware
The **chinese** checker players. Richard Brautigan.—MoGp
The **Chinese** greengrocers. Pat Lowther.—LuZ
Chinese nursery rhymes. See Nursery rhymes—Chinese
Chipmunk ("I saw a little chipmunk") Aileen Fisher.—FiO
Chipmunks
Chipmunk ("I saw a little chipmunk") A. Fisher.—FiO
The chipmunk's song. R. Jarrell.—CoA
"**Chipmunks** jump, and." See Valentine
The **chipmunk's** song. Randall Jarrell.—CoA
Chirping. Aileen Fisher.—FiO

"Christmas is coming, the geese are getting fat." Unknown.—LiCc—LiPch
    Christmas.—BaC
Christmas lights. V. Worth.—LiPch—WoM
Christmas morning ("Christmas bells, awake and ring") H. Behn.—LiCc—LiPch
Christmas morning ("If Bethlehem were here today") E.M. Roberts.—LiCc—LiPch
Christmas 1959 et cetera. G. W. Barrax.—LiO—LiPch
A Christmas package, sels. D. McCord.—McO (Complete)
    1. "I hung up a stocking"
    2. "Here's that little girl who wraps up each gift"
    3. "Asked for another name for Santa Claus"
    4. "Rock candy: hard sweet crystals on a string"
    5. "Alert live reindeer galloping on air"
    6. "Though holly halos hang from many a nail"
    7. "That broken star."—LiPch
    8. "My stocking's where."—LiPch
        Christmas eve.—LiCc
    9. "A collar for Sokko"
Christmas pies. Unknown.—BaC
A Christmas prayer. G. MacDonald.—LiPch
The Christmas pudding. Unknown.—BaC
Christmas secrets. A. Fisher.—FiO
The Christmas star. N.B. Turner.—BaC
The Christmas tree ("The holly's up, the house is all bright") P. Cornelius.—LiPch
Christmas wish. E. S. Lamb.—BaC
The computer's first Christmas card. E. Morgan.—LiPch
Conversation about Christmas, the useful presents. From A child's Christmas in Wales. D. Thomas.—LiPch
Conversation about Christmas, the useless presents. From A child's Christmas in Wales. D. Thomas.—LiPch
The corner newsman. K. Starbird.—HoMp—StC
Country Christmas. A. Fisher.—BaC
The cultivation of Christmas trees. T. S. Eliot.—LiO
"Dame, get up and bake your pies." Unknown.—BaC
"The dark night wakes, the glory breaks." From O little town of Bethlehem. P. Brooks.—BaC
"The darling of the world is come." From A Christmas carol. R. Herrick.—BaC—LiPch
December ("I like days") A. Fisher.—BaC
December fragments. R. Lattimore.—LiPch
Do not open till Christmas. J. S. Tippett.—BaC
"Duckle, duckle, daisy." L. F. Jackson.—BaC
Eerily sweet. E. Coatsworth.—BaC
Ever green. J. Clare.—BaC
Farewell to Christmas. Unknown.—BaC
The first Nowell. Unknown.—LiPch
For Allan. R. Frost.—LiCc

The friendly beasts. Unknown.—BaC—LiPch
Fun and games. From Round about our coal fire. Unknown.—BaC
Gift. C. Freeman.—BaC
    "Christmas morning I."—LiPch
"God bless the master of this house." Unknown.—BaC
Granny winter. Unknown.—BaC
"He comes, the brave old Christmas." Unknown.—BaC
"Heap on more wood, the wind is chill." From Marmion. W. Scott.—LiPch
"Here we come a-wassailing." Unknown.—LiPch
Hog at the manger. N. Farber.—LiPch
"The holly and the ivy." Unknown.—LiO—LiPch
"How cold the snow." From Four Christmas carols. Unknown.—LiPch
"How far is it to Bethlehem." F. Chesterton.—LiPch
A hymn on the nativity of my saviour. B. Jonson.—BaC
    I sing the birth.—BaC
Hymn to joy. J. Cunningham.—LiPch
I saw a stable. M. E. Coleridge.—LiPch
I saw three ships. Unknown.—LiCc
"I wish you a merry Christmas." Unknown.—BaC
"I wonder as I wander." Unknown.—LiPch
In the town. Unknown.—LiPch
In the week that Christmas comes. E. Farjeon.—LiPch
The innkeeper's wife. From The witnesses. C. Sansom.—LiPch
July madness. M. C. Livingston.—LiF
Karma. E. A. Robinson.—LiO
Kid stuff. F. Horne.—LiPch
The kings from the east. H. Heine.—BaC
    "Three holy kings from Morgenland."—LiPch
"Kolyada, kolyada." Unknown.—BaC
Ladybug's Christmas. N. Farber.—LiPch
Lenox Christmas eve 68. S. Cornish.—AdC
A little carol of the Virgin. L. de Vega.—LiPch
The little donkey. F. Jammes.—LiPch
"Little tree." E. E. Cummings.—LiCc
Long, long ago. Unknown.—BaC
"Look, the earth is aflame with delight." From A Christmas carol. P. Brooks.—BaC
Los pastores. E. Agnew.—LiPch
The Magi. From Gospel according to Matthew.—BaC
The mahogany tree. W. M. Thackeray.—BaC
"Man, be merry." Unknown.—BaC
"May each be found thus as the year circles round." Unknown.—BaC
"May God bless your Christmas." Unknown.—BaC
Merry Christmas ("I saw on the snow") A. Fisher.—BaC
Merry Christmas ("M for the music, merry and clear") Unknown.—BaC

"Yule, yule, yule, my belly's full."
Unknown.—BaC

"Yule's come and yule's gone." Unknown.—
BaC

Christmas. See "Christmas is coming, the geese
are getting fat"

Christmas ("My goodness, my goodness")
Marchette Chute.—BaC

Christmas ("The snow is full of silver light")
Faith Baldwin.—BaC

Christmas at Freelands. James Stephens.—BaC

Christmas bells ("I heard the bells on Christmas
day") Henry Wadsworth Longfellow.—
BaC—LiPch (sel.)

Christmas bells ("The singing waits, a merry
throng") John Clare.—BaC

"Christmas bells, awake and ring." See
Christmas morning

Christmas candle. Rachel Field.—BaC

Christmas candles. Aileen Fisher.—BaC

A Christmas carol ("An angel told Mary")
Harry Behn.—LiPch

A Christmas carol ("Before the paling of the
stars") Christina Georgina Rossetti.—BaC

A Christmas carol ("In the bleak midwinter")
Christina Georgina Rossetti.—BaC
"What can I give him."—LiCc (sel.)—LiPch
(sel.)

A Christmas carol, sel. Christina Rossetti
"Thank God, thank God, we do believe."—
LiPch

A Christmas carol, sel. Phillips Brooks
"Look, the earth is aflame with delight."—
BaC

A Christmas carol, sels. Robert Herrick
"The darling of the world is come."—BaC—
LiPch
"What sweeter music can we bring."—LiPch

Christmas chant. Isabel Shaw.—BaC

A Christmas childhood, sel. Patrick Kavanagh
"My father played the melodeon."—LiPch

"Christmas comes, he comes, he comes."
Unknown.—BaC

Christmas day ("Last night in the open
shippen") Andrew Young.—BaC

Christmas eve ("I see some waits awaiting")
David McCord.—McO

Christmas eve ("My stocking's where") See A
Christmas package—"My stocking's where"

Christmas eve ("On a winter night") Marion
Edey and Dorothy Grider.—BaC

"Christmas eve, and twelve of the clock." See
The oxen

Christmas eve legend. Frances Frost.—BaC

A Christmas eve thought. Harriet Brewer
Sterling.—BaC

Christmas goes to sea. Rachel Field.—BaC

A Christmas hymn. Richard Wilbur.—LiO—
LiPch

Christmas in the country. Aileen Fisher.—FiO

"Christmas in the picture book." See Carol for
a New Zealand child

Christmas in the straw. Chad Walsh.—BaC

"Christmas is coming, the geese are getting
fat." Unknown.—LiCc—LiPch
Christmas.—BaC

"Christmas is here." See The mahogany tree

Christmas lights. Valerie Worth.—LiPch—WoM

Christmas morning ("Christmas bells, awake
and ring") Harry Behn.—LiCc—LiPch

Christmas morning ("If Bethlehem were here
today") Elizabeth Madox Roberts.—LiCc—
LiPch

"Christmas morning I." See Gift

Christmas 1959 et cetera. Gerald William
Barrax.—LiO—LiPch

Christmas ornaments. Valerie Worth.—LiPch

A Christmas package, sels. David McCord.—
McO (Complete)
1. "I hung up a stocking"
2. "Here's that little girl who wraps up each
gift"
3. "Asked for another name for Santa Claus"
4. "Rock candy: hard sweet crystals on a
string"
5. "Alert live reindeer galloping on air"
6. "Though holly halos hang from many a
nail"
7. "That broken star."—LiPch
8. "My stocking's where."—LiPch
Christmas eve.—LiCc
9. "A collar for Sokko"

Christmas pies. Unknown.—BaC

A Christmas prayer. George MacDonald.—
LiPch

The Christmas pudding. Unknown.—BaC

Christmas secrets. Aileen Fisher.—FiO

The Christmas star. Nancy Byrd Turner.—BaC

The Christmas tree ("The holly's up, the house
is all bright") Peter Cornelius.—LiPch

Christmas tree ("I'll find me a spruce") Aileen
Fisher.—BaC

Christmas trees
Christmas goes to sea. R. Field.—BaC
Christmas lights. V. Worth.—LiPch
Christmas ornaments. V. Worth.—LiPch
The Christmas tree ("The holly's up, the
house is all bright") P. Cornelius.—LiPch
Christmas tree ("I'll find me a spruce") A.
Fisher.—BaC
Christmas wish. E. S. Lamb.—BaC
City lights ("Into the endless dark") R.
Field.—BaC
Come Christmas. D. McCord.—LiPch—McO
The cultivation of Christmas trees. T. S.
Eliot.—LiO
For Allan. R. Frost.—LiPch
Jubilate herbis. N. Farber.—LiPch
"A little girl marched around her Christmas
tree." From The new nutcracker suite. O.
Nash.—LiPch
"Little tree." E. E. Cummings.—LiPch
The mahogany tree. W. M. Thackeray.—BaC
Phantasus I, 8. A. Holz.—LiPch
"That broken star." From A Christmas
package. D. McCord.—LiPch—McO
To a young wretch. R. Frost.—LiO

Going round in a square. N. Farber.—FaS
The grass, alas. D. Emmons.—BrO
Guide to London. J. Aiken.—AiS
Hydrant. J. Thurman.—ThFo
I hear America griping. M. Bishop.—BrO
"I remember how she sang." R. Penny.—
 AdC
"In the inner city." L. Clifton.—AdC—MoGp
"In the pond in the park." From Water
 picture. M. Swenson.—MoGp
Inner city lullaby. R. Atkins.—AdC
Junior addict. L. Hughes.—AdC
"Just around the corner." D. McCord.—McO
Knock on wood. H. Dumas.—AdC
Lust. W. Matthews.—JaPp
Mannahatta. W. Whitman.—PlG
Minority life. J. Updike.—PlG
"My summer vacation." N. Grimes.—GrS
New York in the spring. D. Budbill.—MoGp
New York sewers. J. Aiken.—AiS
Next door neighbor. A. Fisher.—FiO
O.D. Z. Gilbert.—AdC
Of Dewitt Williams on his way to Lincoln
 cemetery. G. Brooks.—FlA
Of kings and things. L. Morrison.—MoSr
Oil slick. J. Thurman.—MoGp
On watching the construction of a
 skyscraper. B. Raffel.—JaPp
One year to life on the Grand Central
 shuttle. A. Lorde.—AdC
An ordinary evening in Cleveland. L.
 Turco.—FlA
Out of the city. E. Merriam.—MeW
The people upstairs. O. Nash.—BlC
Pigeon ("Do any thing anything you will") E.
 Loftin.—AdC
A poem for Carol. N. Giovanni.—MaP
Pollution ("O, I am mad with the maddest of
 men") M. C. Livingston.—LiF
Pony song. R. Bantista.—LuZ
Prodigal returns. E. Merriam.—MeR
Rainy nights. I. Thompson.—SaM
Rib sandwich. W. J. Harris.—AdC
Schenectady. E. Merriam.—WiP
Scroppo's dog. M. Swenson.—CoG
Sidewalks. V. Worth.—WoM
"The silent cat." D. Kherdian.—KhC
"Standing at the gate." N. Grimes.—GrS
The still voice of Harlem. C. K. Rivers.—AdC
Streetfighter moon. L. Morrison.—MoSr
The streets of town. A. Fisher.—FiO
Suddenly. A. Fisher.—HoMp
Sweet Diane. G. Barlow.—AdC
Thesis, antithesis, and nostalgia. A. Dugan.—
 JaPp
"They're tearing down a town." J. Strunk.—
 BrO
"Those boys that ran together." L. Clifton.—
 AdC
To Desi as Joe the smoky the lover of 115th
 street. A. Lorde.—AdC
To my daughter the junkie on a train. A.
 Lorde.—AdC
Traffic lights. D. McCord.—McSu

Two of a kind. N. Farber.—FaS
Undefeated. R. Froman.—MoGp
Unseen horses. J. B. Grayston.—CoPh
Untitled I. I. Reed.—AdC
Weather. R. Hershon.—LuZ
When you. E. Merriam.—MeB
"Where is the black community." J. C.
 Thomas.—AdC
Whistling Willie. K. Starbird.—BrO
"Who knows if the moon's." E. E.
 Cummings.—HiS
"Who shined shoes in Times Square." L.
 Jeffers.—AdC
Winter news ("The new November wind")
 D. Kherdian.—KhC
The worm. R. Souster.—DoWh
Zebra. J. Thurman.—MoGp
Cities drowned. Henry Newbolt.—PaE
"**Cities** drowned in olden time." See Cities
 drowned
The **city** ("If flowers want to grow") David
 Ignatow.—JaPp
The **city** and Evan. Kaye Starbird.—StC
"**City** asleep." See The city dump
The **city** dump. Felice Holman.—HoA
The **city** in the sea. Edgar Allan Poe.—PaE
City lights ("Into the endless dark") Rachel
 Field.—BaC
Civil War. See United States—History—Civil
 War
Civilization
 Buffalo dusk. C. Sandburg.—PlG
 Civilization ("I've stood here lately, looking
  at the path") M. C. Livingston.—LiF
 "Driving through New England." L.
  Clifton.—PlG
 Everybody tells me everything. O. Nash.—
  BlC
 Inability to depict an eagle. R. Eberhart.—
  PlG
 Like ghosts of eagles. R. Francis.—PlG
 New Mexican mountain. R. Jeffers.—PlG
 The river. H. Crane.—PlG
 To the western world. L. Simpson.—PlG
Civilization ("I've stood here lately, looking at
 the path") Myra Cohn Livingston.—LiF
"**Clack** your beaks you cormorants and
 kittiwakes." See A canticle to the
 waterbirds
Clackety click. Lilian Moore.—MoTs
"**Clad** in thick mail he stumbles down the
 floor." See Divers
Clams
 It's all the same to the clam. S. Silverstein.—
  SiL
Clancy. David Wagoner.—CoPh
Clare, John
 Christmas bells.—BaC
 Ever green.—BaC
Clarence. Shel Silverstein.—SiL
"**Clarence** Lee from Tennessee." See Clarence
Clark, Badger
 The glory trail.—CoPh

Clarke, John Henrik
  Determination.—AdC
Clarke, Pauline
  My name is.—BeR
Class of 19—. Frederic Dec.—JaPp
Classroom. Kenneth Gangemi.—HeB
"Clay." See Playing with clay
Clay, Cassius. See Ali, Muhammad
Clayton, Candyce
  Piano Lessons.—LuZ
"Clean, green, windy billows notching out the
    sky." See Cardigan bay
The **clean** platter. Ogden Nash.—BlC
Clean your room. Jack Prelutsky.—PrR
"Clean your room, my mother said." See Clean
    your room
Cleanliness. See also Bathing
  "An artistic young person of Churt." M. C.
    Livingston.—LiLl
  Clean your room. J. Prelutsky.—PrR
  Crowded tub. S. Silverstein.—SiL
  Getting ready. N. M. Bodecker.—BoHh
  "Little Polly Flinders." Mother Goose.—TrGg
  Messy room. S. Silverstein.—SiL
  Pig ("Pigs are always awfully dirty") W. J.
    Smith.—SmL
  The tiniest man in the washing machine. D.
    Lee.—LeG
Clemmons, Carole Gregory
  Love from my father.—AdC
  Migration.—LuZ
"The clerihew." David McCord.—McO
Clerihews
  "The clerihew." D. McCord.—McO
  War horses. W. Cole.—CoPh
"Click beetle, clack beetle." See Clickbeetle
Clickbeetle. Mary Ann Hoberman.—HoBu
"Clickety clack." See Song of the train
"Clickety clockety clack." See The Bendigo
    track
"The cliff-top has a carpet." See The cliff-top
The **cliff**-top, sel. Robert Bridges
  "The cliff-top has a carpet."—MoF
Cliffs
  "The cliff-top has a carpet." From The
    cliff-top. R. Bridges.—MoF
  The echoing cliff. A. Young.—PaE
  The Irish cliffs of Moher. W. Stevens.—PlL
Clifton, Lucille
  Africa.—AdC
  Breaklight.—LuZ
  Cain.—PlL
  "Driving through New England."—PlG
  Eviction.—MoGp
  For deLawd.—AdC
  God send Easter.—AdC
  Good times.—AdC
  "I went to the valley."—AdC
  "In the inner city."—AdC—MoGp
  July.—LiCc
  "Listen children."—AdC
  Malcolm.—AdC
  Miss Rosie.—AdC
  The raising of Lazarus.—AdC

This morning.—KhI
  "Those boys that ran together."—AdC
  To Bobby Seale.—AdC
The **climbers.** Shel Silverstein.—SiL
Climbing
  The climbers. S. Silverstein.—SiL
  "Every time I climb a tree." From Five
    chants. D. McCord.—McO—PaI
  Penthouse. A. Fisher.—FiO
  A small elegy. R. Snyder.—JaPp
  Timothy Toppin. M. A. Hoberman.—HoY
  The tree and me. K. Kuskin.—KuD
  Up the pointed ladder. D. McCord.—McO
  "When the elm was full." From Autumn
    nature notes. T. Hughes.—HuSs
"Clink." Kazue Mizumura.—MiF
The **clock** ("Here's what I think") Felice
    Holman.—HoA
Clock ("This clock") Valerie Worth.—WiP
"The clock ticks slowly, slowly in the hall." See
    The twenty fourth of December
The **clock** tower. Colleen Thibaudeau.—DoWh
Clockface. Judith Thurman.—ThFo
"Clocks." See Sing song
Clocks and watches
  Alarm clock. E. Merriam.—MoGp—WiP
  The clock ("Here's what I think") F.
    Holman.—HoA
  Clock ("This clock") V. Worth.—WiP
  The clock tower. C. Thibaudeau.—DoWh
  Clockface. J. Thurman.—ThFo
  "Hickory, dickory, dock." Mother Goose.—
    TrGg
  Jim Jay. W. De La Mare.—HiS
  Moon clock. T. Hughes.—HuM
  On a sundial. H. Belloc.—BrO
  "There is a clock." D. Kherdian.—KhC
  Tick tock clock. J. Prelutsky.—PrR
  Tick tock talk. D. McCord.—McO
  Time ("Listen to the clock strike") M. A.
    Hoberman.—HoY
  Where two o'clock came from. K. Patchen.—
    HiS
Cloony the clown. Shel Silverstein.—SiL
"Close in, near to the sand." See Beach
"Close your eyes, feel the." See Haiku for
    Halloween
"Closed, it sleeps." See Safety pin
"A closed window looks down." See Ka'ba
Closet. Judith Thurman.—ThFo
The **closing** of the rodeo. William Jay Smith.—
    PlG
Closing piece. Rainer Maria Rilke.—JaPp
"The clothes that get clean." See L is for
    laundry
Clothing and dress. See also names of clothing,
    as Boots and shoes
  Around my room. W. J. Smith.—SmL
  "An artistic young person of Churt." M. C.
    Livingston.—LiLl
  The bear with the golden hair. K. Kuskin.—
    KuD
  The bohemian. P. L. Dunbar.—BrI

S'no fun.—CoDb
So it goes.—CoDb
Take my advice.—CoDb
War horses.—CoPh
Coleridge, Hartley
    On the death of Echo, a favorite beagle.—
        CoG
Coleridge, Mary Elizabeth
    I saw a stable.—LiPch
Coleridge, Samuel Taylor
    All nature seems at work.—PaB
    "Dear babe, that sleepest cradled by my
        side." See Frost at midnight
    Frost at midnight, sel.
        "Dear babe, that sleepest cradled by my
            side."—PlL
    Icebergs. See The rime of the ancient
        mariner
    The rime of the ancient mariner, sels.
        Icebergs.—PaE
        Water-snakes.—PaE
    Water-snakes. See The rime of the ancient
        mariner
Coleridge, Sara
    "Chill December brings the sleet." See The
        garden year
    The garden year, sel.
        "Chill December brings the sleet."—BaC
"A **collar** for Sokko." See A Christmas package
Collectives
    The squid. O. Nash.—BlC
"**Collie** puppies in a dooryard." See Wonder
The **collier** laddie. Leslie Norris.—NoM
The **collies.** Edward Anthony.—CoG
"**Color** it." See Chromo
Colorado
    Green and blue in Colorado. L. Morrison.—
        MoW
Colors. See also names of colors, as Yellow
    Chameleon. A. Brownjohn.—SaM
    Chromo. S. W. Fabio.—AdC
    Colors for mama. B. Mahone.—AdC
    The colors of night. N. S. Momaday.—MoGd
    Colours ("Red is death, for people who are
        dying") F. Evans.—SaM
    Colours ("What is pink, a rose is pink") C.
        Rossetti.—SaM
    Drawing by Ronnie C., grade one. R.
        Lechlitner.—LuZ
    My coloring book. J. Prelutsky.—PrR
    Oil slick. J. Thurman.—ThFo
    Rainbow writing. E. Merriam.—MeR
    Rhinos purple, hippos green. M. P. Hearn.—
        HeB
    Shade. C. Lynch.—AdC
    Traffic lights. D. McCord.—McSu
    What is pink. C. Rossetti.—WiP
    Yellow ("Green is go") D. McCord.—McO
Colors for mama. Barbara Mahone.—AdC
The **colors** of night. N. Scott Momaday.—MoGd
Colours ("Red is death, for people who are
    dying") Frances Evans.—SaM
Colours ("What is pink, a rose is pink")
    Christina Rossetti.—SaM

Coltrane, John (about)
    After the rain. S. Crouch.—AdC
    Here where Coltrane is. M. S. Harper.—AdC
    John Coltrane an impartial review. A. B.
        Spellman.—AdC
    Sopranosound, memory of John. S. Bourke.—
        AdC
Columbus, sel. Alfred Tennyson
    "Chains, my good Lord, in your raised brows
        I read."—LiO
Columbus ("Inner greet, Greenberg said it")
    Muriel Rukeyser
Columbus ("Once upon a time there was an
    Italian") Ogden Nash.—LiO
Columbus ("Steer on, courageous sailor,
    through mockery and jeering") Friedrich
    von Schiller, tr. fr. the German by Erika
    Gathman Koessler.—LiO
Columbus and the mermaids. Elizabeth
    Coatsworth.—PlG
Columbus, Christopher (about)
    And of Columbus. H. Gregory.—LiO—PlG
    "Chains, my good lord, in your raised brows I
        read." From Columbus. A. Tennyson.—LiO
    Columbus ("Inner greet, Greenberg said it")
        M. Rukeyser.—PlG
    Columbus ("Once upon a time there was an
        Italian") O. Nash.—LiO
    Columbus ("Steer on, courageous sailor,
        through mockery and jeering") F. von
        Schiller.—LiO
    Columbus and the mermaids. E.
        Coatsworth.—PlG
    The discovery. J. C. Squire.—LiO
    May 1506, Christopher Columbus speaking.
        W. T. Scott.—PlG
    Mysterious biography. C. Sandburg.—LiCc—
        LiO
    12 October. M.C. Livingston.—LiCc
    "When my little brother chanted." From
        Religion back home. W. Stafford.—LiCc
    "You, Genoese mariner." W. S. Merwin.—
        PlG
"**Columbus** is remembered by young men."
    See And of Columbus
Comanche. Gary Gildner.—CoPh
Combinations. Mary Ann Hoberman.—HoBu
Come and be my baby. Maya Angelou.—AnO
"**Come** bring with a noise." See The yule log
Come Christmas. David McCord.—LiPch—
    McO
"**Come,** dear children, let us away." See The
    forsaken merman
"**Come,** guard this night the Christmas pie."
    See Stop thief
"**Come** here, Denise." See Denise
"**Come** lasses and lads." See The rural dance
    about the Maypole
"**Come** live with me and be my love." See The
    passionate shepherd to his love
"**Come** now, you supercilious detractors of
    America." See Meredith Phyfe
"**Come** out and climb the garden path." See
    Luriana, Lurilee

"Come play with me." See To a squirrel at Kyle-na-no

"Come, said old Shellover." See Old Shellover

"Come sit down beside me." See Sitting on the fence

Come skating. Shel Silverstein.—SiL

"Come soon." See Letter to a friend

"Come study the names." See The saint's lament

"Come to me broken dreams and all." See The still voice of Harlem

"Come trotting up." See Foal

"Come visit my pancake collection." See The pancake collector

"Come when the nights are bright with stars." See Invitation to love

"Comes the time to blow a double bubble, think." See Bubble gum

"Coming down the mountain in the twilight." See Where the hayfields were

"Coming home late." Kazue Mizumura.—MiF

"Coming home on a summer night." See Small moon

The coming of teddy bears. Dennis Lee.—LeG

"Coming on the morning." See Finders keepers

"Coming over the rise, passing." See On the farm

A common poem. Carolyn M. Rodgers.—AdC

Communes
  For a child gone to live in a commune. W. Stafford.—PlL

Communication. See Conversation; Letters and letter-writing; Speech; Telephones; Talking

Communication I. Maya Angelou.—AnO

Communication II. Maya Angelou
  The student.—AnO
  The teacher.—AnO

Communications. See Radio; Telephones; Television

"The Compact sat in parliament." See 1838

Company. Bobbi Katz.—CoDb

Comparatives. N. Scott Momaday.—MoGd

Comparison ("John is the tallest, he's ever so high") Mary Ann Hoberman.—HoY

Comparison ("The sky of brightest gray seems dark") Paul Laurence Dunbar.—BrI

Compass ("According to") Valerie Worth.—WoSm

Compass song. David McCord.—McO

Compasses
  Compass ("According to") V. Worth.—WoSm
  Compass song. D. McCord.—McO
  Points of the compass. E. Merriam.—MeR

Compensation. Paul Laurence Dunbar.—BrI

Complaint of a young girl. Wang Chung-ju, tr. fr. the Chinese by Kenneth Rexroth.—JaPp

The completion. Lillian Morrison.—MoSr

Complicated thoughts about a small son. E. B. White.—PlL

Computers
  The computer's first Christmas card. E. Morgan.—LiPch
  Epitaph ("Here he lies moulding") L. Mellichamp.—BrO

IBM hired her. W.J.J. Gordon.—BrO

Man of letters. W. Knox.—BrO

Neuteronomy. E. Merriam.—BrO—WiP

No holes marred. S. Douglas.—BrO

The perforated spirit. M. Bishop.—BrO

Think tank. E. Merriam.—BrO

Univac to univac. L. B. Salomon.—BrO

The computer's first Christmas card. Edwin Morgan.—LiPch

Comus, sels. John Milton
  Neptune.—PaE
  Song.—PaE

Conceit. See Pride and vanity

A conceit. Maya Angelou.—AnO

Concerning dragons, sel. Hilary Pepler
  "Are all the dragons dead."—MoF

Concord hymn. Ralph Waldo Emerson.—PlG

Conduct of life. See also Behavior; Etiquette; Proverbs; also names of traits of character, as Perseverance
  The adventures of Isabel. O. Nash.—BlC
  "All that is gold does not glitter." J.R.R. Tolkien.—WiP
  Almost perfect. S. Silverstein.—SiL
  The boy who laughed at Santa Claus. O. Nash.—BlC
  The chambered nautilus. O. W. Holmes.—PaE
  A Christmas prayer. G. MacDonald.—LiPch
  Clean your room. J. Prelutsky.—PrR
  The crow. J. Gardner.—GaCb
  Cry-baby. M. Gardner.—CoI
  Dan Dunder. J. Ciardi.—CoI
  The dreamer ("Temples he built and palaces of air") P. L. Dunbar.—BrI
  Elegy. T. Roethke.—PlL
  Elegy on the death of a mad dog. O. Goldsmith.—CoG
  Epistle to the Olympians. O. Nash.—BlC
  Fare thee well. E. Siegel.—PlG
  "Father says." M. Rosen.—CoI
  The gibbon. E. W. Rudzewicz.—GaCb
  Good and bad. E. A. Parry.—CoI
  Harvey always wins. J. Prelutsky.—PrRh
  The hill. E. Merriam.—MeR
  "I woke up this morning." K. Kuskin.—CoI—WiP
  I'm leery of firms with easy terms. C. S. Jennison.—BrO
  Jack do-good-for-nothing. O. Nash.—BlC
  Jump rope song. K. Starbird.—StC
  Ladies first. S. Silverstein.—SiL
  "Little girl, be careful what you say." C. Sandburg.—WiP
  "Little Jesus of the crib." Unknown.—BaC
  "Long, too long America." W. Whitman.—PlG
  Lord, in my heart. M. Angelou.—AnO
  Love in America. M. Moore.—PlG
  Love necessitates. E. Redmond.—AdC
  Make merry. D. McCord.—McO
  Manners for a child of 1918. E. Bishop.—PlL
  "Mrs. Malone." E. Farjeon.—WiP
  Mother to son. L. Hughes.—LiCc

My mother's sister. C. D. Lewis.—PlL
A near pantoum for a birthday. B. Howes.—PlL
Nobody calls him Jim. J. Prelutsky.—PrRh
On the behavior of Rodney IV who travels in unusual contraptions. L. Phillips.—CoI
The parable of the prodigal son. From Gospel according to Luke.—PlL
A poison tree. W. Blake.—MaP
Protest. F. Holman.—HoA
Put something in. S. Silverstein.—SiL
The python. J. Gardner.—GaCb
Riley. C. Causley.—HiS
Rolling Harvey down the hill. J. Prelutsky.—PrRh
Rough. S. Spender.—MaP
Rules. K. Kuskin.—KuD—WiP
Say nay. E. Merriam.—MeR
Seventy-six. Lao Tsu.—LuZ
Sire. W. S. Merwin.—PlL
The smile. J. Aiken.—AiS
Spider webs. R. Fabrizio.—MaP
Ten kinds. M. M. Dodge.—CoI
A time to talk. R. Frost.—MoGp
The trouble is. M. C. Livingston.—LiF
We must be polite. C. Sandburg.—WiP
We wear the mask. P. L. Dunbar.—BrI
What my Uncle Tony told my sister, Angie, and me. S. J. Ortiz.—LuZ
"A confectioner living in Skittle." Myra Cohn Livingston.—LiLl
Confederate States of America. See United States—History—Civil War
Confession of a glutton. Don Marquis.—CoG
Confessional. Paul Laurence Dunbar.—BrI
"The confines of a city block." See Construction
A confused chameleon. X. J. Kennedy.—KeP
"The congregation rumbles to its feet." See Hymn
Conkling, Hilda
  Easter.—LiCc
  Fairies.—PaI
Connally, Ron
  Formula, tr.—LuZ
Conscience. See also Duty
  Conscience and remorse. P. L. Dunbar.—BrI
  "On the lawn at the villa." L. Simpson.—PlG
  The tiger asks Blake for a bedtime story. N. Willard.—WiV
Conscience and remorse. Paul Laurence Dunbar.—BrI
Conservation
  Unless we guard them well. J. Merchant.—BrO
"Consider the auk." See A caution to everybody
"Consider the sea's listless chime." See The sea-limits
"The consonants laid low." Lillian Morrison.—MoW
"Constantly near you, I never in my entire." See The horse show

Constellations. See also Milky Way
  Constellations. P. St. John.—LuZ
  Orion. D. McCord.—McO
Constellations. Primus St. John.—LuZ
Construction ("The confines of a city block") Karl Shapiro.—JaPp
Construction ("Wham") Virginia Schonberg.—BrO
"A contentious old person named Reagan." William Jay Smith.—SmL
Contentment
  Contentment ("I like the way that the world is made") B. Johnson.—CoG
  Cows ("Half the time they munched the grass, and all the") J. Reeves.—WiP
  Day dreams. W. Canton.—PaB
  Secret talk. E. Merriam.—MeW
  Unsatisfied yearning. R. K. Munkittrick.—CoG
  Valentine for earth. F. Frost.—BrO
Contentment ("I like the way that the world is made") Burges Johnson.—CoG
"The continents in the brain." See Plate tectonics on waking
Conversation
  Butterfly ("Said he didn't know") D. McCord.—McSu
  Conversation ("Mother, may I stay up tonight") D. McCord.—HiS—McO
  Conversation ("Mousie, mousie") R. Fyleman.—WiP
  Cows. J. Reeves.—WiP
  Imaginary dialogues. W. J. Smith.—WiP
  Mister Gaffe. J. Prelutsky.—PrQ
  Puppy and I. A. A. Milne.—WiP
  So that's why. L. Morrison.—MoO
  Tallyho-hum. O. Nash.—CoPh
  Vermont conversation. P. Hubbell.—WiP
Conversation ("Mother may I stay up tonight") David McCord.—HiS—McO
Conversation ("Mousie, mousie") Rose Fyleman.—WiP
Conversation about Christmas, the useful presents. See A child's Christmas in Wales
Conversation about Christmas, the useless presents. See A child's Christmas in Wales
Conversation between Mr. and Mrs. Santa Claus. Rowena Bennett.—BaC
Conversation hearts. Nina Payne.—LiCc
Conversation with Washington. Myra Cohn Livingston.—LiF—LiO
"Coo-oo, coo-oo." Mother Goose.—TrGg
"Cook in a dudgeon, aggrieved against the boss." See Whodunnit
Cook, Joseph
  Boston nursery rhymes, sels.
    Rhyme for a chemical baby.—BrO
    Rhyme for a geological baby.—BrO
    Rhyme for astronomical baby.—BrO
    Rhyme for botanical baby.—BrO
  Rhyme for a chemical baby. See Boston nursery rhymes
  Rhyme for a geological baby. See Boston nursery rhymes

Counting-out rhymes
Counting-out rhyme ("Grimes golden greening yellow transparent") E. Merriam.—MeR
Counting-out rhyme ("Silver bark of beech, and sallow") E. St. V. Millay.—SaM
Counting-out rhyme ("A wasp") M. A. Hoberman.—HoBu
"How many miles to old Norfolk." C. Watson.—WiP

Countries. See names of countries, as Canada
Country. See Country life
The **country** and Nate. Kaye Starbird.—StC
"Country bumpkin." See Father Fox's pennyrhymes
Country cat. Elizabeth Coatsworth.—WiP
Country Christmas. Aileen Fisher.—BaC
Country life. See also Farm life; Village life
Bee tree. R. N. Peck.—PeB
Blueberries lavender. N. D. Watson.—WaB
"Blueberry eyes." N. D. Watson.—WaB
Butterballs. N. D. Watson.—WaB
Christmas in the country. A. Fisher.—FiO
Country cat. E. Coatsworth.—WiP
Country Christmas. A. Fisher.—BaC
Country rain. A. Fisher.—FiO
Country window. A. Fisher.—FiO
Dust ("Around a distant bend the wagon showed") R. N. Peck.—PeB
The errand. H. Behn.—HoMp
Evening song. S. Anderson.—FlA
Finale. From Prairie. C. Sandburg.—FlA
Flutter wheel. R. N. Peck.—PeB
Going to town. F. Lape.—CoPh
Gone. D. McCord.—HoBm—McO
Grand Wood's American landscape. W. T. Scott.—PlG
The harvest moon. T. Hughes.—HuSs
Hello, hello Henry. M. Kumin.—LuZ
Honeybee hill. N. D. Watson.—WaB
Independence day. W. Berry.—LiO
Iowa. M. D. Browne.—FlA
Kansas boy. R. Lechlitner.—FlA
Kentucky Belle. C. F. Woolson.—CoPh
Lamplighter barn. M. C. Livingston.—BeR
Leaves ("Who's killed the leaves") T. Hughes.—HuSs
Lying in a hammock at William Duffy's farm in Pine Island, Minnesota. J. Wright.—FlA
Monkey vines. N. D. Watson.—WaB
Names of horses. D. Hall.—CoPh
Nelly Myers. A. R. Ammons.—KhI
North fence. R. N. Peck.—PeB
On the farm. B. Winder.—CoPh
Out in the boat. L. Morrison.—MoSr
Picking berries. A. Fisher.—FiO
The poultry show. D. McCord.—McO
Psalm of the fruitful field. A. M. Klein.—DoWh
Rutland fair. R. N. Peck.—PeB
September creek. R. N. Peck.—PeB
The seven sorrows. T. Hughes.—HuSs
Snow and snow. T. Hughes.—HuSs
So will I. C. Zolotow.—HoBm

Solstice song. T. Hughes.—HuSs
The star in the pail. D. McCord.—HoBm
Sugar maples. N. D. Watson.—WaB
Three kinds of pleasures. R. Bly.—FlA
A time to talk. R. Frost.—MoGp
A walk for thinking. N. D. Watson.—WaB
White cat. R. Knister.—DoWh
Winter notes. R. N. Peck.—PeB
Wood box ("Behind the old black kitchen stove") R. N. Peck.—PeB
You and me. N. D. Watson.—WaB
Zizzy bee. N. D. Watson.—WaB
Country rain. Aileen Fisher.—FiO
Country window. Aileen Fisher.—FiO
The **couple.** Maya Angelou.—AnO
Couplets
Write me a verse. D. McCord.—McO
Courage. See also Conduct of life; Heroes and heroines; Perseverance
The adventures of Isabel. O. Nash.—BlC
Beware of me. Unknown.—MoGp
Columbus ("Inner greet, Greenberg said it") M. Rukeyser.—PlG
Custard the dragon and the wicked witch. O. Nash.—BlC
Legend. J. Wright.—HiS
The lion. W. Murdoch.—DuSn
Little Giffen. F. O. Ticknor.—PlG
Strange legacies. S. A. Brown.—AdC
The tale of Custard the dragon. O. Nash.—BlC
Tim, an Irish terrier. W. M. Letts.—CoG
"A course in rabbit reading." See Rapid reading
Court trials. See Justice; Law
Courtesy. See Etiquette; Kindness
Courtship. See also Love
"But lo, from forth a copse that neighbours by." From Venus and Adonis. W. Shakespeare.—CoPh
The canal bank. J. Stephens.—YaI
Cecilia. Unknown.—DoWh
Isabel. Unknown.—DoWh
The juniper tree. W. Watson.—DoWh
"Little Jack Dandy-prat was my first suitor." Mother Goose.—TrGg
"Love is the flower of a day." From Variations on a cosmical air. M. Cowley.—YaI
Love me, love my dog. I. V. Crawford.—DoWh
The teapot and the kettle. M. A. Hoberman.—HoY
"There is a girl of our town." Mother Goose.—TrGg
To his mistresse. R. Herrick.—LiO
Cousin Carree's cubic cuisine. X. J. Kennedy.—KeP
The **cove.** David McCord.—McO
"The cove is where the swallows skim." See The cove
Covell, Natalie Ann. See Crossen, Stacy Jo and Covell, Natalie Anne

Coventry carol. Unknown.—LiO—LiPch (at. to Robert Croo)
The **covered** bridge house. Kaye Starbird.—StC
Covers. Nikki Giovanni.—GiV
"The **cow**." See Cow
Cow ("The cow") Valerie Worth.—WiP
The **cow** ("The cow is of the bovine ilk") Ogden Nash.—BlC
Cow ("Cows are not supposed to fly") William Jay Smith.—SmL
"The **cow** has a cud." See Five chants
"The **cow** is of the bovine ilk." See The cow.
Cowboys
  The broncho that would not be broken. V. Lindsay.—CoPh
  The closing of the rodeo. W. J. Smith.—PlG
  The glory trail. B. Clark.—CoPh
  The man from Snowy River. A. B. Paterson.—CoPh
  The outlaw. F. Holman.—CoI
  Ride 'im cowboy. A. L. Freebairn.—CoPh
  Riders ("At four p.m. small fingers moved the dial to one-six-O") L. Peavy.—CoPh
  The zebra dun. Unknown.—CoPh
Cowley, Malcolm
  "Love is the flower of a day." See Variations on a cosmical air
  The mother.—PlL
  Variations on a cosmical air, sel.
    "Love is the flower of a day."—YaI
Cowper, William
  The woodman's dog.—CoG
Cows. See also Calves; Cattle
  At milking. R. N. Peck.—PeB
  The beefalo. J. Gardner.—GaCb
  The birthday cow. E. Merriam.—MeB
  Cow ("The cow") V. Worth.—WiP
  The cow ("The cow is of the bovine ilk") O. Nash.—BlC
  Cow ("Cows are not supposed to fly") W. J. Smith.—SmL
  Cows ("Half the time they munched the grass, and all the") J. Reeves.—WiP
  The crybaby cow. E. Merriam.—MeB
  "Did you feed my cow." Unknown.—WiP
  The discontented cow. X. J. Kennedy.—KeP
  The Halloween cow. E. Merriam.—MeB
  Highway one, movie camera. M. C. Livingston.—LiF
  "I had a little cow." Mother Goose.—WiP
  Miss Casper's cow. K. Starbird.—StC
  One sunny summer's day. D. Lee.—LeG
  The owl cow. E. Merriam.—MeB
  Shaking. S. Silverstein.—SiL
  Winter calf. R. N. Peck.—PeB
  The wise cow enjoys a cloud. N. Willard.—WiV
  "Wooley Foster had a cow." Mother Goose.—TrGg
Cows ("Half the time they munched the grass, and all the") James Reeves.—WiP
"Cows are coming home in Maine." Robert P. Tristram Coffin.—HiD
"Cows are not supposed to fly." See Cow

"Cows graze." See Horses graze
Crab ("The dead crab") Valerie Worth.—WoM
The **crab** ("Never grab a crab") John Gardner.—GaCb
Crab-grass. Ted Hughes.—HuM
Crabapples
  Crabapples ("Sweeten these bitter wild crabapples, Illinois") C. Sandburg.—HoMp
Crabapples ("Sweeten these bitter wild crabapples, Illinois") Carl Sandburg.—HoMp
Crabbe, George
  The borough, sel.
    "Now it is pleasant in the summer-eve."—PaE
  "Now it is pleasant in the summer-eve." See The borough
Crabs
  Crab ("The dead crab") V. Worth.—WoM
  The crab ("Never grab a crab") J. Gardner.—GaCb
Crafter, Susan
  Pig.—DuSn
Crane, Hart
  The river.—PlG
Crashaw, Richard
  An epitaph upon husband and wife, which died, and were buried together.—PlL
Crawford, Isabella V.
  Love me, love my dog.—DoWh
"Crawl, laugh." Issa, tr. fr. the Japanese by Nobuyuki Yuasa.—LiO
Crazy quilt. Jane Yolen.—HeB
Creation
  "And God said, let the waters generate." From Paradise lost. J. Milton.—PaE
  "And God said, let us make man in our image." From Genesis, Bible, Old Testament.—PlL
  Breaking through. J. Thurman.—ThFo
  The camel. J. Gardner.—GaCb
  "I feel me near to some high thing." W. E. Leonard.—MaP
  The invasion of the star streaks. L. Morrison.—MoO
  Makers. N. D. Watson.—WaB
  The opossum. J. Gardner.—GaCb
  Playing with clay. J. Thurman.—ThFo
  The python. J. Gardner.—GaCb
  Scarlett rocks. T. E. Brown.—PaE
  Whale. W. R. Benet.—PaE
  The wise cow makes way, room, and believe. N. Willard.—WiV
Creation. Graeme Turner.—DuSn
Creatures we can do without. Eve Merriam.—MeR
The **cricket** ("And when the rain had gone away") Marjorie Barrows.—PaI
Cricket ("A cricket's ear is in its leg") Mary Ann Hoberman.—HoBu
Cricket ("When a cricket chirps fast, it is hot") David McCord.—McSu
Cricket jackets. Aileen Fisher.—FiO
Cricket song. Aileen Fisher.—FiO

Crickets
Autumn concert. A. Fisher.—FiO
Chirping. A. Fisher.—FiO
The cricket ("And when the rain had gone
away") M. Barrows.—PaI
Cricket ("A cricket's ear is in its leg") M. A.
Hoberman.—HoBu
Cricket ("When a cricket chirps fast, it is
hot") D. McCord.—McSu
Cricket jackets. A. Fisher.—FiO
Cricket song. A. Fisher.—FiO
Crickets ("All busy punching tickets") D.
McCord.—McO
Halloween concert. A. Fisher.—BrIt
Crickets ("All busy punching tickets") David
McCord.—McO
"A **cricket's** ear is in its leg." See Cricket
"The **crickets** in the thickets." See But I
wonder
"**Cried** a maid in the Manor at Foss." Myra
Cohn Livingston.—LiLl
"**Cried** a man on the Salisbury Plain." Myra
Cohn Livingston.—LiLl
Crime and criminals. See also Murder; Thieves
The bloodhound. E. Anthony.—CoG
Inspector Dogbone gets his man. D. Lee.—
LeG
Jesse James, a design in red and yellow for a
nickel library. W. R. Benet.—FlA
The outlaw. F. Holman.—CoI
Whodunnit. E. Merriam.—MeR
Cripples
Foibles. H. Bond.—KhI
The **crisis.** Paul Laurence Dunbar.—BrI
Crispus Attucks. Robert Hayden.—AdC
"**Cristofo** Colombo was a hungry man." See
Mysterious biography
Critics and criticism
To a captious critic. P. L. Dunbar.—BrI
The **crocodial.** Jane Yolen.—YoH
Crocodile ("The crocodile wept bitter tears")
William Jay Smith.—SmL
"The **crocodile** wept bitter tears." See
Crocodile
Crocodiles
Crocodile ("The crocodile wept bitter tears")
W. J. Smith.—SmL
The monkeys and the crocodile. L. E.
Richards.—WiP
The purist. O. Nash.—WiP
Crocuses
"The crocuses are too naked, space shakes
them." From Spring nature notes. T.
Hughes.—HuSs
Looking. A. Fisher.—FiO
"The **crocuses** are too naked, space shakes
them." See Spring nature notes
Croo, Robert
Coventry carol (at.)—LiO—LiPch
"**Crookback** Dick." See Richard III
"**Cross** my heart and hope to die." See From
the kitchen—Pie
The **cross** porpoise. Lillian Morrison.—MoW
"A **cross** porpoise." See The cross porpoise

Crossen, Stacy Jo and Covell, Natalie Anne
Wings.—HoBm
Crossing. Philip Booth.—PlG
Crossing Kansas by train. Donald Justice.—FlA
The **crossing** of Mary of Scotland. William Jay
Smith.—SmL—WiP
"**Crossing** the frontier from dark to light." See
Moon shadow beggars
Crosspatch. Nina Payne.—CoI
Crouch, Stanley
After the rain.—AdC
The **crow** ("By the wave rising, by the wave
breaking") P. K. Page.—DoWh
The **crow** ("The first thing to know") John
Gardner.—GaCb
"**Crow** knows." See Crow wonders
Crow, Mary
Rain in the face.—CoPh
Crow wonders. Lilian Moore.—MoTs
Crowded tub. Shel Silverstein.—SiL
Crows
The answer is no. E. B. White.—PaB
The crow ("By the wave rising, by the wave
breaking") P. K. Page.—DoWh
The crow ("The first thing to know") J.
Gardner.—GaCb
Crow wonders. L. Moore.—MoTs
Crows ("I like to walk") D. McCord.—McO
Crows ("I love crows") W. Witherup.—JaPp
Crows in a winter composition. N. S.
Momaday.—MoGd
Flight. G. Johnston.—DoWh
Fox and crow. W. J. Smith.—SmL
Gnome ("I saw a gnome") H. Behn.—BrIt
Many crows, any owl. D. McCord.—McO
My sister Jane. T. Hughes.—HiS
New notebook. J. Thurman.—ThFo
Riddle-me rhyme. D. McCord.—McSu
"There was an old crow." Mother Goose.—
TrGg
"Tweedledum and tweedledee." Mother
Goose.—TrGg
Crows ("I like to walk") David McCord.—McO
Crows ("I love crows") William Witherup.—
JaPp
Crows in a winter composition. N. Scott
Momaday.—MoGd
Crucifixion. See Easter; Jesus Christ
Cruelty. See Animals—Care
A **crust** of bread. Alfred Starr Hamilton.—KhI
"A **crust** of bread and a corner to sleep in." See
Life
A **crusty** mechanic. N. M. Bodecker.—BoP
Cruz, Victor Hernandez
Chicago, 3 hours.—FlA
Cry-baby. Martin Gardner.—CoI
"A **cry-baby** whimpers wherever she goes." See
Cry-baby
The **crybaby** cow. Eve Merriam.—MeB
Crying
Boy at the window. R. Wilbur.—MaP
The child who cried. F. Holman.—HoBm
Cry-baby. M. Gardner.—CoI
The cry-baby cow. E. Merriam.—MeB

Daisies
  Daisies ("Where the dusty lane") V. Worth.—JaPp
  Daisy world. A. Fisher.—FiO
  Easter daisy. A. Fisher.—FiO
  Park at sundown. M. C. Livingston.—LiF
  "The white daisies." D. Kherdian.—KhC
Daisies ("Where the dusty lane") Valerie Worth.—JaPp
Daisy world. Aileen Fisher.—FiO
Daley's dorg Wattle. W. T. Goodge.—CoG
"Dame, get up and bake your pies." Unknown.—BaC
Dame Hickory. Walter De La Mare.—WaFp
"Dame Hickory, Dame Hickory." See Dame Hickory
Dan Dunder. John Ciardi.—CoI
"Dan Dunder is a blunder." See Dan Dunder
Dana, Doris
  To Noel. tr.—LiPch
Dana, Robert
  Burning the steaks in the rain, reflections on a 46th birthday.—KhI
  Horses.—CoPh
A dance ("One, two") Karla Kuskin.—KuD
The dance of the thirteen skeletons. Jack Prelutsky.—PrN
Dance song 6. Mark Van Doren.—HiD
Dancers. See Dances and dancing
Dances and dancing
  Arabian dance. O. Nash.—BlC
  The artist ("Mr. T bareheaded in a soiled undershirt") W. C. Williams.—LuZ
  A baker in France. N. M. Bodecker.—BoP
  Calico ball. N. D. Watson.—WaB
  Christmas in the straw. C. Walsh.—BaC
  A dance ("One, two") K. Kuskin.—KuD
  The dance of the thirteen skeletons. J. Prelutsky.—PrN
  The dancing seal. W. Gibson.—PaE
  Danse russe. W. C. Williams.—KhI
  The gourd dancer. N. S. Momaday.—MoGd
  The marmalade man makes a dance to mend us. N. Willard.—WiV
  The mistletoe. C. Scollard.—BaC
  The mock turtle's song. From Alice's adventures in wonderland. L. Carroll.—WiP
  New Mexican mountain. R. Jeffers.—PlG
  Ocean dancing. M. C. Livingston.—LiWt
  The old hoofer. L. Morrison.—MoW
  The polka. O. Nash.—BlC
  Russian dance. O. Nash.—BlC
  "A spider danced a cosy jig." I. Layton.—DoWh
  We dance like Ella riffs. C. M. Rodgers.—AdC
  Where the hayfields were. A. MacLeish.—HiD
The dancing seal. Wilfred Gibson.—PaE
Dandelions
  Buttons of gold. A. Fisher.—FiO
  The first dandelion. W. Whitman.—PaB
  For the sewing kit. N. Farber.—FaS

Sun prints. A. Fisher.—FiO
  "Who tossed those golden coins." K. Mizumura.—MiF
"The dandelion's gone to seed." See For the sewing kit
Dandy. Unknown.—BlH
Dangerous condition, sign on inner city house. Russell Atkins.—AdC
Dangerous journey. Joan Aiken.—AiS
Daniel ("Darius the Mede was a king and a wonder") Vachel Lindsay.—WiP
Daniel Boone ("When Daniel Boone goes by, at night") Stephen Vincent Benet.—PlG
Daniel Webster's horses. Elizabeth Coatsworth.—CoPh
Daniell, Rosemary
  Rosemary.—KhI
Daniells, Roy
  The mole.—DoWh
  Noah.—DoWh
Danish nursery rhymes. See Nursery rhymes—Danish
Danner, Margaret
  A grandson is a hoticeberg.—AdC
Danse russe. William Carlos Williams.—KhI
"A dappled horse stood at the edge of the meadow." See The grey horse
"Darby and Joan were dressed in black." Mother Goose.—TrGg
Darcy, M. M.
  Astronaut's choice.—BrO
Dare, Eveline
  "An elephant with a huge trunk."—DuSn
  "If I ever kept a puma."—DuSn
  "If I should take a bath in mud."—DuSn
Dario, Rubén
  The three kings.—BaC—LiPch
"Darius the Mede was a king and a wonder." See Daniel
The dark ("I feared the darkness as a boy") Roy Fuller.—HiD
"Dark is soft, like fur." See Rhyme for night
"The dark night wakes, the glory breaks." See O little town of Bethlehem
The dark way home, survivors. Michael S. Harper.—AdC
The darkling elves. Jack Prelutsky.—PrH
Darkness
  At night ("When night is dark") A. Fisher.—FiO
  Batty. S. Silverstein.—SiL
  The dark ("I feared the darkness as a boy") R. Fuller.—HiD
  "How do you write the dusk." L. Morrison.—MoO
  "It's dark out. M. A. Hoberman.—HoY
  Lady of night. A. Fisher.—FiO
  "On the wall." L. Moore.—MoTs
  Out in the dark. E. Thomas.—PaB
  Rhyme for night. J. Aiken.—AiS—HiD
  Up there in the dark. A. Fisher.—FiO
Darley, George
  The sea ritual.—PaE

"Darling, at the beautician's you buy." See A valentine for a lady

"Darling, my darling, my heart is on the wing." See Morning song of love

"The darling of the world is come." See A Christmas carol

Darr, Ann
The Bagley Iowa poem.—KhI
Self expression.—LuZ

"Darting their lives away." Ann Atwood.—AtH

Daughters
The horse show. W. C. Williams.—PlL
Lessie. E. Greenfield.—GrH
Lyric for the father of a girl. V. R. Lang.—PlL
My father's death. M. Sarton.—PlL
Song for Naomi. I. Layton.—DoWh
To my daughter. S. Spender.—PlL
Where the hayfields were. A. MacLeish.—HiD
A woman mourned by daughters. A. Rich.—PlL

D'Avalos' prayer. John Masefield.—PaE

David and Absalom. See The second book of Samuel

David, King of Israel (about)
David and Absalom. From The second book of Samuel.—PlL

Davidson, Donald
Randall, my son.—PlL

Davies, Jeffrey
The washing machine.—JaPp

Davies, Mary Carolyn
Drums of the rain.—PaI

Davies, W. H.
The cat.—SaM
The dog.—CoG

Davis, Chris
"One day our pets were really sick."—DuSn

Davis, Frank Marshall
Four glimpses of night, sel.
"Peddling from door to door."—RuM
"Peddling from door to door." See Four glimpses of night

Davis, Helen Bayley
Song for a child.—PaI

Dawn. See also Morning
Alba. D. Walcott.—JaPp
At dawn. M. P. Hearn.—HeB
"At dawn the virgin is born." L. de Vega.—LiPch
Awake ("Who is first up") D. McCord.—McSu
By the saltings. T. Walker.—PaE
Dawn ("An angel, robed in spotless white") P. L. Dunbar.—BrI
Daybreak ("Dawn, blinks fawn") D. McCord.—McO
Daybreak in Alabama. L. Hughes.—AdC—MoGp
The horses. T. Hughes.—CoPh
Late starting dawn. R. Brautigan.—JaPp
Very early. K. Kuskin.—KuD

Dawn ("An angel, robed in spotless white") Paul Laurence Dunbar.—BrI

"Dawn, blinks fawn." See Daybreak

"Dawn breaking as I woke." See Alba

"A day." See Wonder

Day. See also Afternoon; Bed-time; Dawn; Evening; Morning; Night
Finders keepers. N. Farber.—FaS
"Hooray." R. Krauss.—ReB
"Rain is so rainy." B. S. De Regniers.—ReB
There came a day. T. Hughes.—HoMp—HuSs—MoGp
Tomorrow ("Tomorrows never seem to stay") D. McCord.—McO

Day. Paul Laurence Dunbar.—BrI

"The day a cricket's jacket." See Cricket jackets

"The day after." Beatrice Schenk De Regniers.—ReB

Day after Halloween. Shel Silverstein.—SiL

Day and night. Aileen Fisher.—FiO

A day at the races. Louis Phillips.—CoPh

"The day dark with rain." Ann Atwood.—AtH

Day dreams. William Canton.—PaB

"Day flows into sea." Ann Atwood.—AtH

"The day grows soft and pink of sky." See At milking

"The day hangs heavy." See Greyday

Day moon. N. M. Bodecker.—BoHh

The day of the dead. D. W. Donzella.—KhI

"The day the peartree started singing." See The man who stopped the birds

The day the T.V. broke. Gerald Jonas.—BrO

"The day was so bright." See A dog in the quarry

"The day we die." Unknown, tr. fr. the Kalahari by Arthur Markowitz.—LuZ

Daybreak. See Dawn

Daybreak ("By that withering oak") Frank Lamont Phillips.—AdC

Daybreak ("Dawn, blinks fawn") David McCord.—McO

Daybreak in Alabama. Langston Hughes.—AdC—MoGp

Days. See Day; Days of the week

Days ("What are days for") Philip Larkin.—LuZ

"The days are short." See January

Days of the week
The greedy man's week. B. S. De Regniers.—ReB
"In Fibruary, any wind's day." D. Orgel.—OrM
"Monday's child is fair of face." Unknown.—LiCc
"On a Fibruary Monday." D. Orgel.—OrM
"On a Fibruary toothday." D. Orgel.—OrM
"On tattersday, come wearing any." D. Orgel.—OrM

Days of the week—Saturday
Rainy rainy Saturday. J. Prelutsky.—PrR
Saturday's child. C. Cullen.—LiO

Days of the week—Sunday
Church poem. J. C. Thomas.—AdC
Homework. R. Hoban.—HoMp—MoGp
Sally Lun Lundy. D. McCord.—McO
"Sunday morning." N. Grimes.—GrS

Those winter Sundays. R. Hayden.—AdC—
 MaP—PlL
"Days that the wind takes over." Karla
 Kuskin.—KuD
De Coccola, Raymond and King, Paul
 Manerathiak's song. trs.—DoWh
 The wind has wings. trs.—DoWh
**De La Mare, Walter (Walter Ramal; Walter
 Rand, pseuds.)**
 At the keyhole.—WiP
 The cupboard.—PaI
 Dame Hickory.—WaFp
 Echoes.—PaE
 An epitaph.—WiP
 Grim.—WaG
 "Here all we see."—PaI
 The huntsmen.—CoPh—HiD
 Jim Jay.—HiS
 Mermaids.—PaE
 Miss T.—WiP
 Mistletoe.—HiS
 No jewel.—SaM
 Old Shellover.—SaM—WiP
 The pool in the rock.—PaE—SaM
 Quack.—WiP
 The rainbow.—SaM
 The ride-by-nights.—HiD
 Santa Claus.—LiPch
 The song of the mad prince.—WiP
 The storm.—PaE
 Sunk Lyonesse.—PaE
 Tillie.—WaGp
 Tom's little dog.—CoG
De Long Peterson, Ruth
 Midwest town.—FlA
De Mille, James
 The gallant highwayman.—DoWh
 "Sweet maiden of Passamaquoddy."—DoWh
De Regniers, Beatrice Schenk
 "The day after."—ReB
 First day of spring.—ReB
 Fourth of July.—ReB
 The greedy man's week.—ReB
 "How old will you be on your birthday."—
 ReB
 "I like winter, spring, summer and fall."—
 BrIt—ReB
 "I think."—ReB
 "I want to."—ReB
 "I want to keep."—ReB
 Late snowfall.—ReB
 "The leaves turn gold."—ReB
 "Let weather be blizzardy, zany."—ReB
 "Monsters do not scare me much."—BrIt—
 ReB
 "Night comes."—ReB
 Ouch, sort of.—ReB
 "Rain is so rainy."—ReB
 "Scare me easy."—ReB
 "Sing the old year out."—ReB
 Snow song.—ReB
 A song to sing over and over.—ReB
 Swell smells.—ReB
 "There are days."—ReB

"This leaf."—ReB
Tooth day.—ReB
"The turkeys."—ReB
A valentine to the wide world.—ReB
"You are."—ReB
De Soto, Hernando (about)
 The distant runners. M. Van Doren.—PlG
Dead. Paul Laurence Dunbar.—BrI
Dead boy. John Crowe Ransom.—PlL
"The **dead** crab." See Crab
"**Dead** heat and windless air." See August
 weather
"The **dead** shall rise again." See The raising of
 Lazarus L. Clifton.—AdC
Deaf Donald. Shel Silverstein.—SiL
"**Deaf** Donald met Talkie Sue." See Deaf
 Donald
Deafness
 Deaf Donald. S. Silverstein.—SiL
 The old wife and the ghost. J. Reeves.—
 WaGp
 "Old woman, old woman, shall we go
 a-shearing." Mother Goose.—YaI
 "Old woman, old woman."—TrGg
"**Dear** babe, that sleepest cradled by my side."
 See Frost at midnight
"**Dear** children, they asked in every town." See
 The kings from the east
"**Dear** critic, who my lightness so deplores."
 See To a captious critic
"**Dear** heart, good-night." See Premonition
"**Dear** Jonno." See A trip on the Staten Island
 ferry
"**Dear** March, come in." See March
"**Dear** parents, I write you this letter." See
 Epistle to the Olympians
"**Dear** Sybil." N. M. Bodecker.—BoHh
Dearmer, Geoffrey
 The Turkish trench dog.—CoG
Death. See also Immortality; Laments; Life—
 Life and death; Love—Love and death
 Abraham's knife. G. Garrett.—PlL
 Adaptation of a theme by Catullus. A. Tate.—
 PlL
 After the killing. D. Randall.—AdC
 Alexander Crummell, dead. P. L. Dunbar.—
 BrI
 Angle of geese. N. S. Momaday.—MoGd
 The assassination ("Do you not find
 something very strange about him") R.
 Hillyer.—LiO
 Assassination ("It was wild") D. L. Lee.—LiO
 At grandmother's. J. Haislip.—LuZ
 At night. R. Eberhart.—PlL
 The banshee. J. Prelutsky.—PrH
 Battle won is lost. P. George.—LuZ
 Before an old painting of the Crucifixion. N.
 S. Momaday.—MoGd
 Belief for JFK. A. R. Ammons.—PlG
 Birmingham 1963. R. R. Patterson.—AdC
 A birthday memorial to Seventh Street. A.
 Lorde.—AdC
 "A black man." S. Cornish.—AdC
 The blessing of the bed. E. Coatsworth.—PlL

Premonition ("Dear heart, good-night") P. L. Dunbar.—BrI

The prophecy of King Tammany. P. Freneau.—PlG

The punishment. J. Aiken.—AiS

The rabbit hunter. R. Frost.—CoG

Rainy mountain cemetery. N. S. Momaday.—MoGd

Rebecca, who slammed doors for fun and perished miserably. H. Belloc.—HiS

"Remembering Grandma filling up this porch." N. Grimes.—GrS

The sea ritual. G. Darley.—PaE

"A sight in camp in the daybreak gray and dim." W. Whitman.—LiO

A sister's grave. R. N. Peck.—PeB

A small elegy. R. Snyder.—JaPp

Song of the giant killer. L. Norris.—NoM

"Sooner or later." S. Cornish.—AdC

The spare quilt. J. P. Bishop.—PlG

The story of a well made shield. N. S. Momaday.—MoGd

Sunk Lyonesse. W. De La Mare.—PaE

Swifts. T. Hughes.—HuSs

That dark other mountain. R. Francis.—LiCc

A threnody. G. T. Lanigan.—DoWh

Thrown away. R. Kipling.—CoPh

To a dead friend. P. L. Dunbar.—BrI

"Today is a very good day to die." N. Wood.—LuZ

Tom McGreevy, in America, thinks of himself as a boy. From Our stars come from Ireland. W. Stevens.—PlG

Twilight's last gleaming. A. W. Monks.—LiO

The twins. C. Bukowski.—KhI

Two figures. N. S. Momaday.—MoGd

Unrealized. T. Hardy.—PlL

A vegetable, I will not be. D. Whitewing.—FlA

"Water wobbling blue sky puddled October." From Autumn nature notes. T. Hughes—HuSs

"Who killed Cock Robin." Mother Goose.—WiP

Winter calf. R. N. Peck.—PeB

Winter verse for his sister. W. Meredith.—PlL

The witnesses. H. W. Longfellow.—PlG

The wolves. G. Kinnell.—LuZ

A woman mourned by daughters. A. Rich.—PlL

Wonder. M. Angelou.—AnO

Words, like spiders. P. Wolny.—JaPp

Writing while my father dies. L. Pastan.—JaPp

"You had to go to funerals." A. Walker.—LuZ

The young dead soldiers. A. MacLeish.—LiO

Death ("Storm and strife and stress") Paul Laurence Dunbar.—BrI

"Death is great." See Closing piece

The death of a soldier. Wallace Stevens.—LiO

Death of Dr. King. Sam Cornish.—AdC—LiO

Death of the cat. Ian Serraillier.—HiS

A death song. Paul Laurence Dunbar.—BrI

"Debbie is in DEBt." See Inside information

Deborah Lee. Yvonne.—AdC

The debt. Paul Laurence Dunbar.—BrI

Dec, Frederick

Bulldozers.—JaPp

Class of 19—.—JaPp

Deceased. Cid Corman.—JaPp

December

"Chill December brings the sleet." From The garden year. S. Coleridge.—BaC

December ("First snow, the flakes") J. Updike.—BaC

December ("I like days") A. Fisher.—BaC

December fragments. R. Lattimore.—LiPch

December river. T. Hughes.—HuSs

"Dimmest and brightest month am I." C. G. Rossetti.—BaC

"I heard a bird sing." O. Herford.—BaC

Snow and snow. T. Hughes.—HuSs

December ("First snow, the flakes") John Updike.—BaC

December ("I like days") Aileen Fisher.—BaC

December fragments. Richmond Lattimore.—LiPch

"December morning melody." See Winter notes

December river. Ted Hughes.—HuSs

Deceptions. Ted Hughes.—HuSs

"Deep beneath the foaming billows." See The kraken

"The deep brown eyes of susans." See Brown eyes are watching

"Deep in my heart that aches with the repression." See Unexpressed

"Deep in the wave is a coral grove." See Coral grove

Deep into winter. Arnold Adoff.—AdE

Deep sea diver. See The diver ("Diver go down")

Deep sea diving

The diver. R. Francis.—PaE

Deep sea diver.—MoGp

Divers. R. H. Schauffler.—PaE

A deep sworn vow. William Butler Yeats.—JaPp

Deer

"Autumn already." A. Atwood.—AtH

Out in the dark. E. Thomas.—PaB

"Over the leaf crisp ground." A. Atwood.—AtH

R is for reindeer. W. J. Smith.—SmL

Simile. N. S. Momaday.—LuZ—MoGd

Song of the deer hunter. Unknown.—MoGp

The stag. T. Hughes.—HuSs

Defeat. See Failure

The defenders. Ted Hughes.—HuSs

Dehn, Paul

"Flight Sergeant Foster flattened Gloucester." See A leaden treasury of English verse

"Geiger, geiger, ticking slow." See A leaden treasury of English verse

How to paint the portrait of a bird. tr.— LuZ

A leaden treasury of English verse, sels.

1. "Ring-a-ring o' neutrons."—BrO

Dehn, Paul—*Continued*
2. "Geiger, geiger, ticking slow."—BrO
3. "Flight Sergeant Foster flattened
Gloucester."—BrO
"Ring-a-ring o' neutrons." See A leaden
treasury of English verse
Delander, Sonja
The octopus.—DuSn
Owls.—DuSn
"The **delicate** shells lay on the shore." See
Each and all
"**Delicate** the toad." Robert Francis.—HiD
"A **delicious** old man of the dunes." See A man
of the dunes
The **delight** song of Tsoai-talee. N. Scott
Momaday.—MoGd
Demille, A. B.
The ice king.—DoWh
Denise. Robert Beverly Hale.—CoG
Dennis, C. J.
A change of air.—DuSn
Woolloomooloo.—DuSn
Dentists
Ruth. K. Starbird.—StC
Tooth trouble. D. McCord.—McO
Derricks. R.R. Cuscaden.—FlA
A **deserted** beach. Robin Smallman.—SaM
Deserts
Abundance. M. Moore.—PaB
Forms of the earth at Abiquiu. N. S.
Momaday.—MoGd
The mummy ("In the darkness of a
sepulcher") J. Prelutsky.—PrH
"This is no place." From Children of the
desert. B. Baylor—MoGp
"**Desire** will come of waiting." See Anywhere is
a street into the night
Despair
All nature seems at work. S. T. Coleridge.—
PaB
Despair ("Let me close the eyes of my soul")
P. L. Dunbar.—BrI
The haunted house. J. Prelutsky.—PrN
Despair ("Let me close the eyes of my soul")
Paul Laurence Dunbar.—BrI
Desserts
"Bananas and cream." D. McCord.—McO
Destruction
The burning. N. S. Momaday.—MoGd
The **detail.** Cid Corman.—JaPp
Determination. John Henrik Clarke.—AdC
"A **determined** young man in Northchapel."
See A man in Northchapel
Detroit. Donald Hall.—FlA
Detroit city. Jill Witherspoon Boyer.—AdC
Detroit, Michigan
Detroit. D. Hall.—FlA
Detroit city. J. W. Boyer.—AdC
Deus ex machina, or, roughly translated, God
only knows what comes out of the
machine. Richard Armour.—BrO
Deutsch, Babette
Fireworks.—LiO
Little catkins. tr.—LiCc—LiO

The mother.—PlL
Need.—JaPp
Phantasus, I, 8. tr.—LiPch
Devil
The devil's pitchfork. R. N. Peck.—PeB
"Did you eever, iver, over." Unknown.—WiP
"Some say the devil's dead." Mother
Goose.—TrGg
The **devil's** pitchfork. Robert Newton Peck.—
PeB
Dew
No jewel. W. De La Mare.—SaM
"The **dew** is gleaming in the grass." See
Among the millet
Dexter. Joan Byers Grayston.—CoPh
Di Caprio, Isabelle
Jabber-whacky, or, on dreaming, after falling
asleep watching TV.—BrO
Dialect—American—Black
A coquette conquered. P. L. Dunbar.—BrI
A death song. P. L. Dunbar.—BrI
Hymn ("O li'l' lamb out in de col' ") P. L.
Dunbar.—BrI
Little brown baby. P. L. Dunbar.—BrI
A negro love song. P. L. Dunbar.—BrI
The real question. P. L. Dunbar.—BrI
Song ("Wintah, summah, snow er shine") P.
L. Dunbar.—BrI
Dialect—Scottish. See entries under Burns,
Robert
Diaries
The book. A. Rich.—PlL
Dickey in Tucson. R. P. Dickey.—KhI
Dickey, James
The hospital window.—PlL
Hunting Civil War relics at Nimblewill
Creek.—PlG
In the tree house at night.—PlL
Dickey, R. P.
Dickey in Tucson.—KhI
Dickey, William
Hope.—CoG
Dickinson, Emily
"Bee, I'm expecting you."—HiS
"Birthday of but a single pang."—LiO
"Dear March, come in." See March
"I know some lonely houses off the road."—
HiS
I'm nobody.—HiS
March, sel.
"Dear March, come in."—HoMp
Moon.—MoGp
"My country need not change her gown."—
PlG
Narrow fellow.—PaB
"She rose to his requirement, dropt."—PlL
To make a prairie.—FlA
Dictionary. William Jay Smith.—SmL
"A **dictionary's** where you can look things up."
See Dictionary
"**Did** an artist weave my." See Who cast my
shadow
"**Did** stegosaurus bellow." See Dinosaur din

"**Did** they send me away from my cat and my wife." See Gunner

"**Did** you eever, iver, over." Unknown.—WiP

"**Did** you ever fight with your sister, yes." See Let her have it

"**Did** you ever see." See Cricket song

"**Did** you feed my cow." Unknown.—WiP

"**Did** you hear 'bout ticklish Tom." See Ticklish Tom

"**Diddle,** diddle, dumpling, my son John." Mother Goose.—TrGg

The **diet.** Susan Mernit.—KhI

Diets and dieting
Adelaide. J. Prelutsky.—PrQ
The diet. S. Mernit.—KhI

Difference ("On paper that's ruled") Aileen Fisher.—FiO

Different dreams. Karla Kuskin.—KuD

A **different** image. Dudley Randall.—AdC

"**Different** people have different 'pinions." Mother Goose.—TrGg

The **difficulty** of living on other planets. Dennis Lee.—LeN

"A **diller,** a dollar." Mother Goose.—TrGg

"**Dilly** dilly piccalilli." Clyde Watson.—WiP

"The **dime** goes in the crocodial." See The crocodial

"**Dimmest** and brightest month am I." Christina Georgina Rossetti.—BaC

The **diners** in the kitchen. James Whitcomb Riley.—CoG

"**Ding-dong,** ding-dong, ding-dong." See A dirge for a righteous kitten

"A **dingo** trapper way out west." Wilbur G. Howcroft.—DuSn

"**Dingty,** diddledy, my mammy's maid." Mother Goose.—LoG—TrGg

"**Dining** with his older daughter." See Waiters

"**Dinner.**" See Corinna

Dinner guest. Shel Silverstein.—SiL

Dinner thought. Arnold Adoff.—AdE

The **dinosaur** ("The dinosaur had two brains") Louis Phillips.—CoDb

The **dinosaur** ("This poem is too small, I fear") Edward Lucie-Smith.—CoDb

"The **dinosaur** died, was consumed by the soil." See Pre-history repeats

Dinosaur din. X. J. Kennedy.—CoDb—KeP

"The **dinosaur** had two brains." See The dinosaur

"**Dinosaur** means terrible lizard." See S'no fun

Dinosaurs ("Dinosaurs do not count") Valerie Worth.—CoDb—WoM

Dinosaurs ("Their feet, planted into tar") Myra Cohn Livingston.—MoGp

Dinosaurs and other prehistoric animals
"Bellowed the ogre." L. Moore.—WaG
Better than a pussycat. W. Cole.—CoDb
Brachiosaurus. M. A. Hoberman.—CoDb—HoY
The brontosaurus. H.A.C. Evans.—CoDb
Company. B. Katz.—CoDb
The dinosaur ("The dinosaur had two brains") L. Phillips.—CoDb

The dinosaur ("This poem is too small, I fear") E. Lucie-Smith.—CoDb
Dinosaur din. X. J. Kennedy.—CoDb—KeP
Dinosaurs ("Dinosaurs do not count") V. Worth.—CoDb—WoM
Dinosaurs ("Their feet, planted into tar") M. C. Livingston.—LiWt—MoGp
The dinosaurs' dinner. D. Lee.—CoDb
The dinosore. J. Yolen.—YoH
Diplodocus holiday. X. J. Kennedy.—KeP
Dudley not cuddly. W. Cole.—CoDb
"The eohippus." W. Cole.—CoDb
"Here he comes." M. Pomeroy.—CoDb
I spy tyrannosaurus. P. Johnson, Jr.—CoDb
Ichthyosaurus. R. S. Oliver.—OlC
"If I had a brontosaurus." S. Silverstein.—CoDb—MoGp
"If you pinch a dinosaur." S. Silverstein.—CoDb
I'm scared. W. Cole.—CoDb
It's all relative. W. Cole.—CoDb
The largest of them all. J. A. Lindon.—CoDb
Lines on a small potato. M. Fishback.—CoDb
Long gone. J. Prelutsky.—CoDb
"The mastodon." M. Braude.—CoDb
My dinosaur's day in the park. E. Winthrop.—CoDb
Next. O. Nash.—BlC
Night voyage. M. Luton.—CoDb
No accounting for tastes. J. A. Lindon.—CoDb
Not me. W. Cole.—CoDb
The only place. W. Cole.—CoDb
Prehistoric. S. Silverstein.—SiL
Pre-history repeats. R. J. McKent.—BrO
The pterodactyl ("Long ago the pterodactyl") H.A.C. Evans.—CoDb
The pterodactyl ("A pterodactyl drove his Edsel") A. M. Ross.—CoDb
S'no fun. W. Cole.—CoDb
So it goes. W. Cole.—CoDb
Take my advice. W. Cole.—CoDb
Time zones. L. Morrison.—CoDb
To the skeleton of a dinosaur in the museum. L. Moore.—CoDb
"The trouble with a dinosaur." X. J. Kennedy.—CoDb
The tyrannosaur. M. Braude.—CoDb
"The tyrannosaurus rex." S. Silverstein.—CoDb
"Tyrannosaurus rex's teeth." X. J. Kennedy.—CoDb—KeP
"The **dinosaurs** are gone, where can you see 'em." See The only place
The **dinosaurs'** dinner. Dennis Lee.—CoDb
"**Dinosaurs** do not count." See Dinosaurs
The **dinosore.** Jane Yolen.—YoH
Diplodocus holiday. X. J. Kennedy.—KeP
"The **diplodocus** weighed twenty ton." See Take my advice

Directions
Compass song. D. McCord.—McO

A **dirge** for a righteous kitten. Vachel Lindsay.—WiP

Dogs

The African wild dog. J. Gardner.—GaCb
The ambiguous dog. A. Guiterman.—CoG
The bath. R. C. Lehmann.—CoG
Beagles. W. R. Rodgers.—CoG
Best of show. B. Howes.—CoG
Beth-Gelert. W. R. Spencer.—CoG
"Big dog." P. Booth.—Cog
Bliss. E. Farjeon.—YaI
The bloodhound. E. Anthony.—CoG
Blue Bell. Unknown.—BlH
"Bow, wow, wow." Mother Goose.—BlH
Boxer pup. G. MacBeth.—MoGp
Brave Rover. M. Beerbohm.—CoG
Buff. Mother Goose.—BlH
Buying a puppy. L. Norris.—NoM
Cachita. C. Pomerantz.—PoT
Canine amenities. Unknown.—CoG
The cat and the dog. J. Gardner.—GaCb
Chums. A. Guiterman.—PaI
The collies. E. Anthony.—CoG
Confession of a glutton. D. Marquis.—CoG
Contentment. B. Johnson.—CoG
D is for dog. W. J. Smith.—SmL
The dachshund. E. Anthony.—CoG
Daley's dorg Wattle. W. T. Goodge.—CoG
Dandy. Unknown.—BlH
"The day was so bright." From A dog in the
    quarry. M. Holub.—CoG
Denise. R. B. Hale.—CoG
The diners in the kitchen. J. W. Riley.—CoG
The dog ("The dog was there, outside her
    door") W. H. Davies.—CoG
Dog ("Dogs are quite a bit like people") W. J.
    Smith.—SmL
A dog ("I am alone") C. Zolotow.—CoG
The dog ("The truth I do not stretch or
    shove") O. Nash.—BlC—CoG
"A dog and a cat went out together."
    Unknown.—WiP
Dog around the block. E. B. White.—CoG
The dog from Malta. Tymnes.—CoG
"The dog has many doggy friends." K.
    Kuskin.—KuR
Dog in the fountain. R. Souster.—CoG
Dog, midwinter. R. Souster.—CoG
The dog parade. A. Guiterman.—CoG
"The doggies went to the mill." Unknown.—
    BlH
The dog's cold nose. A. Guiterman.—CoG
Dog's day. S. Silverstein.—SiL
Dogs of Santiago. E. McCarthy.—CoG
"The dogs of the monks." Unknown.—BlH
A dog's tale. W. Cole.—CoA
The dollar dog. J. Ciardi.—CoG
Early spring. P. Whalen.—HoMp
Elegy on the death of a mad dog. O.
    Goldsmith.—CoG
Epitaph to a dog. Lord Byron.—CoG
Fashions in dogs. E. B. White.—CoG
For a good dog. A. Guiterman.—CoG
For Mugs. M. C. Livingston.—LiF
"For the Fibruary dog show." D. Orgel.—
    OrM

Full of the moon. K. Kuskin.—KuD—RuM
Gluskap's hound. T. G. Roberts.—DoWh
Gone ("I've looked behind the shed") D.
    McCord.—HoBm—McO
The hairy dog. H. Asquith.—PaI—SaM
"Hark, hark, the dogs do bark." Mother
    Goose.—BlH—LoG
Have I got dogs. W. Cole.—CoG
Hector the dog. K. Barnes.—CoG
"Hey diddle, diddle." Mother Goose.—BlH
His Highness's dog. Unknown.—BlH
Hope. W. Dickey.—CoG
The hound. S. Lanier.—CoG
A hound of Cohasset. N. M. Bodecker.—BoP
Hound on the porch roof. R.P.T. Coffin.—
    CoG
The house dog's grave. R. Jeffers.—CoG
"I had a little dog, and his name was Bill."
    Mother Goose.—TrGg
I had a little doggy. Mother Goose.—BlH
I have a lion. K. Kuskin.—KuD
I'm skeleton. L. Moore.—BrIt
The Irish wolf hound. D. F. McCarthy.—CoG
"I've a kisty." Unknown.—BlH
"I've got a dog as thin as a rail." Unknown.—
    CoG
Joggers. D. McCord.—McSu
Little Bingo. Unknown.—BlH
The little black dog. Mother Goose.—BlH
"Little tiny puppy dog." S. Milligan.—CoG
Lone dog. I. R. McLeod.—CoG
Lost dog. F. Rodman.—CoG
Love me, love my dog. I. V. Crawford.—
    DoWh
Luath. R. Burns.—CoG
"A man in our village." L. Norris.—CoG—
    NoM
Me and Samantha. P. Johnson.—CoG
Merlin & the snake's egg. L. Norris.—NoM
Mick. J. Reeves.—CoG
Montgomery, with acknowledgements to T.
    S. Eliot's Macavity. H.A.C. Evans.—CoG
The moon ("My puppy looks at the big old
    moon") A. Fisher.—FiO
Motto for a dog house. A. Guiterman.—CoG
My delicatessen loving dog. X. J. Kennedy.—
    KeP
"My hounds are bred out of the Spartan
    kind." From A midsummer night's dream.
    W. Shakespeare.—CoG
My puppy ("I have a playful") A. Fisher.—
    FiO
My puppy ("It's funny") A. Fisher.—BeR
The needing. R. N. Peck.—PeB
The night hunt. T. MacDonagh.—CoG
Night song. F. Cornford.—CoG
Oh where, oh where. Mother Goose.—BlH
Of an ancient spaniel in her fifteenth year.
    C. Morley.—CoG
Old Blue. Unknown.—CoG
Old dog ("Toward the last in the morning
    she could not") W. Stafford.—CoG
Old dog ("Waddles after") R. Souster.—CoG
Old dog Tray. S. Foster.—CoG

Dogs—*Continued*

The old dog's song. L. Norris.—NoM

"Old farmer Giles." Mother Goose.—BlH

Old man, phantom dog. F. Eckman.—FlA

"Old mother Hubbard." Mother Goose.—BlH

On buying a dog. E. Klauber.—CoG

On the death of Echo, a favorite beagle. H. Coleridge.—CoG

Our Lucy, 1956–1960. P. Goodman.—CoG

"Out on the windy hill." L. Norris.—NoM

Pete the pup at the seashore. D. Marquis.—MoGp

    Pete at the seashore.—CoG

Poetic tale. G. M. Miller.—CoG

"Poor dog Bright." Unknown.—BlH

The porcupine ("Any hound a porcupine nudges") O. Nash.—BlC

The power of the dog. R. Kipling.—CoG

Puppy ("Puppy is one I've failed with, he came too close") F. Lape.—CoG

Puppy and I. A. A. Milne.—WiP

The rabbit hunter. R. Frost.—CoG

Rake. D. U. Ratcliffe.—CoG

Remarks from the pup. B. Johnson.—CoG

"Roon, roon, rosie." Unknown.—BlH

Scroppo's dog. M. Swenson.—CoG

Silly dog. M. C. Livingston.—CoG—LiF

The span of life. R. Frost.—CoG

Stop kicking my dog around. Unknown.—CoG

Sudden assertion. K. Leslie.—CoG

Sunning. J. S. Tippett.—CoG

Suzie's new dog. J. Ciardi.—CoG

"The tamarindo puppy. C. Pomerantz.—PoT

There was a little dog. Mother Goose.—BlH

Tim, an Irish terrier. W. M. Letts.—CoG

Tom's little dog. W. De La Mare.—CoG

The train dogs. P. Johnson.—DoWh

The Turkish trench dog. G. Dearmer.—CoG

Two dogs have I. O. Nash.—CoG

"Two little dogs sat by the fire." Mother Goose.—TrGg

    "Two little dogs."—BlH

Unsatisfied yearning. R. K. Munkittrick.—CoG

Verse for a certain dog. D. Parker.—CoG

A village tale. M. Sarton.—CoG

Whippet. P. Andrew.—CoG

Wonder. B. Raymund.—CoG

The woodman's dog. W. Cowper.—CoG

The young puppy. A. A. Milne.—CoG

"**Dogs** are quite a bit like people." See Dog

The **dog's** cold nose. Arthur Guiterman.—CoG

Dog's day. Shel Silverstein.—SiL

Dogs of Santiago. Eugene McCarthy.—CoG

"The **dogs** of the monks." Unknown.—BlH

"A **dog's** tail." See Tails

A **dog's** tale. William Cole.—CoA

Dolben, D. M.

    A sea song.—PaE

The **dollar** dog. John Ciardi.—CoG

"A **dollar** dog is all mixed up." See The dollar dog

"A **dollar** is a hundred cents." See Centipede

Dolls

The operation. D. Lee.—LeG

Twistable turnable man. S. Silverstein.—SiL

"**Doll's** boy's asleep." E. E. Cummings.—HiD

"**Dolphin** plunge, fountain play." See Invocation

Dolphins and porpoises

The cross porpoise. L. Morrison.—MoW

The porpoise ("I kind of like the playful porpoise") O. Nash.—BlC

"Take the dolphin, as smooth and as slick." From Limericks. D. McCord.—McSu

Domett, Alfred

    A thousand bells.—BaC

Don Larsen's perfect game. Paul Goodman.—LuZ

Done with. Ann Stanford.—LuZ

The **donkey** ("I saw a donkey") Unknown.—CoA

Donkey riding. Unknown.—DoWh

Donkeys

The donkey. Unknown.—CoA

Donkey riding. Unknown.—DoWh

Faith. M. Dunkels.—CoPh

The little donkey. F. Jammes.—LiPch

My donkey. R. Fyleman.—WiP

"A pompous old donkey of Yately." M. C. Livingston.—LiLl

The prayer of the donkey. C. B. de Gasztold.—LiPch

"When the donkey saw the zebra." Unknown.—WiP

Donne, John

An epithalamion, sel.

    "Hail Bishop Valentine, whose day this is."—LiO

"Hail Bishop Valentine, whose day this is." See An epithalamion

A valediction: forbidding mourning.—PlL

The whale.—PaE

Donovan, Rhoda

Ten week wife.—KhI

"**Don't** ask me how he managed." See The worm

Don't cry, darling, it's blood all right. Ogden Nash.—BlC

"**Don't** ever make." See The snake

Don't ever seize a weasel by the tail. Jack Prelutsky.—WiP

"**Don't** go looking for fairies." See Fairies

"**Don't** kill time." See Rune

"**Don't** let them die out." See Now poem for us

"**Don't** tell anybody." Osip Emilevich Mandelstam, tr. by Burton Raffel and Alla Burago.—LuZ

"**Don't** tell me that I talk too much." See Don't you dare

"**Don't** wanna be." Sonia Sanchez.—AdC

"**Don't** waste your time in looking for." See Long gone

"**Don't** write alright, that's wrong." See Like you as it

"**Don't** you care for my love, she said bitterly." See Intimates

Don't you dare. Arnold Spilka.—CoI
"Don't you go too near the sea." See The
 waves of the sea
"Don't you sort of wonder." See Taking a walk
"Don't you think it's probable." See Little talk
Donzella, D. W.
 The day of the dead.—KhI
Doodlebug. Mary Ann Hoberman.—HoBu
"The doodlebug inside its lair." See Doodlebug
"A door." See The poem as a door
Door ("My grandmother's") Valerie Worth.—
 WoSm
The door ("Why is there more") David
 McCord.—McO
"The door is shut fast." See Who's in
Doors
 The alligate. J. Yolen.—YoH
 Door ("My grandmother's") V. Worth.—
  WoSm
 The door ("Why is there more") D.
  McCord.—McO
 Doors ("An open door says come in") C.
  Sandburg.—WiP
 The poem as a door. E. Merriam.—MeR
 Prospective immigrants please note. A.
  Rich.—PlG
 Rebecca, who slammed doors for fun and
  perished miserably. H. Belloc.—HiS
 Two doorbells. X. J. Kennedy.—KeP
Doors ("An open door says, come in") Carl
 Sandburg.—WiP
"The doors are closing." See Indoors
Dorman, Sonya
 Elegy for Bella, Sarah, Rosie, and all the
  others.—PlG
 N. Y. to L. A. by jet plane.—PlG
Dory Miller. Sam Cornish.—AdC
Double barrelled ding dong bat. Unknown.—
 HeB
Double dactyls
 The garden snake. J. Gardner.—GaCb
 The red-headed woodpecker. J. Gardner.—
  GaCb
"The doubles partners quarreled so." See
 Dis-play
Douglas, Suzanne
 No holes marred.—BrO
 Progress.—BrO
Douglass. Paul Laurence Dunbar.—BrI
Douglass, Frederick (about)
 Douglass. P. L. Dunbar.—BrI
 Elegy for Harriet Tubman and Frederick
  Douglass. M. Angelou.—AnO
 Frederick Douglass ("When it is finally ours,
  this freedom, this liberty, this beautiful") R.
  Hayden.—AdC
Dove ("What thing") Norma Farber.—LiPch
Doves. See Pigeons
"The doves stay in their cotes." N. M.
 Bodecker.—BoHh
"Down." See The grasshopper
"Down among the cobwebs, at the roots of
 grass." See Hiding place
"Down away." See Wings

Down below. Joan Aiken.—AiS
"Down by the pool still fishing." See Runover
 rhyme
Down by the sea. David McCord.—McO
"Down by the trickle brook." See Monkey
 vines
"Down comes the winter rain." See Unrealized
"Down dip the branches." Mark Van Doren.—
 HiD
Down in Dallas. X. J. Kennedy.—LiO
"Down in Dallas, down in Dallas." See Down
 in Dallas
"Down in the garden." See Zizzy bee
"Down in the hollow." Aileen Fisher.—PaI
"Down in the meadow." See Peepers in the
 swamp grass
"Down in the silent hallway." See Unsatisfied
 yearning
"Down in the water meadows Riley." See Riley
"Down the star stairs fell." See Dr Klimwell's
 fall
"Down the stream the swans all glide." Spike
 Milligan.—CoA
"Down with the rosemary and bays." See
 Spring cleaning
Dowson, Ernest
 Envoy.—JaPp
"Dozing in the summer sun." See Wake up
The dracula vine. Ted Hughes.—HuM
"The draft of love was cool and sweet." See
 Love's draft
Drafted. Su Wu, tr. fr. the Chinese by Kenneth
 Rexroth.—PlL
Dragon ("A dragon named Ernest Belflour")
 William Jay Smith.—SmL
Dragon flies. See Dragonflies
"A dragon named Ernest Belflour." See Dragon
Dragon night. Jane Yolen.—YoD
The dragon of death. Jack Prelutsky.—PrN
The dragon of Grindly Grun. Shel Silverstein.—
 SiL
Dragonflies
 The dragonfly ("A dragonfly sat") N.
  Giovanni.—GiV
 The dragonfly ("Glassy wings") R. S. Oliver.—
  OlC
 Dragonfly ("You get what you eat with your
  feet when you hunt") M. A. Hoberman.—
  HoBu
 The dragonfly ("A dragonfly sat") Nikki
  Giovanni.—GiV
 The dragonfly ("Glassy wings") Robert S.
  Oliver.—OlC
 Dragonfly ("You get what you eat with your
  feet when you hunt") Mary Ann
  Hoberman.—HoBu
"A dragonfly sat." See The dragonfly
Dragons
 "Are all the dragons dead." From
  Concerning dragons. H. Pepler.—MoF
 Custard the dragon and the wicked witch. O.
  Nash.—BlC
 Dragon ("A dragon named Ernest Belflour")
  W. J. Smith.—SmL

Wild child's lament. J. Yolen.—YoD
The zombie. J. Prelutsky.—PrH
Dreams ("Dream on, for dreams are sweet")
  Paul Laurence Dunbar.—BrI
Dreams ("In my younger years") Nikki
  Giovanni.—AdC
Dreams ("What dreams we have and how they
  fly") Paul Laurence Dunbar.—BrI
Dress. See Clothing and dress
"Dried to a pit of meanness." See Ten week
  wife
Drinking fountain. Marchette Chute.—PaI
Drinks and drinking
  Chocolate milk. J. Prelutsky.—PrR
  Crows ("I love crows") W. Witherup.—JaPp
  Drinking fountain. M. Chute.—PaI
  Lament, for cocoa. J. Updike.—CoPs
  Lemonade ("It's lemonading time again") D.
    McCord.—McO
  Lemonade ("Lemons are all yellow") P.
    Johnson.—CoPs
  "The man in the moon drinks claret."
    Mother Goose.—TrGg
  My papa's waltz. T. Roethke.—MaP
  "Said the monkey to the owl." Unknown.—
    WiP
  The shooting of Dan McGrew. R. W.
    Service.—DoWh
  Song of the pop bottlers. M. Bishop.—CoPs
  "There was an old man in a trunk." O.
    Nash.—BlC
  "Who comes here." Mother Goose.—TrGg
Drinkwater, John
  Snail.—BeR—WiP
The **driver** ("The reins, looped lightly round his
  aged knuckles") Joan Aiken.—AiS
The **driver** ("Someday I'm going to pick up")
  Joel Lueders.—LuZ
"The driver bowed and took my things." See
  Blake's wonderful car delivers us
  wonderfully well
A **driver** from Deering. N. M. Bodecker.—BoP
Drivers and driving
  The driver ("The reins, looped lightly round
    his aged knuckles") J. Aiken.—AiS
  A driver from Deering. N. M. Bodecker.—
    BoP
  Driving to the beach. J. Cole.—HoBm
  "Four-way stop." M. C. Livingston.—LiF
  Out of the city. E. Merriam.—MeW
  A person of Ealing. N. M. Bodecker.—BoP
  A trucker. T. Gunn.—JaPp
  The windshield wipers' song. D. McCord.—
    McSu
"Driving through New England." Lucille
  Clifton.—PlG
Driving to the beach. Joanna Cole.—HoBm
Drowning
  "Belly and Tubs went out in a boat." C.
    Watson.—WiP
  Fear ("Barnabus Browning") S. Silverstein.—
    SiL

"Lord, lord, methought what pain it was to
  drown." From King Richard III. W.
  Shakespeare.—PaE
The mermaid ("A mermaid found a
  swimming lad") W. B. Yeats.—PaE
A **drowsy** day. Paul Laurence Dunbar.—BrI
Drugs. See Drugs and drug use; Medicine
Drugs and drug use
  Junior addict. L. Hughes.—AdC
  O.D. Z. Gilbert.—AdC
  The pusher. M. Angelou.—AnO
  To my daughter the junkie on a train. A.
    Lorde.—AdC
"The drum is our big windowpane." See
  Drums of the rain
Drummers and drums
  Drums of the rain. M. C. Davies.—PaI
  New Mexican mountain. R. Jeffers.—PlG
  "Now Christmas is come." Unknown.—LiPch
  Patapan. B. de la Monnoye.—LiPch
  Percussions. R. Welburn.—AdC
  A portrait of Rudy. J. Cunningham.—AdC
"Drums gather and humble us beyond escape."
  See Belief for JFK
Drums of the rain. Mary Carolyn Davies.—PaI
"Drupaceous fruit." See Jujubes
Dryads. See Fairies
Dryden, John
  Incantation to Oedipus.—LiO
The **duck** ("Behold the duck") Ogden Nash.—
  BlC—LuZ
"The duck has pluck." John Gardner.—GaCb
"The duck is whiter than whey is." See Quack
"Duckle, duckle, daisy." Leroy F. Jackson.—
  BaC
Ducks
  The duck ("Behold the duck") O. Nash.—
    BlC—LuZ
  "The duck has pluck." J. Gardner.—GaCb
  Ducks ("Ducks are lucky") M. A.
    Hoberman.—CoA
  Ducks walking. D. McCord.—McO
  Four little ducks. D. McCord.—McO
  Quack. W. De La Mare.—WiP
  A talented duckling. N. M. Bodecker.—BoP
  A trueblue gentleman. K. Patchen.—HiS
  The turtle. J. Gardner.—GaCb
  The white drake. Unknown.—DoWh
Ducks ("Ducks are lucky") Mary Ann
  Hoberman.—CoA
"Ducks are lucky." See Ducks
Ducks walking. David McCord.—McO
Dudley not cuddly. William Cole.—CoDb
Duet ("I hold her close") Aileen Fisher.—FiO
Dugan, Alan
  Letter to Donald Fall.—KhI
  Thesis, antithesis, and nostalgia.—JaPp
Dugan, Michael
  Discovery.—DuSn
  Food.—DuSn
  Gumble.—DuSn
  My old dad.—DuSn
  Nightening.—DuSn
  "Obsequious Prawn."—DuSn

A song ("Thou art the soul of a summer's day")—BrI

Song ("Wintah, summah, snow er shine")—BrI

The sparrow.—BrI

Spring song.—BrI

The sum.—BrI

A summer's night.—BrI

Sunset.—BrI

Suppose.—BrI

Sympathy.—BrI

Theology.—BrI

Thou art my lute.—BrI

To a captious critic.—BrI

To a dead friend.—BrI

To a lady playing the harp.—BrI

To a violet found on All Saints' Day.—BrI

Twilight.—BrI

Unexpressed.—BrI

Vagrants.—BrI

We wear the mask.—BrI

When all is done.—BrI

"Why fades a dream."—BrI

A winter's day.—BrI

With the lark.—BrI

Dunkels, Marjorie

Faith.—CoPh

Duran, Cheli

Four Christmas carols, sel. tr.

"How cold the snow."—LiPch

Durenda Fair. David McCord.—McO

Durgnat, Raymond

Scrap iron.—JaPp

"**During** the strike, the ponies were brought up." See The ponies

"**Dusk.**" See Swan and shadow

Dusk ("Peeking from her room") Myra Cohn Livingston.—LiF

Dust

Dust ("Around a distant bend the wagon showed") R. N. Peck.—PeB

Laying the dust. D. Levertov.—LuZ—MoGp

Dust ("Around a distant bend the wagon showed") Robert Newton Peck.—PeB

"**Dust** always blowing about the town." See A peck of gold

"**Dust** has a way of hiding." See Mother's helper

"The **dust** of ancient pages." See Communication II—The student

Duty. See also Conduct of life

The shepherd who stayed. T. Garrison.—LiPch

The **dwarf** to her child. Jane Yolen.—YoD

Dwarfs

The dwarf to her child. J. Yolen.—YoD

The **dying** patriot, sel. James Elroy Flecker

"Evening on the olden, the golden sea of Wales."—PaE

E

E is for egg. William Jay Smith.—SmL

Each and all, sel. Ralph Waldo Emerson

"The delicate shells lay on the shore."—PaE

"**Each** house is swept the day before." See Ever green

"**Each** morning when the dawn returns." See The firetender

"**Each** time I see the upside down man." See Reflection

"**Each** year, as spring returns." See Grandfather

The **eagle.** John Gardner.—GaCb

The **eagle-feather** fan. N. Scott Momaday.—MoGd

"The **eagle** is my power." See The eagle-feather fan

"The **eagle**, stooping from yon snow-blown peaks." See Inscription

Eagles

The eagle. J. Gardner.—GaCb

The eagle-feather fan. N. S. Momaday.—MoGd

The eagle's song. Unknown.—PlG

Inability to depict an eagle. R. Eberhart.—PlG

Inscription. J. G. Whittier.—PlG

Like ghosts of eagles. R. Francis.—PlG

The story of a well-made shield. N. S. Momaday.—MoGd

"The **eagles** have practically left America." See Inability to depict an eagle

The **eagle's** song. Unknown, tr. by Mary Austin.—PlG

Early bee. Aileen Fisher.—FiO

"**Early** bee, April bee." See Early bee

Early moon. Aileen Fisher.—FiO

Early snow. Aileen Fisher.—FiO

Early spring. Philip Whalen.—HoMp

"The **early** sunlight quilts the floor." See Crazy quilt

Early supper. Barbara Howes.—HiD

"**Early** this morning." See The strangers

"The **early** wagons left no sign." See The trail into Kansas

Early warning. Shirley Marks.—BrO

Ears

Cricket song. A. Fisher.—FiO

Ears ("Do rabbits and donkeys") A. Fisher.—FiO

Senses. S. Silverstein.—SiL

Shh. E. Merriam.—MeW

Sounds of spring. A. Fisher.—FiO

Transplantitis. L. A. Sobel.—BrO

Ears ("Do rabbits and donkeys") Aileen Fisher.—FiO

"**Ears** cocked wide." See Two at showtime

Earth. See World

"**Earth** and I gave you turquoise." N. Scott Momaday.—MoGd

Egg ("Somehow the hen") Valerie Worth.—
WoSm
Egg thoughts. Russell Hoban.—HeB
Eggs. See also Birds—Eggs and nests
E is for egg. W. J. Smith.—SmL
Easter eggs. H. Behn.—LiCc
The egg ("Let's think of eggs") O. Nash.—
BlC
Egg ("Somehow the hen") V. Worth.—WoSm
Egg thoughts. R. Hoban.—HeB
"Humpty Dumpty sat on a wall." Mother
Goose.—TrGg
If Walt Whitman had written Humpty
Dumpty. F. Jacobs.—CoPs
The importance of eggs. D. McCord.—McO
Meg's egg. M. A. Hoberman.—HoY
Pitcher McDowell. N. M. Bodecker.—BoP
Plymouth Rocks, of course. D. McCord.—
McO
"Sunny side up." A. Adoff.—AdE
Turtle sings an egg song. J. Yolen.—YoD
Written on an egg. E. Morike.—LiCc
Ego-tripping. Eve Merriam.—MeR
Egotists. See Pride and vanity
Eichenthal, Herman
"Three holy kings from Morgenland." tr.—
LiPch
Eight balloons. Shel Silverstein.—SiL
"Eight balloons no one was buyin'." See Eight
balloons
Eighteen flavors. Shel Silverstein.—MoGp
"Eighteen luscious, scrumptious flavors." See
Eighteen flavors
"1863, my great grandmother." See
Generations
1838. Dennis Lee.—LeN
"Eighty feet long was the brachiosaur." See
The largest of them all
Einstein, Albert (about)
Eminent cosmologists ("It did not last, the
Devil howling ho") J. C. Squire.—BrO
"Either I mistake your shape and making
quite." See A midsummer night's dream—
Puck's song
"Either you will." See Prospective immigrants
please note
El-Hajj Malik El-Shabazz, Malcolm X. Robert
Hayden.—AdC
"An elderly hound of Cohasset." See A hound
of Cohasset
Electricity
Circuit breaker. S. Gary.—BrO
Now I set me. R. W. Herman.—BrO
Power lines. M. C. Livingston.—LiF
Elegies. See Laments
Elegy ("Her face like a rain beaten stone on
the day she") Theodore Roethke.—PlL
Elegy for a dead soldier, sel. Karl Shapiro
"Underneath this wooden cross there lies."—
LiO
Elegy for Bella, Sarah, Rosie, and all the others.
Sonya Dorman.—PlG
Elegy for Harriet Tubman and Frederick
Douglass. Maya Angelou.—AnO

Elegy for my father. Howard Moss.—PlL
Elegy on the death of a mad dog. Oliver
Goldsmith.—CoG
The elephant. John Gardner.—GaCb
Elephant ("In his travels, the elephant") David
McFadden.—DoWh
Elephant ("When you put me up on the
elephant's back") William Jay Smith.—SmL
"An elephant with a huge trunk." Eveline
Dare.—DuSn
Elephants
The elephant. J. Gardner.—GaCb
Elephant ("In his travels, the elephant") D.
McFadden.—DoWh
Elephant ("When you put me up on the
elephant's back") W. J. Smith.—SmL
"An elephant with a huge trunk." E. Dare.—
DuSn
"The elephant's nose makes a very good
hose." K. Kuskin.—KuR
The elephant's trunk. D. Burt.—DuSn
Eletephony. L. E. Richards.—WiP
"Here come the elephants, ten feet high." J.
Prelutsky.— CoA
It's all relative. W. Cole.—CoDb
Oliphaunt. From The adventures of Tom
Bombadil. J.R.R. Tolkien.—CoA
"Way down South where bananas grow."
Unknown.—WiP
"The elephant's nose makes a very good hose."
Karla Kuskin.—KuR
The elephant's trunk. Denise Burt.—DuSn
Eletephony. Laura E. Richards.—WiP
"The elevator stops at every floor." See
Neuteronomy
Elevators
Neuteronomy. E. Merriam.—BrO
Ode to a vanished operator in an
automatized elevator. L. Rosenfield.—BrO
The elf and the dormouse. Oliver Herford.—
PaI
"An elf sat on a twig." See The elf singing
The elf singing. William Allingham.—PaI
Eliot, Thomas Stearns
The cultivation of Christmas trees.—LiO
Journey of the Magi.—LiPch
Elm seed blizzard. David McCord.—McO
Elm trees
Elm seed blizzard. D. McCord.—McO
"When the elm was full." From Autumn
nature notes. T. Hughes.—HuSs
Elton, Charles
Luriana, Lurilee.—PaB
Elves. See Fairies
"The elves put out their hats." See Toadstools
Emanuel, James A.
Emmett Till.—AdC
Negritude.—AdC
A small discovery.—MaP
The young ones, flip side.—JaPp
An emergency. Felice Holman.—HoA
Emerson, Ralph Waldo
Concord hymn.—PlG

Emerson, Ralph Waldo—*Continued*
"The delicate shells lay on the shore." See
Each and all
Each and all, sel.
"The delicate shells lay on the shore."—
PaE
Fable.—PaB
Poet.—JaPp
"Why did all manly gifts in Webster fail."—
PlG
Emeruwa, Leatrice W.
Personals.—JaPp
Emigration. See Immigration and emigration
Eminent cosmologists ("It did not last, the
Devil howling ho") John Collings Squire.—
BrO
Eminent cosmologists ("Nature, and nature's
laws lay hid in night") Alexander Pope.—
BrO
Emma. Yvonne.—AdC
Emmett Till ("I hear a whistling") James A.
Emanuel.—AdC
Emmons, Dick
The grass, alas.—BrO
The empty house. Stephen Spender.—JaPp
The enchanted island, sel. Alfred Noyes
"Some would dive in the lagoon."—PaE
Enchantment. See also Charms; Magic
Dragon ("A dragon named Ernest Belflour")
W. J. Smith.—SmL
Fable ("Pity the girl with crystal hair") J.
Aiken.—AiS
The rousing canoe song. H. Fraser.—DoWh
"Thrice the brinded cat hath mew'd." From
Macbeth. W. Shakespeare.—LiO
Encouraged. Paul Laurence Dunbar.—BrI
The end. John Gardner.—GaCb
The end of the Indian poems. Stanley
Plumly.—PlG
The enemy. Myra Cohn Livingston.—LiWt
Energy
The flow, the void. L. Morrison.—MoO
Shiver my timbers. D. McCord.—McO
England
Home thoughts, from abroad. R. Browning.—
PaB
England—History
Henry VIII. E. and H. Farjeon.—WiP
John ("John, John, bad King John") E. and H.
Farjeon.—WiP
Richard III. E. and H. Farjeon.—WiP
Engle, Paul
Notes.—YaI
The tree.—BaC
Water color.—LuZ
The wreath.—BaC
English, Jane. See Gia-fu Feng and English,
Jane, jt. trs.
An Englishman with an atlas or America the
unpronounceable. Morris Bishop.—PlG
"The enigmatic grundiboob." See Homage to
Moose Factory, Ont.
Ennis, Merlin
Preoccupation. tr.—LuZ

"Enough of a day has come to pass." See Inner
city lullaby
Enter this deserted house. Shel Silverstein.—
BrIt
Envoy. Ernest Dowson.—JaPp
Envy. See Jealousy
"The eohippus." William Cole.—CoDb
Epigram on my wedding day. Lord Byron.—
PlL
Epilogue ("My adventures now are ended")
Nancy Willard.—WiV
Epistle to the Olympians. Ogden Nash.—BlC
An epitaph. Walter De La Mare.—WiP
Epitaph ("Here he lies moulding") Leslie
Mellichamp.—BrO
Epitaph for a postal clerk. X. J. Kennedy.—
JaPp
Epitaph to a dog. Lord Byron.—CoG
An epitaph upon husband and wife, which
died, and were buried together. Richard
Crashaw.—PlL
Epitaphs
A dirge for a righteous kitten. V. Lindsay.—
WiP
Epitaph ("Here he lies moulding") L.
Mellichamp.—BrO
An epitaph ("Here lies a most beautiful
lady") W. De La Mare.—WiP
Epitaph for a postal clerk. X. J. Kennedy.—
JaPp
Epitaph to a dog. Lord Byron.—CoG
An epitaph upon husband and wife, which
died, and were buried together. R.
Crashaw.—PlL
To a dead friend. P. L. Dunbar.—BrI
What kind of a guy was he. H. Nemerov.—
JaPp
An epithalamion, sels. John Donne
"Hail Bishop Valentine, whose day this is."—
LiO
"Ere sleep comes down to soothe the weary
eyes." Paul Laurence Dunbar.—BrI
"Erig-ama-role, erig-ama-ree." See Queen Zixi
of Ix
Ernesto Maestas instructs Ynocencia Saavedra
in the art of acting. N. Scott Momaday.—
MoGd
The errand. Harry Behn.—HoMp
Escapes
Runagate runagate. R. Hayden.—AdC
Eskimo chant. Unknown. tr. fr. the Eskimo by
Knud Rasmussen.—DoWh
Eskimo legend. Joan Aiken.—AiS
Eskimos
Eskimo chant. Unknown.—DoWh
Eskimo legend. J. Aiken.—AiS
Heaven and hell. Unknown.—LuZ
Magic words. Unknown.—LuZ
Manerathiak's song. Unknown.—DoWh
Mosquito. Unknown.—MoGp
"Once in the winter." From The forsaken. D.
C. Scott.—DoWh
The train dogs. P. Johnson.—DoWh
The wind has wings. Unknown.—DoWh

Eternity
Forever ("I had not known before") P. L.
Dunbar.—BrI
Ethiopia
#4. D. Long.—AdC
Etiquette
Almost. H. Behn.—WiP
"Dear Sybil." N. M. Bodecker.—BoHh
The hot pizza serenade. F. Jacobs.—CoPs
I am learning. A. Adoff.—AdE
Magic word. M. Gardner.—CoI
My wise old grandpapa. W. G. Howcroft.—
CoPs—DuSn
Peas. D. Barnham.—DuSn
Rules. K. Kuskin.—KuD—WiP
Speak clearly. M. Gardner.—CoPs
Table manners. G. Burgess.—CoPs
We must be polite. C. Sandburg.—WiP
Etter, Dave
Old Dubuque.—FlA
Two beers in Argyle, Wisconsin.—FlA
Euclid (about)
Plane geometry. E. Rounds.—BrO
"Eugene." See Out of the city
Eulogy for Alvin Frost. Audre Lorde.—AdC
Europe. See also names of European countries,
as England
Yonder. R. Eberhart.—PlG
"The **European** bison fell from grace." See The
fall
Evans, Frances
Colours.—SaM
Evans, H.A.C.
The brontosaurus.—CoDb
Montgomery, with acknowledgements to T.
S. Eliot's Macavity.—CoG
The pterodactyl.—CoDb
Evans, Mari
"I am a black woman."—AdC
Langston.—AdC
Uhuru.—AdC
Who can be born black.—AdC
"Even as your progenitors ran." See To a race
horse at Ascot
"Even in summer." See Weather conditions
The **even** sea. May Swenson.—PaE
"Even sunlight dares." See Prisoner
"Even though." See Scat, scitten
Evening. See also Night
"Birds circling at dusk." A. Atwood.—AtH
"Cows are coming home in Maine." R.P.T.
Coffin.—HiD
Day and night. A. Fisher.—FiO
"Down dip the branches." M. Van Doren.—
HiD
Dusk ("Peeking from her room") M. C.
Livingston.—LiF
Early supper. B. Howes.—HiD
Evening ("The sun horse panting and
snorting") M. Singh.—LuZ
Evening ride. J. Hoffman.—CoPh
Friend ("Walking with you") G. Brooks.—
AdC
In winter sky. D. McCord.—McO

Lullaby. F. Holman.—HoA
Lying in a hammock at William Duffy's farm
in Pine Island, Minnesota. J. Wright.—FlA
The park at evening. L. Norris.—HiD—NoM
Plainview: 1. N. S. Momaday.—MoGd
Plenty of time. A. Fisher.—FiO
Sunset ("The river sleeps beneath the sky")
P. L. Dunbar.—BrI
"This is my rock." D. McCord.—BeR—
McO—WiP
Twilight. P. L. Dunbar.—BrI
Twilight song. J. Hunter-Duvar.—DoWh
Vesper. Alcman of Sparta.—LuZ
The warm and the cold. T. Hughes.—HuSs
Evening ("The sun horse panting and
snorting") Mohan Singh, tr. by Balwant
Gargi.—LuZ
"**Evening** on the olden, the golden sea of
Wales." See The dying patriot
Evening ride. Jill Hoffman.—CoPh
Evening song. Sherwood Anderson.—FlA
"**Evening** waddles over the fields like a
turkey." See Bad boy's swan song
"**Ever** been kidnapped." See Kidnap poem
"**Ever** eat a pickled plum." See The song of the
sour plum
"**Ever** eaten Chinese food." See Eating at the
restaurant of How Chow Now
"**Ever,** ever, not ever so terrible." See Castor
oil
Ever green. John Clare.—BaC
"**Ever** heard Bird." See Mellowness and flight
"**Everett** Anderson thinks he'll make." See July
Evergreens
Jubilate herbis. N. Farber.—LiPch
Everson, Ronald
The loaves.—DoWh
Everwine, Peter
For the coming year.—LiO
"**Every** bee." See Bees
"**Every** child who has gardening tools." See
Garden lore
"**Every** February zoo day." Doris Orgel.—OrM
"**Every** game that Harvey plays." See Harvey
always wins
"**Every** kind of a barnyard bird." See Old grey
goose
Every man heart lay down, sel. Lorenz Graham
"And in a far country."—BaC
"**Every** night as I go to bed." See Waltzing
mice
"**Every** time I climb a tree." See Five chants
"**Every** time I come to town." See Stop kicking
my dog around
"**Every** time I visit a strange town." See Outing
"**Every** time I've raced my shadow." See
Shadow race
Everybody has an uncle. Ogden Nash.—BlC
Everybody tells me everything. Ogden Nash.—
BlC
"**Everybody** went to bat three times." See Don
Larsen's perfect game
"**Everybody's** in the ocean." See Down by the
sea

"**Everyone** grumbled, the sky was grey." See Daddy fell into the pond
"**Everyone** is tight asleep." See Morning
"**Everyone's**." See In sympathy, but only for a little longer
"**Everything** is on the run." See Fall wind
"**Everything** King Midas touched." See Squishy touch
Eviction. Lucille Clifton.—MoGp
Evolution
   Anthropoids. M. A. Hoberman.—HoY
   Ocean's edge. L. Morrison.—MoO
   Pre-history repeats. R. J. McKent.—BrO
   Prehistoric. S. Silverstein.—SiL
   Sea-sonnet. V. Sackville-West.—PaE
   The walrus, an evolutionary tale. J. Gardner.—GaCb
"**Evolution** dies out." See Zoo
Ewing, Julia Horatia
   The burial of the linnet.—MoF
   Garden lore.—MoF
Examination. Shel Silverstein.—SiL
"**An excitable** swallow named Will." See The swallow
Excursion. Mary Ann Hoberman.—HoY
The **excursion,** sel. William Wordsworth
   "I have seen."—PaE
Executions. See Hangings
Exit x. David McCord.—McO
Explanations of love. Carl Sandburg.—LuZ
An **explorer** named Bliss. N. M. Bodecker.—BoP
Explorers and exploration. See also names of explorers, as Columbus, Christopher
   And of Columbus. H. Gregory.—PlG
   An explorer named Bliss. N. M. Bodecker.—BoP
   The Mediterranean. A. Tate.—PlG
   The purist. O. Nash.—BlC
   To the western world. L. Simpson.—PlG
"**Extend,** there where you venture and come back." See Walk on the moon
Extinction. See also names of extinct animals, as Auks
   Brachiosaurus ("This dinosaur is now extinct") M. A. Hoberman.—HoY
   Buffalo dusk. C. Sandburg.—PlG
   A caution to everybody. O. Nash.—BlC
   "Consider the auk."—BrO
   The dodo ("Oh when the dodo flourished") I. Wilner.—WiP
   The fall. M. Spark.—Luz
   In the end. D. McCord.—McSu
   Inability to depict an eagle. R. Eberhart.—PlG
   Lines on a small potato. M. Fishback.—CoDb
   Next. O. Nash.—BlC
   The pterodactyl ("A pterodactyl drove his Edsel") A. M. Ross.—CoDb
   To see the rabbit. A. Brownjohn.—WiP
   The turkey. J. Gardner.—GaCb
   When last seen. H. Flexner.—BrO
   Zachary Zed. J. Reeves.—BrO

"The **eye** marvels at the beauty of its whiteness." Ecclesiasticus.—SaM
Eyes
   At night ("When night is dark") A. Fisher.—FiO
   At the keyhole. W. De La Mare.—WiP
   Birds ("Mouths of birds are very strange") A. Fisher.—FiO
   Brown eyes are watching. N. Farber.—FaS
   Gumeye ball. S. Silverstein.—SiL
   Haiku for Halloween. M. C. Livingston.—BrIt
   I have my father's eyes. D. Lee.—LeN
   "Punch and Judy." Unknown.—BeR
   Sea-hawk. R. Eberhart.—PaE
   Senses. S. Silverstein.—SiL
   The silent eye. T. Hughes.—HuM
   True. L. Moore.—WiP
   Your eyes have their silence. G. W. Barrax.—AdC

F

F is for frogboy. William Jay Smith.—SmL
Fabio, Sarah Webster
   Chromo.—AdC
Fable ("The mountain and the squirrel") Ralph Waldo Emerson.—PaB
Fable ("Pity the girl with crystal hair") Joan Aiken.—AiS
Fables
   Fable ("The mountain and the squirrel") R. W. Emerson.—PaB
   Fable ("Pity the girl with crystal hair") J. Aiken.—AiS
   Fox and crow. W. J. Smith.—SmL
   "A spider danced a cosy jig." I. Layton.—DoWh
Fabrizio, Ray
   Rabbits.—SaM
   Spider webs.—MaP
"The **fabulous** wizard of Oz." Unknown.—BrO
Faces
   Captain Blackbeard did what. S. Silverstein.—SiL
   Godmother. P. B. Morden.—PaI
   "He whose face gives no light." From Proverbs of hell. W. Blake.—WiV
   Heredity ("I am the family face") T. Hardy.—PlL
   Me ("My nose is blue") K. Kuskin.—KuD—WiP
   My father's face. H. Carruth.—PlL
   People. W. J. Smith.—SmL
   A person of Haxey. N. M. Bodecker.—BoP
   Someone's face. J. Ciardi.—CoI
   "Sour face Ann." S. Silverstein.—SiL
   Thumb face. S. Silverstein.—SiL
   A valentine for a lady. Lucilius.—LiO
   "What's the horriblest thing you've seen." R. Fuller.—CoI
   "When I was young and foolish." M. A. Hoberman.—HoY

Who ordered the broiled face. S. Silverstein.—SiL

You, tu. C. Pomerantz.—PoT

"The **fact** is." See Some me of beauty

"A **fact** is a fact, lady." See Lady with a lamp

Factories

The foundations of American industry. D. Hall.—PlG

Failure

Failure ("How did it come ungathered, all the sheaved throng") R. Lattimore.—JaPp

Failure ("How did it come ungathered, all the sheaved throng") Richmond Lattimore.—JaPp

Fair, did you wind it. Lillian Morrison.—MoW

"The **fair** maid who, on the first day of May." Unknown.—LiCc

Fair or foul. Lillian Morrison.—MoSr

Fairies

The abominable fairy of Bloor street. D. Lee.—LeN

A big deal for the tooth fairy. X. J. Kennedy.—KeP

The changeling. C. Mew.—PlL

Dame Hickory. W. De La Mare.—WaFp

The darkling elves. J. Prelutsky.—PrH

The elf and the dormouse. O. Herford.—PaI

The elf singing. W. Allingham.—PaI

Fairies ("Don't go looking for fairies") E. Farjeon.—WaFp

Fairies ("I cannot see fairies") H. Conkling.—PaI

The fairies ("Up the airy mountain") W. Allingham.—WaFp

"The fairies have never a penny to spend." R. Fyleman.—WaFp

Fairy fashion. V. Worth.—WaFp

"A fairy went a-marketing." R. Fyleman.—PaI

Gnome ("I saw a gnome") H. Behn.—BrIt

The goblin ("A goblin lives in our house") R. Fyleman.—WiP

The goblin ("There's a goblin as green") J. Prelutsky.—PrI

Goblin feet. J.R.R. Tolkien.—WaFp

Have you watched the fairies. R. Fyleman.—PaI

He who would dream of fairyland. M. P. Hearn.—WaFp

How to tell goblins from elves. M. Shannon.—WaFp

I'd love to be a fairy's child. R. Graves.—WaFp

In black chasms. L. Norris.—NoM

Kennack sands. L. Binyon.—PaE

The leprechaun. R. D. Joyce.—WaFp

The lighthearted fairy. Unknown.—WaFp

The little elf. J. K. Bangs.—PaI

The magic wood. H. Treece.—HiD

"The man from the woods." J. Ciardi.—HiS

Meet on the road. Unknown.—WiP

The mewlips. J.R.R. Tolkien.—HiS

Mister Hoobody. D. Lee.—LeN

Mistletoe. W. De La Mare.—HiS

Overheard on a saltmarsh. H. Monro.—HiS—WiP

The pointed people. R. L. Field.—WaFp

Puck's song. From A midsummer night's dream. W. Shakespeare.—WaFp

Queen Mab. From Romeo and Juliet. W. Shakespeare.—WaFp

The sea-fairies ("Slow sail'd the weary mariners and saw") A. Tennyson.—PaE

Sea fairies ("Look in the caves at the edge of the sea") P. Hubbell.—WaFp

She ("In the darkest part of the forest's heart") J. Prelutsky.—WaFp

Sleep song. S. Kroll.—WaFp

Song ("I like birds, said the Dryad") E. Coatsworth.—WiP

The stars ("Across the dark and quiet sky") N. Giovanni.—GiV

The toadstool wood. J. Reeves.—HiD

Toadstools ("The elves put out their hats") A. Fisher.—FiO

Tolkien on the subway. M. C. Livingston.—LiWt

Wrimples. J. Prelutsky.—PrS

Fairies ("Don't go looking for fairies") Eleanor Farjeon.—WaFp

Fairies ("I cannot see fairies") Hilda Conkling.—PaI

The **fairies** ("Up the airy mountain") William Allingham.—WaFp

"The **fairies** have never a penny to spend." Rose Fyleman.—WaFp

Fairs

Banbury fair. E. G. Millard.—WiP

The poultry show. D. McCord.—McO

"Richard Dick upon a stick." Mother Goose.—TrGg

Rutland fair. R. N. Peck.—PeB

The Summerhill fair. D. Lee.—LeG

Widdecombe fair. Unknown.—CoPh

Fairy fashion. Valerie Worth.—WaFp

"A **fairy** went a-marketing." Rose Fyleman.—PaI

Faith

Belief for JFK. A. R. Ammons.—PlG

By rugged ways. P. L. Dunbar.—BrI

Daniel. V. Lindsay.—WiP

Faith ("I had a donkey") M. Dunkels.—CoPh

For Edwin R. Embree. O. Dodson.—AdC

The forsaken merman. M. Arnold.—PaE

Holy Thursday. W. Blake.—LiO

Religion ("I'm a believer") M. Malloy.—LuZ

The slave singing at midnight. H. W. Longfellow.—PlG

Faith ("I had a donkey") Marjorie Dunkels.—CoPh

Faith and practice. John Balaban.—PlG

Fall. See Autumn

The **fall** ("The European bison fell from grace") Muriel Spark.—LuZ

Fall ("When I go walking in the fall") Karla Kuskin.—KuD

Fall down. Calvin C. Hernton.—AdC

"**Fall** is coming." See September

Fall wind ("Everything is on the run") Aileen Fisher.—FiO

Fall wind ("I scarcely felt a breath of air") Margaret Hillert.—HoMp

Falling asleep. Ian Serraillier.—HiD

"Falling stars shoot quanta." See The invasion of the star streaks

Falling the small drops." See Spell of the rain

"Falls from her heaven the moon, and stars sink burning." See Moon-bathers

Falsehood. See Truth and falsehood

Fame
   The crisis. P. L. Dunbar.—BrI
   May. 1506, Christopher Columbus speaking. W. T. Scott.—PlG
   A New England sampler. J. M. Brinnin.—PlG

"Fame was a claim of uncle Ed's." Ogden Nash.—BlC

Familiar friends. James S. Tippett.—CoA

"Families when a child is born." See On the birth of his son

Family. See also Children and childhood; Home and family life; Married life; Relatives; also names of family members, as Brothers and sisters
   The book. A. Rich.—PlL
   Daddy fell into the pond. A. Noyes.—PaI
   Eviction. L. Clifton.—MoGp
   The family dinner party. Menander.—PlL
   Family portrait. P. Goedicke.—KhI
   The four brothers. C. Pomerantz.—PoT
   The goodnight. L. Simpson.—PlL
   The happy family. J. Ciardi.—HiD
   A household. W. H. Auden.—PlL
   Love don't mean. E. Greenfield.—GrH
   Mag. C. Sandburg.—PlL
   The musk ox. J. Gardner.—GaCb
   New baby. M. C. Livingston.—LiWt
   "Old Mistress McShuttle." Mother Goose.—TrGg
   The primitiae to parents. R. Herrick.—PlL
   "There was a mad man and he had a mad wife." Mother Goose.—TrGg
      "There was a mad man."—LoG
   "You're Mrs. Cobble and I'm Mrs. Frome." M. A. Hoberman.—HoY

The family dinner party. Menander, tr. by C. M. Bowra.—PlL

Family friends. Mary Ann Hoberman.—HoY

"The family gone at last to bed." See The prodigal son

The family of man, sel. Carl Sandburg
   Names.—WiP

Family portrait. Patricia Goedicke.—KhI

"The fanciest dive that ever was dove." See Fancy dive

Fancy dive. Shel Silverstein.—SiL

"Fanfare." Lillian Morrison.—MoW

The fanger. Jane Yolen.—YoH

"The fanger's teeth are widely spaced." See The fanger

Fantasy, for Jennie. Myra Cohn Livingston.—LiWt

Far away. David McCord.—McO

"Far back, related on my mother's side." See Old Salt Kossabone

"Far far away, where ganders are grey." See The witch's balloon

"Far out at sea the mighty tuner." See The tuner fish

Far trek. June Brady.—BrO

"Far undergrounded." See The earth owl

Farber, Norma
   At the ring of a bell.—FaS
   Bandit bee.—FaS
   Blow, wind.—FaS
   Brown eyes are watching.—FaS
   Bye baby walnut.—FaS
   Carousel brunch.—FaS
   Dove.—LiPch
   Finders keepers.—FaS
   For the sewing kit.—FaS
   Forever blowing.—FaS
   Going round in a square.—FaS
   The hatch.—HiS
   Hog at the manger.—LiPch
   How they brought the good news by sea.—LiPch
   I hope she won't grow any more.—FaS
   In a starry orchard.—FaS
   In place of a red carpet.—FaS
   In the park.—FaS
   Jubilate herbis.—LiPch
   Ladybug's Christmas.—LiPch
   Night of the half moon.—FaS
   "The noise of nothing."—FaS
   Praise to the little.—FaS
   The rescue.—FaS
   Spendthrift.—FaS
   Spider.—LiPch
   Sun after rain.—FaS
   Sun for breakfast.—FaS
   Taking turns.—FaS
   Things as they are.—FaS
   Turtle song.—FaS
   Two of a kind.—FaS
   The washer waves.—FaS

Fare thee well. Eli Siegel.—PlG

"Farewell dear babe, my heart's too much content." See In memory of my dear grandchild Elizabeth Bradstreet, who deceased August, 1665, being a year and half old.

"Farewell to an idea, the mother's face." See The auroras of autumn

Farewell to Christmas. Unknown, fr. the French.—BaC

Farewells. See also Parting
   Epilogue ("My adventures now are ended") N. Willard.—WiV
   Farewell to Christmas. Unknown, fr. the French.—BaC

Farjeon, Eleanor
   Alexander to his horse.—CoPh
   Bedtime.—PaI
   Bliss.—YaI
   The brown birds.—BaC
   Catching-song a play rhyme.—WiP

The children's carol.—LiPch
Fairies.—WaFp
"The high skip."—WiP
Holly and mistletoe.—LiPch
In the town. tr.—LiPch
In the week when Christmas comes.—LiPch
"King's cross."—CoI
"Mrs. Malone."—WiP
"Mrs. Peck Pigeon."—BeR
Neptune.—PaE
News, news.—LiCc
"The night will never stay."—MoF—PaI
"Nine-o'clock bell."—MoF
Trees.—WiP
Waves.—PaE
The waves of the sea.—SaM
White horses.—CoPh
A wish.—LiCc
The witch, the witch.—BrIt—WaW
Farjeon, Eleanor and Farjeon, Herbert
Henry VIII.—WiP
John.—WiP
Richard III.—WiP
Farjeon, Herbert. See Farjeon, Eleanor and
Farjeon, Herbert
Farm animals. See Animals; also names of farm
animals, as Cows
The **farm** child's lullaby. Paul Laurence
Dunbar.—BrI
Farm life. See also Country life; Fields;
Harvests and harvesting; also names of
farm animals, as Cows; also names of farm
products, as Wheat
After Christmas. D. McCord.—McO
After supper. H. McNamar.—LuZ
Amanda is shod. M. Kumin.—CoPh
Apple scoop. E. Glen.—MoGp
At milking. R. N. Peck.—PeB
"At quitting time." R. Sund.—LuZ
Barn chores. N. D. Watson.—WaB
Barn fire. N. D. Watson.—WaB
The city and Evan. K. Starbird.—StC
Clancy. D. Wagoner.—CoPh
The cornfield. E. B. White.—PlL
The country and Nate. K. Starbird.—StC
The dark way home, survivors. M. S.
Harper.—AdC
The devil's pitchfork. R. N. Peck.—PeB
"Did you feed my cow." Unknown.—WiP
Familiar friends. J. S. Tippett.—CoA
The farm child's lullaby. P. L. Dunbar.—BrI
Farmer. R. N. Peck.—PeB
The golden boy. T. Hughes.—HuSs
Harvest song. J. Campbell.—LiO
Hay ("The grass is happy") T. Hughes.—HuSs
"I will go with my father a-ploughing." J.
Campbell.—LiO
"I will go with my father a-reaping."—
LiCc (sel.)
Illinois farmer. C. Sandburg.—FlA
Manhood. R. N. Peck.—PeB
Monologue of the rating Morgan in
Rutherford County. C. F. MacIntyre.—
CoPh

More to it than riding. J. A. Lindon.—CoPh
Nest. R. N. Peck.—PeB
"Old farmer Giles." Mother Goose.—BlH
Old gray barn. R. N. Peck.—PeB
On the farm. B. Winder.—CoPh
The pasture. R. Frost.—BeR
Plymouth Rocks, of course. D. McCord.—
McO
The pocket whetstone. R. N. Peck.—PeB
Rabbit track. R. N. Peck.—PeB
Strange legacies. S. A. Brown.—AdC
Tools ("There upon the toolshed wall") R. N.
Peck.—PeB
Vermont conversation. P. Hubbell.—WiP
"What is it this time the dark barn again."
From Sheep. T. Hughes.—HuSs
Where the hayfields were. A. MacLeish.—
HiD
White cat. R. Knister.—DoWh
Winter calf. R. N. Peck.—PeB
Winter worship. R. N. Peck.—PeB
"A **farm** team pitcher, McDowell." See Pitcher
McDowell
Farmer. Robert Newton Peck.—PeB
"The **farmer** knew each time a friend went
past." See Hound on the porch roof
A **farmer** of Cwm. N. M. Bodecker.—BoP
"A **farmer's** neck is red as wind." See Farmer
Farmers. See Farm life
Farms and farming. See Farm life
Farrar, John
Bundles.—BaC
"**Farther** and farther from the three Pa Roads."
See On New Year's eve
Farther and further. David McCord.—McSu
"**Farther** east it wouldn't be on the map." See
Midwest town
"**Farther** is distance and further is time." See
Farther and further
Fashions in dogs. E. B. White.—CoG
Fast and slow. David McCord.—McO
"**Fast** as foxes." See Skiing
Faster than light. A. H. Reginald Buller.—BrO
"**Fat** father robin." David McCord.—McO
"**Fat** polka-dot cat. Betsy Maestro.—MaFp
"**Fat** torpedoes in bursting jackets." See Fourth
of July
Fate
The assassination ("Do you not find
something very strange about him") R.
Hillyer.—LiO
Burying ground by the ties. A. MacLeish.—
PlG
The crisis. P. L. Dunbar.—BrI
"**Father**." See Child dead in old seas
Father ("Carrying my world") Myra Cohn
Livingston.—LiCc
Father ("I dreamed my father flicked") A. R.
Ammons.—PlL
Father and I in the woods. David McCord.—
HiS—McO
"**Father** and I went down to camp." See
Yankee Doodle

Fare thee well. E. Siegel.—PlG
Fear ("Barnabus Browning") S. Silverstein.—SiL
The fear of Bo-talee. N. S. Momaday.—MoGd
The horse that died of shame. N. S. Momaday.—MoGd
It ("I lie in my bed, trying hard to sleep") J. Prelutsky.—PrS
Laly, Laly. M. Van Doren.—HiS
Night ("A wolf") Unknown.—MoGp
A person in Skye. N. M. Bodecker.—BoP
Poem at thirty. S. Sanchez.—AdC
"Scare me easy." B. S. De Regniers.—ReB
Simile. N. S. Momaday.—MoGd
Whatif. S. Silverstein.—SiL
Whooo. L. Moore.—WiP
The will o' the wisp. J. Prelutsky.—PrN
The wind has wings. Unknown.—DoWh
Fear ("Barnabus Browning") Shel Silverstein.—SiL
The fear of Bo-talee. N. Scott Momaday.—MoGd
"The feathers of the willow." See Song
February
"All the Fibruary babies." D. Orgel.—OrM
"Any Fibruary morning." D. Orgel.—OrM
"At the gym in February." D. Orgel.—OrM
The brook in February. C.G.D. Roberts.—DoWh
"By mid-Fibruary moonlight." D. Orgel.—OrM
"Every Fibruary zoo day." D. Orgel.—OrM
February ("The horse, head swinging") B. Winder.—CoPh
February ("The sun rides higher") J. Updike.—LiCc
"For Fibruary fill me up day." D. Orgel.—OrM
"For the Fibruary dog show." D. Orgel.—OrM
"From a Fibruary sandbox." D. Orgel.—OrM
"Here's a Fibruary finding." D. Orgel.—OrM
"If you swim in Fibruary." D. Orgel.—OrM
"In a Fibruary blizzard." D. Orgel.—OrM
"In Aquari-Fibruary." D. Orgel.—OrM
"In dromedary Fibruary." D. Orgel.—OrM
"In Fibruary, any wind's day." D. Orgel.—OrM
"In Fibruary, my canary." D. Orgel—OrM
"In Fibruary, Old MacDonald." D. Orgel.—OrM
"In Fibruary, uncle Harry." D. Orgel.—OrM
"In Fibruary, when it freezes." D. Orgel.—OrM
"In the month of Fibruary." D. Orgel.—OrM
"On a Fibruary Monday." D. Orgel.—OrM
"On a Fibruary thirstday." D. Orgel.—OrM
"On a Fibruary toothday." D. Orgel.—OrM
"On Fibruary fair and foul day." D. Orgel.—OrM
"On Fibruary's loop-de-loop day." D. Orgel.—OrM
"On tattersday, come wearing any." D. Orgel.—OrM

"On the first of Fibruary." D. Orgel.—OrM
"On the last, the twenty-eighth day." D. Orgel.—OrM
"On the third of Fibruary." D. Orgel.—OrM
February ("The horse, head swinging") Barbara Winder.—CoPh
February ("The sun rides higher") John Updike.—LiCc
February 22. John Updike.—PlG
"Fee, fie, fo, fum." See "Fe, fi, fo, fum"
"Feed the wood and have a joyful minute." Johann Wolfgang von Goethe.—BaC
"The feel." See The eel
"Feel free." See To Bobby Seale
"Feeling special." Nikki Grimes.—GrS
Feelings. See also specific emotional states, as Fear; Happiness
Valentine feelings. L. B. Hopkins.—HoMp
Feeney, Leonard
Wind.—PaI
Feet
Barefoot ("After that tight") V. Worth.—WoSm
Barefoot ("Let's pick clovers") A. Fisher.—FiO
"The boy with a wolf's foot." J. Aiken.—AiS
The dinosore. J. Yolen.—YoH
Footprints. J. Aiken.—AiS
Going barefoot. J. Thurman.—ThFo
"Here all we see." W. De La Mare.—PaI
I would like. L. Morrison.—MoW
In search of Cinderella. S. Silverstein.—SiL
Mrs. Button. J. Reeves.—WiP
The quinquaped jikes. P. Wesley-Smith.—DuSn
Shoes ("Shoes are for walking") M. Dugan.—DuSn
Feet. Robert Newton Peck.—PeB
"The feet of the." See Caterpillar
Felicitations. Lillian Morrison.—MoO
Feline lesson. Hugh McNamar.—LuZ
"The fellows up in personnel." See The perforated spirit
Fences
Clackety click. L. Moore.—MoTs
Final stone. R. N. Peck.—PeB
Knotholes. D. McCord.—McO
North fence. R. N. Peck.—PeB
"The pickety fence." From Five chants. D. McCord.—McO—WiP
"Ferdinand De Soto lies." See The distant runners
Ferlinghetti, Lawrence
I am waiting.—PlG
"In Golden Gate Park that day."—LuZ
Fernando. Marci Ridlon.—MoGp
"Fernando has a basketball." See Fernando
Ferries
"Ferry me across the water." C. Rossetti.—WiP
A trip on the Staten Island ferry. A. Lorde.—AdC
"Ferry me across the water." Christina Rossetti.—WiP

"Fire, fire." Unknown.—WiP
  Fire ("Fire, fire, said Mrs Dyer")—BeR
  "Fire, fire, said Mrs McGuire."—TrGg
"Fire, fire, said Mrs Dyer." See "Fire, fire"
"Fire, fire, said Mrs McGuire." See "Fire, fire"
Fire flies. See Fireflies
Fire house. Charlotte Pomerantz.—PoT
"Fire, you handsome creature, shine." See
    When we come home, Blake calls for fire
Fireflies
  All about fireflies all about. D. McCord.—
    McO
  Fireflies ("Fireflies at twilight") M. A.
    Hoberman.—HoBu
  Firefly ("Firefly, firefly in the night") A.
    Fisher.—FiO
  Glowworm. D. McCord.—CoA—McO—MoGp
  Summer stars. A. Fisher.—FiO
  A summer's night. P. L. Dunbar.—BrI
Fireflies ("Fireflies at twilight") Mary Ann
    Hoberman.—HoBu
"Fireflies at twilight." See Fireflies
Firefly ("Firefly, firefly in the night") Aileen
    Fisher.—FiO
"Firefly, airplane, satellite, star." See Back
    yard, July night
"Firefly, firefly in the night." See Firefly
Firehouses
  Fire house. C. Pomerantz.—PoT
Fireman, save my soul. Lillian Morrison.—MoW
The firetender. David McCord.—McO
Firewood. See Wood
Fireworks
  The 5th of July. F. Holman.—HoMp—LiCc
  Fireworks ("First") V. Worth.—LiCc—WoM
  Fireworks ("Not guns, not thunder, but a
    flutter of clouded drums") B. Deutsch.—
    LiO
  Fourth of July night ("The little boat at
    anchor") C. Sandburg.—LiO
  Fourth of July night ("Pin wheels whirling
    round") D. Aldis.—LiCc
  "If I had a firecracker." S. Silverstein.—CoI
  The pinwheel's song. J. Ciardi.—His
Fireworks ("First") Valerie Worth.—LiCc—
    WoM
Fireworks ("Not guns, not thunder, but a flutter
    of clouded drums") Babette Deutsch.—LiO
"First." See Fireworks
The first. Lilian Moore.—MoTs
First and last. David McCord.—McO
The first dandelion. Walt Whitman.—PaB
"The first day of Christmas my true love sent
    to me." See The twelve days of Christmas
The first day of school. Aileen Fisher.—FiO
First day of spring. Beatrice Schenk De
    Regniers.—ReB
"The first drop of rain." Ann Atwood.—AtH
"First, feel, then feel, then." See Young soul
"First grow a moustache." See How to make a
    swing with no rope or board or nails
"First man." See New world
The first Nowell. Unknown.—LiPch

"The first Nowell the angel did say." See The
    first Nowell
First one up. Nancy Dingman Watson.—WaB
"First paint a cage." See How to paint the
    portrait of a bird
The first poem I ever wrote. Naomi Shihab.—
    KhI
"First snow, the flakes." See December
"The first sorrow of autumn." See The seven
    sorrows
First Thanksgiving. Myra Cohn Livingston.—
    LiCc—LiF
"First the melody, clean and hard." See How
    high the moon
"First there were two of us, then there were
    three of us." See The storm
"First, there's the courtship." See Verses versus
    verses
"First, they were too big." See Long johns
"The first thing to know." See The crow
"First time I ever saw a flying change." See
    Flying changes
Fish. See also names of fish, as Guppies; also
    Whales
  The barracuda. J. Gardner.—GaCb
  "The Barrier Reef is a coral puzzle." M.
    Varday.—DuSn
  Comparatives. N. S. Momaday.—MoGd
  "Darting their lives away." A. Atwood.—AtH
  Fish ("Fish have fins") J. Prelutsky.—WiP
  Fish ("Look at the fish") W. J. Smith.—SmL
  Fish ("Look at them flit") M. A. Hoberman.—
    HoY
  Fish on a dish. L. Morrison.—MoW
  "Fishes are finny." K. Kuskin.—KuR
  The flattered flying fish. E. V. Rieu.—HiS
  The guppy ("Whales have calves") O. Nash.—
    BlC—MoGp
  How they brought the good news by sea. N.
    Farber.—LiPch
  I would like. L. Morrison.—MoW
  If I were a. K. Kuskin.—KuD
  "If you swim in Fibruary." D. Orgel.—OrM
  "Mackerel Mack and Halibut Hal." X. J.
    Kennedy.—KeP
  Mackerel song. T. Hughes.—HuSs
  Over the green sands. P. Bennett.—PaE
  "Roger was a razor fish." A. Pittman.—BeR
  "Row, row, row." N. M. Bodecker.—WiP
  Sardines. S. Milligan.—LuZ
  The shirk. J. Yolen.—YoH
  Sky fish. A. Fisher.—FiO
  To fish. L. Hunt.—PaE
  The tuner fish. J. Yolen.—YoH
  Water-snakes. From The rime of the ancient
    mariner. S. T. Coleridge.—PaE
  Whale ("When I swam underwater I saw a
    blue whale") W. J. Smith.—SmL
  "A young man from old Terre Haute." W. J.
    Smith.—SmL
Fish ("Fish have fins") Jack Prelutsky.—WiP
Fish ("Look at the fish") William Jay Smith.—
    SmL

Sky rider.—FiO
Snow on the wind.—FiO
Snow party.—FiO
Snowbirds.—FiO
Snowy benches.—FiO
Sounds of spring.—FiO
Sparkly snow.—FiO
Speaking of leaves.—FiO
Spiderweb.—FiO
Spring.—FiO
Spring joke.—FiO
Spring pictures.—FiO
Stars.—FiO
The streets of town.-—FiO
Suddenly.—HoMp
Summer stars.—FiO
Sun prints.—FiO
Taking a walk.—FiO
Thanksgiving dinner.—FiO
"There goes winter."—FiO
To be a bird.—FiO
To be a clover.—FiO
A toad.—FiO
Toadstools.—FiO
Twice born.—FiO
Under a stone.—FiO
Up there in the dark.—FiO
Walk at night.—FiO
"Waves of the sea."—FiO
When Christmas comes.—BaC
Wind circles.—FiO
Wind music.—FiO
Wings.—FiO
Winter morning.—FiO
Winter stars.—FiO
The witch in the wintry wood.—BrIt
The **fisher** child's lullaby. Paul Laurence
    Dunbar.—BrI
The **fisherman** ("The little boy is fishing")
    David McCord.—McO
The **fisherman** writes a letter to the mermaid.
    Joan Aiken.—AiS
"The **fishermen** say, when your catch is done."
    See The sea wolf
Fishers and fishing
    The boy fishing. E. J. Scovell.—MaP
    A catch. M. A. Hoberman.—HoY
    December river. T. Hughes.—HuSs
    The fisherman ("The little boy is fishing") D.
      McCord.—McO
    The fisherman writes a letter to the
      mermaid. J. Aiken.—AiS
    The lady and the bear. T. Roethke.—HiS
    A lazy day. P. L. Dunbar.—BrI
    "Little Johnny fished all day." Unknown.—
      MoF
    "Now turning homeward." A. Atwood.—AtH
    "Obsequious Prawn." M. Dugan.—DuSn
    "Once in the winter." From The forsaken. D.
      C. Scott.—DoWh
    Out in the boat. L. Morrison.—MoSr
    Runover rhyme. D. McCord.—McO
    The sea wolf. V. McDougal.—PaE
    The silver fish. S. Silverstein.—CoPs

Skip scoop anellie. T. Prideaux.—CoPs
Sky fish. A. Fisher.—FiO
Sunfish ("The sunfish, funny finny one") D.
    McCord.—McO
Where ("Where is that little pond I wish
    for") D. McCord.—McO
"Fishes are finny." Karla Kuskin.—KuR
Fishing. See Fishers and fishing
"Fito is a farmer and he lives in Aguadilla."
    See The four brothers
Fitts, Dudley
    A valentine for a lady. tr.—LiO
Fitzgerald, Edward
    Rubaiyat, sels. tr.
      "They say the lion and the lizard
        keep."—PaB
    "They say the lion and the lizard keep." See
    The Rubaiyat
Fitzgerald, Robert
    July in Indiana.—FlA
    Patrum propositum.—PlG
Five chants. David McCord.—McO (complete)
    "The cow has a cud"
    "Everytime I climb a tree."—PaI
    "Monday morning back to school"
    "The pickety fence."—WiP
    "Thin ice"
"Five doves of autumn." David Kherdian.—
    KhC
"The five-footed jikes." See The quinquaped
    jikes
Five horses. May Swenson.—CoPh
Five little bats. David McCord.—McO
"Five little bats flew out of the attic." See Five
    little bats
Five little chickens. Unknown.—WiP
"Five little monkeys." See The monkeys and
    the crocodile
Five little owls. Unknown.—BeR
"Five little owls in an old elm tree." See Five
    little owls
Five little piggies. Unknown, tr. fr. the Danish
    by N. M. Bodecker.—CoI
Five men against the theme, my name is red
    hot, yo name ain' doodley squat.
    Gwendolyn Brooks.—AdC
"Five minutes, five minutes more, please." See
    Bedtime
"Five-spotted hawk moth." See
    Quinquemaculatus
Flags—United States
    Old glory. M. C. Livingston.—LiF
    Only a little litter. M. C. Livingston.—BrO
Flake on flake. Aileen Fisher.—FiO
"The flame red moon, the harvest moon." See
    The harvest moon
"The flamingo." See Flamingo
Flamingo ("The flamingo") Valerie Worth.—
    WoM
Flamingos
    Flamingo ("The flamingo") V. Worth.—WoM
    Flamingos ("Ah-choo") R. S. Oliver.—OlC
Flamingos ("Ah-choo") Robert S. Oliver.—OlC

"A flash of lightning sparks." K. Mizumura.—MiF

In payment. A. Fisher.—FiO

Indian pipe. M. A. Hoberman.—HoY

"Is it waiting just for me." K. Mizumura.—MiF

Kisses ("Flowers for hours") N. Giovanni.—GiV

Mirrorvm. A. R. Ammons.—JaPp

Next door neighbor. A. Fisher.—FiO

Old florist. T. Roethke.—JaPp

On a bank as I sat fishing. H. Wotton.—PaB

Petals ("Flowers need petals") A. Fisher.—FiO

The sadness of things, for Sappho's sickness. R. Herrick.—PaB

Self-portrait, as a bear. D. Hall.—HiS

Sun flowers. A. Adoff.—AdE

"Tiny wildflowers." B. Maestro.—MaFp

The tuft of flowers. R. Frost.—PaB

"Tulips open one by one." K. Mizumura.—MiF

"Walking in the wind." K. Mizumura.—MiF

"Why are all of these flowers." K. Mizumura.—MiF

"Flowers for hours." See Kisses

"Flowers need petals." See Petals

"The flower's on the bird." See Around and around

Flutter wheel. Robert Newton Peck.—PeB

"The fly is in." Shel Silverstein.—SiL

"The fly made a visit to the grocery store." Unknown.—WiP

The fly nest. Dennis Lee.—LeG

Flying changes. Mary Wood.—CoPh

Flying crooked. Robert Graves.—JaPp—LuZ

"Flying man, flying man." Mother Goose.—LoG

The flying squirrel. John Gardner.—GaCb

"The flying squirrel is crazy." See The flying squirrel

Foal ("Come trotting up") Mary Britton Miller.—CoPh

Fog
  The fog ("Slowly, the fog") F. R. McCreary.—SaM
  Morning fog. N. M. Bodecker.—BoHh
  "There's a bittern that booms in a bog." From Limericks. D. McCord.—McSu

The fog ("Slowly, the fog") F. R. McCreary.—SaM

"The fog fills the air." Ann Atwood.—AtH

"Fog in all the hedges." See Morning fog

Foibles. Harold Bond.—KhI

Foley, J. W.
  Scientific proof.—BrO

Folk, Pat
  Senile.—JaPp

"The folk who live in Backward Town." Mary Ann Hoberman.—HoY

Folk poetry. See Autograph album verses; Counting-out rhymes; Jump-rope rhymes; Mother Goose

Folklore. See Legends; Mythology; Superstitions

"The folks in Little Bickering." See Bickering

"Folks is talkin' 'bout de money, 'bout de silvah an' de gold." See The real question

"Following me all along the road." Kazue Mizumura.—MiF

Fony Baloney. Dennis Lee.—CoI

Food ("Hay is dry") Michael Dugan.—DuSn

Food and drink. David McCord.—McO

Food and eating. See also Cooks and cooking; also names of foods, as Cakes and cookies; also names of meals, as Breakfast
  Accidentally. M. W. Kumin.—CoPs
  Adelaide. J. Prelutsky.—PrQ
  "After covering the continent." A. Adoff.—AdE
  An alarming sandwich. X. J. Kennedy.—CoPs
  Alligator pie. D. Lee.—WiP
  "Amelia mixed the mustard." A. E. Housman.—WiP
  Anna Banana. D. Lee.—CoPs
  Anteater. W. J. Smith.—SmL
  The apple ("Is on top") A. Adoff.—AdE
  Applesauce. M. A. Hoberman.—HoY
  "Arbuckle Jones." P. Wesley-Smith.—CoPs—DuSn
  Artichokes. P. Johnson.—CoPs
  Artie. K. Starbird.—StC
  At the end of summer. A. Adoff.—AdE
  Aunt Nerissa's muffin. W. Irwin.—CoPs
  "The baker wanted me to know." A. Adoff.—AdE
  "Bananas and cream." D. McCord.—McO
  The beefburger. O. Nash.—BlC
  Blunderbore. R. Fuller.—WaG
  The brontosaurus. H.A.C. Evans.—CoDb
  Bubble gum. M. C. Livingston.—LiF
  Burger. A. Adoff.—AdE
  A catch. M. A. Hoberman.—HoY
  Catherine. K. Kuskin.—KuD
  Celery. O. Nash.—BlC—CoPs
  The Chinese greengrocers. P. Lowther.—LuZ
  Chocolate chocolate. A. Adoff.—AdE
  A choosy wolf. X. J. Kennedy.—KeP
  The clean platter. O. Nash.—BlC
  The coach said. A. Adoff.—AdE
  Company. B. Katz.—CoDb
  Confession of a glutton. D. Marquis.—CoG
  Conversation about Christmas, the useless presents. From A child's Christmas in Wales. D. Thomas.—LiPch
  Corn ("Think of months") A. Adoff.—AdE
  The cost of living Mother Goose. D. Richardson.—BrO
  A cucumber's pickle. W. Cole.—CoPs
  Cut out. A. Adoff.—AdE
  The diet. S. Mernit.—KhI
  The diners in the kitchen. J. W. Riley.—CoG
  Dinner thought. A. Adoff.—AdE
  The dinosaurs' dinner. D. Lee.—CoDb
  The discontented cow. X. J. Kennedy.—KeP
  Dividing. D. McCord.—McO
  Early supper. B. Howes.—HiD

"Now thrice welcome Christmas." From Poor Robin's almanack. Unknown.—BaC
"O sliver of liver." M. C. Livingston.—CoPs
"Oak leaf plate." M. A. Hoberman.—HoY
The octopie. J. Yolen.—YoH
Old Christmas returned. Unknown.—BaC
"On a Fibruary thirstday." D. Orgel.—OrM
On eating porridge made of peas. L. Phillips.—CoPs
"Only the onions." A. Adoff.—AdE
Our joyful'st feast. G. Wither.—BaC
The pancake collector. J. Prelutsky.—PrQ
The parsnip. O. Nash.—BlC
Peanut butter batter bread. A. Adoff.—AdE
Peas. D. Barnham.—DuSn
Pease porridge poems. D. McCord.—McO
Peculiar. E. Merriam.—WiP
Periwinkle pizza. D. Lee.—LeG
Pie problem. S. Silverstein.—SiL
Piggy. W. Cole.—CoPs
The pizza ("Look at itsy-bitsy Mitzi") O. Nash.—BlC
Point of view. S. Silverstein.—CoPs
The poodle and the grundiboob. D. Lee.—LeN
"Poor old Mollie Haggarty." D. Barnham.—DuSn
Potato chips. A. E. Gallagher.—CoPs—DuSn
"Poundcake from Ealing." N. M. Bodecker.—BoHh
"Pumberly Pott's unpredictable niece." J. Prelutsky.—PrQ
Rabbit ("A rabbit") M. A. Hoberman.—HoY
"The reason I like chocolate." N. Giovanni.—GiV
Recipe ("I can make a sandwich") B. Katz.—CoPs
Recipe for eats poems. A. Adoff.—AdE
Revenge ("When I find out") M. C. Livingston.—LiF
Rhinoceros stew. M. Luton.—CoPs
Rib sandwich. W. J. Harris.—AdC
"Robbin and Bobbin." Mother Goose.—TrGg
"Round about, round about." Mother Goose.—TrGg
"Said a gluttonous man of New Wales." M. C. Livingston.—LiLl
"Said an old man from Needles-on-Stoor." M. C. Livingston.—LiLl
The sausage. Unknown.—CoPs
Sharing. R. N. Peck.—PeB
Snack. L. Lenski.—HeB
Sneaky Bill. W. Cole.—CoPs
Snowbirds. A. Fisher.—FiO
Song before supper. D. McCord.—McO
The song of the sour plum. Unknown.—PaI
"Spaghetti, spaghetti." J. Prelutsky.—PrR
Speak clearly. M. Gardner.—CoPs
Street song. M. C. Livingston.—LiWt
Sun flowers. A. Adoff.—AdE
Sunday morning toast. A. Adoff.—AdE
Supermarket. F. Holman.—BrO
Sweets. V. Worth.—WoSm
Table manners. G. Burgess.—CoPs

Tableau at twilight. O. Nash.—BlC
Take one apple. A. Adoff.—AdE
Television charmer. From A lot of limericks. X. J. Kennedy.—KeP
Thanksgiving ("In childhood you think") J. N. Morris.—LiO
There is a place. A. Adoff.—AdE
"There was a young lass of south Yarra." W. G. Howcroft.—DuSn
"There was an old lady whose kitchen was bare." D. Lee.—CoPs
Thoughts about oysters. K. Starbird.—CoPs
"A thousand hairy savages." S. Milligan.—CoPs
Three ghostesses. Unknown.—BrIt
"Through the teeth." Unknown.—CoPs
The toaster. W. J. Smith.—SmL
Tom. V. Worth.—WoSm
"Trick or treat, trick or treat." J. Prelutsky.—PrI
Trouble with dinner. J. A. Lindon.—HeB
Two birds with one stone. J. A. Lindon.—CoPs
Uncle Bungle. J. Prelutsky.—PrQ
Vegetables ("Eat a tomato and you'll turn red") S. Silverstein.—CoPs
A visit to the gingerbread house. From A lot of limericks. X. J. Kennedy.—KeP
"A voracious old fellow from Clunes." W. G. Howcroft.—DuSn
Waiters. M. A. Hoberman.—CoPs
The walrus and the carpenter. From Through the looking-glass. L. Carroll.—WiP
When father carves the duck. E. V. Wright.—CoPs
"When good King Arthur ruled this land." Mother Goose.—TrGg
"When you tip the ketchup bottle." Unknown.—CoPs
Who ordered the broiled face. S. Silverstein.—SiL
Wicked witch's kitchen. X. J. Kennedy.—BrIt—WaW
Willie ate a worm. J. Prelutsky.—PrRh
Witches' menu. S. Nikolay.—BrIt—WaW
"The yellow-bellied undersank." B. Giles.—DuSn
Yellow butter. M. A. Hoberman.—HoY
You take the pilgrims, just give me the progress. L. Rosenfield.—BrO
"Your mother." S. Cornish.—AdC
"Yule, yule, yule, my belly's full." Unknown.—BaC
"The **food** of most birds costs them nil." See The pelican
A **fool** and his money. David McCord.—McO
"A **foot** in the stirrup." See Indecision means flexibility
Football
The completion. L. Morrison.—MoSr
In the beginning was the. L. Morrison.—MoSr
Passing fair. L. Morrison.—MoSr

Footprints
Footprints. J. Aiken.—AiS
Trinity Place. D. McCord.—McO
Footprints ("Where did they start, those well marked white") Joan Aiken.—AiS
For a child gone to live in a commune. William Stafford.—PlL
"**For** a fresh start." See Oraga Haru
For a good dog. Arthur Guiterman.—CoG
For a ladybug. Aileen Fisher.—FiO
For a shetland pony brood mare who died in her barren year. Maxine Kumin.—CoPh
"**For** all things black and beautiful." Conrad Kent Rivers.—AdC
For Allan. Robert Frost.—LiCc—LiPch
"**For** an instant the gull." Ann Atwood.—AtH
For black poets who think of suicide. Etheridge Knight.—AdC
"**For** blackmen." See Blackmen, who make morning
"**For** breakfast I had ice cream." See Piggy
For deLawd. Lucille Clifton.—AdC
For each of you. Audre Lorde.—AdC
For Edwin R. Embree. Owen Dodson.—AdC
"**For** February fill me up day." Doris Orgel.—OrM
"**For** hours the princess would not play or sleep." See The yak
"**For** King, for Robert Kennedy." See Words in the mourning time
For Laura. Myra Cohn Livingston.—LiWt
For Malcolm, after Mecca. Gerald W. Barrax.—AdC—LiO
For Malcolm who walks in the eyes of our children. Quincy Troupe.—AdC
For Malcolm X ("All you violated ones with gentle hearts") Margaret Walker.—AdC
For Mattie and eternity. Sterling D. Plumpp.—AdC
"**For** moths and butterflies, it's nice." See Twice born
For Mugs. Myra Cohn Livingston.—LiF
For muh' dear. Carolyn M. Rodgers.—AdC
For my father. Philip Whalen.—KhI
For my people. Margaret Walker.—AdC
"**For** my people everywhere singing their slave songs." See For my people
For my unborn and wretched children. A. B. Spellman.—AdC
"**For** neatness and comfort." N. M. Bodecker.—BoHh
"**For** plate lunch today I have six different choices." See Lunch
For poets. Al Young.—AdC—LuZ
"**For** printed instructions." See No holes marred
For sapphires. Carolyn M. Rodgers.—AdC
"**For** that free grace bringing us past terrible risks." See Minnesota Thanksgiving
For the coming year. Peter Everwine.—LiO
"**For** the Fibruary dog show." Doris Orgel.—OrM
For the old man for drawing, dead at eighty-nine. N. Scott Momaday.—MoGd

For the sewing kit. Norma Farber.—FaS
For the sisters of the Hotel Dieu. A. M. Klein.—DoWh
"**For** the sky, blue, but the six year." See Drawing by Ronnie C., grade one
For the time being, sel. W. H. Auden
At the manger.—LiPch
"**For** this is not the road against which stand enemy lines." See Piyyut for Rosh Hashana
"**For** thou art with me here upon the banks." See Lines composed a few miles above Tintern Abbey
For us, who dare not dare. Maya Angelou.—AnO
"**For** wandering walks." See Joe's snow clothes
"**For** want of a nail, the shoe was lost." Mother Goose.—WiP
"**For** we have seen his star in the east, and are come." See Gospel according to Matthew
"**For** years we've had a little dog." See Two dogs have I
The **forest** greeting. Paul Laurence Dunbar.—BrI
Forests and forestry. See also Trees
Father and I in the woods. D. McCord.—HiS
"The fog fills the air." A. Atwood.—AtH
The grobbles. J. Prelutsky.—PrS
The horses. T. Hughes.—CoPh
The magic wood. H. Treece.—HiD
Out in the dark. E. Thomas.—PaB
The pointed people. R. L. Field.—WaFp
Snow ("The strawberry hill is covered with snow.) N. D. Watson.—WaB
Southern pines. J. P. Bishop.—PlG
Spell of the woods. L. Norris.—NoM
The stag. T. Hughes.—HuSs
"There's a fire in the forest." W.W.E. Ross.—DoWh
The toadstool wood. J. Reeves.—HiD
Under the white pine. D. McCord.—McO
The will o' the wisp. J. Prelutsky.—PrN
The woods at night. M. Swenson.—HiD
Forever ("I had not known before") Paul Laurence Dunbar.—BrI
Forever blowing. Norma Farber.—FaS
Forget it. David McCord.—McO
"**A forgetful** young woman of Tring." Myra Cohn Livingston.—LiLl
Forgetfulness
Forget it. D. McCord.—McO
"I left my head." L. Moore.—WiP
"Mary lost her coat." Unknown.—WiP
Mingram Mo. D. McCord.—McO
Perhaps. D. McCord.—McSu
Something missing. S. Silverstein.—SiL
"**Forgive** me if I have not sent you." See Valentines
Forgive my guilt. Robert P. Tristram Coffin.—MaP
Forgiveness
A penitent considers another coming of Mary. G. Brooks.—LiPch
Fork. Charles Simic.—JaPp
Forks. See Tableware

"Forks." See Breaking through

"Formerly I thought of you twice." See Four notions of love and marriage

Forms of praise. Lillian Morrison.—MoSr

Forms of the earth at Abiquiu. N. Scott Momaday.—MoGd

Formula. Ana Maria Iza, tr. by Ron Connally.—LuZ

The forsaken merman. Matthew Arnold.—PaE

The forsaken, sel. Duncan Campbell Scott
"Once in the winter."—DoWh

Fortune cooky. Myra Cohn Livingston.—LiWt

Fortune telling
Cherrystones. J. Aiken.—AiS
Fortune cooky. M. C. Livingston.—LiWt
"A frightened soothsayer from Ryde." M. C. Livingston.—LiLl

Forty mermaids. Dennis Lee.—LeN

Fossils
The black fern. L. Norris.—NoM
Next. O. Nash.—BlC
The skank. J. Yolen.—YoH

Foster, Stephen
Old dog Tray.—CoG

Foul shot. Edwin A. Hoey.—MoGp

"Found in the garden—dead in his beauty." See The burial of the linnet

The foundations of American industry. Donald Hall.—PlG

A fountain pen poem. N. M. Bodecker.—BoHh

#4. Doughtry Long.—AdC

The four brothers. Charlotte Pomerantz.—PoT

Four Christmas carols, sel. Unknown, tr. fr. the Colombian by Cheli Duran
"How cold the snow."—LiPch

"Four ducks on a pond." See A memory

Four foolish ladies. Jack Prelutsky.—PrQ

Four glimpses of night, sel. Frank Marshall Davis
"Peddling from door to door."—RuM

The four horses. James Reeves.—CoPh

400 meter freestyle. Maxine Kumin.—LuZ

Four little ducks. David McCord.—McO

Four little foxes. Lew Sarett.—WiP

Four notions of love and marriage. N. Scott Momaday.—MoGd

Four of July. Robert Newton Peck.—PeB

"Four stiff-standers." Mother Goose.—TrGg

"Four-way stop." Myra Cohn Livingston.—LiF

The Fourth. Shel Silverstein.—LiCc

Fourth of July
Child. From Song of the banner at daybreak, W. Whitman.—LiCc
The 5th of July. F. Holman.—HoMp—LiCc
Four of July. R. N. Peck.—PeB
The Fourth. S. Silverstein.—LiCc
Fourth of July ("Fat torpedoes in bursting jackets") R. Field.—LiCc
Fourth of July ("We celebrate you") M. C. Livingston.—LiF
Fourth of July ("We will bake independence pie") B. S. De Regniers.—ReB
Fourth of July night ("The little boat at anchor") C. Sandburg.—LiO

Fourth of July night ("Pin wheels whirling round") D. Aldis.—LiCc
Independence day ("Between painting a roof yesterday and the hay") W. Berry.—LiO
July. L. Clifton.—LiCc
"Many ways to spell good night." From Good night. C. Sandburg.—LiCc
Old glory. M. C. Livingston.—LiF
Twilight's last gleaming. A. W. Monks.—LiO

Fourth of July ("Fat torpedoes in bursting jackets") Rachel Field.—LiCc

Fourth of July ("We celebrate you") Myra Cohn Livingston.—LiF

Fourth of July ("We will bake independence pie") Beatrice Schenk De Regniers.—ReB

Fourth of July night ("The little boat at anchor") Carl Sandburg.—LiO

Fourth of July night ("Pin wheels whirling round") Dorothy Aldis.—LiCc

Fox and crow. William Jay Smith.—SmL

"The fox gives warning." Mother Goose.—TrGg

Fox, Siv Cedering
"After good night."—FoB
The blue horse.—FoB
I wonder.—FoB
"If a bad dream comes."—FoB
"In the evening."—FoB
"In the morning."—FoB
"My shoes."—FoB
The names of things.—FoB
Nightmares.—FoB
Northern lights.—FoB
"Once I dreamt I was the snow."—FoB
Shadows.—FoB
Tiger pajamas.—FoB
Waking up.—FoB

Foxes
Four little foxes. L. Sarett.—WiP
Fox and crow. W. J. Smith.—SmL
"The fox gives warning." Mother Goose.—TrGg
A moon manhunt. T. Hughes.—HuM
The three foxes. A. A. Milne.—WiP
"Water wobbling blue sky puddled October." From Autumn nature notes. T. Hughes.—HuSs

Foxgloves. Ted Hughes.—HuM

"Foxgloves on the moon keep to dark caves." See Foxgloves

Foxhunting. See Hunters and hunting

A fragment, sel. James Elroy Flecker
"I have heard a voice of broken seas."—PaE

Fragments. John Masefield.—PaE

Francie. Lillian Morrison.—MoSr

Francis, Robert
Blue jay.—JaPp
Deep sea diver. See Diver
"Delicate the toad."—HiD
Diver.—PaE
Deep sea diver.—MoGp
Like ghosts of eagles.—PlG
Night train.—HiD
That dark other mountain.—LiCc

The **frog** ("The frog sits succulent on his lily
    pad"). Eugene W. Rudzewicz.—GaCb
Frog ("How nice to be") Conrad Aiken.—CoA
Frog ("Pollywiggle") Mary Ann Hoberman.—
    HoY
Frog ("The spotted frog") Valerie Worth.—CoA
Frog in a bog. David McCord.—McO
"The **frog** lay in the step-child's bed." See The
    wooing frog
Frog music. David McCord.—McO
"The **frog** sits succulent on his lily pad." See
    The frog
"**Frogboy** dives in." See F is for frogboy
Frogs. See also Toads; Tree toads
    At the garden gate. D. McCord.—McO
    Bullfrog communique. M. Luton.—CoA
    F is for frogboy. W. J. Smith.—SmL
    The frog ("The frog sits succulent on his lily
        pad"). E. W. Rudzewicz.—GaCb
    Frog ("How nice to be") C. Aiken.—CoA
    Frog ("Pollywiggle") M. A. Hoberman.—HoY
    Frog ("The spotted frog") V. Worth.—CoA
    Frog in a bog. D. McCord.—McO
    Frog music. D. McCord.—McO
    Frogs in spring. A. Fisher.—FiO
    I'm nobody. E. Dickinson.—HiS
    "A noble prince, but very homely." D.
        Orgel.—OrM
    Nocturne. A. Guiterman.—RuM
    Peepers in the swamp grass. N. D. Watson.—
        WaB
    Rebels from fairy tales. H. Hill.—HiS
    Small frogs. L. Norris.—NoM
    Tadpoles. R. Fyleman.—WiP
    Wake up. E. Merriam.—MeB
    The wooing frog. J. Reeves.—HiS
"**Frogs** burrow the mud." See Winter
Frogs in spring. Aileen Fisher.—FiO
"**Frogs** that croak." See Sounds of spring
"**From** a Fibruary sandbox." Doris Orgel.—
    OrM
"**From** breakfast on through all the day." See
    The land of nod
"**From** dusk to dawn." See In search of
    Cinderella
"**From** gable, barn, and stable." Unknown.—
    BaC
"**From** ghoulies and ghosties." Unknown.—LiO
    A Cornish litany.—LiCc
    Ghoulies and ghosties.—WaGp—WaM
    Litany for Halloween.—BrIt
    Prayer for Halloween.—LiF
"**From** Grant's grave Galena." See Old
    Dubuque
"**From** Heaven high I come to you." Martin
    Luther.—LiPch
"**From** here to there." See Going to school
"**From** his wanderings far to eastward." See
    The song of Hiawatha
"**From** hoofbeat to chug-chug to roar of jet."
    See Progress
"**From** my city bed in the dawn I." See S F
"**From** now on kill America out of your mind."
    See Lyric

"**From** out of a wood did a cuckoo fly." See
    The birds
"**From** Paumanok starting I fly like a bird."
    Walt Whitman.—PlG
"**From** such old boards." See Dangerous
    condition, sign on inner city house
"**From** the high deck of Sante Fe's El Capitan."
    See A siding near Chillicothe
From the Japanese. Eve Merriam.—MeR
From the kitchen, sels. David McCord.—McO
    (Complete)
    1. Pie
    2. Macaroon
    3. Fudge
    4. Peanut butter
    5. Cake
    6. Pistachio ice cream
    7. Animal crackers
    8. People crackers
    9. Gingersnaps
    10. Cucumbers vs pickles
From the mailboat passing by. David
    McCord.—McO
"**From** the obscurity of the past we saw." See
    Nat Turner
"**From** the old slave shack I chose my lady."
    See Trellie
From the Persian. David McCord.—McSu
From the window. David Kherdian.—KhC
"**From** whence arrived the praying mantis."
    See The praying mantis
"**From** where I stand now." See 12 October
"**From** winter sleep." See Ladybug's Christmas
"**From** witches and wizards and longtail'd
    buzzards." See A short litany
"**From** you I have been absent in the spring."
    See Sonnets
Froman, Robert
    Easy diver.—CoA
    Puzzle.—MoGp
    Undefeated.—MoGp
Frontier and pioneer life. See also America—
    Settlement; Cowboys; United
    States—History
    Burying ground by the ties. A. MacLeish.—
        PlG
    Comanche. G. Gildner.—CoPh
    First Thanksgiving. M. C. Livingston.—LiCc
    Jamestown ("Let me look at what I was,
        before I die") R. Jarrell.—PlG
    The men of Sudbury. C. Baker.—PlG
    Minnesota Thanksgiving. J. Berryman.—PlG
    A New England sampler. J. M. Brinnin.—PlG
    Peregrine White and Virginia Dare. S. V. and
        R. Benet.—WiP
    The settlers. J. Hemschemeyer.—HiS
    The shooting of Dan McGrew. R. W.
        Service.—DoWh
    The spare quilt. J. P. Bishop.—PlG
    Stanzas on the emigration to America, and
        peopling the western country. P.
        Freneau.—PlG
    The trail beside the River Platte. W.
        Heyen.—PlG

Fyleman, Rose
  The balloon man.—PaI
  Bibbilbonty.—WiP
  Conversation.—WiP
  "The fairies have never a penny to spend."—
    WaFp
  "A fairy went a-marketing.—PaI
  The goblin.—WiP
  Have you watched the fairies.—PaI
  Mice.—PaI
  Momotara, tr.—WaG—WiP
  My donkey.—WiP
  "Stork, stork."—WiP
  Tadpoles.—WiP
  Witch, witch.—BeR—WiP

G

G is for goat. William Jay Smith.—SmL
A **gaggle** of geese, a pride of lions. John
    Moore.—HiD
Galbraith, Georgie Starbuck
  No mixed green salad for me, thanks.—BrO
Gale, Vi
  Orange.—KhI
Gallagher, Anthony E.
  Potato chips.—CoPs—DuSn
Gallagher, Katherine
  Poison ivy.—WaW
The **gallant** highwayman. James De Mille.—
    DoWh
"**Gallop** up the instant stair." See Air on an
    escalator
Galloping ("The rushing, the brushing, the
    wind in your face") Cordelia Chitty.—CoPh
"**Galloping** away to the farthest pasture." See
    Dexter
Galoshes. Rhoda W. Bacmeister.—PaI
Gamblers and gambling
  "One time Henry dreamed the number." D.
    Long.—AdC
Game after supper. Margaret Atwood.—LuZ
The **game** of doublets. David McCord.—McO
Games. See also Nursery play; Play; also names
    of games, as Baseball
  Bobbing for apples. J. Prelutsky.—PrI
  Catching-song a play rhyme. E. Farjeon.—
    WiP
  The chinese checker players. R. Brautigan.—
    MoGp
  The enemy. M. C. Livingston.—LiWt
  The game of doublets. D. McCord.—McO
  Harvey always wins. J. Prelutsky.—PrRh
  Hug o' war. S. Silverstein.—YaI
  "Playing hopscotch on the." K. Mizumura.—
    MiF
The **games** of night. Nancy Willard.—WaGp
"The **game's** the same." See Witch baseball
"**Gamorra** is a dainty steed." See The blood
    horse
Gangemi, Kenneth
  Classroom.—HeB

Garbage
  The city dump. F. Holman.—HoA
  Garbage. V. Worth.—WoSm
  Garbage delight. D. Lee.—LeG
  Only a little litter. M. C. Livingston.—BrO
  Roadside. V. Worth.—WoSm
Garbage. Valerie Worth.—WoSm
Garbage delight. Dennis Lee.—LeG
Garden calendar. N. M. Bodecker.—BoHh
Garden lore. Julia Horatia Ewing.—MoF
The **garden** snake. John Gardner.—GaCb
"**Garden** soil." See Earthworms
Garden song. Austin Dobson.—PaB
Garden toad. Aileen Fisher.—FiO
The **garden** year, sel. Sara Coleridge
  "Chill December brings the sleet."—BaC
The **gardener** ("When Grandpa couldn't hoe or
    spade") Kaye Starbird.—StC
Gardeners. See Gardens and gardening
Gardeners ("So is the child slow stooping beside
    him") David Ignatow.—JaPp
A **gardener's** roses. N. M. Bodecker.—BoP
Gardens and gardening
  After Christmas. M. C. Livingston.—LiWt
  Autumn garden. A. Fisher.—FiO
  The caterpillar. E. Lucie-Smith.—CoA
  Deep into winter. A. Adoff.—AdE
  "Driving through New England." L.
    Clifton.—PlG
  Garden calendar. N. M. Bodecker.—BoHh
  Garden lore. J. H. Ewing.—MoF
  Garden song. A. Dobson.—PaB
  Garden toad. A. Fisher.—FiO
  The gardener ("When Grandpa couldn't hoe
    or spade") K. Starbird.—StC
  Gardeners ("So is the child slow stooping
    beside him") D. Ignatow.—JaPp
  A gardener's roses. N. M. Bodecker.—BoP
  A gard'ner whose plants. N. M. Bodecker.—
    BoP
  "Getting the sweet strawberries." A. Adoff.—
    AdE
  "Late April and you are three, today." From
    Heart's needle. W. D. Snodgrass.—PlL
  Mr Bidery's spidery garden. D. McCord.—
    McO
  Old Shellover. W. De La Mare.—SaM
  Old Tim Toole. D. McCord.—McO
  "Only the onions." A. Adoff.—AdE
  The pole bean tent. K. Starbird.—StC
  Slug ("The slug") V. Worth.—WoSm
  "There was a young farmer of Leeds."
    Unknown.—LoG
  "Unwatch'd, the garden bough shall sway."
    From In memoriam. A. Tennyson.—PaB
  The witch's garden. L. Moore.—WiP
"**Gardens, fields.**" See Snow
Gardner, Isabella
  Not at all what one is used to.—KhI
  Part of the darkness.—FlA
Gardner, John
  The African wild dog.—GaCb
  The alligator.—GaCb
  "Always be kind to animals."—GaCb

Gardner, John—*Continued*
"The armadillo."—GaCb
The baboon.—GaCb
The barracuda.—GaCb
The bear.—GaCb
The beaver.—GaCb
The beefalo.—GaCb
"A bestiary, or book of beasts."—GaCb
The buzzard.—GaCb
The camel.—GaCb
The cat and the dog.—GaCb
The chameleon.—GaCb
The cobra.—GaCb
The cockatoo.—GaCb
The crab.—GaCb
The crow.—GaCb
"The duck has pluck."—GaCb
The eagle.—GaCb
The eel.—GaCb
The elephant.—GaCb
The end.—GaCb
The flying squirrel.—GaCb
The garden snake.—GaCb
The giraffe.—GaCb
The hippopotamus.—GaCb
The house mouse and the church mouse.—
  GaCb
The kangaroo.—GaCb
The leopard.—GaCb
The lion.—GaCb
The lizard.—GaCb
"The lynx."—GaCb
The mole.—GaCb
The mosquito.—GaCb
The moth.—GaCb
The musk ox.—GaCb
The octopus.—GaCb
The opossum.—GaCb
The owl.—GaCb
The panther.—GaCb
The peacock and the great blue heron.—
  GaCb
The penguin.—GaCb
The phoenix.—GaCb
The pig.—GaCb
The python.—GaCb
The red-headed woodpecker.—GaCb
The rhinoceros.—GaCb
The shark.—GaCb
The striped hyena.—GaCb
The swan.—GaCb
The tiger.—GaCb
"The treetoad and the three-toed sloth."—
  GaCb
The turkey.—GaCb
The turtle.—GaCb
The walrus, an evolutionary tale.—GaCb
The wart hog.—GaCb
The wasp and the mud dauber.—GaCb
The water buffalo.—GaCb
The wolf.—GaCb
The yeti.—GaCb
The zebra.—GaCb

Gardner, Lucy
  The whale.—GaCb
Gardner, Martin
  Cry-baby.—CoI
  Magic word.—CoI
  Speak clearly.—CoPs
Gardner, Richard
  Tall stories.—DuSn
A gard'ner whose plants. N. M. Bodecker.—BoP
Gargi, Balwant
  Evening, tr.—LuZ
Gargoyles
  The gargoyle's protest. X. J. Kennedy.—KeP
  The gargoyle's protest. X. J. Kennedy.—KeP
  The garret. Paul Laurence Dunbar.—BrI
Garrett, George
  Abraham's knife.—PlL
Garrison, Theodosia
  The shepherd who stayed.—LiPch
Gary, Sid
  Circuit breaker.—BrO
  Pythagorean razzle dazzle.—BrO
Gasztold, Carmen Bernos de
  The prayer of the donkey.—LiPch
  The prayer of the mouse.—SaM
Gates
  At the garden gate. D. McCord.—McO
Gavenda, Walt
  Eco right.—BrO
Gazelle. Mary Ann Hoberman.—HoY—WiP
Gazelles. See Antelopes
Gebir, sel. Walter Savage Landor
  "I have sinuous shells of pearly hue."—PaE
Geese
  Angle of geese. N. S. Momaday.—MoGd
  Family friends. M. A. Hoberman.—HoY
  Four little ducks. D. McCord.—McO
  A gaggle of geese, a pride of lions. J.
    Moore.—HiD
  "Goodness, gracious, have you heard the
    news." Unknown.—WiP
  The goose ("At the end of the train, in the
    big red caboose") R. S. Oliver.—OlC
  "Gray goose and gander." Mother Goose.—
    TrGg
  "Happy birthday, silly goose." From Father
    Fox's pennyrhymes. C. Watson.—LiCc
  Old grey goose. H. Behn.—CoA
  Puzzling. W. Cole.—CoA
  Something better. D. McCord.—McO
  "Something told the wild geese." R. Field.—
    HoMp
  "V." D. McCord.—McO
"Geiger, geiger, ticking slow." See A leaden
  treasury of English verse
Gems. See Precious stones
General store. Rachel Field.—PaI
Generations. Judy Dothard Simmons.—AdC
A generous man. William Cole.—CoPs
Genesis, sels. Bible—Old Testament
  "And God said, let us make man in our
    image."—PlL
  Cain and Abel.—PlL
The gentled beast. Dilys Laing.—CoPh

"Gentlemen, I love and like you." See Lines to three boys, 8, 6 1/2, and 2 years of age
"Gentlemen owls fly about at night." See Owls
"A genuine anteater." See Anteater
Genus hylobates. Jim Gibbons.—KhI
Geology. See also Rocks and stones
  Rhyme for a geological baby. From Boston nursery rhymes. J. Cook.—BrO
Geometry. See Mathematics
George, Phil
  Battle won is lost.—LuZ
"George Washington, your name is on my lips." See Patriotic poem
Georgia
  Talking to the townsfolk in Ideal, Georgia. I. J. Black.—AdC
"Geraldine now, stop shaking that cow." See Shaking
Geraniums
  Red. L. Moore.—WiP
The germ ("A mighty creature is the germ") Ogden Nash.—BlC
"The German children march along." See German song
German song. Ogden Nash.—BlC
Germany
  German song. O. Nash.—BlC
Geronomo Hacket. N. M. Bodecker.—BoP
"Get on, expecting the worst, a mount like a statue." See The trail horse
"Get out of my way." See Roosters
"Get set, ready now, jump right in." See Rope rhyme
"Get up after a nightmare in which some dead men have." See Things to do around Taos
Get up, get up. Unknown.—CoPs
"Get up, get up, you lazy head." See Get up, get up
Getting ready. N. M. Bodecker.—BoHh
"Getting the sweet strawberries." Arnold Adoff.—AdE
Ghettoes
  And was not improved. L. Bennett.—AdC
  Dangerous condition, sign on inner city house. R. Atkins.—AdC
  "In the inner city." L. Clifton.—AdC—MoGp
  Inner city lullaby. R. Atkins.—AdC
Ghost ("I saw a ghost") Jack Prelutsky.—PrI
Ghost boy. Mark Van Doren.—HiS
The ghost of Caupolican. Unknown, fr. the Araucanian Indian.—WaGp
The ghostly grocer of Grumble Grove. Jack Prelutsky.—WaGp
Ghosts
  A-ha. D. Aldis.—BrIt
  Abraham Lincoln walks at midnight. V. Lindsay.—LiO—PlG
  Attic ghosts. X. J. Kennedy.—KeP
  Autumn ghost sounds. Unknown.—BrIt
  Countdown. J. Prelutsky.—PrI
  Daniel Boone. S. V. Benet.—PlG
  Daniel Webster's horses. E. Coatsworth.—CoPh
  "Do ghouls." L. Moore.—BrIt

"From ghoulies and ghosties." Unknown.—LiO
  A Cornish litany.—LiCc
  Ghoulies and ghosties.—WaGp—WaM
  Litany for Halloween.—BrIt
  Prayer for Halloween.—LiF
The games of night. N. Willard.—WaGp
Ghost ("I saw a ghost") J. Prelutsky.—PrI
Ghost boy. M. Van Doren.—HiS
The ghost of Caupolican. Unknown.—WaGp
The ghostly grocer of Grumble Grove. J. Prelutsky.—WaGp
Ghosts ("A cold and starry darkness moans") H. Behn.—WaGp
The ghoul. J. Prelutsky.—PrN
The glory trail. B. Clark.—CoPh
The great auk's ghost. R. Hodgson.—BrIt
Halloween ("Samantha, call her Sam, OK") D. McCord.—McSu
Halloween ("Stealing white from the withered moon") M. C. Livingston.—LiF—LiO
Haunted ("Black hill black hall") W. Mayne.—WaGp
The haunted house. J. Prelutsky.—PrN
The haunted oven. X. J. Kennedy.—KeP
The headless horseman. J. Prelutsky.—PrH
"Hist whist." E. E. Cummings.—HiS—LiO—WiP
"I like winter, spring, summer, and fall." B. S. De Regniers.—BrIt—ReB
In the old house. J. Aiken.—AiS
"The lady in white." N. M. Bodecker.—BoHh
Long distance. W. Stafford.—HiS
The mini spooks. E. Anderson.—BrIt
"Monsters do not scare me much." B. S. De Regniers.—ReB
Monsters I've met. S. Silverstein.—SiL
The mummy ("In the darkness of a sepulcher") J. Prelutsky.—PrH
No TV. L. Moore.—BrIt
The old ghost. T. L. Beddoes.—WaGp
Old man, phantom dog. F. Eckman.—FlA
The old wife and the ghost. J. Reeves.—BrIt—WaGp
The phantom ice cream man. X. J. Kennedy.—KeP
The phantom ship. M. P. Hearn.—WaGp
The poltergeist ("Something strange is flitting through your hair") J. Prelutsky.—PrH
Pumpkin seeds. D. McCord.—McO
Shadow-bride. J.R.R. Tolkien.—HiS
The shepherd's hut. A. Young.—WaGp
Singing ghost. S. Kroll.—WaGp
Song of two ghosts. Unknown.—WaGp
Southern mansion. A. Bontemps.—AdC
The spectre on the moor. J. Prelutsky.—PrH
Sunk Lyonesse. W. De La Mare.—PaE
The superstitious ghost. A. Guiterman.—BrIt
Teeny tiny ghost. L. Moore.—WaGp
Three ghostesses. Unknown.—BrIt
Tillie. W. De La Mare.—WaGp
"Wailed a ghost in a graveyard at Kew." M. C. Livingston.—LiLl

Ghosts—*Continued*
  Whose boo is whose. X. J. Kennedy.—BrIt—KeP—WaGp
  Widdecombe fair. Unknown.—CoPh
  The wind has wings. Unknown.—DoWh
  Windy nights ("Whenever the moon and stars are set") R. L. Stevenson.—CoPh—RuM
Ghosts ("A cold and starry darkness moans") Harry Behn.—WaGp
The **ghoul.** Jack Prelutsky.—PrN
Ghoulies and ghosties. See "From ghoulies and ghosties"
Gia-fu Feng and English, Jane
  Seventy-six. trs.—LuZ
"The **giant** Blunderbore." See Blunderbore
Giant chants. See Jack the giant killer
"The **giant** Jim." Mother Goose.—LoG
A **giant** named Stanley. Michael Patrick Hearn.—WaG
"**Giant** sunflowers." Betsy Maestro.—MaFp
Giant Thunder. James Reeves.—HiD
"**Giant** Thunder, striding home." See Giant Thunder
The **giant** to his child. Jane Yolen.—YoD
Giants
  The adventures of Isabel. O. Nash.—BlC
  Blunderbore. R. Fuller.—WaG
  "Do what you can to get away." From The history of Jack and the giants. Unknown.—WaG
  "Fe, fi, fo, fum." Mother Goose.—WaG
    "Fee, fie, fo, fum."—TrGg
  Giant chants. From Jack the giant killer. Unknown.—WaG
  "The giant Jim." Mother Goose.—LoG
  A giant named Stanley. M. P. Hearn.—WaG
  Giant Thunder. J. Reeves.—HiD
  The giant to his child. J. Yolen.—YoD
  Giants' delight. S. Kroll.—WaG
  Giant's wife. Unknown.—WaG
  The greedy giant. L. E. Richards.—WaG
  Grim. W. De La Mare.—WaG
  "Hickenthrift and Hickenloop." X. J. Kennedy.—KeP—WaG
  Huffer and Cuffer. J. Prelutsky.—WaG
  In the orchard. J. Stephens.—HiS—WaG
  Like a giant in a towel. D. Lee.—WaG
  Magic story for falling asleep. N. Willard.—WaG
  Me and my giant. S. Silverstein.—WaG
  Momotara. Unknown, tr. by Rose Fyleman.—WaG—WiP
  Shrieks at midnight. D. B. Thompson.—WaG
  A small discovery. J. A. Emanuel.—MaP
  Song of the giant killer. L. Norris.—NoM
  "This leaf." B. S. De Regniers.—ReB
  The towering giant. J. Prelutsky.—PrH
  The up to date giant. X. J. Kennedy.—KeP
Giants' delight. Steven Kroll.—WaG
Giant's wife. Unknown.—WaG
The **gibble.** Jack Prelutsky.—PrS
"The **gibble** is glum and big as a thumb." See The gibble

The **gibbon.** Eugene W. Rudzewicz.—GaCb
"The **gibbon,** as you can tell by his manner." See The gibbon
Gibbons, Jim
  Genus hylobates.—KhI
Gibson, Wilfred
  The dancing seal.—PaE
  Green shag.—PaE
  The ice-cart.—PaE
  The ponies.—CoPh
  Sea-change.—PaE
"A **giddy** young maid in Old Lyme." See A maid in Old Lyme
Gift. Carol Freeman.—BaC
  "Christmas morning I."—LiPch
Gift ("Let me wrap a poem around you") Judith Hemschemeyer.—JaPp
The **gift** ("Older, more generous") N. Scott Momaday.—MoGd
Gift of sight. Robert Graves.—JaPp
The **gift** outright. Robert Frost.—PlG
Gifts and giving. See also Charity; Thankfulness
  The ballad of Befana. P. McGinley.—BaC
  Birthday gifts. H. Asquith.—LiO
  Birthday present. A. Fisher.—FiO
  Carol of the brown king. L. Hughes.—BaC
  A Christmas carol ("In the bleak mid-winter") C. G. Rossetti.—BaC
    "What can I give him."—LiCc (sel.)—LiPch (sel.)
  "Christmas morning I." C. Freeman.—LiPch
  Christmas secrets. A. Fisher.—FiO
  Conversation about Christmas, the useful presents. From A child's Christmas in Wales. D. Thomas.—LiPch
  The corner newsman. K. Starbird.—HoMp—StC
  Do not open till Christmas. J. S. Tippett.—BaC
  For Allan. R. Frost.—LiCc—LiPch
  Gift. C. Freeman.—BaC
    "Christmas morning I."—LiPch
  The gift ("Older, more generous") N. S. Momaday.—MoGd
  "Mrs. Malone." E. Farjeon.—WiP
  My cat. N. D. Watson.—WaB
  "Oh Christmas time is drawing near." Unknown.—BaC
  Otto. G. Brooks.—LiCc
  Overheard on a saltmarsh. H. Monro.—WiP
  The perfect gift. E. V. Cooke.—LiPch
  Shepherd's song at Christmas. L. Hughes.—LiPch
  The three kings. R. Dario.—BaC—LiPch
  The twelve days of Christmas. Unknown.—LiPch
  Waltzing mice. D. McCord.—McO
"A **gigantic** beauty of a stallion, fresh and responsive." See Stallion
"**Gigantic** mills stand stark against the sky." See Steel mills
Gilbert, Alice
  "I ate a ton of sugar."—CoPs

"**Goes** moo moo moo." See The Halloween cow

Goethe, Johann Wolfgang von
"Feed the wood and have a joyful minute."—BaC

Going away. Ann Stanford.—CoPh
Going barefoot. Judith Thurman.—ThFo
Going calling. Aileen Fisher.—FiO
Going round in a square. Norma Farber.—FaS
Going to bed. Marchette Chute.—PaI
Going to school. Karla Kuskin.—HeB
Going to town. Fred Lape.—CoPh
Going too far. William Cole.—CoPs
Going up north. Dennis Lee.—LeN
Gold (color). See Yellow
Gold (metal)
A peck of gold. R. Frost.—HiS
Gold. David McCord.—McSu
Gold-fish. See Goldfish
"The **gold** of her promise." See America
The **gold** tinted dragon. Karla Kuskin.—KuD
The **golden** boy. Ted Hughes.—HuSs
A **golden** day. Paul Laurence Dunbar.—BrI
Golden grain. Helen M. Wright.—CoPh
Goldfinches. Felice Holman.—HoA
Goldfish
My fishes. M. Chute.—CoA
Goldsmith, Oliver
Elegy on the death of a mad dog.—CoG
Golf
Zen and the art of golf with cart. L. Morrison.—MoSr
Golino, Carlo L.
The little trumpet. tr.—LuZ
Gone. David McCord.—HoBm—McO
Good and bad. Edward Abbott Parry.—CoI
"**Good-by** my winter suit." N. M. Bodecker.—BoHh
"**Good-bye,** I said to my conscience." See Conscience and remorse
Good evening, Mr. Soup. Unknown.—CoPs
"**Good** evening, Mr. Soup, Soup, Soup." See Good evening, Mr. Soup
Good for the head. Arnold Adoff.—AdE
Good Friday. Christina Georgina Rossetti.—LiO
"**Good** hunting, aye, good hunting." See The forest greeting
"**Good** King Johan of Bavonia." See King Johan of Bavonia
Good morning ("Good morning to the great trees") Mark Van Doren.—HiD
Good morning America, sel. Carl Sandburg
"Now it's Uncle Sam sitting on top of the world."—LiO
Good morning, love. Paul Blackburn.—KhI
Good-morning poems. See Wake-up poems
"**Good** morning to the great trees." See Good morning
"**Good** morning, tree." See Summer morning
Good news from New England, sel. Edward Johnson
"With hearts revived in conceit, new land and trees they eye."—PlG
Good-night. Paul Laurence Dunbar.—BrI

Good night ("Father puts the paper down") Aileen Fisher.—FiO
"**Good**-night, my love, for I have dreamed of thee." See Absence
Good-night poems. See also Bed-time
Child's game. J. Jerome.—HiD
"Down dip the branches." M. Van Doren.—HiD
Goodnight ("Goodnight Mommy") N. Giovanni.—GiV—RuM
"Now say good night." D. McCord.—McO
Papa bantam's goodnight. J. Yolen.—YoD
Twilight song. J. Hunter-Duvar.—DoWh
Good night, sel. Carl Sandburg
"Many ways to spell good night."—LiCc
"**Good** old Geronomo Hacket." See Geronomo Hacket
"**Good** people all, of every sort." See Elegy on the death of a mad dog
"A **good** time is coming, I wish it were here." See When Santa Claus comes
Good times. Lucille Clifton.—AdC
Good times and no bread. Reginald Lockett.—AdC
"**Good** weather for hay." See Vermont conversation
Goodge, W. T.
Daley's dorg Wattle.—CoG
How we drove the trotter.—CoPh
Goodman, Paul
Don Larsen's perfect game.—LuZ
Our Lucy, 1956–1960.—CoG
Goodness. See Conduct of life
"**Goodness,** gracious, have you heard the news." Unknown.—WiP
Goodnight ("Goodnight Mommy") Nikki Giovanni.—GiV—RuM
The **goodnight** ("He stood still by her bed") Louis Simpson.—PlL
"**Goodnight** Mommy." See Goodnight
Goofus. Dennis Lee.—LeG
Goofy song. Dennis Lee.—LeG
Gooloo. Shel Silverstein.—SiL
"The **gooloo** bird." See Gooloo
Goony bird. William Jay Smith.—SmL
"The **goops** they lick their fingers." See Table manners
The **goose** ("At the end of the train, in the big red caboose") Robert S. Oliver.—OlC
Goose, moose and spruce. David McCord.—McO
Gordon, W.J.J.
IBM hired her.—BrO
Gorillas. See also Monkeys
We must be polite. C. Sandburg.—WiP
Gospel according to Luke, sels. Bible—New Testament
"And some of the Pharisees from among the multitude."—LiPch
"And there were in the same country shepherds."—LiPch
The angels.—BaC (sel.)
The shepherds.—BaC (sel.)
The nativity.—BaC

Gospel according to Luke —*Continued*
  The parable of the prodigal son.—PlL
Gospel according to Matthew, sels. Bible—New
    Testament
  "For we have seen his star in the east, and
    are come."—BaC
  The Magi.—BaC
The **gossip.** Daniel Halpern.—HiS
Gossip
  "It costs little Gossip her income for shoes."
    Mother Goose.—TrGg
  Moon cabbage. T. Hughes.—HuM
Gotlieb, Phyllis
  "How and when and where and why."—
    DoWh
The **gourd** dancer. N. Scott Momaday.—MoGd
Government
  National security. A. MacLeish.—PlG
Govoni, Corrado
  The little trumpet.—LuZ
Graffiti
  To Desi as Joe the smoky the lover of 115th
    street. A. Lorde.—AdC
Graham, Al
  "By rocket, to visit the moon." See
    Interplanetary limericks
  Interplanetary limericks, sels.—BrO
    (Complete)
      "By rocket, to visit the moon"
      "The ladies inhabiting Venus"
      "A Martian named Harrison Harris"
  "The ladies inhabiting Venus." See
    Interplanetary limericks
  "A Martian named Harrison Harris." See
    Interplanetary limericks
Graham, Harry
  Impetuous Samuel.—CoI
Graham, Lorenz
  "And in a far country." See Every man heart
    lay down
  Every man heart lay down, sel.
    "And in a far country."—BaC
Graham, S. J.
  The ballyoons—DuSn
  Pancho Pangolin.—DuSn
  The witch's balloon.—DuSn
Grahame, Kenneth
  Carol. See The wind in the willows
  The song of Mr. Toad. See The wind in the
    willows
  "Villagers all, this frosty tide." See The wind
    in the willows—Carol
  Wind in the willows, sels.
    Carol.—BaC
    "Villagers all, this frosty tide."—LiPch
    The song of Mr. Toad.—WiP
Grain. See names of grain, as Wheat
"A **grand** attempt some amazonian dames." See
    On a fortification at Boston begun by
    women
"The **grand** old Duke of York." Mother
    Goose.—TrGg
Grandfather ("Each year, as spring returns")
    Joan Aiken.—AiS

"A **grandfather** poem." William J. Harris.—
    AdC—MoGp
Grandfathers
  "Any Fibruary morning." D. Orgel.—OrM
  Birdfoot's grampa. J. Bruchac.—MoGp
  The collier laddie. L. Norris.—NoM
  The gardener ("When Grandpa couldn't hoe
    or spade") K. Starbird.—StC
  Grandfather ("Each year, as spring returns")
    J. Aiken.—AiS
  "A grandfather poem. W. J. Harris.—AdC—
    MoGp
  "Granfa' Grig had a pig." Mother Goose.—
    TrGg
  Harmonica man. P. Wolny.—JaPp
  Manners for a child of 1918. E. Bishop.—PlL
  Mosquito. Unknown.—MoGp
  My wise old grandpapa. W. G. Howcroft.—
    CoPs
  Old man playing with children. J. C.
    Ransom.—PlL
  Sire ("Here comes the shadow not looking
    where it is going") W. S. Merwin.—PlL
  So will I. C. Zolotow.—HoBm
  Surprise. S. Silverstein.—SiL
Grandma Ida's cookie dough for apple pie
    crust. Arnold Adoff.—AdE
"**Grandma** sent the hammock." See Hammock
Grandmother ostrich. William Jay Smith.—SmL
"**Grandmother** ostrich goes to bed." See
    Grandmother ostrich
Grandmother, rocking. Eve Merriam.—JaPp—
    MeR
Grandmothers
  Almost ninety. R. Whitman.—JaPp
  Apple scoop. E. Glen.—MoGp
  At grandmother's. J. Haislip.—LuZ
  Big momma. H. R. Madhubuti.—AdC
  "Christmas morning I." C. Freeman.—LiPch
  Constellations. P. St. John.—LuZ
  The cupboard. W. De La Mare.—PaI
  Gift. C. Freeman.—BaC
      "Christmas morning I."—LiPch
  Grandmother, rocking. E. Merriam.—JaPp
  A grandson is a hoticeberg. M. Danner.—
    AdC
  Hammock. S. Silverstein.—SiL
  Jesus drum. P. C. Lomax.—AdC
  The lady in the chair. N. Giovanni.—GiV
  Lineage. M. Walker.—AdC—LuZ
  Love necessitates. E. Redmond.—AdC
  Mr Tom Narrow. J. Reeves.—HiS
  My grandmother ("My grandmother moves
    to my mind in context of sorrow") K.
    Shapiro.—PlL
  A near pantoum for a birthday. B. Howes.—
    PlL
  Old Dubuque. D. Etter.—FlA
  Old people's home. W. H. Auden.—PlL
  "Remembering Grandma filling up this
    porch." N. Grimes.—GrS
  Sestina. E. Bishop.—PlL
  The smile. J. Aiken.—AiS
  There is a place. A. Adoff.—AdE

You take the pilgrims, just give me the
  progress. L. Rosenfield.—BrO
"Grandmother's love." See Love necessitates
Grandpa bear's lullaby. Jane Yolen.—YoD
Grandparents. See Grandfathers; Grandmothers
"A grandson is." See A grandson is a hoticeberg
A grandson is a hoticeberg. Margaret
  Danner.—AdC
"Granfa' Grig had a pig." Mother Goose.—
  TrGg
The granite sentry. Robert Newton Peck.—PeB
Granny winter. Unknown, ad. fr. the Russian
  by Marguerita Rudolph.—BaC
Grant Wood's American landscape. Winfield
  Townley Scott.—PlG
Grapes
  Taste of purple. L. B. Jacobs.—HoMp
"Grapes hang purple." See Taste of purple
Grass
  After a freezing rain. A. Fisher.—FiO
  The beautiful lawn sprinkler. H. Nemerov.—
    JaPp
  Cinderella grass. A. Fisher.—FiO
  The gibble. J. Prelutsky.—PrS
  Grass ("Do you ever think about grass") A.
    Fisher.—FiO
  The grass, alas. D. Emmons.—BrO
  Hay ("The grass is happy") T. Hughes.—HuSs
  Hiding place. N. D. Watson.—WaB
  Lawnmower. V. Worth.—WoM
  Needs. A. R. Ammons.—LuZ
  Summer grass. C. Sandburg.—MoGp
  The tuft of flowers. R. Frost.—PaB
Grass ("Do you ever think about grass") Aileen
  Fisher.—FiO
The grass, alas. Dick Emmons.—BrO
"The grass is happy." See Hay
The grass on the mountain. Unknown, tr. fr.
  the Paiute Indian by Mary Austin.—PlG
"The grass that's fired with finches." See
  Goldfinches
"The grasshopper." See Just now
The grasshopper ("Down") David McCord.—
  CoA—McO—WiP
"Grasshopper green." Nancy Dingman
  Watson.—WaB
Grasshoppers
  The grasshopper ("Down") D. McCord.—
    CoA—McO—WiP
  "Grasshopper green." N. D. Watson.—WaB
  "Little Miss Tuckett." Mother Goose.—BeR—
    CoA—LoG
  My grasshopper. M. C. Livingston.—WiP
  "Way down South where bananas grow."
    Unknown.—WiP
Gratitude. See Thankfulness
"Gratitude to mother earth, sailing through
  night and day." See Prayer for the great
  family
"The grave was three feet long, or less, more
  like." See A sister's grave
Graves. See Tombs
Graves, Robert
  The bedpost.—HiS

Bird of paradise.—PaB
Flying crooked.—JaPp—LuZ
Gift of sight.—JaPp
Henry and Mary.—HiS
The hero.—JaPp
I will write.—JaPp
I'd love to be a fairy's child.—WaFp
Poem, a reminder.—LuZ
The two witches.—HiS
Warning to children.—HiS
What did I dream.—HiD
Graveyards. See Cemeteries
Gray (color)
  What is grey. M. O'Neill.—SaM
"The gray dawn on the mountain top." See
  Day
Gray, Don
  "Jumped off."—LuZ
"Gray goose and gander." Mother Goose.—
  TrGg
"Gray squirrel, standing in the road." See To a
  squirrel
Grayston, Joan Byers
  Dexter.—CoPh
  Unseen horses.—CoPh
The great auk's ghost. Ralph Hodgson.—BrIt
"The great auk's ghost rose on one leg." See
  The great auk's ghost
"Great big gawky Gumbo Cole." See Big
  Gumbo
Great Britain. See England
"Great goblets of pudding powder in milk."
  See Love song
The Great Lakes suite, sels. James Reaney.—
  DoWh (Complete)
  I. Lake Superior
  II. Lake Michigan
  III. Lake Huron
  IV. Lake St. Clair
  V. Lake Erie
  VI. Lake Ontario
The great mother. Gary Snyder.—LiCc
Great mouse. Lilian Moore.—MoTs
"A great oak." See Spell of the seeds
"The great queens, the transatlantic ships." See
  Pleasures of the bath
"The great sword swallower Salomar." See The
  sword swallower
"Greater, he called them, than Homer or
  Chaucer or." See The men of Sudbury
"Greater than memory of Achilles or Ulysses."
  See The Wallabout martyrs
Greed
  Bookworm. M. A. Hoberman.—MoGp
  Confession of a glutton. D. Marquis.—CoG
  The greedy giant. L. E. Richards.—WaG
  "The greedy man is he who sits." Mother
    Goose.—LoG
  The greedy man's week. B. S. De Regniers.—
    ReB
  "Here lies a greedy girl, Jane Bevan."
    Unknown.—CoPs
  Pie problem. S. Silverstein.—SiL
  Piggy. W. Cole.—CoPs

Ground hog day
  Ground hog day ("Ground hog sleeps") L.
    Moore.—MoTs
  Groundhog ("A woodchuck is a groundhog")
    D. McCord.—McSu
Ground hog day. Lilian Moore.—MoTs
"Ground hog sleeps." See Ground hog day
Ground hogs. See Woodchucks
"The ground is white with snow." See
    Resolution
Groundhog ("A woodchuck is a groundhog")
    David McCord.—McSu
Groundhog day. See Ground hog day
Groundhogs. See Woodchucks
Grow up. Unknown.—CoI
"Grow up, grow up." See Grow up
Growing, for Louis. Myra Cohn Livingston.—
    LiWt
Growing up
  The Bagley Iowa poem. A. Darr.—KhI
  Big Gumbo. W. J. Smith.—SmL
  Billy could ride. J. W. Riley.—CoPh
  Birthdays ("If birthdays happened once a
    week") M. A. Hoberman.—HoY
  The birthplace. R. Frost.—LiO
  "Change-up." H. R. Madhubuti.—AdC
  Christening day wishes for my god-child
    Grace Lane Berkley II. R.P.T. Coffin.—LiO
  Comparison. M. A. Hoberman.—HoY
  A cucumber's pickle. W. Cole.—CoPs
  Deborah Lee. Yvonne.—AdC
  Dreams ("In my younger years") N.
    Giovanni.—AdC
  Ed and Sid and Bernard. E. MacDuff.—BrO
  Flying changes. M. Wood.—CoPh
  Growing, for Louis. M. C. Livingston.—LiWt
  Happy birthday to me. E. Merriam.—LiCc
  "Have you ever hurt about baskets." M.
    Altaha.—LuZ
  The hill. E. Merriam.—MeR
  I love to eat. A. Adoff.—AdE
  "I remember." N. Grimes.—GrS
  In the library. M. P. Hearn.—HeB
  John J. M. Angelou.—AnO
  Kid stuff. F. Horne.—LiPch
  Legacies and bastard roses. A. Villanueva.—
    KhI
  Little. D. Aldis.—PaI
    "I am the sister of him."—MoF
  "Long, too long America." W. Whitman.—
    PlG
  Lord, in my heart. M. Angelou.—AnO
  "Mama never understood." N. Grimes.—GrS
  Manhood. R. N. Peck.—PeB
  Minnie Morse. K. Starbird.—CoPh
  Musical career. S. Silverstein.—SiL
  My father's death. M. Sarton.—PlL
  Nowata. D. Ray.—KhI
  "Oh, dearer by far than the land of our
    birth." R. H. Wilde.—PlG
  On relief. R. N. Peck.—PeB
  Order. M. C. Livingston.—LiWt
  "Our blackness did not come to us whole."
    L. B. Bragg.—AdC

Posture. L. Morrison.—MoSr
Question. M. A. Hoberman.—HoY
The question ("People always say to me") K.
  Kuskin.—KuD
Reggie. E. Greenfield.—GrH
Rites of passage. A. Lorde.—AdC
"She sent me out to play again." N.
  Grimes.—GrS
Some me of beauty. C. M. Rodgers.—AdC
Song for Naomi. I. Layton.—DoWh
Song for the newborn. M. Austin.—LiO
"Standing at the gate." N. Grimes.—GrS
"There was a child went forth every day."
  From Leaves of grass. W. Whitman.—PaB
Tomorrow ("It lives there") M. C.
  Livingston.—HoBm
Unwanted. E. Field.—KhI
Wait till then. M. Van Doren.—HiS
"Waiting, Daddy says." N. Grimes.—GrS
What I learned this year. L. Warsh.—KhI
What will you be. D. Lee.—LeG
Whatif. S. Silverstein.—SiL
"When I am a man." Kwakiutl.—LiCc
When I am me. F. Holman.—HoBm
"When I was a little boy, my mother kept
  me in." Mother Goose.—TrGg
"Where did he run to." M. Van Doren.—HiS
Young soul. I. A. Baraka.—AdC
"The grownups say I'm growing tall." See
  Question
"The gruesome ghoul, the grisly ghoul." See
  The ghoul
The grynch. Ogden Nash.—BlC
A guard at Fort Knox. N. M. Bodecker.—BoP
"Guess what happened in the little white
  house." See Custard the dragon and the
  wicked witch
"Guess what I have gone and done." See My
  invention
Guests
  Dinner guest. S. Silverstein.—SiL
Guide to London. Joan Aiken.—AiS
Guinea pigs
  "There was a little guinea pig." Mother
    Goose.—TrGg
  "Three little guinea pigs." Unknown, tr. by
    N. M. Bodecker.—CoA—WiP
Guitars
  My guitar. S. Silverstein.—SiL
  Slim Slater. K. Starbird.—StC
Guiterman, Arthur
  The ambiguous dog.—CoG
  Chums.—PaI
  The dog parade.—CoG
  The dog's cold nose.—CoG
  For a good dog.—CoG
  Motto for a dog house.—CoG
  Nocturne.—RuM
  The superstitious ghost.—BrIt
  What the gray cat sings.—WiP
Gull ("Life is seldom if ever dull") William Jay
  Smith.—SmL

Bobbing for apples. J. Prelutsky.—PrI
Cut out. A. Adoff.—AdE
Day after Halloween. S. Silverstein.—SiL
"From ghoulies and ghosties." Unknown.—
LiO
    A Cornish litany.—LiCc
    Ghoulies and ghosties.—WaGp—WaM
    Litany for Halloween.—BrIt
    Prayer for Halloween.—LiF
Haiku for Halloween. M. C. Livingston.—
BrIt—LiF
Halloween ("Samantha, call her Sam, OK")
D. McCord.—McSu
Halloween ("The sky was yellow") I. O.
Eastwick.—BrIt
Halloween ("Stealing white from the
withered moon") M. C. Livingston.—LiF—
LiO
Halloween ("Tonight is the night") H.
Behn.—BrIt—HoMp—LiCc
Halloween ("Witches flying past on
broomsticks") M. J. Carr.—BrIt
Halloween concert. A. Fisher.—BrIt
The Halloween cow. E. Merriam.—MeB
Halloween witches. F. Holman.—HoA—
LiCc—WaW
Happy Halloween. J. Prelutsky.—PrI
Haunted house ("There's a house") J.
Prelutsky.—PrI
"Hist whist." E. E. Cummings.—HiS—LiCc—
LiO—WaW—WiP
Hitchhiker. D. McCord.—McO
"I like winter, spring, summer, and fall." B.
S. De Regniers.—ReB
It's Halloween. J. Prelutsky.—PrI
The mini spooks. E. Anderson.—BrIt
Mr. Halloween. D. McCord.—McO
Mr Macklin's jack o'lantern. D. McCord.—
BrIt—McO
Mr Macklin's visitor. D. McCord.—McO
"Monsters do not scare me much." B. S. De
Regniers.—BrIt—ReB
"The moon is hiding." K. Mizumura.—MiF
October fun. A. Fisher.—FiO
Old Tim Toole. D. McCord.—McO
On Halloween ("On Halloween I'll go to
town") S. Silverstein.—BrIt
On Halloween ("We mask our faces") A.
Fisher.—FiO
Pamela. D. McCord.—McO
Pumpkin ("After its lid") V. Worth.—BrIt—
LiCc—WoM
Pumpkin ("We bought a fat") J. Prelutsky.—
PrI
Pumpkin head. A. Fisher.—FiO
Pumpkin seeds. D. McCord.—McO
"Scare me easy." B. S. De Regniers.—ReB
Skeleton parade. J. Prelutsky.—PrI
Theme in yellow. C. Sandburg.—MoGp
This is Halloween. D. B. Thompson.—BrIt
Tonight ("Strange shadows out") L. Moore.—
MoTs
Trick ("The people in this house were
mean") J. Prelutsky.—PrI

Trick or treat. D. McCord.—BrIt—McO
"Trick or treat, trick or treat." J. Prelutsky.—
PrI
The trickster. J. Prelutsky.—PrI
"We three." L. Moore.—BrIt—LiCc
What night would it be. J. Ciardi.—BrIt
"What our dame bids us do." From The
masque of queens. B. Jonson.—LiO
Witch's broom notes. D. McCord.—McO
Halloween ("Samantha, call her Sam, OK")
David McCord.—McSu
Halloween ("The sky was yellow") Ivy O.
Eastwick.—BrIt
Halloween ("Stealing white from the withered
moon") Myra Cohn Livingston.—LiF—LiO
Halloween ("Tonight is the night") Harry
Behn.—BrIt—HoMp—LiCc
Halloween ("Witches flying past on
broomsticks") Mary Jane Carr.—BrIt
"Halloween." See Trick or treat
Halloween concert. Aileen Fisher.—BrIt
The Halloween cow. Eve Merriam.—MeB
"Halloween, Halloween." See Trick or treat
Halloween witches. Felice Holman.—HoA—
LiCc—WaW
Halpern, Daniel
    The gossip.—HiS
Hamburger, Mary Ann
    A child is born.—BaC
Hamilton, Alfred Starr
    A crust of bread.—KhI
Hamlet, sels. William Shakespeare
    "Some say that ever 'gainst that season
    comes."—BaC—LiO—LiPch
    "Tomorrow is Saint Valentine's day.—LiCc—
    LiO
Hammock ("Grandma sent the hammock") Shel
Silverstein.—SiL
Hammock ("Our hammock swings between
two trees") David McCord.—McO
Hand over. Joan Aiken.—AiS
Handel's Messiah. See The messiah, sel.
"A handful of wind that I caught with a kite."
See What shall I pack in the box marked
'summer'
Handicapped. See Blind; Cripples; Deafness;
Insanity
Hands
    Daybreak in Alabama. L. Hughes.—AdC
    The eagle-feather fan. N. S. Momaday.—
    MoGd
    Hands ("Inside a cave in a narrow canyon
    near Tassajara") R. Jeffers.—PlG
    The nailbiter. S. Silverstein.—SiL
    Secret hand. E. Merriam.—MeW
Hands ("Inside a cave in a narrow canyon near
Tassajara") Robinson Jeffers.—PlG
"The hands of the sun." See In the sun and
shadow
"The handsomest creature in all the zoo." See
The peacock and the great blue heron
"Handy-spandy." Mother Goose.—LoG
Handyman. Homer Phillips.—BrO

"**Hang** garlands on the bathroom door." See
  The bath
Hangings
  The haunted oak. P. L. Dunbar.—BrI
"**Hannah** Bantry." Mother Goose.—LoG
Hans, Marcie
  "Fueled."—HoMp
Happiness
  Bad day. M. C. Livingston.—LiWt
  Crocodile. W. J. Smith.—SmL
  The delight song of Tsoai-talee. N. S.
    Momaday.—MoGd
  Joy ("In school today") N. Giovanni.—GiV
  Life's tragedy. P. L. Dunbar.—BrI
  My old dad. M. Dugan.—DuSn
  "The reason I like chocolate." N. Giovanni.—
    GiV
  Someone's face. J. Ciardi.—CoI
  Valentine feelings. L. B. Hopkins.—HoMp
"**Happy** birthday, silly goose." See Father Fox's
  pennyrhymes
Happy birthday to me. Eve Merriam.—LiCc
The **happy** family. John Ciardi.—HiD
Happy Halloween. Jack Prelutsky.—PrI
"**Happy** mooday to you." See The birthday cow
"**Hard** and slow." See Turtle song
"A **hard** of hearing herring thought he heard a
  haddock say." See The herring
"**Hard** soft." Arnold Adoff.—AdE
Hardy, Thomas
  Heredity.—PlL
  Over the coffin.—PlL
  The oxen.—BaC—LiPch
  Unrealized.—PlL
  Weathers.—PaB
The **hare** and the tortoise. Ian Serraillier.—HiS
Hares. See Rabbits
"**Hark,** hark, the dogs do bark." Mother
  Goose.—BlH—LoG
Harlem
  "For all things black and beautiful." C. K.
    Rivers.—AdC
  Harlem in January. J. Fields.—AdC
  Juke box love song. L. Hughes.—YaI
  The still voice of Harlem. C. K. Rivers.—AdC
Harlem in January. Julia Fields.—AdC
Harmonica man. P. Wolny.—JaPp
Harper, Michael S.
  Cannon arrested.—AdC
  The dark way home, survivors.—AdC
  Effendi.—AdC
  Here where Coltrane is.—AdC
  Martin's blues.—AdC
The **harpooning.** Ted Walker.—PaE
Harps
  The master-player. P. L. Dunbar.—BrI
  To a lady playing the harp. P. L. Dunbar.—
    BrI
Harriet Beecher Stowe. Paul Laurence
  Dunbar.—BrI
Harriet Tubman. Eloise Greenfield.—GrH
"**Harriet** Tubman didn't take no stuff." See
  Harriet Tubman

Harris, William J.
  Give me five.—AdC
  "A grandfather poem."—AdC—MoGp
  Rib sandwich.—AdC
  They live in parallel worlds.—AdC
  A winter song.—HoMp
Harrison, Frances
  At St. Jerome.—DoWh
Harrison, Jim
  Horse.—CoPh
The **harvest** moon. Ted Hughes.—HuSs
Harvest song. Joseph Campbell.—LiCc—LiO
Harvestman. David McCord.—McO
Harvests and harvesting
  "At quitting time." R. Sund.—LuZ
  The harvest moon. T. Hughes.—HuSs
  Harvest song. J. Campbell.—LiCc—LiO
  Hay ("The grass is happy") T. Hughes.—HuSs
  "I will go with my father a-reaping." From I
    will go with my father a-ploughing. J.
    Campbell.—LiCc
  The reaper. L. H. Allen.—SaM
  "What is it this time the dark barn again."
    From Sheep. T. Hughes.—HuSs
Harvey always wins. Jack Prelutsky.—PrRh
"**Harvey** is a tub of lard." See Harvey never
  shares
"**Harvey** likes to practice knots." See The
  practical joke
Harvey never shares. Jack Prelutsky.—PrRh
"**Harvey** think's he's something." See The race
"**Harvey** whimpers, Harvey whines." See
  Rolling Harvey down the hill
"**Has** anybody seen my mouse." See Missing
"**Has** the sound of over." See Away and ago
The **hat,** the gown and the ring. N. M.
  Bodecker.—BoHh
The **hatch.** Norma Farber.—HiS
Hate
  Artful pose. M. Angelou.—AnO
  I hate Harry. M. Chaikin.—CoI
  A little girl I hate. A. Spilka.—CoI
Hats
  H is for hat. W. J. Smith.—SmL
  Hats ("Round or square") W. J. Smith.—SmL
  "A little bit of this, sir." N. M. Bodecker.—
    BoHh
  The lost cat. S. Silverstein.—SiL
  A man and his hat. L. Parr.—DuSn
  Mr. Smeds and Mr. Spats. S. Silverstein.—SiL
  The trouble was simply that. D. McCord.—
    McO
  "When I was young and foolish." M. A.
    Hoberman.—HoY
Hats ("Round or square") William Jay Smith.—
  SmL
"**Hattie** and Harriet, Hope and Hortense." See
  Four foolish ladies
The **haughty** snail-king. Vachel Lindsay.—HiS
Haunted ("Black hill black hall") William
  Mayne.—WaGp
Haunted house ("Its echoes") Valerie Worth.—
  BrIt—WoM

The **haunted** house ("On a hilltop bleak and bare") Jack Prelutsky.—PrN
Haunted house ("There's a house") Jack Prelutsky.—PrI
The **haunted** oak. Paul Laurence Dunbar.—BrI
The **haunted** oven. X. J. Kennedy.—KeP
"**Have** dinosaurs come back again." See Highway construction
Have fun. Shel Silverstein.—SiL
Have I got dogs. William Cole.—CoG
"**Have** I got dogs, pedigreeds and mutts." See Have I got dogs
"**Have** you ever gone visiting for a weekend of ravelry." See Tallyho-hum
"**Have** you ever hurt about baskets." Marylita Altaha.—LuZ
"**Have** you ever in your life seen a possum play possum." See Opossum
"**Have** you ever reflected on green." From Limericks. David McCord.—McSu
"**Have** you ever smelled summer." See That was summer
"**Have** you heard of the aardwort." See The aardwort
"**Have** you heard the whale sing." See The whale
Have you thanked a green plant today (bumper sticker). Don Anderson.—BrO
Have you watched the fairies. Rose Fyleman.—PaI
"**Have** you watched the fairies when the rain is done." See Have you watched the fairies
Having. William Jay Smith.—SmL
"**Having** a tree growing up out of me." See Headache
"**Having** perceived the connexions, they seek." See Poets and mathematicians
Hawks
    Birds ("The fierce musical cries of a couple of sparrow hawks") R. Jeffers.—PaE
    Buteo regalis. N. S. Momaday.—MoGd
    The osprey ("Now a hungry young osprey named Lee") R. S. Oliver.—OlC
    Sea-hawk. R. Eberhart.—PaE
"The **hawthorne** berries." David Kherdian.—KhC
Hay
    Aster. R. N. Peck.—PeB
    The devil's pitchfork. R. N. Peck.—PeB
    Hay ("The grass is happy") T. Hughes.—HuSs
    Lamplighter barn. M. C. Livingston.—BeR
    Nest. R. N. Peck.—PeB
    The pocket whetstone. R. N. Peck.—PeB
    Where the hayfields were. A. MacLeish.—HiD
Hay ("The grass is happy") Ted Hughes.—HuSs
"**Hay** is dry." See Food
Hay, Sara Henderson
    The curlew.—PaE
    Tidal pool.—PaE
Hayden, Robert
    Beginnings, sel.
        "Plowdens, Finns."—AdC
    Crispus Attucks.—AdC

El-Hajj Malik El-Shabazz, Malcolm X.—AdC
"For King, for Robert Kennedy." See Words in the mourning time
Frederick Douglass.—AdC—PlG
Homage to the empress of the blues.—AdC
"Plowdens, Finns." See Beginnings
Runagate runagate.—AdC
"Sojourner Truth." See Stars
Stars, sel.
    "Sojourner Truth."—AdC
Those winter Sundays.—AdC—MaP—PlL
Words in the mourning time, sel.
    "For King, for Robert Kennedy."—AdC
"**Hayle** holy land wherein our holy lord." See Upon the first sight of New England, June 29, 1638
"**He** always comes on market days." See The balloon man
"**He** bad." See The pusher
"**He** built right on top of the land." See Where she was not born
"**He** came all so still." See A maiden that is makeless
"**He** came apart in the open." See Martin's blues
"**He** came down the old road." See Ghost boy
"**He** came from Malta, and Eumelus says." See The dog from Malta
"**He** can whistle and dance on the walls." See Nimpkin dancing
"**He** comes, the brave old Christmas." Unknown.—BaC
"**He** danced in feathers, with paint across his nose." See Learning about the Indians
"**He** gave silver shoes to the rabbit." See Blake leads a walk on the Milky Way
"**He** had a falcon on his wrist." See Love me, love my dog
"**He** had an idea that gleamed." See Signal
"**He** had been coming a very long time." See For Malcolm who walks in the eyes of our children
"**He** had done for her all that a man could." See I will write
He had his dream. Paul Laurence Dunbar.—BrI
"**He** had his dream, and all through life." See He had his dream
"**He** has no broomstick, but you dare not say." See Mr. Halloween
"**He** has the sign." See Portrait of Malcolm X
"**He** has trained the owl to wake him." See Man and owl
"**He** hinted at times that I was a bastard and I told him to listen." See The twins
"**He** is gone now, he is dead." See For Mugs
"**He** is running like a wasp." See Pole vault
"**He** is that fallen lance that lies as hurled." See The soldier
"**He** is the pond's old father, its brain." See The snapper
"**He** knows my name, Lizette is five." See Lizette
"**He** left the kitchen." See Dory Miller

Henry VIII, King of England (about)
   Henry VIII. E. and H. Farjeon.—WiP
Henry VIII. Eleanor and Herbert Farjeon.—
   WiP
"Henry was a young king." See Henry and
   Mary
The hens. Elizabeth Madox Roberts.—PaI
"Her eyes were gentle, her voice was for soft
   singing." See An old woman remembers
"Her face like a rain beaten stone on the day
   she." See Elegy
Her going. Shirley Kaufman.—JaPp
"Her hand in my hand." See Dance song 6
"Her hand that holds." See Jesus drum
Herbert, A. P.
   The racing man.—CoPh
"Herbert Breeze." Stephen Scheding.—DuSn
Herbert Glerbett. Jack Prelutsky.—CoPs—PrQ
"Herbert Glerbett, rather round." See Herbert
   Glerbett
"Here all we see." Walter De La Mare.—PaI
"Here at the turning of the tide." See Tidal
   pool
"Here come the elephants, ten feet high." Jack
   Prelutsky.—CoA
Here comes. Shel Silverstein.—SiL
"Here comes summer." See Here comes
"Here comes the shadow not looking where it
   is going." See Sire
"Here further up the mountain slope." See The
   birthplace
"Here he comes." Marnie Pomeroy.—CoDb
"Here he lies moulding." See Epitaph
Here I am. Myra Cohn Livingston.—CoI
"Here I am, bully." See Here I am
"Here I am, little jumping Joan." Mother
   Goose.—TrGg
"Here I go riding through my morning self."
   See The landscape inside me
"Here I sit on Honeybee Hill." See Honeybee
   hill
"Here in the dim and the almost dark and the
   warmth of." See The riding stable in
   winter
"Here in this sequester'd close." See Garden
   song
"Here is a fat animal, a bear." See Self-portrait,
   as a bear
"Here is a list." See Sweets
"Here is an apple, ripe and red." See Dividing
"Here is how I eat a fish." See Eating fish
"Here is no place of easy consequence." See
   Abstract: old woman in a room
"Here is the fossil." See The black fern
"Here is the story." See Freddy
"Here lies a greedy girl, Jane Bevan."
   Unknown.—CoPs
"Here lies a most beautiful lady." See An
   epitaph
"Here lies a poor woman who was always
   tired." See On a tired housewife
"Here lies wrapped up tight in sod." See
   Epitaph for a postal clerk

"Here on the river's verge he stood." See
   Bridge
"Here she comes." See Mom's mums
"Here she was wont to go, and here, and
   here." See The sad shepherd—Aeglamour's
   lament
"Here stands a fist." Mother Goose.—TrGg
"Here we bring new water from the well so
   clear." See New Year's water
"Here we come a-wassailing." Unknown.—
   LiPch
"Here we come again, again, and here we
   come again." See The children's carol
"Here we go." Mary Ann Hoberman.—HoY
Here where Coltrane is. Michael S. Harper.—
   AdC
"Here where the wind is always
   north-north-east." See New England
Heredity. See Ancestry
Heredity ("I am the family face") Thomas
   Hardy.—PlL
"Here's a fact that will cause you to frown."
   See Puzzling
"Here's a Fibruary finding." Doris Orgel.—OrM
"Here's a ridiculous riddle for you." See
   Woolloomooloo
"Here's Sulky Sue." See Sulky Sue
"Here's that little girl who wraps each gift."
   See A Christmas package
Here's to adhering. Maya Angelou.—AnO
"Here's to July." See To July
"Here's what I think." See The clock
Herford, Oliver
   The elf and the dormouse.—PaI
   "I heard a bird sing."—BaC
Heritage. See also Ancestry
   Abraham Lincoln walks at midnight. V.
      Lindsay.—PlG
   And of Columbus. H. Gregory.—PlG
   At night. R. Eberhart.—PlL
   Benjamin Franklin Hazard. E. L. Masters.—
      PlG
   The blood horse. B. W. Procter.—CoPh
   The building of the skyscraper. G. Oppen.—
      PlG
   Carriers of the dream wheel. N. S.
      Momaday.—MoGd
   Complicated thoughts about a small son. E.
      B. White.—PlL
   "Driving through New England." L.
      Clifton.—PlG
   The foundations of American industry. D.
      Hall.—PlG
   Heredity ("I am the family face") T.
      Hardy.—PlL
   Indian names. L. H. Sigourney.—PlG
   The Irish cliffs of Moher. W. Stevens.—PlL
   Jamestown ("Let me look at what I was,
      before I die") R. Jarrell.—PlG
   Justice denied in Massachusetts. E. St. V.
      Millay.—PlG
   Like ghosts of eagles. R. Francis.—PlG
   Loneliness ("I was about to go, and said so")
      B. Jenkins.—MaP

The **herring** ("A hard of hearing herring thought he heard a haddock say") Robert S. Oliver.—OlC

Herring-gull. John Hall Wheelock.—PaE

Herrings
The herring ("A hard of hearing herring thought he heard a haddock say") R. S. Oliver.—OlC
The red herring. G. MacBeth.—HiS

Hershon, Robert
Weather.—LuZ

"**He's** the man in the iron pail mask." See The man in the iron pail mask

"**He's** the twistable turnable squeezable pullable." See Twistable turnable man

Hey, bug. Lilian Moore.—WiP

"**Hey**, bug, stay." See Hey, bug

"**Hey**, cat." See Great mouse

"**Hey** diddle diddle, the cat and the fiddle." Mother Goose.—BlH—TrGg

"**Hey** moonface." See Only a little litter

Hey Nonny. David Kherdian.—KhC

"**Hey** there, brontosaurus." See To the skeleton of a dinosaur in the museum

Heyen, William
The snapper.—JaPp
The trail beside the River Platte.—PlG

Hiawatha. See The song of Hiawatha

Hibernation
Grandpa bear's lullaby. J. Yolen.—YoD

"**Hic.**" See Hiccup cure

Hiccup cure. Shel Silverstein.—SiL

"**Hickenthrift** and Hickenloop." X. J. Kennedy.—KeP—WaG

"**Hickory**, dickory, dock." Mother Goose.—TrGg

"**Hide** not, hide not." See The rousing canoe song

Hiding place. Nancy Dingman Watson.—WaB

Hiebert, Paul
Steeds.—DoWh

Higgins, Annie
Waking.—LuZ

"**Higgleby**, piggleby, my black hen." Mother Goose.—TrGg

"**Higgledy**-piggledy." See Twilight's last gleaming

"**Higgledy** piggledy red-headed woodpecker." See The red-headed woodpecker

"**Higgledy** piggledy tongue-flicking garden snake." See The garden snake

"**Higglety**, pigglety, pop." Mother Goose.—TrGg

"**High** in the flowering catalpa trees." See Fox and crow

"**High** in the heavens a single star." See The Christmas star

"**High** on a banyan tree in a row." See Monkey

High on the hog. Julia Fields.—AdC

"The **high** skip." Eleanor Farjeon.—WiP

"**High** up on the ceiling." See U is for up

Higher and lower mathematics. David Kherdian.—KhC

Highway construction. Carol Earle Chapin.—BrO

"The **highway** is full of big cars." See Come and be my baby

Highway one, movie camera. Myra Cohn Livingston.—LiF

"**Highway** turnpike thruway mall." See A charm for our time

Highways. See Roads and streets

The **hiker.** Eve Merriam.—MeR

Hiking. See Camping and hiking

The **hill.** Eve Merriam.—MeR

Hill, Hyacinthe
Rebels from fairy tales.—HiS

Hillert, Margaret
Fall wind.—HoMp
How it happens.—HoMp

Hills. See Mountains

Hillyer, Robert
The assassination.—LiO
Lullaby.—HiD

Hinges ("A bird is full of hinges") Aileen Fisher.—FiO

Hinges ("If we had hinges on our heads") Shel Silverstein.—SiL

"**Hippety**-hop, goes the kangaroo." See Up the hill

Hippopotami
The blame. S. Silverstein.—CoA
The hippopotamus ("Behold the hippopotamus") O. Nash.—BlC
Hippopotamus ("The hippopotamus, hippo for short") W. J. Smith.—SmL
Hippopotamus ("How far from human beauty") M. A. Hoberman.—HoY
The hippopotamus ("Regard the hippopotamus") J. Gardner.—GaCb
Hippo's hope. S. Silverstein.—SiL
I had a hippopotamus. P. Barrington.—WiP

The **hippopotamus** ("Behold the hippopotamus") Ogden Nash.—BlC

Hippopotamus ("The hippopotamus, hippo for short") William Jay Smith.—SmL

Hippopotamus ("How far from human beauty") Mary Ann Hoberman.—HoY

The **hippopotamus** ("Regard the hippopotamus") John Gardner.—GaCb

"The **hippopotamus**, hippo for short." See Hippopotamus

Hippo's hope. Shel Silverstein.—SiL

Hirawa, Yasuko
The song of the sour plum. tr.—PaI

"**His** bridle hung around the post." See Horse

"**His** dinner sits." See While the snake sleeps

"**His** frailty descrete, the rodent turns, looks." See Buteo regalis

"**His** head is tiny because he has few brains." See Whippet

His Highness's dog. Unknown.—BlH

"**His** nightly song will scarce be missed." See Alley cat

"**His** place of birth a solemn angel tells." See Paradise lost

Yellow butter.—HoY
"You were the mother last time."—CoI
"You're Mrs. Cobble and I'm Mrs. Frome."—
  HoY
"The **Hobson**-Jobson children were enamoured
  of the sciences." See Ed and Sid and
  Bernard
Hobson, Rodney
  A man about the kitchen.—BrO
Hochman, Sandra
  Love song for a jellyfish.—LuZ—MoGp
Hodgson, Ralph
  The great auk's ghost.—BrIt
Hoey, Edwin A.
  Foul shot.—MoGp
Hoffman, Jill
  Evening ride.—CoPh
  The stable.—CoPh
  To a horse.—CoPh
Hog at the manger. Norma Farber.—LiPch
Hogg, James
  "Where the pools are bright and deep."—
    MoF
Hogg, Robert
  Song.—DoWh
Hogs. See Pigs
Holahan, Pamela Crawford
  The divorce.—PlL
Holes
  Holes ("Strangest of gaps") L. Morrison.—
    MoO
  Remarks from the pup. B. Johnson.—CoG
Holes ("Strangest of gaps") Lillian Morrison.—
    MoO
Holidays. See also names of holidays, as
    Christmas
  Conversation with Washington. M. C.
    Livingston.—LiF
  The light year. J. Ridland.—LiO
  Once upon a great holiday. A. Wilkinson.—
    DoWh
Hollander, John
  Swan and shadow.—LuZ
Hollands, Sarah
  Snow landscape.—SaM
Holly and mistletoe. Eleanor Farjeon.—LiPch
"The **holly** and the ivy." Unknown.—BaC—
    LiO—LiPch
Holly trees
  "Be links no longer broken." C. Mackay.—
    BaC
  The brown birds. E. Farjeon.—BaC
  "But give me holly, bold and jolly." C. G.
    Rossetti.—BaC
  "Green grow'th the holly." Unknown.—
    BaC—LiPch
  Holly and mistletoe. E. Farjeon.—LiPch
  "The holly and the ivy." Unknown.—BaC—
    LiO—LiPch
"The **holly's** up, the house is all bright." See
    The Christmas tree
Holman, Felice
  At the top of my voice.—HoA
  Bedtime.—HoA

The child who cried.—HoBm
Children and other creatures.—HoA
The city dump.—HoA
The clock.—HoA
Counting birds.—HoA
An emergency.—HoA
The 5th of July.—HoMp—LiCc
Finding out.—HoA
Goldfinches.—HoA
Halloween witches.—HoA—LiCc—WaW
I can fly.—HoA
Invisible.—HoA
Leave me alone.—HoA
Light.—HoA
Lullaby.—HoA
Night sounds.—HoA—RuM
The outlaw.—CoI—HoA
Possibilities.—HoA
Protest.—HoA
Snow.—HoMp
Squirrel.—HoA
Supermarket.—BrO—HoA
They're calling.—HoA
Things that happen.—HoA
Thinking.—HoA
Tiptoe.—HoA
Voices.—HoA
When I am me.—HoBm
Who am I.—HoA
Wild day at the shore.—HoA
Holmes, Oliver Wendell
  The broomstick train, sel.
    "Look out, look out, boys, clear the
      track."—BrIt
  The chambered nautilus.—PaE
  "Look out, look out, boys, clear the track."
    See The broomstick train
  Old Ironsides.—PlG
Holub, Miroslav
  "The day was so bright." See A dog in the
    quarry
  A dog in the quarry, sel.
    "The day was so bright."—CoG
"**Holy** haloes." See Lord, in my heart
Holy Thursday. William Blake.—LiO
Holz, Arno
  Phantasus, I. 8.—LiPch
Homage to Moose Factory, Ont. Dennis Lee.—
    LeN
Homage to the empress of the blues. Robert
    Hayden.—AdC
Home. See Home and family life
"**Home.**" Sam Cornish.—AdC
"**Home.**" See Africa
Home and family life. See also Family;
    Housekeepers and housekeeping
  Alarm ("Mother come quick") X. J.
    Kennedy.—KeP
  Beginnings and endings. P. Koestenbaum.—
    KhI
  The birthplace. R. Frost.—LiO
  The bratty brother, sister. D. Lee.—LeG
  By the shores of Pago Pago. E. Merriam.—
    MeR

Hornets. See Wasps

"A **horrid** old person of Florence." See A person of Florence

Horse ("All fall it stuck") Randy Blasing.—CoPh

Horse ("His bridle hung around the post") Elizabeth Madox Roberts.—CoPh

Horse ("Horse skin, hessian or hard hot silk") Gerard Benson.—CoPh

Horse ("I will not change my horse with any that treads") From Henry V. W. Shakespeare.—CoPh

Horse ("In the stall's gloom") Valerie Worth.—WoSm

Horse ("A quarter horse, no rider") Jim Harrison.—CoPh

The **horse** ("Who is the noblest beast you can name") Shel Silverstein.—CoPh

Horse girl. Henry Petroski.—CoPh

Horse graveyard. Fred Lape.—CoPh

"The **horse**, head swinging." See February

"A **horse** Lord Epsom did bestride." See Lord Epsom

Horse racing. See Rides and riding—Horse

The **horse** show. William Carlos Williams.—PlL

The **horse** show at midnight. Henry Taylor.—CoPh

Horse shows
Faith. M. Dunkels.—CoPh
The horse show at midnight. H. Taylor.—CoPh
Hunter trials. J. Betjeman.—CoPh
Pliny Jane. M. Luton.—CoPh
Two at showtime. S. Brabant.—CoPh

"**Horse** skin, hessian or hard hot silk." See Horse

The **horse** that died of shame. N. Scott Momaday.—MoGd

Horses. See also Rides and riding—Horse
Alexander to his horse. E. Farjeon.—CoPh
Amanda is shod. M. Kumin.—CoPh
The barge horse. S. Jennett.—CoPh
Billy could ride. J. W. Riley.—CoPh
Birth of the foal. F. Juhasz.—CoPh
A blessing. J. Wright.—FlA
The blood horse. B. W. Procter.—CoPh
The blue horse. S. C. Fox.—FoB
The broncho that would not be broken. V. Lindsay.—CoPh
"But lo, from forth a copse that neighbours by." From Venus and Adonis. W. Shakespeare.—CoPh
Catching a horse. B. Winder.—CoPh
The centaur. M. Swenson.—CoPh—HiS
Clancy. D. Wagoner.—CoPh
The closing of the rodeo. W. J. Smith.—PlG
Comanche. G. Gildner.—CoPh
Daniel Webster's horses. E. Coatsworth.—CoPh
Day dreams. W. Canton.—PaB
Dexter. J. B. Grayston.—CoPh
The distant runners. M. Van Doren.—PlG
Dream image. L. Morrison.—MoW
"The eohippus." W. Cole.—CoDb
February. B. Winder.—CoPh

The field ("Somewhere in the field") D. Lawder.—CoPh

Five horses. M. Swenson.—CoPh

Flying changes. M. Wood.—CoPh

Foal ("Come trotting up") M. B. Miller.—CoPh

For a shetland pony brood mare who died in her barren year. M. Kumin.—CoPh

The four horses. J. Reeves.—CoPh

Francie. L. Morrison.—MoSr

"Girls on saddleless horses." R. G. Vliet.—CoPh

The glory trail. B. Clark.—CoPh

Going away. A. Stanford.—CoPh

Going to town. F. Lape.—CoPh

Golden grain. H. M. Wright.—CoPh

The grey horse. J. Reeves.—CoPh

Grog an' Grumble steeplechase. H. Lawson.—CoPh

Haiku, for Cinnamon. L. D. Chaffin.—CoPh

Horse ("All fall it stuck") R. Blasing.—CoPh

Horse ("His bridle hung around the post") E. M. Roberts.—CoPh

Horse ("Horse skin, hessian or hard hot silk") G. Benson.—CoPh

Horse ("In the stall's gloom") V. Worth.—WoSm

Horse ("A quarter horse, no rider") J. Harrison.—CoPh

The horse ("Who is the noblest beast you can name") S. Silverstein.—CoPh

Horse girl. H. Petroski.—CoPh

Horse graveyard. F. Lape.—CoPh

The horse show. W. C. Williams.—PlL

The horse show at midnight. H. Taylor.—CoPh

The horse that died of shame. N. S. Momaday.—MoGd

Horses ("Horses of earth") R. Dana.—CoPh

The horses ("I climbed through the woods in the hour before dawn dark") T. Hughes.—CoPh

The horses ("It has turned to snow in the night") M. Kumin.—HiD

Horses ("The long whip lingers") L. MacNeice.—CoPh

Horses graze. G. Brooks.—AdC

"The horses of the sea." C. Rossetti.—WiP

Hossolalia. M. Luton.—CoPh

How we drove the trotter. W. T. Goodge.—CoPh

The huntsmen. W. De La Mare.—CoPh

"I had a little pony." Mother Goose.—WiP
The bad rider.—CoPh

Jack and his pony, Tom. H. Belloc.—CoPh

Kentucky Belle. C. F. Woolson.—CoPh

Learner. J. A. Lindon.—CoPh

"Lend me your mare to ride a mile." Mother Goose.—TrGg

Little Abigail and the beautiful pony. S. Silverstein.—SiL

The man from Snowy River. A. B. Paterson.—CoPh

The defenders.—HuSs
The dracula vine.—HuM
Earth moon.—HuM
The earth owl.—HuM
Foxgloves.—HuM
The golden boy.—HuSs
The harvest moon.—HuSs
Hay.—HuSs
The horses.—CoPh
"The laburnum top is silent, quite still." See
    Autumn nature notes
Leaves.—HuSs
Mackerel song.—HuSs
A March calf.—HuSs
Moon bells.—HuM
The moon bull.—HuM
Moon cabbage.—HuM
Moon clock.—HuM
Moon cloud gripe.—HuM
Moon dog-daisies.—HuM
Moon freaks.—HuM
The moon haggis.—HuM
A moon hare.—HuM
Moon heads.—HuM
Moon hops.—HuM
Moon horrors.—HuM
The moon hyena.—HuM
A moon lily.—HuM
A moon manhunt.—HuM
The moon mare.—HuM
Moon marriage.—HuM
Moon mirror.—HuM
The moon mourner.—HuM
Moon nasturtiums.—HuM
"The moon-oak."—HuM
Moon ravens.—HuM
Moon roses.—HuM
Moon shadow beggars.—HuM
Moon theatre.—HuM
"Moon thirst."—HuM
Moon thorns.—HuM
Moon tulips.—HuM
Moon walkers.—HuM
Moon ways.—HuM
Moon weapons.—HuM
Moon whales.—HuM
Moon wind.—HuM
Moon wings.—HuM
A moon witch.—HuM
Moon witches.—HuM
Moony art.—HuM
"The mothers have come back." See Sheep
Mushrooms on the moon.—HuM
Music on the moon.—HuM
My sister Jane.—HiS
New year song.—HuSs
    New year's song.—LiO
"An oak tree on the first day of April." See
    Spring nature notes
"Oceanic windy dawn." See Autumn nature
    notes
The river in March.—HuSs
The seven sorrows.—HuSs
The silent eye.—HuM

Sheep, sels.—HuSs (Complete)
    I. "The sheep has stopped crying."
    II. "What is it this time the dark barn
        again."
    III. "The mothers have come back."
"The sheep has stopped crying." See Sheep
Singing on the moon.—HuM
The snail of the moon.—HuM
Snow and snow.—HuSs
Solstice song.—HuSs
"Some people on the moon are so idle."—
    HuM
"Spring bulges the hills." See Spring nature
    notes
Spring nature notes, sels.—HuSs (Complete)
    I. "The sun lies mild and still on the yard
        stones."
    II. "An oak tree on the first day of
        April."
    III. "A spurt of daffodils, stiff and
        quivering."
    IV. "The crocuses are too naked, space
        shakes them."
    V. "Spring bulges the hills."
    VI. "With arms swinging, a tremendous
        skater."
"A spurt of daffodils, stiff and quivering." See
    Spring nature notes
"The sun finally tolerable." See Autumn
    nature notes
"The sun lies mild and still on the yard
    stones." See Spring nature notes
The stag.—HuSs
Swifts.—HuSs
There came a day.—HoMp—HuSs—MoGp
"Three pale foxglove lamp mantles, in full
    flare." See Autumn nature notes
"Through all the orchard's boughs." See
    Autumn nature notes
Tree disease.—HuM
Visiting the moon.—HuM
The warm and the cold.—HuSs
The warrior of winter.—HuSs
"Water wobbling blue sky puddled October."
    See Autumn nature notes
"What is it this time the dark barn again."
    See Sheep
"When the elm was full." See Autumn
    nature notes
"With arms swinging, a tremendous skater."
    See Spring nature notes
Work and play.—HuSs
Hugo, Richard
    A snapshot of the Auxiliary.—KhI
Hugs and kisses. Charlotte Pomerantz.—PoT
Hula eel. Shel Silverstein.—SiL
Human beings. David McCord.—McO
Human body. See Body, Human
Human race
    Anthropoids. M. A. Hoberman.—HoY
    Capsule philosophy. F. Lamport.—BrO

"The **hydrogen** dog and the cobalt cat." See
The space child's Mother Goose
Hyenas
The moon hyena. T. Hughes.—HuM
The striped hyena. J. Gardner.—GaCb
"**Hylas** in the spring." See Wintry
Hymn ("The congregation rumbles to its feet")
Robert Newton Peck.—PeB
A **hymn** ("Lead gently, Lord, and slow") Paul
Laurence Dunbar.—BrI
Hymn ("O li'l' lamb out in de col' ") Paul
Laurence Dunbar.—BrI
Hymn ("When storms arise") Paul Laurence
Dunbar.—BrI
A **hymn** on the nativity of my saviour. Ben
Jonson.—BaC
I sing the birth.—BaC
Hymn to joy. Julia Cunningham.—LiPch
Hymns
Hymn ("The congregation rumbles to its
feet") R. N. Peck.—PeB
A hymn ("Lead gently, Lord, and slow") P.
L. Dunbar.—BrI
Hymn ("O li'l' lamb out in de col' ") P. L.
Dunbar.—BrI
Hymn ("When storms arise") P. L. Dunbar.—
BrI
An Indian hymn of thanks to mother corn.
Unknown.—LiCc

I

"**I**." See Discovery
"**I** ain't one to complain." See A giant named
Stanley
"**I** almost remember." Maya Angelou.—AnO
"**I** always like summer." See Knoxville,
Tennessee
"**I** am a black woman." Mari Evans.—AdC
"**I** am a constant walker." N. M. Bodecker.—
BoHh
"**I** am a feather on the bright sky." See The
delight song of Tsoai-talee
"**I** am a sea-shell flung." See Frutta di mare
"**I** am a sundial, and I make a botch." See On a
sundial
"**I** am alone." See A dog
"**I** am beating breakfast by myself." See
Measuring and mixing
"**I** am cold and alone." See The boy fishing
"**I** am dancing in the water." See Ocean
dancing
"**I** am Gaspar, I have brought frankincense."
See The three kings
"**I** am his Highness's dog at Kew." See His
Highness's dog
"**I** am Lake Superior." See The Great Lakes
suite—Lake Superior
I am learning. Arnold Adoff.—AdE
"**I** am learning how to make a horse go left."
See New skills

"I am lonesome without you seeing me." See
For Laura
"I am looking for a book." Eve Merriam.—MeR
"I am muscles" See Who am I
"I am no priest of crooks nor creeds." See
Religion
"I am off down the road." See Goblin feet
"I am sitting." See The muddy puddle
"I am so little and grey." See The prayer of the
mouse
"I am ten and no one I love has died." See
Deborah Lee
"I am the cat of cats, I am." See Cat of cats
"I am the child fat and contented." See The
diet
"I am the child of the Yei-ie." See Yei-ie's child
"I am the family face." See Heredity
"I am the four in one." See Spell of the
goddess
"I am the magical mouse." See The magical
mouse
"I am the mother of sorrows." See The paradox
"I am the only living thing." See The stallion
"I am the sister of him." See Little
"I am the world's best detective." See The
bloodhound
"I am 32 years old." See Writ on the eve of my
32nd birthday.
"I am turning thirty." See Turning 30 poem
"I am very fond of bugs." See Bugs
I am waiting. Lawrence Ferlinghetti.—PlG
"I am waiting for my case to come up." See I
am waiting
"I arrive Langston." See Do nothing till you
hear from me
"I asked the zebra." See Zebra question
"I ate a ton of sugar." Alice Gilbert.—CoPs
"I ate my sandwich on the rocks." See Ants
and sailboats
"I bear, in sign of love." See Shepherdess'
valentine
"I bought me a parrot in Trinidad." See Parrot
from Trinidad
"I brought my mother buttercups." Aileen
Fisher.—FiO
"I brush my teeth with ocean sand." X. J.
Kennedy.—KeP
"I came to a great door." See The beast
I can fly. Felice Holman.—HoA
"I can fly, of course." See I can fly
"I can make a sandwich." See Recipe
"I can play." See Lamplighter barn
"I can tell you." See How I got ovah
"I can think sharply." See Chameleon
"I cannot see fairies." See Fairies
"I can't afford." See Bored
"I can't fall asleep." See Falling asleep
"I can't forget the second night of the snow."
See The blizzard
"I can't talk." See Give me five
"I chose a pretty stone to love." See After all
"I climbed through woods in the hour before
dawn dark." See The horses

"I have a hot dog for a pet." See Hot dog
I have a lion. Karla Kuskin.—KuD
"I have a little bed." See My bed
"I have a little turtle." See Lost
"I have a pair." See Tiger pajamas
"I have a playful." See My puppy
"I have a purple dragon." See My dragon
"I have a white cat whose name is Moon." See
  Moon
"I have always known." See The way it is
"I have been the planner." See Song in 5 parts
"I have fallen in love with American names."
  See American names
"I have heard a voice of broken seas." See A
  fragment
"I have just come down from my father." See
  The hospital window
I have my father's eyes. Dennis Lee.—LeN
"I have named you queen." See The queen
"I have no name." See Infant joy
"I have no words." See Wild child's lament
"I have nothing new to ask of you." See
  Another year come
"I have seen." See The excursion
"I have sinuous shells of pearly hue." See Gebir
"I have spot resistant trousers." See Summer
  song, after a surfeit of irresistible ads
"I have studied the tight curls on the back of
  your neck." See Movement song
"I have to go now, letter isn't signed." See
  Mystery
"I have two dashing, prancing steeds." See
  Steeds
"I hear a whistling." See Emmett Till
I hear America griping. Morris Bishop.—BrO
"I hear his voice." See Nature dragon
"I heard a bird at dawn." See The rivals
"I heard a bird sing." Oliver Herford.—BaC
"I heard a clash, and a cry." See Middle ages
"I heard about a pole bean tent." See The pole
  bean tent
"I heard of poor." See Poor
"I heard the bells on Christmas day." See
  Christmas bells
"I heard the old, old men say." See The old
  men admiring themselves in the water
"I held Europe in my hand." See Yonder
"I hid the peppermint." See I had to be secret
"I hold her close." See Duet
I hope she won't grow any more. Norma
  Farber.—FaS
"I hope you never contract." See Cactus
  sickness
"I hung up a stocking." See A Christmas
  package
"I imagine the time of our meeting." See
  Forms of the earth at Abiquiu
I is for inkspot. William Jay Smith.—SmL
"I kind of like the playful porpoise." See The
  porpoise
"I knew a tiny sandpiper." See A certain
  sandpiper
"I know a girl." See The canal bank
"I know a lady." Joyce Carol Thomas.—AdC

"I know a little about a lottle." See Fewery,
  mostery, somery
"I know a little cupboard." See The cupboard
"I know a man." See The sand-man
"I know a poem of six lines that no one
  knows." See Anonymous
"I know a pond where frogs repeat." See
  Bullfrog communique
"I know I dreamed again last night." See At
  dawn
"I know I have lost my train." Mother Goose.—
  LoG
"I know my love is true." See Ballad
"I know some lonely houses off the road."
  Emily Dickinson.—HiS
"I know what I feel like." See Changing
"I know what the caged bird feels, alas." See
  Sympathy
"I know what the robin." See Robin song
"I lay down in my grave." See Elegy for
  Harriet Tubman and Frederick Douglass
"I learned to ride with the Colonel." See
  Riding
"I learned two things." See Riding lesson
"I left my head." Lilian Moore.—WiP
"I lie in grass, I gaze content." See Praise to
  the little
"I lie in my bed, trying hard to sleep." See It
"I like birds, said the Dryad." See Song
"I like days." See December
"I like it here just fine." See Girl held without
  bail
"I like it when it shines." See Looking out the
  window
"I like the circling proud old family beech."
  See Beech
"I like the fall." See The mist and all
"I like the park best at evening, on a cool day."
  See The park at evening
"I like the town on rainy nights." See Rainy
  nights
"I like the way the world is made." See
  Contentment
"I like them." See Giraffes
"I like this book, said the King of Spain." See
  The King of Spain
"I like to." See Closet
"I like to go to the stable after supper." See
  White cat
"I like to move, there's such a feeling." See
  Moving
"I like to walk." See Crows
I like to watch the ants at work." See Ants
"I like to watch the clouds roll by." See The
  cherub
"I like winter, spring, summer and fall."
  Beatrice Schenk De Regniers.—BrIt
I like you. Masuhito.—YaI
"I liked growing." Karla Kuskin.—KuD
"I live in an apartment house." See My four
  friends
"I lived on a rooftop." See At first sight
"I look in the mirror, and what do I see." See
  The mirror

I look pretty. Eloise Greenfield.—GrH

"I lose the moments of my day." See Forever blowing

"I love." See Honey, I love

"I love." Eloise Greenfield.—GrH

I love all gravity defiers. Lillian Morrison.—MoSr

"I love crows." See Crows

"I love the baby giant panda." See The panda

I love the world. Paul Wollner.—PaI

"I love thee, Mary, and thou lovest me." See The chemist to his love

"I love this little house because." See Motto for a dog house

I love to eat. Arnold Adoff.—AdE

"I love you." See The people, yes

"I love you." Lillian Morrison.—MoW

"I love you, big world." See I love the world

"I love you, I like you." See Love

"I love you in caves and meadows." David Ignatow.—LuZ

"I love you so." See Chocolate chocolate

"I loved my friend." See Poem

"I made a creature." See My creature

"I met a ghost, but he didn't want my head." See Monsters I've met

"I met a little elf man, once." See The little elf

"I met a man as I went walking." See Puppy and I

"I met a man in an onion bed." See The man in the onion bed

"I never know." See When all the world is full of snow

"I objurgate the centipede." See The centipede

"I often grieve for uncle Hannibal." Ogden Nash.—BlC

"I once knew a bear." See The Great Lakes suite—Lake St. Clair

"I once knew a boy who was odd as could be." See Peculiar

"I once was a seaman stout and bold." See Jolly soldier

"I once went to the beach." See Eating peaches on the beaches

I only watch the bubbles. Nikki Giovanni.—GiV

"I patched my coat with sunlight." See The coat

"I played old country and western." See Jamming with the band at the VFW

"I ponder how He died, despairing once." See Before an old painting of the Crucifixion

"I push the light switch button and, click, the light goes on." See Push button

"I put my honey in her pram." See Excursion

"I put on a pair of overshoes." See Around my room

"I ran along the yellow sand." See Pete the pup at the seashore

"I ran down the steps." See Now

"I ran to the edge of the world." See Finding out

"I read your testimony and I thought." See To Alexander Meiklejohn

"I remember." ("I remember/January") Mae Jackson.—AdC

"I remember." ("I remember/wanting to be big like Mikey") Nikki Grimes.—GrS

"I remember how she sang." Rob Penny.—AdC

"I remember I put on my socks." See Something missing

"I remember or remember hearing." See Once upon a great holiday

"I rise, I rise." Unknown.—FlA

"I rise in the dawn, and I kneel and blow." See The song of the old mother

"I roamed the streets." See Posture

"I rode my pony one summer day." See The errand

"I rowed the boat over to Butterfish Bay." See Butterfish Bay

"I said to myself one morning." See Waking

"I sat as still." See Bumblebee

"I saw a donkey." See The donkey

"I saw a fishing boat steer by." See Christmas goes to sea

"I saw a frieze on whitest marble drawn." See Ecstasy

"I saw a ghost." See Ghost

"I saw a gnome." See Gnome

"I saw a little chipmunk." See Chipmunk

"I saw a little girl I hate." See A little girl I hate

"I saw a proud, mysterious cat." See The mysterious cat

I saw a stable. Mary Elizabeth Coleridge.—LiPch

"I saw a stable, low and very bare." See I saw a stable

"I saw a toad with nobbly warts." See A toad

"I saw an old Indian." See Plainview: 2

"I saw on the snow." See Merry Christmas

"I saw that wizzle bug a wozzle." See Wizzle

"I saw the long line of the vacant shore." See The tides

"I saw the lovely arch." See The rainbow

"I saw the pueblo beneath the blue." See Looking north to Taos

"I saw the two starlings." See The manoeuvre

I saw three ships. Unknown.—LiCc

"I saw three ships come sailing in." See I saw three ships

"I saw two crows upon a tree." See Winter song

"I saw you walking." See At long last

"I say, look up this queer word villanelle." See The villanelle

"I say to you just so." See Ten twice

"I scarcely felt a breath of air." See Fall wind

I scream. Eve Merriam.—MeW

"I see." See Opening the door and entering the barnyard, etc.

"I see a lot of cowboys." See Squaw talk

"I see her against the pearl sky of Dublin." See My mother's sister

"I see now through a rifting cloud." See The sky is turning

"I see some waits awaiting." See Christmas eve

"I see that you're a poetry lover, sweet Diane." See Sweet Diane

"I see the cumulus and sky." Lillian Morrison.—MoW

"I see the moon." See The moon

"I see you're here to sneak some looks." See Gretchen in the kitchen

"I seem to see." See Queer

"I shake shake." See Do not open till Christmas

"I shot an arrow toward the sky." See Arrows

"I sing no song, I spin instead." See Spider

"I sing of a maiden." See A maiden that is makeless

I sing the birth. See A hymn on the nativity of my saviour

"I sing the birth was born tonight." See A hymn on the nativity of my saviour

"I sit in the dusk, I am all alone." See Tableau at twilight

"I sleep." See Locus of a point

"I slip and I slide." See Icy

"I sometimes sit." See Half way dressed

"I spot the hills." See Theme in yellow

I spy tyrannosaurus. Pyke Johnson, Jr.—CoDb

"I stand on the rock." See Beware of me

"I stole brass." Unknown.—WiP

"I swiped my grandma's cigarettes." See Smoking in the cellar

"I swung and swung at empty air." See The abominable baseball bat

"I take on the whole ocean." See Streetfighter moon

"I tarry in days shaped like the high staired street." See A birthday memorial to Seventh Street

"I, the luckiest of stars." See Star of peace

"I think." Beatrice Schenk De Regniers.—ReB

"I think about the elephant and flea." See In the middle

"I think I know just how the notes should sound." See Record

"I think it must be very nice." See Polar bear

"I think mice." See Mice

"I think of forests palaces and swans." See My uncle

"I think of her." See Nelly Myers

I think so, don't you. Unknown.—WiP

"I think that many owls say who—o." See Owls talking

"I thought a horse was gee and whoa." See Learner

"I thought of cards along the mantlepiece." See December fragments

"I thought of life, the outer and the inner." See Scarlett rocks

"I thought of you last night." See Legacies and bastard roses

"I thought that I had wavy hair." See Wavy

"I thought that I knew all there was to know." See Small, smaller

"I thought that I would like to see." See Next

"I told him a tale that I adore." See Andrew's bedtime story

"I took a shell, I shouldn't have, it lay." See The punishment

"I took away the ocean once." See The shell

"I took it to heart." See Triolet

"I took some wood and wire." See My boat

"I took the pail for water when the sun was high." See The star in the pail

"I tried on the farmer's hat." See Tryin' on clothes

"I tried the bell pull." See Visiting the moon

"I tried to catch a cold." See Catching

"I tried to say it, how I tried." See How to learn to say a long, hard word

"I turned on the TV." See Tube time

"I used to dream militant." See Revolutionary dreams

"I used to sit at piano lessons." See Piano lessons

"I used to squash in molehills." See Molehills

"I wake with the rain." See Night rain

"I walk across a tired field." See Old gray barn

"I walk downhill, slow." See Roll call, a land of old folk and children

"I walked a hangover like my death down." See Letter to Donald Fall

"I wandered lonely as a cloud." See Daffodils

"I want something suited to my special needs." See Needs

"I want to." Beatrice Schenk De Regniers.—ReB

"I want to be a carpenter." See Trades

"I want to be buried in an anonymous crater inside the moon." See Unholy missions

"I want to keep." Beatrice Schenk De Regniers.—ReB

"I want to learn to whistle." See Whistles

"I want to write a poem." See Noises

"I want what I want." See Spoiled sister song

I want you to meet. David McCord.—McO—WiP

"I wanted a rib sandwich." See Rib sandwich

"I was about to go, and said so." See Loneliness

"I was angry and mad." See Anger

"I was angry with my friend." See A poison tree

"I was asking for something specific and perfect for my city." See Mannahatta

"I was at a neighbor's farm." See Rabbit track

"I was carried on a platter." See Insomnia

"I was fast asleep, but somehow heard." See Winter calf

"I was mad and I was sad." See The telephone call

"I was not divinely inspired." See The first poem I ever wrote

"I was not; now I am—a few days hence." See The mystery

"I was playing with my hoop along the road." See The turn of the road

"I was raised on the Reservation." See Prospectus

"I was reading." See And then

"I was riding to Poughkeepsie." Mary Ann Hoberman.—HoY

"I'm the man who paints the stripes upon the zebra." See The painter

"I'm the wee wooly witchie of whistlewood way." See The wee woolly witchie of whistlewood way

"Image." Lillian Morrison.—MoW

Imaginary dialogues. William Jay Smith.—WiP

Imagination

    Artie. K. Starbird.—StC

    By myself. E. Greenfield.—GrH

    "Just around the corner." D. McCord.—McO

    Plea. J. Hemschemeyer.—LuZ

    S F. E. Leverett.—BrO

    The toad ("In days of old, those far off times") R. S. Oliver.—OlC

"Immeasurably sad, o long ago." See Loss

Immigrants ("No ship of all that under sail or steam") Robert Frost.—PlG

Immigration and emigration

    Address to the refugees. J. M. Brinnin.—PlG

    Arrival, New York harbor. R. Peters.—PlG

    Burying ground by the ties. A. MacLeish.—PlG

    Elegy for Bella, Sarah, Rosie, and all the others. S. Dorman.—PlG

    Immigrants ("No ship of all that under sail or steam") R. Frost.—PlG

    "Oh, dearer by far than the land of our birth." R. H. Wilde.—PlG

    On being brought from Africa to America. P. Wheatley.—PlG

    Our country. H. D. Thoreau.—PlG

    Prospective immigrants please note. A. Rich.—PlG

    Speech for the repeal of the McCarran Act. R. Wilbur.—PlG

    Stanzas on the emigration to America, and peopling the western country. P. Freneau.—PlG

    Upon the first sight of New England, June 29, 1638. T. Tillam.—PlG

    "With hearts revived in conceit, new land and trees they eye." From Good news from New England. E. Johnson.—PlG

Immortality.

    Anonymous. M. Steingesser.—WiP

    Fragments. J. Masefield.—PaE

    Heaven and hell. Unknown.—LuZ

    The men of Sudbury. C. Baker.—PlG

    "Thou, whose exterior semblance doth belie." From Ode: Intimations of immortality from recollections of early childhood. W. Wordsworth.—PlL

Impatience. See Patience

Impetuous Samuel. Harry Graham.—CoI

The importance of eggs. David McCord.—McO

Importnt. Shel Silverstein.—SiL

"In a boggy old bog." See Frog music

"In a bowl beat 2 eggs." See Sunday morning toast

In a cafe. Richard Brautigan.—JaPp

"In a cottage in Fife." Mother Goose.—LoG

"In a dark, dark wood there was." See In a dark wood

In a dark wood. Unknown.—WaM

"In a darksome dominion." See The towering giant

"In a dreary place." See Ink hats

"In a faraway, faraway forest." See the dragon of death

"In a Fibruary blizzard." Doris Orgel.—OrM

"In a foul and filthy cavern." See The ogre

"In a high wind." See Poem

"In a one button gray wool sweater." See Harmonica man

"In a roostery somewhere near Fen." Myra Cohn Livingston.—LiLl

"In a shady nook one moonlit night." See The leprechaun

"In a snow-enshrouded graveyard." See the dance of the thirteen skeletons

In a starry orchard. Norma Farber.—FaS

"In a storm." See Storm

"In a tub one fine day." See T is for tub

In a word. Eve Merriam.—MeW

"In and out of eaves." Kazue Mizumura.—MiF

"In and out the bushes, up the ivy." See The chipmunk's song

"In Aquari-Fibruary." Doris Orgel.—OrM

"In Baltimore there lived a boy." See The boy who laughed at Santa Claus

In bed ("When I am in bed") Charlotte Zolotow.—HeB

"In Bethlehem is born the holy child." See The messiah

In black chasms. Leslie Norris.—NoM

"In black chasms, in caves where water." See In black chasms

"In broad daylight." See The owl

"In burnished armor." See Starling

"In childhood you think." See Thanksgiving

"In countries where no birds are alive." See For Edwin R. Embree

"In days of old, those far off times." See The toad

"In days of yore the dinosaur." See So it goes

"In death the dead remember their spirit." See Funeral poem

"In dromedary Fibruary." Doris Orgel.—OrM

"In every moon mirror lurks a danger." See Moon mirror

"In February, bring them home." See Conversation hearts

"In Fibruary, any wind's day." Doris Orgel.—OrM

"In Fibruary, my canary." Doris Orgel.—OrM

"In Fibruary, Old MacDonald." Doris Orgel.—OrM

"In Fibruary, uncle Harry." Doris Orgel.—OrM

"In Fibruary, when it freezes." Doris Orgel.—OrM

"In fiction tales we keep performing." See The collies

In-flight meal. From A lot of limericks. X. J. Kennedy.—KeP

"In flowing dress." See The sorceress

"In general I dislike cleaning house, taking stock." See Sabbatical

"In Golden Gate Park that day." Lawrence Ferlinghetti.—LuZ
"In grade school I wondered." See Zimmer in grade school
"In grapes I know there may be seeds." See Answering your question
"In Grumble Grove, near Howling Hop." See The ghostly grocer of Grumble Grove
"In heaven it's allemande left and promenade." See Christmas in the straw
"In his travels, the elephant." See Elephant
"In Italy, a man's name, here a woman's." See How I changed my name, Felice
"In July, the apples on." See Whipping apples
"In jumping and tumbling." Unknown.—MoF
"In Lapland the Lapps." See R is for reindeer
"In late autumn the hound." See Old man, phantom dog
"In Love Lane, in Thistle Grove." See Guide to London
"In March he was buried." See The golden boy
In May. Paul Laurence Dunbar.—BrI
In memoriam, sels. Alfred Tennyson
    "Again at Christmas did we weave."—LiPch
    Ring out, wild bells.—LiO
    "The time draws near the birth of Christ."—LiPch
    "Unwatch'd, the garden bough shall sway."—PaB
    Voices in the mist.—BaC
In memory of my dear grandchild Elizabeth Bradstreet, who deceased August, 1665, being a year and half old. Ann Bradstreet.—PlL
"In mortal combat." See The beefburger
"In my younger years." See Dreams
"In north-west Australia where the iron ore grows." Marguerite Varday.—DuSn
"In ocean's wide domains." See The witnesses
In our tethered boats. Lillian Morrison.—MoW
"In pairs." See For the sisters of the Hotel Dieu
In payment. Aileen Fisher.—FiO
In place of a red carpet. Norma Farber.—FaS
In praise of Neptune. Thomas Campion.—PaE
"In ranges high at Ballyang." See The ballyoons
"In school today." See Joy
"In sea-cold Lyonesse." See Sunk Lyonesse
In search of Cinderella. Shel Silverstein.—SiL
"In some green island of the sea." See Fragments
"In southeast Asia, when you go." See The water buffalo
In space language. Lillian Morrison.—MoO
"In spite of her sniffle." See The sniffle
"In spite of my sad financial state." See I'm leery of firms with easy terms
"In spring, the wind's a sneaky wind." See The wind
"In summer it." See Rosebush
"In summer these." See Two times three
"In Sweden, they say." See Northern lights
In sympathy, but only for a little longer. Ann Menebroker.—KhI

In terms of physics. Lillian Morrison.—MoO
"In the absence of mothballs, the moth." See The moth
In the beginning was the. Lillian Morrison.—MoSr
"In the bleak midwinter." See A Christmas carol
"In the center of the world." See A song to sing over and over
"In the darkest part of the forest's heart." See She
"In the darkling early morning we go milk the Jersey cow." See Barn chores
"In the darkness of a sepulcher." See The mummy
"In the days before the high tide." See A sea song
"In the deep sleep forest." See Alarm clock
"In the desolate depths of a perilous place." See The bogeyman
"In the dust are my father's beautiful hands." See At night
"In the early morning, past the shut houses." See Scroppo's dog
In the end. David McCord.—McSu
"In the engine sound like many people together." See Sky diving
"In the evening." See Autumn concert
"In the evening." Siv Cedering Fox.—FoB
"In the evening, in the windows." See Christmas candles
"In the Ford plant." See The foundations of American industry
"In the ghostly, ghastly silence." See The spectre on the moor
"In the heel of my thumb." See Thumbprint
"In the house." See Teevee
"In the inner city." Lucille Clifton.—AdC—MoGp
In the library. Michael Patrick Hearn.—HeB
"In the long lake's mirror." See From the mailboat passing by
In the middle. David McCord.—McO
"In the middle of a meadow." See Under a stone
"In the midst." See Cat bath
"In the month of Fibruary." Doris Orgel.—OrM
"In the morning." Siv Cedering Fox.—FoB
"In the morning, in the dark." See The night hunt
"In the morning, very early." See Barefoot days
In the motel. X. J. Kennedy.—KeP
"In the muscles of words." See The possessors
In the night. James Stephens.—MaP
"In the numb, numberless days." See The burning
In the old house. Joan Aiken.—AiS
"In the orange tree is the star." See The star that came
In the orchard. James Stephens.—HiS—WaG
In the park ("He who sits in the shade of his tail") Norma Farber.—FaS

In the park ("When you've") Lilian Moore.—FaS

"In the pitch of the night." Lee Bennett Hopkins.—HoBm

"In the pond in the park." See Water picture

"In the reaper's pocket." See The pocket whetstone

"In the rough places." See Weeds

"In the shadows of a mountain." See The abominable snowman

"In the shut drawer, even now, they rave and grieve." See Packet of letters

In the snow or sun. Aileen Fisher.—FiO

"In the stall's gloom." See Horse

"In the street." See Night sounds

In the sun and shadow. Aileen Fisher.—FiO

In the town. Unknown, tr. fr. the French by Eleanor Farjeon.—LiPch

In the tree house at night. James Dickey.—PlL

"In the tug of war between winter and summer." See Eskimo legend

"In the vacant lot." See Barefoot in the clover

"In the very earliest time." See Magic words

In the week when Christmas comes. Eleanor Farjeon.—LiPch

"In the well is well water." See W is for well

"In the wicked afternoon." See Abracadabra

In the wind. Aileen Fisher.—FiO

"In the witch's." See The witch's garden

"In this green month when resurrected flowers." See Memorial wreath

"In this nation." See Of being numerous #24

"In this photo, circa 1934." See A snapshot of the Auxiliary

"In this water, clear as air." See The pool in the rock

In those times. Alan Block.—KhI

"In tight pants, tight skirts." See The young ones, flip side

"In times of calm or hurricane, in days of sun or shower." See The dog parade

"In wildest woods, on treetop shelves." See The darkling elves

"In winter I get up at night." See Bed in summer

In winter sky. David McCord.—McO

"In you, in you I see myself." See Complicated thoughts about a small son

"In your arithmetics." See Who hasn't played gazintas

Inability to depict an eagle. Richard Eberhart.—PlG

Inadequate aqua extremis. Ruth M. Walsh.—BrO

Incantation to Oedipus. John Dryden.—LiO

"Incarnate for our marriage you appeared." See The marriage

Incident in a rose garden. Donald Justice.—LuZ

Indecision means flexibility. Elliot Abhau.—CoPh

Independence
When I am me. F. Holman.—HoBm

Independence day. See Fourth of July

Independence day ("Between painting a roof yesterday and the hay") Wendell Berry.—LiO

"An indescribable earthy smell." See Autumn for me is

"The Indian chief who, fam'd of yore." See The prophecy of King Tammany

An Indian hymn of thanks to mother corn. Unknown.—LiCc

Indian names. Lydia Huntly Sigourney.—PlG

Indian pipe. Mary Ann Hoberman.—HoY

Indian summer. See Autumn

Indian summer. Wilfrid Campbell.—DoWh

Indiana
July in Indiana. R. Fitzgerald.—FlA
Midwest. J. F. Nims.—FlA

"Indiana, no blustering summit or coarse gorge." See Midwest

"The Indians have mostly gone." See Like ghosts of eagles

Indians of the Americas
Ancestors. G. Cohoe.—LuZ
Arrowy dreams. W. Bynner.—PlG
Battle won is lost. P. George.—LuZ
Carriers of the dream wheel. N. S. Momaday.—MoGd
The colors of night. N. S. Momaday.—MoGd
Custer's last stand. From A lot of limericks. X. J. Kennedy.—KeP
The delight song of Tsoai-talee. N. S. Momaday.—MoGd
The discovery. J. C. Squire.—LiO
The eagle-feather fan. N. S. Momaday.—MoGd
The eagle's song. Unknown.—PlG
Earth and I gave you turquoise. N. S. Momaday.—MoGd
The end of the Indian poems. S. Plumly.—PlG
"From his wanderings far to eastward." From The song of Hiawatha. H. W. Longfellow.—PlG
The gourd dancer. N. S. Momaday.—MoGd
The grass on the mountain. Unknown.—PlG
"How busie are the sonnes of men." R. Williams.—PlG
Indian names. L. H. Sigourney.—PlG
Indian pipe. M. A. Hoberman.—HoY
Inscription. J. G. Whittier.—PlG
Isleta Indian girl. K. Wilson.—LuZ
It is mine, this country wide. Unknown.—PlG
Jamestown ("Let me look at what I was, before I die") R. Jarrell.—PlG
Learning about the Indians. M. Oliver.—LuZ
Like ghosts of eagles. R. Francis.—PlG
Long shadows at Dulce. N. S. Momaday.—MoGd
Looking north to Taos. R. Bantista.—LuZ
"Once in the winter." From The forsaken. D. C. Scott.—DoWh
Plainview: 2. N. S. Momaday.—MoGd
Plainview: 4. N. S. Momaday.—MoGd
Pony song. R. Bantista.—LuZ

"Inspire our sons to seek their man shadows."
    See If we cannot live as people
"Instead of counting herds of sheep." See
    Counting birds
Instructions to a princess. Ishmael Reed.—AdC
Insults
    Double barrelled ding dong bat. Unknown.—
        HeB
    Five men against the theme, my name is red
        hot, yo name ain' doodley squat. G.
        Brooks.—AdC
Intelligence
    On the birth of his son. Su Tung-Po.—LiO
Interplanetary limericks, sels. Al Graham.—BrO
    (Complete)
    "By rocket, to visit the moon"
    "The ladies inhabiting Venus"
    "A Martian named Harrison Harris"
Intimates. D. H. Lawrence.—LuZ
Intimations of immortality. See Ode:
    Intimations of immortality from
    recollections of early childhood
"Into my trousers before it was dawn." See
    Four of July
"Into the basin put the plums." See The
    Christmas pudding
"Into the endless dark." See City lights
"Into the house of a Mrs. MacGruder." See The
    outlaw
"Into the station." See Return to nowhere
"An intrepid explorer named Bliss." See An
    explorer named Bliss
The invasion of the star streaks. Lillian
    Morrison.—MoO
Inventors and inventions
    Creation. G. Turner.—DuSn
    The microscope. M. Kumin.—BrO—MoGp—
        WiP
    My invention. S. Silverstein.—BrO
Invisibility
    Invisible. F. Holman.—HoA
Invisible. Felice Holman.—HoA
The invisible beast. Jack Prelutsky.—PrH
Invitation to love. Paul Laurence Dunbar.—BrI
Invitations
    The Queen of the Nile. W. J. Smith.—SmL
Invocation. Louis MacNeice.—HiS
Invocations
    Invocation. L. MacNeice.—HiS
Iowa
    The Bagley Iowa poem. A. Darr.—KhI
    Iowa ("Air as the fuel of owls") M. D.
        Browne.—FlA
    Old Dubuque. D. Etter.—FlA
Iowa ("Air as the fuel of owls") Michael Dennis
    Browne.—FlA
Ireland
    The Irish cliffs of Moher. W. Stevens.—PlL
    Irish tune. L. Morrison.—MoW
    Tom McGreevy, in America, thinks of
        himself as a boy. From Our stars come
        from Ireland. W. Stevens.—PlG
    The westwardness of everything. From Our
        stars come from Ireland. W. Stevens.—PlG

"An iridescent sea horse." Lillian Morrison.—
    MoW
The Irish cliffs of Moher. Wallace Stevens.—PlL
Irish tune. Lillian Morrison.—MoW
The Irish wolf hound. Denis Florence
    McCarthy.—CoG
Iroquois Indians. See Indians of the Americas—
    Iroquois
Irving, Washington
    "Now Christmas is come." See The sketch
        book
    The sketch book, sel.
        "Now Christmas is come."—BaC
Irwin, Wallace
    Aunt Nerissa's muffin.—CoPs
    Science for the young.—BrO
"Is a star." See Summer stars
"Is Easter just a day of hats." See Easter
    morning
"Is hiding." See Dinner thought
"Is it waiting just for me." Kazue Mizumura.—
    MiF
"Is on the top." See The apple
"Is Oz." See Oz
"Is the only arena." See The infinity arena
"Is the total black, being spoken." See Coal
"Is there a place." Lilian Moore.—MoTs
"Is there nothing to be said about the
    cockroach." See Cockroach
"Is this a fast, to keep." See A true Lent
Isabel. Unknown, tr. fr. the French by George
    Lanigan.—DoWh
"Isabel Jones and Curabel Lee." David
    McCord.—McO
"Isabel met an enormous bear." See The
    adventures of Isabel
"Isabel of the lily white hand." See Isabel
Isaiah, sel. Bible—Old Testament
    "The wolf also shall dwell with the lamb."—
        BaC
Islam
    Ka'ba. I. A. Baraka.—AdC
Islands
    Islands in Boston Harbor. D. McCord.—McO
    "Some would dive in the lagoon." From The
        enchanted island. A. Noyes.—PaE
Islands in Boston Harbor. David McCord.—
    McO
Isleta Indian girl. Keith Wilson.—LuZ
"Isn't a breeze." See Listen
Issa
    "Crawl, laugh."—LiO
    "For a fresh start." See Oraga Haru
    Oraga Haru, sel.
        "For a fresh start."—LiO
    "Person after person."—LiO
It ("I lie in my bed, trying hard to sleep") Jack
    Prelutsky.—PrS
"It all happened like this." See My nurse
"It beats me, the way." See Old people
"It came today to visit." See The visitor
"It changes a lot." See M is for mask
"It comes back." See Deceased
"It comes in black." See The telephone

"It costs little Gossip her income for shoes."
  Mother Goose.—TrGg
"It dances." See The newborn colt
"It did not last, the Devil howling ho." See
  Eminent cosmologists
"It doesn't pay to be cross." See The howlery
  growlery room
"It don't matter." Nikki Grimes.—GrS
"It goes fwunkety." See The washing machine
It happened in Montgomery. Phil W. Petrie.—
  MoGp
"It has turned to snow in the night." See The
  horses
"It is a curious thing that you." See The
  kangaroo
"It is a noble country where we dwell." See
  Our country
"It is a slice of moon, they cry." See Abstract
  picture, at the museum
"It is a wonder foam is so beautiful." See Spray
"It is as if a silver chord." See To a dead friend
"It is grey out." Karla Kuskin.—KuD
"It is like the plot of an ol'." See Instructions to
  a princess
"It is midnight." See Poem at thirty
It is mine, this country wide. Unknown.—PlG
"It is not the weight of jewel or plate." See
  The perfect gift
"It is only." See July madness
"It is only when." See So that's why
"It is our hand, the." See Patience of a people
"It is over." See Unspelled
"It is portentous, and a thing of state." See
  Abraham Lincoln walks at midnight
"It is said." See Problems
"It is the calm and solemn night." See A
  thousand bells
"It is the law, our cat has caught a mouse." See
  Cat and mouse
It isn't. Eve Merriam.—MeW
"It isn't a bud." See It isn't
"It keeps eternal whisperings around." See On
  the sea
"It lives there." See Tomorrow
"It may be misery not to sing at all." See Life's
  tragedy
"It neither was the words nor yet the tune."
  See Two girls singing
"It rattles my windows." See Earthquake
"It scurries." See The truth mouse
"It squinted and said." See N is for needle
"It starts out." See The light year
"It takes a good speller." See Spelling bee
"It was a gallant highwayman." See The gallant
  highwayman
"It was a night in winter." See The witnesses—
  The innkeeper's wife
"It was a noon of freedom." See The mother
"It was after the maze and mirth of the
  dance." See The mistletoe
"It was awful, first." See The day the T.V.
  broke
"It was down by the dirty river." See And they
  lived happily ever after for a while

"It was laughing time, and the tall giraffe." See
  Laughing time
"It was lying on the sidewalk." See The snopp
  on the sidewalk
"It was Mama who was partial." See Emma
"It was Thanksgiving." See Fresh meat
"It was there, but I said it couldn't be true in
  daylight." See Nightmare of mouse
"It was touching when I started." See Aunt
  Nerissa's muffin
"It was very pleasant." See A certain peace
"It was wild." See Assassination
"It would be funny." See Hand over
"It's a concert in the bedroom." See The
  bedtime concert
"It's a late starting dawn that breathes my
  vision." See Late starting dawn
"It's a long walk in the dark." See John's song
"It's a very odd thing." See Miss T.
"It's about." See Analysis of baseball
"It's all in." See The poem
It's all relative. William Cole.—CoDb
It's all the same to the clam. Shel Silverstein.—
  SiL
It's already autumn. Elio Pagliarani.—JaPp
"It's already autumn, and I've suffered other
  months." See It's already autumn
"It's awf'lly bad luck on Diana." See Hunter
  trials
"Its breath." See Speaking the poem
"It's Christmas day, I did not get." See Otto
"It's cold, said the cricket." See Halloween
  concert
"It's comforting." Judy Dothard Simmons.—
  AdC
"It's dark out." Mary Ann Hoberman.—HoY
"Its echoes." See Haunted house
"It's full of the moon." See Full of the moon
"It's fun turning somersaults." See Somersaults
"It's funny." See My puppy
"It's funny that smells and sounds return." See
  Scrapbooks
It's Halloween. Jack Prelutsky.—PrI
"It's Halloween, it's Halloween." See It's
  Halloween
"It's hot." Shel Silverstein.—SiL
"It's late and we are sleepy." See Happy
  Halloween
"It's lemonading time again." See Lemonade
"It's live and evil." See The dreadful drawkcab
"It's my birthday." See Happy birthday to me
It's neat. Myra Cohn Livingston.—LiWt
"It's neat, moon." See It's neat
It's never fair weather. Ogden Nash.—BlC
"It's not that I don't care for snakes." See
  Snake problem
"It's queer about my Uncle Frank." See Uncle
  Frank
"It's quiet in the meadow." See A walk for
  thinking
"It's safe to swim." See Have fun
"It's Saturday." See Rainy rainy Saturday
"It's snowing, it's snowing, it's snowing." See
  Snow song

"It's strange about the newsman." See The corner newsman

"It's such a shock, I almost screech." William Cole.—CoPs

"It's summertime." See Reggie

"It's the time of year." See The mini spooks

"It's the world's longest car, I swear." See Longmobile

"It's today." See The way things are

"It's tough being short." See Growing, for Louis

"It's very hard." See Stars

"It's wonderful dogs they're breeding now." See Tim, an Irish terrier

"I've a kisty." Unknown.—BlH

"I've asked professor Swigly Brown." See Write me a verse

"I've been working so hard you just wouldn't believe." See Tired

"I've broken lots of eggs, I guess." See The importance of eggs

"I've caught a fish." See A catch

"I've changed my ways a little, I cannot now." See The house dog's grave

"I've discovered a way to stay friends forever." See Friendship

"I've dropped back to pass." See The completion

"I've got a dog as thin as a rail." Unknown.—CoG

"I've got a secret." See The secret song

"I've got a sort of tying thing." See The fly nest

"I've got three hens, a rooster, no." See Plymouth Rocks, of course

"I've had many a strange occupation." See Occupations

"I've looked behind the shed." See Gone

"I've made me a moon catchin' net." See Moon catchin' net

"I've never been to Heaven." See Rutland fair

"I've never roped a Brahma bull." See Never

"I've stood here lately, looking at the path." See Civilization

Ivory. David McCord.—McO

Ivy

"The holly and the ivy." Unknown.—LiO

Iza, Ana Maria

Formula.—LuZ

J

J is for jack-in-the-box. William Jay Smith.—SmL

"J was Joe Jenkins." Mother Goose.—TrGg

Jabber-whacky, or, on dreaming, after falling asleep watching TV. Isabelle Di Caprio.—BrO

Jack and his pony, Tom. Hilaire Belloc.—CoPh

"Jack be nimble." Mother Goose.—TrGg

Jack do-good-for-nothing. Ogden Nash.—BlC

"Jack had a little pony, Tom." See Jack and his pony, Tom

"Jack Hall." Mother Goose.—WiP

"Jack in the pulpit, where are you Jack." See Spring talk

Jack, Jill, Spratts, and Horner. David McCord.—McO

Jack-o-lanterns. See Halloween; Pumpkins

"Jack rabbit, jackdaw, jaguar." See J's

"Jack Sprat could eat no fat." Mother Goose.—TrGg

Jack the giant killer, sel. Unknown

Giant chants.—WaG

Jack was every inch a sailor. Unknown.—DoWh

Jackson, Angela

Blackmen, who make morning.—AdC

Jackson, Leroy F.

"Duckle, duckle, daisy."—BaC

"Said Simple Sam, does Christmas come."—BaC

Jackson, Mae

"I remember."—AdC

"Jacob Thatcher, out of breath from." See Bee tree

Jacobs, Frank

The hot pizza serenade.—CoPs

If Walt Whitman had written Humpty Dumpty.—CoPs

Jacobs, Leland B.

Katherine tattles.—CoI

Taste of purple.—HoMp

Jacobson, Ethel

Atomic courtesy.—BrO

Jails. See Prisons and prisoners

Jam. David McCord.—WiP

Jamaica

Venus in the tropics. L. Simpson.—KhI

Jamboree. David McCord.—McO

James, Jesse (about)

Jesse James, a design in red and yellow for a nickel library. W. R. Benet.—FlA

"James lives in our neighborhood." See Nobody calls him Jim

Jamestown

Jamestown ("Let me look at what I was, before I die") R. Jarrell.—PlG

Jamestown ("Let me look at what I was, before I die") Randall Jarrell.—PlG

Jammes, Francis

The little donkey.—LiPch

Jamming with the band at the VFW. David Bottoms.—KhI

"Jane gave a leap from her trapeze." X. J. Kennedy.—KeP

Janeczko, Paul B.

After the rain.—JaPp

Lesson for dreamers.—JaPp

January

January ("The days are short") J. Updike.—MoGp

January ("The days are short") John Updike.—MoGp

"January played." See One year

Japanese lesson. David McCord.—McO

Japanese nursery rhymes. See Nursery rhymes—Japanese

Jaques, Florence Page
There once was a puffin.—WiP

Jarrell, Randall
The bird of night.—HiD
The chipmunk's song.—CoA
Gunner.—LiO
Jamestown.—PlG
The mockingbird.—HiD
A sick child.—HiS
A variation on 'to say to go to sleep.'—YaI

Jays
August 28. D. McCord.—McO
Blue jay ("So bandit eyed, so undovelike a bird") R. Francis.—JaPp
Creatures we can do without. E. Merriam.—MeR
J's. R. S. Oliver.—OlC

Jealousy
The valley. S. Moss.—JaPp

"Jean said, no." See Secret

"Jeanie come tie my." Mother Goose.—TrGg

Jeffers, Lance
Breath in my nostrils.—AdC
How high the moon.—AdC
Nina Simone.—AdC
Trellie.—AdC
"Who shined shoes in Times Square.—AdC

Jeffers, Robinson
Birds.—PaE
Hands.—PlG
The house dog's grave.—CoG
New Mexican mountain.—PlG
Shine, republic.—PlG

Jefferson, Thomas (about)
Brave new world. A. MacLeish.—LiO
Monticello. M. Sarton.—PlG

Jellyfish
A jellyfish ("Visible, invisible") M. Moore.—JaPp
The jellyfish ("Who wants my jellyfish") O. Nash.—BlC
Love song for a jellyfish. S. Hochman.—LuZ—MoGp
Skip scoop anellie. T. Prideaux.—CoPs

A **jellyfish** ("Visible, invisible") Marianne Moore.—JaPp

The **jellyfish** ("Who wants my jellyfish") Ogden Nash.—BlC

Jenkins, Brooks
Loneliness.—MaP

Jenkins, John
The long-nosed smelter.—DuSn
The wilderong.—DuSn

Jennens, Charles
"In Bethlehem is born the holy child." See The messiah
The messiah, sel.
"In Bethlehem is born the holy child."—BaC

Jennett, Sean
The barge horse.—CoPh

Jennings, Elizabeth
Rain.—SaM

Jennison, C. S.
I'm leery of firms with easy terms.—BrO

"Jenny had hopes she could sling in the air." See Jenny the juvenile juggler

Jenny the juvenile juggler. Dennis Lee.—HeB

Jerome, Judson
Child's game.—HiD

"Jerry Hall." Mother Goose.—LoG

"A jersey cow exploded." See One sunny summer's day

Jesse James, a design in red and yellow for a nickel library. William Rose Benet.—FlA

"Jesse James was a two gun man." See Jesse James, a design in red and yellow for a nickel library

Jessica, a bird who sings. Nikki Giovanni.—GiV

Jesus Christ. See also Christmas; Easter; God
"And in a far country." From Every man heart lay down. L. Graham.—BaC
"And some of the Pharisees from among the multitude." From Gospel according to Luke.—LiPch
"And there were in the same country shepherds." From Gospel according to Luke.—LiPch
  The angels.—BaC (sel.)
  The shepherds.—BaC (sel.)
An anonymous verse from a Puerto Rican Christmas card. Unknown.—BaC
Ballad of the goodly fere. E. Pound.—LiO
Before an old painting of the Crucifixion. N. S. Momaday.—MoGd
Bethlehem ("A little child") Unknown.—BaC
Calvary. E. A. Robinson.—LiO
The camels, the Kings' camels. L. Norris.—LiPch—NoM
The cherry tree carol ("As Joseph was a-walking")—LiPch
  "As Joseph was a-walking."—BaC
The cherry tree carol ("Joseph was an old man") Unknown.—LiO
Christ is born. Unknown.—BaC
Christmas candle. R. Field.—BaC
A Christmas carol ("An angel told Mary") H. Behn.—LiPch
A Christmas carol ("In the bleak midwinter") C. G. Rossetti.—BaC
  "What can I give him."—LiCc (sel.)—LiPch (sel.)
A Christmas hymn. R. Wilbur.—LiPch
Christmas morning. E. M. Roberts.—LiCc—LiPch
Coventry carol. Unknown.—LiO—LiPch (at. to Robert Croo)
The cultivation of Christmas trees. T. S. Eliot.—LiO
Easter hymn. A. E. Housman.—LiO
"For we have seen his star in the east, and are come." From Gospel according to Matthew.—BaC
The friendly beasts. Unknown.—LiPch

"From Heaven high I come to you." M. Luther.—LiPch

"His place of birth a solemn angel tells." From Paradise lost. J. Milton.—BaC

"The holly and the ivy." Unknown.—LiPch

How they brought the good news by sea. N. Farber.—LiPch

I saw a stable. M. E. Coleridge.—LiPch

"I wonder as I wander." Unknown.—LiPch

"In Bethlehem is born the holy child." From The messiah. C. Jennens.—BaC

The kings from the east. H. Heine.—BaC
    "Three holy kings from Morgenland."—LiPch

Journey of the Magi. T. S. Eliot.—LiPch

Juniper. E. Duggan.—LiPch

"The lamb was bleating softly." J. R. Jiménez.—LiPch

The last supper ("They are gathered, astounded and disturbed") R. M. Rilke.—LiO

"Little Jesus of the crib." Unknown.—BaC

Long, long ago. Unknown.—LiPch

"Look up, you men, men there at the fire." From Annunciation over the shepherds. R. M. Rilke.—LiPch

The Magi. W. B. Yeats.—LiPch

A maiden that is makeless. Unknown.—LiO
    "He came all so still."—LiPch (sel.)

Manger tale. R. N. Peck.—PeB

Mary, mother of Christ. C. Cullen.—LiPch

Mice in the hay. L. Norris.—LiPch—NoM

Morning star. Unknown.—BaC

The nativity. From Gospel according to Luke.—BaC

Oh, my bambino. Unknown.—BaC

One glorious star. Unknown.—BaC

"Out on the windy hill." L. Norris.—NoM

Pieta. R. M. Rilke.—LiO

The prayer of the donkey. C. B. de Gasztold.—LiPch

Resurrection ("Some of us") F. Horne.—LiO

Shepherd's song at Christmas. L. Hughes.—BaC—LiPch

Song ("Why do bells for Christmas sing") E. Field.—BaC

The stable cat. L. Norris.—NoM

"This crosse-tree here." R. Herrick.—LiO

The three kings ("I am Gaspar, I have brought frankincense") R. Dario—BaC—LiPch

Three kings ("Three kings came out of Indian land") Unknown.—BaC

"The wolf also shall dwell with the lamb." From Isaiah.—BaC

Jesus drum. Pearl Cleage Lomax.—AdC

"Jesus our brother, strong and good." See The friendly beasts

Jetliner. Naoshi Koriyama.—LuZ

Jewelry
    "Ride a cock horse to Coventry Cross." Mother Goose.—TrGg
    Song of the marble earrings. L. Morrison.—MoW

Jewels. See Precious stones

Jigsaw puzzle. Russell Hoban.—MoGp

"Jill Withers had a farthingale." John Becker.—WiP

Jim Jay. Walter De La Mare.—HiS

Jim, who ran away from his nurse, and was eaten by a lion. Hilaire Belloc.—WiP

Jiménez, Juan Ramón
    "The lamb was bleating softly."—LiPch
    The star that came.—BaC
    You light.—BaC

"Jiminy jiminy jukebox, wheatcakes, crumbs." See Mole

Jingle. Eve Merriam.—MeB

Jittery Jim. William Jay Smith.—SmL

Joans, Ted
    Love tight.—AdC—YaI

Job, sel. Bible—Old Testament
    Leviathan.—PaE
    The war horse.—CoPh

Joe ("We feed the birds in winter") David McCord.—McO

Joe's snow clothes. Karla Kuskin.—KuD
    "For wandering walks."—WiP

Joggers ("To see his jogs") David McCord.—McSu

Jogging. See Runners and running

John ("John comes in with a basket") David McCord.—McO

John ("John could take his clothes off") N. M. Bodecker.—BeR

John ("John, John, bad King John") Eleanor and Herbert Farjeon.—WiP

John Anderson my jo. Robert Burns.—PlL

"John Anderson my jo, John." See John Anderson my jo

John Coltrane an impartial review. A. B. Spellman.—AdC

"John comes in with a basket." See John

"John could take his clothes off." See John

"John is the tallest, he's ever so high." See Comparison

John J. Maya Angelou.—AnO

"John, John, bad King John." See John

"Johnny cake and venison and sassafras tea." See Plainview: 4

"Johnny came from England." See The pair of pants

"Johnny made a custard." See Some cook

"Johnny reading in his comic." See Any day now

John's song. Joan Aiken.—AiS—HiD

"John's words were the words." See After the rain

Johnson, Burges
    Contentment.—CoG
    Remarks from the pup.—CoG

Johnson, Edward
    Good news from New England, sel.
        "With hearts revived in conceit, new land and trees they eye."—PlG
    "With hearts revived in conceit, new land and trees they eye." See Good news from New England

"**Just** at dusk." See The owl on the aerial
Just because. David McCord.—McO
"**Just** look at this ocean I made." See Bathtub
Just now. David Kherdian.—KhC
"**Just** off the highway to Rochester, Minnesota."
    See A blessing
"**Just** so it goes, the day, the night." See An
    ordinary evening in Cleveland
"**Just** so you shouldn't have to ask again." See
    What kind of a guy was he
"**Just** when winter spreads out." Arnold
    Adoff.—AdE
Justice
    Justice denied in Massachusetts. E. St. V.
       Millay.—PlG
Justice denied in Massachusetts. Edna St.
    Vincent Millay.—PlG
Justice, Donald
    Crossing Kansas by train.—FlA
    Incident in a rose garden.—LuZ
Juxtaposing. Eve Merriam.—MeR

K

K is for king. William Jay Smith.—SmL
Ka'ba. Imamu Amiri Baraka.—AdC
Kaddish, sel. Allen Ginsburg
    "Another year, I left NY, on west coast in."—
       PlL
Kafu Hoh
    The sky. tr.—LuZ
Kai-yu Hsu
    White butterfly. tr.—LuZ
"**Kamaoktunga,** I am afraid and I tremble." See
    Manerathiak's song
The **kangaroo** ("It is a curious thing that you")
    Elizabeth Coatsworth.—CoA
Kangaroo ("Kangaroo hopped to the pink
    tureen") Robert S. Oliver.—OlC
The **kangaroo** ("The kangaroo is of course by
    nature") John Gardner.—GaCb
The **kangaroo** ("O kangaroo, O kangaroo")
    Ogden Nash.—BlC
Kangaroo ("A tough kangaroo named Hopalong
    Brown") William Jay Smith.—SmL
"**Kangaroo** hopped to the pink tureen." See
    Kangaroo
"The **kangaroo** is of course by nature." See The
    kangaroo
Kangaroos
    Jumpety-bumpety-hop. Unknown.—CoA
    The kangaroo ("It is a curious thing that
       you") E. Coatsworth.—CoA
    Kangaroo ("Kangaroo hopped to the pink
       tureen") R. S. Oliver.—OlC
    The kangaroo ("The kangaroo is of course by
       nature") J. Gardner.—GaCb
    The kangaroo ("O kangaroo, O kangaroo") O.
       Nash.—BlC
    Kangaroo ("A tough kangaroo named
       Hopalong Brown") W. J. Smith.—SmL

"**Said** a restless young person of Yew." M. C.
    Livingston.—LiLl
"**This** animal is a kangaroo." K. Kuskin.—KuR
The toad and the kangaroo. S. Silverstein.—
    SiL
Wish. M. A. Hoberman.—HoY
Kansas
    "And in the cold, bleak winter time." From
       Moonlight. W. G. Vincent.—FlA
    Crossing Kansas by train. D. Justice.—FlA
    Kansas boy. R. Lechlitner.—FlA
    The trail into Kansas. W. S. Merwin.—PlG
Kansas boy. Ruth Lechlitner.—FlA
"**Karen** can canter, Karen can." See Horse girl
Karma ("Christmas was in the air and all was
    well") Edwin Arlington Robinson.—LiO
Katawumpus. Edward Abbott Parry.—CoI
"**Kate's** on for two, Elise is three." See Balloons
Katherine tattles. Leland B. Jacobs.—CoI
Katz, Bobbi
    Company.—CoDb
    Recipe.—CoPs
    Samuel.—MoGp
    Spring is.—MoGp
    What shall I pack in the box marked
       'summer.'—HoMp
Kaufman, Bob
    Blues note.—AdC
    Unholy missions.—AdC
    When we hear the eye open.—AdC
Kaufman, Shirley
    Her going.—JaPp
Kavanagh, Patrick
    A Christmas childhood, sel.
       "My father played the melodeon."—
          LiPch
    "My father played the melodeon." See A
       Christmas childhood
Keats, John
    On the sea.—PaE
    Sonnet to a cat.—PaB
    To autumn.—PaB
    To my brothers.—PlL
"**Keep** your whiskers crisp and clean." See The
    king of cats sends a postcard to his wife
Keepsake. Eloise Greenfield.—GrH
Kell, Richard
    Husband and wife.—PlL
    Pigeons.—LuZ
Kemp, Lysander
    The three kings. tr.—LiPch
Kennack sands. Laurence Binyon.—PaE
Kennedy, John Fitzgerald (about)
    Belief for JFK. A. R. Ammons.—PlG
    Down in Dallas. X. J. Kennedy.—LiO
Kennedy, Mary
    The newborn colt.—CoPh
Kennedy, X. J.
    The abominable baseball bat.—KeP
    Alarm.—KeP
    An alarming sandwich.—CoPs
    "At Mount Rushmore I looked up into one."
       See Edgar's story
    Attic ghosts.—KeP

A meditation. H. Melville.—PlG
Problems. L. Morrison.—MoO
"True kindness is a pure divine affinity." H. D. Thoreau.—PlL
Kindness to animals. Laura E. Richards.—CoA
King, Dorothy
Billy boy.—WiP
King Edward's prayer book, sel.
The stork, a Christmas ballad.—BaC
King Henry V, sel. William Shakespeare
The horse.—CoPh
King Henry IV, sel. William Shakespeare
"Yea, there thou makest me sad and makest me sin."—PlL
King Johan of Bavonia. N. M. Bodecker.—BoP
King lives. Jill Witherspoon Boyer.—AdC
King, Martin Luther (about)
Assassination ("It was wild") D. L. Lee.—LiO
Death of Dr. King. S. Cornish.—AdC—LiO
King lives. J. W. Boyer.—AdC
Martin Luther King Jr. ("A man went forth with gifts") G. Brooks.—AdC
Martin's blues. M. S. Harper.—AdC
The **king** of cats orders an early breakfast. Nancy Willard.—WiV
The **king** of cats sends a postcard to his wife. Nancy Willard.—WiV
The **King** of Spain. William Jay Smith.—SmL
The **King** of Umpalazzo. Mary Ann Hoberman.—HoY
King, Paul. See De Coccola, Raymond and King, Paul, jt. trs.
King Richard III, sel. William Shakespeare
"Lord, lord, methought what pain it was to drown."—PaE
King Rufus. Y. Y. Segal, tr. fr. the Yiddish by A. M. Klein.—DoWh
"The **king** sent for his wise men all." See W
"**King** still lives." See King lives
"The **king** whose crown was upside down." N. M. Bodecker.—BoHh
Kings. See Rulers; also names of kings, as David, King of Israel
"**King's** cross." Eleanor Farjeon.—CoI
The **kings** from the east. Heinrich Heine.—BaC
"Three holy kings from Morgenland." tr. by Herman Eichenthal—LiPch
Kinnell, Galway
The wolves.—LuZ
Kipling, Rudyard
The power of the dog.—CoG
Thrown away.—CoPh
The white seal's lullaby.—PaE
A **kirgize** in a yurt. N. M. Bodecker.—BoP
"A **kirgize** who lived in a yurt." See A kirgize in a yurt
Kisses ("Flowers for hours") Nikki Giovanni.—GiV
Kisses ("Two") Judith Thurman.—ThFo
Kissing
Hugs and kisses. C. Pomerantz.—PoT
Kisses ("Flowers for hours") N. Giovanni.—GiV
Kisses ("Two") J. Thurman.—ThFo

The mistletoe. C. Scollard.—BaC
Mistletoe. W. De La Mare.—HiS
Under the mistletoe. C. Cullen.—BaC—LiPch
Kisvardai, Anthony
Eating peaches on the beaches.—DuSn
Kit, six years old, standing by the dashboard keeping daddy awake on a trip home from the beach. William Stafford.—LuZ
"The **kitchen** in its readiness." See This winter day
"The **kitchen** today is so full of appliances." See Deus ex machina, or, roughly translated, God only knows what comes out of the machine
Kitchens
Deus ex machina, or, roughly translated, God only knows what comes out of the machine. R. Armour.—BrO
How not to have to dry the dishes. S. Silverstein.—SiL
A man about the kitchen. R. Hobson.—BrO
The teapot and the kettle. M. A. Hoberman.—HoY
This winter day. M. Angelou.—AnO
The toaster. W. J. Smith.—SmL
You take the pilgrims, just give me the progress. L. Rosenfield.—BrO
Kite ("I flew my kite") David McCord.—McO
Kite ("The kite, kept") Valerie Worth.—WoSm
"The **kite,** kept." See Kite
"**Kite** on the end of the twine." See Three signs of spring
Kites
Kite ("I flew my kite") D. McCord.—McO
Kite ("The kite, kept") V. Worth.—WoSm
"There's a lift up aloft for the wing." From Limericks. D. McCord.—McSu
Kitten ("The black kitten") Valerie Worth.—WoM
The **kitten** ("The trouble with a kitten is") Ogden Nash.—BlC
Kittens. See Cats
"**Kittens** have paws they don't have pawses." See Just because
"**Kittle** kittle me." See You and me
Klauber, Edgar
On buying a dog.—CoG
Klein, A. M.
Bandit.—DoWh
For the sisters of the Hotel Dieu.—DoWh
King Rufus. tr.—DoWh
Orders.—DoWh
Psalm of the fruitful field.—DoWh
"**Knee** deep in coldness, muzzle buried white." See Wisdom
Knight, Etheridge
For black poets who think of suicide.—AdC
The idea of ancestry.—AdC
Portrait of Malcolm X.—AdC
"A **knight** of Cales, a gentleman of Wales." Mother Goose.—TrGg
Knights and knighthood
Custard the dragon and the wicked witch. O. Nash.—BlC

Sitting in the sand.—KuD
The snake.—KuD
"The snake is long."—KuR
Snow.—KuD
Spring.—HoMp—KuD—WiP
"Spring again."—KuD
Square as a house.—KuD
"Take a word like cat."—KuD
"This animal is a kangaroo."—KuR
"This cat."—KuD
"This is a tiger."—KuR
Thistles.—KuD—WiP
"Thoughts that were put into words."—KuD
Tiptoe.—KuD
The tree and me.—KuD
Very early.—KuD
When I went out.—KuD
"Where have you been dear."—HoBm—KuD
Where would you be.—KuD
William's toys.—KuD
The witches' ride.—KuD—WaW
"Write about a radish."—KuD
Kwakiutl Indians. See Indians of the
    Americas—Kwakiutl

L

L is for laundry. William Jay Smith.—SmL
Labor. See Work
Laborers. See Work
"The **laburnum** top is silent, quite still." See
    Autumn nature notes
Ladders
    Up the pointed ladder. D. McCord.—McO
Ladies first. Shel Silverstein.—SiL
"**Ladies,** hens, and all you chicks." See Papa
    bantam's goodnight
"The **ladies** inhabiting Venus." See
    Interplanetary limericks
The **lady** and the bear. Theodore Roethke.—
    HiS
Lady-birds. See Beetles
Lady-bugs. See Beetles
"A **lady** came to a bear by a stream." See The
    lady and the bear
A **lady** comes to an inn. Elizabeth
    Coatsworth.—HiS
"The **lady** in gold." N. M. Bodecker.—BoHh
A **lady** in Madrid. N. M. Bodecker.—BoP
A **lady** in Plummer. N. M. Bodecker.—BoP
The **lady** in the chair. Nikki Giovanni.—GiV
"The **lady** in white." N. M. Bodecker.—BoHh
"The **lady** in yellow." N. M. Bodecker.—BoHh
Lady of night. Aileen Fisher.—FiO
A **lady** of Venice. N. M. Bodecker.—BoP
"**Lady** Santa Ana." See An anonymous verse
    from a Puerto Rican Christmas card
"A **lady** who lived in Madrid." See A lady in
    Madrid
"A **lady** who lived in Uganda." See The panda
Lady with a lamp. Myra Cohn Livingston.—LiF
"**Ladybird,** ladybird." Ivy O. Eastwick.—WiP

Ladybirds. See Beetles
Ladybug. Mary Ann Hoberman.—HoBu
Ladybug ("We say ladybug") David McCord.—
    McSu
"**Ladybug** red, when you fly away home." See
    Ladybug
Ladybugs. See Beetles
Ladybug's Christmas. Norma Farber.—LiPch
Laing, Dilys
    The gentled beast.—CoPh
Lake Erie. See The Great Lakes suite
"**Lake Erie** is weary." See The Great Lakes
    suite—Lake Erie
Lake Huron. See The Great Lakes suite
Lake Michigan. See The Great Lakes suite
Lake Ontario. See The Great Lakes suite
Lake St. Clair. See The Great Lakes suite
Lake Superior. See The Great Lakes suite
Lakes and ponds
    The cove. D. McCord.—McO
    Four little ducks. D. McCord.—McO
    From the mailboat passing by. D. McCord.—
      McO
    Lake Erie. From The Great Lakes suite. J.
      Reaney.—DoWh
    Lake Huron. From The Great Lakes suite. J.
      Reaney.—DoWh
    Lake Michigan. From The Great Lakes suite.
      J. Reaney.—DoWh
    Lake Ontario. From The Great Lakes suite. J.
      Reaney.—DoWh
    Lake St. Clair. From The Great Lakes suite.
      J. Reaney.—DoWh
    Lake Superior. From The Great Lakes suite.
      J. Reaney.—DoWh
Laly, Laly. Mark Van Doren.—HiS
Lamb, Elizabeth Searle
    Christmas wish.—BaC
"The **lamb** was bleating softly." Juan Ramón
    Jiménez, tr. by Robert Bly.—LiPch
Lambs. See also Sheep
    "A discerning young lamb of Long Sutton."
      M. C. Livingston.—LiLl
    Hymn ("O li'l lamb out in de col' ") P. L.
      Dunbar.—BrI
    "The lamb was bleating softly." J. R.
      Jiménez.—LiPch
    "The mothers have come back." From
      Sheep. T. Hughes.—HuSs
    New year song. T. Hughes.—HuSs
      New year's song.—LiO
    "The sheep has stopped crying." From
      Sheep. T. Hughes.—HuSs
"**Lambs** bleat." See Speak up
Lament, for cocoa. John Updike.—CoPs
Laments. See also Death
    Adaptation of a theme by Catullus. A. Tate.—
      PlL
    Alexander Crummell, dead. P. L. Dunbar.—
      BrI
    Dead boy. J. C. Ransom.—PlL
    Elegy ("Her face like a rain beaten stone on
      the day she") T. Roethke.—PlL

The last cry of the damp fly. Dennis Lee.—LeG

The last day of the year. Su Tung P'o, tr. fr. the Chinese by Kenneth Patchen.—LiCc

"Last night did Christ the sun rise from the dark." See Easter Sunday

"Last night I dreamed of an old lover." See Grandmother, rocking

"Last night I watched my brothers play." See The brothers

"Last night in the open shippen." See Christmas day

"Last night the sky was reckless." See Sparkly snow

"Last night we anchored in." See Arrival, New York harbor

"Last night when I got up." See Roaches

"Last night, while I lay thinking here." See Whatif

The last quatrain of the ballad of Emmett Till. Gwendolyn Brooks.—AdC

Last snow. Andrew Young.—SaM

"The last snow is going." See Spring

"Last summer I couldn't swim at all." See A year later

The last supper ("They are gathered, astounded and disturbed") Rainer Maria Rilke, tr. fr. the German by M. D. Herter Norton.—LiO

"The last time I kissed her." See Almost ninety

"The last time I was home." See Mothers

The last waltz. Robert Newton Peck.—PeB

The last word of a bluebird as told to a child. Robert Frost.—HoMp
  The last word of a bluebird.—HiS

"Late afternoon, clouds make a hole." See In winter sky

"Late April and you are three, today." See Heart's needle

"Late last night, at wildwitchhall." See Wild witches' ball

"Late pretty late." See The windshield wipers' song

Late snowfall. Beatrice Schenk De Regniers.—ReB

Late starting dawn. Richard Brautigan.—JaPp

Lattimore, Richmond
  December fragments.—LiPch
  Failure.—JaPp
  The lonely swimmers.—PaE
  My uncle.—PlL
  Reports of midsummer girls.—JaPp
  Scene from the working class.—PlL
  A siding near Chillicothe.—FlA

Laughing child. Carl Sandburg.—JaPp

Laughing time. William Jay Smith.—SmL

Laughter
  After the rain. P. B. Janeczko.—JaPp
  The biggest laugh. M. C. Livingston.—LiF
  Cloony the clown. S. Silverstein.—SiL
  Daddy fell into the pond. A. Noyes.—PaI
  Laughing time. W. J. Smith.—SmL
  Laughter ("We are light") M. Waddington.—DoWh

Moochie. E. Greenfield.—GrH
  "The tickle tiger." D. Lee.—LeG
  A ticklish recipe. X. J. Kennedy.—KeP
  Ticklish Tom. S. Silverstein.—SiL

Laughter ("We are light") Miriam Waddington.—DoWh

"Laughter of children brings." See Early supper

Laundresses and laundrymen. See Laundry

Laundromat ("You'll find me in the laundromat, just me and shirts and stuff") David McCord.—McO

Laundry
  L is for laundry. W. J. Smith.—SmL
  Laundromat ("You'll find me in the laundromat, just me and shirts and stuff") D. McCord.—McO
  Our washing machine. P. Hubbell.—PaI
  The shepherd's hut. A. Young.—WaGp
  Wash day wonder. D. Faubion.—BrO

Laurel, Alicia Bay. See Sender, Ramon and Laurel, A. B.

Lavender's blue. Mother Goose.—YaI

"Lavender's blue, dilly, dilly, lavender's green." See Lavender's blue

Law. See also Justice
  Benjamin Franklin Hazard. E. L. Masters.—PlG

"The law says you and I belong to each other, George." See Two strangers breakfast

Lawder, Douglas
  The field.—CoPh

Lawns and lawn care. See Grass

"The lawn is full of footprints." See Sun prints

"The lawnmower." See Lawnmower

Lawnmower. Valerie Worth.—WoM

Lawrence, D. H.
  Intimates.—LuZ
  Sea-weed.—PaE
  Spray.—PaE
  Things men have made.—JaPp

Lawson, Henry
  Grog an' Grumble steeplechase.—CoPh

"Lay me down beneaf de willers in de grass." See A death song

Laying the dust. Denise Levertov.—LuZ—MoGp

Layton, Irving
  Song for Naomi.—DoWh
  "A spider danced a cosy jig."—DoWh

Laziness
  "A lazy old grocer of Eyer." M. C. Livingston.—LiLl
  "Lazy witch." M. C. Livingston.—WaW

A lazy day. Paul Laurence Dunbar.—BrI

"A lazy old grocer of Eyer." Myra Cohn Livingston.—LiLl

"Lazy witch." Myra Cohn Livingston.—WaW

"Lead gently, Lord, and slow." See A hymn

Leadbelly gives an autograph. Imamu Amiri Baraka.—AdC

A leaden treasury of English verse, sels. Paul Dehn
  1. "Ring-a-ring o' neutrons."—BrO

The saint's lament.—LeN
"A sasquatch from Saskatchewan."—LeG
The secret song.—LeG
Skindiver.—LeG
Smelly Fred.—LeG
"The snuggle bunny."—LeG
A song for Nimpkin.—LeN
Spadina.—LeN
Summer song.—LeG
The Summerhill fair.—LeG
"Suzy grew a moustache."—LeG
The swing.—LeG
There was a man.—LeN
"There was an old lady whose kitchen was bare."—CoPs
The thing.—LeN
"The tickle tiger."—LeG
The tiniest man in the washing machine.—LeG
To recognize the lesser glunk.—LeN
Tongue twister.—WiP
Tony Baloney.—CoI
Wellington the skeleton.—LeN
What will you be.—LeG
Winter song.—LeN
With my foot in my mouth.—LeN
Worm.—LeG
You too lie down.—LeN
Lee, Don L. See Madhubuti, Haki R.
Leeuwenhoek, Anton (about)
The microscope. M. W. Kumin.—BrO—MoGp—WiP
"Left like water in glasses overnight." See Love from my father
"Left, right, march the waves." See The Great Lakes suite—Lake Ontario
"The left side of her world is gone." See Strokes
Legacies and bastard roses. Alma Villanueva.—KhI
The legacy. Marge Piercy.—KhI
Legend ("The blacksmith's boy went out with a rifle") Judith Wright.—HiS
Legends. See also Mythology
The colors of night. N. S. Momaday.—MoGd
Legend. J. Wright.—HiS
Legs
The centipede ("I objurgate the centipede") O. Nash.—BlC
Centipede ("This centipede has fifty legs") D. McCord.—McO
Legs. D. McCord.—McSu
The octopus. O. Nash.—BlC
Legs ("When I asked the class, how many legs") David McCord.—McSu
Lehmann, R. C.
The bath.—CoG
Lemonade ("It's lemonading time again") David McCord.—McO
Lemonade ("Lemons are all yellow") Pyke Johnson.—CoPs
"Lemons are all yellow." See Lemonade
"Lend me your mare to ride a mile." Mother Goose.—TrGg

L'Engle, Madeleine
O simplicitas. See Three songs of Mary
Three songs of Mary, sel.
O simplicitas.—LiPch
Lenox Christmas eve '68. Sam Cornish.—AdC
Lenski, Lois
"Old Santa is an active man."—BaC
Snack.—HeB
Leonard, William Ellery
"I feel me near to some high thing."—MaP
The leopard. John Gardner.—GaCb
"The leopard, animal trainers say." See The leopard
Leopards
The leopard. J. Gardner.—GaCb
The leprechaun. Robert Dwyer Joyce.—WaFp
Leslie, Kenneth
Sudden assertion.—CoG
"The lesser glunk has two in front." See To recognize the lesser glunk
Lessie. Eloise Greenfield.—GrH
Lesson for dreamers. Paul B. Janeczko.—JaPp
Lester, Richard
"My cello big and fat."—MoF
"Let Christmas celebrate greenly, for the fir is king." See Jubilate herbis
Let her have it. William Cole.—HeB
"Let me close the eyes of my soul." See Despair
"Let me dry you, says the desert." See Earth song
"Let me fetch sticks." See Bliss
"Let me live with marriage." June Jordan.—PlL
"Let me look at what I was, before I die." See Jamestown
"Let me tell to you the story." See Los pastores
"Let me tell you all about me." Karla Kuskin.—KuD—YaI
"Let me weigh what to say of the bat." From Limericks. David McCord.—McSu
"Let me wrap a poem around you." See Gift
"Let the rain kiss you." See April rain song
"Let them keep it." See And was not improved
"Let us abandon then our gardens and go home." See Justice denied in Massachusetts
"Let us contemplate the sad fate." See A cucumber's pickle
"Let us do justice to the skink." See The skink
"Let us scoot, zip out." See In our tethered boats
"Let us sing praise of the bold and determined mosquito." See The mosquito
"Let weather be blizzardy, zany." Beatrice Schenk De Regniers.—ReB
"Let x be this." See Exit x
"Let's buy pan de agua, daughter." See My Mami takes me to the bakery
Let's dress up. Mary Ann Hoberman.—HoY
"Let's dress up in grown up clothes." See Let's dress up
"Let's give a party." See Snow party
"Let's go see old Abe." See Lincoln monument, Washington

"**Let's** hang up some suet." See Country
  Christmas
"**Let's** pick clovers." See Barefoot
"**Let's** straighten this out, my little man." See
  To a small boy standing on my shoes while
  I am wearing them
"**Let's** think of eggs." See The egg
Letter to a friend. Lilian Moore.—HoMp
Letter to Donald Fall. Alan Dugan.—KhI
Letter to Lord Byron, sel. W. H. Auden
  "My father's forebears were all Midland
    yeomen."—PlL
Letters and letter writing
  Deceased. C. Corman.—JaPp
  Epistle to the Olympians. O. Nash.—BlC
  The fisherman writes a letter to the
    mermaid. J. Aiken.—AiS
  I will write. R. Graves.—JaPp
  The king of cats sends a postcard to his wife.
    N. Willard.—WiV
  Letter to a friend. L. Moore.—HoMp
  Mystery. D. McCord.—McSu
  Packet of letters. L. Bogan.—JaPp
  "Too slow." L. Morrison.—MoW
  "A white bird." L. Morrison.—MoW
  Words, like spiders. P. Wolny.—JaPp
Letters of the alphabet. See Alphabet
Letts, W. M.
  Tim, an Irish terrier.—CoG
Leunig, Michael
  Sitting on the fence.—DuSn
Leverett, Ernest
  S F.—BrO
Levertov, Denise
  Laying the dust.—LuZ—MoGp
  A little carol of the Virgin. tr.—LiPch
  Salamander.—MoGp
  The secret.—LuZ
Leviathan ("Canst thou draw out leviathan with
  an hook, or his"). See Job
Leviathan ("Leviathan drives the eyed prow of
  his face") Peter Quennell.—PaE
"**Leviathan** drives the eyed prow of his face."
  See Leviathan
"**Levinia** was a simple child, to whom words
  meant just." See A word or two on Levinia
Lewis, C. Day
  My mother's sister.—PlL
Lewis has a trumpet. Karla Kuskin.—KuD
Liberty. See also Freedom
  Address to the refugees. J. M. Brinnin.—PlG
  The garret. P. L. Dunbar.—BrI
  "I read your testimony and I thought." From
    To Alexander Meiklejohn. J. Beecher.—PlG
  Liberty ("When liberty is headlong girl") A.
    MacLeish.—PlG
  Ode ("God save the rights of man") P.
    Freneau.—PlG
  Refugee in America. L. Hughes.—PlG
  Stanzas on the emigration to America, and
    peopling the western country. P.
    Freneau.—PlG
  Sympathy. P. L. Dunbar.—BrI

Liberty ("When liberty is headlong girl")
  Archibald MacLeish.—PlG
Libraries and librarians
  In the library. M. P. Hearn.—HeB
  Overdues. S. Silverstein.—SiL
  The plaque in the reading room for my
    classmates killed in Korea. F. D. Reeve.—
    PlG
Life
  Alba. D. Walcott.—JaPp
  "All that is gold does not glitter." J.R.R.
    Tolkien.—WiP
  "And the days are not full enough." E.
    Pound.—JaPp
  Another year come. W. S. Merwin.—JaPp—
    LiO
  Anywhere is a street into the night. N. S.
    Momaday.—MoGd
  At sunset time. P. L. Dunbar.—BrI
  Bad day. M. C. Livingston.—LiWt
  "Behold the child among his new born
    blisses." From Ode: Intimations of
    immortality from recollections of early
    childhood. W. Wordsworth.—PlL
  A birthday memorial to Seventh Street. A.
    Lorde.—AdC
  "Birthday of but a single pang." E.
    Dickinson.—LiO
  "The boy with a wolf's foot." J. Aiken.—AiS.
  Breaklight. L. Clifton.—LuZ
  By rugged ways. P. L. Dunbar.—BrI
  By the stream. P. L. Dunbar.—BrI
  A charm for our time. E. Merriam.—BrO
  Cognation. L. Morrison.—MoO
  Comparatives. N. S. Momaday.—MoGd
  Comparison. P. L. Dunbar.—BrI
  A day at the races. L. Phillips.—CoPh
  The delight song of Tsoai-talee. N. S.
    Momaday.—MoGd
  Dreams ("Dream on, for dreams are sweet")
    P. L. Dunbar.—BrI
  Dreams ("What dreams we have and how
    they fly") P. L. Dunbar.—BrI
  Envoy. E. Dowson.—JaPp
  Fair or foul. L. Morrison.—MoSr
  For each of you. A. Lorde.—AdC
  For my people. M. Walker.—AdC
  For my unborn and wretched children. A. B.
    Spellman.—AdC
  The foundations of American industry. D.
    Hall.—PlG
  The garret. P. L. Dunbar.—BrI
  He had his dream. P. L. Dunbar.—BrI
  "Hello and goodbye." M. A. Hoberman.—
    HoY
  Honey, I love. E. Greenfield.—GrH
  The horse show. W. C. Williams.—PlL
  How many, how much. S. Silverstein.—SiL
  I am waiting. L. Ferlinghetti.—PlG
  If. P. L. Dunbar.—BrI
  "I'm sorry says the machine." E. Merriam.—
    MeR
  In a cafe. R. Brautigan.—JaPp
  In our tethered boats. L. Morrison.—MoW

In terms of physics. L. Morrison.—MoO
Inability to depict an eagle. R. Eberhart.—PlG
The infinity arena. L. Morrison.—MoO
It's all the same to the clam. S. Silverstein.—SiL
"It's comforting." J. D. Simmons.—AdC
Jigsaw puzzle. R. Hoban.—MoGp
Juxtaposing. E. Merriam.—MeR
Krasnopresnenskaya station. N. S. Momaday.—MoGd
Life ("A crust of bread and a corner to sleep in") P. L. Dunbar.—BrI
Life's tragedy. P. L. Dunbar.—BrI
Locus of a point. L. Morrison.—MoO
Mag. C. Sandburg.—PlL
"Make music with your life." B. O'Meally.—AdC
"A man in our village." L. Norris.—NoM
May 1506, Christopher Columbus speaking. W. T. Scott.—PlG
Mementos, 1. W. D. Snodgrass.—PlL
The mosquito. J. Gardner.—GaCb
Mother to son. L. Hughes.—HiS
Mothers ("The last time I was home") N. Giovanni.—AdC
Motorway reflection. J. Aiken.—AiS
Movement song. A. Lorde.—AdC
Mundus et infans. W. H. Auden.—PlL
My life. W. Stafford.—KhI
Myself when I am real. A. Young.—AdC
The mystery. P. L. Dunbar.—BrI
A near pantoum for a birthday. B. Howes.—PlL
New and old gospel. N. Mackey.—AdC
New year song. T. Hughes.—HuSs
    New year's song.—LiO
Nine triads. L. Morrison.—MoSr
No present like the time. D. McCord.—McO
Ocean's edge. L. Morrison.—MoO
The paradox. P. L. Dunbar.—BrI
Points of the compass. E. Merriam.—MeR
Possibilities. L. Morrison.—MoO
Preoccupation. Unknown.—LuZ
The real question. P. L. Dunbar.—BrI
Religion ("I'm a believer") M. Malloy.—LuZ
Reverses. M. Angelou.—AnO
Sabbatical. J. Randall.—KhI
"Sawing the wood." A. Saroyan.—KhI
Scene from the working class. R. Lattimore.—PlL
Science lesson. L. Morrison.—MoO
Sestina. E. Bishop.—PlL
Ships that pass in the night. P. L. Dunbar.—BrI
Slow through the dark. P. L. Dunbar.—BrI
Small moon. H. Nemerov.—JaPp
Some lives. L. Morrison.—MoO
A song for Nimpkin. D. Lee.—LeN
Song in 5 parts. W. P. Root.—KhI
The song of the mad prince. W. De La Mare.—WiP
The sparrow. P. L. Dunbar.—BrI
Street window. C. Sandburg.—JaPp

Summer song. D. Lee.—LeN
Survivor. J. D. Simmons.—AdC
Take time out. M. Angelou.—AnO
Terra cotta. K. C. Lyle.—AdC
That's the way it is. L. Morrison.—MoO
"There is obviously a complete lack of understanding." O. Nash.—BlC
These damned trees crouch. J. Barnes.—KhI
Things ("Went to the corner") E. Greenfield.—GrH
Things that happen. F. Holman.—HoA
Things to do around Taos. K. McCullough.—KhI
Tight rope. I. A. Baraka.—AdC
Time of the mad atom. V. Brasier.—BrO
The trip. W. Stafford.—JaPp
Troubled woman. L. Hughes.—JaPp
The tuft of flowers. R. Frost.—PaB
Turning 30 poem. J. Brandi.—KhI
"Unwatch'd, the garden bough shall sway." From In memoriam. A. Tennyson.—PaB
Vagrants. P. L. Dunbar.—BrI
The valley. S. Moss.—JaPp
Verses versus verses. M. Bell.—KhI
The walnut tree. D. McCord.—McO
Warning to children. R. Graves.—HiS
The way things are. M. C. Livingston.—LiWt
What I learned this year. L. Warsh.—KhI
When we hear the eye open. B. Kaufman.—AdC
Who am I. F. Holman.—HoA
Who, where. L. Morrison.—MoW
"Why fades a dream." P. L. Dunbar.—BrI
A wish. E. Farjeon.—LiCc
You and me and P. B. Shelley. O. Nash.—BlC
Youth ("A young Apollo, golden haired") F. Cornford.—JaPp
Life—Conduct of life. See Conduct of life
Life—Life after death. See Immortality
Life—Life and death
  Almost ninety. R. Whitman.—JaPp
  And of Columbus. H. Gregory.—LiO—PlG
  "Another year, I left NY, on west coast in." From Kaddish. A. Ginsberg.—PlL
  Beyond the years. P. L. Dunbar.—BrI
  Beginnings and endings. P. Koestenbaum.—KhI
  Behind the arras. P. L. Dunbar.—BrI
  Black. J. Chester.—SaM
  The burial. A. MacLeish.—PlL
  Burying ground by the ties. A. MacLeish.—PlG
  Cornelia's song. From The white devil. J. Webster.—PaB
  The cultivation of Christmas trees. T. S. Eliot.—LiO
  "The day was so bright." From A dog in the quarry. M. Holub.—CoG
  Days ("What are days for") P. Larkin.—LuZ
  The eagle's song. Unknown.—PlG
  Elegy for Harriet Tubman and Frederick Douglass. M. Angelou.—AnO
  The end of the Indian poems. S. Plumly.—PlG

"I like winter, spring, summer, and fall." B. S. De Regniers.—ReB

I'd like to. M. A. Hoberman.—HoY

Lasagna. X. J. Kennedy.—CoPs

Peculiar. E. Merriam.—WiP

A person of Florence. N. M. Bodecker.—BoP

Rathers. D. McCord.—McSu

"The reason I like chocolate." N. Giovanni.— GiV

Song ("I like birds, said the Dryad") E. Coatsworth.—WiP

Tee-vee enigma. S. Raskin.—BrO

The **likes** and looks of letters. David McCord.— McO

Lilies

A moon lily. T. Hughes.—HuM

Orange lilies. J. Reaney.—DoWh

Tiger lily. D. McCord.—McO

"Lilies are white." Unknown.—PaB

"Lilies will languish, violets look ill." See The sadness of things, for Sappho's sickness

Limericks

"An affectionate fellow in Cheddar." M. C. Livingston.—LiLl

"An artist who set up his easel." From Limericks. D. McCord.—McSu

"An artistic young person of Churt." M. C. Livingston.—LiLl

"Ask a squirrel, when he's cracking a nut." From Limericks. D. McCord.—McSu

A baker in France. N. M. Bodecker.—BoP

A boa from Goa. N. M. Bodecker.—BoP

Bookworm ("A bookworm of curious breed") M. A. Hoberman.—MoGp

A bride of North Conway. N. M. Bodecker.— BoP

A bright idea. From A lot of limericks. X. J. Kennedy.—KeP

"By rocket, to visit the moon." From Interplanetary limericks. A. Graham.—BrO

"Called a boatman at Charing Cross Pier." M. C. Livingston.—LiLl

"A certain old widow of Chipping." M. C. Livingston.—LiLl

"A confectioner living in Skittle." M. C. Livingston.—LiLl

"A contentious old person named Reagan." W. J. Smith.—SmL

A cook whose dishes. N. M. Bodecker.—BoP

The cougar. R. S. Oliver.—OlC

"Cried a maid in the Manor at Foss." M. C. Livingston.—LiLl

"Cried a man on the Salisbury Plain." M. C. Livingston.—LiLl

A crusty mechanic. N. M. Bodecker.—BoP

Custer's last stand. From A lot of limericks. X. J. Kennedy.—KeP

"A discerning young lamb of Long Sutton." M. C. Livingston.—LiLl

A driver from Deering. N. M. Bodecker.— BoP

"An elephant with a huge trunk." E. Dare.— DuSn

An explorer named Bliss. N. M. Bodecker.— BoP

A farmer of Cwm. N. M. Bodecker.—BoP

Faster than light. A.H.R. Buller.—BrO

"A fine lady of Gorley on Thames." M. C. Livingston.—LiLl

First day of spring. B. S. De Regniers.—ReB

"A forgetful young woman of Tring." M. C. Livingston.—LiLl

Fourth of July. B. S. De Regniers.—ReB

"A frightened soothsayer from Ryde." M. C. Livingston.—LiLl

A gardener's roses. N. M. Bodecker.—BoP

A gard'ner whose plants. N. M. Bodecker.— BoP

Geronomo Hacket. N. M. Bodecker.—BoP

A guard at Fort Knox. N. M. Bodecker.—BoP

"Have you ever reflected on green." From Limericks. D. McCord.—McSu

A hound of Cohasset. N. M. Bodecker.—BoP

"I like winter, spring, summer, and fall." B. S. De Regniers.—ReB

IBM hired her. W.J.J. Gordon.—BrO

"In a roostery somewhere near Fen." M. C. Livingston.—LiLl

In-flight meal. From A lot of limericks. X. J. Kennedy.—KeP

"Just a mouse in the wainscot, they say." From Limericks. D. McCord.—McSu

"A kind woman quite near Barnby Moor." M. C. Livingston.—LiLl

King Johan of Bavonia. N. M. Bodecker.— BoP

A kirgize in a yurt. N. M. Bodecker.—BoP

"The ladies inhabiting Venus." From Interplanetary limericks. A. Graham.—BrO

A lady in Madrid. N. M. Bodecker.—BoP

A lady in Plummer. N. M. Bodecker.—BoP

A lady of Venice. N. M. Bodecker.—BoP

A lass from Milwaukee. N. M. Bodecker.— BoP

A lass on Ben Nevis. N. M. Bodecker.—BoP

Late snowfall. B. S. De Regniers.—ReB

"A lazy old grocer of Eyer." M. C. Livingston.—LiLl

"Let me weigh what to say of the bat." From Limericks. D. McCord.—McSu

"Let weather be blizzardy, zany." B. S. De Regniers.—ReB

A maid in New York. N. M. Bodecker.—BoP

A maid in Old Lyme. N. M. Bodecker.—BoP

A maid of Great Baddow. N. M. Bodecker.— BoP

A man in a suit. N. M. Bodecker.—BoP

A man in a tree. N. M. Bodecker.—BoP

A man in Guam. N. M. Bodecker.—BoP

A man in Karachi. N. M. Bodecker.—BoP

A man in Northchapel. N. M. Bodecker.— BoP

A man of Cologne. N. M. Bodecker.—BoP

A man of Pennang. N. M. Bodecker.—BoP

"A man on the Isle of Wight." M. C. Livingston.—LiLl

Limericks—*Continued*

"A Martian named Harrison Harris." From Interplanetary limericks. A. Graham.—BrO

"A meticulous person of Grange." M. C. Livingston.—LiLl

"Monsters do not scare me much." B. S. De Regniers.—ReB

Murdoch of Mugg. N. M. Bodecker.—BoP

"An obnoxious old person named Hackett." W. J. Smith.—SmL

Odd bird. From A lot of limericks. X. J. Kennedy.—KeP

The old man and the bee. E. Lear.—WiP

"An old man from Okefenokee." W. J. Smith.—SmL

On reading, four limericks. M. C. Livingston.—LiF

"One egg in the nest of that crow." From Limericks. D. McCord.—McSu

The osprey ("Now a hungry young osprey named Lee") R. S. Oliver.—OlC

Ouch, sort of. B. S. De Regniers.—ReB

The panda. W. J. Smith.—SmL

A person from Aruba. N. M. Bodecker.—BoP

A person from Britain. N. M. Bodecker.—BoP

A person in Corning. N. M. Bodecker.—BoP

A person in Rome. N. M. Bodecker.—BoP

A person in Skye. N. M. Bodecker.—BoP

A person in Spain. N. M. Bodecker.—BoP

A person in Stirling. N. M. Bodecker.—BoP

A person named Briggs. N. M. Bodecker.—BoP

A person of Deeping. N. M. Bodecker.—BoP

A person of Ealing. N. M. Bodecker.—BoP

A person of Florence. N. M. Bodecker.—BoP

A person of Haxey. N. M. Bodecker.—BoP

A person of Keene. N. M. Bodecker.—BoP

A person of Nigg. N. M. Bodecker.—BoP

A person of Pinsk. N. M. Bodecker.—BoP

A person of Rame. N. M. Bodecker.—BoP

"A person of Stow-on-the-Wold." M. C. Livingston.—LiLl

Pitcher McDowell. N. M. Bodecker.—BoP

"A pompous old donkey of Yately." M. C. Livingston.—LiLl

A poor man whose pajamas. N. M. Bodecker.—BoP

"A ribald old parrot of Cuffley." M. C. Livingston.—LiLl

"Said a gluttonous man of New Wales." M. C. Livingston.—LiLl

"Said a guide walking round Lacock Abbey." M. C. Livingston.—LiLl

"Said a poor girl from Southend-on-Sea." M. C. Livingston.—LiLl

"Said a restless young person of Yew." M. C. Livingston.—LiLl

"Said a serious scholar from Leech." M. C. Livingston.—LiLl

"Said a three-day-old infant in Leek." M. C. Livingston.—LiLl

"Said an old man from Needles-on-Stoor." M. C. Livingston.—LiLl

A sheik from Riff. N. M. Bodecker.—BoP

Sloth. M. A. Hoberman.—HoY

"A small mouse in Middleton Stoney." M. C. Livingston.—LiLl

Snow song. B. S. De Regniers.—ReB

"So you found some fresh tracks in the snow." From Limericks. D. McCord.—McSu

"So your phone discontinues to buzz." From Limericks. D. McCord.—McSu

Sticky situation. From A lot of limericks. X. J. Kennedy.—KeP

The swallow ("An excitable swallow named Will") R. S. Oliver.—OlC

"Take the dolphin, as smooth and as slick." From Limericks. D. McCord.—McSu

A talented duckling. N. M. Bodecker.—BoP

Television charmer. From A lot of limericks. X. J. Kennedy.—KeP

Tennis clinic. L. Morrison.—MoSr

"There was a fat man of Bombay." Unknown.—LoG

"There was a young farmer of Leeds." Unknown.—LoG

"There was a young fellow of Stroud." M. C. Livingston.—LiLl

"There was a young lady named Harris." O. Nash.—BlC

"There was a young lady named Rose." W. J. Smith.—SmL

"There was a young lass of south Yarra." W. G. Howcroft.—DuSn

"There was a young person named Crockett." W. J. Smith.—SmL

"There was a young woman of Brighton." M. C. Livingston.—LiLl

"There was an old lady named Brown." W. J. Smith.—SmL

"There was an old lady named Crockett." W. J. Smith.—SmL

"There was an old lady named Hart." W. J. Smith.—SmL

"There was an old man from Luray." W. J. Smith.—SmL

"There was an old man in a trunk." O. Nash.—BlC

"There was an old person of Ware." E. Lear.—WiP

"There was an old woman named Piper." W. J. Smith.—SmL

"There was life in the dead tree that fell." From Limericks. D. McCord.—McSu

"There was once a young fellow of Wall." M. C. Livingston.—LiLl

"There's a bittern that booms in a bog." From Limericks. D. McCord.—McSu

"There's a lift up aloft for the wing." From Limericks. D. McCord.—McSu

"There's an ant on the front windowsill." From Limericks. D. McCord.—McSu

"Think of darkness, then think of the mole." From Limericks. D. McCord.—McSu

"Though the termite be sharp as they come." From Limericks. D. McCord.—McSu

Tooth day. B. S. De Regniers.—ReB

A traveler for Dakota. N. M. Bodecker.—BoP

Travelers lugging valises. N. M. Bodecker.—BoP

"The turtle, of course, has a shell." From Limericks. D. McCord.—McSu

The tutor. C. Wells.—WiP

"A venturesome woman of Kent." M. C. Livingston.—LiLl

A viper named Sam. N. M. Bodecker.—BoP

A visit to the gingerbread house. From A lot of limericks. X. J. Kennedy.—KeP

"A voracious old fellow from Clunes." W. G. Howcroft.—DuSn

"Wailed a ghost in a graveyard at Kew." M. C. Livingston.—LiLl

A woman of Ware. N. M. Bodecker.—BoP

Write me a verse. D. McCord.—McO

The young lady of Lynn. Unknown.—WiP

"A young man from old Terre Haute." W. J. Smith.—SmL

The young puppy. A. A. Milne.—CoG

Limericks. David McCord

"An artist who set up his easel."—McSu

"Ask a squirrel when he's cracking a nut."—McSu

"Have you ever reflected on green."—McSu

"Just a mouse in the wainscot, they say."—McSu

"Let me weigh what to say of the bat."—McSu

"One egg in the nest of that crow."—McSu

"So you found some fresh tracks in the snow."—McSu

"So your phone discontinues to buzz."—McSu

"Take the dolphin, as smooth and as slick."—McSu

"There was life in the dead tree that fell."—McSu

"There's a bittern that booms in a bog."—McSu

"There's a lift up aloft for the wing."—McSu

"There's an ant on the front windowsill."—McSu

"Think of darkness, then think of the mole."—McSu

"Though the termite be sharp as they come."—McSu

"The turtle, of course, has a shell."—McSu

Lincoln. Paul Laurence Dunbar.—BrI

Lincoln, Abraham (about)

Abraham Lincoln. R. and S. V. Benet.—LiCc

Abraham Lincoln walks at midnight. V. Lindsay.—LiO—PlG

Anne Rutledge. E. L. Masters.—LiO

"At Mount Rushmore I looked up into one." From Edgar's story. X. J. Kennedy.—LiO

Booth killed Lincoln. Unknown.—LiO

Lincoln. P. L. Dunbar.—BrI

Lincoln monument, Washington. L. Hughes.—LiCc—LiO

O captain, my captain. W. Whitman.—PlG

"There was a darkness in this man, an immense and hollow." From Lincoln. J. G. Fletcher.—LiO

To meet Mr. Lincoln. E. Merriam.—LiCc

"Up from the log cabin to the Capitol." From Lincoln, the man of the people. E. Markham.—LiO

"When lilacs last in the dooryard bloom'd." sel. W. Whitman.—LiO

Lincoln monument, Washington. Langston Hughes.—LiCc—LiO

Lincoln, sel. John Gould Fletcher

"There was a darkness in this man, an immense and hollow."—LiO

Lincoln, the man of the people, sel. Edwin Markham

"Up from the log cabin to the Capitol."—LiO

"Lincoln was a long man." See Abraham Lincoln

Lindon, J. A.

The largest of them all.—CoDb

Learner.—CoPh

More to it than riding.—CoPh

No accounting for tastes.—CoDb

Trouble with dinner.—HeB

Two birds with one stone.—CoPs

Lindsay, Norman

The magic pudding, sel.

"On Tuesday morn as it happened by chance."—DuSn

"On Tuesday morning as it happened by chance." See The magic pudding

Lindsay, Vachel

Abraham Lincoln walks at midnight.—LiO—PlG

The broncho that would not be broken.—CoPh

Daniel.—WiP

A dirge for a righteous kitten.—WiP

The haughty snail-king.—HiS

The little turtle.—PaI

"The moon's the north wind's cooky."—PaI—RuM

The mysterious cat.—WiP

Lineage. Margaret Walker.—AdC—LuZ

"Lines." See New notebook

Lines composed a few miles above Tintern Abbey, sel. William Wordsworth

"For thou art with me here upon the banks."—PlL

Lines on a small potato. Margaret Fishback.—CoDb

Lines to three boys, 8, 6 1/2, and 2 years of age. Franklin Pierce Adams.—PlL

Link rhymes. See Build-on rhymes

The lion ("Altho' the lion seems to wink") Walter Murdoch.—DuSn

Lion ("The beast that is most fully dressed") William Jay Smith.—SmL

The lion ("A lion is fierce") Spike Milligan.—CoA

The lion ("Oh, weep for Mr. and Mrs. Bryan") Ogden Nash.—BlC

The lion ("The old father lion") John
    Gardner.—GaCb
"The lion and the unicorn." Mother Goose.—
    TrGg
"Lion hunger, tiger leap." See The way of
    Cape Race
"A lion is fierce." See The lion
Lions
    I have a lion. K. Kuskin.—KuD
    "If a lion comes to visit." K. Kuskin.—KuR
    Jim, who ran away from his nurse, and was
        eaten by a lion. H. Belloc.—WiP
    The lion ("Altho' the lion seems to wink") W.
        Murdoch.—DuSn
    Lion ("The beast that is most fully dressed")
        W. J. Smith.—SmL
    The lion ("A lion is fierce") S. Milligan.—CoA
    The lion ("Oh, weep for Mr. and Mrs.
        Bryan") O. Nash.—BlC
    The lion ("The old father lion") J. Gardner.—
        GaCb
    "The lion and the unicorn." Mother Goose.—
        TrGg
    Lions ("Bars, wire") V. Worth.—WoM
    "One thing you can say about roaring." K.
        Kuskin.—KuD
Lions ("Bars, wire") Valerie Worth.—WoM
Listen ("Isn't a breeze") Aileen Fisher.—FiO
"Listen children." Lucille Clifton.—AdC
Listen, everything. Aileen Fisher.—FiO
"Listen for noises." See How to tell a tornado
"Listen, the trees are singing." See Spell of the
    woods
"Listen, the wind is still." See Spring thunder
"Listen to the clock strike." See Time
"Listening to the man." See Poem for Otis
    Redding
Litany for Halloween. See "From ghoulies and
    ghosties"
Litter. See Garbage
Little ("I am the sister of him") Dorothy
    Aldis.—PaI
    "I am the sister of him."—MoF
Little ("Little wind, little sun") David
    McCord.—McO
Little Abigail and the beautiful pony. Shel
    Silverstein.—SiL
"Little anna, brown anna." See Anna
"The little bat hangs upside down." See Point
    of view
Little Bingo. Unknown.—BlH
"The little bird sits in the nest and sings." See
    Preparation
"A little bird, with plumage brown." See The
    sparrow
"A little bit of this, sir." N. M. Bodecker.—
    BoHh
The little black dog. Mother Goose.—BlH
"The little black dog ran round the house." See
    The little black dog
"Little Bo-Peep." See The space child's Mother
    Goose
"Little bo-peepals." See Boston nursery rhymes
    —Rhyme for botanical baby

"The little boat at anchor." See Fourth of July
    night
"The little boy." See Junior addict
The little boy and the old man. Shel
    Silverstein.—SiL
"The little boy is fishing." See The fisherman
"Little boy, little boy." Unknown.—WiP
"Little boys and little maidens." See Little
    catkins
"Little boys are like." See Snowflakes
Little brown baby. Paul Laurence Dunbar.—
    BrI
"Little brown baby wif spa'klin' eyes." See
    Little brown baby
"Little Bru and little Chris." See The lady in
    the chair
A little carol of the Virgin. Lope de Vega, tr.
    by Denise Levertov.—LiPch
"The little caterpillar creeps." See Cocoon
Little catkins. Alexander Blok, tr. fr. the
    Russian by Babette Deutsch.—LiO
"Little children skip." Thomas Hood.—MoF
"Little Clotilda, well and hearty." Mother
    Goose.—LoG
"A little colt broncho loaned to the farm." See
    The broncho that would not be broken
"The little cousin is dead, by foul subtraction."
    See Dead boy
Little Dimity. William Jay Smith.—SmL
"Little dog sitting by the fireside." See A dog's
    tale
The little donkey. Francis Jammes, tr. by Lloyd
    Alexander.—LiPch
"The little donkey pulls its cart." See The little
    donkey
"A little dreaming by the way." See The sum
Little elegy. Elinor Wylie.—YaI
The little elf. John Kendrick Bangs.—PaI
Little Fan. James Reeves.—HiS
"Little flame mouths." See Dragon night
"Little ghost." See No TV
Little Giffen. Francis Orray Ticknor.—PlG
"Little girl, be careful what you say." Carl
    Sandburg.—WiP
A little girl I hate. Arnold Spilka.—CoI
"Little girl, little girl, where have you been."
    Mother Goose.—WiP
"A little girl marched around her Christmas
    tree." See The new nutcracker suite
Little girl speakings. Maya Angelou.—AnO
"Little Jack Dandy-prat was my first suitor."
    Mother Goose.—TrGg
"Little Jesus of the crib." Unknown.—BaC
"Little Johnny fished all day." Unknown.—MoF
"Little kangaroos I think." See houses
"Little ladybug." Betsy Maestro.—MaFp
Little league. David McCord.—McO
"Little Lenore." Kaye Starbird.—StC
"A little lonely child am I." See The
    moon-child
"Little lowly people of the earth." See
    Mushrooms
A little lullaby to be read a little bit out loud.
    Charlotte Pomerantz.—PoT

Little, Malcolm. See Malcolm X.
"Little Martha piggy-wig." Clyde Watson.—WiP
"Little Miss Lilly." Mother Goose.—LoG
"Little Miss Limberkin." Mary Mapes Dodge.—CoA
"Little Miss Muffet." Mother Goose.—TrGg
"Little Miss Tuckett." Mother Goose.—CoA—LoG
"Little Miss Tuckett." Unknown.—BeR
"Little mouse." See Race prejudice
"The little newt." See The newt
"A little old lady in Plummer." See A lady in Plummer
"A little old lady of Venice." See A lady of Venice
"A little old man of Derby." Mother Goose.—TrGg
"A little old person of Nigg." See A person of Nigg
"A little pig found a fifty dollar note." Mother Goose.—TrGg
Little piggy. Thomas Hood.—WiP
"Little Polly Flinders." Mother Goose.—TrGg
"The little priest of Felton." Mother Goose.—TrGg
"The little rain." Judith Thurman.—ThFo
"The little red hen does not write with a pen." See Hen
"Little Shon a Morgan." Mother Goose.—TrGg
"The little shrew is soricine." See Shrew
"Little sister." Nikki Grimes.—GrS
"Little square of earth." See Undefeated
Little talk. Aileen Fisher.—PaI
"Little Tee Wee." Mother Goose.—LoG—TrGg
Little things, Importance of
    Little ("Little wind, little sun") D. McCord.—McO
    Praise to the little. N. Farber.—FaS
    The small. T. Roethke.—HiS
"Little tiny puppy dog." Spike Milligan.—CoG
"Little tree." E. E. Cummings.—LiCc—LiPch
The little trumpet. Corrado Govoni, tr. by Carlo L. Golino.—LuZ
The little turtle. Vachel Lindsay.—PaI
"The little white birches." See Little white birches
Little white birches. Aileen Fisher.—FiO
"Little wind, little sun." See Little
"Live lizard, dead lizard." See Witches' menu
Livesay, Dorothy
    Abracadabra.—DoWh
Livingston, Myra Cohn
    Abstract picture, at the museum.—LiWt
    "An affectionate fellow in Cheddar."—LiLl
    After Christmas.—LiWt
    "An artistic young person of Churt."—LiLl
    August.—HoMp
    Bad day.—LiWt
    Bathtub.—LiWt
    Beach.—LiWt
    Bedtime.—LiF
    The biggest laugh.—LiF
    Bubble gum.—LiF

Buildings.—BeR
"Called a boatman at Charing Cross Pier."—LiLl
Car wash.—LiWt
"A certain old widow of Chipping."—LiLl
Civilization.—LiF
"A confectioner living in Skittle."—LiLl
Conversation with Washington.—LiF—LiO
"Cried a maid in the Manor at Foss."—LiLl
"Cried a man on the Salisbury Plain."—LiLl
"Curiosity's not in me head." See On reading
Dinosaurs.—LiWt—MoGp
"A discerning young lamb of Long Sutton."—LiLl
Dusk.—LiF
Earthquake.—LiWt
The enemy.—LiWt
Fantasy, for Jennie.—LiWt
Father.—LiCc
"A fine lady of Gorley on Thames."—LiLl
First Thanksgiving.—LiCc—LiF
For Laura.—LiWt
For Mugs.—LiF
"A forgetful young woman of Tring."—LiLl
Fortune cooky.—LiWt
"Four-way stop."—LiF
Fourth of July.—LiF
Friend.—LiWt
"A frightened soothsayer from Ryde."—LiLl
"Give me a book."—LiF
Growing, for Louis.—LiWt
Haiku for Halloween.—BrIt—LiF
Halloween.—LiF—LiO
Here I am.—CoI
Highway one, movie camera.—LiF
History.—LiWt
"If you don't know the meaning of snook." See On reading
"If you're apt to be ravenous, look." See On reading
I'm sorry.—LiWt
"In a roostery somewhere near Fen."—LiLl
It's neat.—LiWt
July madness.—LiF
"A kind woman quite near Barnby Moor."—LiLl
Lady with a lamp.—LiF
Lamplighter barn.—BeR
"A lazy old grocer of Eyer."—LiLl
"Lazy witch."—WaW
Like Thor.—LiWt
Lonesome.—LiWt
"A man on the Isle of Wight."—LiLl
"A meticulous person of Grange."—LiLl
Morning.—WiP
Mountain.—LiWt
Moving clouds.—LiF
Mummy.—LiWt
My box.—LiWt
My grasshopper.—WiP
Names.—LiWt
Natural history museum.—LiWt
New baby.—LiWt
New year's eve.—HoMp

Lomax, Pearl Cleage
  Jesus drum.—AdC
  Mississippi born.—AdC
  Poem.—AdC
London, England
  Guide to London. J. Aiken.—AiS
  "Oh London bridge what made me start."
    Mother Goose.—TrGg
Lone dog. Irene Rutherford McLeod.—CoG
Loneliness
  Alone ("Lying, thinking") M. Angelou.—AnO
  "At Mount Rushmore I looked up into one."
    From Edgar's story, X. J. Kennedy.—LiO
  Chicken-licken. M. Angelou.—AnO
  Danse russe. W. C. Williams.—KhI
  The dark ("I feared the darkness as a boy")
    R. Fuller.—HiD
  A dog. C. Zolotow.—CoG
  Dog, midwinter. R. Souster.—CoG
  The empty house. S. Spender.—JaPp
  For Laura. M. C. Livingston.—LiWt
  Greyday. M. Angelou.—AnO
  John's song. J. Aiken.—AiS—HiD
  Krasnopresnenskaya station. N. S.
    Momaday.—MoGd
  Loneliness ("I was about to go, and said so")
    B. Jenkins.—MaP
  Lonesome. M. C. Livingston.—LiWt
  The moon-child. W. Sharp.—PaE
  On New Year's eve. Ts'uei T'u.—LiO
  Small moon. H. Nemerov.—JaPp
  Snowy benches. A. Fisher.—FiO
  The tuft of flowers. R. Frost.—PaB
  Up in the pine. N. D. Watson.—WaB
  "The world is not a pleasant place to be." N.
    Giovanni.—JaPp
Loneliness ("I was about to go, and said so")
    Brooks Jenkins.—MaP
"A **lonely** sparrow." Kazue Mizumura.—MiF
The **lonely** swimmers. Richmond Lattimore.—
    PaE
"A **lonely** young viper named Sam." See A
    viper named Sam
Lonesome. Myra Cohn Livingston.—LiWt
"**Lonesome** all alone." See Lonesome
"**Long** ago." See The bear with the golden hair.
"**Long** ago the pterodactyl." See The
    pterodactyl
"The **long** canoe." See Lullaby
Long, Charles C.
  Yei-ie's child.—LuZ
Long distance. William Stafford.—HiS
Long, Doughtry
  #4.—AdC
  "One time Henry dreamed the number."—
    AdC
  Poem no. 21.—AdC
Long gone. Jack Prelutsky.—CoDb
A **long**-haired griggle. Alice Gilbert.—WaM
"A **long**-haired griggle from the land of
    Grunch." See A long-haired griggle
"The **long**-haired yak has long black hair." See
    Yak
Long johns. N. M. Bodecker.—BoHh

Long, long ago. Unknown.—BaC—LiPch
The **long**-nosed smelter. John Jenkins.—DuSn
"The **long** rolling. See The main deep
Long shadows at Dulce. N. Scott Momaday.—
    MoGd
Long story. Lilian Moore.—MoTs
"**Long** time ago, we two set out." See Vagrants
"A **long** time since it seems today." See A New
    Year letter
"**Long,** too long America." Walt Whitman.—
    PlG
"The **long** whip lingers." See Horses
Longfellow, Henry Wadsworth
  Christmas bells.—BaC
    "I heard the bells on Christmas day."—
      LiPch (sel.)
  "From his wanderings far to eastward." See
    The song of Hiawatha
  "I heard the bells on Christmas day." See
    Christmas bells
  One glorious star. tr.—BaC
  Seaweed.—PaE
  The slave singing at midnight.—PlG
  The song of Hiawatha, sel.
    "From his wanderings far to
      eastward."—PlG
  The sound of the sea.—PaE
  "The tide rises, the tide falls."—SaM
  The tides.—PaE
  The witnesses.—PlG
Longing. Paul Laurence Dunbar.—BrI
Longmobile. Shel Silverstein.—SiL
Look. David McCord.—McSu
"**Look.**" Mary Ann Hoberman.—HoY
"**Look,** a house is being moved." See House
    moving
The **look** and sound of words. David
    McCord.—McO
"**Look** at it rain." See Country window
"**Look** at itsy-bitsy Mitzi." See The pizza
"**Look** at the fish." See Fish
"**Look** at the mare of farmer Giles." See The
    mare
"**Look** at them flit." See Fish
"**Look** at us." See Bike ride
"**Look** in the caves at the edge of the sea." See
    Sea fairies
Look not too deep, sel. Laurence Binyon
    "Sleeplessly circle the waves."—PaE
"**Look** one way and the sun is going down."
    See The mockingbird
"**Look** out for the platform." Joan Aiken.—AiS
"**Look** out, look out, boys, clear the track." See
    The broomstick train
"**Look,** the earth is aflame with delight." See A
    Christmas carol
"**Look** there at the star." See Shepherd's song
    at Christmas
"**Look,** there is nothing to see." See Tooth day
"**Look** up, you men, men there at the fire." See
    Annunciation over the shepherds
Look, what am I. David McCord.—McO
Looking ("We poke around and pry about")
    Aileen Fisher.—FiO

How many, how much. S. Silverstein.—SiL

"How much do you love me." Unknown.—WiP

"Huckleberry, gooseberry, raspberry pie." From Father fox's pennyrhymes. C. Watson.—LiCc

Husband and wife. R. Kell.—PlL

I like you. Masuhito.—YaI

"I love." E. Greenfield.—GrH

I love the world. P. Wollner.—PaI

"I love you." From The people, yes. C. Sandburg.—LiCc

"I love you." L. Morrison.—MoW

"I love you in caves and meadows." D. Ignatow.—LuZ

I would like. L. Morrison.—MoW

If. P. L. Dunbar.—BrI

If she sang. G. W. Barrax.—AdC

In May. P. L. Dunbar.—BrI

In space language. L. Morrison.—MoO

In the tree house at night. J. Dickey.—PlL

Inspiration. P. L. Dunbar.—BrI

Instructions to a princess. I. Reed.—AdC

Intimates. D. H. Lawrence.—LuZ

Invitation to love. P. L. Dunbar.—BrI

It's already autumn. E. Pagliarani.—JaPp

Juke box love song. L. Hughes.—YaI

Kidnap poem. N. Giovanni.—YaI

Kisses. J. Thurman.—ThFo

Lesson for dreamers. P. B. Janeczko.—JaPp

"Let me live with marriage." J. Jordan.—PlL

Life's tragedy. P. L. Dunbar.—BrI

"Lilies are white." Unknown.—PaB

Lines to three boys, 8, 6 1/2, and 2 years of age. F. P. Adams.—PlL

The little donkey. F. Jammes.—LiPch

Little elegy. E. Wylie.—YaI

Love ("I love you, I like you") W. J. Smith.—SmL

Love ("A life was mine full of the close concern") P. L. Dunbar.—BrI

Love ("Ricky was "L" but he's home with the flu") S. Silverstein.—YaI

Love don't mean. E. Greenfield.—GrH

"Love is the flower of a day." From Variations on a cosmical air. M. Cowley.—YaI

Love letters, unmailed. E. Merriam.—MeR

Love lyric, II. Unknown.—YaI

Love me, love my dog. I. V. Crawford.—DoWh

Love poem. R. Bly.—JaPp

A love song ("Ah, love, my love is like a cry in the night") P. L. Dunbar.—BrI

Love tight. T. Joans.—AdC—YaI

Love's apotheosis. P. L. Dunbar.—BrI

Love's castle. P. L. Dunbar.—BrI

Love's draft. P. L. Dunbar.—BrI

Love's humility. P. L. Dunbar.—BrI

Love's phases. P. L. Dunbar.—BrI

Love's seasons. P. L. Dunbar.—BrI

Lyrics of love and sorrow. P. L. Dunbar.—BrI

"A man in our village." L. Norris.—CoG

The man in the onion bed. J. Ciardi.—CoPs

Man thinking about woman. H. R. Madhubuti.—AdC

The marriage ("Incarnate for our marriage you appeared") Y. Winters.—PlL

The master-player. P. L. Dunbar.—BrI

The masters. P. L. Dunbar.—BrI

Mementos, 1. W. D. Snodgrass.—PlL

The mermaid. A. Tennyson.—PaE

The merman. A. Tennyson.—PaE

Mi maestro. A. Castillo.—LuZ

Miss Rosie. L. Clifton.—AdC

Morning song. H. Blakely.—AdC

Morning song of love. P. L. Dunbar.—BrI

Movement song. A. Lorde.—AdC

Mundus et infans. W. H. Auden.—PlL

"Music, when soft voices die." P. B. Shelley.—JaPp

A musical. P. L. Dunbar.—BrI

My mother's sister. C. D. Lewis.—PlL

My uncle ("I think of forests palaces and swans") R. Lattimore.—PlL

My valentine ("I will make you brooches and toys for your delight") R. L. Stevenson.—LiO—YaI

Myself when I am real. A. Young.—AdC

A near pantoum for a birthday. B. Howes.—PlL

Need. B. Deutsch.—JaPp

A negro love song. P. L. Dunbar.—BrI

Nelly Myers. A. R. Ammons.—KhI

New and old gospel. N. Mackey.—AdC

Noises. F. Johnson.—AdC

Now long ago. M. Angelou.—AnO

Number theory. L. Morrison.—MoO

Observations. L. Morrison.—MoO

The old flame. R. Lowell.—PlL

On being introduced to you. E. Merriam.—MeR

"One time Henry dreamed the number." D. Long.—AdC

Outing. J. Aiken.—AiS

Overheard in a bubble chamber. L. Morrison.—MoO

The owl and the pussy-cat. E. Lear.—WiP

Passing time. M. Angelou.—AnO

The passionate shepherd to his love. C. Marlowe.—PaB

A pavane for the nursery. W. J. Smith.—HiD—YaI

Pigeon ("Do any thing anything you will") E. Loftin.—AdC

Poem ("I loved my friend") L. Hughes.—LuZ—MaP

Poem ("You said") P. C. Lomax.—AdC

The power of the dog. R. Kipling.—CoG

"A pretty little girl in a round-eared cap." Mother Goose.—TrGg

Psyche with the candle. A. MacLeish.—JaPp

"Pull yourself together, Michael." L. Morrison.—MoW

The queen. P. Neruda.—YaI

"The real people loves one another." R. Penny.—AdC

"Love don't mean all that kissing." See Love
   don't mean
Love fifteen. Lillian Morrison.—MoSr
Love from my father. Carole Gregory
   Clemmons.—AdC
"Love hath the wings of the butterfly." See
   Love's phases
"The love I chased has turned to laurel." See
   Apollo and Daphne
Love in America. Marianne Moore.—PlG
"Love is fair you wind it." See Fair, did you
   wind it
"Love is the flower of a day." See Variations on
   a cosmical air
Love letters, unmailed. Eve Merriam.—MeR
Love lyric, II. Unknown, tr. fr. the Egyptian by
   Noel Stock.—YaI
"Love me, I care not what the circling years."
   See Love's apotheosis
"Love me, I love you." See A mother's song
Love me, love my dog. Isabella V. Crawford.—
   DoWh
Love necessitates. Eugene Redmond.—AdC
Love poem. Robert Bly.—JaPp
A love song ("Ah, love, my love is like a cry in
   the night") Paul Laurence Dunbar.—BrI
Love song ("Great goblets of pudding powder
   in milk") Arnold Adoff.—AdE
Love-song ("If death should claim me for her
   own to-day") Paul Laurence Dunbar.—BrI
Love song for a jellyfish. Sandra Hochman.—
   LuZ—MoGp
Love tight. Ted Joans.—AdC—YaI
"Love which is the most difficult mystery." See
   Psyche with the candle
"Lovely Fia was the summer queen." See A
   mare
Love's apotheosis. Paul Laurence Dunbar.—BrI
Love's castle. Paul Laurence Dunbar.—BrI
Love's draft. Paul Laurence Dunbar.—BrI
Love's humility. Paul Laurence Dunbar.—BrI
Love's labour's lost, sel. William Shakespeare
   "When daisies pied and violets blue."—PaB
Love's phases. Paul Laurence Dunbar.—BrI
Love's philosophy, sel. Percy Bysshe Shelley
   "See the mountains kiss high heaven."—YaI
Love's seasons. Paul Laurence Dunbar.—BrI
"Loving care." See Leave me alone
"Loving looks the large eyed cow." See A
   Christmas prayer
Lowe, Yvonne
   Anger.—CoI
Lowell, Amy
   Sea shell.—SaM
   Trades.—PaI
Lowell, James Russell
   "And they who do their souls no wrong."—
      BaC
   "Never to see a nation born." See Under the
      old elm tree
   Sixty eighth birthday.—JaPp
   Under the old elm, sel.
      "Never to see a nation born."—PlG

Lowell, Robert
   Between the porch and the altar, sel.
      "Meeting his mother makes him lose ten
         years."—PlL
   "Meeting his mother makes him lose ten
      years." See Between the porch and the
      altar
   The old flame.—PlL
Lowther, Pat
   The Chinese greengrocers.—LuZ
Luath. Robert Burns.—CoG
Lucas, F. L.
   Vesper, tr.—LuZ
Lucas Park, St. Louis. Paul Southworth Bliss.—
   FlA
Lucie-Smith, Edward
   The caterpillar.—CoA
   The dinosaur.—CoDb
   The parrot.—HiS
   The shark.—CoA
Lucilius
   A valentine for a lady.—LiO
Lueders, Edward
   Two ways to wake a sleepwalker.—LuZ
Lueders, Joel
   The driver.—LuZ
Luke, Saint. See Gospel according to Luke
Lullabies
   Carol ("I saw a sweet, a seemly sight")
      Unknown.—BaC
   Caterpillar's lullaby. J. Yolen.—YoD
   Coventry carol. Unknown.—LiO—LiPch (at.
      to Robert Croo)
   Dragon night. J. Yolen.—YoD
   The dwarf to her child. J. Yolen.—YoD
   The farm child's lullaby. P. L. Dunbar.—BrI
   Father wolf's midnight song. J. Yolen.—YoD
   The fisher child's lullaby. P. L. Dunbar.—BrI
   The giant to his child. J. Yolen.—YoD
   Good-night. P. L. Dunbar.—BrI
   Grandpa bear's lullaby. J. Yolen.—YoD
   Hale's lullaby. J. Yolen.—YoD
   "Hush my baby, don't say a word."
      Unknown.—WiP
   Inner city lullaby. R. Atkins.—AdC
   A little lullaby to be read a little bit out loud.
      C. Pomerantz.—PoT
   Lullaby ("The long canoe") R. Hillyer.—HiD
   Lullaby ("The trees now look scary") F.
      Holman.—HoA
   Mermaid's lullaby. J. Yolen.—YoD
   Mother worm's hum. J. Yolen.—YoD
   Sleep song. S. Kroll.—WaFp
   The troll to her children. J. Yolen.—YoD
   The white seal's lullaby. R. Kipling.—PaE
Lullaby ("The long canoe") Robert Hillyer.—
   HiD
Lullaby ("The trees now look scary") Felice
   Holman.—HoA
"Lully, lulla, thou little tiny child." See
   Coventry carol
"The lumber camp was quiet, it was noon." See
   The cornering

"**Lumbering** carefully over stone and earth."
  See Tortoise
Lumps. Judith Thurman.—MoGp—ThFo
"**Lumpy** chases pigeons." Jack Prelutsky.—
  PrRh
Lumpy is my friend. Jack Prelutsky.—PrRh
"**Lumpy** likes to pick his nose." See Lumpy is
  my friend
Lumumba, Patrice (about)
  Lumumba's grave. L. Hughes.—AdC
"**Lumumba** was black." See Lumumba's grave
Lumumba's grave. Langston Hughes.—AdC
Lunch ("For plate lunch today I have six
  different choices") Katy Hall.—HeB
Luriana, Lurilee. Charles Elton.—PaB
The **lurpp** is on the loose. Jack Prelutsky.—PrS
Lust. William Matthews.—JaPp
"**Luther** B stepped from his air conditioned
  house." See I hear America griping
Luther, Martin
  "From Heaven high I come to you."—LiPch
Luton, Mildred
  Bullfrog communique.—CoA
  Hossolalia.—CoPh
  Night voyage.—CoDb
  Pliny Jane.—CoPh
  Rhinoceros stew.—CoPs
Lying in a hammock at William Duffy's farm in
  Pine Island, Minnesota. James Wright.—
  FlA
"**Lying,** thinking." See Alone
Lyle, K. Curtis
  Terra cotta.—AdC
Lyme, New Hampshire. David Kherdian.—KhC
Lynch, Charles
  If we cannot live as people.—AdC
  Shade.—AdC
Lynchings. See Hangings
The **lynx.** ("The lynx has never seen the
  sphinx") Robert S. Oliver.—OlC
"**The lynx.**" John Gardner.—GaCb
Lynxes
  The lynx ("The lynx has never seen the
  sphinx") R. S. Oliver.—OlC
  "The lynx." J. Gardner.—GaCb
Lyric ("From now on kill America out of your
  mind") James Agee.—PlG
Lyric for the father of a girl. V. R. Lang.—PlL
Lyrics of love and sorrow. Paul Laurence
  Dunbar.—BrI

M

"**M** for the music, merry and clear." See Merry
  Christmas
M is for mask. William Jay Smith.—SmL
Macaroon. See From the kitchen—Macaroon
"**The macaroon** is quite a chewy cookie." See
  From the kitchen—Macaroon
MacBeth, George
  Boxer pup.—MoGp
  The red herring.—HiS

Macbeth, sels. William Shakespeare
  The making of a charm ("Round about the
  cauldron go")—WaW
  "Thrice the brinded cat hath mew'd."—LiO
McCaig, Ronald and Stuart, Isla
  The pelican.—DuSn
McCarthy, Denis Florence
  The Irish wolf hound.—CoG
McCarthy, Eugene
  Dogs of Santiago.—CoG
McCord, David
  The adventure of Chris.—McO
  Afreet.—McO
  After Christmas.—McO
  Alarm.—McO
  "Alert live reindeer galloping on air." See
    Christmas package
  All about fireflies all about.—McO
  All day long.—McO
  Alley cat.—McO
  Alphabet eta z.—McO
  Animal crackers. See From the kitchen
  Answering your question.—McO
  Ants and sailboats.—McO
  Any day now.—BrO
  "An artist who set up his easel." See
    Limericks
  "Ask a squirrel when he's cracking a nut."
    See Limericks
  "Asked for another name for Santa Claus."
    See Christmas package
  Asleep and awake.—McO
  At low tide.—McO
  At the garden gate.—McO
  August 28.—McO
  Awake.—McSu
  Away and ago.—McO
  The ballade.—McO
  Ballade, an easy one.—McO
  Balloons.—McO
  "Bananas and cream."—McO
  Beech.—McO
  Big question.—McO
  Birds in the rain.—McO
  Boo moo.—McO
  Books.—McO
  "Books fall open."—McO
  Breakfast.—McO
  Bumblebee.—McO
  Butterfly.—McSu
  Cake. See From the kitchen
  Castor oil.—McO
  The cellar hole.—McO
  Centipede.—McO
  Christmas eve. See A Christmas package—
    "My stocking's where"
  A Christmas package, sels.—McO (Complete)
    1. "I hung up a stocking"
    2. "Here's that little girl who wraps up
      each gift"
    3. "Asked for another name for Santa
      Claus"
    4. "Rock candy: hard sweet crystals on a
      string"

5. "Alert live reindeer galloping on air"
6. "Though holly halos hang from many a nail"
7. "That broken star"—LiPch
8. "My stocking's where"—LiPch Christmas eve.—LiCc
9. "A collar for Sokko"
The cinquain.—McO
Circus ("Caleb likes a good sad clown")—McO
"The clerihew."—McO
The clouds.—McO
Cocoon.—McO—WiP
"A collar for Sokko." See Christmas package
Come Christmas.—LiPch—McO
Compass song.—McO
Conversation.—HiS—McO
Corinna.—McO
The cove.—McO
"The cow has a cud." See Five chants
Cricket.—McSu
Crickets.—McO
Crows.—McO
Cucumbers vs pickles. See From the kitchen
Daybreak.—McO
Dividing.—McO
The doctor.—McO
Dr Klimwell's fall.—McO
Dr Ping and Mr Pong.—McO
The door.—McO
Down by the sea.—McO
Ducks walking.—McO
Durenda fair.—McO
Earth song.—McO
Earwig.—McSu
Easter morning, sels.—McO (Complete)
1. "Question, What kind of rabbit can an Easter rabbit be"
2. "Mr Rabbit, a basket on his arm"
3. "Is Easter just a day of hats"—LiCc (sel.)
Eating at the restaurant of How Chow Now.—McO
Elm seed blizzard.—McO
"Every time I climb a tree." See Five chants
Exit x.—McO
Far away.—McO
Farther and further.—McSu
Fast and slow.—McO
"Fat father robin."—McO
Father and I in the woods.—HiS—McO
Figures of speech.—McO
The firetender.—McO
First and last.—McO
The fisherman.—McO
Five chants
"The cow has a cud."—McO
"Every time I climb a tree."—McO—PaI
"Monday morning back to school."—McO
"The pickety fence."—McO—WiP
"Thin ice."—McO
Five little bats.—McO
Flicker.—McO

Food and drink.—McO
A fool and his money.—McO
Forget it.—McO
Four little ducks.—McO
Fred.—McO
Frog in a bog.—McO
Frog music.—McO
From the kitchen, sels.—McO (Complete)
1. Pie
2. Macaroon
3. Fudge
4. Peanut butter
5. Cake
6. Pistachio ice cream
7. Animal crackers
8. People crackers
9. Gingersnaps
10. Cucumbers vs pickles
From the mailboat passing by.—McO
From the Persian.—McSu
The frost pane.—McO
Fudge. See From the kitchen
The game of doublets.—McO
Gingersnaps. See From the kitchen
Glowworm.—CoA—MoGp—McO
Gold.—McSu
Gone.—HoBm—McO
Goose, moose and spruce.—McO
The grasshopper.—CoA—McO—WiP
Groundhog.—McSu
Haiku.—McO
Halloween.—McSu
Hammock.—McO
Harvestman.—McO
"Have you ever reflected on green." See Limericks
"Here's that little girl who wraps up each gift." See Christmas package
Hitchhiker.—BrIt—McO
Hot line to the nursery.—McO
How tall.—McO
How to draw a monkey.—McO
How to learn to say a long, hard word.—McSu
Human beings.—McO
The hunter.—McO
I have a book.—McO
"I hung up a stocking." See Christmas package
I want you to meet.—McO—WiP
The importance of eggs.—McO
In the end.—McSu
In the middle.—McO
In winter sky.—McO
Innuendo.—McO
Inside information.—McO
"Is Easter just a day of hats." See Easter morning
"Isabel Jones and Curabel Lee."—McO
Islands in Boston Harbor.—McO
Ivory.—McO
Jack, Jill, Spratts, and Horner.—McO
Jam.—WiP
Jamboree.—McO

Rain song.—McO
The rainbow.—McO
Rapid reading.—McO
Rathers.—McSu
Rhyme.—McO
Riddle-me rhyme.—McSu
"Rock candy: Hard sweet crystals on a
    string." See Christmas package
Roller coaster.—McSu
Runover rhyme.—McO
Sailor John.—McO
Sally Lun Lundy.—McO
Says Tom to me.—McO
Scat, scitten.—McO
Secret.—McO
The shell.—McO
Shiver my timbers.—McO
Shrew.—McO
Sing song.—McO
Singular indeed.—McO
Skyviews.—McSu
"Smart Mr. Doppler."—McO
Snail.—McO
Snake.—McO
Snowflakes.—HoMp—McO
Snowman.—McO
So run along and play.—McO
"So you found some fresh tracks in the
    snow." See Limericks
"So your phone discontinues to buzz." See
    Limericks
Something better.—McO
Sometimes.—McO
Song.—McO
Song before supper.—McO
Song of the train.—McO
Speak up.—McSu
Spelling bee.—McO
Spike spoke spook.—McO
Spittlebug.—McSu
Spring talk.—McO
Squaw talk.—McO
The star in the pail.—HoBm—McO
The starfish.—McO
Starling.—McO
Suddenly.—McO—MoGp
Summer shower.—McO
Sunfish.—McO
Take sky.—McO
"Take the dolphin, as smooth and as slick."
    See Limericks
Ten nights before Christmas.—McO
Ten twice.—McO
The tercet.—McO
"That broken star." See Christmas package
That's not.—McO
"There was life in the dead tree that fell."
    See Limericks
"There's a bittern that booms in a bog." See
    Limericks
"There's a lift up aloft for the wing." See
    Limericks
"There's an ant on the front windowsill." See
    Limericks

Thin ice. See Five chants
"Think of darkness, then think of the mole."
    See Limericks
"This is my rock."—BeR—McO—WiP
Those double z's.—McSu
"Though holly halos hang from many a nail."
    See Christmas package
"Though the termite be sharp as they come."
    See Limericks
Three signs of spring.—McO
Through the window.—McO
Tick tock talk.—McO
Tiger lily.—McO
Tiggady Rue.—McO
Tim.—McO
"To walk in warm rain."—McSu
Tom and Joe.—McO
Tomorrow.—McO
Tooth trouble.—McO
Traffic lights.—McSu
Trick or treat.—BrIt—McO
Trinity Place.—McO
The trouble was simply that.—McO
Trouble with pies.—McO
Turtle.—McO
"The turtle, of course, has a shell." See
    Limericks
Two times three.—McO
Under the white pine.—McO
Up from down under.—McO
Up the pointed ladder.—McO
"V."—McO
The villanelle.—McO
The walnut tree.—McO
Waltzing mice.—McO
Watching the moon.—McO
The wave.—McO
What am I up to.—McO
"What are pockets for."—McO
When I would travel.—McO
When monkeys eat bananas.—McO
Where.—McO
Whistle.—McO
The white ships.—McO
Who can say.—McSu
Who hasn't played gazintas.—McO
"Who wants a birthday."—McO
The wind.—McO
The windshield wipers' song.—McSu
Wintry.—McO
Wishful.—McO
Witch's broom.—McSu
Witch's broom notes.—BrIt—McO
Wizzle.—McO
Word music.—McSu
A word or two on Levinia.—McO
Worm.—McSu
Write me a verse.—McO
X and Y.—McO
Yellow.—McO
Yellow jacket.—McO
"You mustn't call it hopsichord."—McO
Young Sammy.—McO
Z.—McO

McCreary, F. R.
  The fog.—SaM
McCullough, Ken
  Things to do around Taos.—KhI
MacDonagh, Thomas
  The night hunt.—CoG
MacDonald, George
  A Christmas prayer.—LiPch
  The wind and the moon.—MoF
MacDonald, John
  The cuckoo.—DuSn
MacDonald, Mary
  The alligator.—DuSn
McDougal, Violet
  The sea wolf.—PaE
MacDuff, Edward
  Ed and Sid and Bernard.—BrO
McFadden, David
  Elephant.—DoWh
McFingal, sel. John Trumbull
  "Rise then, ere ruin swift surprize."—PlG
McGinley, Phyllis
  The ballad of Befana.—BaC
  The giveaway.—LuZ
McGonigle's tail. Dennis Lee.—LeG
McGrath, Thomas
  The landscape inside me.—KhI
Machinery. See also names of machines, as
    Clocks
  The ballad of Newington Green. J. Aiken.—
    AiS
  The clock. F. Holman.—HoA
  Deus ex machina, or, roughly translated, God
    only knows what comes out of the
    machine. R. Armour.—BrO
  Handyman. H. Phillips.—BrO
  Highway construction. C. E. Chapin.—BrO
  Homework machine. S. Silverstein.—SiL
  "I'm sorry says the machine." E. Merriam.—
    MeR
  Laundromat. D. McCord.—BrO
  Lawnmower. V. Worth.—WoM
  Our washing machine. P. Hubbell.—PaI—
    WiP
  Tick tock clock. J. Prelutsky.—PrR
  Wash day wonder. D. Faubion.—BrO
  The washing machine. J. Davies.—JaPp
MacIntyre, C. F.
  Monologue of the rating Morgan in
    Rutherford County.—CoPh
Mackay, Charles
  "Be links no longer broken."—BaC
Mackay, Helen
  Autumn for me is.—SaM
McKent, Robert J.
  Pre-history repeats.—BrO
"Mackerel Mack and Halibut Hal." X. J.
    Kennedy.—KeP
Mackerel song. Ted Hughes.—HuSs
Mackerels
  Mackerel song. T. Hughes.—HuSs
Mackey, Nate
  New and old gospel.—AdC

MacLeish, Archibald
  Brave new world.—LiO
  The burial.—PlL
  Burying ground by the ties.—PlG
  Liberty.—PlG
  National security.—PlG
  Psyche with the candle.—JaPp
  The snow fall.—MoGp
  Unfinished history.—PlL
  Where the hayfields were.—HiD
  The young dead soldiers.—LiO
McLennan, William
  Cecilla. tr.—DoWh
McLeod, Irene Rutherford
  Lone dog.—CoG
McMahon, Michael Beirne
  Once upon a nag.—CoPh
McNamar, Hugh
  After supper.—LuZ
  Feline lesson.—LuZ
MacNeice, Louis
  Horses.—CoPh
  Invocation.—HiS
"The mad queen in red." See Q is for queen
Madhubuti, Haki R.
  African poems, sel.
    "We're an Africanpeople."—AdC
  Assassination.—LiO
  Big momma.—AdC
  "Change-up."—AdC
  Man thinking about woman.—AdC
  "We're an Africanpeople." See African
    poems
Maestro, Betsy
  "Black and white kitten."—MaFp
  "Brown furry rabbit."—MaFp
  "Fat polka-dot cat.—MaFp
  "Giant sunflowers."—MaFp
  "Little ladybug."—MaFp
  "Quiet cardinal."—MaFp
  "Raindrops like bubbles."—MaFp
  "Slow-moving turtle."—MaFp
  "Some small smooth shells have."—MaFp
  "These flat stones are coins."—MaFp
  "Three baby raccoons."—MaFp
  "Tiny chickadee."—MaFp
  "Tiny wildflowers."—MaFp
  "We ate a kumquat."—MaFp
  "You greedy starlings."—MaFp
Mag. Carl Sandburg.—PlL
"Maggie and Milly and Molly and May." E. E.
    Cummings.—HoMp
Magi
  At the manger. From For the time being. W.
    H. Auden.—LiPch
  The ballad of Befana. P. McGinley.—BaC
  Carol of the brown king. L. Hughes.—BaC—
    LiPch
  Carol of the three kings. W. S. Merwin.—
    LiPch
  "For we have seen his star in the east, and
    are come." From Gospel according to
    Matthew.—BaC
  Journey of the Magi. T. S. Eliot.—LiPch

The kings from the east. H. Heine.—BaC
"Three holy kings from Morgenland."—
LiPch
The magi ("Now as at all times I can see in
the mind's eye") W. B. Yeats.—LiO—LiPch
The magi ("When they had heard the king,
they departed") From Gospel according to
Matthew.—BaC
"My father played the melodeon." From A
Christmas childhood. P. Kavanagh.—LiPch
The perfect gift. E. V. Cooke.—LiPch
The three kings ("I am Gaspar, I have
brought frankincense") R. Dario.—BaC—
LiPch
Three kings ("Three kings came out of
Indian land") Unknown.—BaC
"We three kings of Orient are." J. H.
Hopkins.—LiPch
The magi ("Now as at all times I can see in the
mind's eye") William Butler Yeats.—LiO—
LiPch
The magi ("When they had heard the king,
they departed") From Gospel according to
Matthew.—BaC
Magic. See also Charms; Enchantment
Amanda is shod. M. Kumin.—CoPh
The cat and the wizard. D. Lee.—LeN
Magic carpet. S. Silverstein.—SiL
Magic words. Unknown.—LuZ
The magical mouse. K. Patchen.—HiS
Merlin & the snake's egg. L. Norris.—NoM
The wizard ("The wizard, watchful, waits
alone") J. Prelutsky.—PrN
Magic carpet. Shel Silverstein.—SiL
Magic jellybean. Jack Prelutsky.—PrR
"The magic of the day is the morning." See
Ballad of the morning streets
The magic pudding, sel. Norman Lindsay
"On Tuesday morn as it happened by
chance."—DuSn
Magic story for falling asleep. Nancy Willard.—
WaG
The magic wood. Henry Treece.—HiD
Magic word. Martin Gardner.—CoI
Magic words. Unknown, fr. the Netsilik
Eskimo, tr. by Edward Field.—LuZ
The magical mouse. Kenneth Patchen.—HiS
"Magical prognosticator." See Halloween
witches
Magnet. Valerie Worth.—MoGp—WoM
Magnetism
Magnet. V. Worth.—MoGp—WoM
Magnifying glass. Valerie Worth.—WoM
The mahogany tree. William Makepeace
Thackeray.—BaC
Mahone, Barbara
Colors for mama.—AdC
Sugarfields.—AdC
A maid in New York. N. M. Bodecker.—BoP
A maid in Old Lyme. N. M. Bodecker.—BoP
A maid of Great Baddow. N. M. Bodecker.—
BoP
The maiden. Rochelle Ratner.—JaPp
A maiden that is makeless. Unknown.—LiO

Mail carriers
The lion. S. Milligan.—CoA
The main-deep. James Stephens.—PaE—SaM
Maine
"Cows are coming home in Maine." R.P.T.
Coffin.—HiD
The rain in Maine. N. M. Bodecker.—BoHh
"Make a joyful noise unto the Lord, all ye
lands." See Psalms—Psalm 100
Make-believe
"After covering the continent." A. Adoff.—
AdE
Butterfish Bay. M. A. Hoberman.—HoY
Closet. J. Thurman.—ThFo
Forty mermaids. D. Lee.—LeN
Frost. E. J. Pratt.—DoWh
"Here we go." M. A. Hoberman.—HoY
Kidnapped. S. Silverstein.—SiL
"Look out for the platform." J. Aiken.—AiS
Man for Mars. D. McCord.—McO
Mrs. Caribou. W. J. Smith.—SmL
Moon theatre. T. Hughes.—HuM
Night landscape. J. Aiken.—AiS—HiD—RuM
"Oak leaf plate." M. A. Hoberman.—HoY
Pad and pencil. D. McCord.—McO
"Pretending to sleep." J. Thurman.—HoBm
Riders. L. Peavy.—CoPh
Sailor John. D. McCord.—McO
The ships of Yule. B. Carman.—DoWh
A sick child. R. Jarrell.—HiS
They're calling. F. Holman.—HoA
This bridge. S. Silverstein.—SiL
Wings. S. J. Crossen and N. A. Covell.—
HoBm
The wise cow makes way, room, and believe.
N. Willard.—WiV
"You're Mrs. Cobble and I'm Mrs. Frome."
M. A. Hoberman.—HoY
Make merry. David McCord.—McO
"Make merry, child, make merry." See Make
merry
"Make music with your life." Bob O'Meally.—
AdC
"Make the bed." See The blessing of the bed
Makers. Nancy Dingman Watson.—WaB
The making of a charm. See Macbeth
Making work for father. X. J. Kennedy.—KeP
Makley, Mike
The new kid.—MoGp
Malcolm ("Nobody mentioned war") Lucille
Clifton.—AdC
Malcolm, a thousandth poem. Conrad Kent
Rivers.—AdC
Malcolm X (about)
Aardvark. J. Fields.—AdC—LiO
El-Hajj Malik El-Shabazz, Malcolm X. R.
Hayden.—AdC
For Malcolm, after Mecca. G. W. Barrax.—
AdC—LiO
For Malcolm who walks in the eyes of our
children. Q. Troupe.—AdC
For Malcolm X ("All you violated ones with
gentle hearts") M. Walker.—AdC
"I remember." M. Jackson.—AdC

Malcolm X —*Continued*
    Malcolm ("Nobody mentioned war") L.
        Clifton.—AdC
    Malcolm, a thousandth poem. C. K. Rivers.—
        AdC
    Malcolm X ("Original") G. Brooks.—AdC—
        LiO
    Portrait of Malcolm X. E. Knight.—AdC
    The pusher. M. Angelou.—AnO
Malcolm X ("Original") Gwendolyn Brooks.—
    AdC—LiO
The **Maldive** shark. Herman Melville.—PaE
Malloy, Merrit
    Religion.—LuZ
"**Mama** never understood." Nikki Grimes.—GrS
"**Mama's** cooking pots of couscous." See By the
    shores of Pago Pago
"**Mama's** shiny purple coat." See I look pretty
"**Mami**, how long will you be away." See Hugs
    and kisses
Man. See Human race
A **man** about the kitchen. Rodney Hobson.—
    BrO
A **man** and his hat. Letitia Parr.—DuSn
Man and owl. Joan Aiken.—AiS
"**Man**, be merry." Unknown.—BaC
A **man** for all seasonings. Richard Armour.—
    CoPs
Man for Mars. David McCord.—McO
The **man** from Snowy River. A. B. "Banjo"
    Paterson.—CoPh
"The **man** from the woods." John Ciardi.—HiS
A **man** in a suit. N. M. Bodecker.—BoP
A **man** in a tree. N. M. Bodecker.—BoP
A **man** in Guam. N. M. Bodecker.—BoP
A **man** in Karachi. N. M. Bodecker.—BoP
A **man** in Northchapel. N. M. Bodecker.—BoP
Man in orbit. D. O. Pitches.—LuZ
"A **man** in our village." Leslie Norris.—CoG—
    NoM
The **man** in the iron pail mask. Shel
    Silverstein.—SiL
"The **man** in the marmalade hat." See The
    man in the marmalade hat arrives
The **man** in the marmalade hat arrives. Nancy
    Willard.—WiV
"The **man** in the moon drinks claret." Mother
    Goose.—TrGg
The **man** in the onion bed. John Ciardi.—
    CoPS—HiS
"The **man** in the wilderness asked me." Mother
    Goose.—TrGg
"A **man** is born gentle and weak." See
    Seventy-six
"**Man** moped along, his moped said." See
    Moped
"The **man** next door gave me a cat." See My
    cat
A **man** of Cologne. N. M. Bodecker.—BoP
Man of letters. Warren Knox.—BrO
"A **man** of low degree was sore oppressed." See
    The crisis
A **man** of Pennang. N. M. Bodecker.—BoP
A **man** of the dunes. N. M. Bodecker.—BoP

"A **man** on the Isle of Wight." Myra Cohn
    Livingston.—LiLl
Man on wheels. Karl Shapiro.—JaPp
Man thinking about woman. Haki R.
    Madhubuti.—AdC
"A **man** went a-hunting at Reigate." Mother
    Goose.—TrGg
"A **man** went forth with gifts." See Martin
    Luther King Jr.
The **man** who stopped the birds. Joan Aiken.—
    AiS
Manatees
    Columbus and the mermaids. E.
        Coatsworth.—PlG
    "With hearts revived in conceit, new land
        and trees they eye." From Good news
        from new England. E. Johnson.—PlG
Mandelbaum, Allen
    Through the vines.—PlL
Mandelstam, Osip Emilevich
    "Don't tell anybody."—LuZ
    "Tartars, Uzbeks, Samoyeds."—LuZ
Manerathiak's song. Unknown, tr. fr. the
    Eskimo by Raymond De Coccola and Paul
    King.—DoWh
Manfred, Freya
    "Moon light."—CoPh
    Projected view of 2000.—KhI
Manger tale. Robert Newton Peck.—PeB
Manhood. Robert Newton Peck.—PeB
"A **manhunt** on the moon is full of horrible
    sights." See A moon manhunt
Mannahatta. Walt Whitman.—PlG
Manners
    The boar and the dromedar. H. Beissel.—
        DoWh
    The gallant highwayman. J. De Mille.—
        DoWh
    Ladies first. S. Silverstein.—SiL
    Manners for a child of 1918. E. Bishop.—PlL
    "Of a little take a little." Mother Goose.—
        TrGg
    The primitiae to parents. R. Herrick.—PlL
    Trouble with dinner. J. A. Lindon.—HeB
Manners for a child of 1918. Elizabeth
    Bishop.—PlL
The **manoeuvre.** William Carlos Williams.—
    JaPp
"**Many** as the troubles upon the old moon are."
    See The armies of the moon
Many crows, any owl. David McCord.—McO
"**Many** horses ran." See Dream image
"**Many** remember the learned professor." See
    If
"**Many** ways to spell good night." See Good
    night
"**Map** of a city with streets meeting at center."
    See Puzzle
Maple trees
    A small elegy. R. Snyder.—JaPp
    Sugar maples. N. D. Watson.—WaB
Maps
    The cloud-mobile. M. Swenson.—HiS

Marble
"I see the cumulus and sky." L. Morrison.—
MoW
Song of the marble earrings. L. Morrison.—
MoW
March
"Dear March, come in." From March. E.
Dickinson.—HoMp
March ("A blue day") E. Coatsworth.—HoMp
The March bee. E. Blunden.—PaB
Muddy March. A. Fisher.—FiO
March ("A blue day") Elizabeth Coatsworth.—
HoMp
The **March** bee. Edmund Blunden.—PaB
A **March** calf. Ted Hughes.—HuSs
March, sel. Emily Dickinson
"Dear March, come in."—HoMp
Marching. See Parades
The **mare** ("Look at the mare of farmer Giles")
Herbert Asquith.—CoA—CoPh
A **mare** ("Lovely Fia was the summer queen")
Kate Barnes.—CoPh
Mare ("When the mare shows you") Judith
Thurman.—CoPh—ThFo
"The **mare** roamed soft about the slope." See
Orchard
Mari Rosa and the butterfly. Charlotte
Pomerantz.—PoT
Marine. Rolfe Humphries.—PaE
"**Mariposa**, butterfly." See Mari Rosa and the
butterfly
Marisol. Charlotte Pomerantz.—PoT
"**Mark** Antony would now rouse fears." See
Transplantitis
Markets and marketing. See also Grocery
stores; Shops and shopkeepers
Banbury fair. E. G. Millard.—WiP
Billy boy. D. King.—WiP
The cost of living Mother Goose. D.
Richardson.—BrO
Mrs. Golightly. J. Reeves.—WiP
My Mami takes me to the bakery. C.
Pomerantz.—PoT
Saturday shopping. K. Edelman.—PaI
Supermarket. F. Holman.—BrO—HoA
There was an old woman ("As I've heard
tell") Mother Goose.—WiP
"Tomorrow's the fair." Unknown.—LiCc
Whistling Willie. K. Starbird.—BrO
"Your mother." S. Cornish.—AdC
Markham, Edwin
Lincoln, the man of the people, sel.
"Up from the log cabin to the
Capitol."—LiO
"Up from the log cabin to the Capitol." See
Lincoln, the man of the people
Markowitz, Arthur
"The day we die." tr.—LuZ
Marks, Shirley
Early warning.—BrO
Marlowe, Christopher
The passionate shepherd to his love.—PaB
The **marmalade** man makes a dance to mend
us. Nancy Willard.—WiV

Marmion, sel. Sir Walter Scott
"Heap on more wood, the wind is chill."—
BaC—LiPch
Marquis, Don
Confession of a glutton.—CoG
Pete at the seashore. See Pete the pup at the
seashore
Pete the pup at the seashore.—MoGp
Pete at the seashore.—CoG
Marriage. See also Brides and bridegrooms;
Courtship; Married life
After ever happily. I. Serraillier.—HiS
A black wedding song. G. Brooks.—AdC
"Who would marry a mineral." L.
Morrison.—MoW
The **marriage** ("Incarnate for our marriage you
appeared") Yvor Winters.—PlL
"**Marriage** on the moon is rather strange." See
Moon marriage
Married life
Addict. J. Montgomery.—BrO
April [sixty-eight] 68. S. Cornish.—AdC
Banjo tune. W. J. Smith.—SmL
A certain peace. N. Giovanni.—AdC
Conversation between Mr. and Mrs. Santa
Claus. R. Bennett.—BaC
Epigram on my wedding day. Lord Byron.—
PlL
An epitaph upon husband and wife, which
died, and were buried together. R.
Crashaw.—PlL
Haiku ("There are things sadder") S.
Sanchez.—LuZ
Henry VIII. E. and H. Farjeon.—WiP
Housewife. J. Miles.—JaPp
Husband and wife. R. Kell.—PlL
"Husband, husband, cease your strife." R.
Burns.—PlL
"In Golden Gate Park that day." L.
Ferlinghetti.—LuZ
"Jack Sprat could eat no fat." Mother
Goose.—TrGg
John Anderson my jo. R. Burns.—PlL
"Let me live with marriage." J. Jordan.—PlL
Mag. C. Sandburg.—PlL
A man and his hat. L. Parr.—DuSn
The marriage ("Incarnate for our marriage
you appeared") Y. Winters.—PlL
Migration. C. G. Clemmons.—LuZ
Moon marriage. T. Hughes.—HuM
My rules. S. Silverstein.—LuZ
Natural tears. T. Hood.—PlL
Old and new. Unknown.—PlL
"Old Ben Golliday." M. Van Doren.—HiS
The old flame. R. Lowell.—PlL
"One time Henry dreamed the number." D.
Long.—AdC
Over the coffin. T. Hardy.—PlL
Rift tide. R. M. Walsh.—BrO
The river-merchant's wife, a letter.
Rihauku.—YaI
Sarah's saga. L. Morrison.—MoW
"She rose to his requirement, dropt." E.
Dickinson.—PlL

"You must wake and call me early, call me early." From The May queen. A. Tennyson.—LiCc

May ("Now children may") John Updike.—HoMp

May be. William Cole.—CoDb

May day. See May

"May each be found thus as the year circles round." Unknown.—BaC

May 1506, Christopher Columbus speaking. Winfield Townley Scott.—PlG

May fly. Mary Ann Hoberman.—HoBu

"May God bless your Christmas." Unknown, fr. the Swedish.—BaC

"May he have new life like the fall." See John Coltrane an impartial review

The May queen, sel. Alfred Lord Tennyson "You must wake and call me early, call me early."—LiCc

"May your large intestine freeze in a knot like a skate-lace." See Curse, on a driver who splashed his new pants when he could have just as easily driven around the puddle

"May your tree." See Christmas wish

"Maybe they're glad." See Frogs in spring

The Mayflower Immigration. R. Frost.—PlG

Mayne, William Haunted.—WaGp

The maze. Lillian Morrison.—MoO

Me ("My nose is blue") Karla Kuskin.—KuD—WiP

Me and my giant. Shel Silverstein.—WaG

Me and Samantha. Pyke Johnson.—CoG

"A meadow sculpture." Ann Atwood.—AtH

Meadows. See Fields

The meal. Karla Kuskin.—KuD

Meals. See Breakfast; Food and eating

Mean song. Eve Merriam.—CoI

Measuring and mixing. Arnold Adoff.—AdE

Meat. See Food and eating

Medicine Castor oil. D. McCord.—McO Transplantitis. L. A. Sobel.—BrO

Meditation Sarah's saga. L. Morrison.—MoW

A meditation ("How often in the years that close") Herman Melville.—PlG

The Mediterranean. Allen Tate.—PlG

Mediterranean sea The Mediterranean. A. Tate.—PlG

The meehoo with an exactlywatt. Shel Silverstein.—SiL

"Meekly the sea." See The even sea

"Meet ladybug." See I want you to meet

"Meet me my love, meet me my love." See The juniper tree

Meet on the road. Unknown.—WiP

"Meeting his mother makes him lose ten years." See Between the porch and the altar

"Meg." See Meg's egg

Meg's egg. Mary Ann Hoberman.—HoY

Melancholy Sometimes. J. Prelutsky.—PrR

"Melissa Finnan Haddie." See Miss M.F.H.E.I.I. Jones

Mellichamp, Leslie Epitaph.—BrO

Mellowness and flight. George Barlow.—AdC

Melville, Herman The Maldive shark.—PaE A meditation.—PlG

"Melvin Martin Riley Smith." David McCord.—McO

Mementos, 1. W. D. Snodgrass.—PlL

Memorial ode. Chief John Buck, fr. the Iroquois Indian.—PlG

Memorial wreath. Dudley Randall.—AdC

Memories. See also Childhood recollections Ballade of the old time engine. E. H. Vines.—BrO A birthday memorial to Seventh Street. A. Lorde.—AdC Bulldozers. F. Dec.—JaPp Cities drowned. H. Newbolt.—PaE "Don't tell anybody." O. E. Mandelstam.—LuZ Elegy for Bella, Sarah, Rosie, and all the others. S. Dorman.—PlG Failure. R. Lattimore.—JaPp Father ("I dreamed my father flicked") A. R. Ammons.—PlL The 5th of July. F. Holman.—HoMp Grandfather ("Each year, as spring returns") J. Aiken.—AiS Grandmother, rocking. E. Merriam.—JaPp—MeR The horses. T. Hughes.—CoPh "I almost remember." M. Angelou.—AnO "I wandered lonely as a cloud." From Daffodils. W. Wordsworth.—PaB Mementos, 1. W. D. Snodgrass.—PlL Memories ("How sweet the silent backward tracings") W. Whitman.—JaPp A memory. W. Allingham.—PaB Minority report. J. Updike.—PlG Miss Rosie. L. Clifton.—AdC "My father remembers." J. Aiken.—AiS Now poem for us. S. Sanchez.—AdC The old flame. R. Lowell.—PlL Old man, phantom dog. F. Eckman.—FlA An old woman remembers. S. A. Brown.—AdC Plainview: 2. N. S. Momaday.—MoGd Reports of midsummer girls. R. Lattimore.—JaPp Scrapbooks. N. Giovanni.—AdC So will I. C. Zolotow.—HoBm The span of life. R. Frost.—CoG The stallion. A. Porter.—CoPh That was summer. M. Ridlon.—HoMp Tom McGreevy, in America, thinks of himself as a boy. From Our stars come from Ireland. W. Stevens.—PlG When you are old. W. B. Yeats.—JaPp

Polyglot.—MeR
Portmanteaux.—MeW
Postcards.—MeR
Prodigal returns.—MeR
Puzzle.—MeB
Rainbow writing.—MeR
Reply to the question, how can you become
  a poet.—MeR
Say nay.—MeR
Schenectady.—WiP
A secret.—LiCc
Secret hand.—MeW
Secret talk.—MeW
Shh.—MeW
Silly speak.—MeB
Some uses for poetry.—JaPp
"The summer night."—MoGp
Summer solstice.—MeR
"Supermarket, supermarket."—MeW
Teevee.—BrO
"Tell me a story."—MeW
Think tank.—BrO
Thumbprint.—MaP
To meet Mr. Lincoln.—LiCc
Tube time.—MeW
Two people.—MeW
Twogether.—MeR
Un-negative.—MeR
Wake up.—MeB
Ways of composing.—MeR
What goes with what.—MeB
What is a rhyme.—MeW
When you.—MeB
Where oh where.—MeB
Which Washington.—LiCc
"Who."—MeB
Whodunnit.—MeR
Will you.—MeB
A word or two with you.—MeW
Merrill, Boynton, Jr.
  The stallion.—CoPh
Merry Christmas ("I saw on the snow") Aileen
  Fisher.—BaC
Merry Christmas ("M for the music, merry and
  clear") Unknown.—BaC
Merry-go-round ("Horses in front of me") Mark
  Van Doren—HiS
Merry-go-round ("I climbed up on the
  merry-go-round") Dorothy W. Baruch.—
  PaI
"**Merry**-go-round on the pepper mill." See
  Carousel brunch
Merry-go-rounds
  Carousel brunch. N. Farber.—FaS
  Horses ("The long whip lingers") L.
    MacNeice.—CoPh
  Merry-go-round ("Horses in front of me") M.
    Van Doren.—HiS
  Merry-go-round ("I climbed up on the
    merry-go-round") D. W. Baruch.—PaI
Merwin, W. (William) S. (Stanley)
  Another year come.—JaPp—LiO
  "At dawn the virgin is born." tr.—LiPch
  Carol of the three kings.—LiPch

Separation.—JaPp—LuZ
Sire.—PlL
The trail into Kansas.—PlG
The unwritten.—LuZ
"You, Genoese mariner."—PlG
The **messiah**, sel. Charles Jennens
  "In Bethlehem is born the holy child."—BaC
"A **messy** old man in Guam." See A man in
  Guam
Messy room. Shel Silverstein.—SiL
"**Metamorphosis**." See Butterfly
Metempsychosis. Kenneth Rexroth.—PlL
Meteors
  The invasion of the star streaks. L.
    Morrison.—MoO
  "There's a lady in Washington Heights." M.
    Bishop.—BrO
Methuselah. Unknown.—BrO
"**Methuselah** ate what he found on his plate."
  See Methuselah
"A **meticulous** person of Grange." Myra Cohn
  Livingston.—LiLl
Mew, Charlotte
  The changeling.—PlL
The **mewlips.** J.R.R. Tolkien.—HiS
Meyer, Bert
  Funeral.—JaPp
Mezey, Robert
  My mother.—KhI
  My stars. tr.—LiO
Mezey, Robert and Starkman, Shula
  Birth. trs.—LiO
Mi maestro. Ana Castillo.—LuZ
Mice
  The cat ("One gets a wife, one gets a house")
    O. Nash.—BlC
  Cat and mouse. R. N. Peck.—PeB
  The cat who aspired to higher things. X. J.
    Kennedy.—KeP
  Conversation. R. Fyleman.—WiP
  Difference. A. Fisher.—FiO
  Feline lesson. H. McNamar.—LuZ
  Great mouse. L. Moore.—MoTs
  "Hickory, dickory, dock." Mother Goose.—
    TrGg
  The house mouse and the church mouse. J.
    Gardner.—GaCb
  "The house of the mouse." L. S. Mitchell.—
    PaI
  "Jack Hall." Mother Goose.—WiP
  "Just a mouse in the wainscot, they say."
    From Limericks. D. McCord.—McSu
  "Little Miss Limberkin." M. M. Dodge.—CoA
  "The little priest of Felton." Mother Goose.—
    TrGg
  The magical mouse. K. Patchen.—HiS
  Merry Christmas. A. Fisher.—BaC
  Mice ("I dropped a pea in the larder") J.
    Aiken.—AiS
  Mice ("I think mice") R. Fyleman.—PaI
  Mice ("Mice find places") V. Worth.—WoSm
  Mice and cat. C. Sansom.—CoA
  "Mice are nice." N. M. Bodecker.—BoHh
  Mice in the hay. L. Norris.—LiPch—NoM

Milton, John
 "And God said, let the waters generate." See
  Paradise lost
 "At thy nativity a glorious quire." See
  Paradise regained
 "But peaceful was the night." See On the
  morning of Christ's nativity
 Comus, sel.
  Neptune.—PaE
  Song.—PaE
 "His place of birth a solemn angel tells." See
  Paradise lost
 Neptune. See Comus
 On the morning of Christ's nativity, sel.
  "But peaceful was the night."—BaC
 Paradise lost, sels.
  "And God said, let the waters
   generate."—PaE
  "His place of birth a solemn angel
   tells."—BaC
  "Two of far nobler shape, erect and
   tall."—PlL
 Paradise regained, sel.
  "At thy nativity a glorious quire."—
   LiPch
 Song. See Comus
 "Two of far nobler shape, erect and tall." See
  Paradise lost
Milton Trimmer. N. M. Bodecker.—BoHh
"Milton Trimmer, ardent swimmer." See
 Milton Trimmer
Mind. See also Wisdom
 By the stream. P. L. Dunbar.—BrI
 My uncle. R. Lattimore.—PlL
 The sky is turning. L. Morrison.—MoO
"Mind your own business." Unknown.—CoI
Minerals
 "I see the cumulus and sky." L. Morrison.—
  MoW
 "Who would marry a mineral." L.
  Morrison.—MoW
Miners. See Mines and mining
Mines and mining
 The black fern. L. Norris.—NoM
 The collier laddie. L. Norris.—NoM
 The pit ponies. L. Norris.—NoM
 The ponies. W. Gibson.—CoPh
Mingram Mo. David McCord.—McO
The mini spooks. Eloise Anderson.—BrIt
Minnesota
 The dark way home, survivors. M. S.
  Harper.—AdC
 Minnesota Thanksgiving. J. Berryman.—PlG
Minnesota Thanksgiving. John Berryman.—PlG
Minnie Morse. Kaye Starbird.—CoPh
Minority report. John Updike.—PlG
Mintz, Ruth Finer
 Piyyut for Rosh Hashana. tr.—LiO
The mirror ("I look in the mirror, and what do
 I see") William Jay Smith.—SmL
"Mirror." Lillian Morrison.—MoW
"Mirror, mirror on the wall." See Wicked witch
 admires herself
Mirrorment. A. R. Ammons.—JaPp

Mirrors. See also Reflections (mirrored)
 Intimates. D. H. Lawrence.—LuZ
 The mirror ("I look in the mirror, and what
  do I see") W. J. Smith.—SmL
 "Mirror." L. Morrison.—MoW
 Mirrorment. A. R. Ammons.—JaPp
 Mirrors ("The sun must have a lot of fun") A.
  Fisher.—FiO
 Moon mirror. T. Hughes.—HuM
 Wicked witch admires herself. X. J.
  Kennedy.—KeP
Mirrors ("The sun must have a lot of fun")
 Aileen Fisher.—FiO
Misapprehension. Paul Laurence Dunbar.—BrI
"Mischievous monkey, behavior cantankerous."
 See The monkey
Misnomer. Eve Merriam.—MeR
Miss Casper's cow. Kaye Starbird.—StC
"Miss Dickinson is gone." See A New England
 sampler
"Miss Flynn has over thirty cats." See The cat
 lady
Miss M.F.H.E.I.I. Jones. Karla Kuskin.—WiP
Miss Rosie. Lucille Clifton.—AdC
"Miss Samantha Ballantine." Wilbur G.
 Howcroft.—DuSn
Miss T. Walter De La Mare.—WiP
"Missak is dancing." See Victims 3 cat 0
"Missak on his." See Cat
Missing. A. A. Milne.—PaI
"Mississauga rattlesnakes." See Rattlesnake
 skipping song
Mississippi
 Mississippi born. P. C. Lomax.—AdC
 The song turning back into itself. A.
  Young.—AdC
Mississippi born. Pearl Cleage Lomax.—AdC
Mississippi river
 The river ("Stick your patent name on a
  signboard") H. Crane.—PlG
Mist. See also Fog
 The mist and all. D. Willson.—PaI
The mist and all. Dixie Willson.—PaI
"The mist has left the greening plain." See
 Morning
Mr Bidery's spidery garden. David McCord.—
 McO
"Mr Frost's barn." See Barn fire
Mister Gaffe. Jack Prelutsky.—PrQ
"Mister Gaffe is quite peculiar." See Mister
 Gaffe
Mr Halloween. David McCord.—McO
Mister Hoobody. Dennis Lee.—LeN
"Mr Macklin takes his knife." See Mr Macklin's
 jack o'lantern
"Mr Macklin's back in town." See Mr Macklin's
 visitor
Mr Macklin's jack o'lantern. David McCord.—
 BrIt—McO
Mr Macklin's visitor. David McCord.—McO
"Mister Malachi O'Malley." See Swept off his
 pins
Mr Mixup tells a story. David McCord.—McO
Mr Mulligan's window. Jack Prelutsky.—PrRh

Mister rabbit. Unknown.—WiP

"Mr Rabbit, a basket on his arm." See Easter morning

"Mister rabbit, mister rabbit." See Mister rabbit

Mr Smeds and Mr Spats. Shel Silverstein.—SiL

Mr Smith. William Jay Smith.—SmL

Mr Spade and Mr Pail. David McCord.—McO

"Mr Spade and Mr Pail and Mr Henry Digger." See Mr Spade and Mr Pail

"Mr Spats." See Mr Smeds and Mr Spats

"Mr T bareheaded in a soiled undershirt." See The artist

Mr Tom Narrow. James Reeves.—HiS

Mistletoe
  Holly and mistletoe. E. Farjeon.—LiPch
  The mistletoe ("It was after the maze and mirth of the dance") C. Scollard.—BaC
  Under the mistletoe. C. Cullen.—BaC—LiPch

The mistletoe ("It was after the maze and mirth of the dance") Clinton Scollard.—BaC

Mistletoe ("Sitting under the mistletoe") Walter De La Mare.—HiS

Mistral, Gabriela
  The stable.—BaC
  To Noel.—LiPch

Mrs Button. James Reeves.—WiP

Mrs Caribou. William Jay Smith.—SmL

Mrs Golightly. James Reeves.—WiP

"Mrs Golightly's galoshes." See Mrs. Golightly

"Mrs Goose had a family of gay little geese." See Family friends

"Mrs McTwitter the baby-sitter." See The sitter

"Mrs Malone." Eleanor Farjeon.—WiP

Mistress Mary. William Jay Smith.—SmL

"Mistress Mary, quite contrary." See Mistress Mary

"Mrs Peck Pigeon." Eleanor Farjeon.—BeR

Mrs Utter. James Reeves.—WiP

A misty day. Paul Laurence Dunbar.—BrI

Mitchell, Lucy Sprague
  "The house of the mouse."—PaI

"The mite." Eugene W. Rudzewicz.—GaCb

"Mix in a large bowl." See Grandma Ida's cookie dough for apple pie crust

"Mix in a large bowl." See Peanut butter batter bread

"A mixture a mingle." See Jingle

Mizumura, Kazue
  "Again and again."—MiF
  "All through the long night."—MiF
  "Behind her misty veil."—MiF
  "Clink."—MiF
  "Coming home late."—MiF
  "A flash of lightning sparks."—MiF
  "Following me all along the road."—MiF
  "In and out of eaves."—MiF
  "Is it waiting just for me."—MiF
  "A lonely sparrow."—MiF
  "The moon is hiding."—MiF
  "Moon, you look so cool."—MiF
  "O moon, who looks in."—MiF
  "The party is over."—MiF
  "Playing hopscotch on the."—MiF

  "Please bird, don't go yet."—MiF
  "Snow makes a new land."—MiF
  "Snowflowers blossom."—MiF
  "So soon the apple blossoms."—MiF
  "The spring snowflakes tickle."—MiF
  "Squeals of children."—MiF
  "Then it came up."—MiF
  "Tulips open one by one."—MiF
  "Walking in the wind."—MiF
  "White petals falling."—MiF
  "Who tossed those golden coins."—MiF
  "Why are all of these flowers."—MiF
  "Wind rustles the trees."—MiF
  "The wind sweeps away."—MiF
  "With the frenzied wind."—MiF

The MJQ. Joyce Carol Thomas.—AdC

"Mo memorized the dictionary." See Memorizin' Mo

Mobile ("Our little mobile hangs and swings") David McCord.—McO

Mobiles
  Mobile ("Our little mobile hangs and swings") D. McCord.—McO

The mock turtle's song. See Alice's adventures in wonderland

The mockingbird ("Look one way and the sun is going down") Randall Jarrell.—HiD

Mockingbirds
  The mockingbird ("Look one way and the sun is going down") R. Jarrell.—HiD

Modern life. See also Atomic age
  And they lived happily ever after for a while. J. Ciardi.—LuZ
  Push button. S. Silverstein.—SiL

"A modest but talented duckling." See A talented duckling

Moffett, Judith
  Plaint of the summer vampires.—LuZ

Moffit, John
  "To look at any thing."—MaP

Mohr, Howard
  How to tell a tornado.—LuZ

Mole ("Jiminy jiminy jukebox, wheatcakes, crumbs") William Jay Smith.—SmL

The mole ("The mole, it may have been vole, I can't distinguish") Roy Daniells.—DoWh

The mole ("Three cheers for the mole") John Gardner.—GaCb

"The mole, it may have been vole, I can't distinguish." See The mole

Molehills. Nancy Dingman Watson.—WaB

Moles (animals)
  "Fat father robin." D. McCord.—McO
  Mole ("Jiminy jiminy jukebox, wheatcakes, crumbs") W. J. Smith.—SmL
  The mole ("The mole, it may have been vole, I can't distinguish") R. Daniells.—DoWh
  The mole ("Three cheers for the mole") J. Gardner.—GaCb
  Molehills. N. D. Watson.—WaB
  "Think of darkness, then think of the mole." From Limericks. D. McCord.—McSu

Molly Mock-Turtle. William Jay Smith.—SmL

"Molly Mock-Turtle of Ocean View." See Molly Mock-Turtle

Momaday, N. Scott
  Abstract: old woman in a room.—MoGd
  Angle of geese.—MoGd
  Anywhere is a street into the night.—MoGd
  The bear.—MoGd
  Before an old painting of the Crucifixion.— MoGd
  The burning.—MoGd
  Buteo regalis.—MoGd
  Carriers of the dream wheel.—MoGd
  The colors of night.—MoGd
  Comparatives.—MoGd
  Crows in a winter composition.—MoGd
  The delight song of Tsoai-talee.—MoGd
  The eagle-feather fan.—MoGd
  "Earth and I gave you turquoise."—MoGd
  Ernesto Maestas instructs Ynocencia Saavedra in the art of acting.—MoGd
  The fear of Bo-talee—MoGd
  For the old man for drawing, dead at eighty-nine.—MoGd
  Forms of the earth at Abiquiu.—MoGd
  Four notions of love and marriage.—MoGd
  The gift.—MoGd
  The gourd dancer.—MoGd
  Headwaters.—MoGd
  The horse that died of shame.—MoGd
  Krasnopresnenskaya station.—MoGd
  Long shadows at Dulce.—MoGd
  The monoliths.—MoGd
  New world.—MoGd
  North Dakota, north light.—MoGd
  Pit viper.—MoGd
  Plainview: 1.—MoGd
  Plainview: 2.—MoGd
  Plainview: 3.—MoGd
  Plainview: 4.—MoGd
  Rainy mountain cemetery.—MoGd
  Simile.—LuZ—MoGd
  The stalker.—MoGd
  The story of a well-made shield.—MoGd
  That woman and this woman.—MoGd
  To a child running with outstretched arms in Canyon de Chelly.—MoGd
  Two figures.—MoGd
  Walk on the moon.—MoGd
  Winter holding off the coast of North America.—MoGd
  The wound.—MoGd
"Momma cooks with a wok." Arnold Adoff.— AdE
"Mommy did you bring my flippers." See Tommy's mommy
"Mommy watches the soap." See I only watch the bubbles
Momotara. Unknown, tr. fr. the Japanese by Rose Fyleman.—WaG—WiP
Mom's mums. David McCord.—McO
"Monday morning back to school." See Five chants
"Monday's child is fair of face." Unknown.— LiCc

Money
  Coins ("Coins are pleasant") V. Worth.—WiP
  The debt. P. L. Dunbar.—BrI
  "The fairies have never a penny to spend." R. Fyleman.—WaFp
  A fool and his money. D. McCord.—McO
  A guard at Fort Knox. N. M. Bodecker.—BoP
  Hand over. J. Aiken.—AiS
  "If I'd as much money as I could spend." Mother Goose.—TrGg
  I'm leery of firms with easy terms. C. S. Jennison.—BrO
  "A little pig found a fifty dollar note." Mother Goose.—TrGg
  Money ("Workers earn it") R. Armour.—WiP
  Penny song. N. M. Bodecker.—BoHh
  The real question. P. L. Dunbar.—BrI
  "These flat stones are coins." B. Maestro.— MaFp
  Tony and the quarter. J. Prelutsky.—PrRh
Money ("Workers earn it") Richard Armour.— WiP
Monkey ("High on a banyan tree in a row") William Jay Smith.—SmL
The monkey ("Mischievous monkey, behavior cantankerous") Robert S. Oliver.—OlC
Monkey vines. Nancy Dingman Watson.—WaB
Monkeys. See also Gorillas
  Anthropoids. M. A. Hoberman.—HoY
  The baboon. J. Gardner.—GaCb
  Brothers. W. Cole.—CoA
  Genus Hylobates. J. Gibbons.—KhI
  How to draw a monkey. D. McCord.—McO
  Monkey ("High on a banyan tree in a row") W. J. Smith.—SmL
  The monkey ("Mischievous monkey, behavior cantankerous") R. S. Oliver.—OlC
  The monkeys and the crocodile. L. E. Richards.—WiP
  When monkeys eat bananas. D. McCord.— McO
The monkeys and the crocodile. Laura E. Richards.—WiP
Monks, Arthur W.
  Twilight's last gleaming.—LiO
Monnoye, Bernard de la
  Patapan.—LiPch
The monoliths. N. Scott Momaday.—MoGd
Monologue of the rating Morgan in Rutherford County. C. F. MacIntyre.—CoPh
Monro, Harold
  Milk for the cat.—PaB
  Overheard on a saltmarsh.—HiS—WiP
"A monster." See Cloud shadow
The monster in my closet. Elizabeth Winthrop.—WaM
Monster menu. Florence Parry Heide.—WaM
"A monster moved into my closet." See The monster in my closet
Monsters
  The abominable snowman. J. Prelutsky.—PrH
  The adaptable mountain dugong. T. Hughes.—HuM
  The alligate. J. Yolen.—YoH

At the sandpile. A. Fisher.—FiO
"Behind her misty veil." K. Mizumura.—MiF
The burrow wolf. T. Hughes.—HuM
Crab-grass. T. Hughes.—HuM
Day and night. A. Fisher.—FiO
Day moon. N. M. Bodecker.—BoHh
Dusk ("Peeking from her room") M. C. Livingston.—LiF
Early moon. A. Fisher.—FiO
Earth moon. T. Hughes.—HuM
Eskimo chant. Unknown.—DoWh
The first. L. Moore.—MoTs
"Following me all along the road." K. Mizumura.—MiF
Full of the moon. K. Kuskin.—KuD—RuM
The harvest moon. T. Hughes.—HuSs
I hope she won't grow any more. N. Farber.—FaS
It's neat. M. C. Livingston.—LiWt
Moon ("I have a white cat whose name is Moon") W. J. Smith.—SmL
The moon ("I see the moon") D. Lee.—LeG
Moon ("Moon have you met my mother") K. Kuskin.—KuD
Moon ("The moon was but a chin of gold") E. Dickinson.—MoGp
The moon ("My puppy looks at the big old moon") A. Fisher.—FiO
Moon-bathers. J. Freeman.—PaE
Moon catchin' net. S. Silverstein.—SiL
A moon hare. T. Hughes.—HuM
The moon hyena. T. Hughes.—HuM
"Moon light." F. Manfred.—CoPh
Moon nasturtiums. T. Hughes.—HuM
"The moon-oak." T. Hughes.—HuM
Moon poem ("Ouu gee whiz") S. Sharp.—BrO
"Moon thirst." T. Hughes.—HuM
Moon thorns. T. Hughes.—HuM
Moon ways. T. Hughes.—HuM
Moon weapons. T. Hughes.—HuM
Moon whales. T. Hughes.—HuM
Moon wind. T. Hughes.—HuM
Moon witches. T. Hughes.—HuM
"Moon, you look so cool." K. Mizumura.—MiF
"The moon's the north wind's cooky." V. Lindsay.—PaI—RuM
Moonstruck. A. Fisher.—FiO
Mushrooms on the moon. T. Hughes.—HuM
Music on the moon. T. Hughes.—HuM
Night game. L. Morrison.—MoSr
Night of the half moon. N. Farber.—FaS
Night song. F. Cornford.—CoG
Nocturn cabbage. C. Sandburg.—HiD
"O moon, who looks in." K. Mizumura.—MiF
Only a little litter. M. C. Livingston.—BrO
"The party is over." K. Mizumura.—MiF
Pi in the sky. J. Aiken.—AiS
Singing on the moon. T. Hughes.—HuM
Skyviews. D. McCord.—McSu
Slug ("The slug") V. Worth.—WoSm
The snail of the moon. T. Hughes.—HuM

"Some people on the moon are so idle." T. Hughes.—HuM
Spell of the moon. L. Norris.—NoM
"Stay, June, stay." From Stay, June, stay. C. Rossetti.—HoMp
Streetfighter moon. L. Morrison.—MoSr
"The summer night." E. Merriam.—MoGp
The sun and moon circus soothes the wakeful guests. N. Willard.—WiV
"Then it came up." K. Mizumura.—MiF
"There is a black field." L. Morrison.—MoW
Two of a kind. N. Farber.—FaS
"Two things the moon steals." A. Atwood.—AtH
Visiting the moon. T. Hughes.—HuM
Watching the moon. D. McCord.—McO
"A weightless balloon." A. Atwood.—AtH
What they say. L. Morrison.—MoW
"Who knows if the moon's." E. E. Cummings.—HiS
The wind and the moon. G. MacDonald.—MoF
Winter moon ("How thin and sharp is the moon tonight") L. Hughes.—HiD
Moon ("I have a white cat whose name is Moon") William Jay Smith.—SmL
The moon ("I see the moon") Dennis Lee.—LeG
Moon ("Moon have you met my mother") Karla Kuskin.—KuD
Moon ("The moon was but a chin of gold") Emily Dickinson.—MoGp
The moon ("My puppy looks at the big old moon") Aileen Fisher.—FiO
"Moon." See The first
"Moon and her mother." See I hope she won't grow any more
Moon-bathers. John Freeman.—PaE
Moon bells. Ted Hughes.—HuM
The moon bull. Ted Hughes.—HuM
Moon cabbage. Ted Hughes.—HuM
Moon catchin' net. Shel Silverstein.—SiL
The moon-child. William Sharp.—PaE
Moon clock. Ted Hughes.—HuM
Moon cloud gripe. Ted Hughes.—HuM
"Moon cloud gripe first shows." See Moon cloud gripe
Moon dog-daisies. Ted Hughes.—HuM
Moon freaks. Ted Hughes.—HuM
The moon haggis. Ted Hughes.—HuM
"The moon haggis has a crazy." See The moon haggis
A moon hare. Ted Hughes.—HuM
"Moon have you met my mother." See Moon
Moon heads. Ted Hughes.—HuM
Moon hops. Ted Hughes.—HuM
Moon horrors. Ted Hughes.—HuM
The moon hyena. Ted Hughes.—HuM
"The moon hyena's laughter." See The moon hyena
"The moon is a dusty place." See Moon witches
"The moon is haunted by a crying." See The moon mourner
"The moon is hiding." Kazue Mizumura.—MiF

"The **moon** is up." See Old Moll
"**Moon** light." Freya Manfred.—CoPh
A **moon** lily. Ted Hughes.—HuM
A **moon** manhunt. Ted Hughes.—HuM
The **moon** mare. Ted Hughes.—HuM
"The **moon** mare runs." See The moon mare
Moon marriage. Ted Hughes.—HuM
Moon mirror. Ted Hughes.—HuM
The **moon** mourner. Ted Hughes.—HuM
"The **moon** moved over last night." See The
    5th of July
Moon nasturtiums. Ted Hughes.—HuM
"The **moon**-oak." Ted Hughes.—HuM
Moon poem ("Ouu gee whiz") Saundra
    Sharp.—BrO
Moon ravens. Ted Hughes.—HuM
Moon roses. Ted Hughes.—HuM
Moon shadow beggars. Ted Hughes.—HuM
Moon theatre. Ted Hughes.—HuM
"**Moon** thirst." Ted Hughes.—HuM
Moon thorns. Ted Hughes.—HuM
Moon tulips. Ted Hughes.—HuM
Moon walkers. Ted Hughes.—HuM
"The **moon** was but a chin of gold." See Moon
Moon ways. Ted Hughes.—HuM
Moon weapons. Ted Hughes.—HuM
Moon whales. Ted Hughes.—HuM
Moon wind. Ted Hughes.—HuM
Moon wings. Ted Hughes.—HuM
A **moon** witch. Ted Hughes.—HuM
"A **moon** witch is no joke." See A moon witch
Moon witches. Ted Hughes.—HuM
"**Moon,** you look so cool." Kazue Mizumura.—
    MiF
Moonlight, sel. W. G. Vincent
    "And in the cold, bleak winter time."—FlA
"**Moonlight** washes the west side of the house."
    See Winter verse for his sister
"The **moon's** roads are treacherous." See Moon
    ways
"The **moon's** roses are very odd." See Moon
    roses
"The **moon's** the north wind's cooky." Vachel
    Lindsay.—PaI—RuM
"The **moon's** thorns." See Moon thorns
Moonstruck. Aileen Fisher.—FiO
Moony art. Ted Hughes.—HuM
Moore, Clement C.
    A visit from St. Nicholas.—LiPch
Moore, John
    A gaggle of geese, a pride of lions.—HiD
Moore, Jonathan
    The rain reminds me.—MoGp
Moore, Lilian
    "Bellowed the ogre."—WaG
    Bike ride.—MoTs
    Clackety click.—MoTs
    Cloud shadow.—MoTs
    Crow wonders.—MoTs
    "Did an artist weave my." See Who cast my
        shadow
    "Do ghouls."—BrIt
    The first.—MoTs
    "Go with the poem."—MoGp

Great mouse.—MoTs
Ground hog day.—MoTs
Hey, bug.—WiP
"I left my head."—WiP
"I'm lumpish." See Who cast my shadow
I'm skeleton.—BrIt
In the park.—MoTs
"Is there a place."—MoTs
Letter to a friend.—HoMp
Long story.—MoTs
The monster's birthday.—WaM
The monster's pet.—WaM
No TV.—BrIt
"On the wall."—MoTs
Partners.—MoTs
Recess.—MoTs
Red.—WiP
"A shadow bird." See Who cast my shadow
"The shadow of a tree."—MoTs
Squirrel.—HoMp
Teeny tiny ghost.—WaGp
Telling time.—MoTs
To the skeleton of a dinosaur in the
    museum.—CoDb
Tonight.—MoTs
True.—WiP
"Until I saw the sea."—HoBm
Wake up, shadows.—MoTs
"We three."—BrIt—LiCc
Who cast my shadow, sels.—MoTs (Complete)
    1. "I'm lumpish"
    2. "Did an artist weave my"
    3. "A shadow bird"
Whooo.—WiP
Winter dark.—HoMp
Witch goes shopping.—WaW
The witch's garden.—WiP
Moore, Marianne
    Abundance.—PaB
    A jellyfish.—JaPp
    Love in America.—PlG
    St. Valentine.—LiO
Moore, Rosalie
    Cats sleep fat.—MoGp
Mooses
    Family friends. M. A. Hoberman.—HoY
Moped. David McCord.—McSu
Morden, Phyllis B.
    Godmother.—PaI
"**More** jam, said Rosie to her Mom." See Magic
    word
More or less. David McCord.—McO
"**More** shower than shine." See Valentines to
    my mother
More to it than riding. J. A. Lindon.—CoPh
"The **more** you heap." Mother Goose.—TrGg
Moreland, Jane P.
    Pony girl.—CoPh
Morgan, Edwin
    The computer's first Christmas card.—LiPch
Morgans in October. Suzanne Brabant.—CoPh
Morike, Edward
    Written on an egg.—LiCc

Morley, Christopher
Of an ancient spaniel in her fifteenth year.—CoG
Song for a little house.—PaI
"The **morn** of life is past." See Old dog Tray
"**Morning**." See By the sea
Morning. See also Wake-up poems
After the storm. From Resolution and independence. W. Wordsworth.—SaM
Alarm clock. E. Merriam.—LuZ
Among the millet. A. Lampman.—DoWh
Ballad of the morning streets. I. A. Baraka.—AdC
Barefoot days. R. Field.—PaI
Carousel brunch. N. Farber.—FaS
Christmas morning. H. Behn.—LiPch
Day. P. L. Dunbar.—BrI
Dog in the fountain. R. Souster.—CoG
First one up. N. D. Watson.—WaB
Frosty morning. A. Fisher.—FiO
Going to school. K. Kuskin.—HeB
Good morning ("Good morning to the great trees") M. Van Doren.—HiD
Good morning, love. P. Blackburn.—KhI
Housewife. J. Miles.—JaPp
"I heard a bird at dawn." From The rivals. J. Stephens.—MoF
"I woke up this morning." K. Kuskin.—CoI—KuD
"In the morning." S. C. Fox.—FoB
Morning ("The mist has left the greening plain") P. L. Dunbar.—BrI
Morning song. H. Blakely.—AdC
Mother worm's hum. J. Yolen.—YoD
The night hunt. T. MacDonagh.—CoG
"Oceanic windy dawn." From Autumn nature notes. T. Hughes.—HuSs
"Once a year, at Easter." A. Fisher.—FiO
"Only the onions." A. Adoff.—AdE
The owl ("When cats run home and light is come") A. Tennyson.—PaB
Plate tectonics on waking. L. Morrison.—MoO
Polyglot. E. Merriam.—MeR
Skiing. R. Burgunder.—HoMp
The song of the old mother. W. B. Yeats.—PlL
The strangers. A. A. Brown.—DoWh
Summer morning. M. C. Livingston.—LiF
Sun for breakfast. N. Farber.—FaS
This morning. L. Clifton.—KhI
Those winter Sundays. R. Hayden.—AdC—MaP—PlL
Unseen horses. J. B. Grayston.—CoPh
Wake up, shadows. L. Moore.—MoTs
Waking ("I said to myself one morning") A. Higgins.—LuZ
What did I dream. R. Graves.—HiD
Winter morning ("A tablecloth all snowy white") A. Fisher.—FiO
With the lark. P. L. Dunbar.—BrI
"The year's at the spring." From Pippa passes. R. Browning.—MoF
Pippa's song.—PaB

Zebra. J. Thurman.—MoGp—ThFo
Morning ("Everyone is tight asleep") Myra Cohn Livingston.—WiP
Morning ("The mist has left the greening plain") Paul Laurence Dunbar.—BrI
"The **morning** after winter." See The chickadee
Morning fog. N. M. Bodecker.—BoHh
"**Morning,** morning will produce." See Breakfast
Morning song. Henry Blakely.—AdC
Morning song of love. Paul Laurence Dunbar.—BrI
Morning star. Unknown.—BaC
"**Morning** star, O cheering sight." See Morning star
"**Mornings** before breakfast." See First one up
Morris, John N.
Thanksgiving.—LiO
Morris, William
The earthly paradise, sel.
"Under a bent when the night was deep."—LiPch
"Under a bent when the night was deep." See The earthly paradise
Morrison, Lillian
After all.—MoW
The angels of motion.—MoSr
Astronomical note.—MoO
At first sight.—MoW
At the beach.—MoW
Axiom.—MoW
Beautiful Ben.—MoSr
"Blow a curve."—MoO
The boxer.—MoSr
Burning bright.—MoW
Chico.—MoSr
Coastline olympics.—MoSr
Cognation.—MoO
The completion.—MoSr
"The consonants laid low."—MoW
The cross porpoise.—MoW
Cycle.—MoO
Dis-play.—MoSr
Dream image.—MoW
Fair, did you wind it.—MoW
Fair or foul.—MoSr
"Fanfare."—MoW
Felicitations.—MoO
Fireman, save my soul.—MoW
Fish on a dish.—MoW
The flow, the void.—MoO
Forms of praise.—MoSr
Francie.—MoSr
F's and g's dancing.—MoW
Girl child.—MoSr
Green and blue in Colorado.—MoW
Holes.—MoO
House call.—MoO
"How do you write the dusk."—MoO
I love all gravity defiers.—MoSr
"I love you."—MoW
"I see the cumulus and sky."—MoW
I would like.—MoW

The **mother** ("It was a noon of freedom")
  Malcolm Cowley.—PIL
Mother ("My mother says") Kaye Starbird.—
  StC
The **mother** ("On the hilltop, close to the house
  of the empress') Babette Deutsch.—PIL
Mother cat. Aileen Fisher.—FiO
Mother cat's purr. Jane Yolen.—YoD
"**Mother** come quick." See Alarm
"**Mother**, dear, was it just a year." See The
  divorce
Mother Goose. See also Nursery rhymes—
  Chinese;—Danish;—French;—Japanese;—
  Scottish
  "Alas, alas, for Miss Mackay."—LoG
  "An apple a day."—TrGg
  "Arthur O'Bower has broken his band."—
    TrGg
  "As I was going out one day."—LoG
  "As I was going to Darby."—TrGg
  "As I went over the water."—TrGg
  "Aunt Elise."—LoG
  "Baby, baby, naughty baby."—TrGg
  The bad rider. See "I had a little pony"
  "Barber, barber, shave a pig."—TrGg
  "Bat, bat, come under my hat."—TrGg
  "Bell-horses, bell-horses."—TrGg
  "Bow, wow, wow."—BlH
  Buff.—BlH
  "Charley, barley, buck and rye."—TrGg
  "Charley, Charley."—LoG
  "Cheese and bread for gentlemen."—TrGg
  Christmas. See "Christmas is coming, the
    geese are getting fat"
  "Christmas is coming, the geese are getting
    fat."—LiC—LiPch
      Christmas.—BaC
  "Coo-oo, coo-oo."—TrGg
  "Darby and Joan were dressed in black."—
    TrGg
  "Diddle, diddle, dumpling, my son John."—
    TrGg
  "Different people have different 'pinions."—
    TrGg
  "A diller, a dollar."—TrGg
  "Dingty diddledy, my mammy's maid."—
    LoG—TrGg
  "Doctor Foster went to Glo'ster.—TrGg
  "Fe, fi, fo, fum."—WaG
    "Fee, fie, fo, fum."—TrGg
  "Fee, fie, fo, fum." See "Fe, fi, fo, fum"
  Fire ("Fire, fire, said Mrs. Dyer"). See "Fire,
    fire"
  "Fire, fire."—WiP
    Fire ("Fire, fire, said Mrs. Dyer")—BeR
    "Fire, fire, said Mrs. McGuire."—TrGg
  "Fire, fire, said Mrs. McGuire." See "Fire,
    fire"
  "Flying man, flying man."—LoG
  "For want of a nail, the shoe was lost."—WiP
  "Four stiff-standers."—TrGg
  "The fox gives warning."—TrGg
  "The giant Jim."—LoG
  "The grand old Duke of York."—TrGg

  "Granfa' Grig had a pig."—TrGg
  "Gray goose and gander."—TrGg
  "The greedy man is he who sits."—LoG
  "Gregory Griggs, Gregory Griggs."—LoG
  "Handy-spandy."—LoG
  "Hannah Bantry."—LoG
  "Hark, hark, the dogs do bark."—BlH—LoG
  "Hector Protector was dressed all in
    green."—TrGg
  "A hedge between."—TrGg
  "Here I am, little jumping Joan."—TrGg
  "Here stands a fist."—TrGg
  "Hey diddle diddle, the cat and the
    fiddle."—BlH—TrGg
  "Hickory, dickory, dock."—TrGg
  "Higgleby, piggleby, my black hen."—TrGg
  "Higglety, pigglety, pop."—TrGg
  "How many miles to Dover-town."—TrGg
  "Humpty Dumpty sat on a wall."—TrGg
  "I had a little cow."—WiP
  "I had a little dog, and his name was Bill."—
    TrGg
  I had a little doggy.—BlH
  "I had a little hen."—WiP
  "I had a little pony."—WiP
    The bad rider.—CoPh
  "I know I have lost my train."—LoG
  "If all the seas were one sea."—WiP
  "If I'd as much money as I could spend."—
    TrGg
  "If you would see a church miswent."—TrGg
  "I'll sing you a song."—TrGg
  "I'm the king of the castle."—TrGg
  "In a cottage in Fife."—LoG
  "It costs little Gossip her income for
    shoes."—TrGg
  "J was Joe Jenkins."—TrGg
  "Jack be nimble."—TrGg
  "Jack Hall."—WiP
  "Jack Sprat could eat no fat."—TrGg
  "Jeanie come tie my."—TrGg
  "Jerry Hall."—LoG
  "A knight of Cales, a gentleman of Wales."—
    TrGg
  Lavender's blue.—YaI
  "Lend me your mare to ride a mile."—TrGg
  "The lion and the unicorn."—TrGg
  The little black dog.—BlH
  "Little Clotilda, well and hearty."—LoG
  "Little girl, little girl, where have you
    been."—WiP
  "Little Jack Dandy-prat was my first
    suitor."—TrGg
  "Little Miss Lilly."—LoG
  "Little Miss Muffet."—TrGg
  "Little Miss Tuckett."—BeR—CoA—LoG
  "A little old man of Derby."—TrGg
  "A little pig found a fifty dollar note."—TrGg
  "Little Polly Flinders."—TrGg
  "The little priest of Felton."—TrGg
  "Little Shon a Morgan."—TrGg
  "Little Tee Wee."—LoG—TrGg
  "The man in the moon drinks claret."—TrGg

"Mother, may I stay up tonight." See Conversation

"Mother, may I take a swim." Unknown.—WiP

Mother owl's song. Jane Yolen.—YoD

"A mother skunk all black and white." See How many

Mother to son. Langston Hughes.—HiS—LiCc

"Mother wave sings soft to sleep." See Ocean at night

"Mother why have you brought me here, oh, where is father." See My brother's dream

Motherhood. See Mothers and motherhood

Mother worm's hum. Jane Yolen.—YoD

Mothers and motherhood. See also Home and family life; Love—Maternal

All the little animals. M. Rukeyser.—PlL

"Another year, I left NY, on west coast in." From Kaddish. A. Ginsberg.—PlL

At night. R. Eberhart.—PlL

The bloody show. J. Murray.—KhI

The burial. A MacLeish.—PlL

Colors for mama. B. Mahone.—AdC

Country cat. E. Coatsworth.—WiP

Dance song 6. M. Van Doren.—HiD

Daybreak. F. L. Phillips.—AdC

"Earth fills her lap with pleasures of her own." From Ode: Intimations of immortality from recollections of early childhood. W. Wordsworth.—PlL

Elegy for Bella, Sarah, Rosie, and all the others. S. Dorman.—PlG

Emma. Yvonne.—AdC

Falling asleep. I. Serraillier.—HiD

"Farewell to an idea, the mother's face." From The auroras of autumn. W. Stevens.—PlL

For deLawd. L. Clifton.—AdC

For muh' dear. C. M. Rodgers.—AdC

For sapphires. C. M. Rodgers.—AdC

Generations. J. D. Simmons.—AdC

The great mother. G. Snyder.—LiCc

"Here we go." M. A. Hoberman.—HoY

The horse show. W. C. Williams.—PlL

"I brought my mother buttercups." A. Fisher.—FiO

"I love you." From The people, yes. C. Sandburg.—LiCc

"If there are any heavens my mother will (all by herself) have. E. E. Cummings.—PlL

In the old house. J. Aiken.—AiS

John J. M. Angelou.—AnO

A leave taking. Y. Winters.—PlL

"Little Polly Flinders." Mother Goose.—TrGg

"Mama never understood." N. Grimes.—GrS

Marthe, the mar, la mer, la mere, tram, he, rath, mare, hear my mere, my mart. C. Inez.—KhI

Mary, mother of Christ. C. Cullen.—LiPch

"Meeting his mother makes him lose ten years." From Between the porch and the altar. R. Lowell.—PlL

"Momma cooks with a wok." A. Adoff.—AdE

The mother ("It was a noon of freedom") M. Cowley.—PlL

Mother ("My mother says") K. Starbird.—StC

The mother ("On the hilltop, close to the house of the emperor") B. Deutsch.—PlL

Mother cat. A. Fisher.—FiO

Mother to son. L. Hughes.—HiS—LiCc

Mothers ("The last time I was home") N. Giovanni.—AdC

Mothers ("Oh mother") A. Sexton.—PlL

"The mothers have come back." From Sheep. T. Hughes.—HuSs

Mother's helper. A. Fisher.—FiO

Mother's nerves. X. J. Kennedy.—CoI

Mother's pig. X. J. Kennedy.—KeP

A mother's song. C. Rossetti.—PaI

My brother's dream. J. Aiken.—AiS

"My father which art in earth." From Changing mind. C. Aiken.—PlL

My mother. R. Mezey.—KhI

"My mother's mad for bargain sales." X. J. Kennedy.—KeP

My mother's sister. C. D. Lewis.—PlL

O simplicitas. From Three songs of Mary. M. L'Engle.—LiPch

"Once in the winter." From The forsaken. D. C. Scott.—DoWh

"Our blackness did not come to us whole." L. B. Bragg.—AdC

Outing. J. Aiken.—AiS

Sam's world. S. Cornish.—AdC—LiCc

Self expression. A. Darr.—LuZ

"She sent me out to play again." N. Grimes.—GrS

"The sheep has stopped crying." From Sheep. T. Hughes.—HuSs

Sometimes I think of Maryland. J. Braxton.—AdC

The song of the old mother. W. B. Yeats.—PlL

The spare quilt. J. P. Bishop.—PlG

Sugarfields. B. Mahone.—AdC

Tommy's mommy. N. Giovanni.—GiV

Unrealized. T. Hardy.—PlL

Valentines to my mother. C. G. Rossetti.—LiO

The waves of the sea. E. Farjeon.—SaM

The way it is. G. Oden.—AdC

"Where have you been dear." K. Kuskin.—HoBm—KuD

The winter of the separation. P. Booth.—PlL

A woman mourned by daughters. A. Rich.—PlL

Women ("They were women then") A. Walker.—PlG

"Your mother." S. Cornish.—AdC

Mothers ("The last time I was home") Nikki Giovanni.—AdC

Mothers ("Oh mother") Anne Sexton.—PlL

"The mothers have come back." See Sheep, sels.

Mother's helper. Aileen Fisher.—FiO

Mother's nerves. X. J. Kennedy.—CoI

Mother's pig. X. J. Kennedy.—KeP

A mother's song. Christina Rossetti.—PaI

My Mami takes me to the bakery. Charlotte Pomerantz.—PoT
My mother. Robert Mezey.—KhI
"My mother groan'd, my father wept." See Infant sorrow
"My mother has a spotted pig." See Mother's pig
My mother said. Unknown.—WiP
"My mother said, I never should." See My mother said
"My mother said, if just once more." See Mother's nerves
"My mother says." See Mother
"My mother she wore." See The hat, the gown and the ring
My mother takes my wife's side. David Kherdian.—KhI
"My mother took my hand in hers." See I have my father's eyes
"My mother writes from Trenton." See My mother
"My mother's mad for bargain sales." X. J. Kennedy.—KeP
My mother's sister. C. Day Lewis.—PlL
"My mouth stays shut." Arnold Adoff.—AdE
My name. Lee Bennett Hopkins.—LiCc
My name is. Pauline Clarke.—BeR
"My name is Sluggery-wuggery." See My name is
"My neighbor in the country, Henry Manley." See Hello, hello Henry
"My north stonefence is down, it begs my tend." See North fence
"My nose is blue." See Me
"My nose is green." Mother Goose.—TrGg
My nurse. Stephen Shu Ning Liu.—KhI
My old dad. Michael Dugan.—DuSn
"My old flame, my wife." See The old flame
My own room. Nancy Dingman Watson.—RuM—WaB
My papa's waltz. Theodore Roethke.—MaP
"My parents kept me from children who were rough." See Rough
"My pen is a thermometer." See House call
"My pet dinosaur got in trouble." See My dinosaur's day in the park
"My pretty little seashell." See My seashell
My puppy ("I have a playful") Aileen Fisher.—FiO
My puppy ("It's funny") Aileen Fisher.—BeR
"My puppy looks at the big old moon." See The moon
"My rocket engine burned." See In space language
My rules. Shel Silverstein.—LuZ
My seashell. Agnia Barto, tr. by M. Morton.—SaM
"My shoes." Siv Cedering Fox.—FoB
My sister Jane. Ted Hughes.—HiS
"My sister says." See Rhinos purple, hippos green
My stars. Abraham Ibn Ezra, tr. fr. the Spanish by Robert Mezey.—LiO
"My stegosaur." See Abiding question

"My stocking's where." See Christmas eve
"My summer vacation." Nikki Grimes.—GrS
My uncle ("I think of forests palaces and swans") Richmond Lattimore.—PlL
My uncle Jack. David Amey.—PaI
"My uncle Jack collects door knobs." See My uncle Jack
My valentine. Robert Louis Stevenson.—LiO—YaI
"My whole life has been a chronology of changes." See For Malcolm, after Mecca
My wise old grandpapa. Wilbur G. Howcroft.—CoPs—DuSn
"My, you're a tiny little runt." See It's all relative
Myrtle. Theodore Roethke.—CoI
"Myself, I rather like the bat." See The bat
Myself when I am real. Al Young.—AdC
Mysterious biography. Carl Sandburg.—LiCc—LiO
The mysterious cat. Vachel Lindsay.—WiP
Mystery ("I have to go now, letter isn't signed") David McCord.—McSu
The mystery ("I was not; now I am—a few days hence") Paul Laurence Dunbar.—BrI
The mystic sea. Paul Laurence Dunbar.—BrI
Mythology. See also names of mythical beings, as Neptune, Unicorns
   "I have heard a voice of broken seas." From A fragment. J. E. Flecker.—PaE
   Like Thor. M. C. Livingston.—LiWt
   The mother. B. Deutsch.—PlL
   The phoenix. J. Gardner.—GaCb
   Song. From Comus. J. Milton.—PaE

N

N is for needle. William Jay Smith.—SmL
N. Y. to L. A. by jet plane. Sonya Dorman.—PlG
Nada. Charlotte Pomerantz.—PoT
"Nada is nothing." See Nada
The nailbiter. Shel Silverstein.—SiL
Nails
   "For want of a nail, the shoe was lost." Mother Goose.—WiP
Name and place. Madeline Tiger Bass.—KhI
"Name in a footnote, faceless name." See Crispus Attucks
"A name like Egbert, that's a blast." See Names
Names. See also Christenings
   American names. S. V. Benet.—PlG
   The animal song. Unknown.—CoA
   Carriers of the dream wheel. N. S. Momaday.—MoGd
   Five men against the theme, my name is red hot, yo name ain' doodley squat. G. Brooks.—AdC
   The four brothers. C. Pomerantz.—PoT
   Genus hylobates. J. Gibbons.—KhI
   A giant named Stanley. M. P. Hearn.—WaG
   The gourd dancer. N. S. Momaday.—MoGd

The shark.—BlC
The shrimp.—BlC
The skink.—BlC
The sniffle.—BlC
The squid.—BlC
Sweet dreams.—BlC
Tableau at twilight.—BlC—CoPs
The tale of Custard the dragon.—BlC
Tallyho-hum.—CoPh
The termite.—BlC
"There is obviously a complete lack of
    understanding."—BlC
"There was a young lady named Harris."—
    BlC
"There was a young lady of Rome."—BrO
"There was an old man in a trunk."—BlC
To a small boy standing on my shoes while I
    am wearing them.—BlC
The toucan.—BlC
The turkey.—BlC
The turtle.—BlC
Two dogs have I.—CoG
The wapiti.—BlC
A watched example never boils.—BlC
"The wendigo."—BlC
Winter morning.—BlC
The wombat.—BlC
You and me and P. B. Shelley.—BlC
"Nasturtiums on earth are small and seething
    with." See Moon nasturtiums
"Nasturtiums with." See Rainbow writing
Nat Turner ("From the obscurity of the past
    we saw") Samuel Allen.—AdC
Nate's song. Joan Aiken.—AiS
National security. Archibald MacLeish.—PlG
The nativity. See Gospel according to Luke
Natural history museum. Myra Cohn
    Livingston.—LiWt
Natural tears. Thomas Hood.—PlL
Naturally. Audre Lorde.—AdC
Nature. See also Country life
    All day long. D. McCord.—McO
    All nature seems at work. S. T. Coleridge.—
        PaB
    April birthday. T. Hughes.—HuSs
    By Frazier Creek Falls. G. Snyder.—PlG
    Eminent cosmologists ("It did not last, the
        Devil howling ho") J. C. Squire.—BrO
    Eminent cosmologists ("Nature, and nature's
        laws lay hid in night") A. Pope.—BrO
    "Go out." E. Mathias.—SaM
    June ("Now is the ox-eyed daisy out") J.
        Reaney.—DoWh
    "Look." M. A. Hoberman.—HoY
    A man in a tree. N. M. Bodecker.—BoP
    Nature dragon. L. Morrison.—MoW
    New world. N. S. Momaday.—MoGd
    On a bank as I sat fishing. H. Wotton.—PaB
    "Once we felt at home with nature if we
        knew the nomenclature." From Progress.
        F. Lamport.—BrO
    Other talk. A. Fisher.—FiO
    "Out in the dark and daylight." A. Fisher.—
        FiO

    Overlooking. A. Fisher.—FiO
    The painter. S. Silverstein.—SiL
    Plenty of time. A. Fisher.—FiO
    Psalm of the fruitful field. A. M. Klein.—
        DoWh
    Song ("I like birds, said the Dryad") E.
        Coatsworth.—WiP
    Song ("The owl is abroad") Unknown.—PaB
    "The sun finally tolerable." From Autumn
        nature notes. T. Hughes.—HuSs
    Swifts. T. Hughes.—HuSs
    To a mouse. R. Burns.—PaB
    Tryin' on clothes. S. Silverstein.—SiL
    The tuft of flowers. R. Frost.—PaB
    "Unwatch'd, the garden bough shall sway."
        From In memoriam. A. Tennyson.—PaB
    The warm and the cold. T. Hughes.—HuSs
    Wild strawberries. S. Silverstein.—SiL
"Nature, and nature's laws lay hid in night."
    See Eminent cosmologists
Nature dragon. Lillian Morrison.—MoW
Navajo Indians. See Indians of the Americas—
    Navajo
Naval battles. See Warships
A near pantoum for a birthday. Barbara
    Howes.—PlL
"Near this spot." See Epitaph to a dog
Need ("What do we need for love, a midnight
    fire") Babette Deutsch.—JaPp
The needing. Robert Newton Peck.—PeB
"A needle and thread." See What goes with
    what
Needles and pins. Mark Van Doren.—HiS
Needs. A. R. Ammons.—LuZ
Negritude. James A. Emanuel.—AdC
A Negro love song. Paul Laurence Dunbar.—
    BrI
Negroes. See Blacks
Neighbors
    Family friends. M. A. Hoberman.—HoY
    Frying pan in the moving van. E. Merriam.—
        MeW
    Hello, hello Henry. M. Kumin.—LuZ
    Neighbors ("The Cobbles live in the house
        next door") M. A. Hoberman.—HeB
    Next door neighbor. A. Fisher.—FiO
Neighbors ("The Cobbles live in the house next
    door") Mary Ann Hoberman.—HeB
Nelly Myers. A. R. Ammons.—KhI
Nemerov, Howard
    The beautiful lawn sprinkler.—JaPp
    Small moon.—JaPp
    Snowflakes.—JaPp
    What kind of a guy was he.—JaPp
Neptune (god)
    In praise of Neptune. T. Campion.—PaE
    Neptune ("As Pluto ruled the underworld")
        E. Farjeon.—PaE
    Neptune ("Neptune, besides the sway") From
        Comus. J. Milton.—PaE
Neptune (planet)
    The nineteenth moon of Neptune beasts. X.
        J. Kennedy.—KeP

Neptune ("As Pluto ruled the underworld")
    Eleanor Farjeon.—PaE
"Neptune, besides the sway." See Comus—
    Neptune
Neruda, Pablo
    The queen.—YaI
Nest. Robert Newton Peck.—PeB
Neuteronomy. Eve Merriam.—BrO—WiP
Nevada ("Some cowpoke named her Nevada")
    Stanley Noyes.—CoPh
Never. Shel Silverstein.—SiL
"Never ending turning round on." See
    True-love knot valentine
"Never, ever let them know." N. M.
    Bodecker.—BoHh
"Never grab a crab." See The crab
"Never mind the rain." N. M. Bodecker.—
    BoHh
"Never talk down to a glowworm." See
    Glowworm
"Never tickle." See Prickled pickles don't smile
"Never to see a nation born." See Under the
    old elm
New and old gospel. Nate Mackey.—AdC
New baby. Myra Cohn Livingston.—LiWt
"New cakes of soap." See Soap
New England
    Address to the scholars of New England. J. C.
        Ransom.—PlG
    "Driving through New England." L.
        Clifton.—PlG
    New England ("Here where the wind is
        always north-north-east") E. A. Robinson.—
        PlG
    Upon the first sight of New England, June
        29, 1638. T. Tillam.—PlG
    "With hearts revived in conceit, new land
        and trees they eye." From Good news
        from New England. E. Johnson.—PlG
New England ("Here where the wind is always
    north-north-east") Edwin Arlington
    Robinson.—PlG
New England Protestant. Richard Eberhart.—
    PlL
A New England sampler. John Malcolm
    Brinnin.—PlG
"A new family's coming to live next door to
    me." See Frying pan in the moving van
New Hampshire
    Lyme, New Hampshire. D. Kherdian.—KhC
The new kid. Mike Makley.—MoGp
New Mexican mountain. Robinson Jeffers.—PlG
New Mexico
    Forms of the earth at Abiquiu. N. S.
        Momaday.—MoGd
    New Mexican mountain. R. Jeffers.—PlG
    The sand painters. B. Belitt.—PlG
    Things to do around Taos. K. McCullough.—
        KhI
New notebook. Judith Thurman.—ThFo
"The new November wind." See Winter news
The new nutcracker suite, sel. Ogden Nash
    "A little girl marched around her Christmas
        tree."—LiPch

"A new pail." See Pail
The new pants. Arnold Adoff.—AdE
New season. Lillian Morrison.—MoSr
New shoes. Marjorie Seymour Watts.—PaI
New skills. Naomi Shihab Nye.—CoPh
New world. N. Scott Momaday.—MoGd
New Year. See also Rosh Hashana
    Another year come. W. S. Merwin.—LiO
    "Both my child." Teitoku.—LiO
    "For a fresh start." From Oraga Haru. Issa.—
        LiO
    For the coming year. P. Everwine.—LiO
    "God bless the master of this house."
        Unknown.—BaC
    The last day of the year. Su Tung P'o.—LiCc
    New year song. T. Hughes.—HuSs
        New year song.—LiO
    New Year's eve ("We got a broom like father
        said") M. C. Livingston.—HoMp
    New Year's water. Unknown.—LiCc—LiO
    News, news. E. Farjeon.—LiCc
    On New Year's eve. Ts'uei T'u.—LiO
    Resolution. T. Berrigan.—LiO
    Ring out, wild bells. From In memoriam. A.
        Tennyson.—LiO
    "The roads are very dirty, my boots are very
        thin." Unknown.—LiCc
    "Sing the old year out." B. S. De Regniers.—
        ReB
    Spring thoughts. Huang-fu Jan.—LiO
    "This is the autumn and our harvest." From
        New year's. C. Reznikoff.—LiO
    A wish. E. Farjeon.—LiCc
    "You'll find whenever the New Year comes."
        Unknown.—LiCc
A New Year letter, sel. W. H. Auden
    "A long time since it seems today."—PlG
New year song. Ted Hughes.—HuSs
    New Year's song.—LiO
New year's, sel. Charles Reznikoff
    "This is the autumn and our harvest."—LiO
New Year's eve ("We got a broom like father
    said") Myra Cohn Livingston.—HoMp
New Year's water. Unknown.—LiCc—LiO
New York city
    Arrival, New York harbor. R. Peters.—PlG
    Central Park West. S. Moss.—JaPp
    Langston. M. Evans.—AdC
    A maid in New York. N. M. Bodecker.—BoP
    Mannahatta. W. Whitman.—PlG
    New York in the spring. D. Budbill.—MoGp
    New York sewers. J. Aiken.—AiS
    One year to life on the Grand Central
        shuttle. A. Lorde.—AdC
    To Desi as Joe the smoky the lover of 115th
        street. A. Lorde.—AdC
    To the statue. M. Swenson.—PlG
    A trip on the Staten Island ferry. A. Lorde.—
        AdC
    "Who shined shoes in Times Square." L.
        Jeffers.—AdC
New York in the spring. David Budbill.—MoGp
New York sewers. Joan Aiken.—AiS

Noah

The dog's cold nose. A. Guiterman.—CoG
Noah ("They gathered around and told him not to do it") R. Daniells.—DoWh
Noah's ark ("The mice squeak") S. Silverstein.—CoA
Old Noah's ark. Unknown.—CoA
Noah ("They gathered around and told him not to do it") Roy Daniells.—DoWh
Noah's ark ("The mice squeak") Shel Silverstein.—CoA
"A **noble** prince, but very homely." Doris Orgel.—OrM
Nobody ("Nobody loves me") Shel Silverstein.—SiL
"**Nobody** but me can know the sorrow that wrings me." See Complaint of a young girl
Nobody calls him Jim. Jack Prelutsky.—PrRh
"**Nobody** here but us birds." See Family portrait
"**Nobody** knows." See Night out
"**Nobody** knows what's there but me." See My box
"**Nobody** loves me." See Nobody
"**Nobody** mentioned war." See Malcolm
Nocturn cabbage. Carl Sandburg.—HiD
Nocturne ("The three-toed tree toad") Arthur Guiterman.—RuM
"**Noel** is leaving us." See Farewell to Christmas
"**Noel** of the marvelous night." See To Noel
Noise. See Sounds
"The **noise** of nothing." Norma Farber.—FaS
Noises ("I want to write a poem") Fred Johnson.—AdC
Noises ("We play that we are soldiers") Aileen Fisher.—FiO
"**Noises** coming down the stairs." See Rest hour
Noises new to sea and land." See The big tent under the roof
The **noisy** wrens. Aileen Fisher.—FiO
Nomenclature. Peter Wesley-Smith.—CoI
Nonsense. See also Limericks; also entries under Carroll, Lewis and Lear, Edward
Adelaide. J. Prelutsky.—PrQ
An adventure story. F. Maurice.—DuSn
"Alas, alas, for Miss Mackay." Mother Goose.—LoG
"All the Fribruary babies." D. Orgel.—OrM
Always sprinkle pepper. S. Silverstein.—SiL
"As I was going out one day." Mother Goose.—LoG
Aunt Samantha. J. Prelutsky.—PrQ
Backward Bill. S. Silverstein.—SiL
The ballyoons. S. J. Graham.—DuSn
"Bat, bat, come under my hat." Mother Goose.—TrGg
Bath song. D. Lee.—LeG
Bibbilbonty. R. Fyleman.—WiP
Bickering. N. M. Bodecker.—BoHh
The big molice pan and the bertie dumb. D. Lee.—LeG
The bluffalo. J. Yolen.—YoH
"By mid-Fribruary moonlight." D. Orgel.—OrM

The centerpede. J. Yolen.—YoH
"Cheese and bread for gentlemen." Mother Goose.—TrGg
A child's song. D. Lee.—LeN
Chook chook. D. Barnham.—DuSn
Cow. W. J. Smith.—SmL
The crocodial. J. Yolen.—YoH
Crosspatch. N. Payne.—CoI
The curly-wigs. L. Parr.—DuSn
The cyclone visitors. D. Lee.—LeN
The difficulty of living on other planets. D. Lee.—LeN
"Dilly dilly piccalilli." C. Watson.—WiP
"A dingo trapper way out west." W. G. Howcroft.—DuSn
Do it yourself. J. Aiken.—AiS
"A dog and a cat went out together." Unknown.—WiP
Double barrelled ding dong bat. Unknown.—HeB
Dumbly Humpty. R. Tillack.—DuSn
Eating peaches on the beaches. A. Kisvardai.—DuSn
The edgehog. J. Yolen.—YoH
"Father, may I go to war." Unknown.—WiP
The fax. J. Yolen.—YoH
The floor and the ceiling. W. J. Smith.—SmL
"The fly is in." S. Silverstein.—SiL
"The folk who live in Backward Town." M. A. Hoberman.—HoY
"For neatness and comfort." N. M. Bodecker.—BoHh
Four foolish ladies. J. Prelutsky.—PrQ
"The frummick and the frelly." J. Prelutsky.—PrS
Garden calendar. N. M. Bodecker.—BoHh
Goofus. D. Lee.—LeG
Goofy song. D. Lee.—LeG
"The grand old Duke of York." Mother Goose.—TrGg
Gretchen in the kitchen. J. Prelutsky.—PrQ
The happy family. J. Ciardi.—HiD
Having. W. J. Smith.—SmL
"Hello, Bill." Unknown.—WiP
"Herbert Breeze." S. Scheding.—DuSn
Herbert Glerbett. J. Prelutsky.—PrQ
"Here stands a fist." Mother Goose.—TrGg
"Hey diddle diddle, the cat and the fiddle." Mother Goose.—TrGg
"Higglety, pigglety, pop." Mother Goose.—TrGg
How to make a swing with no rope or board or nails. S. Silverstein.—SiL
I think so, don't you. Unknown.—WiP
"I went to the river." Unknown.—WiP
If ("If I had wheels instead of feet") S. Silverstein.—SiL
"If all the seas were one sea." Mother Goose.—WiP
"I'll sing you a song." Mother Goose.—TrGg
"In Aquari-Fribruary." D. Orgel.—OrM
"In Fribruary, Old MacDonald." D. Orgel.—OrM
"In Fribruary, uncle Harry." D. Orgel.—OrM

Norris, Leslie
  The black fern.—NoM
  "The boy in the stone."—NoM
  Buying a puppy.—NoM
  The camels, the Kings' camels.—LiPch—NoM
  The collier laddie.—NoM
  In black chasms.—NoM
  Kevin scores.—NoM
  "A man in our village."—CoG—NoM
  Merlin & the snake's egg.—NoM
  Mice in the hay.—LiPch—NoM
  The old dog's song.—NoM
  "Out on the windy hill."—NoM
  The park at evening.—HiD—NoM
  The pit ponies.—NoM
  "The quiet-eyed cattle."—LiPch—NoM
  The sand rose.—NoM
  Sea and sand.—NoM
  Small frogs.—NoM
  Song of the giant killer.—NoM
  Spell of the goddess.—NoM
  Spell of the moon.—NoM
  Spell of the rain.—NoM
  Spell of the raingods.—NoM
  Spell of the seeds.—NoM
  Spell of the woods.—NoM
  The stable cat.—LiPch—NoM
  Swan.—NoM
North Dakota, north light. N. Scott
    Momaday.—MoGd
North fence. Robert Newton Peck.—PeB
North pole. See Polar regions
"North, south, east, and west." See Compass
    song
The north wind doth blow. Mother Goose.—
    CoA
Northern lights
  Northern lights ("In Sweden, they say") S. C.
    Fox.—FoB
  Northern lights ("In Sweden, they say") Siv
    Cedering Fox.—FoB
Norton, M. D. Herter
  Annunciation over the shepherds, sel. tr.
    "Look up, you men, men there at the
      fire."—LiPch
  The last supper. tr.—LiO
  "Look up, you men, men there at the fire."
    See Annunciation over the shepherds
  Pieta. tr.—LiO
"The nose becomes a triangular history." See
    Terra cotta
"Nose, nose, jolly red nose." Mother Goose.—
    LoG
Noses
  The bloodhound. E. Anthony.—CoG
  But I wonder. A. Fisher.—FiO
  The dog's cold nose. A. Guiterman.—CoG
  "I am a constant walker." N. M. Bodecker.—
    BoHh
  A lass on Ben Nevis. N. M. Bodecker.—BoP
  The long-nosed smelter. J. Jenkins.—DuSn
  "My nose is green." Mother Goose.—TrGg
  "Nose, nose, jolly red nose." Mother Goose.—
    LoG

A person in Stirling. N. M. Bodecker.—BoP
"Peter White will ne'er go right." Mother
    Goose.—LoG—TrGg
Senses. S. Silverstein.—SiL
Sneezing ("Air comes in tickly") M. L.
    Allen.—PaI
"There was a young lady named Rose." W. J.
    Smith.—SmL
"Not a cowboy after all." See Francie
"Not all those who pass." See The great mother
"Not always sure what things called sins may
    be." See Forgive my guilt
Not at all what one is used to. Isabella
    Gardner.—KhI
"Not born to the forest are we." See Twelfth
    night
"Not even dried-up leaves." See Thesis,
    antithesis, and nostalgia
"Not guns, not thunder, but a flutter of
    clouded drums." See Fireworks
Not lost in the stars. Bruce Bliven.—BrO
Not me ("The iguanodon looked like our
    iguanas") William Cole.—CoDb
Not me ("The slithergadee has crawled out of
    the sea") Shel Silverstein.—WaM
"Not me but cows walk up and beg to." Arnold
    Adoff.—AdE
"Not sickroom still, but often deathly pale."
    See Winter worship
"Not slowly wrought, nor treasured for their
    form." See Snowflakes
"Not too abruptly, now." See Two ways to
    wake a sleepwalker
Note ("Straw, feathers, dust") William
    Stafford.—MoGp
Notes. Paul Engle.—YaI
Nothing
  Nada. C. Pomerantz.—PoT
  "The noise of nothing." N. Farber.—FaS
  Nothing. B. Giles.—DuSn
Nothing. Barbara Giles.—DuSn
Nothing at all. Donald Finkel.—LuZ
"Nothing in the sky is high." See Asleep and
    awake
"Nothing is ever lost." See The flow, the void
"Nothing is less." See Sparrow
"Nothing, nothing can keep me from my love."
    See Love lyric, II
"Nothing sings from these orange trees." See
    On watching the construction of a
    skyscraper
Notice ("I have a dog") David McCord.—McO
Notions. Eve Merriam.—MeR
November
  "November bares the robin's nest." D.
    McCord.—McO
  The stag. T. Hughes.—HuSs
"November bares the robin's nest." David
    McCord.—McO
"November snow had come and drifted,
    almost." See The needing
Now. Nancy Dingman Watson.—WaB
"Now a hungry young osprey named Lee." See
    The osprey

"**Now** a man in Oodnadatta." See A change of air

"**Now** as at all times I can see in the mind's eye." See The Magi

"**Now** as the train bears west." See Night journey

"**Now** birds that sleep in brittle trees." See Wood's litany

"**Now** blocks to cleave." See Poor Robin's almanack

"**Now** children may." See May

"**Now** Christmas comes." See The wreath

"**Now** Christmas is come." See The sketch book

"**Now** Christmas is come." Unknown.—LiPch

"**Now** come to think of it, you say." See Figures of speech

"**Now** dreams." See Oppression

"**Now** everything is ready, child, and ready I'm for you." See Song before supper

Now have good day. Unknown.—BaC

"**Now** have good day, now have good day." See Now have good day

"**Now** he takes his mark." See Jetliner

"**Now** I lay me down to sleep." See Prayer of the selfish child

Now I set me. Reinhold W. Herman.—BrO

"**Now**, I'm not the one." See Garbage delight

"**Now** in the dawn before it dies, the eagle swings." See The story of a well-made shield

"**Now** in white." See The tree

"**Now** is my misery full, and namelessly." See Pieta

"**Now** is the ox-eyed daisy out." See June

"**Now** it is pleasant in the summer-eve." See The borough

"**Now** it's Uncle Sam sitting on top of the world." See Good morning America

"**Now**, listen, ye who established the Great League." See Memorial ode

Now long ago. Maya Angelou.—AnO

"**Now**, not a tear begun." See A woman mourned by daughters

Now poem for us. Sonia Sanchez.—AdC

"**Now** pray, where are you going, child." See Meet on the road

"**Now** rock the boat to a fare thee well." See Rites of passage

"**Now** say good night." David McCord.—McO

"**Now** sleep the mountain summits, sleep the glens." See Vesper

"**Now** that he's left the room." See Univac to univac

"**Now** that the time has come wherein." See Poor Robin's almanack

"**Now** that's what I call a real mountain." See Mountain

"**Now** the gardens grow on trees." See Autumn garden

"**Now** the mouse goes to his hole." See Bedtime

"**Now** the river is rich, but her voice is low." See The river in March

"**Now**, the showground is quiet." See Horse show at midnight

"**Now** the snow is vanished clean." See Quebec May

"**Now** the summer is grown old." See Autumn

"**Now** there comes." See New Year's song

"**Now** think of words, take sky." See Take sky

"**Now** thrice welcome Christmas." See Poor Robin's almanack

"**Now** touch the air softly." See A pavane for the nursery

"**Now** turning homeward." Ann Atwood.—AtH

"**Now**, twas twenty five or thirty years since Jack first saw the light." See Jack was every inch a sailor

"**Now** when we leave the windows of hay." See To a horse

"**Now**, wouldn't it be funny." See Wouldn't it be funny

Nowata. David Ray.—KhI

Nowlan, Alden
The palomino stallion.—CoPh

Noyes, Alfred
Daddy fell into the pond.—PaI
The enchanted island, sel.
      "Some would dive in the lagoon."—PaE
The rock pool.—PaE
Seagulls on the serpentine.—PaE
"Some would dive in the lagoon." See The enchanted island

Noyes, Stanley
Nevada.—CoPh

Number theory. Lillian Morrison.—MoO

Numberot. Oscar Mendelsohn.—DuSn

Numbers. Aliki Barnstone.—LuZ

Numbers
Rhyme ("The bee thrives") D. McCord.—McO

"**Nunaptigne**, in our land, ahe, ahe, ee, ee, iee." See The wind has wings

Nuns
For the sisters of the Hotel Dieu. A. M. Klein.—DoWh

Nursery play
"Here stands a fist." Mother Goose.—TrGg
"I'm the king of the castle." Mother Goose.—TrGg

Nursery rhymes—American and English. See Mother Goose

Nursery rhymes—Chinese
"You'll find whenever the New Year comes." Unknown.—LiCc

Nursery rhymes—Danish
Five little piggies. Unknown.—CoI
"Three little guinea pigs." Unknown, tr. by N. M. Bodecker.—CoA—WiP

Nursery rhymes—English and American. See Mother Goose

Nursery rhymes—French
"Baby, baby, naughty baby." Mother Goose.—TrGg
The goblin. Unknown, tr. by R. Fyleman.—WiP

Nursery rhymes—Japanese
  Momotara. Unknown, tr. by R. Fyleman.—
    WaG—WiP
Nursery rhymes—Scottish
  "I've a kisty." Unknown.—BlH
  "Roon, roon, rosie." Unknown.—BlH
  "What's in there." Unknown.—WiP
Nurses and nursing
  My nurse. S. Shu Ning Liu.—KhI
  Nurse's song. W. Blake.—MoF
Nurse's song. William Blake.—MoF
Nursing. See Nurses and nursing
Nuts and nutting. See names of nuts, as
    Walnuts
"**Nuts** to you, and nuts to me." Mary Ann
    Hoberman.—CoI
Nye, Naomi Shihab
  New skills.—CoPh
"**Nymph,** nymph, what are your beads." See
    Overheard on a saltmarsh

O

"**Oh.**" See The Fourth
"**O** beautiful for spacious skies." See America
    the beautiful
"**Oh** blue blows the lilac and green grows the
    corn." See Nate's song
"**Oh,** Bonnie is the little cow." See Midnight in
    Bonnie's stall
O captain, my captain. Walt Whitman.—PlG
"**O** captain, my captain, our fearful trip is
    done." See O captain, my captain
"**Oh** Christmas time is drawing near."
    Unknown.—BaC
O clouds. Elizabeth Coatsworth.—WiP
"**O** clouds, so white against the sky." See O
    clouds
O.D. Jack Gilbert.—AdC
"**Oh,** dearer by far than the land of our birth."
    Richard Henry Wilde.—PlG
"**Oh** do not bring the wart hog here." See The
    wart hog
"**Oh,** do not needle porcupin." See The
    porcupin
"**Oh,** do not tease the bluffalo." See The
    bluffalo
"**Oh** for the breath of the briny deep." See A
    sailor's song
"**O** gaze on the graceful gazelle as it grazes."
    See Gazelle
"**Oh** give me a pup." See Poetic tale
"**O** God, who made me." See The prayer of the
    donkey
"**Oh,** grim and gloomy." See Grim and gloomy
Oh have you heard. Shel Silverstein.—HoMp—
    LiCc
"**Oh** have you heard it's time for vaccinations."
    See Oh have you heard
"**Oh,** he did whistle and she did sing." See
    Bells

"**Oh,** he was a handsome trotter, and he
    couldn't be." See How we drove the
    trotter
"**Oh,** hear you a horn, mother, behind the hill."
    See The horn
"**Oh** Humpty, O Dumpty, you've had a fearful
    spill." See If Walt Whitman had written
    Humpty Dumpty
"**Oh,** hush thee, my baby, the night is behind
    us." See The white seal's lullaby
"**O,** I am mad with the maddest of men." See
    Pollution
"**Oh,** I can laugh and I can sing." See Whistling
"**O,** I have been walking." See Street song
O is for owl. William Jay Smith.—SmL
"**Oh,** it poured and it rained." See Fudge
"**Oh,** it will be fine." See Valentine for earth
"**O** Jean Baptiste, pourquoi." See Pourquoi
"**O** kangaroo, O kangaroo." See The kangaroo
"**O** li'l' lamb out in de col.' " See Hymn
O little town of Bethlehem, sel. Phillips Brooks
    "The dark night wakes, the glory breaks."—
    BaC
"**Oh** London bridge what made me start."
    Mother Goose.—TrGg
"**O** lonesome sea-gull, floating far." See
    Sea-birds
"**Oh,** long, long." See The grass on the
    mountain
"**O** Lord, the hard-won miles." See A prayer
"**Oh,** mighty America, hast thou come to this."
    See Fare thee well
"**O** Mrs. Mosquito, quit biting me, please." See
    Mosquito
"**O** moon, who looks in." Kazue Mizumura.—
    MiF
"**Oh** mother." See Mothers
"**Oh** murdering Jack." See Suspense
Oh, my bambino. Unknown, tr. fr. the Italian
    by Laura Mincieli Ross.—BaC
"**O,** o, o." See The ocean of vowels
"**Oh** our mother the earth oh our father the
    sky." See Song of the sky loom
"**O** penguin, do you ever try." See Penguin
"**O** prairie mother, I am one of your boys." See
    Prairie—Finale
"**O** ptarmigan, O ptarmigan." See Ptarmigan
"**O** reapers and gleaners." See Harvest song
"**O** sailor, come ashore." Christina Rossetti.—
    WiP
"**O** say can you up." See Old glory
"**Oh,** see the octopie inert." See The octopie
O simplicitas. See Three songs of Mary
"**Oh,** sing a song of phosphates." See Boston
    nursery rhymes — Rhyme for a chemical
    baby
"**O** sixteen hundred and ninety one." See The
    two witches
"**O** sliver of liver." Myra Cohn Livingston.—
    CoPs
"**Oh,** the blithery, blathery pirate." See The
    pirate
"**O** the King of Umpalazzo." See The King of
    Umpalazzo

"Oh the little bird is rocking in the cradle of the wind." See The farm child's lullaby

O the little rusty dusty miller." Mother Goose.—TrGg

"Oh the lurpp is on the loose, the loose." See the lurpp is on the loose

"Oh, then, I see Queen Mab hath been with you." See Romeo and Juliet—Queen Mab

"Oh, there once was a puffin." See There once was a puffin

"Oh, to be in England." See Home thoughts, from abroad

"Oh to have you in May." See In May

"Oh, weep for Mr. and Mrs. Bryan." See The lion

"Oh what a beautiful thing." See First day of spring

"Oh, what a party." See The monster's birthday

"Oh what are they a-doing of, the sirens on the rocks." See Socks for the sirens

"Oh, what if the Easter bunny." See What if

"Oh when the dodo flourished." See The dodo

Oh where, oh where. Mother Goose.—BlH

"Oh where, oh where has my little dog gone." See Oh where, oh where

"Oh, who is so merry, so merry, heigh ho." See The lighthearted fairy

"Oh, who is the Lord of the land of life." See The masters

"Oh, wind of the spring-time, oh, free wind of May." See Roses

"Oh, wouldn't it be a most wondrous thing." See My guitar

"O wrap yourself round in calico bright." See Calico ball

"O you merry, merry souls." See Round about our coal fire—Fun and games

"O you so long dead." See To my brother

The oak and the rose. Shel Silverstein.—SiL

"The oak is a railway station." See Deceptions

"Oak leaf plate." Mary Ann Hoberman.—HoY

"An oak tree and a rosebush grew." See The oak and the rose

"An oak tree on the first day of April." See Spring nature notes

Oak trees

The California oaks. Y. Winters.—PlG

Deceptions. T. Hughes.—HuSs

The haunted oak. P. L. Dunbar.—BrI

The oak and the rose. S. Silverstein.—SiL

"An oak tree on the first day of April." From Spring nature notes. T. Hughes.—HuSs

"An **obnoxious** old person named Hackett." William Jay Smith.—SmL

"**Obsequious** Prawn." Michael Dugan.—DuSn

Observations. Lillian Morrison.—MoO

"**Occasional** mornings when an early fog." See Housewife

Occupations. See also names of occupations, as Fishers and fishing

Adventures of a frisbee. S. Silverstein.—SiL

Columbus. O. Nash.—LiO

A crusty mechanic. N. M. Bodecker.—BoP

Handyman. H. Phillips.—BrO

Never. S. Silverstein.—SiL

Occupations ("I've had many a strange occupation") N. M. Bodecker.—BoHh

Ode to a vanished operator in an automatized elevator. L. Rosenfield.—BrO

Old florist. T. Roethke.—JaPp

Order. M. C. Livingston.—LiWt

Personals. L. W. Emeruwa.—JaPp

Occupations ("I've had many a strange occupation") N. M. Bodecker.—BoHh

Ocean. See also Mediterranean sea; Seashore; Tides; Waves

"All day I hear the noise of waters." From Chamber music. J. Joyce.—SaM

By the sea ("Morning") E. Merriam.—MeR

By the sea ("Why does the sea moan evermore") C. Rossetti.—PaE

Cardigan bay. J. Masefield.—PaE

The cataclysm. E. Shanks.—PaE

Cities drowned. H. Newbolt.—PaE

The city in the sea. E. A. Poe.—PaE

Columbus and the mermaids. E. Coatsworth.—PlG

The coral grove. J. G. Percival.—PaE—SaM

"Day flows into sea." A. Atwood.—AtH

The diver. R. Francis.—PaE

Deep sea diver.—MoGp

Divers ("Clad in thick mail he stumbles down the floor") R. H. Schauffler.—PaE

Echoes. W. De La Mare.—PaE

"Evening on the olden, the golden sea of Wales." From The dying patriot. J. E. Flecker.—PaE

"Full fathom five thy father lies." From The tempest. W. Shakespeare.—PaE Ariel's dirge.—WiP

Gull. W. J. Smith.—SmL

The herring ("A hard of hearing herring thought he heard a haddock say") R. S. Oliver.—OlC

How they brought the good news by sea. N. Farber.—LiPch

"I brush my teeth with ocean sand." X. J. Kennedy.—KeP

"I have heard a voice of broken seas." From A fragment. J. E. Flecker.—PaE

"I have seen." From the excursion. W. Wordsworth.—PaE

In praise of Neptune. T. Campion.—PaE

"Inside the lab." J. Ryder.—HeB

"An iridescent sea horse." L. Morrison.—MoW

Islands in Boston Harbor. D. McCord.—McO

The kraken ("Below the thunders of the upper deep") A. Tennyson.—PaE

The kraken ("Deep beneath the foaming billows") J. Prelutsky.—PrH

"Mackerel Mack and Halibut Hal." X. J. Kennedy.—KeP

Mackerel song. T. Hughes.—HuSs

The main-deep. J. Stephens.—PaE—SaM

The Maldive shark. H. Melville.—PaE

Marine. R. Humphries.—PaE

The song of the old mother. W. B. Yeats.—
PlL
The span of life. R. Frost.—CoG
Strokes. W. Stafford.—JaPp
Sunning. J. S. Tippett.—CoG
Survivor. J. D. Simmons.—AdC
"There was an old woman lived under the
hill." Mother Goose.—TrGg
To Catlin. R. N. Peck.—PeB
Unfinished history. A. MacLeish.—PlL
The valley. S. Moss.—JaPp
When you are old. W. B. Yeats.—JaPp
Old and new. Unknown, tr. by Arthur Waley.—
PlL
"Old Ben Golliday." Mark Van Doren.—HiS
"An old billy goat." See G is for goat
Old Blue. Unknown.—CoG
"The old buccaneer." See P is for pirate
Old Christmas returned. Unknown.—BaC
"Old daddy longlegs, harvestman." See
Harvestman
Old dog ("Toward the last in the morning she
could not") William Stafford.—CoG
Old dog ("Waddles after") Raymond Souster.—
CoG
"The old dog barks backward without getting
up." See The span of life
"Old dog lay in the summer sun." See Sunning
Old dog Tray. Stephen Foster.—CoG
The old dog's song. Leslie Norris.—NoM
Old Dubuque. Dave Etter.—FlA
"Old farmer Giles." Mother Goose.—BlH
"The old father lion." See The lion
The old flame. Robert Lowell.—PlL
Old florist. Theodore Roethke.—JaPp
"Old friend of man, and made." See Look,
what am I
The old ghost. Thomas Lovell Beddoes.—WaGp
Old glory. Myra Cohn Livingston.—LiF
Old gray barn. Robert Newton Peck.—PeB
Old grey goose. Harry Behn.—CoA
"Old he was but not yet wax." See My father's
face
The old hoofer. Lillian Morrison.—MoW
Old Ironsides. Oliver Wendell Holmes.—PlG
"Old Jumpety-bumpety-hop-and-go-one." See
Jumpety-bumpety-hop
"Old King Cole was a merry old soul." Mother
Goose.—TrGg
"The old King of Dorchester." See The
ceremonial band
"The old man." See Birdfoot's grampa
The old man and the bee. Edward Lear.—WiP
"An old man came to church one day." See
The stranger
"An old man from Okefenokee." William Jay
Smith.—SmL
Old man, phantom dog. Frederick Eckman.—
FlA
Old man playing with children. John Crowe
Ransom.—PlL
"The old man walks December's crust." See An
old man's crust
An old man's crust. Robert Newton Peck.—PeB

"An old man's son was killed far away in the
staked." See The colors of night
"Old men." See Lucas Park, St. Louis
The old men. Cid Corman.—JaPp
The old men admiring themselves in the
water. William Butler Yeats.—JaPp
"Old men stand." See Bulldozers
"Old Mrs Caribou lives by a lake." See Mrs.
Caribou
"Old Mistress McShuttle." Mother Goose.—
TrGg
"Old Mog comes in and sits on the
newspaper." See Cat
Old Moll. James Reeves.—WaW
"Old mother Hubbard." Mother Goose.—BlH
"Old Noah once he built an ark." See Old
Noah's ark
Old Noah's ark. Unknown.—CoA
Old people. Myra Cohn Livingston.—LiWt
"The old people speak of death." Quincy
Troupe.—AdC
Old people's home. W. H. Auden.—PlL
"Old Saint Nicholas comes so speedily."
Unknown, fr. the German.—BaC
Old Salt Kossabone. Walt Whitman.—PlL
"Old Santa is an active man." Lois Lenski.—
BaC
Old Shellover. Walter De La Mare.—SaM—
WiP
Old snake has gone to sleep. Margaret Wise
Brown.—WiP
"Old Tillie Turveycombe." See Tillie
Old Tim Toole. David McCord.—McO
"Old Tom." See Tom
"Old tree." See Visitor
The old wife and the ghost. James Reeves.—
BrIt—WaGp
"Old woman, old woman, shall we go a
shearing." Mother Goose.—YaI
"Old woman, old woman."—TrGg
An old woman remembers. Sterling A.
Brown.—AdC
"The old women, like the oaks and the red
clay of that land." See The old women still
sing
The old women still sing. Charles H. Rowell.—
AdC
"An old, worn harp that had been played." See
The master-player
"Older, more generous." See The gift
Oliphaunt. See The adventures of Tom
Bombadil
Oliver, Mary
Learning about the Indians.—LuZ
Oliver, Robert S.
Ants.—OlC
Bees.—OlC
The cougar.—OlC
The dragonfly.—OlC
The eel.—OlC
Flamingos.—OlC
The goose.—OlC
The herring.—OlC
Ichthyosaurus.—OlC

On the skateboard. Lillian Morrison.—MoGp
On the slope. David McCord.—McSu
"On the springs in a chair." See S is for springs
"On the third of Fibruary." Doris Orgel.—OrM
"On the threshold of the stable smelling." See The stable
"On the twelfth day of July." See Orange lilies
"On the wall." Lilian Moore.—MoTs
"On the wave-washed scarp of crag." See Green shag
"On the wind-beaten plains." See Ancestors
"On this day in Sicily." See The day of the dead
"On tiptoe." See Tiptoe
"On Tuesday morn as it happened by chance." See The magic pudding
On watching the construction of a skyscraper. Burton Raffel.—JaPp
"On wool soft feet he peeps and creeps." See Santa Claus
"Once a big molice pan." See The big molice pan and the bertie dumb
"Once a dream did weave a shade." See Dream
"Once a snowflake fell." See Winter poem
"Once a year." See The slummings
"Once a year, at Easter." Aileen Fisher.—FiO
"Once, dwarfs ran in cavernous mountains." See Tolkien on the subway
"Once from a big, big building." See A visit to the asylum
"Once, I didn't mean to." See Accidentally
"Once I dreamt I was the snow." Siv Cedering Fox.—FoB
"Once I was jealous of lovers, now I am." See The valley
"Once in the winter." See The forsaken
"Once more around should do it, the man confided." See Flight of the roller-coaster
"Once the long season had us in its reach." See Orange
"Once there was a kindhearted lad named." See Jack do-good-for-nothing
"Once there was a man who owned a fine hunting." See The horse that died of shame
"Once there was an elephant." See Eletephony
"Once there was an onion." See The sad sliced onion
"Once upon." See Alexander Soames, his poems
Once upon a great holiday. Anne Wilkinson.—DoWh
Once upon a nag. Michael Beirne McMahon.—CoPh
"Once upon a time there was a person." See Earth moon
"Once upon a time there was an Italian." See Columbus
"Once upon a time there were three little foxes." See The three foxes
"Once upon a train track." See The ombley-gombley

"Once we felt at home with nature if we knew the nomenclature." See Progress
"Once when the snow of the year was beginning to fall." See The runaway
"One afternoon, my cousin Ben." See On relief
"One afternoon, while sitting in a tree." See The python
"One by one the leaves fall down." See The leaves fall down
"One day a boy went walking." See Who ever sausage a thing
"One day a boy went walking." Mother Goose.—LoG
"One day, a fine day, a high-flying-sky day." See The cat heard the cat-bird
"One day, having nothing much to do, God." See The opossum
"One day in March." See Almost spring
"One day our pets were really sick." Chris Davis.—DuSn
"One day when I was walking out." See Pig
"One egg in the nest of that crow." From Limericks. David McCord.—McSu
"One ewe." See Shepherd's night count
"One frosty evening." See Sunflowers
"One gets a wife, one gets a house." See The cat
One glorious star. Unknown, tr. by Henry Wadsworth Longfellow.—BaC
"One if by land." See Early warning
"One innocent spring." See Now long ago
"One little duck." See Four little ducks
"One locust alone doesn't make any trouble." See Locust
"One misty, moisty morning." Mother Goose.—TrGg
"One morning in a spelling test." See The spelling test
"One morning when I went over to Bournemouth." See Venus in the tropics
"One mouse adds up to many mice." See Singular indeed
"One mouse, two mice." See Mice and cat
"One night I couldn't fall asleep." See Night voyage
"One night in a dark museum." See Diplodocus holiday
"One of the things you never see." See Proverbs
"One of their horses was Nancy Hanks." See Going to town
"One ounce of truth benefits." Nikki Giovanni.—AdC
"One picture puzzle piece." See Picture puzzle piece
"One side of his world is always missing." See Riding a one eyed horse
"One summer night a little raccoon." See Raccoon
One sunny summer's day. Dennis Lee.—LeG
"One thing you can say about roaring." Karla Kuskin.—KuD
"One thing you left with us, Jack Johnson." See Strange legacies

Orion (constellation)

Orion ("Orion in the cold December sky") D. McCord.—McO

"Orion in the cold December sky." See Orion

Orphans

Autobiographia literaria. F. O'Hara.—KhI

Ortiz, Simon J.

What my Uncle Tony told my sister, Angie, and me.—LuZ

Osage Indians. See Indians of the Americas—Osage

The osprey ("Now a hungry young osprey named Lee") Robert S. Oliver.—OlC

Ospreys. See Hawks

The ostrich ("The ostrich roams the great Sahara") Ogden Nash.—BlC

"The ostrich roams the great Sahara." See The ostrich

Ostriches

Grandmother ostrich. W. J. Smith.—SmL

The ostrich ("The ostrich roams the great Sahara") O. Nash.—BlC

"Other acquainted years." See On reaching forty

"Other birds soar in the clouds." See Pigeons

Other talk. Aileen Fisher.—FiO

"Others because you did not keep." See A deep sworn vow

Otherwise. Aileen Fisher.—PaI

Otto ("It's Christmas day, I did not get") Gwendolyn Brooks.—LiCc—LiPch

Otto ("He was the youngest son of a strange brood") Theodore Roethke.—PlL

"Ouch." See Yellowjackets

Ouch, sort of. Beatrice Schenk De Regniers.—ReB

Ough. David McCord.—McO

"Our anchor's too big for our ship." See Anchored

"Our baseball team never did very much." See The new kid

"Our birth is but a sleep and a forgetting." See Ode: Intimations of immortality from recollections of early childhood

"Our blackness did not come to us whole." Linda Brown Bragg.—AdC

"Our car was fierce enough." See The trip

"Our cat turns up her nose at mice." See The cat who aspired to higher things

Our country. Henry David Thoreau.—PlG

"Our daughter, Alicia." See Hot line

"Our dog Fred." See The diners in the kitchen

"Our half of the earth has tipped away from you." See Being of the sun—Winter solstice chant

"Our hammock swings between two trees." See Hammock

"Our household gods our parents be." See The primitiae to parents

Our joyful'st feast. George Wither.—BaC

"Our lawn has a jacket." See Buttons of gold

"Our little mobile hangs and swings." See Mobile

"Our lives are loops." See Fair or foul

Our Lucy, 1956–1960. Paul Goodman.—CoG

"Our Mr. Toad." David McCord.—McO

Our stars come from Ireland, sels. Wallace Stevens.—PlG (Complete)

I. Tom McGreevy, in America, thinks of himself as a boy

II. The westwardness of everything

"Our turtle did not eat today." See Turtle

Our washing machine. Patricia Hubbell.—PaI—WiP

"Our washing machine went whisity whirr." See Our washing machine

"Our wrens are back." See The noisy wrens

"Out from the beach the ships I see." See The white ships

"Out here in Ringoes." See Rural recreation

Out in the boat. Lillian Morrison.—MoSr

Out in the dark. Edward Thomas.—PaB

"Out in the dark and daylight." Aileen Fisher.—FiO

"Out in the dark over the snow." See Out in the dark

"Out in the sky the great dark clouds are massing." See Ships that pass in the night

"Out in the wilds of south Australia." Marguerite Varday.—DuSn

Out in the winter wind. Aileen Fisher.—FiO

"Out of him that I loved." See Our stars come from Ireland—Tom McGreevy, in America, thinks of himself as a boy

"Out of me, unworthy and unknown." See Anne Rutledge

"Out of my heart, one day, I wrote a song." See Misapprehension

Out of season. Aileen Fisher.—FiO

Out of the city. Eve Merriam.—MeW

"Out of the dark." See The open door

"Out of the focal and foremost fire." See Little Giffen

"Out of the gargoyle's throat of stone." See The gargoyle's protest

"Out of the lamplight." See Mice in the hay

"Out of the night and the north." See The train dogs

"Out on the windy hill." Leslie Norris.—NoM

Outdoor life. See Camping and hiking; Country life; Nature; Roads and trails; also names of outdoor activities, as Hunters and hunting

Outer space. See Space and space travel

Outing. Joan Aiken.—AiS

The outlaw. Felice Holman.—CoI—HoA

Outlaws. See Crime and criminals

"Outside, I want to play." Nikki Grimes.—GrS

Outside or underneath. Shel Silverstein.—SiL

"Outside our ways you found." See For a child gone to live in a commune

"Outside the rain upon the street." See A musical

"Ouu gee whiz." See Moon poem

Over and under. William Jay Smith.—WiP

"Over by my bedroom wall." See The ugstabuggle

"Over every elm, the." See You too lie down

"Over hills." See The witches' ride

Water color. L. Morrison.—MoW
The **pair** of pants. Dennis Lee.—LeG
Paiute Indians. See Indians of the Americas—
Paiute
Palace cook's tale. Joan Aiken.—AiS
Palen, Jennie M.
To a race horse at Ascot.—CoPh
The **palomino** stallion. Alden Nowlan.—CoPh
Pamela. David McCord.—McO
"**Pamela** Purse yelled, ladies first." See Ladies
first
"**Pamela,** you may call her that." See Pamela
The **pancake** collector. Jack Prelutsky.—PrQ
Pancho Pangolin. S. J. Graham.—DuSn
The **panda** ("I love the baby giant panda")
Ogden Nash.—BlC
The **panda** ("A lady who lived in Uganda")
William Jay Smith.—SmL
Pandas
The panda ("I love the baby giant panda") O.
Nash.—BlC
The panda ("A lady who lived in Uganda")
W. J. Smith.—SmL
"Yolande the panda." N. Giovanni.—GiV
Pandora
Pandora's box. E. Merriam.—MeR
Pandora's box. Eve Merriam.—MeR
The **panther** ("Lock your doors when the
panther roars") John Gardner.—GaCb
The **panther** ("The panther is like a leopard")
Ogden Nash.—BlC—MoGp
"The **panther** is like a leopard." See The
panther
Panthers
The panther ("Lock your doors when the
panther roars") J. Gardner.—GaCb
The panther ("The panther is like a leopard")
O. Nash.—BlC—MoGp
Papa bantam's goodnight. Jane Yolen.—YoD
Papago Indians. See Indians of the Americas—
Papago
Paper
Paper I. C. Sandburg.—WiP
Paper II. C. Sandburg.—WiP
"**Paper** is two kinds, to write on, to wrap with."
See Paper I
Paper I. Carl Sandburg.—WiP
Paper II. Carl Sandburg.—WiP
The **parable** of the prodigal son. See Gospel
according to Luke
Parables
The parable of the prodigal son. From
Gospel according to Luke.—PlL
"**Parade.**" Lillian Morrison.—MoW
Parades
"Bring the comb and play upon it." R. L.
Stevenson.—MoF
"Parade." L. Morrison.—MoW
Skeleton parade. J. Prelutsky.—PrI
Paradise. See Heaven
Paradise lost, sels. John Milton
"And God said, let the waters generate."—
PaE

"His place of birth a solemn angel tells."—
BaC
"Two of far nobler shape, erect and tall."—
PlL
Paradise regained, sel. John Milton
"At thy nativity a glorious quire."—LiPch
Paradox, sel. Angelus Silesius
"Now simple we must grow."—BaC
The **paradox** ("I am the mother of sorrows")
Paul Laurence Dunbar.—BrI
The **parakeet** trail. Lillian Morrison.—MoO
Parakeets
The parakeet trail. L. Morrison.—MoO
"This is Elmer Johnson." N. M. Bodecker.—
BoHh
The **parent** ("Children aren't happy with
nothing to ignore") Ogden Nash.—BlC
Parentheses. Eve Merriam.—MeR
Parents and parenthood. See also Family;
Fathers and fatherhood; Home and family
life; Mothers and motherhood
Beth-Gelert. W. R. Spencer.—CoG
Epistle to the Olympians. O. Nash.—BlC
For sapphires. C. M. Rodgers.—AdC
Lines to three boys, 8, 6 1/2, and 2 years of
age. F. P. Adams.—PlL
Manerathiak's song. Unknown.—DoWh
The parent ("Children aren't happy with
nothing to ignore") O. Nash.—BlC
The primitiae to parents. R. Herrick.—PlL
Tableau at twilight. O. Nash.—BlC
Through the vines. A. Mandelbaum.—PlL
Two people. E. Merriam.—MeW
The **park** at evening. Leslie Norris.—HiD—
NoM
Park at sundown. Myra Cohn Livingston.—LiF
Parker, Charlie (about)
Mellowness and flight. G. Barlow.—AdC
Yardbird's skull. O. Dodson.—AdC
Parker, Dorothy
Verse for a certain dog.—CoG
Parking lot full. Eve Merriam.—MeR
"A **parking** meter told me." See The
abominable fairy of Bloor street
Parks
Cannon Park. M. St. Germain.—JaPp
In the park. L. Moore.—MoTs
Lucas Park, St. Louis. P. S. Bliss.—FlA
"Mama never understood." N. Grimes.—GrS
My dinosaur's day in the park. E.
Winthrop.—CoDb
The park at evening. L. Norris.—HiD—NoM
Park at sundown. M. C. Livingston.—LiF
Snowy benches. A. Fisher.—FiO
"**Parque** de bombas, boom boo." See Fire house
Parr, Letitia
The curly-wigs.—DuSn
A man and his hat.—DuSn
The **parrot.** Edward Lucie-Smith.—HiS
Parrot from Trinidad. William Jay Smith.—SmL
Parrot from Zambezi. William Jay Smith.—SmL
"A **parrot** I bought in Zambezi." See Parrot
from Zambezi
"The **parrot** is a thief." See The parrot

Dust.—PeB
Farmer.—PeB
Feet.—PeB
Final stone.—PeB
Flutter wheel.—PeB
Four of July.—PeB
The granite sentry.—PeB
Hymn.—PeB
The last waltz.—PeB
Manger tale.—PeB
Manhood.—PeB
Mushrooms.—PeB
The needing.—PeB
Nest.—PeB
North fence.—PeB
Old gray barn.—PeB
An old man's crust.—PeB
On relief.—PeB
The pocket whetstone.—PeB
Rabbit track.—PeB
Rutland fair.—PeB
Sarah's wondrous thing.—PeB
September creek.—PeB
Sharing.—PeB
Shoeing up the mare.—PeB
A sister's grave.—PeB
Sumac whistle.—PeB
Summer sump.—PeB
To Catlin.—PeB
To leather.—PeB
Tools.—PeB
Whipping apples.—PeB
Winter calf.—PeB
Winter notes.—PeB
Winter worship.—PeB
Wood box.—PeB
Peckin'. Shel Silverstein.—SiL
Peculiar. Eve Merriam.—WiP
"The **pedal** on our school piano squeaks." See
　Fun
Peddlers and venders
The balloon man. R. Fyleman.—PaI
"The chestnut vendor." K. Szelki.—JaPp
The corner newsman. K. Starbird.—HoMp—
　StC
The ice-cart. W. Gibson.—PaE
The ice cream man. R. Field.—PaI
Lemonade. D. McCord.—McO
Mr. Tom Narrow. J. Stephens.—HiS
Mom's mums. D. McCord.—McO
Needles and pins. M. Van Doren.—HiS
"Peddling from door to door." From Four
　glimpses of night. F. M. Davis.—RuM
Shoeshine men. A. Lorde.—MoGp
"Who shined shoes in Times Square." L.
　Jeffers.—AdC
"**Peddling** from door to door." See Four
　glimpses of night
"**Peeking** from her room." See Dusk
Peepers in the swamp grass. Nancy Dingman
　Watson.—WaB
The **pelican** ("The food of most birds costs
　them nil") Ronald McCaig and Isla
　Stuart.—DuSn

Pelicans
The pelican ("The food of most birds costs
　them nil") R. McCaig and I. Stuart.—DuSn
Pencils
The unwritten. W. S. Merwin.—LuZ
Penguin ("O penguin, do you ever try") Mary
　Ann Hoberman.—HoY
The **penguin** ("The penguin is often compared,
　wrongly") John Gardner.—GaCb
Penguin ("The polar bear never makes his
　bed") William Jay Smith.—SmL
"The **penguin** is often compared, wrongly." See
　The penguin
Penguins
Penguin ("O penguin, do you ever try") M.
　A. Hoberman.—HoY
The penguin ("The penguin is often
　compared, wrongly") J. Gardner.—GaCb
Penguin ("The polar bear never makes his
　bed") W. J. Smith.—SmL
Polar bear. W. J. Smith.—SmL
A **penitent** considers another coming of Mary.
　Gwendolyn Brooks.—LiPch
"**Penny** pincher." See Penny song
Penny, Rob
"I remember how she sang."—AdC
"The real people loves one another."—AdC
Penny song. N. M. Bodecker.—BoHh
Penthouse. Aileen Fisher.—FiO
People
Cat. W. J. Smith.—SmL
Dog. W. J. Smith.—SmL
Grant Wood's American landscape. W. T.
　Scott.—PlG
Holes ("Strangest of gaps") L. Morrison.—
　MoO
"It don't matter." N. Grimes.—GrS
Man and owl. J. Aiken.—AiS
Mannahatta. W. Whitman.—PlG
Mr. Smith. W. J. Smith.—SmL
Observations. L. Morrison.—MoO
Of being numerous #24. G. Oppen.—PlG
Our country. H. D. Thoreau.—PlG
People ("Hour after hour") W. J. Smith.—
　SmL
A short directory of Kent. J. Aiken.—AiS
Some lives. L. Morrison.—MoO
"There was an old lady named Hart." W. J.
　Smith.—SmL
The trip. W. Stafford.—JaPp
We wear the mask. P. L. Dunbar.—BrI
"Wear you a hat or wear you a crown."
　Mother Goose.—TrGg
Work and play. T. Hughes.—HuSs
People—Portraits. See also Boys and boyhood;
　Girls and girlhood
Creatures we can do without. E. Merriam.—
　MeR
Notions. E. Merriam.—MeR
"Word face." L. Morrison.—MoW
People—Portraits—Men
Benjamin Franklin Hazard. E. L. Masters.—
　PlG
The couple. M. Angelou.—AnO

Peregrine White and Virginia Dare. Rosemary and Stephen Vincent Benet.—WiP
The **perfect** gift. Edmund Vance Cooke.—LiPch
"A **perfect** rainbow, a wide." See The storm
Perfection
    Almost perfect. S. Silverstein.—SiL
    Life's tragedy. P. L. Dunbar.—BrI
The **perforated** spirit. Morris Bishop.—BrO
Perhaps ("Perhaps I didn't") David McCord.—McSu
"**Perhaps** I didn't." See Perhaps
"**Perhaps** the children of a future day." See Unless we guard them well
Periwinkle pizza. Dennis Lee.—LeG
"**Permitted** to assist you, let me see." See St. Valentine
Perry, Jillian D.
    To an old cat.—SaM
Perseverance
    He had his dream. P. L. Dunbar.—BrI
    Slow through the dark. P. L. Dunbar.—BrI
A **person** from Britain. N. M. Bodecker.—BoP
A **person** in Aruba. N. M. Bodecker.—BoP
A **person** in Corning. N. M. Bodecker.—BoP
A **person** in Rome. N. M. Bodecker.—BoP
A **person** in Skye. N. M. Bodecker.—BoP
A **person** in Spain. N. M. Bodecker.—BoP
A **person** in Stirling. N. M. Bodecker.—BoP
A **person** named Briggs. N. M. Bodecker.—BoP
A **person** of Deeping. N. M. Bodecker.—BoP
A **person** of Ealing. N. M. Bodecker.—BoP
A **person** of Florence. N. M. Bodecker.—BoP
A **person** of Haxey. N. M. Bodecker.—BoP
A **person** of Keene. N. M. Bodecker.—BoP
A **person** of Nigg. N. M. Bodecker.—BoP
A **person** of Pinsk. N. M. Bodecker.—BoP
A **person** of Rame. N. M. Bodecker.—BoP
"A **person** of Stow-on-the-Wold." Myra Cohn Livingston.—LiLl
"A **person** of taste in Aruba." See A person in Aruba
Personal beauty. See Beauty, personal
Personals. Leatrice W. Emeruwa.—JaPp
Pessimism. See Despair; Melancholy
Petals ("Flowers need petals") Aileen Fisher.—FiO
Pete the pup at the seashore. Don Marquis.—MoGp
    Pete at the seashore.—CoG
"**Peter** is often the first one up." See The first day of school
"**Peter,** Peter, pumpkin eater." Mother Goose.—TrGg
"**Peter** was a pilot." Dennis Lee.—LeG
Peter White will ne'er go right." Mother Goose.—LoG—TrGg
"**Peterboo** and Prescott." See Almost
Peters, Robert
    Arrival, New York harbor.—PlG
Petrie, Phil W.
    It happened in Montgomery.—MoGp
Petroski, Henry
    Horse girl.—CoPh

Pets. See also names of pets, as Cats
    Albert. D. Abse.—MaP
    The animal store. R. Field.—PaI
    Cat bath. V. Worth.—WoSm
    "Chang McTang McQuarter cat." J. Ciardi.—WiP
    The collies. E. Anthony.—CoG
    The dog ("The truth I do not stretch or shove") O. Nash.—BlC—CoG
    The dog parade. A. Guiterman.—CoG
    The dracula vine. T. Hughes.—HuM
    Dudley not cuddly. W. Cole.—CoDb
    Duet. A. Fisher.—FiO
    Fashions in dogs. E. B. White.—CoG
    For a good dog. A. Guiterman.—CoG
    For Mugs. M. C. Livingston.—LiF
    Gone. D. McCord.—HoBm—McO
    Have I got dogs. W. Cole.—CoG
    Hot dog. S. Silverstein.—SiL
    The hound. S. Lanier.—CoG
    Hula eel. S. Silverstein.—SiL
    I had a hippopotamus. P. Barrington.—WiP
    I have a lion. K. Kuskin.—KuD
    I'd like to. M. A. Hoberman.—HoY
    "If I ever kept a puma." E. Dare.—DuSn
    Kindness to animals. L. E. Richards.—CoA
    Lost dog. F. Rodman.—CoG
    Man and owl. J. Aiken.—AiS
    Missing. A. A. Milne.—PaI
    The monster's pet. L. Moore.—WaM
    My cat and I. A. Fisher.—FiO
    My dinosaur's day in the park. E. Winthrop.—CoDb
    My puppy ("It's funny") A. Fisher.—BeR
    Of an ancient spaniel in her fifteenth year. C. Morley.—CoG
    Old dog Tray. S. Foster.—CoG
    The old dog's song. L. Norris.—NoM
    "One day our pets were really sick." C. Davis.—DuSn
    The power of the dog. R. Kipling.—CoG
    Samuel. B. Katz.—MoGp
    Silly dog. M. C. Livingston.—LiF
    Suzie's new dog. J. Ciardi.—CoG
    Tim, an Irish terrier. W. M. Letts.—CoG
    Tom's little dog. W. De La Mare.—CoG
    Turtle ("Our turtle did not eat today") S. Silverstein.—SiL
    Two dogs have I. O. Nash.—CoG
    Wild strawberries. S. Silverstein.—SiL
Phantasus, I, 8. Arno Holz, tr. by Babette Deutsch.—LiPch
The **phantom** ice cream man. X. J. Kennedy.—KeP
The **phantom** ship. Michael Patrick Hearn.—WaGp.
Phantoms. See Ghosts
Phillips, Frank Lamont
    Daybreak.—AdC
Phillips, Homer
    Handyman.—BrO
Phillips, Louis
    A day at the races.—CoPh
    The dinosaur.—CoDb

The pig ("The pig, if I am not mistaken") O. Nash.—BlC

Pig ("Pigs are always awfully dirty") W. J. Smith.—SmL

A pig tale. J. Reeves.—WiP

Pigs ("Pigs are stout") J. Prelutsky.—PrQ

The piguana. J. Yolen.—YoH

"There once was a pig." M. A. Hoberman.—HoY

"There was a lady loved a swine." Mother Goose.—WiP

"This little pig built a spaceship." From The space child's Mother Goose. F. Winsor.—BrO

Pigs ("Pigs are stout") Jack Prelutsky.—PrQ

"**Pigs** are always awfully dirty." See Pig

"**Pigs** are stout." See Pigs

The **piguana**. Jane Yolen.—YoH

Pilgrims
First Thanksgiving. M. C. Livingston.—LiF

Pillbug. Mary Ann Hoberman.—HoBu

"A **pillbug** when excited will roll up into a ball." See Pillbug

"The **pillows** wet our faces with." See New and old gospel

Pilots and piloting. See Fliers and Flight

"**Pin** wheels whirling round." See Fourth of July night

Pine trees
Southern pines. J. P. Bishop.—PlG
Under the white pine. D. McCord.—McO
Up in the pine. N. D. Watson.—HoBm

Ping pong
Dr Ping and Mr Pong. D. McCord.—McO

Pink
The groaning board.—CoPs

"**Pinky** Pauper picked my pocket." Clyde Watson.—WiP

Pins
Safety pin. V. Worth.—WoM

The **pinwheel's** song. John Ciardi.—HiS

Pioneer life. See Frontier and pioneer life

Pippa passes, sel. Robert Browning
"The year's at the spring."—MoF
Pippa's song.—PaB

Pippa's song. See Pippa passes

The **pirate** ("Oh, the blithery, blathery pirate") Shel Silverstein.—SiL

Pirate captain Jim. Shel Silverstein.—WiP

Pirates
Captain Blackbeard did what. S. Silverstein.—SiL
P is for pirate. W. J. Smith.—SmL
The pirate ("Oh, the blithery, blathery pirate") S. Silverstein.—SiL
Pirate captain Jim. S. Silverstein.—WiP
The reformed pirate. T. G. Roberts.—DoWh
The tale of Custard the dragon. O. Nash.—BlC

Pistachio ice cream. See From the kitchen—Pistachio ice cream

"**Pistachio** ice cream, all green." See From the kitchen—Pistachio ice cream

The **pit** ponies. Leslie Norris.—NoM

Pit viper. N. Scott Momaday.—MoGd

Pitcher McDowell. N. M. Bodecker.—BoP

Pitches, D. O.
Man in orbit.—LuZ

Pittman, Al
"Roger was a razor fish."—BeR

"**Pity** the girl with crystal hair." See Fable

Piyyut for Rosh Hashana, Chaim Guri, tr. fr. the Israeli by Ruth Finer Mintz.—LiO

The **pizza** ("Look at itsy-bitsy Mitzi") Ogden Nash.—BlC

"**Place** a foot upon a pedal." See Bike twister

"**Place** your hand." See Love tight

Places. See also names of places, as Vermont
American names. S. V. Benet.—PlG
An Englishman with an atlas or America the unpronounceable. M. Bishop.—PlG
"From Paumanok starting I fly like a bird." W. Whitman.—PlG
Mice ("Mice find places") V. Worth.—WoSm
N. Y. to L. A. by jet plane. S. Dorman.—PlG
Our country. H. D. Thoreau.—PlG
The river. H. Crane.—PlG

Plaint of the summer vampires. Judith Moffet.—LuZ

Plainview: 1. N. Scott Momaday.—MoGd

Plainview: 2. N. Scott Momaday.—MoGd

Plainview: 3. N. Scott Momaday.—MoGd

Plainview: 4. N. Scott Momaday.—MoGd

Plane geometry. Emma Rounds.—BrO

Plane thinking. Joan Aiken.—AiS

Planets. See Moon; Space and space travel; World

"**Planted** in rows." See C is for cabbages

Plants and planting. See also Gardens and gardening; also names of plants, as Dandelions
Apollo and Daphne. J. Aiken.—AiS
The black fern. L. Norris.—NoM
Crab-grass. T. Hughes.—HuM
The defenders. T. Hughes.—HuSs
Done with. A. Stanford.—LuZ
The dracula vine. T. Hughes.—HuM
Foxgloves. T. Hughes.—HuM
"Fueled." M. Hans.—HoMp
The golden boy. T. Hughes.—HuSs
Have you thanked a green plant today (bumper sticker). D. Anderson.—BrO
The house plants. E. Coatsworth.—MaP
Jubilate herbis. N. Farber.—LiPch
Moon dog-daisies. T. Hughes.—HuM
Moon hops. T. Hughes.—HuM
Moon roses. T. Hughes.—HuM
"My great corn plants." Unknown.—MoGp
"The sun finally tolerable." From Autumn nature notes. T. Hughes.—HuSs
Surprises are happening. J. C. Soule.—HoMp
"Three pale foxglove lamp mantles, in full flare." From Autumn nature notes. T. Hughes.—HuSs
You can't get rags from ragweed. K. Starbird.—StC

The **plaque** in the reading room for my
　　classmates killed in Korea. F. D. Reeve.—
　　PlG
Plate tectonics on waking. Lillian Morrison.—
　　MoO
Plath, Sylvia
　　Mushrooms, sel.
　　　　"So many of us."—MoGp
　　"So many of us." See Mushrooms
Play. See also Counting-out rhymes; Games;
　　Jump-rope rhymes; Make-believe; Nursery
　　play
　　Andrew's bedtime story. I. Serraillier.—HiD
　　Applesauce. M. A. Hoberman.—HoY
　　Around my room. W. J. Smith.—SmL
　　At the sandpile. A. Fisher.—FiO
　　"Bring the comb and play upon it." R. L.
　　　　Stevenson.—MoF
　　Catching-song a play rhyme. E. Farjeon.—
　　　　WiP
　　Catherine. K. Kuskin.—KuD
　　The cellar hole. D. McCord.—McO
　　The centaur. M. Swenson.—CoPh—HiS
　　"Here I am, little jumping Joan." Mother
　　　　Goose.—TrGg
　　"Here we go." M. A. Hoberman.—HoY
　　Hydrant. J. Thurman.—ThFo
　　In the park. L. Moore.—MoTs
　　Let's dress up. M. A. Hoberman.—HoY
　　Love ("Ricky was "L" but he's home with
　　　　the flu") S. Silverstein.—YaI
　　Monkey vines. N. D. Watson.—WaB
　　Moochie. E. Greenfield.—GrH
　　The muddy puddle. D. Lee.—LeG
　　My boat. J. Prelutsky.—PrR
　　My coloring book. J. Prelutsky.—PrR
　　Noises ("We play that we are soldiers") A.
　　　　Fisher.—FiO
　　Nurse's song. W. Blake.—MoF
　　Oil slick. J. Thurman.—ThFo
　　The outlaw. F. Holman.—CoI
　　"Outside, I want to play." N. Grimes.—GrS
　　Pick me up. W. J. Smith.—WiP
　　"Playing hopscotch on the." K. Mizumura.—
　　　　MiF
　　The pole bean tent. K. Starbird.—StC
　　Rain ("What a day, does it rain, is it rainy")
　　　　D. McCord.—McSu
　　Rainy rainy Saturday. J. Prelutsky.—PrR
　　Recess. L. Moore.—MoTs
　　Rhinoceros. W. J. Smith.—SmL
　　Rural recreation. L. Morrison.—MoSr
　　A sandpile town. A. Fisher.—FiO
　　"She sent me out to play again." N.
　　　　Grimes.—GrS
　　The ships of Yule. B. Carman.—DoWh
　　Snow ("We'll play in the snow") K. Kuskin.—
　　　　KuD
　　So run along and play. D. McCord.—McO
　　Somersaults. J. Prelutsky.—PrR
　　Song ("I'd much rather sit there in the sun")
　　　　R. Krauss.—HiS
　　Spring. K. Kuskin.—HoMp—KuD—WiP
　　Strawberry patches. N. Giovanni.—GiV

Tired. S. Silverstein.—SiL
"Waiting for someone to play with." N.
　　Grimes.—GrS
Whenever. M. A. Hoberman.—HoY
"Where the pools are bright and deep." J.
　　Hogg.—MoF
Whipping apples. R. N. Peck.—PeB
Will you. E. Merriam.—MeB
Wings. S. J. Crossen and N. A. Covell.—
　　HoBm
"You were the mother last time." M. A.
　　Hoberman.—CoI
"You're Mrs Cobble and I'm Mrs Frome." M.
　　A. Hoberman.—HoY
Play ball. Shel Silverstein.—SiL
"The **play** street." See Hydrant
"**Playing** hopscotch on the." Kazue
　　Mizumura.—MiF
Playing with clay. Judith Thurman.—ThFo
Plea. Judith Hemschemeyer.—LuZ
"**Please** bird, don't go yet." Kazue Mizumura.—
　　MiF
Please, Johnny. John Ciardi.—WaM
Pleasures of the bath. Eve Merriam.—MeR
Plenty of time. Aileen Fisher.—FiO
Pliny Jane. Mildred Luton.—CoPh
"**Plowdens,** Finns." See Beginnings
Plumly, Stanley
　　The end of the Indian poems.—PlG
Plumpp, Sterling D.
　　For Mattie and eternity.—AdC
"**Plunk** a plunk, plunk a plunk." See Banjo
　　tune
"A **plus** or a minus." See Shall I consider you
Plymouth Rocks, of course. David McCord.—
　　McO
Po Chu-i
　　To his brother Hsing-Chien.—PlL
Pocahontas (about)
　　Jamestown ("Let me look at what I was,
　　　　before I die") R. Jarrell.—PlG
The **pocket** whetstone. Robert Newton Peck.—
　　PeB
Pockets
　　"What are pockets for." D. McCord.—McO
Poe, Edgar Allan
　　The city in the sea.—PaE
Poem ("I loved my friend") Langston
　　Hughes.—LuZ—MaP
Poem ("In a high wind") A. R. Ammons.—
　　MoGp
The **poem** ("It's all in") William Carlos
　　Williams.—JaPp
Poem ("You said") Pearl Cleage Lomax.—AdC
Poem, a reminder. Robert Graves.—LuZ
A **poem** about beauty, blackness, poetry, and
　　how to be all three. Linda Brown Bragg.—
　　AdC
The **poem** as a door. Eve Merriam.—MeR
Poem at thirty. Sonia Sanchez.—AdC
A **poem** for Carol. Nikki Giovanni.—MaP
A **poem** for heroes. Julia Fields.—AdC
Poem for Otis Redding. Joyce Carol Thomas.—
　　AdC

Points of view
  Point of view. S. Silverstein.—CoPs
Poison ivy
  Poison ivy ("A wicked witch") K.
    Gallagher.—WaW
  The witch's garden. L. Moore.—WiP
Poison ivy ("A wicked witch") Katherine
  Gallagher.—WaW
A poison tree. William Blake.—MaP
Poland
  The polka. O. Nash.—BlC
Polar bear ("I think it must be very nice")
  William Jay Smith.—SmL
"The polar bear never makes his bed." See
  Penguin
Polar regions. See also Eskimos
  Charter flight. J. Aiken.—AiS
  The ice-cart. W. Gibson.—PaE
  The ice king. A. B. Demille.—DoWh
  Manerathiak's song. Unknown.—DoWh
  "Once in the winter." From The forsaken. D.
    C. Scott.—DoWh
  Penguin ("The polar bear never makes his
    bed") W. J. Smith.—SmL
  Polar bear ("I think it must be very nice") W.
    J. Smith.—SmL
  The shooting of Dan McGrew. R. W.
    Service.—DoWh
  The train dogs. P. Johnson.—DoWh
  The wind has wings. Unknown.—DoWh
The pole bean tent. Kaye Starbird.—StC
Pole vault. Shiro Murano, tr. by Satoru Sato
  and Constance Urdang.—LuZ
Police
  Inspector Dogbone gets his man. D. Lee.—
    LeG
  Lust. W. Matthews.—JaPp
"Policeman, policeman." See Stop thief
Politeness. See Etiquette
The polka. Ogden Nash.—BlC
Pollution
  And they lived happily ever after for a while.
    J. Ciardi.—LuZ
  Like ghosts of eagles. R. Francis.—PlG
  Pollution ("O, I am mad with the maddest of
    men") M. C. Livingston.—LiF
  "There was a young lady of Rome." O.
    Nash.—BrO
Pollution ("O, I am mad with the maddest of
  men") Myra Cohn Livingston.—LiF
"Polly put the kettle on." Mother Goose.—
  TrGg
"Polly Vole." See Shiver my timbers
"Pollywiggle." See Frog
The poltergeist ("Something strange is flitting
  through your hair") Jack Prelutsky.—PrH
Polyglot. Eve Merriam.—MeR
Pome. David McCord.—McO
Pomerantz, Charlotte
  Cachita.—PoT
  Fire house.—PoT
  The four brothers.—PoT
  Hugs and kisses.—PoT

  A little lullaby to be read a little bit out
    loud.—PoT
  Mari Rosa and the butterfly.—PoT
  Marisol.—PoT
  "My fat cat."—PoT
  My Mami takes me to the bakery.—PoT
  Nada.—PoT
  "The tamarindo puppy."—PoT
  The tea party.—PoT
  You, tu.—PoT
Pomeroy, Marnie
  "Here he comes."—CoDb
"A pompous old donkey of Yately." Myra Cohn
  Livingston.—LiLl
Ponds. See Lakes and ponds; Puddles
Ponies. See Horses
The ponies ("During the strike, the ponies
  were brought up") Wilfrid Gibson.—CoPh
"The pony air, wild wheat." See The end of
  the Indian poems
Pony girl. Jane P. Moreland.—CoPh
Pony song. Rudy Bantista.—LuZ
"A poodle and a grundiboob." See The poodle
  and the grundiboob
The poodle and the grundiboob. Dennis Lee.—
  LeN
The pool. Paul Laurence Dunbar.—BrI
The pool in the rock. Walter De La Mare.—
  PaE—SaM
Poor. Myra Cohn Livingston.—LiWt
"A poor but good woman of Ware." See A
  woman of Ware
"Poor dinosore, his body's big." See The
  dinosore
"Poor dog Bright." Unknown.—BlH
"Poor giant, I see you still don't know." See
  Song of the giant killer
Poor girl. Maya Angelou.—AnO
"A poor, honest baker in France." See A baker
  in France
"Poor Jane Higgins." See A pig tale
"Poor little pigeon-toed Dimity Drew." See
  Little Dimity
A poor man whose pajamas. N. M. Bodecker.—
  BoP
"Poor Mrs. Utter." See Mrs. Utter
"Poor munster cheese monster." See The
  munster cheese monster
"Poor old Mr Bidery." See Mr Bidery's spidery
  garden
"Poor old Mollie Haggarty." Dorothy
  Barnham.—DuSn
"Poor old Penelope." Jack Prelutsky.—PrQ
Poor Robin's almanack, sels. Unknown
  "Now blocks to cleave."—BaC
  "Now that the time has come wherein."—
    BaC
  "Now thrice welcome Christmas."—BaC
The poor snail. J. M. Westrup.—CoA
"Poor song." See The tape
"Pop bottles pop bottles." See Song of the pop
  bottlers
Pope, Alexander
  Eminent cosmologists.—BrO

"**Poplars** are standing there still as death." See
Southern mansion
The **porcupin**. Jane Yolen.—YoH
The **porcupine** ("Any hound a porcupine
nudges") Ogden Nash.—BlC
The **porcupine** ("I watched a weeping
porcupine") Karla Kuskin.—KuD
The **porcupine** ("A porcupine looks somewhat
silly") Karla Kuskin.—CoA—LiCc
"A **porcupine** looks somewhat silly." See The
porcupine
Porcupines
Curious Clyde. J. Prelutsky.—PrQ
The porcupin. J. Yolen.—YoH
The porcupine ("Any hound a porcupine
nudges") O. Nash.—BlC
The porcupine ("I watched a weeping
porcupine") K. Kuskin.—KuD
The porcupine ("A porcupine looks
somewhat silly") K. Kuskin.—CoA—LiCc
The **porpoise** ("I kind of like the playful
porpoise") Ogden Nash.—BlC
Porpoises. See Dolphins and porpoises
Porter, Alan
The stallion.—CoPh
The **portly** object. Karla Kuskin.—KuD
Portmanteaux. Eve Merriam.—MeW
Portrait ("A big young bareheaded woman")
William Carlos Williams.—MoGp
Portrait of Malcolm X. Etheridge Knight.—AdC
A **portrait** of Rudy. Jim Cunningham.—AdC
Portraits. See Paintings and pictures; also
People—Portraits
Possessions. See Wealth
"**Possessions** tie him to his grave." See I have
The **possessors**. Lillian Morrison.—MoSr
Possibilities ("Possibilities, possibilities,
possibilities, possibilities") Felice Holman.—
HoA
Possibilities ("Since we're patterns") Lillian
Morrison.—MoO
"**Possibilities**, possibilities, possibilities,
possibilities." See Possibilities
Possums. See Opossums
Postcards. Eve Merriam.—MeR
"The **poster** with my picture on it." See
Unwanted
"The **postman** comes when I am still in bed."
See A sick child
Postmen. See Mail carriers
Posture. Lillian Morrison.—MoSr
"A **potato** chip is something." See Potato chips
Potato chips. Anthony E. Gallagher.—CoPs—
DuSn
Potatoes
Potato chips. A. E. Gallagher.—CoPs—DuSn
Pottery. See Tableware
Poughkeepsie, New York (about)
"I was riding to Poughkeepsie." M. A.
Hoberman.—HoY
Poultry. See also names of kinds of poultry, as
Chickens
The poultry show. D. McCord.—McO
The **poultry** show. David McCord.—McO

Pound, Ezra
"And the days are not full enough."—JaPp
Ballad of the goodly fere.—LiO
The river-merchant's wife, a letter. tr.—YaI
"**Poundcake** from Ealing." N. M. Bodecker.—
BoHh
Pourquoi. Unknown.—CoG
Poverty
Bored. S. Silverstein.—SiL
Eviction. L. Clifton.—MoGp
Good times. L. Clifton.—AdC
Mrs Utter. J. Reeves.—WiP
Poor. M. C. Livingston.—LiWt
The real question. P. L. Dunbar.—BrI
Street window. C. Sandburg.—JaPp
Power lines. Myra Cohn Livingston.—LiF
The **power** of the dog. Rudyard Kipling.—CoG
The **practical** joke. Jack Prelutsky.—PrRh
Prairie, sel. Carl Sandburg
Finale.—FlA
Prairies
Finale. From Prairie. C. Sandburg.—FlA
To make a prairie. E. Dickinson.—FlA
Praise of a good woman. See Proverbs, sel.
Bible—Old Testament
The **praise** of Christmas, sel. Unknown
"When Christmas-tide comes in like a
bride."—BaC
Praise to the little. Norma Farber.—FaS
Pratt, E. J.
Frost.—DoWh
The shark.—DoWh
The way of Cape Race.—DoWh
Pratt, William W.
Same old trick.—BrO
"**Pray**, what can dreams avail." See Dream
song II
"**Pray** why are you so bare, so bare." See The
haunted oak
A **prayer** ("O Lord, the hard-won miles") Paul
Laurence Dunbar.—BrI
A **prayer** for Halloween. See "From ghoulies
and ghosties"
Prayer for the great family. Gary Snyder, fr.
the Mohawk Indian.—LiO
The **prayer** of the donkey. Carmen Bernos de
Gasztold, tr. by Rumer Godden.—LiPch
The **prayer** of the mouse. Carmen Bernos de
Gasztold, tr. by Rumer Godden.—SaM
Prayer of the selfish child. Shel Silverstein.—SiL
"**Prayer** unsaid, and mass unsung." See The
sea ritual
Prayers. See also Hymns; Psalms
D'Avalos' prayer. J. Masefield.—PaE
"From ghoulies and ghosties." Unknown.—
LiO
A Cornish litany.—LiCc
Ghoulies and ghosties.—WaGp—WaM
Litany for Halloween.—BrIt
A prayer for Halloween.—BrIt
A prayer ("O Lord, the hard-won miles") P.
L. Dunbar.—BrI
A short litany. Unknown.—WaW

Willie ate a worm.—PrRh
The witch.—PrN
The wizard.—PrN
The wozzit.—PrS
Wrimples.—PrS
The yak.—WiP
The zombie.—PrH
Premonition ("Dear heart, good-night") Paul
  Laurence Dunbar.—BrI
Premonitions. See Omens; Prophecies
Preoccupation. Unknown, tr. fr. the Mbundu
  by Merlin Ennis.—LuZ
Preparation. Paul Laurence Dunbar.—BrI
Present. Sonia Sanchez.—AdC
Presents. See Gifts and giving
Presidents. See names of presidents, as Lincoln,
  Abraham
"Pretending to sleep." Judith Thurman.—
  HoBm—ThFo
"A pretentious old man of the Bosporus." See A
  bright idea
"A pretty little girl in a round-eared cap."
  Mother Goose.—TrGg
"Pretty, that's what daddy." Nikki Grimes.—
  GrS
"A pretty young maid in New York." See A
  maid in New York
Prevert, Jacques
  How to paint the portrait of a bird.—LuZ
Prickled pickles don't smile. Nikki Giovanni.—
  GiV
Pride and vanity
  The flattered flying fish. E. V. Rieu.—HiS
  Girl child. L. Morrison.—MoSr
  The hare and the tortoise. I. Serraillier.—HiS
  I'm sorry. M. C. Livingston.—LiWt
  The mysterious cat. V. Lindsay.—WiP
  The purist. O. Nash.—BlC—WiP
  The race. J. Prelutsky.—PrRh
Prideaux, Tom
  Skip scoop anellie.—CoPs
The primitiae to parents. Robert Herrick.—PlL
"Princes and kings decay and die." See Stanzas
  on the decease of Thomas Paine, who died
  at New York on the 8th day of June, 1809
Princes and princesses
  After ever happily. I. Serraillier.—HiS
  Palace cook's tale. J. Aiken.—AiS
  The yak. V. Sheard.—DoWh
Prisoner. Maya Angelou.—AnO
Prisons and prisoners
  Girl held without bail. M. Walker.—AdC
  The idea of ancestry. E. Knight.—AdC
  If we cannot live as people. C. Lynch.—AdC
  Prisoner. M. Angelou.—AnO
  To Bobby Seale. L. Clifton.—AdC
Privacy
  My box. M. C. Livingston.—LiWt
The prize in the sky. X. J. Kennedy.—KeP
Probability and birds. Russell Atkins.—AdC
"The probability in the yard." See Probability
  and birds
"Probable-Possible, my black hen." See The
  space child's Mother Goose

The problem of wild horses. Barbara Winder.—
  CoPh
Problems ("It is said") Lillian Morrison.—MoO
Procter, Bryan Waller
  The blood horse.—CoPh
  The stormy petrel.—PaE
Prodigal returns. Eve Merriam.—MeR
The prodigal son. Theodore Spencer.—PlL
Professions. See names of professions, as
  Doctors
Progress
  Ballade of the old time engine. E. H.
    Vines.—BrO
  Blast off. From Progress. F. Lamport.—BrO
  The building of the skyscraper. G. Oppen.—
    PlG
  Civilization ("I've stood here lately, looking
    at the path") M. C. Livingston.—LiF
  Construction ("Wham") V. Schonberg.—BrO
  Far trek. J. Brady.—BrO
  Highway construction. C. E. Chapin.—BrO
  "If all the thermo-nuclear warheads." K.
    Burke.—BrO
  Kid stuff. F. Horne.—LiPch
  Meredith Phyfe. E. L. Masters.—PlG
  Miss Casper's cow. K. Starbird.—StC
  Ode to a vanished operator in an
    automatized elevator. L. Rosenfield.—BrO
  "Once we felt at home with nature if we
    knew the nomenclature." From Progress.
    F. Lamport.—BrO
  Progress ("From hoofbeat to chug-chug to
    roar of jet") S. Douglas.—BrO
  Progress ("There are two ways now") E.
    Agnew.—LuZ
  Same old trick. W. W. Pratt.—BrO
  Southern pines. J. P. Bishop.—PlG
  Stanzas on the emigration to America, and
    peopling the western country. P.
    Freneau.—PlG
  "They're tearing down a town." J. Strunk.—
    BrO
  Unless we guard them well. J. Merchant.—
    BrO
  Whistling Willie. K. Starbird.—BrO
  You take the pilgrims, just give me the
    progress. L. Rosenfield.—BrO
Progress ("From hoofbeat to chug-chug to roar
  of jet") Suzanne Douglas.—BrO
Progress ("There are two ways now") Edith
  Agnew.—LuZ
Progress, sels. Felicia Lamport
  Blast off.—BrO
  "Once we felt at home with nature if we
    knew the nomenclature."—BrO
A project for freight trains. David Young.—LuZ
Projected view of 2000. Freya Manfred.—KhI
"Promise not to tell." See The secret
Pronunciation
  An englishman with an atlas, or America the
    unpronounceable. M. Bishop.—PlG
  Ough. D. McCord.—McO

"**Pure** fasted faces draw unto this feast." See Easter communion

"**Pure** gold, they said in her praise." See Around Thanksgiving

The **purist**. Ogden Nash.—BlC—WiP

Purple (color)
Taste of purple. L. B. Jacobs.—HoMp

Push button. Shel Silverstein.—SiL

The **pusher**. Maya Angelou.—AnO

"**Pushing** heavy." See From the window

"**Pussy** cat, pussy cat, where have you been." Mother Goose.—TrGg

Pussy willows. See Willow trees

Pussy willows ("Willow buds come early") Aileen Fisher.—FiO

Put something in. Shel Silverstein.—SiL

Puzzle ("Map of a city with streets meeting at center") Robert Froman.—MoGp

Puzzle ("My best friend's name is Billy") Arnold Spilka.—CoI

Puzzle ("What can you do with a lap") Eve Merriam.—MeB

Puzzles
Jigsaw puzzle. R. Hoban.—MoGp
Picture puzzle piece. S. Silverstein.—SiL
Puzzle ("Map of a city with streets meeting at center") R. Froman.—MoGp
Puzzle ("What can you do with a lap") E. Merriam.—MeB
Rebus valentine. Unknown.—YaI

Puzzling. William Cole.—CoA

"The **pygmy** shrew is very small." See The shrew

Pythagorean razzle dazzle. Sid Gary.—BrO

The **python** ("One afternoon, while sitting in a tree") John Gardner.—GaCb

The **pythong**. Jane Yolen.—YoH

"The **pythong** ties itself in knots." See The pythong

Pythons
The python ("One afternoon, while sitting in a tree") J. Gardner.—GaCb

Q

Q is for queen. William Jay Smith.—SmL

Quack. Walter De La Mare.—WiP

"**Quack**, said the billy goat." Charles Causley.—BeR—CoA

"The **quality** of these trees, green height, of the sky, shining." See Shine, republic

Quarrels. See Fights

"A **quarter** horse, no rider." See Horse

Quatrains
Write me a verse. D. McCord.—McO

Quebec, Canada
Donkey riding. Unknown.—DoWh
Quebec May. E. Birney.—DoWh

Quebec May. Earle Birney.—DoWh

The **queen**. Pablo Neruda, tr. fr. the Spanish by Donald D. Walsh.—YaI

Queen Mab. See Romeo and Juliet

"The **queen** of ants she lays the eggs." See Ant song

The **Queen** of Eene. Jack Prelutsky.—PrQ

"The **Queen** of Eene is such a goose." See The Queen of Eene

The **Queen** of the Nile. William Jay Smith.—SmL

Queen Zixi of Ix, sel. L. Frank Baum
Witches' spells.—WaW

Queens. See Rulers

Queer. David McCord.—McO

Queer story of the fowse or fox. David McCord.—McO

Quennell, Peter
The divers.—PaE
Leviathan.—PaE

Question ("The grownups say I'm growing tall") Mary Ann Hoberman.—HoY

The **question** ("If I could teach you how to fly") Dennis Lee.—LeN

The **question** ("People always say to me") Karla Kuskin.—KuD

Question ("Who says, but one month more") David McCord.—McO

"**Question**, What kind of rabbit can an Easter rabbit be." See Easter morning

Questions
Answering your question. D. McCord.—McO
Applesauce. M. A. Hoberman.—HoY
Dictionary. W. J. Smith.—SmL
John ("John comes in with a basket") D. McCord.—McO
"The man in the wilderness asked me." Mother Goose.—TrGg
The question ("People always say to me") K. Kustin.—KuD
Question ("Who says, but one month more") D. McCord.—McO
Questions at night. L. Untermeyer.—RuM
"Where have you been dear." From Near the window tree. K. Kuskin.—HoBm
Why ("Why do apricots look like eggs") W. J. Smith.—SmL
Zebra question. S. Silverstein.—SiL

Questions at night. Louis Untermeyer.—RuM

"**Quick**." See Blue alert

"**Quick**, quick, said Jack." See Jack, Jill, Spratts, and Horner

Quick trip. Shel Silverstein.—SiL

"**Quiet** cardinal." Betsy Maestro.—MaFp

"The **quiet-eyed** cattle." Leslie Norris.—LiPch—NoM

"**Quiet**, my horse, be quiet." See Alexander to his horse

"A **quiet** old farmer of Cwm." See A farmer of Cwm

The **quiet** shining sun. Aileen Fisher.—FiO

"**Quietly** down the sky." See Lady of night

"**Quietness** clings to the air." See The snow fall

Quilts
Crazy quilt. J. Yolen.—HeB
The spare quilt. J. P. Bishop.—PlG

The **quinquaped** jikes. Peter Wesley-Smith.—DuSn

Railroads

Ballade of the old time engine. E. H. Vines.—BrO

The Bendigo track. O. Mendelsohn.—DuSn

Burying ground by the ties. A. MacLeish.—PlG

Crossing. P. Booth.—PlG

Crossing Kansas by train. D. Justice.—FlA

Derricks. R. R. Cuscaden.—FlA

Evening song. S. Anderson.—FlA

The goose ("At the end of the train, in the big red caboose") R. S. Oliver.—OlC

The green train. E. V. Rieu.—HiS

"I know I have lost my train." Mother Goose.—LoG

The locomotive sloth. X. J. Kennedy.—KeP

"Look out for the platform." J. Aiken.—AiS

Night journey. T. Roethke.—PlG

Night landscape. J. Aiken.—AiS—HiD—RuM

Night train. R. Francis.—HiD

The ombley-gombley. P. Wesley-Smith.—WaM

A project for freight trains. D. Young.—LuZ

Return to nowhere. J. Aiken.—AiS

Riding on the train. E. Greenfield.—GrH

The river. H. Crane.—PlG

A siding near Chillicothe. R. Lattimore.—FlA

Song of the train. D. McCord.—McO

Whistle. D. McCord.—McO

Rain

After a freezing rain. A. Fisher.—FiO

After a rain. A. Fisher.—FiO

April fool ("April started out to cry") A. Fisher.—FiO

April rain song. L. Hughes.—HoMp

Birds in the rain. D. McCord.—McO

Country rain. A. Fisher.—FiO

Country window. A. Fisher.—FiO

"The day dark with rain." A. Atwood.—AtH

"Do ghouls." L. Moore.—BrIt

"Doctor Foster went to Glo'ster." Mother Goose.—TrGg

"The doves stay in their cotes." N. M. Bodecker.—BoHh

A drowsy day. P. L. Dunbar.—BrI

Drums of the rain. M. C. Davies.—PaI

"The first drop of rain." A. Atwood.—AtH

For a ladybug. A. Fisher.—FiO

Fudge. J. Prelutsky.—PrR

Like a giant in a towel. D. Lee.—WaG

"The little rain." J. Thurman.—ThFo

Magic jellybean. J. Prelutsky.—PrR

"Nicely, nicely, nicely, nicely there away in the east." Unknown.—MoGp

"Nicely while it is raining." Unknown.—MoGp

Night rain. A. Stanford.—LuZ

A person in Spain. N. M. Bodecker.—BoP

Rain ("Beautiful rain") E. Jennings.—SaM

Rain ("Rain hits over and over") A. Stoutenberg.—MoGp

Rain ("What a day, does it rain, is it rainy") D. McCord.—McSu

The rain in Maine. N. M. Bodecker.—BoHh

Rain in the night. A. J. Burr.—PaI

The rain reminds me. J. Moore.—MoGp

Rain song. D. McCord.—McO

Rain songs. P. L. Dunbar.—BrI

Raindrops ("How brave a ladybug must be") A. Fisher.—FiO

"Raindrops like bubbles." B. Maestro.—MaFp

Rainy nights. I. Thompson.—SaM

Rainy rainy Saturday. J. Prelutsky.—PrR

Samurai and hustlers. J. Johnson.—AdC

Silly dog. M. C. Livingston.—CoG

Spell of the rain. L. Norris.—NoM

Spell of the raingods. L. Norris.—NoM

Spring rain. M. Chute.—PaI

The streets of town. A. Fisher.—FiO

Summer grass. C. Sandburg.—MoGp

Summer shower. D. McCord.—McO

Sun after rain. N. Farber.—FaS

The telephone call. J. Prelutsky.—PrR

"Through the window." N. Koriyama.—LuZ

"To walk in warm rain." D. McCord.—McSu

Wager. M. A. Hoberman.—HoY

The walrust. J. Yolen.—YoH

"The wind I love the best." From The spring wind. C. Zolotow.—HoMp

The windshield wipers' song. D. McCord.—McSu

Rain ("Beautiful rain") Elizabeth Jennings.—SaM

Rain ("Rain hits over and over") Adrien Stoutenberg.—MoGp

Rain ("What a day, does it rain, is it rainy") David McCord.—McSu

"The **rain** falls in my face." See Rain in the face

"**Rain** hits over and over." See Rain

The **rain** in Maine. N. M. Bodecker.—BoHh

Rain in the face. Mary Crow.—CoPh

Rain in the night. Amelia Josephine Burr.—PaI

"The **rain** is driving silver nails." See Rain song

"The **rain** is over." See Birth

"**Rain** is so rainy." Beatrice Schenk De Regniers.—ReB

"**Rain**, rain, went away." See Sun after rain

The **rain** reminds me. Jonathan Moore.—MoGp

"The **rain** reminds me of my father." See The rain reminds me

Rain song. David McCord.—McO

Rain songs. Paul Laurence Dunbar.—BrI

"The **rain** streams down like harp-strings from the sky." See Rain songs

"**Rain**, with a silver flail." See Whale

The **rainbow** ("I saw the lovely arch") Walter De La Mare.—SaM

The **rainbow** ("The rainbow arches in the sky") David McCord.—McO

"The **rainbow** arches in the sky." See The rainbow

Rainbow writing. Eve Merriam.—MeR

Rainbows

Legend. J. Wright.—HiS

The rainbow ("I saw the lovely arch") W. De La Mare.—SaM

Red (color)
  King Rufus. Y. Y. Segal.—DoWh
  Red ("All day") L. Moore.—WiP
  When Sue wears red. L. Hughes.—AdC
Red ("All day") Lilian Moore.—WiP
Red birds
  "Quiet cardinal." B. Maestro.—MaFp
  Thistles. K. Kuskin.—WiP
The red-headed woodpecker. John Gardner.—
  GaCb
The red herring. George MacBeth.—HiS
"Red is death, for people who are dying." See
  Colours
"A red salamander." See Salamander
"Red sky at night." Unknown.—SaM
Redbirds. See Red birds
Redcloud, Prince
  And then.—HoMp
  Spring.—HoMp
Redding, Otis (about)
  Poem for Otis Redding. J. C. Thomas.—AdC
Redmond, Eugene
  Love necessitates.—AdC
Reed, Ishmael
  Beware, do not read this poem.—AdC
  Instructions to a princess.—AdC
  The reactionary poet.—AdC
  Untitled I.—AdC
Reeve, F. D.
  The plaque in the reading room for my
    classmates killed in Korea.—PlG
Reeves, James
  The black pebble.—MaP—WiP
  The ceremonial band.—WiP
  Cows.—WiP
  The four horses.—CoPh
  Giant Thunder.—HiD
  The grey horse.—CoPh
  Grim and gloomy.—SaM
  The horn.—HiS
  Little Fan.—HiS
  Mick.—CoG
  Mr Tom Narrow.—HiS
  Mrs Button.—WiP
  Mrs Golightly.—WiP
  Mrs Utter.—WiP
  Old Moll.—WaW
  The old wife and the ghost.—BrIt—WaGp
  A pig tale.—WiP
  The sea.—SaM
  Shiny.—SaM
  The snail.—SaM
  The toadstool wood.—HiD
  W.—MoGp
  The wooing frog.—HiS
  Zachary Zed.—BrO
"Reflect upon the dinosaur." See Lines on a
  small potato
Reflection. Shel Silverstein.—SiL
Reflections (mirrored)
  By the stream. P. L. Dunbar.—BrI
  From the mailboat passing by. D. McCord.—
    McO
  I wonder. S. C. Fox.—FoB

"In the pond in the park." From Water
  picture. M. Swenson.—MoGp
The mirror ("I look in the mirror, and what
  do I see") W. J. Smith.—SmL
Mirrors ("The sun must have a lot of fun") A.
  Fisher.—FiO
Reflection ("Each time I see the upside down
  man") S. Silverstein.—SiL
Sky fish. A. Fisher.—FiO
The star in the pail. D. McCord.—HoBm
The reformed pirate. T. G. Roberts.—DoWh
Refugee in America. Langston Hughes.—
  LiCc—PlG
The refusal to be wrecked. Lillian Morrison.—
  MoW
"Regard the hippopotamus." See The
  hippopotamus
Reggie. Eloise Greenfield.—GrH
"The reins, looped lightly round his aged
  knuckles." See The driver
"Rejoice and be glad." Unknown, fr. the
  Armenian.—BaC
Relatives. See also names of relatives, as Uncles
  The four brothers. C. Pomerantz.—PoT
  "Pumberly Pott's unpredictable niece." J.
    Prelutsky.—PrQ
Relativity. Kathleen Millay.—BrO
Relax, it's sonic boom. See Sonic boom
"Relentless rat-tat-tat." See The boxer
Religion. See also Churches; also names of
  religions, as Christianity
  Address to the scholars of New England. J. C.
    Ransom.—PlG
  Arrival, New York harbor. R. Peters.—PlG
  The house mouse and the church mouse. J.
    Gardner.—GaCb
  "How busie are the sonnes of men." R.
    Williams.—PlG
  On being brought from Africa to America. P.
    Wheatley.—PlG
  Religion ("I am no priest of crooks nor
    creeds") P. L. Dunbar.—BrI
  The saint's lament. D. Lee.—LeN
  Upon the first sight of New England, June
    29, 1638. T. Tillam.—PlG
  "With hearts revived in conceit, new land
    and trees they eye." From Good news
    from New England. E. Johnson.—PlG
Religion ("I am no priest of crooks nor creeds")
  Paul Laurence Dunbar.—BrI
Religion ("I'm a believer") Merrit Malloy.—LuZ
Religion back home, sel. William Stafford
  "When my little brother chanted."—LiCc
Religions. See Christianity; Islam; Judaism;
  Mythology
Remarks from the pup. Burges Johnson.—CoG
"Remember whistling Willie's market." See
  Whistling Willie
"Remembering Grandma filling up this porch."
  Nikki Grimes.—GrS
Reply to the question: how can you become a
  poet. Eve Merriam.—MeR
Reports of midsummer girls. Richmond
  Lattimore.—JaPp

Richardson, Dow
  The cost of living Mother Goose.—BrO

Riches. See Wealth
"Ricky was 'L' but he's home with the flu."
  See Love

Riddle ("Their name is where they like to
  live") Mary Ann Hoberman.—HoBu
The riddle ("Why does a chicken cross the
  road") Kaye Starbird.—StC
A riddle. See "Two legs sat upon three legs"
"Riddle cum diddle cum dido." See Kindness
  to animals
"Riddle me no." See Fiddle faddle

Riddle-me rhyme. David McCord.—McSu
"Riddle-me, riddle-me, ree." See Riddle-me
  rhyme

Riddles
  "Arthur O'Bower has broken his band."
    Mother Goose.—TrGg
  "Flower of England, fruit of Spain."
    Unknown.—BaC
  "Four stiff-standers." Mother Goose.—TrGg
  "Humpty Dumpty sat on a wall." Mother
    Goose.—TrGg
  "I see the cumulus and sky." L. Morrison.—
    MoW
  "I'm banged and chopped and sliced." L.
    Morrison.—MoW
  "An iridescent sea horse." L. Morrison.—
    MoW
  It isn't. E. Merriam.—MeW
  "Look, what am I." D. McCord.—McO
  Rat riddles. C. Sandburg.—HiS
  Riddle ("Their name is where they like to
    live") M. A. Hoberman.—HoBu
  The riddle ("Why does the chicken cross the
    road") K. Starbird.—StC
  Riddle-me rhyme. D. McCord.—McSu
  The toaster. W. J. Smith.—SmL
  "Two brothers we are, great burdens we
    bear." Mother Goose.—TrGg
  "Two legs sat upon three legs." Mother
    Goose.—TrGg
    A riddle.—BlH
  "What is the rhyme for porringer." Mother
    Goose.—WiP
  "What the stars in the street puddles say." L.
    Morrison.—MoW
  "A white bird." L. Morrison.—MoW
  Who cast my shadow. L. Moore.—MoTs
  "A worthless article." L. Morrison.—MoW
  Written on an egg. E. Morike.—LiCc
The ride. Kaye Starbird.—StC
"Ride a cock-horse to Coventry Cross." Mother
  Goose.—TrGg
The ride-by-nights. Walter De La Mare.—HiD
Ride 'im cowboy, A. L. Freebairn.—CoPh
"Ride 'im cowboy, ride 'im." See Ride 'im
  cowboy

Riders ("At four p.m. small fingers moved the
  dial to one-six-O") Linda Peavy.—CoPh

Rides and riding—Horse
  Billy could ride. J. W. Riley.—CoPh
  Bronco busting, event #1. M. Swenson.—
    CoPh
  Buckin' bronco. S. Silverstein.—SiL
  The centaur. M. Swenson.—CoPh—HiS
  Dexter. J. B. Grayston.—CoPh
  The errand. H. Behn.—HoMp
  Evening ride. J. Hoffman.—CoPh
  Flying changes. M. Wood.—CoPh
  Galloping ("The rushing, the brushing, the
    wind in your face") C. Chitty.—CoPh
  The gentled beast. D. Laing.—CoPh
  The grey horse. J. Reeves.—CoPh
  Grog an' Grumble steeplechase. H.
    Lawson.—CoPh
  The headless horseman. J. Prelutsky.—PrH
  Horse ("Horse skin, hessian or hard hot silk")
    G. Benson.—CoPh
  The horse ("I will not change my horse with
    any that treads") From King Henry V. W.
    Shakespeare.—CoPh
  Hossolalia. M. Luton.—CoPh
  How we drove the trotter. W. T. Goodge.—
    CoPh
  The huntsmen ("Three jolly gentlemen") W.
    De La Mare.—HiD
  "If I had a pony." A. Fisher.—FiO
  Indecision means flexibility. E. Abhau.—CoPh
  Learner. J. A. Lindon.—CoPh
  Lord Epsom. H. Belloc.—CoPh
  The man from Snowy River. A. B.
    Paterson.—CoPh
  "Moon light." F. Manfred.—CoPh
  Nevada. S. Noyes.—CoPh
  New skills. N. S. Nye.—CoPh
  On dressing to go hunting. Unknown.—CoPh
  On the farm. B. Winder.—CoPh
  The racing man. A. P. Herbert.—CoPh
  The ride. K. Starbird.—StC
  "Ride a cock-horse to Coventry Cross."
    Mother Goose.—TrGg
  Ride 'im cowboy. A. L. Freebairn.—CoPh
  Riding ("I learned to ride with the Colonel")
    F. Grossman.—CoPh
  Riding a one eyed horse. H. Taylor.—CoPh
  Riding lesson. H. Taylor.—CoPh—LuZ—
    MoGp
  The riding stable in winter. J. Tagliabue.—
    CoPh
  Tallyho-hum. O. Nash.—CoPh
  To a horse. J. Hoffman.—CoPh
  The trail horse. D. Wagoner.—CoPh
  Windy nights. R. L. Stevenson.—CoPh—RuM
  The zebra dun. Unknown.—CoPh
Riding ("I learned to ride with the Colonel")
  Florence Grossman.—CoPh
Riding a one eyed horse. Henry Taylor.—CoPh
Riding lesson. Henry Taylor.—CoPh—LuZ—
  MoGp
Riding on the train. Eloise Greenfield.—GrH
The riding stable in winter. John Tagliabue.—
  CoPh

Ridland, John
 The assassin. See Assassination poems
 Assassination poems.—LiO (Complete)
  The assassin
  The friends
  Knowing it
  The nation
  Not believing it
  Not wanting to believe it
 The friends. See Assassination poems
 Knowing it. See Assassination poems
 The light year.—LiO
 The nation. See Assassination poems
 Not believing it. See Assassination poems
 Not wanting to believe it. See Assassination
  poems
Ridlon, Marci
 Fernando.—MoGp
 That was summer.—HoMp
Rieu, E. (Emile) V. (Victor)
 The flattered flying fish.—HiS
 The green train.—HiS
 The paint box.—HiS
 Tony the turtle.—HiS
Rift tide. Ruth M. Walsh.—BrO
"**Right** after our Thanksgiving feast." See The
 skeleton walks
"**Right** from the start he is dressed in his best,
 his blacks and his whites." See A March
 calf
The **right** place. Myra Cohn Livingston.—LiWt
"**Right** reverend and worshipful and my right
 wellbeloved." See Unto my valentine
Rihauku
 The river-merchant's wife, a letter.—YaI
Riley. Charles Causley.—HiS
Riley, James Whitcomb
 Billy could ride.—CoPh
 The diners in the kitchen.—CoG
Rilke, Rainer Maria
 Annunciation over the shepherds, sel.
  "Look up, you men, men there at the
   fire."—LiPch
 Closing piece.—JaPp
 The last supper.—LiO
 "Look up, you men, men there at the fire."
  See Annunciation over the shepherds
 Pieta.—LiO
The **rime** of the ancient mariner, sels. Samuel
 Taylor Coleridge.
 Icebergs.—PaE
 Water-snakes.—PaE
"**Ring**-a-ring o' neutrons." See A leaden
 treasury of English verse
Ring out, wild bells. See In memoriam
"**Ring** out, wild bells, to the wild sky." See In
 memoriam—Ring out, wild bells
"**Ring** out ye bells." Paul Lawrence Dunbar.—
 BaC
Rings. See Jewelry
Riots
 April 68. S. Cornish.—AdC
 An old woman remembers. S. A. Brown.—
  AdC

"**Rise** at 7:15." See Good morning, love
Rise, shepherds. Unknown.—BaC
"**Rise,** shepherds, though the night is deep."
 See Rise, shepherds
"**Rise** then, ere ruin swift surprize." See
 McFingal
"**Rise** up and look." See Sun for breakfast
Rites of passage. Audre Lorde.—AdC
The **rivals,** sel. James Stephens
 "I heard a bird at dawn."—MoF
The **river** ("Stick your patent name on a
 signboard") Hart Crane.—PlG
The **river** in March. Ted Hughes.—HuSs
The **river**-merchant's wife, a letter. Rihauku, tr.
 by Ezra Pound.—YaI
River night. Frances Frost.—RuM
"The **river** sleeps beneath the sky." See Sunset
Rivers. See also names of rivers, as Mississippi
 river
 Bridge ("Here on the river's verge he stood")
  J. Aiken.—AiS
 "The brook moves slowly." A. Atwood.—AtH
 December river. T. Hughes.—HuSs
 Detroit. D. Hall.—FlA
 Headwaters. N. S. Momaday.—MoGd
 History among the rocks. R. P. Warren.—PlG
 Like ghosts of eagles. R. Francis.—PlG
 Midsummer. D. McCord.—McSu
 The rapid ("All peacefully gliding") C.
  Sangster.—DoWh
 The river ("Stick your patent name on a
  signboard") H. Crane.—PlG
 The river in March. T. Hughes.—HuSs
 River night. F. Frost.—RuM
 Song. From Comus. J. Milton.—PaE
 The trail beside the River Platte. W.
  Heyen.—PlG
Rivers, Conrad Kent
 "For all things black and beautiful."—AdC
 Malcolm, a thousandth poem.—AdC
 The still voice of Harlem.—AdC
"The **river's** high, the clouds are low." See
 Midsummer
Roaches ("Last night when I got up") Peter
 Wild.—LuZ
"The **road** is full of saucers." See Country rain
"The **road** runs straight with no turning, the
 circle." See Black people, this is our
 destiny
Roads and streets. See also Trails
 Country rain. A. Fisher.—FiO
 Highway construction. C. E. Chapin.—BrO
 "Moon light." F. Manfred.—CoPh
 Moon ways. T. Hughes.—HuM
 Night sounds. F. Holman.—RuM
 Oil slick. J. Thurman.—MoGp
 The riddle ("Why does the chicken cross the
  road") K. Starbird.—StC
 Roadside. V. Worth.—WoSm
 The streets of town. A. Fisher.—FiO
 Suddenly. A. Fisher.—HoMp
 The way things are. M. C. Livingston.—LiWt
 "What the stars in the street puddles say." L.
  Morrison.—MoW

"The **roads** are very dirty, my boots are very thin." Unknown.—LiCc

"The **roads** to the beach." See On our bikes

Roadside. Valerie Worth.—WoSm

"**Roast** me a wren to start with." See The king of cats orders an early breakfast

"**Robbin** and Bobbin." Mother Goose.—TrGg

Robert Gould Shaw. Paul Laurence Dunbar.—BrI

Roberts, Charles G. D.
  The brook in February.—DoWh
  Ice.—DoWh

Roberts, Elizabeth Madox
  Christmas morning.—LiCc—LiPch
  The circus.—LiCc
  Father's story.—LiCc
  The hens.—PaI
  Horse.—CoPh
  Mumps.—WiP
  The woodpecker.—PaI

Roberts, T. G.
  Gluskap's hound.—DoWh
  The reformed pirate.—DoWh

Robeson, Paul (about)
  Paul Robeson ("That time") G. Brooks.—AdC

Robin song ("I know what the robin") Aileen Fisher.—FiO

Robins
  Betsy Robin. W. J. Smith.—SmL
  "Fat father robin." D. McCord.—McO
  The north wind doth blow. Mother Goose.—CoA
  "November bares the robin's nest." D. McCord.—McO
  Robin song ("I know what the robin") A. Fisher.—FiO
  "Who killed Cock Robin." Mother Goose.—WiP
  Worm ("That lonely worm upon the lawn") D. McCord.—McSu

Robinson, Edwin Arlington
  Calvary.—LiO
  Karma.—LiO
  New England.—PlG

"**Rock** candy, hard sweet crystals on a string." See A Christmas package

Rock 'n' roll band. Shel Silverstein.—SiL

The **rock** pool ("Bright as a fallen fragment of the sky") Alfred Noyes.—PaE

The **rock** pool ("This is the sea, in these uneven walls") Edward Shanks.—PaE

Rockabye. Shel Silverstein.—SiL

"**Rockabye** baby, in the treetop." See Rockabye

Rockets
  "Fueled." M. Hans.—HoMp

Rocks and stones
  The black pebble. J. Reeves.—MaP—WiP
  "The boy in the stone." L. Norris.—NoM
  The detail. C. Corman.—JaPp
  Final stone. R. N. Peck.—PeB
  The friendly rock. S. N. Pulsifer.—PaI
  Inscription. J. G. Whittier.—PlG
  The monoliths. N. S. Momaday.—MoGd
  North fence. R. N. Peck.—PeB

  Rocks ("Big rocks into pebbles") F. P. Heide.—HoBm—MoGp
  Rocks ("They say no") V. Worth.—WoSm
  The sand rose. L. Norris.—NoM
  "These flat stones are coins." B. Maestro.—MaFp
  "This is my rock." D. McCord.—BeR—McO

Rocks ("Big rocks into pebbles") Florence Parry Heide.—HoBm—MoGp

Rocks ("They say no") Valerie Worth.—WoSm

Rodeos
  Bronco busting, event #1. M. Swenson.—CoPh
  Ride 'im cowboy. A. Freebairn.—CoPh

Rodgers, Carolyn M.
  A common poem.—AdC
  For muh' dear.—AdC
  For sapphires.—AdC
  How I got ovah.—AdC
  Some me of beauty.—AdC
  We dance like Ella riffs.—AdC

Rodgers, W. R.
  Beagles.—CoG

Rodman, Frances
  Lost dog.—CoG

Roethke, Theodore
  The bat.—BrIt—SaM
  The beast.—HiS
  Elegy.—PlL
  The lady and the bear.—HiS
  My papa's waltz.—MaP
  Myrtle.—CoI
  Night journey.—PlG
  Old florist.—JaPp
  Otto.—PlL
  The small.—HiS
  Wish for a young wife.—PlL

"**Roger** was a razor fish." Al Pittman.—BeR

Roll call, a land of old folk and children. Isaac J. Black.—AdC

"**Roll** on, thou deep and dark blue ocean—roll." See The ocean

Roller coaster ("These roller-coaster cars, some said") David McCord.—McSu

Roller-coasters
  Flight of the roller-coaster. R. Souster.—DoWh—HiS
  Roller coaster ("These roller-coaster cars, some said") D. McCord.—McSu

"**Rolling** and tossing out sparkles like roses." See Night landscape

"**Rolling** away from Chicago." See Derricks

Rolling Harvey down the hill. Jack Prelutsky.—PrRh

Roman mythology. See Mythology

Romance. See also Adventure and adventurers; Courtship; Knights and knighthood
  The couple. M. Angelou.—AnO
  Notes. P. Engle.—YaI
  Pickin em up and layin em down. M. Angelou.—AnO
  Shadow-bride. J.R.R. Tolkien.—HiS

Romeo and Juliet, sel. William Shakespeare
  Queen Mab.—WaFp

The gibbon.—GaCb
The gnat.—GaCb
"The mite."—GaCb
Rugs
Magic carpet. S. Silverstein.—SiL
Rukeyser, Muriel
All the little animals.—PlL
Columbus.—PlG
Rulers. See also Princes and princesses; also
names of rulers, as Mary, Queen of Scots
Carol of the brown king. L. Hughes.—BaC—
LiPch
Henry and Mary. R. Graves.—HiS
The ice king. A. B. Demille.—DoWh
John ("John, John, bad King John") E. and H.
Farjeon.—WiP
Journey of the Magi. T. S. Eliot.—LiPch
K is for king. W. J. Smith.—SmL
King Johan of Bavonia. N. M. Bodecker.—
BoP
The King of Spain. W. J. Smith.—SmL
The King of Umpalazzo. M. A. Hoberman.—
HoY
King Rufus. Y. Y. Segal.—DoWh
"The king whose crown was upside down."
N. M. Bodecker.—BoHh
"King's cross." E. Farjeon.—CoI
The kings from the east. H. Heine.—BaC
"Three holy kings from Morgenland."—
LiPch
Lavender's blue. Mother Goose.—YaI
"Old King Cole was a merry old soul."
Mother Goose.—TrGg
Orange lilies. J. Reaney.—DoWh
Q is for queen. W. J. Smith.—SmL
The Queen of Eene. J. Prelutsky.—PrQ
The Queen of the Nile. W. J. Smith.—SmL
A threnody. G. T. Lanigan.—DoWh
When kings wore crowns. N. M. Bodecker.—
BoHh
The yak ("For hours the princess would not
play or sleep") V. Sheard.—DoWh
Rules
The mules. O. Nash.—BlC
Rules. K. Kuskin.—KuD—WiP
Rules. Karla Kuskin.—KuD—WiP
"The **rumps** of horses." See On rears
"**Run,** little wild ones." See Christmas in the
country
"**Run** seaward, launch upon the air, and sound
your desolate cry." See Herring-gull
Runagate runagate. Robert Hayden.—AdC
The **runaway.** Robert Frost.—CoPh
Rune. Lillian Morrison.—MoW
Runners and running. See also Races and
racing—Foot
Joggers ("To see his jogs") D. McCord.—
McSu
Lessie. E. Greenfield.—GrH
Runover rhyme. David McCord.—McO
"**Runs** falls rises stumbles on from darkness into
darkness." See Runagate runagate
Ruptured recipes. Barbara Giles.—DuSn

The **rural** dance about the Maypole, sel.
Unknown.
"Come lasses and lads."—LiCc
Rural recreation. Lillian Morrison.—MoSr
"The **rushing,** the brushing, the wind in your
face." See Galloping
Russia
"Kolyada, kolyada." Unknown.—BaC
Krasnopresnenskaya station. N. Scott
Momaday.—MoGd
Russian dance. O. Nash.—BlC
Russian dance. Ogden Nash.—BlC
"The **Russian** moujik is made for music." See
Russian dance
Rust
The walrust. J. Yolen.—YoH
Ruth. Kaye Starbird.—StC
Rutland fair. Robert Newton Peck.—PeB
Rutledge, Anne (about)
Anne Rutledge ("Out of me, unworthy and
unknown") E. L. Masters.—LiO
Ryder, Joanne
"Inside the lab."—HeB

S

S F. Ernest Leverett.—BrO
S is for springs. William Jay Smith.—SmL
Sabbatical. Julia Randall.—KhI
"**Sabrina** fair." See Comus—Song
Sacco and Vanzetti (about)
Justice denied in Massachusetts. E. St. V.
Millay.—PlG
Sackville-West, V.
Sea-sonnet.—PaE
Sacrifices
Incantation to Oedipus. J. Dryden.—LiO
The **sad** child's song. Mark Van Doren.—HiS
The **sad** shepherd, sel. Ben Jonson.
Aeglamour's lament.—PaB
The **sad** sliced onion. Margaret Wise Brown.—
WiP
"**Saddest** of all things on the moon is the snail
without." See The snail of the moon
"The **saddest** thing I ever did see." See Peckin'
"**Sadie.**" See Personals
The **sadness** of things, for Sappho's sickness.
Robert Herrick.—PaB
Safety
The mole. R. Daniells.—DoWh
Safety pin. Valerie Worth.—WoM
"**Said** a gluttonous man of New Wales." Myra
Cohn Livingston.—LiLl
"**Said** a guide walking round Lacock Abbey."
Myra Cohn Livingston.—LiLl
"**Said** a mouthful of Mighty Mump cereal." See
Television charmer
"**Said** a poor girl from Southend-on-Sea." Myra
Cohn Livingston.—LiLl
"**Said** a restless young person of Yew." Myra
Cohn Livingston.—LiLl

"Said a serious scholar from Leech." Myra Cohn Livingston.—LiLl

"Said a three-day-old infant in Leek." Myra Cohn Livingston.—LiLl

"Said an old man from Needles-on-Stoor." Myra Cohn Livingston.—LiLl

"Said Dr Ping to Mr Pong." See Dr Ping and Mr Pong

"Said he didn't know." See Butterfly

"Said little a to big G." See Importnt

"Said Marcia Brown to Carlos Baker." See Imaginary dialogues

"Said Simple Sam, does Christmas come." Leroy F. Jackson.—BaC

"Said the cat to the owl." See A witch flies by

"Said the eagle." See The eagle's song

"Said the engineer, radio waves." See Not lost in the stars

"Said the first little chicken." See Five little chickens

"Said the fur coated dame to the hairless pup." See Canine amenities

"Said the little boy, sometimes I drop my spoon." See The little boy and the old man

"Said the monkey to the owl." Unknown.—WiP

"Said the Queen of the Nile." See The Queen of the Nile

"Said the shark to the flying fish over the phone." See The flattered flying fish

"Said the teapot to the kettle." See The teapot and the kettle

"Said the toad to the kangaroo." See The toad and the kangaroo

"Said the wife to her husband." See Rift tide

"Said the wind to the moon." See The wind and the moon

Sailing. See Boats and boating; Ships

Sailing, sailing. Lillian Morrison.—MoSr

Sailor John. David McCord.—McO

Sailors. See Seafaring life

A sailor's song. Paul Laurence Dunbar.—BrI

"Saint Bridget was." See The giveaway

St. Germain, Mark
  Cannon Park.—JaPp

St. John, Primus
  Constellations.—LuZ

"St. John tells how, at Cana's wedding feast." See A wedding toast

St. Louis, Missouri
  Lucas Park, St. Louis. P. S. Bliss.—FlA

Saint Nicholas. See Santa Claus

"Saint Nicholas, my dear good friend." Unknown.—BaC

St. Valentine ("Permitted to assist you, let me see") Marianne Moore.—LiO

Saint Valentine's day
  Conversation hearts. N. Payne.—LiCc
  "Country bumpkin." From Father Fox's pennyrhymes. C. Watson.—LiCc
  "Hail Bishop Valentine, whose day this is." From An epithalamion. J. Donne.—LiO
  "I bear, in sign of love." From Shepherdess' valentine. F. Andrewes.—LiO
  "I think." B. S. De Regniers.—ReB

My valentine. R. L. Stevenson.—LiO—YaI

Rebus valentine. Unknown.—YaI

St. Valentine ("Permitted to assist you, let me see") M. Moore.—LiO

A secret. E. Merriam.—LiCc

To his mistresse. R. Herrick.—LiO

"Tomorrow is Saint Valentine's day." From Hamlet. W. Shakespeare.—LiCc

Unto my valentine. M. Brews.—LiO

Valentine ("Chipmunks jump, and") D. Hall.—JaPp—YaI

Valentine feelings. L. B. Hopkins.—HoMp

A valentine for a lady. Lucilius.—LiO

Valentine for earth. F. Frost.—BrO

A valentine to the wide world. B. S. De Regniers.—ReB

Valentines ("Forgive me if I have not sent you") H. Dumas.—LiCc

Valentines to my mother. C. G. Rossetti.—LiO

"You are." B. S. De Regniers.—ReB

Saints. See names of saints, as Luke, Saint

The saint's lament. Dennis Lee.—LeN

Salamander ("A red salamander") Denise Levertov.—MoGp

Salamanders
  "The newt." R. S. Oliver.—OlC
  The newt ("The little newt") D. McCord.—McO
  Salamander ("A red salamander") D. Levertov.—MoGp
  Samuel. B. Katz.—MoGp

Sally Lun Lundy. David McCord.—McO

"Sally over the water." Unknown.—WiP

Salmon
  December river. T. Hughes.—HuSs

Salomon, Louis B.
  Univac to univac.—BrO

"Sam had spirits naught could check." See Impetuous Samuel

"Samantha, call her Sam, OK." See Halloween

"Samantha the golden retriever." See Me and Samantha

Same old trick. William W. Pratt.—BrO

Sampson, Judith
  While the snake sleeps.—LuZ

"Sampt'e drew the string back and back until he felt." See The stalker

"Sam's mother has." See Sam's world

Sam's world. Sam Cornish.—AdC—LiCc

Samuel. Bobbi Katz.—MoGp

Samurai and hustlers. Joe Johnson.—AdC

Sanchez, Sonia
  "Don't wanna be."—AdC
  Haiku.—LuZ
  Now poem for us.—AdC
  Poem at thirty.—AdC
  Present.—AdC

Sand
  At the sandpile. A Fisher.—FiO
  Beaches ("There are reaches of beaches") K. Kuskin.—KuD
  Rocks ("Big rocks into pebbles") F. P. Heide.—HoBm—MoGp

The sand rose. L. Norris.—NoM
A sandpile town. A. Fisher.—FiO
Sitting in the sand. K. Kuskin.—KuD
The washer waves. N. Farber.—FaS
The **sand**-man. Paul Laurence Dunbar.—BrI
The **sand** painters. Ben Belitt.—PlG
The **sand** rose. Leslie Norris.—NoM
Sandburg, Carl
  Broken sky.—JaPp
  Buffalo dusk.—PlG
  Crabapples.—HoMp
  Doors.—WiP
  Explanations of love.—LuZ
  The family of man, sel.
        Names.—WiP
  Finale. See Prairie
  Fourth of July night.—LiO
  Good morning America, sel.
        "Now it's Uncle Sam sitting on top of the
          world."—LiO
  Good night, sel.
        "Many ways to spell good night."—LiCc
  "I love you." See The people, yes
  Illinois farmer.—FlA
  Laughing child.—JaPp
  "Little girl, be careful what you say."—WiP
  Mag.—PlL
  "Many ways to spell good night." See Good
    night
  Mysterious biography.—LiCc—LiO
  Names. See The family of man
  "Now it's Uncle Sam sitting on top of the
    world." See Good morning America
  Nocturn cabbage.—HiD
  Paper I.—WiP
  Paper II.—WiP
  The people, yes, sel.
        "I love you."—LiCc
  Prairie, sel.
        Finale.—FlA
  Rat riddles.—HiS
  Sea-wash.—WiP
  Stars.—WiP
  Street window.—JaPp
  Summer grass.—MoGp
  Theme in yellow.—MoGp
  Two strangers breakfast.—PlL
  Washington monument by night.—LiO
        "The wind bit hard at Valley Forge one
          Christmas."—LiCc (sel.)
  We must be polite.—WiP
  "The wind bit hard at Valley Forge." See
    Washington Monument by night
  Wingtip.—JaPp
  Worms and the wind.—LuZ—WiP
A **sandpile** town. Aileen Fisher.—FiO
The **sandpiper** ("Across the narrow beach we
  flit") Celia Thaxter.—PaE
The **sandpiper** ("Along the sea-edge, like a
  gnome") Witter Bynner.—PaE
Sandpipers
  A certain sandpiper. X. J. Kennedy.—KeP
  The sandpiper ("Across the narrow beach we
    flit") C. Thaxter.—PaE

The **sandpiper** ("Along the sea-edge, like a
  gnome") W. Bynner.—PaE
Sangster, Charles
  The rapid.—DoWh
Sansom, Clive
  Mice and cat.—CoA
  The witnesses, sel.
        The innkeeper's wife.—LiPch
Santa Claus
  The boy who laughed at Santa Claus. O.
    Nash.—BlC
  A Christmas eve thought. H. B. Sterling.—
    BaC
  Conversation between Mr. and Mrs. Santa
    Claus. R. Bennett.—BaC
  For Allan. R. Frost.—LiPch
  "My stocking's where." From A Christmas
    package. D. McCord.—LiPch—McO
  "Old Saint Nicolas comes so speedily."
    Unknown.—BaC
  "Old Santa is an active man." L. Lenski.—
    BaC
  "Saint Nicholas, my dear good friend."
    Unknown.—BaC
  Santa Claus ("He comes in the night, he
    comes in the night") Unknown.—BaC
  Santa Claus ("On wool soft feet he peeps and
    creeps") W. de la Mare.—LiPch
  Stocking song on Christmas eve. M. M.
    Dodge.—BaC
  Ten nights before Christmas. D. McCord.—
    McO
  To Noel. G. Mistral.—LiPch
  A visit from St. Nicholas. C. C. Moore.—
    LiPch
  When Santa Claus comes. Unknown.—BaC
Santa Claus ("He comes in the night, he comes
  in the night") Unknown.—BaC
Santa Claus ("On wool soft feet he peeps and
  creeps") Walter de la Mare.—LiPch
"**Sarah** is our tabby cat." See Sarah's wondrous
  thing
"**Sarah** sagged." See Sarah's saga
Sarah's saga. Lillian Morrison.—MoW
Sarah's wondrous thing. Robert Newton
  Peck.—PeB
Sardines. Spike Milligan.—LuZ
Sarett, Lew
  Four little foxes.—WiP
Saroyan, Aram
  "Sawing the wood."—KhI
Sarton, May
  Monticello.—PlG
  My father's death.—PlL
  A village tale.—CoG
"A **sasquatch** from Saskatchewan." Dennis
  Lee.—LeG
The **sasquatch** quashes a rumor. X. J.
  Kennedy.—KeP
Sassoon, Siegfried
  Middle Ages.—HiS
Satan. See Devil
"The **satin** sea lions." See Sea lions

Satoru Sato and Urdang, Constance
  Pole vault. jt. trs.—LuZ
Saturday. See Days of the week—Saturday
Saturday shopping. Katherine Edelman.—PaI
Saturday's child. Countee Cullen.—LiO
The **sausage.** Unknown.—CoPs
"The **sausage** is a cunning bird." See The
  sausage
"The **savage** tribes that have their lairs." See
  Moon bells
Savannah, Georgia
  "My father remembers." J. Aiken.—AiS
"**Sawing** the wood." Aram Saroyan.—KhI
Sawyer, Ruth
  Words from an old Spanish carol.—LiPch
Say nay. Eve Merriam.—MeR
"**Say** of them." See To the veterans of the
  Abraham Lincoln brigade
"**Says** the humpbacked zebu." See Z is for zebu
"**Says** the prancing french poodle." See D is for
  dog
Says Tom to me. David McCord.—McO
"**Says** Tom to me, I slept the sleep of the just."
  See Says Tom to me
"A **scandalous** man." See Mr. Tom Narrow
"**Scant** is the holly." See The brown birds
"**Scare** me easy." Beatrice Schenk De
  Regniers.—ReB
Scarecrows
  Crow wonders. L. Moore.—MoTs
Scarlett rocks. T. E. Brown.—PaE
Scat, scitten. David McCord.—McO
Scene from the working class. Richmond
  Lattimore.—PlL
Schauffler, Robert Haven
  Divers.—PaE
Scheding, Stephen
  "Herbert Breeze."—DuSn
Schenectady. Eve Merriam.—WiP
Schiller, Frederich von
  Columbus.—LiO
Schonberg, Virginia
  Construction.—BrO
School. See also Teachers and teaching
  Back to school. A. Fisher.—FiO
  Class of 19—. F. Dec.—JaPp
  Classroom. K. Gangemi.—HeB
  Communication II—The student. M.
    Angelou.—AnO
  The first day of school. A. Fisher.—FiO
  Going to school. K. Kuskin.—HeB
  The hero. R. Graves.—JaPp
  History. M. C. Livingston.—LiWt
  Homework ("Homework sits on top of
    Sunday, squashing Sunday flat") R.
    Hoban.—HoMp—MoGp
  Homework ("What is it about homework") J.
    Yolen.—HeB
  Homework machine. S. Silverstein.—SiL
  "I don't understand." N. Grimes.—GrS
  Indoors. R. Burgunder.—HoMp
  "Inside the lab." J. Ryder.—HeB
  Jittery Jim. W. J. Smith.—SmL
  Joy ("In school today") N. Giovanni.—GiV

  Learning about the Indians. M. Oliver.—LuZ
  Legs. D. McCord.—McSu
  "Monday morning back to school." From
    Five chants. D. McCord.—McO
  "Nine-o'clock bell." E. Farjeon.—MoF
  The shadow on the map. J. Aiken.—AiS
  The spelling test. K. Starbird.—StC
  Sweet Diane. G. Barlow.—AdC
  "Waiting for lunchtime." N. Grimes.—GrS
  "Waiting for summer to end." N. Grimes.—
    GrS
  Wings. S. J. Crossen and N. A. Covell.—
    HoBm
  Zimmer in grade school. P. Zimmer.—KhI
  Zimmer's head thudding against the
    blackboard. P. Zimmer.—JaPp
"A **school** bus driver from Deering." See A
  driver from Deering
Schulz, Lillian
  "Fuzzy wuzzy, creepy crawly."—PaI
Science
  Astronaut's choice. M. M. Darcy.—BrO
  The bat and the scientist. J. S. Bigelow.—BrO
  The beefalo. J. Gardner.—GaCb
  Ed and Sid and Bernard. E. MacDuff.—BrO
  Eminent cosmologists ("It did not last, the
    Devil howling ho") J. C. Squire.—BrO
  Eminent cosmologists ("Nature, and nature's
    laws lay hid in night") A. Pope.—BrO
  "The fabulous wizard of Oz." Unknown.—
    BrO
  "Inside the lab." J. Ryder.—HeB
  The microscope. M. Kumin.—WiP
  "Once we felt at home with nature if we
    knew the nomenclature." From Progress.
    F. Lamport.—BrO
  Relativity. K. Millay.—BrO
  Science for the young. W. Irwin.—BrO
  Science lesson. L. Morrison.—MoO
  Scientific proof. J. W. Foley.—BrO
  Some quarks have a strange flavor. L.
    Morrison.—MoO
Science for the young. Wallace Irwin.—BrO
Science lesson. Lillian Morrison.—MoO
Scientific proof. J. W. Foley.—BrO
"The **scientists** sit long of nights." See
  Astronaut's choice
"**Scolding.**" See Squirrel
Scollard, Clinton
  The mistletoe.—BaC
Scott, Duncan Campbell
  The forsaken, sel.
    "Once in the winter."—DoWh
  "Once in winter." See The forsaken
Scott, Elizabeth Manson
  My bed.—PaI
Scott, Geoffrey
  Frutta di mare.—PaE
Scott, Sir Walter
  "Heap on more wood, the wind is chill." See
    Marmion
  Marmion, sel.
    "Heap on more wood, the wind is
      chill."—BaC—LiPch

Scott, Winfield Townley
Grant Wood's American landscape.—PlG
May 1506, Christopher Columbus speaking.—PlG
Scottish dialect. See Burns, Robert
Scottish nursery rhymes. See Nursery rhymes—Scottish
Scottus, Sedulius
Easter Sunday.—LiO
Scovell, E. J.
The boy fishing.—MaP
Scrap iron. Raymond Durgnat.—JaPp
Scrapbooks. Nikki Giovanni.—AdC
"Scraw." See Creatures we can do without
Scroppo's dog. May Swenson.—CoG
Sculpture and sculpturing. See also Statues
"The boy in the stone." L. Norris.—NoM
Playing with clay. J. Thurman.—ThFo
"The scum has come." See Lament, for cocoa
Sea. See Mediterranean sea; Ocean
The sea ("The sea is a hungry dog") James Reeves.—SaM
Sea and sand. Leslie Norris.—NoM
"The sea awoke at midnight from its sleep." See The sound of the sea
Sea-birds. Elizabeth Akers.—PaE
Sea-change. Wilfred Gibson.—PaE
Sea cows. See Manatees
Sea fairies ("Look in the caves at the edge of the sea") Patricia Hubbell.—WaFp
The sea-fairies ("Slow sail'd the weary mariners and saw") Lord Alfred Tennyson.—PaE
Sea gull ("The sea gull curves his wings") Elizabeth Coatsworth.—WiP
"The sea gull curves his wings." See Sea gull
Sea gulls. See Gulls
Sea-hawk. Richard Eberhart.—PaE
Sea horses
"An iridescent sea horse." L. Morrison.—MoW
"The sea is a hungry dog." See The sea
"The sea is a-roarin', the sea gulls they screech." See Captain Blackbeard did what
"The sea laments. See Echoes
Sea life. See names of kinds of sea life, as Whales
The sea-limits. Dante Gabriel Rossetti.—PaE
Sea lions ("The satin sea lions") Valerie Worth.—MoGp—WoM
Sea longing. Sara Teasdale.—PaE
The sea ritual. George Darley.—PaE
Sea shell. Amy Lowell.—SaM
"Sea shell, sea shell." See Sea shell
A sea song. D. M. Dolben.—PaE
Sea-sonnet. V. Sackville-West.—PaE
Sea-wash. Carl Sandburg.—WiP
"The sea-wash never ends." See Sea-wash
Sea-weed. D. H. Lawrence.—PaE
"Sea-weed sways and sways and swirls." See Sea-weed
The sea wolf. Violet McDougal.—PaE

Seafaring life. See also Fishers and fishing; Pirates; Ships
Atlantis ("There was an island in the sea") C. Aiken.—PaE
Columbus and the mermaids. E. Coatsworth.—PlG
D'Avalos' prayer. J. Masefield.—PaE
Donkey riding. Unknown.—DoWh
The fisher child's lullaby. P. L. Dunbar.—BrI
"Full fathom five." From The tempest. W. Shakespeare.—PaE
Ariel's dirge.—WiP
Jack was every inch a sailor. Unknown.—DoWh
Jolly soldier. Unknown.—LiO
Kansas boy. R. Lechlitner.—FlA
"Little Tee Wee." Mother Goose.—TrGg
"O sailor, come ashore." C. Rossetti.—WiP
Old Salt Kossabone. W. Whitman.—PlL
The reformed pirate. T. G. Roberts.—DoWh
A sailor's song. P. L. Dunbar.—BrI
The sea-fairies. A. Tennyson.—PaE
The sea ritual. G. Darley.—PaE
Sea-sonnet. V. Sackville-West.—PaE
The stormy petrel. B. W. Procter.—PaE
To my father. R. L. Stevenson.—PlL
Venus in the tropics. L. Simpson.—KhI
"You, Genoese mariner." W. S. Merwin.—PlG
Seagulls on the serpentine. Alfred Noyes.—PaE
Seal ("See how he dives") William Jay Smith.—PaE—SmL
Seale, Bobby (about)
To Bobby Seale. L. Clifton.—AdC
"Sealed wax cells." See Honeycomb
A sealess world. Joan Campbell.—PaE
Seals (animals)
The dancing seal. W. Gibson.—PaE
The moon-child. W. Sharp.—PaE
Sea lions. V. Worth.—MoGp—WoM
Seal ("See how he dives") W. J. Smith.—PaE—SmL
The white seal's lullaby. R. Kipling.—PaE
Seamen. See Seafaring life
"Search carefully on the trunk of." See Underwing moth
"Search thou my heart." See Confessional
Seashells. See Shells
Seashore. See also Ocean
Afternoon, Amagansett beach. J. H. Wheelock.—PaE
At low tide. D. McCord.—McO
At night. R. Eberhart.—PlL
At the beach. L. Morrison.—MoW
Beach ("Close in, near to the sand") M. C. Livingston.—LiWt
Beaches ("There are reaches of beaches") K. Kuskin.—KuD
The black pebble. J. Reeves.—MaP—WiP
"The boy in the foam." A. Atwood.—AtH
By the saltings. T. Walker.—PaE
Carol for a New Zealand child. D. N. White.—BaC
A certain sandpiper. X. J. Kennedy.—KeP

A secret ("Somebody rang the bell") Eve
    Merriam.—LiCc
The secret ("Two girls discover") Denise
    Levertov.—LuZ
Secret hand. Eve Merriam.—MeW
The secret sits. Robert Frost.—MoGp
The secret song ("I've got a secret") Dennis
    Lee.—LeG
The secret song ("Who saw the petals")
    Margaret Wise Brown.—WiP
Secret talk. Eve Merriam.—MeW
Secrets
    Christmas secrets. A. Fisher.—FiO
    "Don't tell anybody." O. E. Mandelstam.—
        LuZ
    Frutta di mare. G. Scott.—PaE
    I had to be secret. M. Van Doren.—HiS
    My box. M. C. Livingston.—LiWt
    Secret ("Jean said, no") D. McCord.—McO
    The secret ("Promise not to tell") M. C.
        Livingston.—LiF
    A secret ("Somebody rang the bell") E.
        Merriam.—LiCc
    The secret ("Two girls discover") D.
        Levertov.—LuZ
    The secret sits. R. Frost.—MoGp
    The secret song ("I've got a secret") D.
        Lee.—LeG
    The secret song ("Who saw the petals") M.
        W. Brown.—WiP
    "Seems I'm never old enough." N. Grimes.—
        GrS
    "This is my rock." D. McCord.—McO
"Secrets long and secrets wide." See Christmas
    secrets
"See how he dives." See Seal
"See, see, what shall I see." Mother Goose.—
    TrGg
"See the chariot at hand here of love." See The
    triumph of Charis
"See, the mother corn comes hither, making
    all." See An Indian hymn of thanks to
    mother corn
"See the mountains kiss high heaven." See
    Love's philosophy
"See what a lovely shell." See The shell
Seeds
    After Christmas. M. C. Livingston.—LiWt
    Cut out. A. Adoff.—AdE
    Elm seed blizzard. D. McCord.—McO
    "Fueled." M. Hans.—HoMp
    The golden boy. T. Hughes.—HuSs
    Spell of the seeds. L. Norris.—NoM
    Sun flowers. A. Adoff.—AdE
    Tillie. W. De La Mare.—WaGp
"Seeing the snowman standing all alone." See
    Boy at the window
"Seems I'm never old enough." Nikki
    Grimes.—GrS
"Seen my lady home las' night." See A negro
    love song
Segal, Y. Y.
    King Rufus.—DoWh
    Rhymes.—DoWh

Sekula, Irene
    Mother Goose (Circa 2054)—BrO
Self
    Ancestors. R. Fuller.—PlL
    By myself. E. Greenfield.—GrH
    Changing ("I know what I feel like") M. A.
        Hoberman.—HoY
    Cold term. I. A. Baraka.—AdC
    Ego-tripping. E. Merriam.—MeR
    Finding out. F. Holman.—HoA
    "I love." E. Greenfield.—GrH
    If she sang. G. W. Barrax.—AdC
    The landscape inside me. T. McGrath.—KhI
    A near pantoum for a birthday. B. Howes.—
        PlL
    Some me of beauty. C. M. Rodgers.—AdC
    Song in 5 parts. W. P. Root.—KhI
    Thumbprint. E. Merriam.—MaP
    "Under my hat is my hair." N. M.
        Bodecker.—BoHh
    Unholy missions. B. Kaufman.—AdC
    What I learned this year. L. Warsh.—KhI
    When I am me. F. Holman.—HoBm
    When we hear the eye open. B. Kaufman.—
        AdC
    "Where have you been dear." K. Kuskin.—
        HoBm—KuD
    Who am I ("I am muscles") L. Morrison.—
        MoW
    Who am I ("The trees ask me") F. Holman.—
        HoA
    Who, where. L. Morrison.—MoW
Self expression. Ann Darr.—LuZ
Self-portrait, as a bear. Donald Hall.—HiS
Selfishness
    Harvey never shares. J. Prelutsky.—PrRh
    Prayer of the selfish child. S. Silverstein.—SiL
Sender, Ramon and Laurel, Alicia Bay
    Being of the sun, sel.
        Winter solstice chant.—BaC
    Winter solstice chant. See Being of the sun
Senile. Pat Folk.—JaPp
"A senior wizard." See The cat and the wizard
Senses. See also Odors; Sight; Sounds; Taste;
    Touch
    Queer. D. McCord.—McO
    Senses. S. Silverstein.—SiL
Senses. Shel Silverstein.—SiL
Senses of insecurity. Maya Angelou.—AnO
Separation. W. S. Merwin.—JaPp—LuZ
September
    September ("Fall is coming") M. C.
        Livingston.—HoMp
    September ("Fall is coming") Myra Cohn
        Livingston.—HoMp
    September creek. Robert Newton Peck.—PeB
"September evenings such as these." See
    Watching the moon
"September is a long." See Long shadows at
    Dulce
"September rain falls on the house." See
    Sestina
"Serene when the moon's in winter quarters."
    See Socks and shoes

"My hounds are bred out of the Spartan
    kind."—CoG
Puck's song.—WaFp
You spotted snakes.—PaB
"My gentle Puck, come hither, thou
    rememberest." See A midsummer night's
    dream
"My hounds are bred out of the Spartan
    kind." See A midsummer night's dream
Puck's song. See A midsummer night's dream
Queen Mab. See Romeo and Juliet
Romeo and Juliet, sel.
    Queen Mab.—WaFp
"Some say that ever 'gainst that season
    comes." See Hamlet
Sonnets, sel.
    "From you I have been absent in the
        spring."—PaB
The tempest, sels.
    Ariel's song.—PaB
    "Full fathom five thy father lies."—PaE
    Ariel's dirge.—WiP
"Thrice the brinded cat hath mew'd." See
    Macbeth
"Tomorrow is Saint Valentine's day." See
    Hamlet
Venus and Adonis, sel.
    "But lo, from forth a copse that
        neighbours by."—CoPh
"When daisies pied and violets blue." See
    Love's labour's lost
"Yea, there thou makest me sad and makest
    me sin." See King Henry IV
You spotted snakes. See A midsummer
    night's dream
Shaking. Shel Silverstein.—SiL
"Shall hog with holy child converse." See Hog
    at the manger
Shall I consider you. Lillian Morrison.—MoO
"Shall I dig a hole." See Applesauce
"Shall I tell you who will come." See Words
    from an old Spanish carol
Shan Mei
    The green spring.—SaM
Shanks, Edward
    The cataclysm.—PaE
    The rock pool.—PaE
Shannon, Monica
    How to tell goblins from elves.—WaFp
    Uncle Frank.—PaI
"Shapely, sharp Durenda Fair." See Durenda
    Fair
Shapes. Shel Silverstein.—SiL
Shapiro, Karl
    Construction.—JaPp
    Elegy for a dead soldier, sel.
        "Underneath this wooden cross there
            lies."—LiO
    Man on wheels.—JaPp
    My grandmother.—PlL
    Party in winter.—JaPp
    The twins.—PlL
    "Underneath this wooden cross there lies."
        See Elegy for a dead soldier

Sharing. Robert Newton Peck.—PeB
The shark ("He seemed to know the harbour")
    E. J. Pratt.—DoWh
The shark ("How many scientists have
    written") Ogden Nash.—BlC
The shark ("My dear, let me tell you about the
    shark") John Ciardi.—LuZ
The shark ("The shark has rows") Edward
    Lucie-Smith.—CoA
The shark ("The shark is a trifle crazy") John
    Gardner.—GaCb
"The shark has rows." See The shark
"The shark is a trifle crazy." See The shark
Sharks
    "Beat me and bite me." D. Lee.—LeG
    Have fun. S. Silverstein.—SiL
    The Maldive shark. H. Melville.—PaE
    The shark ("He seemed to know the
        harbour") E. J. Pratt.—DoWh
    The shark ("How many scientists have
        written") O. Nash.—BlC
    The shark ("My dear, let me tell you about
        the shark") J. Ciardi.—LuZ
    The shark ("The shark has rows") E.
        Lucie-Smith.—CoA
    The shark ("The shark is a trifle crazy") J.
        Gardner.—GaCb
Sharp, Saundra
    Moon poem.—BrO
"Sharp sting of sand, saltwater stain." See
    House on Cape Cod
Sharp, William
    The moon-child.—PaE
Shaw, Isabel
    Christmas chant.—BaC
Shaw, Nate (about)
    The music. E. Hoagland.—AdC
Shaw, Robert Gould (about)
    Robert Gould Shaw. P. L. Dunbar.—BrI
She ("In the darkest part of the forest's heart")
    Jack Prelutsky.—WaFp
"She always has a treasure." See Next door
    neighbor
"She comes by night, in fearsome flight." See
    The witch
"She gave me a rose." Paul Laurence
    Dunbar.—BrI
"She lay in bed on the second floor." See At
    grandmother's
"She owns a corner by the fire." See To an old
    cat
"She pops their flanks with a rawhide whip."
    See Pony girl
"She reads the paper." See Two people
"She rose to his requirement, dropt." Emily
    Dickinson.—PlL
"She sent me out to play again." Nikki
    Grimes.—GrS
"She shared the lettered strivings." See
    Communication II—The teacher
"She shouted down the seashore she saw the
    shark." See Six tongue twisters
"She stands." See Troubled woman

"**She** stood hanging wash before sun." See
  Migration
"**She** told the story, and the whole world
  wept." See Harriet Beecher Stowe
"**She** walks alone." See The spearthrower
"**She** wanted to play the piano." See Musical
  career
"**She** was afraid of men." See Chicken-licken
"**She** was never a dog that had much sense."
  See Of an ancient spaniel in her fifteenth
  year
"**She** was opening up her umbrella." See Snap
"**She** went up the mountain to pluck wild
  herbs." See Old and new
"**She** wished of him a lover's kiss and." See
  Communication I
Sheard, Virna
  The yak.—DoWh
Sheep. See also Lambs; Shepherds
  "As I was going to Darby." Mother Goose.—
    TrGg
  "Little Bo-Peep." From The space child's
    Mother Goose. F. Winsor.—BrO
  "The mothers have come back." From
    Sheep. T. Hughes.—HuSs
  "The sheep has stopped crying." From
    Sheep. T. Hughes.—HuSs
  Shepherd's night count. J. Yolen.—YoD
  "What is it this time the dark barn again."
    From Sheep. T. Hughes.—HuSs
  Where it starts. M. C. Livingston.—LiF
Sheep, sels. Ted Hughes.—HuSs (Complete)
  I. "The sheep has stopped crying."
  II. "What is it this time the dark barn again."
  III. "The mothers have come back."
"The **sheep** are brown." See Where it starts
"The **sheep** has stopped crying." See Sheep,
  sels.
A **sheik** from Riff. N. M. Bodecker.—BoP
"A **sheik** from the mountains of Riff." See A
  sheik from Riff
The **shell** ("And then I pressed the shell")
  James Stephens.—PaE
The **shell** ("I took away the ocean once") David
  McCord.—McO
The **shell** ("See what a lovely shell") Lord
  Alfred Tennyson.—PaE
The **shell** ("What has the sea swept up") Mary
  Webb.—PaE
The **shell** ("Who could devise") Vernon
  Watkins.—PaE
Shellfish. See names of shellfish, as Lobsters
Shelley, Percy Bysshe
  Love's philosophy, sel.
      "See the mountains kiss high heaven."—
        YaI
  "Music, when soft voices die."—JaPp
  "See the mountains kiss high heaven." See
    Love's philosophy
  A widow bird sate mourning.—PaB
Shelley, Percy Bysshe (about)
  You and me and P. B. Shelley. O. Nash.—BlC
Shells
  The black pebble. J. Reeves.—MaP—WiP

The chambered nautilus. O. W. Holmes.—
  PaE
The coral grove. J. G. Percival.—PaE
"The delicate shells lay on the shore." From
  Each and all. R. W. Emerson.—PaE
Ecstasy. W. J. Turner.—PaE
Frutta di mare. G. Scott.—PaE
"I have seen." From The excursion. W.
  Wordsworth.—PaE
"I have sinuous shells of pearly hue." From
  Gebir. W. S. Landor.—PaE
My seashell. A. Barto.—SaM
"O sailor, come ashore." C. Rossetti.—WiP
On some shells found inland. T. Stickney.—
  PaE
The punishment. J. Aiken.—AiS
Scarlett rocks. T.E. Brown.—PaE
The sea-limits. D. G. Rossetti.—PaE
Sea shell. A. Lowell.—SaM
The shell ("And then I pressed the shell.") J.
  Stephens.—PaE
The shell ("I took away the ocean once") D.
  McCord.—McO
The shell ("See what a lovely shell") A.
  Tennyson.—PaE
The shell ("What has the sea swept up") M.
  Webb.—PaE
The shell ("Who could devise") V. Watkins.—
  PaE
Snail ("Snail upon the wall") J. Drinkwater.—
  WiP
"Some small smooth shells have." B.
  Maestro.—MaFp
The **shepherd** who stayed. Theodosia
  Garrison.—LiPch
Shepherdess' valentine, sel. Francis Andrewes
  "I bear, in sign of love."—LiO
Shepherds. See also Sheep
  About the field. Unknown.—BaC
  "And there were in the same country
    shepherds." From Gospel according to
    Luke.—LiPch
      The shepherds.—BaC (sel.)
  Bring your pipes. Unknown.—BaC
  "How simple we must grow." From Paradox.
    A. Silesius.—BaC
  "I bear, in sign of love." From Shepherdess'
    valentine. F. Andrewes.—LiO
  "Little Bo-Peep." From The space child's
    Mother Goose. F. Winsor.—BrO
  "Look up, you men, men there at the fire."
    From Annunciation over the shepherds. R.
    M. Rilke.—LiPch
  Los pastores. E. Agnew.—LiPch
  The passionate shepherd to his love. C.
    Marlowe.—PaB
  Rise, shepherds. Unknown.—BaC
  The shepherd who stayed. T. Garrison.—
    LiPch
  The shepherd's hut. A. Young.—WaGp
  "The shepherds knew." Unknown.—BaC
  Shepherd's night count. J. Yolen.—YoD
  Shepherd's song at Christmas. L. Hughes.—
    BaC—LiPch

"Under a bent when the night was deep."
From The earthly paradise. W. Morris.—
LiPch
The **shepherds**. See Gospel according to
Luke—"And there were in the same
country shepherds"
The **shepherd's** hut. Andrew Young.—WaGp
"The **shepherds** knew." Unknown.—BaC
Shepherd's night count. Jane Yolen.—YoD
Shepherd's song at Christmas. Langston
Hughes.—BaC—LiPch
"**She's** taught me that I mustn't bark." See
Remarks from the pup
Shh. Eve Merriam.—MeW
Shihab, Naomi
The first poem I ever wrote.—KhI
Shine, republic. Robinson Jeffers.—PlG
"**Shining** in his stickiness and glistening with
honey." See The friendly cinnamon bun
"**Shining** like lamps and light as balloons." See
Moon heads
Shiny. James Reeves.—SaM
"**Shiny** are the chestnut leaves." See Shiny
"The **ship** moves." William Carlos Williams.—
MoGp
Ships. See also Shipwrecks; Warships
Aunt Nerissa's muffin. W. Irwin.—CoPs
Down below. J. Aiken.—AiS
Immigration. R. Frost.—PlG
Jack was every inch a sailor. Unknown.—
DoWh
The Mediterranean. A. Tate.—PlG
My father's death. M. Sarton.—PlL
The phantom ship. M. P. Hearn.—WaGp
River night. F. Frost.—RuM
"The ship moves." W. C. Williams.—MoGp
Ships that pass in the night. P. L. Dunbar.—
BrI
The way of Cape Race. E. J. Pratt.—DoWh
The white ships. D. McCord.—McO
The **ships** of Yule. Bliss Carman.—DoWh
Ships that pass in the night. Paul Laurence
Dunbar.—BrI
Shipwrecks
Cardigan bay. J. Masefield.—PaE
"Lord, lord, methought what pain it was to
drown." From King Richard III. W.
Shakespeare.—PaE
The witnesses. H. W. Longfellow.—PlG
The **shirk**. Jane Yolen.—YoH
Shiver my timbers. David McCord.—McO
The **shlepard**. Jane Yolen.—YoH
Shoeing up the mare. Robert Newton Peck.—
PeB
"**Shoelaces**." See Notions
Shoes. See Boots and shoes
Shoes ("Shoes are for walking") Michael
Dugan.—DuSn
Shoes ("Shoes on our feet") Aileen Fisher.—FiO
Shoes ("Which to prefer") Valerie Worth.—
WoM
"**Shoes** and socks and underwear." See The
right place
"**Shoes** are for walking." See Shoes

"**Shoes** on our feet." See Shoes
Shoeshine men. Audre Lorde.—MoGp
The **shooting** of Dan McGrew. Robert W.
Service.—DoWh
Shopping. See Markets and marketing;
Peddlers and venders; Shops and
shopkeepers
Shops and Shopkeepers. See also names of
shops and shopkeepers, as Barbers and
barbershops
Air on an escalator. J. Aiken.—AiS
Alligator on the escalator. E. Merriam.—WiP
The Chinese greengrocers. P. Lowther.—LuZ
Excursion. M. A. Hoberman.—HoY
"The fly made a visit to the grocery store."
Unknown.—WiP
General store. R. Field.—PaI
"A lazy old grocer of Eyer." M. C.
Livingston.—LiLl
Street window. C. Sandburg.—JaPp
Suddenly. A. Fisher.—HoMp
"Tommy kept a chandler's shop." Mother
Goose.—TrGg
Whistling Willie. K. Starbird.—BrO
Shore. See Seashore
Short, Clarice
The owl on the aerial.—LuZ
A **short** directory of Kent. Joan Aiken.—AiS
A **short** litany. Unknown.—WaW
"The **shortest** fight." See The knockout
Should all of this come true. X. J. Kennedy.—
KeP
"The **shreek** is a shiverous beast." See Please,
Johnny
Shrew ("The little shrew is soricine") David
McCord.—McO
The **shrew** ("The pygmy shrew is very small")
Jack Prelutsky.—WiP
Shrews
Shrew ("The little shrew is soricine") D.
McCord.—McO
The shrew ("The pygmy shrew is very
small") J. Prelutsky.—WiP
Small, smaller. R. Hoban.—MoGp
Shrieks at midnight. Dorothy Brown
Thompson.—WaG
The **shrimp**. Ogden Nash.—BlC
"A **shrimp** who sought his lady shrimp." See
The shrimp
Shu Ning Liu, Stephen
My nurse.—KhI
"**Shut**, closet door." See Bedtime
Sicily
The day of the dead. D. W. Donzella.—KhI
A **sick** child. Randall Jarrell.—HiS
Sickness. See also names of diseases, as Mumps
Breakfast ("Morning, morning will produce")
D. McCord.—McO
Cactus sickness. T. Hughes.—HuM
Can I get you a glass of water, or please close
the glottis after you. O. Nash.—BlC
Catching. S. Silverstein.—SiL
The crossing of Mary of Scotland. W. J.
Smith.—WiP

Hot dog.—SiL
How many, how much.—SiL
How not to have to dry the dishes.—SiL
How to make a swing with no rope or board or nails.—SiL
Hug o' war.—YaI
Hula eel.—SiL
Hurk.—SiL
If.—SiL
"If I had a brontosaurus."—CoDb—MoGp
"If I had a firecracker."—CoI
"If you pinch a dinosaur."—CoDb
Importnt.—SiL
In search of Cinderella.—SiL
It's all the same to the clam.—SiL
"It's hot."—SiL
Jumping rope.—HeB
Kidnapped.—SiL
Ladies first.—SiL
A light in the attic.—SiL
Little Abigail and the beautiful pony.—SiL
The little boy and the old man.—SiL
Longmobile.—SiL
The lost cat.—SiL
Love.—YaI
Magic carpet.—SiL
The man in the iron pail mask.—SiL
Me and my giant.—WaG
The meehoo with an exactlywatt.—SiL
Memorizin' Mo.—SiL
Messy room.—SiL
Mr. Smeds and Mr. Spats.—SiL
Monsters I've met.—SiL
Moon catchin' net.—SiL
Musical career.—SiL
My guitar.—SiL
My invention.—BrO
My rules.—LuZ
The nailbiter.—SiL
Never.—SiL
Noah's ark.—CoA
Nobody.—SiL
Not me.—WaM
Oh have you heard.—HoMp—LiCc
The oak and the rose.—SiL
On Halloween.—BrIt
One two.—SiL
Outside or underneath.—SiL
Overdues.—SiL
The painter.—SiL
Peckin'.—SiL
Picture puzzle piece.—SiL
Pie problem.—SiL
The pirate.—SiL
Pirate captain Jim.—WiP
Play ball.—SiL
Poemsicle.—SiL
Point of view.—CoPs
Prayer of the selfish child.—SiL
Prehistoric.—SiL
Push button.—SiL
Put something in.—SiL
Quick trip.—SiL
Reflection.—SiL

Rhino pen.—SiL
Rock 'n' roll band.—SiL
Rockabye.—SiL
Senses.—SiL
Shadow race.—SiL
Shaking.—SiL
Shapes.—SiL
Signals.—SiL
The silver fish.—CoPs
The sitter.—SiL
Skin stealer.—SiL
Snake problem.—SiL
Snap.—SiL
Some day.—CoPh
Somebody has to.—SiL
Something missing.—SiL
"Sour face Ann."—SiL
Spelling bee.—SiL
Squishy touch.—SiL
"Standing is stupid."—SiL
Stop thief.—SiL
Strange wind.—SiL
Superstitious.—SiL
Surprise.—SiL
Suspense.—SiL
The sword swallower.—SiL
"They've put a brassiere on the camel."—SiL
This bridge.—SiL
Thumb face.—SiL
Ticklish Tom.—SiL
Tired.—SiL
The toad and the kangaroo.—SiL
Tree house.—BeR
Tryin' on clothes.—SiL
Turtle.—SiL
Tusk, tusk.—SiL
Twistable turnable man.—SiL
"The tyrannosaurus rex."—CoDb
Union for children's rights.—SiL
Unscratchable itch.—SiL
Vegetables.—CoPs.
Wavy.—SiL
What did.—SiL
Whatif.—SiL
Who ordered the broiled face.—SiL
Wild strawberries.—SiL
The worst.—CoI
Zebra question.—SiL

Simic, Charles
　Fork.—JaPp
Simile. N. Scott Momaday.—LuZ—MoGd
Simmons, Judy Dothard
　Alabama.—AdC
　Generations.—AdC
　"It's comforting."—AdC
　Survivor.—AdC
Simone, Nina (about)
　Nina Simone ("This brown woman's voice") L. Jeffers.—AdC
"Simple and fresh and fair from winter's close emerging." See The first dandelion
Simple song. Marge Piercy.—LuZ—MaP
Simpson, Louis
　The goodnight.—PlL

"As I was going to Darby." Mother Goose.—TrGg

"Big dog." P. Booth.—CoG

The brontosaurus. H.A.C. Evans.—CoDb

The dinosaur ("This poem is too small, I fear") E. Lucie-Smith.—CoDb

For a ladybug. A. Fisher.—FiO

"The frummick and the frelly." J. Prelutsky.—PrS

The gibble. J. Prelutsky.—PrS

"Here he comes." M. Pomeroy.—CoDb

How big. A. Fisher.—FiO

It's all relative. W. Cole.—CoDb

The largest of them all. J. A. Lindon.—CoDb

Lines on a small potato. M. Fishback.—CoDb

Mice ("Mice find places") V. Worth.—WoSm

The monumental meath. J. Prelutsky.—PrS

The oak and the rose. S. Silverstein.—SiL

Small, smaller. R. Hoban.—MoGp

Take my advice. W. Cole.—CoDb

Teeny tiny ghost. L. Moore.—WaGp

"There was a little guinea pig." Mother Goose.—TrGg

A thought. M. A. Hoberman.—HoY

The tigirth. J. Yolen.—YoH

Whale ("A whale is stout about the middle") M. A. Hoberman.—HoY

The skank. Jane Yolen.—YoH

Skateboards and skateboarding

On the skateboard. L. Morrison.—MoGp

The sidewalk racer. L. Morrison.—MoSr

Skating

Come skating. S. Silverstein.—SiL

Sidewalks. V. Worth.—WoM

Suddenly. D. McCord.—McO

"A **skeleton** called Wellington." See Wellington the skeleton

"A **skeleton** once in Khartoum." Unknown.—BrIt

Skeleton parade. Jack Prelutsky.—PrI

The **skeleton** walks. X. J. Kennedy.—BrIt

Skeletons

The dance of the thirteen skeletons. J. Prelutsky.—PrN

I'm skeleton. L. Moore.—BrIt

"The mastodon." M. Braude.—CoDb

"A skeleton once in Khartoum." Unknown.—BrIt

Skeleton parade. J. Prelutsky.—PrI

The skeleton walks. X. J. Kennedy.—BrIt

Wellington the skeleton. D. Lee.—LeN

"The **skeletons** are out tonight." See Skeleton parade

"**Skeletons**, spirits and haunts." See Day after Halloween

The **sketch** book, sel. Washington Irving "Now Christmas is come."—BaC

Skiing

Skiing ("Fast as foxes") R. Burgunder.—HoMp

The world's best hopper. K. Starbird.—StC

Skiing ("Fast as foxes") Rose Burgunder.—HoMp

Skimmers. Paul Baker Newman.—PaE

"**Skimming**." See On the skateboard

"**Skimming** an asphalt sea." See The sidewalk racer

Skin

Skin stealer. S. Silverstein.—SiL

The **skin** spinners. Joan Aiken.—AiS

Skin stealer. Shel Silverstein.—SiL

Skindiver. Dennis Lee.—LeG

The **skink.** Ogden Nash.—BlC

Skinned knee. Judith Thurman.—ThFo

Skip scoop anellie. Tom Prideaux.—CoPs

Skipping

"The high skip." E. Farjeon.—WiP

"Little children skip." T. Hood.—MoF

Rattlesnake skipping song. D. Lee.—WiP

"**Skittery** two year olds." See Morgans in October

"**Skittish**." See The women's 400 meters

Skunks

How many. M. A. Hoberman.—HoY

The skank. J. Yolen.—YoH

Sky

All that sky. A. Fisher.—FiO

Back yard, July night. W. Cole.—LuZ

Blue alert. E. Merriam.—MeR

Broken sky. C. Sandburg.—JaPp

Brooms ("On stormy days") D. Aldis.—PaI

Clouds ("All my life, I guess, I've loved the clouds") D. McCord.—McO

Clouds ("These clouds are soft fat horses") J. Reaney.—DoWh

Footprints. J. Aiken.—AiS.

The hatch. N. Farber.—HiS

In winter sky. D. McCord.—McO

Questions at night. L. Untermeyer.—RuM

"Red sky at night." Unknown.—SaM

The sky ("The sky at night is like a big city") Unknown.—LuZ

The sky is turning. L. Morrison.—MoO

Sky skimmers. M. C. Livingston.—LiF

Skyviews. D. McCord.—McSu

Song of the sky loom. Unknown.—MoGp

Take sky. D. McCord.—McO

"There was an old woman tossed in a blanket." Mother Goose.—TrGg

"There was an old woman tossed up in a basket." Mother Goose.—LoG

Wake up, shadows. L. Moore.—MoTs

What they say. L. Morrison.—MoW

The **sky** ("The sky at night is like a big city") Unknown, tr. fr. the Ewe by Kafu Hoh.—LuZ

"The **sky** at night is like a big city." See The sky

Sky diving

Sky diving ("In the engine sound like many people together") R. Taylor.—LuZ

Volare. L. Morrison.—MoSr

Sky diving ("In the engine sound like many people together") Rod Taylor.—LuZ

Sky fish. Aileen Fisher.—FiO

"The **sky** is a dead fish." See The plaque in the reading room for my classmates killed in Korea

The sky is turning. Lillian Morrison.—MoO
"The sky of brightest gray seems dark." See Comparison
"The sky of gray is eaten in six places." See Broken sky
Sky rider. Aileen Fisher.—FiO
Sky skimmers. Myra Cohn Livingston.—LiF
"The sky was yellow." See Halloween
Skylarks. See Larks
Skyviews. David McCord.—McSu
The slave singing at midnight. Henry Wadsworth Longfellow.—PlG
Slavery
    Aunt Sue's stories. L. Hughes.—HiD
    Breath in my nostrils. L. Jeffers.—AdC
    Burying ground by the ties. A. MacLeish.—PlG
    Child dead in old seas. M. Angelou.—AnO
    Frederick Douglass ("When it is finally ours, this freedom, this liberty, this beautiful") R. E. Hayden.—PlG
    Harriet Tubman. E. Greenfield.—GrH
    Nat Turner. S. Allen.—AdC
    Nina Simone. L. Jeffers.—AdC
    On being brought from Africa to America. P. Wheatley.—PlG
    Refugee in America. L. Hughes.—PlG
    Runagate runagate. R. Hayden.—AdC
    The slave singing at midnight. H. W. Longfellow.—PlG
    "Sojourner Truth." From Stars. R. Hayden.—AdC
    Song for the old ones. M. Angelou.—AnO
    Southern mansion. A. Bontemps.—AdC
    Strong men. S. A. Brown.—AdC
    Trellie. L. Jeffers.—AdC
    "Why did all manly gifts in Webster fail." R. W. Emerson.—PlG
    The witnesses. H. W. Longfellow.—PlG
Sleds and sleighs
    On the slope. D. McCord.—McSu
Sleep. See also Bed-time; Dreams; Lullabies
    Alarm clock. E. Merriam.—MoGp
    Asleep and awake. D. McCord.—McO
    Bears. E. Coatsworth.—CoA
    The cat ("Within that porch, across the way") W. H. Davies.—SaM
    The city and Evan. K. Starbird.—StC
    The country and Nate. K. Starbird.—StC
    "Doll's boy's asleep." E. E. Cummings.—HiD
    Goodnight ("Goodnight Mommy") N. Giovanni.—GiV—RuM
    "I want to." B. S. De Regniers.—ReB
    "I want to keep." B. S. De Regniers.—ReB
    Insomnia. L. Morrison.—MoW
    Insomnia the gem of the ocean. J. Updike.—BrO
    The land of nod. R. L. Stevenson.—PaI
    Mother cat's purr. J. Yolen.—YoD
    Night sounds. F. Holman.—HoA—RuM
    Night train. R. Francis.—HiD
    A person in Corning. N. M. Bodecker.—BoP
    "Pretending to sleep." J. Thurman.—HoBm—ThFo

Rhyme for night. J. Aiken.—AiS
Says Tom to me. D. McCord.—McO
Sleep song. S. Kroll.—WaFp
The sleepers. K. Starbird.—StC
The sun and moon circus soothes the wakeful guests. N. Willard.—WiV
Sweet dreams. O. Nash.—BlC
"There was a young woman of Brighton." M. C. Livingston.—LiLl
Tunnel. J. Thurman.—ThFo
Turtle sings an egg song. J. Yolen.—YoD
Two ways to wake a sleepwalker. E. Lueders.—LuZ
Vesper. Alcman of Sparta.—LuZ
Wild child's lament. J. Yolen.—YoD
The wise cow enjoys a cloud. N. Willard.—WiV
"Sleep, my hundred young ones." See Turtle sings an egg song
Sleep song. Steven Kroll.—WaFp
"Sleep sweetly in your humble graves." See Ode
"Sleep the half sleep." See Mother cat's purr
"Sleep will come." See Mother owl's song
"Sleep, young wriggler." See Mother worm's hum
The sleepers. Kaye Starbird.—StC
"Sleeplessly circle the waves." See Look not too deep
"Sleepy Betsy from her pillow." See The bedpost
Slim Slater. Kaye Starbird.—StC
"Slim Slater lives in a camper." See Slim Slater
"The slithergadee has crawled out of the sea." See Not me
Sloth ("A tree's a trapeze for a sloth") Mary Ann Hoberman.—HoY
Sloths
    Sloth ("A tree's a trapeze for a sloth") M. A. Hoberman.—HoY
    "The treetoad and the three-toed sloth." J. Gardner.—GaCb
"The slow death of love." See Juxtaposing
"Slow moves the pageant of a climbing race." See Slow through the dark
"Slow-moving turtle." Betsy Maestro.—MaFp
"Slow sail'd the weary mariners and saw." See The sea-fairies
Slow through the dark. Paul Laurence Dunbar.—BrI
"Slowly, slowly, he cruises." See The barracuda
"Slowly, the fog." See The fog
"Slowly with bleeding nose and aching wrists." See The hero
"The slug." See Slug
Slug. Valerie Worth.—WoSm
"Slug-a-bed." Mother Goose.—TrGg
Slugs
    Slug. V. Worth.—WoSm
The slummings. Jane Yolen.—YoH
The small. Theodore Roethke.—HiS
"Small as a fox and like." See Our Lucy, 1956-1960
"The small birds swirl around." See The small

"Small, busy flames play through the fresh laid coals." See To my brothers
"Small comfort the candle." See Small dirge
Small dirge. Isabel Wilner.—WiP
A small discovery. James A. Emanuel.—MaP
A small elegy. Richard Snyder.—JaPp
Small frogs. Leslie Norris.—NoM
"Small grains." See Magnifying glass
"Small hands I lift to You who once were small." See Christmas candle
Small moon. Howard Nemerov.—JaPp
"A small mouse in Middleton Stoney." Myra Cohn Livingston.—LiLl
Small, smaller. Russell Hoban.—MoGp
"A small woolly llama." See A is for alpaca
Smallman, Robin
    A deserted beach.—SaM
"Smart Mr. Doppler." David McCord.—McO
"The smear of blue peat smoke." See The shepherd's hut
"The smell of clover." See Clover field
"The smell of sage." See Church poem
"The smell of the sea in my nostrils." See The mystic sea
Smells. See Odors
Smelly Fred. Dennis Lee.—LeG
The smile ("My grandmother, I've discovered") Joan Aiken.—AiS
Smith, Bessie (about)
    Homage to the empress of the blues. R. Hayden.—AdC
Smith, Iain Crichton
    Two girls singing.—LuZ
Smith, John (about)
    Jamestown ("Let me look at what I was, before I die") R. Jarrell.—PlG
Smith, William Jay
    A is for alpaca.—SmL
    Alice.—SmL
    Anteater.—SmL
    Antelope.—SmL
    Apples.—SmL
    Around my room.—SmL
    B is for bats.—SmL
    Bad boy's swan song.—CoI
    Banjo tune.—SmL
    Betsy Robin.—SmL
    Big and little.—SmL
    Big Gumbo.—SmL
    Butterfly.—SmL
    C is for cabbages.—SmL
    Camel.—SmL
    Cat.—SmL
    The closing of the rodeo.—PlG
    Coati-mundi.—SmL
    "A contentious old person named Reagan."—SmL
    Cow.—SmL
    Crocodile.—SmL
    The crossing of Mary of Scotland.—SmL—WiP
    D is for dog.—SmL
    Dictionary.—SmL
    Dog.—SmL

Dragon.—SmL
E is for egg.—SmL
Elephant.—SmL
F is for frogboy.—SmL
Fish.—SmL
The floor and the ceiling.—SmL—WiP
Fox and crow.—SmL
G is for goat.—SmL
Giraffe.—SmL
Goony bird.—SmL
Grandmother ostrich.—SmL
Gull.—SmL
H is for hat.—SmL
Hats.—SmL
Having.—SmL
Hen.—SmL
Hippopotamus.—SmL
I is for inkspot.—SmL
Imaginary dialogues.—WiP
J is for jack-in-the-box.—SmL
Jittery Jim.—SmL
K is for king.—SmL
Kangaroo.—SmL
The King of Spain.—SmL
L is for laundry.—SmL
The land of Ho-Ho-Hum.—SmL
Laughing time.—SmL
Lion.—SmL
Little Dimity.—SmL
Love.—SmL
M is for mask.—SmL
The mirror.—SmL
Mr. Smith.—SmL
Mrs. Caribou.—SmL
Mistress Mary.—SmL
Mole.—SmL
Molly Mock-Turtle.—SmL
Monkey.—SmL
Moon.—SmL
My body.—SmL
N is for needle.—SmL
O is for owl.—SmL
"An obnoxious old person named Hackett."—SmL
"An old man from Okefenokee."—SmL
Opossum.—CoA—SmL
Over and under.—WiP
The owl.—SmL
P is for pirate.—SmL
The panda ("A lady who lived in Uganda")—SmL
Parrot from Trinidad.—SmL
Parrot from Zambezi.—SmL
A pavane for the nursery.—HiD—YaI
Penguin.—SmL
People.—SmL
Pick me up.—SmL—WiP
Pig.—SmL
Polar bear.—SmL
"Puptents and pebbles."—SmL
Q is for queen.—SmL
The Queen of the Nile.—SmL
R is for reindeer.—SmL
Raccoon.—SmL—WiP

The **sniffle.** Ogden Nash.—BlC

S'no fun. William Cole.—CoDb

Snodgrass, W. D.
   April inventory.—KhI
   "Child of my winter, born." See Heart's needle
   Heart's needle, sels.
      "Child of my winter, born."—PlL
      "Late April and you are three, today."—PlL
   "Late April and you are three, today." See Heart's needle
   Mementos, 1.—PlL

The **snopp** on the sidewalk. Jack Prelutsky.—PrS

Snoring
   Abiding question. S. Kroll.—CoDb
   An emergency. F. Holman.—HoA

"**Snout** too little." See The piguana

Snow. See also Winter
   And then. Prince Redcloud.—HoMp
   Blizzard ("The big city is rude to snow") J. Thurman.—ThFo
   The blizzard ("I can't forget the second night of the snow") K. Starbird.—StC
   Boy at the window. R. Wilbur.—MaP
   December ("First snow, the flakes") J. Updike.—BaC
   Early snow. A. Fisher.—FiO
   Flake on flake. A. Fisher.—FiO
   The horses ("It has turned to snow in the night") M. Kumin.—HiD
   "How cold the snow." From Four Christmas carols. Unknown.—LiPch
   Joe's snow clothes. K. Kuskin.—KuD
      "For wandering walks.—WiP
   Last snow. A. Young.—SaM
   Late snowfall. B. S. De Regniers.—ReB
   Like a giant in a towel. D. Lee.—WaG
   "A lonely sparrow." K. Mizumura.—MiF
   Merry Christmas. A. Fisher.—BaC
   Monkey. W. J. Smith.—SmL
   On the slope. D. McCord.—McSu
   "Once I dreamt I was the snow." S. C. Fox.—FoB
   The open door. E. Coatsworth.—HiD
   Out in the winter wind. A. Fisher.—FiO
   "Please bird, don't go yet." K. Mizumura.—MiF
   Rabbit track. R. N. Peck.—PeB
   Runaway. R. Frost.—CoPh
   Small, smaller. R. Hoban.—MoGp
   S'no fun. W. Cole.—CoDb
   Snow ("Gardens, fields") V. Worth.—WoSm
   Snow ("Snow") M. A. Hoberman.—HoY
   Snow ("Softly") F. Holman.—HoMp
   Snow ("The strawberry hill is covered with snow") N. D. Watson.—WaB
   Snow ("We'll play in the snow") K. Kuskin.—KuD
   Snow and snow. T. Hughes.—HuSs
   The snow fall. A. MacLeish.—MoGp
   Snow landscape. S. Hollands.—SaM

"Snow makes a new land." K. Mizumura.—MiF
   Snow on the wind. A. Fisher.—FiO
   Snow party. A. Fisher.—FiO
   Snow song. B. S. De Regniers.—ReB
   Snow woman. N. D. Watson.—WaB
   Snowflakes ("Little boys are like") N. Giovanni.—GiV
   Snowflakes ("Not slowly wrought, nor treasured for their form.") H. Nemerov.—JaPp
   Snowflakes ("Sometime this winter if you go") D. McCord.—HoMp—McO
   "Snowflowers blossom." K. Mizumura.—MiF
   Snowy benches. A. Fisher.—FiO
   "So you found some fresh tracks in the snow." From Limericks. D. McCord.—McSu
   Sparkly snow. A. Fisher.—FiO
   "The spring snowflakes tickle." K. Mizumura.—MiF
   Trinity Place. D. McCord.—McO
   When all the world is full of snow. N. M. Bodecker.—BoHh
   "The wind sweeps away." K. Mizumura.—MiF
   Winter is tacked down. N. Weygant.—HoMp
   Winter morning ("A tablecloth all snowy white") A. Fisher.—FiO
   Winter poem. N. Giovanni.—LuZ
   "With the frenzied wind." K. Mizumura.—MiF

Snow ("Gardens, fields") Valerie Worth.—WoSm

Snow ("Snow") Mary Ann Hoberman.—HoY

Snow ("Softly") Felice Holman.—HoMp

Snow ("The strawberry hill is covered with snow") Nancy Dingman Watson.—WaB

Snow ("We'll play in the snow") Karla Kuskin.—KuD

"**Snow.**" See Snow

Snow and snow. Ted Hughes.—HuSs

The **snow** fall. Archibald MacLeish.—MoGp

"**Snow** has carpeted the ground." See Granny winter

"The **snow** in the sugar bush is up to my knees." See Sugar maples

"The **snow** is full of silver light." See Christmas

"**Snow** is sometimes a she, a soft one." See Snow and snow

Snow landscape. Sarah Hollands.—SaM

"The **snow** lies sprinkled on the beach." Robert Bridges.—PaE

"**Snow** makes a new land." Kazue Mizumura.—MiF

Snow on the wind. Aileen Fisher.—FiO

Snow party. Aileen Fisher.—FiO

Snow song. Beatrice Schenk De Regniers.—ReB

Snow woman. Nancy Dingman Watson.—WaB

"**Snow** woman snow woman." See Snow woman

Snowbirds. Aileen Fisher.—FiO

Snowflakes ("Little boys are like") Nikki Giovanni.—GiV

Snowflakes ("Not slowly wrought, nor treasured for their form") Howard Nemerov.—JaPp
Snowflakes ("Sometime this winter if you go") David McCord.—HoMp—McO
"Snowflowers blossom." Kazue Mizumura.—MiF
Snowman ("My little snowman has a mouth") David McCord.—McO
"The snowman's buttons are undone." See April
Snowmen
  "All through the long night." K. Mizumura.—MiF
  April ("The snowman's buttons are undone") A. Fisher.—FiO
  "I'm lumpish." From Who cast my shadow. L. Moore.—MoTs
  Snowman ("My little snowman has a mouth") D. McCord.—McO
Snowy benches. Aileen Fisher.—FiO
"A snowy field, a stable piled." See Christmas at Freelands
"A snowy path for squirrel and fox." See The brook in February
"The snuggle bunny." Dennis Lee.—LeG
Snyder, Gary
  By Frazier Creek Falls.—PlG
  The great mother.—LiCc
  Prayer for the great family.—LiO
Snyder, Richard
  A small elegy.—JaPp
"So bandit eyed, so undovelike a bird." See Blue jay
So come we running. Unknown.—BaC
"So come we running to the crib." See So come we running
"So I run out, I am holding a hare." See A moon hare
"So is the child slow stooping beside him." See Gardeners
So it goes. William Cole.—CoDb
"So it has come to this." See The ambition bird
"So many of us." See Mushrooms
So run along and play. David McCord.—McO
"So small a thing." See Mummy
"So, some tempestuous morn in early June." See Thyrsis
"So soon the apple blossoms." Kazue Mizumura.—MiF
So that's why. Lillian Morrison.—MoO
"So when the bugs take over." See In the end
So will I. Charlotte Zolotow.—HoBm
"So you found some fresh tracks in the snow." From Limericks. D. McCord.—McSu
"So your phone discontinues to buzz." From Limericks. D. McCord.—McSu
"So you're playing." See Identities
Soap
  I only watch the bubbles. N. Giovanni.—GiV
  Soap ("New cakes of soap") J. Thurman.—ThFo
  Soap bubble. V. Worth.—WoM
Soap ("New cakes of soap") Judith Thurman.—ThFo

Soap bubble. Valerie Worth.—WoM
"The soap bubble's." See Soap bubble
Sobel, Lester A.
  Transplantitis.—BrO
Soccer
  Kevin scores. L. Norris.—NoM
Socks and shoes. Joan Aiken.—AiS
Socks for the sirens. Joan Aiken.—AiS
"Soft." See Sopranosound, memory of John
"Softly." See Snow
"Softly, softly, day and night." See Flake on flake
"Sojourner Truth." See Stars
Sold. R. R. Cuscaden.—FlA
The soldier ("He is that fallen lance that lies as hurled") Robert Frost.—LiO
Soldiers. See also War
  The death of a soldier. W. Stevens.—LiO
  Dory Miller. S. Cornish.—Adc
  Drafted. Su Wu.—PlL
  Gunner. R. Jarrell.—LiO
  Jamming with the band at the VFW. D. Bottoms.—KhI
  Jolly soldier. Unknown.—LiO
  Kentucky Belle. C. F. Woolson.—CoPh
  The locust swarm. Hsu Chao.—LuZ
  "A sight in camp in the daybreak gray and dim." W. Whitman.—LiO
  The soldier ("He is that fallen lance that lies as hurled") R. Frost.—LiO
  To the veterans of the Abraham Lincoln brigade. G. Taggard.—LiO
  "Underneath this wooden cross there lies." From Elegy for a dead soldier. K. Shapiro.—LiO
  "Who comes here." Mother Goose.—WiP
  The young dead soldiers. A. MacLeish.—LiO
"Solemn pastors." See The MJQ
Solitude. See also Loneliness; Silence
  On the sea. J. Keats.—PaE
  Sitting on the fence. M. Leunig.—DuSn
  Up in the pine. N. D. Watson.—HoBm
  The wasp and the mud dauber. J. Gardner.—GaCb
"Solomon Grundy." See The space child's Mother Goose
Solstice song. Ted Hughes.—HuSs
"Some are teethed on a silver spoon." See Saturday's child
Some cook. John Ciardi.—CoPs
"Some cowpoke named her Nevada." See Nevada
Some day. Shel Silverstein.—CoPh
"Some day." See What someone said when he was spanked on the day before his birthday
"Some day I'll have a war horse." See Some day
"Some day I'm going to have a store." See General store
"Some days the moon comes early." See Early moon
"Some days, when the sun is high." See Day moon
"Some dogs are brats." See For a good dog

"**Some** farms have graveyards tucked upon a knoll." See Horse graveyard
"**Some** have a dog." See Human beings
Some lives. Lillian Morrison.—MoO
Some me of beauty. Carolyn M. Rodgers.—AdC
"**Some** of us." See Resurrection
"**Some** people manicure their nails." See The nailbiter
"**Some** people on the moon are so idle." Ted Hughes.—HuM
"**Some** people say that apples are red." See Apples
"**Some** people stop hunting because they get tired." See On dressing to go hunting
"**Some** people think a worm is rude." See Worm
"**Some** primal termite knocked on wood." See The termite
Some quarks have a strange flavor. Lillian Morrison.—MoO
"**Some** say that ever 'gainst that season comes." See Hamlet
"**Some** say the devil's dead." Mother Goose.—TrGg
"**Some** say the nightmare." See Nightmares
"**Some** singers sing of women's eyes." See The clean platter
"**Some** small smooth shells have." Betsy Maestro.—MaFp
"**Some** things will never change although." See Far trek
"**Some** travelers lugging valises." See Travelers lugging valises
Some uses for poetry. Eve Merriam.—JaPp
"**Some** whales." See Tall stories
"**Some** would dive in the lagoon." See The enchanted island
Somebody has to. Shel Silverstein.—SiL
"**Somebody** has to go polish the stars." See Somebody has to
"**Somebody** rang the bell." See A secret
"**Someday** I'll go to Winnipeg." See Tongue twister
"**Someday** I'm going to pick up." See The driver
"**Somehow** the hen." See Egg
Someone's face. John Ciardi.—CoI
"**Someone's** face was all frowned shut." See Someone's face
Somersaults. Jack Prelutsky.—PrR
"**Somethin'** else and." See Cannon arrested
"**Somethin** is lost in me." See Man thinking about woman
Something better. David McCord.—McO
"**Something** I want to communicate to you." See With the door open
Something missing. Shel Silverstein.—SiL
"**Something** strange is flitting through your hair. See The poltergeist
"**Something** told the wild geese." Rachel Field.—HoMp
"**Sometime** this winter if you go." See Snowflakes

Sometimes ("The clouds are full of new blue sky") David McCord.—McO
Sometimes ("Sometimes I simply have to cry") Jack Prelutsky.—PrR
"**Sometimes** I simply have to cry." See Sometimes
Sometimes I think of Maryland. Jodi Braxton.—AdC
"**Sometimes** it is like a beast." See A trucker
"**Sometimes** my mind is crazy." See Goofus
"**Sometimes**, riding in a car, in Wisconsin." See Three kinds of pleasures
"**Sometimes** when." See I wonder
"**Sometimes** when I." See New York in the spring
"**Sometimes** when you watch the fire." See Long distance
"**Somewhere** cities burn." See April 68
"**Somewhere** in the field." See The field
"**Son**." See Father and I in the woods
Song ("Ask me no more where Jove bestows") Thomas Carew.—PaB
Song ("The feathers of the willow") R. W. Dixon.—PaB
Song ("I like birds, said the Dryad") Elizabeth Coatsworth.—WiP
Song ("I'd much rather sit there in the sun") Ruth Krauss.—HiS
Song ("My heart to thy mercy") Paul Laurence Dunbar.—BrI
Song ("The owl is abroad") Unknown.—PaB
Song ("A spirit haunts the year's last hours") Alfred Tennyson.—PaB
Song ("The sun is mine") Robert Hogg.—DoWh
A **song** ("Thou art the soul of a summer's day") Paul Laurence Dunbar.—BrI
Song ("Why do bells for Christmas sing") Eugene Field.—BaC
Song ("Wind and wave and star and sea") David McCord.—McO
Song ("Wintah, summah, snow er shine") Paul Laurence Dunbar.—BrI
Song before supper. David McCord.—McO
Song by Lady Happy, as a sea-goddess. M. Cavendish.—PaE
Song for a child. Helen Bayley Davis.—PaI
Song for a little house. Christopher Morley.—PaI
Song for Naomi. Irving Layton.—DoWh
A **song** for Nimpkin. Dennis Lee.—LeN
Song for the newborn. Mary Austin.—LiO
Song for the old ones. Maya Angelou.—AnO
Song in 5 parts. William Pitt Root.—KhI
"A **song** is but a little thing." See The poet and his song
"The **song** of canaries." See The canary
The **song** of Hiawatha, sel. Henry Wadsworth Longfellow
  "From his wanderings far to eastward."—PlG
The **song** of Mr. Toad. Kenneth Grahame.—WiP
Song of Sitting Bull. Unknown.—PlG

Soup
   Beautiful soup. From Alice's adventures in
      wonderland. L. Carroll.—WiP
   Good evening, Mr. Soup. Unknown.—CoPs
   This winter day. M. Angelou.—AnO
"Sour face Ann." Shel Silverstein.—SiL
Souster, Raymond
   "All animals like me."—DoWh
   Dog in the fountain.—CoG
   Dog, midwinter.—CoG
   Flight of the roller-coaster.—DoWh—HiS
   Old dog.—CoG
   The worm.—DoWh
The South
   For my people. M. Walker.—AdC
   Kentucky Belle. C. F. Woolson.—CoPh
   "My father remembers." J. Aiken.—AiS
   The song turning back into itself. A.
      Young.—AdC
   Southeast Arkanasia. M: Angelou.—AnO
   Southern mansion. A. Bontemps.—AdC
   Southern pines. J. P. Bishop.—PlG
   The southern road. D. Randall.—AdC
   Trellie. L. Jeffers.—AdC
"South African bloodstone." Quincy Troupe.—
   AdC
Southeast Arkanasia. Maya Angelou.—AnO
Southern mansion. Arna Bontemps.—AdC
Southern pines. John Peale Bishop.—PlG
The **southern** road. Dudley Randall.—AdC
Space and space travel
   Astronaut's choice. M. M. Darcy.—BrO
   The burrow wolf. T. Hughes.—HuM
   "By rocket, to visit the moon." From
      Interplanetary limericks. A. Graham.—BrO
   Capsule philosophy. F. Lamport.—BrO
   Christmas 1959 et cetera. G. W. Barrax.—
      LiO—LiPch
   "The crocuses are too naked, space shakes
      them." From Spring nature notes. T.
      Hughes.—HuSs
   Far trek. J. Brady.—BrO
   Felicitations. L. Morrison.—MoO
   The first. L. Moore.—MoTs
   In space language. L. Morrison.—MoO
   "The ladies inhabiting Venus." From
      Interplanetary limericks. A. Graham.—BrO
   The light year. J. Ridland.—LiO
   Man in orbit. D. O. Pitches.—LuZ
   "A Martian named Harrison Harris." From
      Interplanetary limericks. A. Graham.—BrO
   Moon poem ("Ouu gee whiz") S. Sharp.—
      BrO
   Mushrooms on the moon. T. Hughes.—HuM
   The nineteenth moon of Neptune beasts. X.
      J. Kennedy.—KeP
   Not lost in the stars. S. Bliven.—BrO
   Only a little litter. M. C. Livingston.—BrO
   Relativity. K. Millay.—BrO
   Rocks ("They say no") V. Worth.—WoSm
   S F. E. Leverett.—BrO
   Same old trick. W. W. Pratt.—BrO
   "Solomon Grundy." From The space child's
      Mother Goose. F. Winsor.—BrO

   "This little pig built a spaceship." From The
      space child's Mother Goose. F. Winsor.—
      BrO
   Time zones. L. Morrison.—CoDb—MoW
   Valentine for earth. F. Frost.—BrO
The **space** child's Mother Goose, sels. Frederick
   Winsor
   1. "Probable-Possible, my black hen."—BrO
   5. "Little Bo-Peep."—BrO
   10. "This little pig built a spaceship."—BrO
   22. "Solomon Grundy."—BrO
   35. "The hydrogen dog and the cobalt
      cat."—BrO
"**Spaced** in a helmet." See Man for Mars
Spadina. Dennis Lee.—LeN
"**Spaghetti,** spaghetti." Jack Prelutsky.—PrR
The **span** of life. Robert Frost.—CoG
"The **spangled** pandemonium." Palmer
   Brown.—WaM
Spanish language
   Cachita. C. Pomerantz.—PoT
   Fire house. C. Pomerantz.—PoT
   The four brothers. C. Pomerantz.—PoT
   Hugs and kisses. C. Pomerantz.—PoT
   A little lullaby to be read a little bit out loud.
      C. Pomerantz.—PoT
   Mari Rosa and the butterfly. C. Pomerantz.—
      PoT
   Marisol. C. Pomerantz.—PoT
   "My fat cat." C. Pomerantz.—PoT
   My Mami takes me to the bakery. C.
      Pomerantz.—PoT
   Nada. C. Pomerantz.—PoT
   "The tamarindo puppy." C. Pomerantz.—
      PoT
   The tea party. C. Pomerantz.—PoT
   You, tu. C. Pomerantz.—PoT
The **spare** quilt. John Peale Bishop.—PlG
Spark, Muriel
   The fall.—LuZ
Sparkly snow. Aileen Fisher.—FiO
The **sparrow.** Paul Laurence Dunbar.—BrI
Sparrow ("Nothing is less") Valerie Worth.—
   WoM
Sparrows
   The sparrow. P. L. Dunbar.—BrI
   Sparrow ("Nothing is less") V. Worth.—WoM
   Sparrows ("A hummingbird hums") K.
      Starbird.—StC
   Spill. J. Thurman.—ThFo
Sparrows ("A hummingbird hums") Kaye
   Starbird.—StC
"**Sparrows** sniffed the air, and hung." See
   Spadina
Speak clearly. Martin Gardner.—CóPs
"**Speak** gently, spring, and make no sudden
   sound." See Four little foxes
Speak up. David McCord.—McSu
"**Speaking** of Joe, I should have said." See Fred
Speaking of leaves. Aileen Fisher.—FiO
Speaking the poem. Lillian Morrison.—MoW
"The **spearmen** heard the bugle sound." See
   Beth-Gelert
The **spearthrower.** Lillian Morrison.—MoSr

Spring. See also March; April; May; also Seasons
  Aeglamour's lament. From The sad shepherd. B. Jonson.—PaB
  All nature seems at work. S. T. Coleridge.—PaB
  Almost. D. Kherdian.—KhC
  Almost spring. J. Thurman.—ThFo
  "April winter." D. Kherdian.—KhC
  "Bee, I'm expecting you." E. Dickinson.—HiS
  The brook in February. C.G.D. Roberts.—DoWh
  Changing time. P. L. Dunbar.—BrI
  The chickadee ("The morning after winter") A. Fisher.—FiO
  Clover field. A. Fisher.—FiO
  "The crocuses are too naked, space shakes them." From Spring nature notes. T. Hughes.—HuSs
  "Dear March, come in." From March. E. Dickinson.—HoMp
  Deceptions. T. Hughes.—HuSs
  Early bee. A. Fisher.—FiO
  Early spring. P. Whalen.—HoMp
  Easter daisy. A. Fisher.—FiO
  Elm seed blizzard. D. McCord.—McO
  The first dandelion. W. Whitman.—PaB
  First day of spring. B. S. De Regniers.—ReB
  "A flash of lightning sparks." K. Mizumura.—MiF
  Flutter wheel. R. N. Peck.—PeB
  Four little foxes. L. Sarett.—WiP
  Frogs in spring. A. Fisher.—FiO
  "From you I have been absent in the spring." From Sonnets. W. Shakespeare.—PaB
  A gaggle of geese, a pride of lions. J. Moore.—HiD
  "Good-by my winter suit." N. M. Bodecker.—BoHh
  The green spring. Shan Mei.—SaM
  Home thoughts, from abroad. R. Browning.—PaB
  "I heard a bird sing." O. Herford.—BaC
  "If I had a pony." A. Fisher.—FiO
  In the wind. A. Fisher.—FiO
  June bug. M. A. Hoberman.—HoBu
  Leaf buds. A. Fisher.—FiO
  Letter to a friend. L. Moore.—HoMp
  Letter to Donald Fall. A. Dugan.—KhI
  Lighthearted William. W. C. Williams.—HiS
  Listen, everything. A. Fisher.—FiO
  Looking. A. Fisher.—FiO
  Lyme, New Hampshire. D. Kherdian.—KhC
  The man in the marmalade hat arrives. N. Willard.—WiV
  March ("A blue day") E. Coatsworth.—HoMp
  The March bee. E. Blunden.—PaB
  May ("Now children may") J. Updike.—HoMp
  A memory. W. Allingham.—PaB
  Muddy March. A. Fisher.—FiO
  New season. L. Morrison.—MoSr
  New year song. T. Hughes.—HuSs
    New year's song.—LiO

  New York in the spring. D. Budbill.—MoGp
  The noisy wrens. A. Fisher.—FiO
  On a bank as I sat fishing. H. Wotton.—PaB
  Pussy willows ("Willow buds come early") A. Fisher.—FiO
  Quebec May. E. Birney.—DoWh
  Sarah's wondrous thing. R. N. Peck.—PeB
  Shoeing up the mare. R. N. Peck.—PeB
  "So, some tempestuous morn in early June." From Thyrsis. M. Arnold.—PaB
  Sounds of spring. A. Fisher.—FiO
  Spring ("How pleasing") Prince Redcloud.—HoMp
  Spring ("I'm shouting") K. Kuskin.—HoMp—KuD—WiP
  Spring ("The last snow is going") H. Behn.—WiP
  Spring ("When you see a daffodil") A. Fisher.—FiO
  "Spring again." K. Kuskin.—KuD
  "Spring bulges the hills." From Spring nature notes. T. Hughes.—HuSs
  Spring cleaning. R. Herrick.—BaC
  "Spring goeth all in white." R. Bridges.—SaM
  Spring is. B. Katz.—MoGp
  Spring joke. A. Fisher.—FiO
  Spring nature notes. T. Hughes.—HuSs
  Spring pictures. A. Fisher.—FiO
  "The spring snowflakes tickle." K. Mizumura.—MiF
  Spring song ("A blue-bell springs upon the ledge") P. L. Dunbar.—BrI
  Spring song ("Spring is coming, spring is coming") Unknown.—SaM (at. to William Blake)
  Spring talk. D. McCord.—McO
  Spring thoughts. Huang-fu Jan.—LiO
  Spring thunder. M. Van Doren.—MoGp
  "A spurt of daffodils, stiff and quivering." From Spring nature notes. T. Hughes.—HuSs
  "The sun lies mild and still on the yard stones." From Spring nature notes. T. Hughes.—HuSs
  Surprises are happening. J. C. Soule.—HoMp
  "There goes winter." A. Fisher.—FiO
  "There was a child went forth every day." From Leaves of grass. W. Whitman.—PaB
  Three signs of spring. D. McCord.—McO
  Today ("Today, though spring was overdue") K. Starbird.—StC
  "Tulips open one by one." K. Mizumura.—MiF
  "When daisies pied and violets blue." From Love's labour's lost. W. Shakespeare.—PaB
  The wind ("In spring, the wind's a sneaky wind") K. Starbird.—StC
  "The wind I love the best." From The spring wind. C. Zolotow.—HoMp
  The worm ("Don't ask me how he managed") R. Souster.—DoWh
  "The year's at the spring." From Pippa passes. R. Browning.—MoF
    Pippa's song.—PaB

Spring ("How pleasing") Prince Redcloud.—HoMp

Spring ("I'm shouting") Karla Kuskin.—HoMp—KuD—WiP

Spring ("The last snow is going") Harry Behn.—WiP

Spring ("When you see a daffodil") Aileen Fisher.—FiO

"Spring again." Karla Kuskin.—KuD

"Spring bulges the hills." See Spring nature notes

Spring cleaning. Robert Herrick.—BaC

Spring diet. Nancy Dingman Watson.—WaB

"Spring goeth all in white." Robert Bridges.—SaM

Spring is. Bobbi Katz.—MoGp

"Spring is coming, spring is coming." See Spring song

"Spring is when." See Spring is

Spring joke. Aileen Fisher.—FiO

Spring nature notes, sels. Ted Hughes.—HuSs (Complete)
  I. "The sun lies mild and still on the yard stones."
  II. "An oak tree on the first day of April."
  III. "A spurt of daffodils, stiff and quivering."
  IV. "The crocuses are too naked, space shakes them."
  V. "Spring bulges the hills."
  VI. "With arms swinging, a tremendous skater."

"Spring paints pictures in the town." See Spring pictures

Spring pictures. Aileen Fisher.—FiO

Spring rain. Marchette Chute.—PaI

"The spring snowflakes tickle." Kazue Mizumura.—MiF

Spring song ("A blue-bell springs upon the ledge") Paul Laurence Dunbar.—BrI

Spring song ("Spring is coming, spring is coming") Unknown.—SaM (at. to William Blake)

Spring talk. David McCord.—McO

Spring thoughts. Huang-fu Jan, tr. fr. the Chinese by Witter Bynner.—LiO

Spring thunder. Mark Van Doren.—MoGp

The spring wind, sel. Charlotte Zolotow
  "The wind I love the best."—HoMp

The sprinters. Lillian Morrison.—MoSr

"A spruce-covered mountain against the sky." See Green and blue in Colorado

"A spurt of daffodils, stiff and quivering." See Spring nature notes

Square as a house. Karla Kuskin.—KuD

"The square heeled boat sets off for the statue." See To the statue

"The square of the hypotenuse of the right triangle." See Pythagorean razzle dazzle

"A square was sitting quietly." See Shapes

Squaw talk. David McCord.—McO

"Squeals of children." Kazue Mizumura.—MiF

Squid
  The squid ("What happy appellations these") O. Nash.—BlC

The squid ("What happy appellations these") Ogden Nash.—BlC

"Squiggly wiggly wriggly jiggly higgly piggly worm." See Worm

Squire, John Collings
  The discovery.—LiO
  Eminent cosmologists.—BrO

Squirrel ("Scolding") Felice Holman.—HoA

Squirrel ("The squirrel in the hickory tree's a") Lilian Moore.—HoMp

"The squirrel in the hickory tree's a." See Squirrel

Squirrels
  "Ask a squirrel, when he's cracking a nut." From Limericks. D. McCord.—McSu
  Fable. R. W. Emerson.—PaB
  The flying squirrel. J. Gardner.—GaCb
  Fred. D. McCord.—McO
  In the park. N. Farber.—FaS
  Joe. D. McCord.—McO
  Squirrel ("Scolding") F. Holman.—HoA
  Squirrel ("The squirrel in the hickory tree's a") L. Moore.—HoMp
  To a squirrel. M. C. Livingston.—LiWt
  To a squirrel at Kyle-na-no. W. B. Yeats.—SaM
  "Whisky, frisky."—PaI

Squishy touch. Shel Silverstein.—SiL

The stable ("On the threshold of the stable smelling") Jill Hoffman.—CoPh

The stable ("When midnight came") Gabriela Mistral, tr. fr. the Spanish by Langston Hughes.—BaC

The stable cat. Leslie Norris.—LiPch—NoM

"A stable lamp is lighted." See A Christmas hymn

Stafford, William
  Cold.—MoGp
  Father's voice.—PlL
  For a child gone to live in a commune.—PlL
  Kit, six years old, standing by the dashboard keeping daddy awake on a trip home from the beach.—LuZ
  Long distance.—HiS
  My life.—KhI
  Note.—MoGp
  Old dog.—CoG
  Religion back home, sel.
    "When my little brother chanted."—LiCc
  Strokes.—JaPp
  The trip.—JaPp
  "When my little brother chanted." See Religion back home
  Which.—MoGp

The stag. Ted Hughes.—HuSs

"The stained." See Garbage

Stairs
  Dr Klimwell's fall. D. McCord.—McO
  Halfway down. A. A. Milne.—HiS

The stalker. N. Scott Momaday.—MoGd

"The stall so tight he can't raise heels or knees." See Bronco busting, event #1

Stallion ("A gigantic beauty of a stallion, fresh and responsive") Walt Whitman.—CoPh

The **stallion** ("The grey grass in the early winter") Alan Porter.—CoPh

The **stallion** ("I am the only living thing") Boynton Merrill, Jr.—CoPh

"**Stand**, the ground's your own, my braves." See Warren's address at Bunker Hill

"**Standing** at the gate." Nikki Grimes.—GrS

"**Standing** is stupid." Shel Silverstein.—SiL

"**Standing** on 127th the." See Langston

"**Standing** up on lifted, folded rock." See By Frazier Creek Falls

Stanford, Ann

Done with.—LuZ

Going away.—CoPh

Night rain.—LuZ

Stanzas on the decease of Thomas Paine, who died at New York on the 8th day of June, 1809. Philip Freneau.—PlG

Stanzas on the emigration to America, and peopling the western country. Philip Freneau.—PlG

"**Star**-face Lightfoot, sired by the Fox." See Monologue of the rating Morgan in Rutherford County

The **star** in the pail. David McCord.—HoBm—McO

Star of peace. Myra Cohn Livingston.—LiF

"A **star** rose in the sky." See Carol of the birds

The **star** that came. Juan Ramon Jimenez.—BaC

Starbird, Kaye

The ant in the windmill.—StC

Artie.—StC

"As soon as the stars are suburbs."—StC

The birds.—StC

The blizzard.—StC

The cat lady.—StC

The city and Evan.—StC

The corner newsman.—HoMp—StC

The country and Nate.—StC

The covered bridge house.—StC

Eat-it-all Elaine.—CoPs—WiP

Eddie wasn't ready.—StC

The gardener.—StC

"I dreamed I visited Buzzard's Bay."—StC

Jump rope song.—StC

"Little Lenore."—StC

Loring.—StC

Minnie Morse.—CoPh

Miss Casper's cow.—StC

Mother.—StC

Patsy Doolin.—CoI

The pole bean tent.—StC

The riddle.—StC

The ride.—StC

Ruth.—StC

The sleepers.—StC

Slim Slater.—StC

Sparrows.—StC

The spelling test.—StC

The stranger.—StC

That morning in June.—StC

Thoughts about oysters.—CoPs

Today.—StC

The twins.—StC

Watch out.—StC

Wendy in winter.—StC

Whistling Willie.—BrO

The wind.—StC

The world's best hopper.—StC

You can't get rags from ragweed.—StC

Starfish

The starfish ("When I see a starfish") D. McCord.—McO

The **starfish** ("When I see a starfish") David McCord.—McO

Starkman, Shula. See Mezey, Robert and Starkman, Shula

Starling ("In burnished armor") David McCord.—McO

Starlings

The manoeuvre. W. C. Williams.—JaPp

Starling ("In burnished armor") D. McCord.—McO

"You greedy starlings." B. Maestro.—MaFp

Stars

"As soon as the stars are suburbs." K. Starbird.—StC

Astronomical note. L. Morrison.—MoO

Blake leads a walk on the Milky Way. N. Willard.—WiV

Christmas ("The snow is full of silver light") F. Baldwin.—BaC

The Christmas star. N. B. Turner.—BaC

Come Christmas. D. McCord.—LiPch

Constellations. P. St. John.—LuZ

Dr Klimwell's fall. D. McCord.—McO

In a starry orchard. N. Farber.—FaS

The invasion of the star streaks. L. Morrison.—MoO

The kings from the east. H. Heine.—BaC

"Three holy kings from Morgenland.—LiPch

Morning star. Unknown.—BaC

My stars. A. Ibn Ezra.—LiO

The names of things. S. C. Fox.—FoB

One glorious star. Unknown.—BaC

Orion. D. McCord.—McO

Sky fish. A. Fisher.—FiO

Somebody has to. S. Silverstein.—SiL

The star in the pail. D. McCord.—HoBm—McO

Star of peace. M. C. Livingston.—LiF

The star that came. J. R. Jiménez.—BaC

The stars ("Across the dark and quiet sky") N. Giovanni.—GiV

Stars ("It's very hard") A. Fisher.—FiO

Stars ("The stars are too many to count") C. Sandburg.—WiP

Stars ("While we") V. Worth.—WoSm

Summer stars. A. Fisher.—FiO

Taking turns. N. Farber.—FaS

"There is one glory of the sun, and another glory." From Corinthians.—BaC

The three kings. R. Dario.—BaC—LiPch

Artie. K. Starbird.—StC
Aunt Sue's stories. L. Hughes.—HiD
The bedpost. R. Graves.—HiS
Father's story. E. M. Roberts.—LiCc
The red herring. G. MacBeth.—HiS
Suspense. S. Silverstein.—SiL
"Tell me a story." E. Merriam.—MeW
The tiger asks Blake for a bedtime story. N.
    Willard.—WiV
The **stork**, a Christmas ballad. See King
    Edward's prayer book
"The **stork** she rose on Christmas eve." See
    King Edward's prayer book—The stork, a
    Christmas ballad
"**Stork**, stork." Rose Fyleman.—WiP
Storks
    The stork, a Christmas ballad. From King
        Edward's prayer book.—BaC
    "Stork, stork." R. Fyleman.—WiP
The **storm** ("First there were two of us, then
    there were three of us") Walter De La
    Mare.—PaE
Storm ("In a storm") Adrien Stoutenberg.—
    MoGp
The **storm** ("A perfect rainbow, a wide")
    William Carlos Williams.—JaPp
"**Storm** and strife and stress." See Death
"The **storm** came up so very quick." See Spring
    rain
"The **storm** is on." See Like Thor
Storms. See also Rain; Snow; Weather; Winds
    Like Thor. M. C. Livingston.—LiWt
    Nothing at all. D. Finkel.—LuZ
    "Once in the winter." From The forsaken. D.
        C. Scott.—DoWh
    Spring thunder. M. Van Doren.—MoGp
    The storm ("First there were two of us, then
        there were three of us") W. De La Mare.—
        PaE
    Storm ("In a storm") A. Stoutenberg.—MoGp
    The storm ("A perfect rainbow, a wide") W.
        C. Williams.—JaPp
    The voice in the storm. Lillian Morrison.—
        MoO
    A watched example never boils. O. Nash.—
        BlC
The **stormy** petrel. Bryan Waller Procter.—PaE
The **story** of a well-made shield. N. Scott
    Momaday.—MoGd
Storytelling. See Stories and storytelling
Stoutenberg, Adrien
    The bear who came to dinner.—HiS
    Rain.—MoGp
    Storm.—MoGp
    Tornado season.—MoGp
"**Stowaway** in a fold." See The witnesses
Stowe, Harriet Beecher (about)
    Harriet Beecher Stowe. P. L. Dunbar.—BrI
Strange legacies. Sterling A. Brown.—AdC
"**Strange** shadows out." See Tonight
Strange wind. Shel Silverstein.—SiL
The **stranger** ("An old man came to church one
    day") Kaye Starbird.—StC

The **stranger** in the pumpkin. John Ciardi.—
    BrIt
"The **stranger** in the pumpkin said." See The
    stranger in the pumpkin
The **strangers**. Audrey Alexandra Brown.—
    DoWh
"**Strangest** of gaps." See Holes
"**Straw**, feathers, dust." See Note
Strawberries
    "Getting the sweet strawberries." A. Adoff.—
        AdE
    "I liked growing." K. Kuskin.—KuD
    "Never, ever let them know." N. M.
        Bodecker.—BoHh
    Strawberry patches. N. Giovanni.—GiV
    Wild strawberries. S. Silverstein.—SiL
"The **strawberry** hill is covered with snow." See
    Snow
Strawberry patches. Nikki Giovanni.—GiV
Streams
    The brook in February. C. G. D. Roberts.—
        DoWh
    Flutter wheel. R. N. Peck.—PeB
    September creek. R. N. Peck.—PeB
Street cries
    "If I'd as much money as I could spend."
        Mother Goose.—TrGg
Street demonstration. Margaret Walker.—AdC
Street song. Myra Cohn Livingston.—LiWt
Street window. Carl Sandburg.—JaPp
Streetfighter moon. Lillian Morrison.—MoSr
Streets. See Roads and streets
The **streets** of town. Aileen Fisher.—FiO
Strength
    The crisis. P. L. Dunbar.—BrI
    "I am a black woman." M. Evans.—AdC
"**Stretching** her head toward the stars." See
    Pliny Jane
"**Strike**, strike for children's rights." See Union
    for children's rights
String
    Three signs of spring. D. McCord.—McO
The **striped** hyena. John Gardner.—GaCb
"The **striped** hyena never combs his hair." See
    The striped hyena
Strokes. William Stafford.—JaPp
Strong men. Sterling A. Brown.—AdC
Strunk, Jud
    "They're tearing down a town."—BrO
Stuart, Isla. See McCaig, Ronald and Stuart, Isla
"**Stuffed** away into." See Rags
Su Tung P'o
    The last day of the year.—LiCc
    On the birth of his son.—LiO
Su Wu
    Drafted.—PlL
Submarines
    Sardines. S. Milligan.—LuZ
Subways
    One year to life on the Grand Central
        shuttle. A. Lorde.—AdC
    To my daughter the junkie on a train. A.
        Lorde.—AdC

Light ("Light through white organdy") F. Holman.—HoA

Locus of a point. L. Morrison.—MoO

Marisol. C. Pomerantz.—PoT

Mirrors. A. Fisher.—FiO

Partners. L. Moore.—MoTs

The quiet shining sun. A. Fisher.—FiO

Recess. L. Moore.—MoTs

Shiver my timbers. D. McCord.—McO

Skyviews. D. McCord.—McSu

Sun ("The sun") V. Worth.—MoGp—WiP

The sun ("Sunsets are so pretty") N. Giovanni.—GiV

Sun after rain. N. Farber.—FaS

The sun and moon circus soothes the wakeful guests. N. Willard.—WiV

"The sun finally tolerable." From Autumn nature notes. T. Hughes.—HuSs

Sun prints. A. Fisher.—FiO

Sun song. L. Hughes.—AdC

Telling time. L. Moore.—MoTs

"This is my rock." D. McCord.—BeR

A true account of talking to the sun at Fire Island. F. O'Hara.—KhI

What they say. L. Morrison.—MoW

Winter solstice chant. From Being of the sun. R. Sender and A. B. Laurel.—BaC

Sun ("The sun") Valerie Worth.—MoGp—WiP

The sun ("Sunsets are so pretty") Nikki Giovanni.—GiV

"The sun." See Sun

Sun after rain. Norma Farber.—FaS

The sun and moon circus soothes the wakeful guests. Nancy Willard.—WiV

"Sun and softness." See Sun song

"The sun appearing: a pendant." See Plainview: 3

"The sun descending in the west." See Night

"The sun finally tolerable." See Autumn nature notes

Sun flowers. Arnold Adoff.—AdE

Sun for breakfast. Norma Farber.—FaS

"The sun horse panting and snorting." See Evening

"Sun in the back yard." See Back yard

"The sun is mine." See Song

"Sun is ringing a golden bell." See At the ring of a bell

"The sun is shining in my backdoor." See Myself when I am real

"The sun is the nearest star." See Astronomical note

"The sun lies mild and still on the yard stones." See Spring nature notes

"The sun must have a lot of fun." See Mirrors

Sun prints. Aileen Fisher.—FiO

"The sun rides higher." See February

"Sun shining bright on the mountain rock." See Old snake has gone to sleep

Sun song. Langston Hughes.—AdC

"The sun, they say, is very big." See How big

"The sun was shining on the sea." See Through the looking-glass—The walrus and the carpenter

"The sun was warm but the wind was chill." From Two tramps in mud time

"The sun woke me this morning loud." See A true account of talking to the sun at Fire Island

Sund, Robert

"At quitting time."—LuZ

Bee.—MoGp

Sunday. See Days of the week—Sunday

"Sunday morning." See An emergency

"Sunday morning." Nikki Grimes.—GrS

"Sunday morning and her mother's hands." See Birmingham 1963

Sunday morning toast. Arnold Adoff.—AdE

"Sundays too my father got up early." See Those winter Sundays

Sundials

On a sundial. H. Belloc.—BrO

Telling time. L. Moore.—MoTs

Sunfish ("The sunfish, funny finny one") David McCord.—McO

"The sunfish, funny finny one." See Sunfish

Sunflowers

Ah, sunflower. W. Blake.—PaB

"Giant sunflowers." B. Maestro.—MaFp

Sunflowers ("One frosty evening) N. M. Bodecker.—BoHh

Two sunflowers move into the yellow room. N. Willard.—WiV

Sunflowers ("One frosty evening") N. M. Bodecker.—BoHh

Sunk Lyonesse. Walter De La Mare.—PaE

"Sunlit sea." See Comparatives

Sunning. James S. Tippett.—CoG

"Sunny side up." Arnold Adoff.—AdE

Sunset ("The river sleeps beneath the sky") Paul Laurence Dunbar.—BrI

"Sunsets are so pretty." See The sun

Supermarket. Felice Holman.—BrO—HoA

"Supermarket, supermarket." Eve Merriam.—MeW

Supernatural. See Fairies; Ghosts; Witches

Superstitions. See also Fortune telling

Black cat ("A cat as black") J. Prelutsky.—PrI

People once believed that, sels. Unknown.—BaC

Superstitious ("If you are superstitious you'll never step on cracks") S. Silverstein.—SiL

Superstitious ("If you are superstitious you'll never step on cracks") Shel Silverstein.—SiL

The superstitious ghost. Arthur Guiterman.—BrIt

Suppose. Paul Laurence Dunbar.—BrI

"Suppose you met a witch. . . there's one I know." See Suppose you met a witch

Suppose you met a witch, sel. Ian Serraillier

"Suppose you met a witch. . . there's one I know."—LiCc

"Surely a dead moth's." See Funeral

"Surely silly Sharon sells sharp sheep shears, Susan." See Six tongue twisters

Surf. Lillian Morrison.—MoSr

The telephone ("It comes in black") M.
  Angelou.—AnO
The telephone ("When I was just as far as I
  could walk") R. Frost.—HiS
The telephone call. J. Prelutsky.—PrR
"We could be friends." M. C. Livingston.—
  LiWt—YaI
Television
  Addict. J. Montgomery.—BrO
  The biggest laugh. M. C. Livingston.—LiF
  Channels. S. Silverstein.—SiL
  Clarence. S. Silverstein.—SiL
  The day the T.V. broke. G. Jonas.—BrO
  Jabber-whacky, or, on dreaming, after falling
    asleep watching TV. I. Di Caprio.—BrO
  Let her have it. W. Cole.—HeB
  No TV. L. Moore.—BrIt
  Squaw talk. D. McCord.—McO
  Summer song, after a surfeit of irresistible
    ads. W. W. Watt.—BrO
  Tee-vee enigma. S. Raskin.—BrO
  Teevee. E. Merriam.—BrO
  The television ("Unaccustomed") G.
    Godbey.—LuZ
  Television charmer. From A lot of limericks.
    X. J. Kennedy.—KeP
  Tube time. E. Merriam.—MeW
The **television** ("Unaccustomed") Geoffrey
  Godbey.—LuZ
Television charmer. From A lot of Limericks.
  X. J. Kennedy.—KeP
"**Tell** me a story." Eve Merriam.—MeW
"**Tell** me, O octopus, I begs." See The octopus
"**Tell** me, tell me, Sarah Jane." Charles
  Causley.—WiP
"**Tell** me then." See Rhino pen
Telling time. Lilian Moore.—MoTs
The **tempest**, sels. William Shakespeare
  Ariel's song.—PaB
    "Full fathom five thy father lies."—PaE
    Ariel's dirge.—WiP
"**Temples** he built and palaces of air." See The
  dreamer
Ten kinds. Mary Mapes Dodge.—CoI
"**Ten** little tadpoles playing in a pool." See
  Tadpoles
Ten nights before Christmas. David McCord.—
  McO
Ten twice. David McCord.—McO
Ten week wife. Rhoda Donovan.—KhI
Tennis
  Dis-play. L. Morrison.—MoSr
  A lady of Venice. N. M. Bodecker.—BoP
  Love fifteen. L. Morrison.—MoSr
  Tennis clinic. L. Morrison.—MoSr
Tennis clinic. Lillian Morrison.—MoSr
Tennyson, Alfred, Lord
  "Again at Christmas did we weave." See In
    memoriam
  "Chains, my good lord, in your raised brows I
    read." See Columbus
  Columbus, sel.
    "Chains, my good lord, in your raised
      brows I read."—LiO

In memoriam, sels.
  "Again at Christmas did we weave."—
    LiPch
  Ring out, wild bells.—LiO
  "The time draws near the birth of
    Christ."—LiPch
  "Unwatch'd, the garden bough shall
    sway."—PaB
  Voices in the mist.—BaC
The kraken.—PaE
The May queen, sel.
  "You must wake and call me early, call
    me early."—LiCc
The mermaid.—PaE
The merman.—PaE
The owl.—PaB
"Ring out, wild bells." See In memoriam
The sea-fairies.—PaE
The shell.—PaE
Song.—PaB
"The time draws near the birth of Christ."
  See In memoriam
"Unwatch'd, the garden bough shall sway."
  See In memoriam
Voices in the mist. See In memoriam
"You must wake and call me early, call me
  early." See The May queen
"A tense ancestor of the skunk." See The skank
The **tercet**. David McCord.—McO
"A **tercet** is a stanza of three lines." See The
  tercet
Tercets
  The tercet. D. McCord.—McO
"**Terence** McDiddler." Mother Goose.—LoG—
  TrGg
The **termite** ("Some primal termite knocked on
  wood") Ogden Nash.—BlC
Termite ("The termite is a decent sort") Mary
  Ann Hoberman.—HoBu
"The **termite** is a decent sort." See Termite
Termites
  The termite ("Some primal termite knocked
    on wood") O. Nash.—BlC
  Termite ("The termite is a decent sort") M.
    A. Hoberman.—HoBu
  "Though the termite be sharp as they come."
    From Limericks. D. McCord.—McSu
  Xylophagous insects. R. S. Oliver.—OlC
Terra cotta. K. Curtis Lyle.—AdC
"The **terrible** giant had a wife." See Giant's
  wife
Terrible troll's trollbridge. X. J. Kennedy.—KeP
Tessimond, A. S. J.
  A hot day.—SaM
The **testament** of perpetual change. William
  Carlos Williams.—PlG
Tewa Indians. See Indians of the Americas—
  Tewa
Thackeray, William Makepeace
  The mahogany tree.—BaC
"**Thank** God, thank God, we do believe." See A
  Christmas carol

"There are monsters everywhere." See
  Monsters everywhere
"There are no more monsters, I have to
  confess." See May be
"There are reaches of beaches." See Beaches
"There are several attitudes towards
  Christmas." See The cultivation of
  Christmas trees
"There are songs and sounds in stillness." See
  Voices
"There are ten ghosts." See Countdown
"There are things sadder." See Haiku
"There are three names." See National security
"There are two ways now." See Progress
"There are weapons on the moon." See Moon
  weapons
"There are words like freedom." See Refugee
  in America
"There at the top of the world." See Harlem in
  January
"There, by the curb." See Oil slick
There came a day. Ted Hughes.—HoMp—
  HuSs—MoGp
"There came a day that caught the summer."
  See There came a day
"There goes the wapiti." See The wapiti
"There goes winter." Aileen Fisher.—FiO
"There in the hollow of the hills I see." See
  Plainview: 1
"There is a black field." Lillian Morrison.—
  MoW
"There is a clock." David Kherdian.—KhC
"There is a cool river." See Detroit
"There is a face upon my thumb." See Thumb
  face
"There is a girl of our town." Mother Goose.—
  TrGg
"There is a heaven, for ever, day by day." See
  Theology
"There is a man who says he may." See
  Pumpkin seeds
There is a place. Arnold Adoff.—AdE
"There is a place where love begins and a
  place." See Explanations of love
"There is a song to be sung at night." See The
  middle of the night
"There is a spot that you can't scratch." See
  Unscratchable itch
"There is a sudden little wind that grieves."
  See October wind
"There is joy in." See Eskimo chant
"There is more." See Mosquito
"There is no impeding." See Sailing, sailing
"There is no wind on the moon at all." See
  Moon wind
"There is not a poem in sight." See Writing
  while my father dies
"There is nothing more fair." See Passing fair
"There is nothing more perky." See The turkey
"There is obviously a complete lack of
  understanding." Ogden Nash.—BlC
"There is one glory of the sun, and another
  glory." See Corinthians

"There is only one horse on the earth." See
  The family of man—Names
"There is sorrow enough in the natural way."
  See The power of the dog
"There must be magic." See Otherwise
"There must be other kind of talk." See Other
  talk
"There once was a fat little pig named Alice."
  See Alice
"There once was a giant." See The greedy
  giant
"There once was a girl named Myrtle." See
  Myrtle
"There once was a hippo who wanted to fly."
  See Hippo's hope
"There once was a man who was elephant
  strong." See An adventure story
"There once was a pig." Mary Ann
  Hoberman.—HoY
There once was a puffin. Florence Page
  Jaques.—WiP
"There she is, out in the rain." See Silly dog
"There the black river, boundary to hell." See
  The southern road
"There they were." See A day at the races
"There upon the toolshed wall." See Tools
"There was a bald person in Rome." See A
  person in Rome
"There was a boy whose name was Jim." See
  Jim, who ran away from his nurse, and was
  eaten by a lion
"There was a child went forth every day." See
  Leaves of grass
"There was a crooked man, and he went a
  crooked mile." Mother Goose.—TrGg
"There was a darkness in this man, an immense
  and hollow." See Lincoln
"There was a farmer had a dog." See Little
  Bingo
"There was a fat man of Bombay." Unknown.—
  LoG
"There was a giant by the orchard wall." See
  In the orchard
"There was a girl named Abigail." See Little
  Abigail and the beautiful pony
"There was a gray rat looked at me." See Rat
  riddles
"There was a Jewish bandit who lived in a
  wood." See Bandit
"There was a lady loved a swine." Mother
  Goose.—WiP
There was a little dog. Mother Goose.—BlH
"There was a little dog, and he had a little
  tail." See There was a little dog
"There was a little guinea pig." Mother
  Goose.—TrGg
"There was a little turtle." See The little turtle
"There was a mad man." See "There was a
  mad man and he had a mad wife"
"There was a mad man and he had a mad
  wife." Mother Goose.—TrGg
  "There was a mad man."—LoG
"There was a maid on Scrabble Hill." Mother
  Goose.—LoG

There was a man. Dennis Lee.—LeN
"There was a man in our town." Mother Goose.—TrGg
"There was a man named Mingram Mo." See Mingram Mo
"There was a man who dwelt alone." See Shadow-bride
"There was a man who never was." See There was a man
"There was a man who was so fat." See The portly object
"There was a poor man whose pajamas." See A poor man whose pajamas
"There was a roaring in the wind all night." See Resolution and independence—After the storm
"There was a tailor built a house." See Blake tells the tiger the tale of the tailor
"There was a witch." See Two witches
"There was a witch who knitted things." See Knitted things
"There was a witch who met an owl." See Hitchhiker
"There was a young bride of North Conway." See A bride of North Conway
"There was a young farmer of Leeds." Unknown.—LoG
"There was a young fellow of Stroud." Myra Cohn Livingston.—LiLl
"There was a young lady named Bright." See Faster than light
"There was a young lady named Harris." Ogden Nash.—BlC
"There was a young lady named Rose." William Jay Smith.—SmL
"There was a young lady of Lynn." See The young lady of Lynn
"There was a young lady of Newington Green." See The ballad of Newington Green
"There was a young lady of Rome." Ogden Nash.—BrO
"There was a young lass of south Yarra." Wilbur G. Howcroft.—DuSn
"There was a young lass on Ben Nevis." See A lass on Ben Nevis
"There was a young man from Port Jervis." See Tennis clinic
"There was a young man in a suit." See A man in a suit
"There was a young person in Skye." See A person in Skye
"There was a young person named Briggs." See A person named Briggs
"There was a young person named Crockett." William Jay Smith.—SmL
"There was a young person of Pinsk." See A person of Pinsk
"There was a young puppy called Howard." See The young puppy
"There was a young woman of Brighton." Myra Cohn Livingston.—LiLl
"There was an if upon a stair." See Timely
"There was an Indian, who had known no change." See The discovery

"There was an island in the sea." See Atlantis
"There was an old crow." Mother Goose.—TrGg
"There was an old crusty mechanic." See A crusty mechanic
"There was an old gard'ner whose plants." See A gard'ner whose plants
"There was an old lady." See Godmother
"There was an old lady named Brown." William Jay Smith.—SmL
"There was an old lady named Crockett." William Jay Smith.—SmL
"There was an old lady named Hart." William Jay Smith.—SmL
"There was an old lady whose kitchen was bare." Dennis Lee.—CoPs
"There was an old man." See A man and his hat
"There was an old man from Luray." William Jay Smith.—SmL
"There was an old man in a tree." See The old man and the bee
"There was an old man in a trunk." Ogden Nash.—BlC
"There was an old man named Michael Finnegan." Mother Goose.—LoG
"There was an old man of Cologne." See A man of Cologne
"There was an old mess cook whose dishes." See A cook whose dishes
"There was an old person from Britain." See A person from Britain
"There was an old person of Ware." Edward Lear.—WiP
"There was an old wife and she lived all alone." See The old wife and the ghost
There was an old woman ("As I've heard tell") Mother Goose.—WiP
"There was an old woman lived under the hill." Mother Goose.—TrGg
"There was an old woman lived under the hill, she put a mouse in a bag." Mother Goose.—TrGg
"There was an old woman named Piper." William Jay Smith.—SmL
"There was an old woman tossed in a blanket." Mother Goose.—TrGg
"There was an old woman tossed up in a basket." Mother Goose.—LoG
"There was an old woman who lived in a shoe." Mother Goose.—TrGg
"There was life in the dead tree that fell." From Limericks. D. McCord.—McSu
"There was movement at the station, for the word had passed around." See The man from Snowy River
"There was never any worry about bread or even butter." See Not at all what one is used to
"There was once a high wall, a bare wall, and." See The red herring
"There was once a swing in a walnut tree." See The walnut tree

"There was once a thin cougar named Sean."
See The cougar

"There was once a young fellow of Wall." Myra
Cohn Livingston.—LiLl

"There was this Spike who simply could not
fit." See Spike spoke spook

"There went three children down to the
shore." See The black pebble

"There were lots on the farm." See After
Christmas

"There were the roses, in the rain." See The
act

"There were the useful presents, engulfing
mufflers." See A child's Christmas in
Wales—Conversation about Christmas, the
useful presents

"There were three jovial huntsmen." Mother
Goose.—TrGg

"There were two great trees." See Laly, Laly

"There's a bittern that booms in a bog." From
Limericks. David McCord.—McSu

"There's a cat out there." See Alarm

"There's a deep secret place, dark in the hold
of this ship." See Down below

"There's a fellow I know." See Silly speak

"There's a fire in the forest." W.W.E. Ross.—
DoWh

"There's a friendly rock down by the shore."
See The friendly rock

"There's a goblin as green." See The goblin

"There's a grubby sort of fairy." See Mister
Hoobody

"There's a house." See Haunted house

"There's a lady in Washington Heights." Morris
Bishop.—BrO

"There's a lift up aloft for the wing." From
Limericks. David McCord.—McSu

"There's a light in the attic." See A light in the
attic

"There's a long-legged girl." See Pickin em up
and layin em down

"There's a place the man always say." See
Where

"There's a polar bear." See Bear in there

"There's a strange new dye." See The hot pizza
serenade

"There's a tree by the meadow." See The tree
and me

"There's a wozzit in the closet." See The
wozzit

"There's an ant on the front windowsill." From
Limericks. David McCord.—McSu

"There's an eyeball in the gumball machine."
See Gumeye ball

"There's big waves and little waves." See
Waves

"There's lots of funny goings on the public
don't suspect." See Montgomery, with
acknowledgements to T. S. Eliot's Macavity

"There's no better dog nor Hardcastle's Rake."
See Rake

"There's only one phoenix in the world at a
time." See The phoenix

"There's room in the bus." See Jittery Jim

"There's someone at the door, said gold
candlestick." See Green candles

"There's something up there on the wall." See
Look

"There's too many kids in this tub." See
Crowded tub

"These are also." See O.D.

"These are my murmur-laden shells that keep."
See On some shells found inland

"These are the ashes of fiery weather." See
Our stars come from Ireland—The
westwardness of everything

"These are the nights when the geese." See A
gaggle of geese, a pride of lions

"These clouds are soft fat horses." See Clouds

These damned trees crouch. Jim Barnes.—KhI

"These damned trees crouch heavy under
heaven." See These damned trees crouch

"These figures moving in my rhyme." See Two
figures

"These flat stones are coins." Betsy Maestro.—
MaFp

"These lizards, toads and turtles, dear, with
which you love to play." See Prehistoric

"These roller-coaster cars, some said." See
Roller coaster

"These sourpusses, says Aunt Jill." See A
ticklish recipe

Thesis, antithesis, and nostalgia. Alan Dugan.—
JaPp

"They are all gathered, astounded and
disturbed." See The last supper

"They are not long, the weeping and the
laughing." See Envoy

"They are so beautiful." See Sun flowers

"They come like the ghosts of horses, shyly."
See The pit ponies

"They could have sung me just one song." See
Dog's day

"They did it, George, they did it." See
Conversation with Washington

"They dragged you from the homeland." See
Strong men

"They gathered around and told him not to do
it." See Noah

"They hop o'er your plate." See Cheese
jumpers

"They live." See They live in parallel worlds

They live in parallel worlds. William J.
Harris.—AdC

"They live their days in a fragrance." See The
Chinese greengrocers

"They married us when they put." See Drafted

"They may take strange." See Fairy fashion

"They never stop asking me." See What will
you be

"They paddle with staccato feet." See Pigeons

"They please me not, these solemn songs." See
A choice

"They plough through the moon stuff." See
Moon whales

"They said come skating." See Come skating

"They said, 'You are no longer a lad.' " See
Battle won is lost

"This far roaming lass from Milwaukee." See A lass from Milwaukee

"This gentleman the charming duck." See A trueblue gentleman

"This inn belongs to William Blake." See William Blake's inn for innocent and experienced travelers

"This is." See The cinquain

"This is a game that Lewis Carroll played." See The game of doublets

"This is a song to be sung at night." See The middle of the night

"This is a tiger." Karla Kuskin.—KuR

"This is an." See My mother takes my wife's side

"This is before electricity." See Game after supper

"This is Elmer Johnson." N. M. Bodecker.— BoHh

This is Halloween. Dorothy Brown Thompson.—BrIt

"This is my rock." David McCord.—BeR— McO—WiP

"This is no green bird, but gray with bright red." See The gossip

"This is no place." See Children of the desert

"This is not real, this is the shape of a dream spun." See Grant Wood's American landscape

"This is the age." See Time of the mad atom

"This is the autumn and our harvest." See New year's

"This is the debt I pay." See The debt

This is the key. Mother Goose.—WiP

"This is the lapping world." See Ocean's edge

"This is the sea, in these uneven walls." See The rock pool

"This is the ship of pearl, which, poets feign." See The chambered nautilus

"This is the story of timid Tim." See The witch in the wintry wood

"This is the time of the crit, the creeple, and the makeiteer." See Five men against the theme, my name is red hot, yo name ain' doodley squat

"This is the weather the cuckoo likes." See Weathers

"This is the week when Christmas comes." See In the week when Christmas comes

"This is the wheel of dreams." See Carriers of the dream wheel

"This is the wind's doing." See Partners

"This Kansas boy who never saw the sea." See Kansas boy

"This late drawing." See For the old man for drawing, dead at eight-nine

"This leaf." Beatrice Schenk De Regniers.— ReB

"This legendary house, this dear enchanted tomb." See Monticello

"This letter combination makes it tough." See Ough

"This little man lived all alone." Mother Goose.—LoG

"This little pig built a spaceship." See The space child's Mother Goose

"This love is a rich cry over." See A black wedding song

"This manhole cover's just as neat." See Two of a kind

"This middle aged person of Keene." See A person of Keene

This morning. Lucille Clifton.—KhI

"This morning." See This morning

"This morning at five I awoke with a cough." See Ants

"This morning I got kidnapped." See Kidnapped

"This morning I held Harriet in my head against an orange." See True love

"This morning the snow." See Crows in a winter composition

"This poem came out." See A fountain pen poem

"This poem is too small, I fear." See The dinosaur

"This small." See Magnet

"This started out as a." See Jumping rope

"This sticky trail." See Snail

"This strange thing must have crept." See Fork

This thing. Michael Patrick Hearn.—WaM

"This turtle moved his house across the street." See Turtle

"This water is so clear." See The fisherman writes a letter to the mermaid

"This wind brings all dead things to life." See A windy day

This winter day. Maya Angelou.—AnO

"This woman vomiten her." See Present

Thistles
  "Theophilus Thistle, the successful thistle sifter." Mother Goose.—LoG
  Thistles ("Thirty thirsty thistles") K. Kuskin.—KuD—WiP
  Thistles ("Thirty thirsty thistles") Karla Kuskin.—KuD—WiP

Thomas, Dylan
  A child's Christmas in Wales, sels.
    Conversation about Christmas, the useful presents.—LiPch
    Conversation about Christmas, the useless presents.—LiPch
  Conversation about Christmas, the useful presents. See A child's Christmas in Wales
  Conversation about Christmas, the useless presents. See A child's Christmas in Wales

Thomas, Edward
  Out in the dark.—PaB

Thomas, Joyce Carol
  Church poem.—AdC
  "I know a lady."—AdC
  The MJQ.—AdC
  Poem for Otis Redding.—AdC
  "Where is the black community."—AdC

Thompson, Dorothy Brown
  Shrieks at midnight.—WaG
  This is Halloween.—BrIt

Thompson, Irene
  Rainy nights.—SaM
Thoreau, Henry David
  Our country.—PlG
  "True kindness is a pure divine affinity."—
    PlL
"Those boys that ran together." Lucille
    Clifton.—AdC
Those double z's. David McCord.—McSu
"Those eager little leaguers." See Little league
Those last, late hours of Christmas eve. Lou
    Ann Welte.—LiPch
Those winter Sundays. Robert Hayden.—AdC—
    MaP—PlL
"Those words." See Swearing
Thou art my lute. Paul Laurence Dunbar.—BrI
"Thou art my lute, by thee I sing." See Thou
    art my lute
"Thou art the soul of a summer's day." See A
    song
"Thou descended from the stars." See Oh, my
    bambino
"Thou who hast slept all night upon the
    storm." See To the man-of-war bird
"Thou, whose exterior semblance doth belie."
    See Ode: Intimations of immortality from
    recollections of early childhood
"Though He be Lord of all." Unknown.—BaC
"Though he purrs, the cat's only partly here."
    See The cat and the dog
"Though holly halos hang from many a nail."
    See A Christmas package
"Though no kin to those fine glistening." See
    Christening day wishes for my god-child
    Grace Lane Berkley II
"Though the barn is so warm." See The
    palomino stallion
"Though the termite be sharp as they come."
    From Limericks. David McCord.—McSu
"Though Timmy is a pleasant boy. See The
    twins
Thought. See also Mind
  Beetle thoughts. A. Fisher.—FiO
  Dinner thought. A. Adoff.—AdE
  Plane thinking. J. Aiken.—AiS
  Ratio. L. Morrison.—MoO
  Signal. L. Morrison.—MoW
  Speech for the repeal of the McCarran Act.
    R. Wilbur.—PlG
  The telephone. R. Frost.—HiS
  "There is a black field." L. Morrison.—MoW
  Thinking. F. Holman.—HoA
  "Thoughts that were put into words." K.
    Kuskin.—KuD
  Unexpressed. P. L. Dunbar.—BrI
  "Where have you been dear." K. Kuskin.—
    HoBm—KuD
  "Why fades a dream." P. L. Dunbar.—BrI
A thought. Mary Ann Hoberman.—HoY
"Thoughtful little Willie Frazer." See Science
    for the young
"The thoughtful old walrus with the mournful
    eyes." See The walrus
Thoughts about oysters. Kaye Starbird.—CoPs

"Thoughts like slow fish move upward, while
    the plane." See Plane thinking
"Thoughts that were put into words." Karla
    Kuskin.—KuD
A thousand bells. Alfred Domett.—BaC
"A thousand hairy savages." Spike Milligan.—
    CoPs
"A thousand miles beyond this sun-steeped
    wall." See Sea longing
"A thousand miles from land are we." See The
    stormy petrel
"Three baby raccoons." Betsy Maestro.—MaFp
"Three boys, American, in dungarees." See
    February 22
"Three carriers of suspense." See Nine triads
"Three cheers for the mole." See The mole
"Three days we had." See First Thanksgiving
"Three excellent wishes." See Nine triads
The three foxes. A. A. Milne.—WiP
Three ghostesses. Unknown.—BrIt
"Three glides of satisfaction." See Nine triads
"Three gooses, geese." See Goose, moose and
    spruce
"Three grand arcs." See Nine triads
"Three Halloween tricksters are we." See The
    tricksters
"Three holy kings from Morgenland." See The
    kings from the east
"Three jolly gentlemen." See The huntsmen
Three kinds of pleasures. Robert Bly.—FlA
The three kings ("I am Gaspar, I have brought
    frankincense") Rubén Dario, tr. by
    Lysander Kemp.—BaC—LiPch
Three kings ("Three kings came out of Indian
    land") Unknown.—BaC
"Three kings came out of Indian land." See
    Three kings
"Three little birds." Laura E. Richards.—CoA
"Three little ghostesses. See Three ghostesses
"Three little guinea pigs." Unknown, tr. fr. the
    Danish by N. M. Bodecker.—CoA—WiP
"Three of us here on the hill." See The hill
"Three pale foxglove lamp mantles, in full
    flare." See Autumn nature notes
Three percussion pieces. Lillian Morrison.—
    MoW
"Three pleasurable curves." See Nine triads
Three riddles. See Who cast my shadow
"Three shots requiring skill." See Nine triads
Three signs of spring. David McCord.—McO
Three songs of Mary, sel. Madeleine L'Engle
    O simplicitas.—LiPch
"Three strange men came to the inn." See A
    lady comes to an inn
"Three swift arrivals to admire." See Nine
    triads
"Three swishes that lift the heart." See Nine
    triads
"The three-toed tree toad." See Nocturne
"Three vital sounds." See Nine triads
"Three wise men of Gotham." Mother Goose.—
    TrGg
A threnody. George T. Lanigan.—DoWh

"Thrice the brinded cat hath mew'd." See
   Macbeth
Thrift
   The debt. P. L. Dunbar.—BrI
"Through all the orchard's boughs." See
   Autumn nature notes
"Through darkening trees." Ann Atwood.—AtH
"Through jaggedy cliffs of snow, along
   sidewalks of glass." See Party in winter
"Through the automatic carwash." Robert Vas
   Dias.—LuZ
"Through the green clover and white tipped
   violets." See Strawberry patches
"Through the hayseed meadows." See Walking
   with the goats
Through the looking-glass, sel. Lewis Carroll
   The walrus and the carpenter.—WiP
"Through the revolving door." See Alligator on
   the escalator
"Through the teeth." Unknown.—CoPs
Through the vines. Allen Mandelbaum.—PlL
Through the window. David McCord.—McO
"Through the window." Naoshi Koriyama.—
   LuZ
Thrown away. Rudyard Kipling.—CoPh
Thumb face. Shel Silverstein.—SiL
"The thumb, for a summer's promise." See The
   sand painters
Thumbprint. Eve Merriam.—MaP
Thumbs
   Thumb face. S. Silverstein.—SiL
Thunder
   Over and under. W. J. Smith.—WiP
   Spring thunder. M. Van Doren.—MoGp
Thurman, Judith
   Almost spring.—ThFo
   Balloons.—ThFo
   Blizzard.—ThFo
   Breaking through.—ThFo
   Campfire.—ThFo
   Clockface.—ThFo
   Closet.—ThFo
   Flashlight.—MoGp—ThFo
   Going barefoot.—ThFo
   Hydrant.—ThFo
   Kisses.—ThFo
   "The little rain."—ThFo
   Lumps.—MoGp—ThFo
   Mare.—CoPh—ThFo
   New notebook.—ThFo
   Oil slick.—MoGp—ThFo
   Playing with clay.—ThFo
   "Pretending to sleep."—HoBm—ThFo
   Rags.—ThFo
   Skinned knee.—ThFo
   Soap.—ThFo
   Spill.—ThFo
   Tunnel.—ThFo
   Turning the corner.—ThFo
   Zebra.—MoGp—ThFo
"Thus piteously love closed what he begat."
   George Meredith.—PlL
"Thus she had lain." See Africa

"Thy tones are silver melted into sound." See
   To a lady playing the harp
Thyrsis, sel. Matthew Arnold
   "So, some tempestuous morn in early
   June."—PaB
"Tick-a-loc rock-a-bye." See Child's game
"Tick tock." See Tick tock clock
Tick tock clock. Jack Prelutsky.—PrR
Tick tock talk. David McCord.—McO
"The ticket said, to SFO." See Man of letters
The tickle rhyme. Ian Serraillier.—BeR—CoA—
   MoGp—SaM—WiP
"The tickle tiger." Dennis Lee.—LeG
A ticklish recipe. X. J. Kennedy.—KeP
Ticklish Tom. Shel Silverstein.—SiL
Ticknor, Francis Orray
   Little Giffen.—PlG
Tidal pool. Sara Henderson Hay.—PaE
"The tide rises, the tide falls." Henry
   Wadsworth Longfellow.—SaM
The tides. Henry Wadsworth Longfellow.—PaE
Tides
   At low tide. D. McCord.—McO
   Mr Spade and Mr Pail. D. McCord.—McO
   The pool in the rock. W. De La Mare.—PaE
   Tidal pool. S. H. Hay.—PaE
   "The tide rises, the tide falls." H. W.
   Longfellow.—SaM
Tietjens, Eunice
   Moving.—PaI
Tiger ("A hunter cried out when he spotted a
   tiger.") William Jay Smith.—SmL
Tiger ("I'm a tiger") Mary Ann Hoberman.—
   BeR—CoI—HoY
The tiger ("The tiger has swallowed") Valerie
   Worth.—MoGp
The tiger ("The tiger is a perfect saint") John
   Gardner.—GaCb
The tiger ("Tiger, tiger, burning bright")
   William Blake.—PaB
The tiger asks Blake for a bedtime story. Nancy
   Willard.—WiV
"The tiger has swallowed." See The tiger
"The tiger is a perfect saint." See The tiger
Tiger lily. David McCord.—McO
"The tiger lily is a panther." See Tiger lily
Tiger pajamas. Siv Cedering Fox.—FoB
"Tiger, sunflowers, king of cats." See The
   marmalade man makes a dance to mend us
"Tiger, tiger, burning bright." See The tiger
Tigers
   The cougar. R. S. Oliver.—OlC
   "This is a tiger." K. Kuskin.—KuR
   "The tickle tiger." D. Lee.—LeG
   Tiger ("A hunter cried out when he spotted
   a tiger.") W. J. Smith.—SmL
   Tiger ("I'm a tiger") M. A. Hoberman.—
   BeR—CoI—HoY
   The tiger ("The tiger has swallowed") V.
   Worth.—MoGp
   The tiger ("The tiger is a perfect saint") J.
   Gardner.—GaCb
   The tiger ("Tiger, tiger, burning bright") W.
   Blake.—PaB

Tigers—*Continued*
   Tiger pajamas. S. C. Fox.—FoB
   The tigirth. J. Yolen.—YoH
Tiggady Rue. David McCord.—McO
Tight rope. Imamu Amiri Baraka.—AdC
The **tigirth**. Jane Yolen.—YoH
"The **tigirth** weights an awful lot." See The
   tigirth
Till, Emmett (about)
   Emmett Till ("I hear a whistling") J. A.
      Emanuel.—AdC
   The last quatrain of the ballad of Emmett
      Till. G. Brooks.—AdC
Tillack, Ronald
   Dumbly Humpty.—DuSn
Tillam, Thomas
   Upon the first sight of New England, June
      29, 1638.—PlG
Tillie. Walter De La Mare.—WaGp
Tim ("When Tim was six or seven or eight")
   David McCord.—McO
Tim, an Irish terrier. W. M. Letts.—CoG
Time. See also Change
   "And the days are not full enough." E.
      Pound.—JaPp
   Another year come. W. S. Merwin.—JaPp—
      LiO
   At sunset time. P. L. Dunbar.—BrI
   "Bell-horses, bell-horses." Mother Goose.—
      TrGg
   Beyond the years. P. L. Dunbar.—BrI
   Clockface. J. Thurman.—ThFo
   Cycle. L. Morrison.—MoO
   Days ("What are days for") P. Larkin.—LuZ
   "A diller, a dollar." Mother Goose.—TrGg
   Failure. R. Lattimore.—JaPp
   Farther and further. D. McCord.—McSu
   Figures of speech. D. McCord.—McO
   Finale. From Prairie. C. Sandburg.—FlA
   For Edwin R. Embree. O. Dodson.—AdC
   Forever ("I had not known before") P. L.
      Dunbar.—BrI
   "How far." M. A. Hoberman.—HoY
   Jim Jay. W. De La Mare.—HiS
   The light year. J. Ridland.—LiO
   Make merry. D. McCord.—McO
   May fly. M. A. Hoberman.—HoBu
   "Meeting his mother makes him lose ten
      years." From Between the porch and the
      altar. R. Lowell.—PlL
   Moon clock. T. Hughes.—HuM
   Movement song. A. Lorde.—AdC
   The mystic sea. P. L. Dunbar.—BrI
   No present like the time. D. McCord.—McO
   Now long ago. M. Angelou.—AnO
   On a sundial. H. Belloc.—BrO
   Passing time. M. Angelou.—AnO
   Relativity. K. Millay.—BrO
   Rune. L. Morrison.—MoW
   The sea-limits. D.G. Rossetti.—PaE
   Ships that pass in the night. P. L. Dunbar.—
      BrI
   Song for Naomi. I. Layton.—DoWh
   Telling time. L. Moore.—MoTs

   Time ("Listen to the clock strike") M. A.
      Hoberman.—HoY
   "Time is looking at you." L. Morrison.—MoO
   A time to talk. R. Frost.—MoGp
   Time zones. L. Morrison.—MoW
   Two figures. N. S. Momaday.—MoGd
   Walk on the moon. N. S. Momaday.—MoGd
   The walrus, an evolutionary tale. J.
      Gardner.—GaCb
   Where two o'clock came from. K. Patchen.—
      HiS
   Wonder. M. Angelou.—AnO
Time ("Listen to the clock strike") Mary Ann
   Hoberman.—HoY
"The **time** draws near the birth of Christ." See
   In memoriam
"**Time** is looking at you." Lillian Morrison.—
   MoO
Time of the mad atom. Virginia Brasier.—BrO
"**Time** ticks." See Telling time
A **time** to talk. Robert Frost.—MoGp
Time zones. Lillian Morrison.—CoDb—MoW
Timely. Barbara Giles.—DuSn
"**Timothy** Tompkins had turnips and tea." See
   The meal
Timothy Toppin. Mary Ann Hoberman.—HoY
"**Timothy** Toppin climbed up a tree." See
   Timothy Toppin
Timrod, Henry
   Ode.—PlG
"**Ting**-a-ling-a-ling." See Listen, everything
"The **tiniest** man." See The tiniest man in the
   washing machine
The **tiniest** man in the washing machine.
   Dennis Lee.—LeG
"**Tiny** chickadee." Betsy Maestro.—MaFp
"**Tiny** wildflowers." Betsy Maestro.—MaFp
"The **tiny** young hunter arose with the morn."
   See The hunter
Tippett, James S.
   Do not open till Christmas.—BaC
   Familiar friends.—CoA
   Sunning.—CoG
Tiptoe ("On tiptoe") Felice Holman.—HoA
Tiptoe ("Yesterday I skipped all day") Karla
   Kuskin.—KuD
Tired. Shel Silverstein.—SiL
"A **tiresome** person in Corning." See A person
   in Corning
" 'Tis better to sit here beside the sea." See
   Silence
Tishler, Joseph
   Cheese jumpers.—DuSn
To a captious critic. Paul Laurence Dunbar.—
   BrI
To a child running with outstretched arms in
   Canyon de Chelly. N. Scott Momaday.—
   MoGd
To a dead friend. Paul Laurence Dunbar.—BrI
To a horse. Jill Hoffman.—CoPh
"**To** a king who had." See King Rufus
To a lady playing the harp. Paul Laurence
   Dunbar.—BrI
To a mouse. Robert Burns.—PaB

To a race horse at Ascot. Jennie M. Palen.—CoPh

To a small boy standing on my shoes while I am wearing them. Ogden Nash.—BlC

To a squirrel. Myra Cohn Livingston.—LiWt

To a squirrel at Kyle-na-no. William Butler Yeats.—SaM

To a tiger swallowtail butterfly. Mary Ann Hoberman.—HoBu

To a violet found on All Saints' Day. Paul Laurence Dunbar.—BrI

To a young wretch. Robert Frost.—LiO

To Alexander Meiklejohn, sel. John Beecher "I read your testimony and I thought."—PlG

To an old cat. Jillian D. Perry.—SaM

To auntie. Robert Louis Stevenson.—PlL

To autumn. John Keats.—PaB

To be a bird. Aileen Fisher.—FiO

To be a clover. Aileen Fisher.—FiO

"To be is to be the value." See Number theory

"To bed, to bed." Mother Goose.—WiP

To Bobby Seale. Lucille Clifton.—AdC

To Catlin. Robert Newton Peck.—PeB

"To clothe the fiery thought." See Poet

"To count myself." See Counting

To Desi as Joe the smoky the lover of 115th street. Audre Lorde.—AdC

"To draw a monkey, don't begin." See How to draw a monkey

"To dream." See Formula

To E.B.B., sel. Robert Browning "What were seen, none knows, none ever shall know."—PlL

To fish. Leigh Hunt.—PaE

To his brother dead. Catullus, tr. fr. the Latin by Aubrey Beardsley.—PlL

To his brother Hsing-Chien. Po Chu-i, tr. fr. the Chinese by Arthur Waley.—PlL

To his excellency George Washington. Phillis Wheatley.—LiO

To his mistresse. Robert Herrick.—LiO

To his wife. Theodore Spencer.—PlL

"To hit a bump is what I like." See Making work for father

To July. Unknown.—HoMp

To leather. Robert Newton Peck.—PeB

"To look at any thing." John Moffitt.—MaP

"To make a knothole." See Knotholes

To make a prairie. Emily Dickinson.—FlA

"To make a prairie it takes a clover and one bee." See To make a prairie

"To market, to market." See The cost of living Mother Goose

To meet Mr. Lincoln. Eve Merriam.—LiCc

"To move my chop." See I am learning

To my brother. Louise Bogan.—PlL

To my brothers. John Keats.—PlL

To my daughter. Stephen Spender.—PlL

To my daughter the junkie on a train. Audre Lorde.—AdC

To my dear and loving husband. Anne Bradstreet.—PlL

To my father ("Peace and her huge invasion to these shores") Robert Louis Stevenson.—PlL

"To my friend." See Plea

"To my valentine." See Rebus valentine

To Noel. Gabriela Mistral, tr. from the Spanish by Doris Dana.—LiPch

"To paint without a palette." See Some uses for poetry

To recognize the lesser glunk. Dennis Lee.—LeN

To say to go to sleep. See A variation on 'to say to go to sleep.'

"To see his jogs." See Joggers

To see the rabbit. Alan Brownjohn.—WiP

"To smash the simple atom." See Atomic courtesy

To the man-of-war bird. Walt Whitman.—PaE

To the skeleton of a dinosaur in the museum. Lilian Moore.—CoDb

To the statue. May Swenson.—PlG

To the veterans of the Abraham Lincoln brigade. Genevieve Taggard.—LiO

To the western world. Louis Simpson.—PlG

"To these whom death again did wed." See An epitaph upon husband and wife, which died, and were buried together

"To 350 degrees and grease." See Turn the oven on

"To try to say it." See I'm sorry

"To walk in warm rain." David McCord.—McSu

"To western woods, and lonely plains." See Stanzas on the emigration to America, and peopling the western country

"To whit." See The owl

A toad ("I saw a toad with nobbly warts") Aileen Fisher.—FiO

The toad ("In days of old, those far off times") Robert S. Oliver.—OlC

Toad ("When the flowers") Valerie Worth.—WoM

The toad and the kangaroo. Shel Silverstein.—SiL

Toads. See also Frogs; Tree toads

    The adventure of Chris. D. McCord.—McO

    Birdfoot's grampa. J. Bruchac.—MoGp

    "Delicate the toad." R. Francis.—HiD

    Garden toad. A. Fisher.—FiO

    "Our Mr. Toad." D. McCord.—McO

    Prehistoric. S. Silverstein.—SiL

    Prickled pickles don't smile. N. Giovanni.—GiV

    The song of Mr. Toad. K. Grahame.—WiP

    A toad ("I saw a toad with nobbly warts") A. Fisher.—FiO

    The toad ("In days of old, those far off times") R. S. Oliver.—OlC

    Toad ("When the flowers") V. Worth.—WoM

    The toad and the kangaroo. S. Silverstein.—SiL

The toadstool wood. James Reeves.—HiD

"The toadstool wood is dark and mouldy." See The toadstool wood

Travelers lugging valises. N. M. Bodecker.—
  BoP
The tree ("Now in white") Paul Engle.—BaC
The tree and me. Karla Kuskin.—KuD
Tree disease. Ted Hughes.—HuM
Tree house ("A tree house, a free house") Shel
  Silverstein.—BeR
"A tree house, a free house." See Tree house
"A tree may be laughter in the spring." See
  Winter night
Tree toads
  Peepers in the swamp grass. N. D. Watson.—
    WaB
  "The treetoad and the three-toed sloth." J.
    Gardner.—GaCb
Treece, Henry
  The magic wood.—HiD
Treehouses
  In the tree house at night. J. Dickey.—PlL
  Tree house ("A tree house, a free house") S.
    Silverstein.—BeR
Trees. See also Forests and forestry; also names
    of trees, as Oak trees
  Brooms ("On stormy days") D. Aldis.—PaI
  "The chestnut splits its padded cell." From
    Autumn nature notes. T. Hughes.—HuSs
  Christmas lights. V. Worth.—LiPch
  Counting-out rhyme. E. St. V. Millay.—SaM
  "Every time I climb a tree." D. McCord.—
    PaI
  "If you stood with your feet in the earth." K.
    Kuskin.—KuD
  In the park. L. Moore.—MoTs
  Juniper. E. Duggan.—LiPch
  "The laburnum top is silent, quite still."
    From Autumn nature notes. T. Hughes.—
    HuSs
  "Little tree." E. E. Cummings.—LiCc
  Lullaby. F. Holman.—HoA
  Midwinter. N. M. Bodecker.—BoHh
  "The shadow of a tree." L. Moore.—MoTs
  Small dirge. I. Wilner.—WiP
  Spell of the woods. L. Norris.—NoM
  Spendthrift. N. Farber.—FaS
  There came a day. T. Hughes.—HuSs
  Trees ("The birch is a fountain") E.
    Farjeon.—WiP
  "Under this autumn sky." A. Adoff.—AdE
  "Wassail the trees, that they may bear."
    From Ceremonies for Christmas. R.
    Herrick.—LiPch
  Watching the moon. D. McCord.—McO
  "We ate a kumquat." B. Maestro.—MaFp
  "White petals falling." K. Mizumura.—MiF
  Winter night. C. Hutchison.—BaC
Trees. Eleanor Farjeon.—WiP
"A tree's a trapeze for a sloth." See Sloth
"The trees are down, but the leaves are up."
  See Old Tim Toole
"The trees ask me." See Who am I
"The trees bend down along the stream." See
  A lazy day
"The trees now look scary." See Lullaby
"Treetalk and windsong are." See Sugarfields

"The treetoad and the three-toed sloth." John
  Gardner.—GaCb
Trellie. Lance Jeffers.—AdC
Triads
  Nine triads. L. Morrison.—MoSr
"Tribolite, grapholite, nautilus pie." See Boston
  nursery rhymes—Rhyme for a geological
  baby
Trick ("The people in this house were mean")
  Jack Prelutsky.—PrI
Trick or treat. David McCord.—BrIt—McO
"Trick or treat, trick or treat." Jack
  Prelutsky.—PrI
"A trick that everyone abhors." See Rebecca,
  who slammed doors for fun and perished
  miserably
The tricksters. Jack Prelutsky.—PrI
Trifles. See Little things, importance of
Trinity Place. David McCord.—McO
Triolet. Lillian Morrison.—MoW
Triolets
  Triolet. L. Morrison.—MoW
  Write me a verse. D. McCord.—McO
The trip ("Our car was fierce enough") William
  Stafford.—JaPp
A trip on the Staten Island ferry. Audre
  Lorde.—AdC
The triumph of Charis. Ben Jonson.—PaB
The troll ("Be wary of the loathsome troll")
  Jack Prelutsky.—BrIt—PrN
"Troll sat alone on his seat of stone." See The
  stone troll
The troll to her children. Jane Yolen.—YoD
Troll trick. B. J. Lee.—BrIt
Trollope's journal, sel. Elizabeth Bishop
  "As far as statues go, so far there's not."—
    PlG
Trolls. See Monsters
The trouble is. Myra Cohn Livingston.—LiF
"The trouble is no one appreciates me." See
  The trouble is
The trouble was simply that. David McCord.—
  McO
"The trouble with a dinosaur." X. J.
  Kennedy.—CoDb
"The trouble with a kitten is." See The kitten
Trouble with dinner. J. A. Lindon.—HeB
Trouble with pies. David McCord.—McO
Troubled woman. Langston Hughes.—JaPp
Troupe, Quincy
  For Malcolm who walks in the eyes of our
    children.—AdC
  "The old people speak of death."—AdC
  "South African bloodstone."—AdC
  Transformation.—Adc
A trucker. Thom Gunn.—JaPp
Trucks
  A trucker. T. Gunn.—JaPp
True ("When") Lilian Moore.—WiP
A true account of talking to the sun at Fire
  Island. Frank O'Hara.—KhI
"True kindness is a pure divine affinity." Henry
  David Thoreau.—PlL
A true Lent. Robert Herrick.—LiO

"The turtle's always been inclined." See The
 turtle
Tusk, tusk. Shel Silverstein.—SiL
Tusser, Thomas
 "At Christmas, play and make good cheer."—
 BaC
The tutor. Carolyn Wells.—WiP
"A tutor who tooted the flute." See The tutor
"Twango twango, zing zong." See Pancho
 Pangolin
" 'Twas Brillo, and the G.E. stoves." See
 Jabber-whacky, or, on dreaming, after
 falling asleep watching TV
" 'Twas Euclid, and the theorem pi." See Plane
 geometry
" 'Twas late on an eve in midsummer." See He
 who would dream of fairyland
" 'Twas mercy brought me from my pagan
 land." See On being brought from Africa
 to America
" 'Twas on a Holy Thursday, their innocent
 faces clean." See Holy Thursday
" 'Twas the night before Christmas, when all
 through the house." See A visit from St.
 Nicholas
"Tweedledum and Tweedledee." Mother
 Goose.—TrGg
Twelfth night. Elizabeth Coatsworth.—BaC
The twelve days of Christmas. Unknown.—
 LiPch
12 October. Myra Cohn Livingston.—LiCc
"Twelve snails went walking after night." See
 The haughty snail-king
The twenty fourth of December. Unknown.—
 BaC
"21 and 21." See Numberot
Twice born. Aileen Fisher.—FiO
Twilight. Paul Laurence Dunbar.—BrI
Twilight song. John Hunter-Duvar.—DoWh
Twilight's last gleaming. Arthur W. Monks.—
 LiO
Twins
 The twins ("Likeness has made them animal
 and shy") K. Shapiro.—PlL
 The twins ("Though Timmy is a pleasant
 boy") K. Starbird.—StC
 The twins ("He hinted at times that I was a
 bastard and I told him to listen") Charles
 Bukowski.—KhI
 The twins ("Likeness has made them animal
 and shy") Karl Shapiro.—PlL
 The twins ("Though Timmy is a pleasant boy")
 Kaye Starbird.—StC
" 'Twixt a smile and a tear." See Twilight
" 'Twixt the coastline and the border lay the
 town of Grog an' Grumble." See Grog an'
 Grumble steeplechase
Twistable turnable man. Shel Silverstein.—SiL
"Two." See Kisses
Two at showtime. Suzanne Brabant.—CoPh
Two beers in Argyle, Wisconsin. Dave Etter.—
 FlA
Two birds with one stone. J. A. Lindon.—CoPs

"Two brothers we are, great burdens we bear."
 Mother Goose.—TrGg
"Two cats were sitting in a tree." N. M.
 Bodecker.—WiP
Two dogs have I. Ogden Nash.—CoG
Two doorbells. X. J. Kennedy.—KeP
"Two doorbells glowered out at me." See Two
 doorbells
Two figures. N. Scott Momaday.—MoGd
"Two ghosts I know once traded heads." See
 Whose boo is whose
Two girls. Charles Reznikoff.—JaPp
"Two girls discover." See The secret
"Two girls of twelve or so at a table." See Two
 girls
Two girls singing. Iain Crichton Smith.—LuZ
"The two gray kits." Mother Goose.—TrGg
Two in bed. Abram Bunn Ross.—PaI
 "When my brother Tommy."—MoF
"Two legs sat upon three legs." Mother
 Goose.—TrGg
 A riddle.—BlH
"Two little dogs." See "Two little dogs sat by
 the fire"
"Two little dogs sat by the fire." Mother
 Goose.—TrGg
 "Two little dogs."—BlH
"The two little princesses." See Palace cook's
 tale
"Two months old, already." See
 Metempsychosis
"Two nasty little houses back to back." See
 Scene from the working class
Two of a kind. Norma Farber.—FaS
"Two of far nobler shape, erect and tall." See
 Paradise lost
Two people. Eve Merriam.—MeW
"Two people asked." See He'd just come from
 the churchyard
"Two pigeons on the stoop." See Higher and
 lower mathematics
Two postures beside a fire. James Wright.—PlL
"Two respectable rhymes." See Rhymes
"Two separate words." See Portmanteaux
"Two sets of DNA are we." See Felicitations
Two strangers breakfast. Carl Sandburg.—PlL
Two sunflowers move into the yellow room.
 Nancy Willard.—WiV
"Two things fly in the dark of the night." See
 Night travel
"Two things the moon steals." Ann Atwood.—
 AtH
Two times three. David McCord.—McO
"Two track stars ran a race." See Photo finish
Two tramps in mud time, sel. Robert Frost
 "The sun was warm but the wind was
 chill."—HoMp
Two ways to wake a sleepwalker. Edward
 Lueders.—LuZ
The two witches ("O sixteen hundred and
 ninety-one") Robert Graves.—HiS
Two witches ("There was a witch") Alexander
 Resnikoff.—BrIt
Twogether. Eve Merriam.—MeR

Tymnes
   The dog from Malta.—CoG
Tynan, Katharine
   August weather.—SaM
"Typewriter." See Ways of composing
"Typing doesn't disturb anyone." See What I
   learned this year
The tyrannosaur. Michael Braude.—CoDb
"Tyrannosaur remains are found." See The
   tyrannosaur
"The tyrannosaurus rex." Shel Silverstein.—
   CoDb
"Tyrannosaurus rex's teeth." X. J. Kennedy.—
   CoDb—KeP

U

U is for up. William Jay Smith.—SmL
"Ugly babies." Mother Goose.—TrGg
"An ugly face with triangle eyes." See Cut out
The ugstabuggle. Peter Wesley-Smith.—WaM
Uhuru. Mari Evans.—AdC
Umbrellas
   The elf and the dormouse. O. Herford.—PaI
   Snap. S. Silverstein.—SiL
Un-natural history. Ronald Oliver Brierley.—
   DuSn
Un-negative. Eve Merriam.—MeR
"Unaccustomed." See The television
"Unbuttoned button." See Skyviews
Unclaimed. Florida Watts Smyth.—CoPh
Uncle Bungle. Jack Prelutsky.—PrQ
"Uncle Bungle, now deceased." See Uncle
   Bungle
Uncle Frank. Monica Shannon.—PaI
Uncles
   Everybody has an uncle. O. Nash.—BlC
   "Fame was a claim of uncle Ed's." O.
      Nash.—BlC
   "I often grieve for uncle Hannibal." O.
      Nash.—BlC
   My uncle ("I think of forests palaces and
      swans") R. Lattimore.—PlL
   My uncle Jack. D. Amey.—PaI
   New England Protestant. R. Eberhart.—PlL
   "Pumberly Pott's unpredictable niece." J.
      Prelutsky.—PrQ
   Uncle Bungle. J. Prelutsky.—PrQ
   Uncle Frank. M. Shannon.—PaI
Undefeated. Robert Froman.—MoGp
"Under a bent when the night was deep." See
   The earthly paradise
"Under a plant in my garden." See Garden
   toad
Under a stone. Aileen Fisher.—FiO
"Under a toadstool." See The elf and the
   dormouse
"Under my hat is my hair." N. M. Bodecker.—
   BoHh
"Under the dying sun." See The reaper
Under the mistletoe. Countee Cullen.—BaC—
   LiPch

Under the old elm, sel. James Russsell Lowell
   "Never to see a nation born."—PlG
"Under the rabbit there, I saw a tree." See Mr
   Mixup tells a story
Under the sea. Alan Butterfield.—SaM
Under the white pine. David McCord.—McO
"Under this autumn sky." Arnold Adoff.—AdE
"Underneath the water." See Way down deep
"Underneath this wooden cross there lies." See
   Elegy for a dead soldier
The underwing moth. Robert S. Oliver.—OlC
"Unexpectedly descending things." See Moon
   wings
Unexpressed. Paul Laurence Dunbar.—BrI
Unfinished history. Archibald MacLeish.—PlL
Unholy missions. Bob Kaufman.—AdC
Unicorn. William Jay Smith.—HiS—SmL
"The unicorn with the long white horn." See
   Unicorn
Unicorns
   "The lion and the unicorn." Mother Goose.—
      TrGg
   Once upon a great holiday. A. Wilkinson.—
      DoWh
   The strangers. A. A. Brown.—DoWh
   Unicorn. W. J. Smith.—HiS—SmL
Union for children's rights. Shel Silverstein.—
   SiL
United States. See also America
   An Englishman with an atlas or America the
      unpronounceable. M. Bishop.—PlG
   "From Paumanok starting I fly like a bird."
      W. Whitman.—PlG
   Grant Wood's American landscape. W. T.
      Scott.—PlG
   "Now it's Uncle Sam sitting on top of the
      world." From Good morning America. C.
      Sandburg.—LiO
   O captain, my captain. W. Whitman.—PlG
   Our country. H. D. Thoreau.—PlG
   Patriotic poem. D. Wakowski.—LiO
United States—History. See also Frontier and
   pioneer life; Immigration and emigration
   The distant runners. M. Van Doren.—PlG
   February 22. J. Updike.—PlG
   The foundations of American industry. D.
      Hall.—PlG
   It happened in Montgomery. P. W. Petrie.—
      MoGp
   "A long time since it seems today." From A
      New Year letter, W. H. Auden.—PlG
   Meredith Phyfe. E. L. Masters.—PlG
   On a fortification at Boston begun by
      women. B. Tompson.—PlG
   The prophecy of King Tammany. P.
      Freneau.—PlG
   The river. H. Crane.—PlG
   Speech for the repeal of the McCarran Act.
      R. Wilbur.—PlG
United States—History—Civil War
   Cannon Park. M. St. Germain.—JaPp
   History among the rocks. R. P. Warren.—PlG
   Hunting Civil War relics at Nimblewill
      Creek. J. Dickey.—PlG

V

Work and play. T. Hughes.—HuSs
Vacation time. Nikki Giovanni.—GiV
Vagabonds. See Gypsies; Wayfaring life
Vagrants. Paul Laurence Dunbar.—BrI
A **valediction:** forbidding mourning. John
    Donne.—PlL
Valentine ("Chipmunks jump, and") Donald
    Hall.—JaPp—YaI
Valentine feelings. Lee Bennett Hopkins.—
    HoMp
A **valentine** for a lady, Lucilius, tr. fr. the Latin
    by Dudley Fitts.—LiO
Valentine for earth. Frances Frost.—BrO
A **valentine** to the wide world. Beatrice Schenk
    De Regniers.—ReB
Valentines ("Forgive me if I have not sent
    you") Henry Dumas.—LiCc
Valentine's day. See Saint Valentine's day
Valentines to my mother. Christina Georgina
    Rossetti.—LiO
The **valley.** Stanley Moss.—JaPp
The **vampire** ("The night is still and somber")
    Jack Prelutsky.—PrN
"The **vampire** bats all wear bright purple hats."
    See Vampires
Vampires. See Monsters
Vampires ("The vampire bats all wear bright
    purple hats") Robert S. Oliver.—OlC
Van Doren, Mark
    Carl.—PlL
    Dance song 6.—HiD
    The distant runners.—PlG
    "Down dip the branches."—HiD
    Ghost boy.—HiS
    Good morning.—HiD
    I had to be secret.—HiS
    Laly, Laly.—HiS
    Merry-go-round.—HiS
    Needles and pins.—HiS
    "Old Ben Golliday."—HiS
    The sad child's song.—HiS
    Spring thunder.—MoGp
    Wait till then.—HiS
    "Where did he run to."—HiS
Varday, Marguerite
    "The Barrier Reef is a coral puzzle."—DuSn
    "In north-west Australia where the iron ore
        grows."—DuSn
    "Out in the wilds of south Australia."—DuSn
A **variation** on 'to say to go to sleep.' Randall
    Jarrell, ad. fr. Rainer Maria Rilke.—YaI
Variations on a cosmical air, sel. Malcolm
    Cowley
    "Love is the flower of a day."—YaI
Vas Dias, Robert
    "Through the automatic carwash."—LuZ
"**Vats** of soup." See Giants' delight
"The **vaulter** suspended." See I love all gravity
    defiers
Vega, Lope de
    "At dawn the virgin is born."—LiPch
    A little carol of the Virgin.—LiPch
A **vegetable,** I will not be. Donna Whitewing.—
    FlA

Vegetables. See also Food and eating; Gardens
    and gardening; also names of vegetables, as
    Potatoes
    Artichokes. P. Johnson.—CoPs
    Celery. O. Nash.—CoPs
    "On Tuesday morn as it happened by
        chance." From The magic pudding. N.
        Lindsay.—DuSn
    Rabbit ("A rabbit") M. A. Hoberman.—HoY
    Vegetables ("Eat a tomato and you'll turn
        red") S. Silverstein.—CoPs
Vegetables ("Eat a tomato and you'll turn red")
    Shel Silverstein.—CoPs
Venders. See Peddlers and venders
"A **venturesome** woman of Kent." Myra Cohn
    Livingston.—LiLl
Venus and Adonis, sel. William Shakespeare
    "But lo, from forth a copse that neighbours
        by."—CoPh
Venus in the tropics. Louis Simpson.—KhI
Vermont
    The granite sentry. R. N. Peck.—PeB
    Rutland fair. R. N. Peck.—PeB
Vermont conversation. Patricia Hubbell.—WiP
Verse. See Poets and poetry
Verse for a certain dog. Dorothy Parker.—CoG
Verses versus verses. Marvin Bell.—KhI
"**Vertical** light." See You light.
Very early. Karla Kuskin.—KuD
"**Very** thin." See Snake
Vesey, Paul. See Allen, Samuel
Vesper. Alcman of Sparta, tr. by F. L. Lucas.—
    LuZ
Victims 3 cat 0. David Kherdian.—KhC
Village life. See also Towns
    Calico ball. N. D. Watson.—WaB
    Carol. From The wind in the willows. K.
        Grahame.—BaC
        "Villagers all, this frosty tide."—LiPch
    The granite sentry. R. N. Peck.—PeB
    "A man in our village." L. Norris.—CoG
    Midwest town. R. De Long Peterson.—FlA
    A village tale. M. Sarton.—CoG
A **village** tale. May Sarton.—CoG
"**Villagers** all, this frosty tide." See Wind in the
    willows
The **villanelle.** David McCord.—McO
Villanelles
    The villanelle. D. McCord.—McO
Villanueva, Alma
    Legacies and bastard roses.—KhI
Vincent, W. G.
    "And in the cold, bleak winter time." See
        Moonlight
    Moonlight, sel.
        "And in the cold, bleak winter time."—
            FlA
Vines, Eda H.
    Ballade of the old time engine.—BrO
Violets
    To a violet found on All Saints' Day. P. L.
        Dunbar.—BrI
Violinists. See Fiddlers and fiddling
A **viper** named Sam. N. M. Bodecker.—BoP

Virgin Mary. See Mary, Virgin
Virginia
"I went to the valley."—AdC
"**Visible,** invisible." See A jellyfish
The **vision** of the mermaids, sel. Gerard Manley
Hopkins
"Mermaids six or seven."—PaE
Visions. See also Dreams
The brothers. E. Muir.—PlL
The dreamer ("Temples he built and palaces
of air") P. L. Dunbar.—BrI
"From his wanderings far to eastward."
From The song of Hiawatha. H. W.
Longfellow.—PlG
"Image." L. Morrison.—MoW
Nine triads. L. Morrison.—MoSr
Roses and revolutions. D. Randall.—AdC
A **visit** from St. Nicholas. Clement C. Moore.—
LiPch
A **visit** to the asylum. Edna St. Vincent
Millay.—HiS
A **visit** to the gingerbread house. From A lot of
limericks. X. J. Kennedy.—KeP
Visiting the moon. Ted Hughes.—HuM
The **visitor.** Jack Prelutsky.—CoI—PrQ
Visitor ("Old tree") Myra Cohn Livingston.—
LiF
Vliet, R. G.
"Girls on saddleless horses."—CoPh
The **voice** in the storm. Lillian Morrison.—MoO
Voices
Clean your room. J. Prelutsky.—PrR
Ecstasy. W. H. Turner.—PaE
Voices ("There are songs and sounds in
stillness") F. Holman.—HoA
Voices of heroes overheard in a churchyard
dedicated to the memory of 1776. H.
Gregory.—LiO
Voices in the mist. From In memoriam. A.
Tennyson.—BaC
Voices of heroes, overheard in a churchyard
dedicated to the memory of 1776. Horace
Gregory.—LiO
Voices ("There are songs and sounds in
stillness") Felice Holman.—HoA
Volare. Lillian Morrison.—MoSr
Volcanoes
V is for volcano. W. J. Smith.—SmL
Voodoo
The zombie. J. Prelutsky.—PrH
"A **voracious** old fellow from Clunes." Wilbur
G. Howcroft.—DuSn
Vultures
The buzzard. J. Gardner.—GaCb

W

W. James Reeves.—MoGp
W is for well. William Jay Smith.—SmL
"The **wackiest** bird." See The muddleheaded
messer

Waddell, Helen
Easter Sunday. tr.—LiO
Waddington, Miriam
Laughter.—DoWh
Rhymes. tr.—DoWh
"**Waddles** after." See Old dog
Wager. Mary Ann Hoberman.—HoY
Wagoner, David
Clancy.—CoPh
Snake hunt.—LuZ
The trail horse.—CoPh
"**Wailed** a ghost in a graveyard at Kew." Myra
Cohn Livingston.—LiLl
Wait till then. Mark Van Doren.—HiS
Waiters. Mary Ann Hoberman.—CoPs—HoY
Waiting
Before Christmas. A. Fisher.—FiO
Christmas secrets. A. Fisher.—FiO
I am waiting. L. Ferlinghetti.—PlG
Waiters. M. A. Hoberman.—HoY
"Waiting, Daddy says." N. Grimes.—GrS
"Waiting for lunchtime." N. Grimes.—GrS
"Waiting for someone to play with." N.
Grimes.—GrS
"Waiting for summer to end." N. Grimes.—
GrS
"**Waiting,** Daddy says." Nikki Grimes.—GrS
"**Waiting** for lunchtime." Nikki Grimes.—GrS
"**Waiting** for someone to play with." Nikki
Grimes.—GrS
"**Waiting** for summer to end." Nikki Grimes.—
GrS
"**Waiting** in this great mansion, Tom Tiddler's
ground." See As good as a feast
Wake up. Eve Merriam.—MeB
Wake up ("If my brain were a bugle to blast
you") Lillian Morrison.—MoW
Wake-up poems. See also Morning
Asleep and awake. D. McCord.—McO
Awake ("Who is first up") D. McCord.—McSu
An emergency. F. Holman.—HoA
Get up, get up. Unknown.—CoPs
"I woke up this morning." K. Kuskin.—
KuD—WiP
Morning ("Everyone is tight asleep") M. C.
Livingston.—WiP
Very early. K. Kuskin.—KuD
Wake up ("If my brain were a bugle to blast
you") L. Morrison.—MoW
Waking ("I said to myself one morning") A.
Higgins.—LuZ
Waking up ("What, oh") S. C. Fox.—FoB
Wake up, shadows. Lilian Moore.—MoTs
Waking ("I said to myself one morning") Annie
Higgins.—LuZ
Waking from a nap on the beach. May
Swenson.—JaPp
Waking up ("What, oh") Siv Cedering Fox.—
FoB
Wakowski, Diane
Patriotic poem.—LiO
Walcott, Derek
Alba.—JaPp
Waldheim cemetery. Robert Sward.—FlA

Waley, Arthur
Old and new. tr.—PlL
On the birth of his son. tr.—LiO
To his brother Hsing-Chien. tr.—PlL
Walk at night. Aileen Fisher.—FiO
A **walk** for thinking. Nancy Dingman
Watson.—WaB
Walk on the moon. N. Scott Momaday.—MoGd
"**Walk** the plank, says pirate Jim." See Pirate
captain Jim
Walker, Alice
Women.—PlG
"You had to go to funerals."—LuZ
Walker, Margaret
For Malcolm X.—AdC
For my people.—AdC
Girl held without bail.—AdC
Lineage.—AdC—LuZ
Street demonstration.—AdC
Walker, Ted
By the saltings.—PaE
The harpooning.—PaE
Walking
The clock tower. C. Thibaudeau.—DoWh
Coati-mundi. W. J. Smith.—SmL
Fall. K. Kuskin.—KuD
"I am a constant walker." N. M. Bodecker.—
BoHh
Ice-creepers. E. Merriam.—MeR
In the sun and shadow. A. Fisher.—FiO
Joe's snow clothes. K. Kuskin.—KuD
"For wandering walks."—WiP
A lass from Milwaukee. N. M. Bodecker.—
BoP
Meet on the road. Unknown.—WiP
Puppy and I. A. A. Milne.—WiP
Sidewalks. V. Worth.—WoM
So run along and play. D. McCord.—McO
"Some people on the moon are so idle." T.
Hughes.—HuM
Street song. M. C. Livingston.—LiWt
Taking a walk. A. Fisher.—FiO
That morning in June. K. Starbird.—StC
Tiptoe ("On tiptoe") F. Holman.—HoA
Tiptoe ("Yesterday I skipped all day") K.
Kuskin.—KuD
"To walk in warm rain." D. McCord.—McSu
Walk at night. A. Fisher.—FiO
A walk for thinking. N. D. Watson.—WaB
Walking ("When daddy") G. Glaubitz.—PaI
When you. E. Merriam.—MeB
Walking ("When daddy") Grace Glaubitz.—PaI
"**Walking** in the wind." Kazue Mizumura.—
MiF
Walking with the goats. Nancy Dingman
Watson.—WaB
"**Walking** with you." See Friend
The **Wallabout** martyrs. Walt Whitman.—PlG
Walls
The tickle rhyme. I. Serraillier.—BeR
"**Walnut** in a walnut shell." See Bye baby
walnut
The **walnut** tree. David McCord.—McO

Walnut trees
The walnut tree. D. McCord.—McO
Walnuts
Bye baby walnut. N. Farber.—FaS
The **walrus**, an evolutionary tale. John
Gardner.—GaCb
"The **walrus** got braces." See Tusk, tusk
Walruses
Tusk, tusk. S. Silverstein.—SiL
The walrus, an evolutionary tale. J.
Gardner.—GaCb
The walrus and the carpenter. From
Through the looking-glass. L. Carroll.—WiP
The **walrust**. Jane Yolen.—YoH
Walsh, Chad
Christmas in the straw.—BaC
Walsh, Donald D.
The queen. tr.—YaI
Walsh, Ruth M.
Inadequate aqua extremis.—BrO
Rift tide.—BrO
Waltzing mice. David McCord.—McO
Wang Chung-ju
Complaint of a young girl.—JaPp
The **wapiti**. Ogden Nash.—BlC
War. See also Peace; Soldiers; Warships; also
subdivisions under countries, as United
States—History—Civil War
The armies of the moon. T. Hughes.—HuM
Battle won is lost. P. George.—LuZ
Early warning. S. Marks.—BrO
Faith and practice. J. Balaban.—PlG
"Father, may I go to war." Unknown.—WiP
Gunner. R. Jarrell.—LiO
Hunting Civil War relics at Nimblewill
Creek. J. Dickey.—PlG
Little Giffen. F. O. Ticknor.—PlG
A meditation. H. Melville.—PlG
National security. A. MacLeish.—PlG
"On the lawn at the villa." L. Simpson.—PlG
"A sight in camp in the daybreak gray and
dim." W. Whitman.—LiO
The soldier ("He is that fallen lance that lies
as hurled") R. Frost.—LiO
To the veterans of the Abraham Lincoln
brigade. G. Taggard.—LiO
The Turkish trench dog. G. Dearmer.—CoG
Voices of heroes overheard in a churchyard
dedicated to the memory of 1776. H.
Gregory.—LiO
"When brothers forget." J. W. Boyer.—AdC
The young dead soldiers. A. MacLeish.—LiO
The **war** horse. See Job
War horses. William Cole.—CoPh
Ward, Sherry
The wind.—SaM
The **warm** and the cold. Ted Hughes.—HuSs
Warning to children. Robert Graves.—HiS
"A **warning** wind finds out my resting place."
See The March bee
Warnings
Alarm. D. McCord.—McO
Warning to children. R. Graves.—HiS

"**Water** wobbling blue sky puddled October."
    See Autumn nature notes
Waterfalls
    By Frazier Creek Falls. G. Snyder.—PlG
Watermelons
    Two birds with one stone. J. A. Lindon.—
    CoPs
Water's edge. Lillian Morrison.—MoW
Watkins, Vernon
    The shell.—PaE
Watson, Clyde
    "Apples for the little ones." See Father Fox's
    pennyrhymes
    "Belly and Tubs went out in a boat."—WiP
    "Country bumpkin." See Father Fox's
    pennyrhymes
    "Dilly dilly piccalilli."—WiP
    Father Fox's pennyrhymes, sels.
        "Apples for the little ones."—LiCc
        "Country bumpkin."—LiCc
        "Happy birthday, silly goose."—LiCc
        "Huckleberry, gooseberry, raspberry
        pie."—LiCc
    "Happy birthday, silly goose." See Father
    Fox's pennyrhymes
    "How many miles to old Norfolk."—WiP
    "Huckleberry, gooseberry, raspberry pie."
    See Father Fox's pennyrhymes
    "Little Martha piggy-wig."—WiP
    "Pinky Pauper picked my pocket."—WiP
Watson, Nancy Dingman
    Barn chores.—WaB
    Barn fire.—WaB
    Blueberries lavender.—WaB
    "Blueberry eyes."—WaB
    Butterballs.—WaB
    Calico ball.—WaB
    First one up.—WaB
    "Grasshopper green."—WaB
    Hiding place.—WaB
    Honeybee hill.—WaB
    Makers.—WaB
    Molehills.—WaB
    Monkey vines.—WaB
    My cat.—WaB
    My own room.—RuM—WaB
    Now.—WaB
    Peepers in the swamp grass.—WaB
    Rooster rue.—WaB
    Snow.—WaB
    Snow woman.—WaB
    Spotter and swatter—WaB
    Spring diet.—WaB
    Sugar maples.—WaB
    Up in the pine.—HoBm—WaB
    A walk for thinking.—WaB
    Walking with the goats.—WaB
    You and me.—WaB
    Zizzy bee.—WaB
Watson, Wilfred
    The juniper tree.—DoWh
Watt, W. W.
    Summer song, after a surfeit of irresistible
    ads.—BrO

Watts, Marjorie Seymour
    New shoes.—PaI
The **wave**. David McCord.—McO
"**Wave** swashes." See Water's edge
Waves
    The even sea." M. Swenson.—PaE
    "The horses of the sea." C. Rossetti.—WiP
    Marine. R. Humphries.—PaE
    Sea and sand. L. Norris.—NoM
    "Sleeplessly circle the waves." From Look
    not too deep. L. Binyon.—PaE
    Spray. D. H. Lawrence.—PaE
    The washer waves. N. Farber.—FaS
    Waves ("There's big waves and little waves")
    E. Farjeon.—PaE
Waves ("There's big waves and little waves")
    Eleanor Farjeon.—PaE
"The **waves** come in on pearly toes." See The
    washer waves
"The **waves** lined up." See Sea and sand
"**Waves** of the sea." Aileen Fisher.—FiO
The **waves** of the sea. Eleanor Farjeon.—SaM
"The **waves** reach up." See Coastline olympics
"**Waves** that are white far out." See Marine
"**Waves** want." See Surf
Wavy. Shel Silverstein.—SiL
Way down deep. Mary Ann Hoberman.—HoY
Way down in the music. Eloise Greenfield.—
    GrH
"**Way** down South where bananas grow."
    Unknown.—WiP
"**Way** high up the Mogollons." See The glory
    trail
The **way** it is. Gloria Oden.—AdC
The **way** of Cape Race. E. J. Pratt.—DoWh
"The **way** the cooked shoes sizzle." See
    Amanda is shod
The **way** things are. Myra Cohn Livingston.—
    LiWt
The **way** to the zoo. Unknown.—CoI
Wayfaring life
    The river. H. Crane.—PlG
Ways of composing. Eve Merriam.—MeR
"**We** all look on with anxious eyes." See When
    father carves the duck
"**We** are flakes." See Cognation
"**We** are going to see the rabbit." See To see
    the rabbit
"**We** are in Chicago's Waldheim cemetery."
    See Waldheim cemetery
"**We** are landless dream farmers." See Dream
    farmer
"**We** are light." See Laughter
"**We** are the frogs who will not turn to
    princes." See Rebels from fairy tales
"**We** are the raingods, we are the clouds." See
    Spell of the raingods
"**We** ate a kumquat." Betsy Maestro.—MaFp
"**We** bought a fat." See Pumpkin
"**We** bought a pumpkin big and round." See
    Pumpkin head
"**We** bought him at auction, tranquillized to a
    drooping halt." See Clancy

"We broke Mister Mulligan's window." See Mr. Mulligan's window
"We brought a rug for sitting on." See The picnic
"We called him Mr. Catlin, he was old." See To Catlin
"We can't find the cat." See The lost cat
"We celebrate you." See Fourth of July
"We climbed a tree." See Penthouse
"We climbed to the pond." See Small frogs
"We could be friends." Myra Cohn Livingston.—LiWt—YaI
We dance like Ella riffs. Carolyn M. Rodgers.—AdC
"We dance round in a ring and suppose." See The secret sits
"We feed the birds in winter." See Joe
"We found a nest of sparrows." See Baby birds
"We got a broom like father said." See New year's eve
"We had better conserve our water." See Inadequate aqua extremis
"We had red earth once to smear on our cheeks." See Arrowy dreams
"We have a nice clean new green lawn." See Something better
"We have forgot, who safe in cities dwell." See Sea-sonnet
"We have loved each other in this time twenty years." See Unfinished history
"We have the statue for it, Liberty." See Address to the refugees
"We have these drums." See Percussions
"We heard a jay." See In the wind
"We jeer." See Tee-vee enigma
"We live in a bubble chamber." See In terms of physics
"We live in fragments." See Tight rope
"We lived in language all our black selves." See When the wine was gone
"We mask our faces." See On Halloween
"We might have been hall or wall of a stately palace." See Song of the marble earrings
"We move very fast and smoothly." See Good times and no bread
We must be polite. Carl Sandburg.—WiP
"We never gave each other groceries." See Marthe, the mar, la mer, la mere, tram, he, rath, mare, hear my mere, my mart
"We play that we are soldiers." See Noises
"We poke around and pry about." See Looking
"We put more coal on the big red fire." See Father's story
"We saw a city of daisies." See Daisy world
We saw a light. Unknown.—BaC
"We saw a light shine out afar." See We saw a light
"We saw a young little." See Sky rider
"We say ladybug." See Ladybug
"We sing, and plan." See Before Christmas
"We sit outside." See Death of Dr. King
"We three." Lilian Moore.—BrIt—LiCc
"We three kings of Orient are." John H. Hopkins.—LiPch

"We watched slant eyes." See Feline lesson
We wear the mask. Paul Laurence Dunbar.—BrI
"We wear the mask that grins and lies." See We wear the mask
"We were camped on the plains at the head of the Cimarron." See The zebra dun
"We will bake independence pie." See Fourth of July
"We will kill." See After the killing
Wealth. See also Money
  "The fairies have never a penny to spend." R. Fyleman.—WaFp
  I have. J. Aiken.—AiS
  "Melvin Martin Riley Smith." D. McCord.—McO
  Notice ("I have a dog") D. McCord.—McO
"A wealthy dromedar." See The boar and the dromedar
Weapons. See Arms and armor; also names of weapons, as Guns
"Wear you a hat or wear you a crown." Mother Goose.—TrGg
Weasels
  The cornering. R. N. Peck.—PeB
  Don't ever seize a weasel by the tail. J. Prelutsky.—WiP
Weather. See also Clouds; Dew; Fog; Mist; Rain; Rainbows; Seasons; Snow; Storms; Winds
  Earth song. D. McCord.—McO
  It's never fair weather. O. Nash.—BlC
  "Let weather be blizzardy, zany." B. S. De Regniers.—ReB
  The mole. J. Gardner.—GaCb
  "Never mind the rain." N. M. Bodecker.—BoHh
  "On Fribruary fair and foul day." D. Orgel.—OrM
  "Rain is so rainy." B. S. De Regniers.—ReB
  "Red sky at night." Unknown.—SaM
  Song ("Wind and wave and star and sea") D. McCord.—McO
  "The sun was warm but the wind was chill." From Two tramps in mud time. R. Frost.—HoMp
  Take sky. D. McCord.—McO
  "This little man lived all alone." Mother Goose.—LoG
  Tornado season. A. Stoutenberg.—MoGp
  Two times three. D. McCord.—McO
  A watched example never boils. O. Nash.—BlC
  Weather ("On sunny afternoons") R. Hershon.—LuZ
Weather ("On sunny afternoons") Robert Hershon.—LuZ
Weather conditions. Myra Cohn Livingston.—LiF
"The weather is so very mild." See A watched example never boils
Weathers. Thomas Hardy.—PaB
Weavers and weaving
  Song of the sky loom. Unknown.—MoGp

What the gray cat sings. A. Guiterman.—WiP

Webb, Mary
 The shell.—PaE

Webster, Daniel (about)
 Daniel Webster's horses. E. Coatsworth.—CoPh
 "Why did all manly gifts in Webster fail." R. W. Emerson.—PlG

Webster, John
 Cornelia's song. See The white devil
 The white devil, sel.
  Cornelia's song.—PaB

"We'd have a old car, the kind that gets." See Kit, six years old, standing by the dashboard keeping daddy awake on a trip home from the beach

A **wedding** toast. Richard Wilbur.—PlL

Weddings. See Brides and bridegrooms; Marriages

"**Wee,** sleekit, cow'rin', tim'rous beastie." See To a mouse

The **wee** woolly witchie of whistlewood way. Jack Prelutsky.—WaW

Weeds
 Undefeated. R. Froman.—MoGp
 Weeds ("In the rough places") V. Worth.—WoM
 Weeds ("In the rough places") Valerie Worth.—WoM

The **weevil** ("Alfalfa, rice, and especially boll, the") Robert S. Oliver.—OlC

Wegant, Noemi
 Winter is tacked down.—HoMp

"A **weightless** balloon." Ann Atwood.—AtH

Welburn, Ron
 Percussions.—AdC

"**Welcome** be thou, heavenly king." Unknown.—BaC

"**Welcome** be ye that are here." Unknown.—BaC

"**Welcome,** Christmas, heel and toe." See Stocking song on Christmas eve

"**Well,** here you are." See Who ordered the broiled face.

"**Well** I'm going down the road." See Goofy song

"**We'll** play in the snow." See Snow

"**Well,** son, I'll tell you." See Mother to son

Wellington the skeleton. Dennis Lee.—LeN

Wells
 The grasshopper. D. McCord.—CoA—McO—WiP
 "The man from the woods." J. Ciardi.—HiS
 W is for well. W. J. Smith.—SmL

Wells, Carolyn
 The tutor.—WiP

Welte, Lou Ann
 Those last, late hours of Christmas eve.—LiPch

"The **wendigo.**" Ogden Nash.—BlC

Wendy in winter. Kaye Starbird.—StC

"**Went** to the corner." See Things

"**We're** an Africanpeople." See African poems

"**We're** going for a ride on the smelter's nose." See The long-nosed smelter

"**We're** hoping to be arrested." See Street demonstration

"**We're** sleeping in the woods." See Campfire

"**Were** you ever in Quebec." See Donkey riding

The **werewolf.** Jack Prelutsky.—PrN

Wesley-Smith, Peter
 "Arbuckle Jones."—CoPs—DuSn
 Nomenclature.—CoI
 The octopus.—DuSn
 The ombley gombley.—WaM
 The quinquaped jikes.—DuSn
 The ugstabuggle.—WaM

"**West** is the springtime." See Points of the compass

"The **west** wind plays a merry tune." See Wind music

Westrup, J. M.
 The poor snail.—CoA

The **westwardness** of everything. See Our stars come from Ireland

"**We've** been caught by the quick digesting Gink." See Quick trip

Wevill, David
 Birth of the foal. tr.—CoPh

Weygant, Noemi
 Winter is tacked down.—HoMp

The **whale** ("At every stroke his brazen fins do take") John Donne.—PaE

The **whale** ("Have you heard the whale sing") Lucy Gardner.—GaCb

Whale ("Rain, with a silver flail.") William Rose Benet.—PaE

Whale ("A whale is stout about the middle") Mary Ann Hoberman.—HoY—WiP

Whale ("When I swam underwater I saw a blue whale") William Jay Smith.—SmL

"A **whale** is stout about the middle" See Whale

Whalen, Philip
 Early spring.—HoMp
 For my father.—KhI

Whalers. See Whales and whaling

Whales and whaling
 Hale's lullaby. J. Yolen.—YoD
 The harpooning. T. Walker.—PaE
 The huge leviathan. E. Spenser.—PaE
 If you ever. Unknown.—WiP
 Jack was every inch a sailor. Unknown.—DoWh
 Leviathan ("Canst thou draw out leviathan with an hook, or his") From Job, Bible, Old Testament.—PaE
 Leviathan ("Leviathan drives the eyed prow of his face") P. Quennell.—PaE
 Moon whales. T. Hughes.—HuM
 Nate's song. J. Aiken.—AiS
 Tall stories. R. Gardner.—DuSn
 A thought. M. A. Hoberman.—HoY
 The whale ("At every stroke his brazen fins do take") J. Donne.—PaE
 The whale ("Have you heard the whale sing") L. Gardner.—GaCb

"**Whatever** it is, it's a passion." See Love in America

"**Whatever** you want on the moon." See Moony art

Whatif. Shel Silverstein.—SiL

"**What's** in there." Unknown.—WiP

"**What's** that." Florence Parry Heide.—WaM

"**What's** the good of a wagon." See The gold tinted dragon

"**What's** the good of breathing." See The frost pane

"**What's** the horriblest thing you've seen." Roy Fuller.—CoI

"**What's** the news of the day." Mother Goose.— TrGg

"**What's** your name." See Pudden Tame

Wheat
The golden boy. T. Hughes.—HuSs
A vegetable, I will not be. D. Whitewing.— FlA

"**Wheatfields** of chiffon." See Best of show

Wheatley, Phillis
On being brought from Africa to America.— PlG
To his excellency George Washington.—LiO

Wheelock, John Hall
Afternoon, Amagansett beach.—PaE
Herring-gull.—PaE

"**When.**" See True

"**When** a cricket chirps fast, it is hot." See Cricket

"**When** a friend calls to me from the road." See A time to talk

"**When** a great wave disturbs the ocean cold." See The cataclysm

"**When** a missile goes over the moon, I'm a guy." See Same old trick

"**When** active dinosaur children." See I spy tyrannosaurus

When all is done. Paul Laurence Dunbar.—BrI

"**When** all is done, and my last word is said." See When all is done

"**When** all is zed and done." See Z

When all the world is full of snow. N. M. Bodecker.—BoHh

"**When** Aunt Emily died, her husband would not look." See New England Protestant

"**When** black people are." A. B. Spellman.— AdC

"**When** brothers build a city." See Malcolm, a thousandth poem

"**When** brothers forget." Jill Witherspoon Boyer.—AdC

When candy was chocolate. William Jay Smith.—SmL

"**When** candy was chocolate and bread was white." See When candy was chocolate

"**When** cats run home and light is come." See The owl

"**When** Christ was born in Bethlehem." See One glorious star

When Christmas comes. Aileen Fisher.—BaC

"**When** Christmas-tide comes in like a bride." See The praise of Christmas

"**When** daddy." See Walking

"**When** daisies pied and violets blue." See Love's labour's lost

"**When** Daniel Boone goes by, at night." See Daniel Boone

"**When** descends on the Atlantic." See Seaweed

"**When** dreams like stars collide." See Lesson for dreamers

"**When** dusk is done." See Different dreams

"**When** Evan went to town from the farm." See The city and Evan

When father carves the duck. E. V. Wright.— CoPs

"**When** first I presented him to you." See Sharing

"**When** frost unlocks the last stiff leaf." See The phantom ice cream man

"**When** good King Arthur ruled this land." Mother Goose.—TrGg

"**When** Grandpa couldn't hoe or spade." See The gardener

"**When** he has dined, the man-eating tiger leaves." See Moon horrors

"**When** he takes a bath, the antelope." See Antelope

"**When** he's riding." See On the behavior of Rodney IV who travels in unusual contraptions

"**When** I am a man." Kwakiutl, tr. fr. the American Indian by Frank Boaz.—LiCc

"**When** I am bad, my father gets." See Patsy Doolin

"**When** I am in bed." See In bed

When I am me. Felice Holman.—HoBm

"**When** I am walking down the street." See New shoes

"**When** I asked the class, how many legs." See Legs

"**When** I climb up." See Drinking fountain

"**When** I fill in my coloring book." See My coloring book

"**When** I find out." See Revenge

"**When** I flop down." See My cat and I

"**When** I get to be a composer." See Daybreak in Alabama

"**When** I go walking in the fall." See Fall

"**When** I invite the giraffe to dine." See Giraffe

"**When** I lay me down to sleep." See Insomnia the gem of the ocean

"**When** I see a starfish." See The starfish

"**When** I see the dentist." See Tooth trouble

"**When** I stamp." See At the top of my voice

"**When** I swam underwater I saw a blue whale." See Whale

"**When** I tried." See The maze

"**When** I wake in the early mist." See Very early

"**When** I was a child." See Autobiographia literaria

"**When** I was a little boy, my mother kept me in." Mother Goose.—TrGg

"**When** I was a rider." See The names of things

"**When** I was but a little chap." See My wise old grandpapa

Who am I ("The trees ask me") Felice Holman.—HoA

"Who are you." See To Desi as Joe the smoky the lover of 115th street

"Who are you." Mother Goose.—LoG

Who can be born black. Mari Evans.—AdC

"Who can find a virtuous woman." See Proverbs, sel. Bible, Old Testament—Praise of a good woman

Who can say. David McCord.—McSu

Who cast my shadow, sels. Lilian Moore.— MoTs (Complete)
1. "I'm lumpish."
2. "Did an artist weave my."
3. "A shadow bird."

"Who comes here." Mother Goose.—TrGg— WiP

"Who could devise." See The shell

"Who does not love the juniper tree." See Juniper

Who ever sausage a thing. Unknown.—CoPs

"Who has a big and smiling mouth." See October fun

"Who has seen the wind." Christina Rossetti.— WiP

Who hasn't played gazintas. David McCord.— McO

"Who in the world would ever have guessed." See Easter eggs

"Who is first up." See Awake

"Who is my father in this world, in this house." See The Irish cliffs of Moher

Who is sad. Elizabeth Coatsworth.—WiP

"Who is sad and who is sorry." See Who is sad

"Who is that in the tall grasses singing." See Song for Naomi

"Who is the noblest beast you can name." See The horse

"Who is this." See The ghost of Caupolican

"Who killed Cock Robin." Mother Goose.—WiP

"Who knows." See Shoeshine men

"Who knows if the moon's." E. E. Cummings.—HiS

"Who lives on Neptune's nineteenth moon." See The nineteenth moon of Neptune beasts

Who ordered the broiled face. Shel Silverstein.—SiL

"Who said, peacock pie." See The song of the mad prince

"Who saw the petals." See The secret song

"Who says, but one month more." See Question

"Who shined shoes in Times Square." Lance Jeffers.—AdC

"Who so late." See At the garden gate

"Who tossed those golden coins." Kazue Mizumura.—MiF

"Who wanted to see how I wrote." See For Allan

"Who wants a birthday." David McCord.— McO

"Who wants my jellyfish." See The jellyfish

"Who wants to go to the poultry show." See The poultry show

Who, where. Lillian Morrison.—MoW

"Who would be." See The merman

"Who would marry a mineral." Lillian Morrison.—MoW

"Who would suspect, or even know." See A vegetable, I will not be

"Whodunit." See Spilt milk, whodunit

Whodunnit. Eve Merriam.—MeR

"Whoever shall this trumpet blow." See Jack the giant killer—Giant chants

"Whoever's the new baby around here." See New baby

"Who'll solve my problem, asks the moon." See Pi in the sky

Whooo. Lillian Moore.—WiP

"Whooooo." See The owl cow

Who's in. Elizabeth Fleming.—SaM—WiP

"Who's killed the leaves." See Leaves

"Who's that great vandal of a child you carry." See Dangerous journey

"Who's that ringing at the front door bell." Mother Goose.—WiP

"Who's that tickling my back, said the wall." See The tickle rhyme

Whose boo is whose. X. J. Kennedy.—BrIt— KeP—WaGp

"Whosever room this is should be ashamed." See Messy room

Why ("Why do apricots look like eggs") William Jay Smith.—SmL

"Why are all of these flowers." Kazue Mizumura.—MiF

"Why are our ancestors." See Ancestors

"Why are you called butterfly." See To a tiger swallowtail butterfly

"Why can't I dig with my spoon and make." See Trouble with dinner

"Why did all manly gifts in Webster fail." Ralph Waldo Emerson.—PlG

"Why did the woman want to kill one dog." See A village tale

"Why do apricots look like eggs." See Why

"Why do bells for Christmas sing." See Song

"Why do peas roll off the fork." See Peas

"Why do two and two make four." See That's the way it is

"Why do we walk every street, every block." See The thing

"Why do you lose things this way." See Big question

"Why does a chicken cross the road." See The riddle

"Why does the sea moan evermore." See By the sea

"Why fades a dream." Paul Laurence Dunbar.—BrI

"Why, I often wondered." See A crust of bread

"Why, is the sky." See Questions at night

"Why is there more." See The door

"Why, sit down, so I let myself settle." See A visit to the gingerbread house

"Willow buds come early." See Pussy willows
Willow trees
  Pussy willows ("Willow buds come early") A. Fisher.—FiO
  Song ("The feathers of the willow") R. W. Dixon.—PaB
Willson, Dixie
  The mist and all.—PaI
Wilner, Isabel
  The dodo.—WiP
  The prudent rodent.—WiP
  Small dirge.—WiP
Wilson, Keith
  Isleta Indian girl.—LuZ
Wind
  "Again and again." K. Mizumura.—MiF
  Among the millet. A. Lampman.—DoWh
  The apple. A. Adoff.—AdE
  "Arthur O'Bower has broken his band." Mother Goose.—TrGg
  Blow, wind. N. Farber.—FaS
  Clouds ("White sheep, white sheep") C. Rossetti.—PaI
  "The day we die." Unknown.—LuZ
  "Days that the wind takes over." K. Kuskin.—KuD
  Echoes. W. De La Mare.—PaE
  Fall wind ("Everything is on the run") A. Fisher.—FiO
  Fall wind ("I scarcely felt a breath of air") M. Hillert.—HoMp
  "In Fibruary, any wind's day." D. Orgel.—OrM
  In the wind. A. Fisher.—FiO
  Like a giant in a towel. D. Lee.—WaG
  Listen ("Isn't a breeze") A. Fisher.—FiO
  Moon wind. T. Hughes.—HuM
  "The moon's the north wind's cooky." V. Lindsay.—PaI—RuM
  Motorway reflection. J. Aiken.—AiS
  The north wind doth blow. Mother Goose.—CoA
  Note ("Straw, feathers, dust") W. Stafford.—MoGp
  O clouds. E. Coatsworth.—WiP
  "Oceanic windy dawn." From Autumn nature notes. T. Hughes.—HuSs
  October wind. D. McCord.—McO
  Out in the winter wind. A. Fisher.—FiO
  Partners. L. Moore.—MoTs
  A peck of gold. R. Frost.—HiS
  Poem. A. R. Ammons.—MoGp
  The quiet shining sun. A. Fisher.—FiO
  Rags. J. Thurman.—ThFo
  Rain songs. P. L. Dunbar.—BrI
  Roses ("Oh, wind of the spring-time, oh, free wind of May") P. L. Dunbar.—BrI
  The sand rose. L. Norris.—NoM
  Snow on the wind. A. Fisher.—FiO
  Song ("A spirit haunts the year's last hours") A. Tennyson.—PaB
  Storm ("In a storm") A. Stoutenberg.—MoGp
  Strange wind. S. Silverstein.—SiL
  Tornado season. A. Stoutenberg.—MoGp
  Turning the corner. J. Thurman.—ThFo
  "Who has seen the wind." C. Rossetti.—WiP
  The wind ("Blow, wind, blow today") S. Ward.—SaM
  The wind ("In spring, the wind's a sneaky wind") K. Starbird.—StC
  The wind ("Wind in the garden") D. McCord.—McO
  Wind ("Wind is to show") L. Feeney.—PaI
  The wind ("The wind, it is a ghostly hand") N. Carey.—SaM
  The wind and the moon. G. MacDonald.—MoF
  Wind circles. A. Fisher.—FiO
  "The wind has such a rainy sound." C. Rossetti.—WiP
  The wind has wings. Unknown.—DoWh
  "The wind I love the best." From The spring wind. C. Zolotow.—HoMp
  Wind music. A. Fisher.—FiO
  "The wind sweeps away." K. Mizumura.—MiF
  A windy day. A. Young.—SaM
  Windy nights ("Whenever the moon and stars are set") R. L. Stevenson.—CoPh--RuM
  Worms and the wind. C. Sandburg.—LuZ—WiP
The wind ("Blow, wind, blow today") Sherry Ward.—SaM
The wind ("In spring, the wind's a sneaky wind") Kaye Starbird.—StC
The wind ("Wind in the garden") David McCord.—McO
Wind ("Wind is to show") Leonard Feeney.—PaI
The wind ("The wind, it is a ghostly hand") N. Carey.—SaM
The wind and the moon. George MacDonald.—MoF
"Wind and wave and star and sea." See Song
"The wind bit hard at Valley Forge one Christmas." See Washington monument by night
Wind circles. Aileen Fisher.—FiO
"Wind-flicked and ruddy her young body glowed." See Sea-change
"The wind has such a rainy sound." Christina Rossetti.—WiP
The wind has wings. Unknown, tr. fr. the Eskimo by Raymond De Coccola and Paul King.—DoWh
"The wind I love the best." See The spring wind
"Wind in the garden." See The wind
Wind in the willows, sels. Kenneth Grahame Carol.—BaC
  "Villagers all, this frosty tide."—LiFch
  The song of Mr. Toad.—WiP
"The wind is out in its rage to-night." See The fisher child's lullaby
"The wind is standing still and we are moving." See Motorway reflection
"Wind is to show." See Wind

The turn of the road. J. Stephens.—HiS

A visit to the gingerbread house. From A lot of limericks. X. J. Kennedy.—KeP

The two witches ("O sixteen hundred and ninety-one") R. Graves.—HiS

Two witches ("There was a witch") A. Resnikoff.—BrIt

The wee woolly witchie of whistlewood way. J. Prelutsky.—WaW

"What our dame bids us do." From The masque of queens. B. Johnson.—LiO

What the gray cat sings. A. Guiterman.—WiP

Wicked witch admires herself. X. J. Kennedy.—KeP

Wicked witch's kitchen. X. J. Kennedy.—BrIt—WaW

Wild witches' ball. J. Prelutsky.—WaW

The witch ("She comes by night, in fearsome flight") J. Prelutsky.—PrN

Witch baseball. S. Kroll.—WaW

A witch flies by. E. H. Sechrist.—BrIt

Witch goes shopping. L. Moore.—WaW

The witch in the wintry wood. A. Fisher.—BrIt

The witch, the witch. E. Farjeon.—BrIt—WaW

Witch, witch. R. Fyleman.—BeR—WiP

Witches' menu. S. Nikolay.—BrIt—WaW

The witches' ride. K. Kuskin.—KuD—WaW

Witches' spells. From Queen Zixi of Ix. L. F. Baum.—WaW

The witch's balloon. S. J. Graham.—DuSn

Witch's broom. D. McCord.—McSu

Witch's broom notes. D. McCord.—BrIt—McO

The witch's cat. I. Serraillier.—HiS

The witch's garden. L. Moore.—WiP

"Witches flying past on broomsticks." See Halloween

Witches' menu. Sonja Nikolay.—BrIt—WaW

The witches' ride. Karla Kuskin.—KuDs—WaW

Witches' spells. See Queen Zixi of Ix

The witch's balloon. S. J. Graham.—DuSn

Witch's broom. David McCord.—McSu

Witch's broom notes. David McCord.—BrIt—McO

The witch's cat. Ian Serraillier.—HiS

The witch's garden. Lilian Moore.—WiP

"With a sadness curtained." See The maiden

"With arms swinging, a tremendous skater." See Spring nature notes

"With company coming." See Thanksgiving dinner

"With hearts revived in conceit, new land and trees they eye." See Good news from New England

"With light enough on clean fresh fallen snow." See Trinity Place

"With many a scowl." See Troll trick

With my foot in my mouth. Dennis Lee.—LeN

"With shoes on." See Going barefoot

"With the apple in his strength." See The defenders

With the door open. David Ignatow.—LuZ

"With the frenzied wind." Kazue Mizumura.—MiF

With the lark. Paul Laurence Dunbar.—BrI

"With the stars." See For the coming year

"With the wind at my back." See Turning the corner

"With two 60's stuck on the scoreboard." See Foul shot

Wither, George

Our joyful'st feast.—BaC

Witherup, William

Crows.—JaPp

"Within a London garret high." See The garret

"Within that porch, across the way." See The cat

"Without a pen." See Wind circles

"Without the door let sorrow lie." See Christmas pies

"Withouten you." See Little elegy

The witnesses ("In ocean's wide domains") Henry Wadsworth Longfellow.—PlG

The witnesses ("Stowaway in a fold") X. J. Kennedy.—LiPch

The witnesses, sel. Clive Sansom

The innkeeper's wife.—LiPch

Wives. See Married life

The wizard ("The wizard, watchful, waits alone") Jack Prelutsky.—PrN

"The wizard, watchful, waits alone." See The wizard

Wizards

"Bellowed the ogre." L. Moore.—WaG

The cat and the wizard. D. Lee.—LeN

The elf singing. W. Allingham.—PaI

Merlin & the snake's egg. L. Norris.—NoM

The wizard ("The wizard, watchful, waits alone") J. Prelutsky.—PrN

Wizzle. David McCord.—McO

"A wolf." See Night

The wolf. John Gardner.—GaCb

"The wolf also shall dwell with the lamb." See Isaiah

"The wolf is a very good watchdog, it's true." See The wolf

Wolfe, Humbert

Green candles.—HiS—WiP

Wollner, Paul

I love the world.—PaI

Wolny, P.

Harmonica man.—JaPp

Words, like spiders.—JaPp

Wolves

The burrow wolf. T. Hughes.—HuM

A choosy wolf. X. J. Kennedy.—KeP

Father wolf's midnight song. J. Yolen.—YoD

Night ("A wolf") Unknown.—MoGp

The train dogs. P. Johnson.—CoG

The wolf. J. Gardner.—GaCb

The wolves ("Last night knives flashed, LeChien cried") G. Kinnell.—LuZ

The wolves ("Last night knives flashed, LeChien cried") Galway Kinnell.—LuZ

Woman me. Maya Angelou.—AnO

Misnomer. E. Merriam.—MeR
More or less. D. McCord.—McO
Mystery. D. McCord.—McSu
Only. D. McCord.—McO
Ough. D. McCord.—McO
Parking lot full. E. Merriam.—MeR
The parrot. E. Lucie-Smith.—HiS
Poem, a reminder. R. Graves.—LuZ
Poemsicle. S. Silverstein.—SiL
Polyglot. E. Merriam.—MeR
Portmanteaux. E. Merriam.—MeW
The possessors. L. Morrison.—MoSr
Possibilities. F. Holman.—HoA
Postcards. E. Merriam.—MeR
A project for freight trains. D. Young.—LuZ
Ptarmigan. D. McCord.—McO
"Puptents and pebbles." W. J. Smith.—SmL
The purist. O. Nash.—BlC
Puzzling. W. Cole.—CoA
Queer story of the fowse or fox. D.
  McCord.—McO
Rapid reading. D. McCord.—McO
Rathers. D. McCord.—McSu
Refugee in America. L. Hughes.—LiCc
Rhymes ("Two respectable rhymes") Y. Y.
  Segal.—DoWh
Sailing, sailing. L. Morrison.—MoSr
Scat, scitten. D. McCord.—McO
Should all of this come true. X. J. Kennedy.—
  KeP
Simple song. M. Piercy.—MaP
Singular indeed. D. McCord.—McO
Snail ("This sticky trail") D. McCord.—McO
Some quarks have a strange flavor. L.
  Morrison.—MoO
Sometimes. D. McCord.—McO
Speaking the poem. L. Morrison.—MoW
Spike spoke spook. D. McCord.—McO
The suspense of the coming word. L.
  Morrison.—MoO
"Take a word like cat." K. Kuskin.—KuD
Ten twice. D. McCord.—McO
Those double z's. D. McCord.—McSu
"Thoughts that were put into words." K.
  Kuskin.—KuD
Three percussion pieces. L. Morrison.—MoW
Timely. B. Giles.—DuSn
Twogether. E. Merriam.—MeR
Un-negative. E. Merriam.—MeR
The unwritten. W. S. Merwin.—LuZ
Up from down under. D. McCord.—McO
Verses versus verses. M. Bell.—KhI
What am I up to. D. McCord.—McO
What did. S. Silverstein.—SiL
What is a rhyme. E. Merriam.—MeW
When monkeys eat bananas. D. McCord.—
  McO
When the wine was gone. A. Aubert.—AdC
"Word face." L. Morrison.—MoW
Word music. D. McCord.—McSu
A word or two on Levinia. D. McCord.—
  McO
A word or two with you. E. Merriam.—MeW
Words, like spiders. P. Wolny.—JaPp

"A worthless article." L. Morrison.—MoW
Writing while my father dies. L. Pastan.—
  JaPp
"You mustn't call it hopsichord." D.
  McCord.—McO
Young Sammy. D. McCord.—McO
Your eyes have their silence. G. W. Barrax.—
  AdC
Words from an old Spanish carol. Ruth
  Sawyer.—LiPch
Words in the mourning time, sel. Robert
  Hayden
    "For King, for Robert Kennedy."—AdC
Words, like spiders. P. Wolny.—JaPp
Wordsworth, William
  After the storm. See Resolution and
    independence
  "Behold the child among his newborn
    blisses." See Ode: Intimations of
    immortality from recollections of early
    childhood
  Daffodils, sel.
      "I wandered lonely as a cloud."—PaB
  "Earth fills her lap with pleasures of her
    own." See Ode: Intimations of immortality
    from recollections of early childhood
  The excursion, sel.
      "I have seen."—PaE
  "For thou art with me here upon the banks."
    See Lines composed a few miles above
    Tintern Abbey
  "I have seen." See The excursion
  "I wandered lonely as a cloud." See Daffodils
  Lines composed a few miles above Tintern
    Abbey, sel.
      "For thou art with me here upon the
        banks."—PlL
  Ode: Intimations of immortality from
    recollections of early childhood, sels.
      V. "Our birth is but a sleep and a
        forgetting."—PlL
      VI. "Earth fills her lap with pleasures of
        her own."—PlL
      VII. "Behold the child among his new
        born blisses."—PlL
      VIII. "Thou, whose exterior semblance
        doth belie."—PlL
  "Our birth is but a sleep and a forgetting."
    See Ode: Intimations of immortality from
    recollections of early childhood
  Resolution and independence, sel.
      After the storm.—SaM
  "Thou, whose exterior semblance doth
    belie." See Ode: Intimations of immortality
    from recollections of early childhood
Wordsworth, William (about)
  "The child is father to the man." G. M.
    Hopkins.—PlL
Work
  "At quitting time." R. Sund.—LuZ
  Burying ground by the ties. A. MacLeish.—
    PlG
  The foundations of American industry. D.
    Hall.—PlG

"**Worlds** and words." See Fantasy, for Jennie
The **world's** best hopper. Kaye Starbird.—StC
The **worm** ("Don't ask me how he managed")
    Raymond Souster.—DoWh
Worm ("Some people think a worm is rude")
    Dennis Lee.—LeG
Worm ("Squiggly wiggly wriggly jiggly higgly
    piggly worm") Mary Ann Hoberman.—WiP
Worm ("That lonely worm upon the lawn")
    David McCord.—McSu
Worms. See also Caterpillars; Centipedes
    Earthworms ("Garden soil") V. Worth.—WoM
    "Fat father robin." D. McCord.—McO
    "It's such a shock, I almost screech." W.
        Cole.—CoPs
    Mother worm's hum. J. Yolen.—YoD
    "Night crawler." N. M. Bodecker.—BoHh
    Old Shellover. W. De La Mare.—WiP
    Willie ate a worm. J. Prelutsky.—PrRh
    The worm ("Don't ask me how he
        managed") R. Souster.—DoWh
    Worm ("Some people think a worm is rude")
        D. Lee.—LeG
    Worm ("Squiggly wiggly wriggly jiggly higgly
        piggly worm") M. A. Hoberman.—WiP
    Worm ("That lonely worm upon the lawn")
        D. McCord.—McSu
    Worms and the wind. C. Sandburg.—LuZ—
        WiP
Worms and the wind. Carl Sandburg.—LuZ—
    WiP
"**Worms** would rather be worms." See Worms
    and the wind
"**Wormy** apples at the grocery." See Eco right
The **worst.** Shel Silverstein.—CoI
Worth, Valerie
    Acorn.—WoM
    Back yard.—WoSm
    Barefoot.—WoSm
    Bell.—WoSm
    Cat bath.—WoSm
    Caterpillar.—WoM
    Christmas lights.—LiPch—WoM
    Christmas ornaments.—LiPch
    Clock.—WiP
    Coins.—WiP
    Compass ("According to")—WoSm
    The cow.—WiP
    Crab.—WoM
    Daisies.—JaPp
    Dinosaurs.—CoDb—WoM
    Door.—WoSm
    Earthworms.—WoM
    Egg.—WoSm
    Fairy fashion.—WaFp
    Fireworks.—LiCc—WoM
    Flamingo.—WoM
    Frog.—CoA
    Garbage.—WoSm
    Haunted house.—BrIt—WoM
    Honeycomb.—WoSm
    Horse.—WoSm
    Hose.—WoM
    Kite.—WoSm

    Kitten.—WoM
    Lawnmower.—WoM
    Lions.—WoM
    Magnet.—MoGp—WoM
    Magnifying glass.—WoM
    Mice.—WoSm
    Mosquito.—WoM
    Mushroom.—WoSm
    Pail.—WoSm
    Pigeons.—WoSm
    Pumpkin.—BrIt—LiCc—WoM
    Rags.—WoSm
    Roadside.—WoSm
    Rocks ("They say no")—WoSm
    Rosebush.—WoSm
    Safety pin.—WoM
    Sea lions.—MoGp—WoM
    Shoes.—WoM
    Sidewalks.—WoM
    Slug.—WoSm
    Snow.—WoSm
    Soap bubble.—WoM
    Sparrow.—WoM
    Stars.—WoSm
    Sun.—MoGp—WiP
    Sweets.—WoSm
    The tiger.—MoGp
    Toad.—WoM
    Tom.—WoSm
    Turtle.—WoSm
    Weeds.—WoM
"A **worthless** article." Lillian Morrison.—MoW
Wotton, Sir Henry
    On a bank as I sat fishing.—PaB
"**Wouldn't** it be fun." See Walk at night
"**Wouldn't** it be funny." Pixie O'Harris.—DuSn
"**Wouldn't** you love." See Lasagna
"**Wouldn't** you think." See All that sky
The **wound.** N. Scott Momaday.—MoGd
"The **wound** gaped open." See The wound
The **wounded** cupid. Robert Herrick.—LiO
The **wozzit.** Jack Prelutsky.—PrS
The **wreath.** Paul Engle.—BaC
Wrens
    The noisy wrens. A. Fisher.—FiO
Wright, E. V.
    When father carves the duck.—CoPs
Wright, Helen M.
    Golden grain.—CoPh
Wright, James
    A blessing.—FlA
    Lying in a hammock at William Duffy's farm
        in Pine Island, Minnesota.—FlA
    Two postures beside a fire.—PlL
Wright, Judith
    Legend.—HiS
Wrimples. Jack Prelutsky.—PrS
Writ on the eve of my 32nd birthday. Gregory
    Corso.—KhI
"**Write** about a radish." Karla Kuskin.—KuD
Write me a verse. David McCord.—McO

X

Y

The yeti. J. Gardner.—GaCb
"Yickity-yackity, yickity-yak." See The yak
"Yolande the panda." Nikki Giovanni.—GiV
Yolen, Jane
  The aardwort.—YoH
  The alligate.—YoH
  The bluffalo.—YoH
  The canterpillar.—YoH
  Caterpillar's lullaby.—YoD
  The centerpede.—YoH
  Crazy quilt.—HeB
  The crocodial.—YoH
  The dinosore.—YoH
  Dragon night.—YoD
  The dwarf to her child.—YoD
  The edgehog.—YoH
  The fanger.—YoH
  Father wolf's midnight song.—YoD
  The fax.—YoH
  The giant to his child.—YoD
  Grandpa bear's lullaby.—YoD
  Hale's lullaby.—YoD
  Homework.—HeB
  Mermaid's lullaby.—YoD
  Mother cat's purr.—YoD
  Mother owl's song.—YoD
  Mother worm's hum.—YoD
  The octopie.—YoH
  Papa bantam's goodnight.—YoD
  The piguana.—YoH
  The porcupin.—YoH
  The pythong.—YoH
  Shepherd's night count.—YoD
  The shirk.—YoH
  The shlepard.—YoH
  The skank.—YoH
  The slummings.—YoH
  The tigirth.—YoH
  The troll to her children.—YoD
  The tuner fish.—YoH
  Turtle sings an egg song.—YoD
  The walrust.—YoH
  Wild child's lament.—YoD
Yolka, sel. Marguerita Rudolph
  "What merriment, what merriment."—BaC

Yom Kippur
  Yom Kippur, fasting. R. Whitman.—LiO
Yom Kippur, fasting. Ruth Whitman.—LiO
Yonder. Richard Eberhart.—PlG
"Yonder they are coming." See It is mine, this
  country wide
"Yoohoo, yoohoo." See The Great Lakes suite—
  Lake Huron
You and me. Nancy Dingman Watson.—WaB
You and me and P. B. Shelley. Ogden Nash.—
  BlC
"You are." Beatrice Schenk De Regniers.—ReB
"You are." See Overheard in a bubble chamber
"You are blind, you see." See Ernesto Maestas
  instructs Ynocencia Saavedra in the art of
  acting
"You are French, je suis." See Innuendo

"You are, in 1925, my father." See Rowing in
  Lincoln Park
"You are lost in the desolate forest." See The
  will o' the wisp
"You are not pregnant, said the man." See All
  the little animals
"You are old, Father William, the young man
  said." See Alice's adventures in wonderland
"You are small and intense." See To a child
  running with outstretched arms in Canyon
  de Chelly
"You are you." See You, tu
"You ask for a civilized animal." See The
  African wild dog
"You built the new court house, Spoon River."
  See Benjamin Franklin Hazard
"You can go in the stall, it's a mare and her
  first colt." See Unclaimed
"You can talk about yer sheep dorgs, said the
  man." See Daley's dorg Wattle
"You can't catch me." See Catching-song a play
  rhyme
You can't get rags from ragweed. Kaye
  Starbird.—StC
"You can't race me, said Johnny the hare." See
  The hare and the tortoise
"You clumsy bumbling beast of night." See
  June bug
"You come." See On the naming day
"You find out a lot about friends." See Friend
"You, Genoese mariner." W. S. Merwin.—PlG
"You get what you eat with your feet when
  you hunt." See Dragonfly
"You greedy starlings." Betsy Maestro.—MaFp
"You had to go to funerals." Alice Walker.—
  LuZ
"You have a magic carpet." See Magic carpet
"You have anti-freeze in the car." See Solstice
  song
"You have seen the world, you have seen the
  zoo." See Swan
"You, hiding there in your words." See The
  book
"You know no Persian words." See From the
  Persian
"You know the word cathedral." See The look
  and sound of words
"You lie now in many coffins." See For
  Malcolm, after Mecca
You light. Juan Ramón Jiménez.—BaC
"You may hang your hat on the nose of the
  rhinoceros." See Rhinoceros
"You may leave the clam on the ocean's floor."
  See It's all the same to the clam
"You mean, if I'd keep my room clean." See
  Order
"You might think I was in the way." See So
  run along and play
"You must remember." See Circuit breaker
"You must wake and call me early, call me
  early." See The May queen
"You mustn't call it hopsichord." David
  McCord.—McO
"You said." See Poem

"**You** say you want to fight me." See Bloody
Bill
"**You** see this Christmas tree all silver gold."
See Come Christmas
"**You** should never squeeze a weasel." See
Don't ever seize a weasel by the tail
You spotted snakes. See A midsummer night's
dream
"**You** spotted snakes, with double tongue." See
A midsummer night's dream—You spotted
snakes
"**You** strange, astonish'd-looking, angle-faced."
See To fish
You take the pilgrims, just give me the
progress. Loyd Rosenfield.—BrO
You too lie down. Dennis Lee.—LeN
You, tu. Charlotte Pomerantz.—PoT
"**You** were always a one to." See Foibles
"**You** were the mother last time." Mary Ann
Hoberman.—CoI
"**You**'ll find me in the laundromat, just me and
shirts and stuff." See Laundromat
"**You**'ll find whenever the New Year comes."
Unknown.—LiCc
Young, Al
For poets.—AdC—LuZ
Identities.—KhI
Myself when I am real.—AdC
The song turning back into itself.—AdC
Young, Andrew
Christmas day.—BaC
The echoing cliff.—PaE
Last snow.—SaM
The shepherd's hut.—WaGp
A windy day.—SaM
"A **young** Apollo, golden haired." See Youth
Young, David
A project for freight trains.—LuZ
The **young** dead soldiers. Archibald
MacLeish.—LiO
"The **young** dead soldiers do not speak." See
The young dead soldiers
The **young** lady of Lynn. Unknown.—WiP
"A **young** man from old Terre Haute." William
Jay Smith.—SmL
The **young** ones, flip side. James A. Emanuel.—
JaPp
"A **young** person of precious precocity." See
On reading, four limericks
The **young** puppy. A. A. Milne.—CoG
Young Sammy. David McCord.—McO
"**Young** Sammy, when he was no more." See
Young Sammy
Young soul. Imamu Amiri Baraka.—AdC
"**Young** Stephen has a young friend John." See
Sailor John
"**Your** absence has gone through me." See
Separation
"**Your** archival voice." See The music
"**Your** birthday comes to tell me this." E. E.
Cummings.—LiCc
"**Your** dog, what dog, you mean it, that." See
Suzie's new dog

Your eyes have their silence. Gerald W.
Barrax.—AdC
"**Your** eyes have their silence in giving words."
See Your eyes have their silence
"**Your** hand." See Love letters, unmailed
"**Your** lips were so laughing." See Langston
blues
"**Your** mother." Sam Cornish.—AdC
"**Your** skin like dawn." See Passing time
"**Your** sleep will be." See Caterpillar's lullaby
"**Your** smile." See After the rain
"**Your** smile, delicate." See Woman me
"**Your** spoken words are roses fine and sweet."
See Roses and pearls
"**Your** voice sister." See Mississippi born
"**You**'re in the mood for freaky food." See
Wicked witch's kitchen
"**You**'re Mrs. Cobble and I'm Mrs. Frome."
Mary Ann Hoberman.—HoY
"**You**'re not supposed to roast a ghost." See The
haunted oven
"**You**'re old enough to know, my son." See
Speak clearly
"**You**'re right." See In the library
"**Yours** is the hair of a golden girl." See
October
Youth. See also Boys and boyhood; Childhood
recollections; Girls and girlhood; Youth and
age
   "Our birth is but a sleep and a forgetting."
   From Ode: Intimations of immortality from
   recollections of early childhood. W.
   Wordsworth.—PlL
Youth ("A young Apollo, golden haired")
Frances Cornford.—JaPp
Youth and age. See also Birthdays; Childhood
recollections; Old age; Youth
   The act. W. C. Williams.—LuZ
   April inventory. W. D. Snodgrass.—KhI
   Aunt Roberta. E. Greenfield.—GrH
   Birdfoot's grampa. J. Bruchac.—MoGp
   Burning the steaks in the rain, reflections on
   a 46th birthday. R. Dana.—KhI
   "Children's children are the crown of old
   men." From Proverbs, Bible, Old
   Testament.—PlL
   The chinese checker players. R. Brautigan.—
   MoGp
   The cultivation of Christmas trees. T. S.
   Eliot.—LiO
   The dark ("I feared the darkness as a boy")
   R. Fuller.—HiD
   Envoy. E. Dowson.—JaPp
   Father's voice. W. Stafford.—PlL
   Frozen dream. S. Silverstein.—SiL
   Grandfather ("Each year, as spring returns")
   J. Aiken.—AiS
   Grandmother, rocking. E. Merriam.—MeR
   Harmonica man. P. Wolny.—JaPp
   Jamming with the band at the VFW. D.
   Bottoms.—KhI
   John Anderson my jo. R. Burns.—PlL
   The legacy. M. Piercy.—KhI

The little boy and the old man. S.
  Silverstein.—SiL
Loneliness ("I was about to go, and said so")
  B. Jenkins.—MaP
Make merry. D. McCord.—McO
Nelly Myers. A. R. Ammons.—KhI
New Mexican mountain. R. Jeffers.—PlG
The niece at the deathbed. T. Spencer.—PlL
No present like the time. D. McCord.—McO
Old man playing with children. J. C.
  Ransom.—PlL
Old people. M. C. Livingston.—LiWt
On reaching forty. M. Angelou.—AnO
Outing. J. Aiken.—AiS
Reports of midsummer girls. R. Lattimore.—
  JaPp
Sestina. E. Bishop.—PlL
The song of the old mother. W. B. Yeats.—
  PlL
To the veterans of the Abraham Lincoln
  brigade. G. Taggard.—LiO
Two postures beside a fire. J. Wright.—PlL
Vacation time. N. Giovanni.—GiV
Writ on the eve of my 32nd birthday. G.
  Corso.—KhI
"You are old, Father William, the young man
  said." From Alice's adventures in
  wonderland. L. Carroll.—WiP
The young ones, flip side. J. A. Emanuel.—
  JaPp
Youth ("A young Apollo, golden haired") F.
  Cornford.—JaPp
"You've got another love." See Poor girl
"You've no need to light a night light."
  Unknown.—RuM
Yuasa, Nobuyuki
  "Both my child." tr.—LiO
  "Crawl, laugh." tr.—LiO
  "For a fresh start." See Oraga Haru
  Oraga Haru, sels.
    "For a fresh start." tr.—LiO
    "Person after person." tr.—LiO
  "Person after person." See Oraga Haru
Yukon. See Polar regions
The yule log. Robert Herrick.—BaC
"Yule, yule, yule." Unknown.—BaC
"Yule, yule, yule, my belly's full." Unknown.—
  BaC
"Yule's come and yule's gone." Unknown, fr.
  the Scottish.—BaC
Yvonne
  Deborah Lee.—AdC
  Emma.—AdC
  Where she was not born.—AdC

Z

Z. David McCord.—McO
Z is for zebu. William Jay Smith.—SmL
Zachary Zed. James Reeves.—BrO
"Zachary Zed was the last man." See Zachary
  Zed
Zebra ("Are zebras black with broad white
  stripes") William Jay Smith.—SmL

Zebra ("White sun") Judith Thurman.—MoGp—
  ThFo
The zebra ("The zebra is of course") John
  Gardner.—GaCb
The zebra dun. Unknown.—CoPh
"The zebra is of course." See The zebra
Zebra question. Shel Silverstein.—SiL
Zebras
  "When the donkey saw the zebra."
    Unknown.—WiP
  Zebra ("Are zebras black with broad white
    stripes") W. J. Smith.—SmL
  Zebra ("White sun") J. Thurman.—MoGp—
    ThFo
  The zebra ("The zebra is of course") J.
    Gardner.—GaCb
  Zebra question. S. Silverstein.—SiL
The zebu ("Although it's hard to understand")
  Robert S. Oliver.—OlC
Zebus
  Z is for zebu. W. J. Smith.—SmL
  The zebu ("Although it's hard to
    understand") R. S. Oliver.—OlC
Zen and the art of golf with cart. Lillian
  Morrison.—MoSr
Zimmer in grade school. Paul Zimmer.—KhI
Zimmer, Paul
  Zimmer in grade school.—KhI
  Zimmer's head thudding against the
    blackboard.—JaPp
Zimmer's head thudding against the
  blackboard. Paul Zimmer.—JaPp
Zizzy bee. Nancy Dingman Watson.—WaB
Zolotow, Charlotte
  Autumn.—HoMp
  A dog.—CoG
  In bed.—HeB
  "No one would believe."—MoGp
  So will I.—HoBm
  The spring wind, sel.
    "The wind I love the best."—HoMp
  "The wind I love the best." See The spring
    wind
The zombie. Jack Prelutsky.—PrH
Zoo ("Evolution dies out") Michael Allin.—LuZ
Zoo manners. Eileen Mathias.—CoA
"Zoom." See Three percussion pieces
Zoos
  Anthropoids. M. A. Hoberman.—HoY
  The carcajou and the kincajou. O. Nash.—
    BlC
  The eagle. J. Gardner.—GaCb
  The elephant. J. Gardner.—GaCb
  "Every Fibruary zoo day." D. Orgel.—OrM
  Lions ("Bars, wire") V. Worth.—WoM
  Nimpkin and the animals. D. Lee.—LeN
  Sea lions. V. Worth.—MoGp—WoM
  "The spangled pandemonium." P. Brown.—
    WaM
  Swan. W. J. Smith.—SmL
  Tails. M. C. Livingston.—CoA
  To see the rabbit. A. Brownjohn.—WiP
  Wouldn't it be funny. P. O'Harris.—DuSn
  Zoo ("Evolution dies out") M. Allin.—LuZ
  Zoo manners. E. Mathias.—CoA

DIRECTORY OF PUBLISHERS
AND DISTRIBUTORS

Addison-Wesley. Addison-Wesley Publishing Company Inc., Reading, MA 01867

Atheneum. Atheneum Publishers, 597 Fifth Ave., New York, NY 10017

Bradbury. Bradbury Press Inc., 2 Overhill Rd., Scarsdale, NY 10583

Clarion. Clarion Books, 52 Vanderbilt Ave., New York, NY 10017

Collins. William Collins Sons & Company Ltd., 14 St. James's Place, London SW1A 1PS England

Coward. Coward-McCann / Putnam Publishing Group, 200 Madison Ave., New York, NY 10016

Crowell. Thomas Y. Crowell / Harper & Row Publishers Inc., 10 East 53rd St., New York, NY 10022

Delacorte. Delacorte Press / Dell Publishing Company Inc., 1 Dag Hammarskjold Plaza, 245 East 47th St., New York, NY 10017

Dell. Dell Publishing Company Inc., 1 Dag Hammarskjold Plaza, 245 East 47th St., New York, NY 10017

Dial. The Dial Press / Dell Publishing Company Inc., 1 Dag Hammarskjold Plaza, 245 East 47th St., New York, NY 10017

Dutton. E. P. Dutton Inc., 2 Park Ave., New York, NY 10016

Farrar. Farrar Straus & Giroux Inc., 19 Union Square West, New York, NY 10003

Follett. Follett Publishing Company, 1010 West Washington Blvd., Chicago, IL 60607

Four Winds. Four Winds Press / Scholastic Inc., 730 Broadway, New York, NY 10003

Godine. David R. Godine Publisher Inc., 306 Dartmouth St., Boston, MA 02116

Greenwillow. Greenwillow Books / William Morrow & Company Inc., 105 Madison Ave., New York, NY 10016

Harcourt. Harcourt Brace Jovanovich Inc., 757 Third Ave., New York, NY 10017

Harper. Harper & Row Publishers Inc., 10 East 53rd St., New York, NY 10022

Holiday House. Holiday House Inc., 18 East 53rd St., New York, NY 10022

Holt. Holt Rinehart & Winston General Books, 521 Fifth Ave., New York, NY 10175

Houghton. Houghton Mifflin Company, 1 Beacon St., Boston, MA 02108

Knopf. Alfred A. Knopf Inc., 201 East 50th St., New York, NY 10022

Lippincott. J. B. Lippincott Company, East Washington Square, Philadelphia, PA 19105

Little. Little Brown & Company, 34 Beacon St., Boston, MA 02106

Lothrop. Lothrop Lee & Shepard / William Morrow & Company Inc., 105 Madison Ave., New York, NY 10016

McGraw-Hill. McGraw-Hill Inc., 1221 Avenue of the Americas, New York, NY 10020

Macmillan. The Macmillan Publishing Company Inc., 866 Third Ave., New York, NY 10022

Methuen. Methuen Inc., 733 Third Ave., New York, NY 10017

Morrow. William Morrow & Company Inc., 105 Madison Ave., New York, NY 10016

Oxford. Oxford University Press Inc., 200 Madison Ave., New York, NY 10016

Parents. Parents Magazine Press, 685 Third Ave., New York, NY 10017

Philomel. Philomel Books, 51 Madison Ave., New York, NY 10010

Prentice-Hall. Prentice-Hall Inc., Englewood Cliffs, NJ 07632

Press Pacifica. Press Pacifica, P.O. Box 1227, Kailua, HI 96734

Putnam. Putnam Publishing Group, 200 Madison Ave., New York, NY 10016

Random House. Random House Inc., 201 East 50th St., New York, NY 10022

Scribner. The Scribner Book Companies Inc., 597 Fifth Ave., New York, NY 10017

Seabury. Seabury Press, 815 Second Ave., New York, NY 10017

Viking. Viking Press, 40 West 23rd St., New York, NY 10010

Walker. Walker & Company, 720 Fifth Ave., New York, NY 10019

Warne. Frederick Warne & Company Inc., 2 Park Ave., New York, NY 10016

THE SURE THING

WARREN MURPHY

PINNACLE BOOKS
WINDSOR PUBLISHING CORP.

For Riley and Shane and Joel,
for Margaret and Winifred
and especially and always,
for the kid from the mushroom mine.

PINNACLE BOOKS

are published by

Windsor Publishing Corp.
475 Park Avenue South
New York, NY 10016

First printing: November, 1988

Printed in the United States of America

HE PROBABLY HAD
A HALF HOUR AT BEST.

Against the wall of the Installation's computer lab were a row of metal cabinets. Matt opened them and saw row after row of ten and twenty gigabyte metal discs. It was obvious they held information that came from the huge Chrin 210D computer, and Matt knew his next step was to break into the machine and drain its brain. Then he heard a shout from the hallway outside and the lab door burst open.

In the first flash of surprise Matt experienced a feeling of stunned anger that he had come this far only to be discovered at the last minute.

And then a feeling he had not known since Vietnam.

The knowledge that he would kill if he had to.

And ask no questions of himself afterward!

PINNACLE BRINGS YOU THE FINEST IN FICTION

THE HAND OF LAZARUS   (100-2, $4.50)
by Warren Murphy & Molly Cochran
The IRA's most bloodthirsty and elusive murderer has chosen the
small Irish village of Ardath as the site for a supreme act of terror
destined to rock the world: the brutal assassination of the Pope!
From the bestselling authors of GRANDMASTER!

LAST JUDGMENT   (114-2, $4.50)
by Richard Hugo
Only former S.A.S. agent James Ross can prevent a centuries-old
vision of the Apocalypse from becoming reality . . . as the malevolent instrument of Adolf Hitler's ultimate revenge falls into the
hands of the most fiendish assassin on Earth!
                   "RIVETING...A VERY FINE BOOK"
                          —*NEW YORK TIMES*

TRUK LAGOON   (121-5, $3.95)
Mitchell Sam Rossi
Two bizarre destinies inseparably linked over forty years unleash a
savage storm of violence on a tropic island paradise—as the most
incredible covert operation in military history is about to be uncov-
ered at the bottom of TRUK LAGOON!

THE LINZ TESTAMENT   (117-6, $4.50)
Lewis Perdue
An ex-cop's search for his missing wife traps him a terrifying secret
war, as the deadliest organizations on Earth battle for possession
of an ancient relic that could shatter the foundations of Western
religion: the Shroud of Veronica, irrefutable evidence of a second
Messiah!

*Available wherever paperbacks are sold, or order direct from the
Publisher. Send cover price plus 50¢ per copy for mailing and handling to Zebra Books, Dept. 129 , 475 Park Avenue South, New
York, N.Y. 10016. Residents of New York, New Jersey and Pennsylvania must include sales tax. DO NOT SEND CASH.*

"There are only two sure things—death and taxes."

—Attributed to Benjamin Franklin

CHAPTER ONE

For Matt Taylor, Monday night in a Los Angeles hotel was like this.

A knockout Oriental hooker came into the lobby bar but passed him up to go talk to some bald guy sitting at a table in the corner; five minutes later, they left together and Matt hoped they both had AIDS.

The bartender brought him a Chivas Regal on the rocks, put a paper umbrella in the damned drink, and said it was his own personal statement in the never-ending expansion of the art of mixology.

A strolling accordionist came into the bar, stood right behind Matt's stool, and played "Lady of Spain" all the way to its dismal conclusion.

Then a movie actor came in, a fat man with a shaved-bald head, parked himself on the stool next to Matt's, got the house telephone and started bellowing at people in a loud attempt to prove how important he was. Matt wanted to ask him if he was so important, how was it that he was reduced to doing guest spots on "Circus of the Stars."

But instead, Matt just moved away to a seat at the far end of the bar, picked up the copy of the *Los Angeles Times* that someone had left there and began to leaf through the pages.

And there it was, on page one of an inside section, and Matt stifled a small groan.

It happened every year. As April drew close, some idiot headline writer on some newspaper somewhere would lead off a story on income tax returns with "April: the Cruelest Month," or some variation of that theme, under the cretinous assumption that no one had ever been clever enough before to think of doing just that.

And every time Matt Taylor saw that headline, he would get depressed and stay depressed until perhaps the middle of June when the worst of it was over. He often thought that if T. S. Eliot really wanted to know how cruel April could be, he should have worked for the Internal Revenue Service.

The bartender saw him reading the story.

"I hate income taxes," he said.

"I work for the I.R.S.," Matt Taylor said.

"But taxes are the price we pay for civilization," the bartender said.

"I'll be sure to mention that thought to our Audit Division," Taylor said and picked up his drink and took it up to his room. God, he hated Los Angeles. But he was stuck with it at least once a year on business, because when Uncle Sam said go, Matt Taylor got up and went.

He had a long title with the Internal Revenue Service but basically it boiled down to being the chief troubleshooting analyst. Which meant that whenever the I.R.S. computer system got screwed up—as it did every spring—it was his job to unscrew it. And every year as the system grew more complicated, the job got harder. The glitches started appearing the day after New Year's, and by the first week in April at least half the processing centers around the country were in a state of complete electronic nervous breakdown.

And there they stayed—with Taylor holding it all together somehow—until mid-June when almost all the year's tax returns had been fed through the machines and filed. Then Taylor spent the rest of the year trying to make sure the breakdowns

8

did not occur again, but they did the following Spring, just like clockwork.

He had put in a long weekend trying to clean up Los Angeles' act and he was not in the mood for snooty hookers, shouting actors, accordion players, and bartenders who put paper umbrellas in Scotch, so he went back to his room just in time for his boss to call and tell him to hurry back to Washington, D. C.

It was nine o'clock in Los Angeles, and for a moment he thought of calling his wife to tell her that his trip had been cut short. He reached for the telephone receiver, then stayed his hand. Although it was midnight back in Washington, D.C., his wife was probably not home and if she wasn't, he didn't really want to know about it.

Three hours later, he was airborne out of Los Angeles. After he got off the red-eye in New York and while he was waiting for the shuttle to Washington, he finally got around to calling his apartment. He let the phone ring a long time before hanging up. Perhaps Melanie had left the apartment early to go to work. He didn't feel much like going home himself, so when he got to D.C., he took a cab from the airport right to his office.

He needed a shower and a shave and a chance to brush his teeth and that all made him feel awful. He always felt that way when he was not neatly turned out, and he couldn't decide whether that was just the way a computer man's mind worked or if it was the result of the three years he had spent in the Marine Corps when he was a kid. On the one hand, the Marine Corps had been a long time ago—fourteen years—and he should have gotten over their dress code by now. On the other hand, most systems analysts dressed as if they found their clothing in a charity container in a suburban shopping mall.

So why was he different? Who knew? Another great unsolved mystery to go with the other great unsolved mysteries. Like where was his wife?

Taylor let himself into his office. It was standard government middle-management grade with wooden furniture, a carpet on

9

the floor, and a window overlooking the parking lot. He pulled out the bottom desk drawer, lowered himself into his chair and leaned back, resting his feet in the drawer. He shut his eyes and thought—first about how worthless the whole data processing network was and how it was a wonder that anything ever got done—and about the endless flights, hopping around the country, trying to patch the whole damned thing together for one more tax season. He thought about flying—which he hated and feared—and then he thought about going home to Melanie—which he was starting to hate and fear almost as much as flying.

"Are you awake?"

Matt Taylor looked up. Walt Fluory, the boss who had called him back from Los Angeles the night before, was standing just inside the door.

"Sure. Come on in, Walt. Just don't come too close. I haven't had a chance to shower yet."

Fluory closed the door softly behind him and walked toward Taylor's desk. He was a dapper, smallish man, perhaps five feet nine but looking smaller because he seemed to have frail bones and an unmasculine delicacy about his build. His dark blond hair was swept in a deep wave across his forehead and he had wide-set green eyes. He had a square jaw and a habit of grinning but never really smiling.

"Little spot of trouble, old boy," he said.

"Some day, Walt, you're going to come in here and tell me that everything's fine," Taylor said.

"Don't hold your breath waiting."

"And I'm going to die of a heart attack. What is it today?"

"Well, the big thing is, like I told you on the phone last night, you've got to get up to Philadelphia. They're all discombobulated up there."

"Yeah, you said that on the phone. That's the big thing. What's the small thing? Why don't you give it to me all at once? I hate being nickeled and dimed to death. And sit down, please."

"It's this gang of Japs," Fluory said. He had been standing and he finally sat in the chair next to Taylor's desk.

"What gang of Japs?"

"They're visiting hotshots from Japan's tax service. They've come here to see how our system works during a time of stress."

"They picked the right time," Taylor said. He took his feet out of the desk drawer and swiveled around to face his boss and almost-friend.

"And Larry Wu won't show them around," Fluory said. "Something about Chunking. Do you know what the hell he's talking about?"

"Chunking makes chop suey," Taylor said. "It's Nanking."

"What's the difference? Chunking, Nanking, doesn't your old frat brother like chop suey anymore?"

Despite himself, Taylor smiled. He and Larry Wu had studied at Carnegie-Mellon together and Wu had told him the story of Nanking many times. Two years before World War II started for the rest of the world, the Japanese had invaded China. Nanking was a large southern city that had been foolish enough or brave enough to offer resistance. Western missionaries later claimed that the Japanese troops were unleashed by their commanders with orders to rape, pillage, and murder. The best estimates said that the Japanese had killed a quarter of a million Chinese in the first three days of their occupation and another quarter-million in the next three weeks. Larry Wu's grandparents were among the dead.

Taylor shook his head.

"He just doesn't like the Japanese," he said.

"Yeah, well, war is hell. But it's over. You know, time to forgive and forget. The little bastards are our friends now."

"Not Larry's friends," Taylor said.

"I've figured that all out by now," Fluory said. "So you've got to be a good guy and take the damned Nips through Larry's section. Just punch up a couple of returns on the terminal, show them how we make random checks and then kiss them all *Say-*

11

onara and tell them not to forget their cameras on the way out."

Taylor thought about protesting, decided it wasn't worth it and said, "Sure, why not?"

"Great, great. See you later and we'll talk about Philadelphia. They'll be here in about ten minutes."

Without hanging around for an argument, Fluory was gone.

Taylor started to ask what the big Philadelphia computer emergency was that was bigger than the big Los Angeles computer emergency but gave up on the effort. It would wait and maybe the longer the better. Instead he took his shaving kit from his suitcase and went down the hall to the men's room to try to clean up.

When he got back to his office, the Japanese visitors were waiting for him. There were six of them, all dressed in dark blue suits, white shirts, and rep ties. They did not all look alike, Taylor thought, but he would have had one hell of a hard time describing their differences. They all smiled broadly when he greeted them and shook his hand with the moderately respectful fifteen-degree bow from the waist. Two of them wore Nikons around their necks and one of them did the speaking for the rest. He seemed to be the only one who spoke or understood English.

Taylor ushered the group down the hall and into one of the return-checking centers. Ordinarily, he told them, the Washington headquarters did not handle this sort of work; it was usually done by the regional offices, but this time the computer systems in Philadelphia and New York which handled most of the traffic for the mid-Atlantic states were in a state of nearly total breakdown, and so Washington was picking up some of the slack.

He walked to one of the supervisor's terminals and waited for the visitors to gather around. When they had, he turned to the translator.

"This is where we do the preliminary checks on tax returns that come through here." He turned and typed something on the computer keypad.

12

"What I've done now is to order the computer to reach in and pull out an income tax return at random," he said. As he spoke, the yellow-green letters and numbers formed on the screen and Taylor pointed to it.

"What we're looking at now is the basic information on the income tax return filed by ... hmmm ... a Fred Kohler of ... let's see ... Harker's Furnace, Pennsylvania. That's up north of us. Now let's make a quick check of his return."

As he typed in another short instruction, he heard the translator softly explaining what he had said to the other five men.

The screen rolled and flashed up a new string of figures. "What we've got showing now, next to Mr. Kohler's return, are the national average figures for each of the deductions he claims. This is the quickest preliminary way to pick up any hint of fraud or tax evasion." He waited again for the translator, and then leaned over and pointed to the screen as the men moved in close around him.

"For example, Mr. Kohler claims an income of $20,000 and he claims charitable deductions last year of $650. Now if that is ... say, more than twenty-five per cent above the national average, the computer would flag this return and pass it on to a human auditor to check for possible fraud. So let's check. For Mr. Kohler's income level, the average annual donation to charity is ... $650. He's exactly average." Matt Taylor tried a small smile on his guest. "It's unusual," he said, "but some people *are* exactly average. Now let's see if he made any contributions to his retirement account. Let's see. Mr. Kohler contributed $1,897 and the national average is ... $1,897."

He paused and said," That's interesting," as much to himself as to the Japanese visitors. "Let's check out his other deductions. Hmmmm. He made $14 in political campaign contributions and the national average is ... $14. His interest payments ... $2,950 and the national average is ... $2,950."

The translator was talking rapidly as Taylor turned to the men and said, "We seem to have come up with a most unusual

13

man. He is exactly average in all ways, and I don't think that I've ever seen that happen before."

The guide translated what Taylor had said and the others laughed politely. Taylor glanced at his watch. There was still five minutes left on their scheduled time with him and he could think of nothing else to say.

"Are there any questions?" he asked, and was surprised when no one spoke. That was not the way he had heard of the Japanese acting. He shuffled his feet for a moment and said, "Maybe we'll try another tax return."

The Japanese all nodded. Perhaps they understood English better than he thought they did.

Taylor typed into the computer instructions to pull out the return following that of Fred Kohler. In a moment, it appeared. The name at the top was that of Clyde Stallbarn, but with a quick scanning, Taylor could see that in all other respects, it was an exact duplicate of Fred Kohler's return. Even the return address was the same: care of White Pine Cabins, R.D. 47, Harker's Furnace, Pennsylvania. And all the financial entries were the same too.

Matt Taylor let out a low whistle. "Well, I'll be double damned," he said.

The odds against this happening were even more than astronomical. It was just damned impossible. Taylor had already forgotten that he was playing host to some Japanese visitors. He rolled out the chair at the desk, sat down in it, and typed some more instructions into the computer, calling for the next item in the file. He waited a couple of seconds and a third return from Harker's Furnace appeared on the screen. This one was for an Andrew McCabe and was an exact duplicate of the other two returns, except for the name on the top.

Taylor leaned back in the chair, watching the screen and thinking. Two identical returns from one town, each mirroring the national averages, was impossible. Three was unthinkable.

Taylor heard a slight murmur, remembered the Japanese,

14

and turned to look at their translator. The man seemed embarrassed.

"What is it?" Taylor asked.

"They want to know if this is usual."

Taylor did not answer for a moment. The Japanese were sharp; they had obviously noticed his agitation. "Tell them it sure doesn't happen every day," he said.

The translator repeated that and was answered with a round of polite smiles.

Taylor heard someone clearing his throat at the door to the room. He looked up and saw Walt Fluory.

"Are our friends all done here, Matt?" he asked. "I want to take them up to see the director."

It took Taylor a moment to focus his mind on the question, then he said, "Yeah, sure. They're finished."

He unhooked his long legs from under the desk and rose to his full height. At six feet four, he towered over the Japanese, even though he had not noticed it back in his office. He turned to the visitors, shook hands with each of them, attempted a slight bow, even as he said a prayer of thanksgiving that they were going.

As soon as they had followed Fluory from the room, he sat down at the desk again to examine the third return.

It had disappeared. The screen was blank.

Taylor cursed softly to himself and punched away at the keyboard, ordering the computer to display the information on Andrew McCabe again. Nothing happened.

Taylor waited and still nothing happened.

He swore, aloud this time, and retyped the request. The screen stayed blank. There were no instructions or warnings displayed. He tried to call up Clyde Stallbarn's return, the second one he had checked, and still the display screen stayed empty.

"What the hell is this?" he muttered.

"Having problems, pal?" a voice behind him said.

15

He twisted in his seat and saw Larry Wu standing in the doorway.

"I'm not sure what's happening," Taylor said. He explained about the three identical returns.

"Try Fred Kohler again," Wu said.

Taylor typed in the name and the location, Harker's Furnace, Pennsylvania. This time, letters started appearing on the screen.

They read: "No returns exist for that name at that address."

CHAPTER TWO

Matt Taylor pulled the blinds on the large single window in his office, turned off his overhead light, tilted his chair back, and again rested his feet inside the desk drawer.

When the door opened, he did not bother to stir.

"You asleep again?" a voice asked, lightly, bantering.

"Naaah. Just checking my eyelids for holes," Taylor said but moved his feet to a more businesslike position.

As he flicked the overhead light switch, Walt Fluory chuckled and Taylor decided the man chuckled more than most. Maybe that was the secret of his success.

Not as a bureaucrat though. Definitely not that. Even though Fluory held a high Civil Service position with Internal Revenue, everybody knew that was not his real job. That was just to give him space to operate from. Fluory was one of the administration's golden boys, the political protege and chief hatchetman for the head of the I.R.S. himself, Anthony Plevris.

Fluory had two thick folders in his arms and as he dropped them onto Taylor's desk, he said, "We ought to talk about Philadelphia."

Taylor sat up straight and stretched. He was soft-looking—the way a lot of big men are who spend too much time behind a desk—but on closer look, it was obvious that he was still in pretty decent shape, even though it might be more attributable to genetic memory than any effort at physical conditioning.

"I'm all ears," he said.

"Mind if I sit down?" Fluory asked. That was like him, too, Taylor thought. Polite in all the small things. And ruthless in all the big ones.

Taylor nodded and Fluory sat neatly in the chair alongside the desk. "Philadelphia's all screwed up," he said.

"I've been here eight years," Taylor said. "Philly's always all screwed up."

"Even worse this time. You'll see when you look in those folders. And April 15th is drawing nigh," Fluory said. "What day is this?"

"Almost April. Almost All Fools' Day," Taylor said.

"Now if anything deserves to be a national holiday, that one does. No, I mean what day of the week?"

"Tuesday," Taylor said.

"Yeah. That's what I thought. Matt, would Melanie mind too much if I sent you up to Philly for a couple of days?"

Taylor felt his face stiffen at the mention of his wife's name. Why would she mind, he thought. She would probably be glad to get rid of him for a while longer so she could cat around or do whatever it was she did when she wasn't running her little specialty gift shop.

He ignored the question. "When would you want me to go?" he said.

"I was thinking of the day after tomorrow. Would that be too soon for you? I wouldn't ask except ..." Fluory let his voice trail off.

Taylor knew. The media had been having a field day with the problems in the Philadelphia I.R.S. office. Newsmen and editorial writers seemed to get no end of enjoyment out of sticking it to an administration that had won office largely by promising efficient government. Taylor sometimes thought it was lucky that the press didn't understand that things at other

18

I.R.S. regional offices were even more screwed up than at Philadelphia.

"I can make it," Taylor said after flipping through his desk calendar. He used a desk pen to mark in his departure for Thursday. "In the morning?"

Fluory nodded. "I've made reservations for us." He got up to leave.

Taylor shrugged and said, "Walt, you know I've already taken their system apart and put it back together twice."

"I know," Fluory said, pausing by the chair. "Maybe I shouldn't be saying this. Hey, what the hell. You know and I know that what's going on up there is just bad management. So some people higher up want to see how you handle the problem. It might be an opportunity. Talk is that there's a new top-level assignment opening up."

"Yeah? What kind of assignment?" Taylor asked.

"More I cannot say," Fluory said. He grinned again.

"I'll only believe it," Taylor said, "if this comes from your political goombah."

"The man upstairs?" Fluory said, jabbing an index finger upward, as if in the direction of the office of Walter Plevris, head of the I.R.S.

Taylor nodded and Fluory said, "Maybe even higher than that. Listen. The president's on television tonight. Watch him. You'll find it interesting."

He turned and strolled, casually dramatic, toward the door. He stopped with his hand on the knob.

"And, Matt. Get the hell out of here. Take those files home if you want and get some sleep." He chuckled. "If I had a wife who was the prettiest woman in Washington, I sure wouldn't hang around here any more than I had to."

Taylor mumbled to himself, "That's assuming she's home," but Fluory was already on his way out the door and did not hear him.

He sat looking at the file and wondering what Fluory was

hinting at. Something was going on. Fluory was too close to Plevris to hint at things that wouldn't transpire. But what?

Plevris had been in the news lately more often than heads of the I.R.S. usually were. Three years earlier, the man had been the campaign director for the vice president, Charles Garner Barkley, and now he was in the paper most days as the chief mediator in the administration between the forces still loyal to lameduck president Tom Chesney and those who had already switched loyalties to the vice president.

It was a tough choice and a tough way to make a living, Taylor thought. On the one hand, President Chesney was your big boss; on the other hand, Vice President Barkley was going to run for President and somebody with ambition might be well advised to get on his bandwagon now.

Taylor often considered himself lucky that he did not have to play that game. Politics was something for the big boys with more to lose than he had. All Matt Taylor had to do was to be a good technician, leave the policy making and the politics to men like Fluory who seemed to be better at it and maybe even seemed to enjoy it.

As he opened up the file folders and started to look through the reports on Philadelphia's current problem, he remembered that he forgotten to tell Fluory about the peculiar returns he had retrieved from Harker's Furnace, Pennsylvania.

Taylor shuffled through the files until almost noon, when he stuffed them into his Kluge travel bag, then stopped by Larry Wu's cubicle as he was leaving the office.

He paused in the entranceway. The slim young Chinese was pounding away at his computer keyboard, oblivious to what was going on around him.

Taylor cleared his throat. Wu waved a hand impatiently over his head, still without looking up. He watched a string of letters and numbers chasing themselves across the terminal's screen. After a moment, he stopped watching and pounded his fist on the desk. When he turned and saw Taylor, he said, "Dammit, Matt. Somebody sure as hell slammed that door tight after you walked through there this morning."

"Harker's Furnace? Those wacky returns?" Taylor said.

Wu nodded. "Closed tight." He got up and took his jacket down from a clothes tree standing in a corner of his workspace.

It was a lightweight dark blue silk with pinstripes of three colors running through it. The tailoring was exceptional, a reminder of earlier days when Larry Wu had been conspicuously rich, a multimillionaire whiz kid industrialist.

Wu was thirty-five years old, two years younger than Taylor. He had studied at Carnegie-Mellon with Taylor, but after getting his doctorate, had gone to work for one of those hot new software manufacturers. Then one day, he had decided to stop making money for someone else and start making it for himself. He took his savings, moved back to San Francisco with his mother and father, and worked up a program that could just about manage a whole hospital by itself. That was the beginning. Inside three years, he had a company that was producing income in the seven figures. He got an ulcer. To relax, he started doing cocaine. Brain-fried, he lost his business. And two years back, he had come to Washington to see his old friend, Matt Taylor.

He still loved computers, Larry had said, and he loved programming them. But he couldn't handle the pressures of running his own business anymore and he didn't think he could produce fast enough to work for someone else's business. That seemed to leave government service. Could Taylor find him a job?

"Let's get this straight, Larry," Taylor had said. "You can't deal with the pressure of your own business and you think you're too slow to work in private industry. In other words, you're saying you're just incompetent enough to work for the feds. Is that it?"

"Something like that," Larry had jovially agreed. "Look at

21

the bright side. I know more about computers than all but five or six guys in the world, not counting you. I'm a steal."

"Aaaah, I guess you're good enough for government work," Taylor had said and gotten him a job as a section chief in the I.R.S.'s computer auditing division. He never regretted it. Wu was still the best computer man he had ever known, and on a half dozen occasions, Taylor had been forced to call him in to help solve some problem that had him totally stymied. The cocaine was far behind him now and Taylor fully expected that one day, Larry would tell him he was leaving and then go back into private industry and make another fortune.

Wu slipped into his jacket and said, "You buying me lunch?"

"Actually I was on my way home," he said.

"What's home? Buy me lunch. But we've got to make a stop first."

"For what?" Taylor asked.

"I want to buy a map."

"Hey, this is the I.R.S. The federal government. Requisition a map. Why buy one?"

"Because I want it this year," Wu said.

"All right. We'll buy one."

"And you pay," Wu said. When Taylor started to object, the Chinese said, "Don't forget, my friend. You make the big bucks now."

They ate their lunch at a McDonald's across from a little park that was filled with trees that were hurrying the spring season a little and already had begun to bud. After bribing a couple of surly winos to vacate a bench, Wu spread out a handful of napkins and dumped two cartons of French fries on them, then doused the fries with salt and catsup.

"This stuff will kill us," Taylor complained.

"So will water if you drink too much of it."

Taylor gulped down a fistful of fries and followed it with a slug of chocolate milkshake.

Larry was shuffling the map around on the bench.

"The question for today is where the hell is Harker's Furnace, PA," he said.

"That's why you had me lay out two bucks for a map?" Taylor asked.

"Right."

"Idiot. I could tell you where Harker's is. It's about twenty miles from my hometown. Iron City."

"What a stupid name for a city. I've been there. There's no iron there and it isn't even a city. Just a wide spot in the road. It says here that Harker's Furnace is at C-5 on the map."

"Does it say how big?" Taylor asked.

"There's an asterisk."

"Which means?"

"Which means," said Wu, trying to find the legend on the map, "which means fewer than two hundred-fifty people."

The map started to blow away as Wu tried to fold it to the C-5 section.

"Any year now," Taylor said sarcastically.

"You westerners are always impatient," Wu said. "Wisdom takes time. Remember that. That is the eightfold path to true enlightenment and happiness." He kept struggling with the map.

"Right, right, right. And Rome wasn't built in a day and haste makes waste. I know all that. Here. Give me the damned map and you eat your junk food."

While Wu dug into the French fries, Taylor finished folding the map and studied it for a while.

"What's so interesting?" Wu asked.

"I told you. Harker's Furnace is about twenty miles from my hometown. But what's interesting is that it isn't any nearer to anything else. It looks like it's right in the middle of the Allegheny National Forest."

He started to hand the map to Wu who shrugged and waved it away. "One map's just like another map to me," he said.

"You keep it. You mention anything about those funny returns to our peerless leader?"

"No. I forgot. Damn it, he wants me to go to Philly again. Same old mess with the system."

"How'd Melanie take that news?" Wu asked.

"I haven't told her yet," Taylor said. He kicked the side of his suitcase. "Truth is I haven't even been home yet." He laughed bitterly. "I don't know if Melanie has either."

Larry Wu sighed. "Someday, my old friend, you're going to come to you senses and dump that woman and marry my sister, Katie."

"Fat chance," Taylor said

"And what's wrong with my sister, Round Eyes?"

"Your folks would just love it, wouldn't they? Katie marrying a westerner."

"They'd make an exception in your case, Matt. First of all, they've met you and they know you don't smell funny like most whites. And second of all, Katie's going around with a lot of people, white guys, black guys, even a Nip or two, and you'd certainly be an improvement over that. And besides, they'd figure since we both work at the same place, if you married Katie, you'd have to see that I got a big raise. Chinese family traditions, you know. And then, with us up so high in the I.R.S., nobody in the family would ever have to pay taxes again because we'd fix the computers for them. I tell you, Matt, my folks would be a piece of cake. Marry Katie."

"I should have," Taylor said. "Her. Or somebody. Anybody but who I did marry."

"It's come to that, huh?"

"Pretty much. Damn it, Larry. We don't see each other any more. We don't talk. She's always out on the party circuit. For all I know, she's slept in every bed in town. When I'm out of town and call, she's never home. Or at least she never answers. Aaaah." He shrugged as if to dismiss the subject.

"And you just keep taking it," Larry said. "Let me ask you a question. What does it take to get you pissed off enough just to pack your clothes and walk? What does it take to get you pissed off at anything? Or have I asked you that before?"

"You've got to be Zen," Taylor said with a wry grin. "Anger never solves anything. And besides, there's an old rule. 'Better the devil you know than the devil you don't know.' "

"And best, no devil at all," Wu said. "And don't give me that 'no anger' bullshit. You didn't spend all that time in Vietnam, being Rambo, without having a good mad on for somebody."

Taylor shook his head. "I joined the Marines out of spite. I didn't ask to go to Nam and when I got there, I wasn't mad at anybody. I just got a little annoyed later when I saw the way Charlie was treating our POWs. And when I was done, I left Nam and I haven't thought about it since. Getting angry's not my style."

"And neither is getting happy, I guess," Wu said.

"Drop it, Larry."

"It's dropped."

They sat silently, finishing the MacDonald's meal, and as they were cleaning up to leave, Wu said, "You know, you may be on to something with those Harker's Furnace returns."

"Like what?" Taylor asked.

"I don't know yet."

"What do you mean 'yet'? "

Larry Wu grinned. "I don't like unsolved puzzles."

CHAPTER THREE

It was unseasonably warm for late March—a preview of the steambath that Washington would become during the summer—and Taylor decided to walk home from his office.

He thought of the lunchtime conversation with Larry Wu. Larry just did not understand about Vietnam. Maybe no one did who had not been there.

Taylor had spent the better part of two years in Nam. He was one of a small team of Marine raiders who had volunteered to drop behind enemy lines to free captured Americans before the Viet Cong had a chance to transfer them to concentration camps back in the North. Taylor had gone in a hundred and fifty times; he had been wounded four times; he had been awarded six medals; he and his group had saved the lives of six hundred American GIs and when he had been discharged and returned to the States, his left arm still in bandages from a shrapnel burst he had taken, a woman walked up to him at Los Angeles Airport, spat in his face and screamed at him, "Baby killer!"

Nothing had prepared him for that kind of a homecoming. Yes, he'd killed in Nam. But not babies; not civilians; he had killed enemy soldiers in wartime, in rescue missions behind enemy lines. Maybe he hadn't expected a brass band for his homecoming, but he hadn't expected spit in the face either.

He had looked at the woman in the airport, her frizzy pseudo-black hair, her leather earrings, her elegantly faded blue jeans with the butterfly applique near the crotch, and he had said simply: "Lady. Go fuck yourself."

He had walked away and left her screaming after him, "Coward. Baby killer. Coward. Baby killer."

Maybe, he thought, that was when he decided, "Why bother?" Why fight? There were precious few things worth fighting about. Maybe the best revenge wasn't living well; it was just living.

He was soaked with perspiration when he got back to his apartment at the Elysian.

The building dated back to the mid-1920s and in the past few years had been written up many times as a masterpiece of the Art Deco style of that time. It was a massive white brick thing that Taylor thought was the ugliest building he had ever seen. It was set at the edge of a city park that until lately had been the domain of pushers and hookers but had recently become trendily respectable. Less than a block from the building, there was an entrance to the Metro's Green Line subway.

Inside the lobby, the Elysian was elaborately, almost overwhelmingly decorated, like something out of a poof's pipe dream. Even when Taylor had trouble accepting the decor, though, he had to admit that the building was clean, the apartments were large, well lighted and airy and that the elevators always worked. Federal government, please note, he thought, and acknowledged that the primary reason he disliked the place was that they could afford to live there only because of the income from Melanie's gift shop. They could not have handled it on Taylor's salary alone. Just another little slice of resentment.

The shades in his apartment were pulled and the place smelled of Melanie and the thick musky perfume she liked to splash on her body before they made love.

Even though it was his apartment, too, Taylor paused inside

27

the doorway and called out to her, all the while thinking that he should have phoned first. But there was no answer from inside the apartment and he walked down the long hallway into the spacious living room.

Nothing had changed since he had left a week before. A couple of large, comfortable sofas, a coffee table, four lamp tables were placed precisely around the room, while scattered here and there were a dozen or so things from Melanie's shop, *Imaginating*. Melanie called them thingamajigs and they could be almost anything that struck her fancy: an apothecary jar filled with glass marbles; an ivory skeleton; a piece of old Chinese jade sculpture—some of them selling for a dollar, some for five thousand times that. Whatever they were, Melanie had done well in marketing them and her downtown shop had become a hangout for interior decorators and liberated, thirty-five-year-old female bureaucrats, the kind who spent all their time telling each other how fulfilled and happy they were and how they didn't really need, much less want, a husband and/or child and would settle for a nice wooden nicknack instead. The place also seemed to attract a lot of young Congressmen and Congressional staffers who seemed clearly, to Taylor, to be just young guys on the make.

He dropped his garment bag in the middle of the Persian rug and tossed his jacket over the back of one of the sofas. Taylor entered their bedroom. A king-sized bed took up most of the floor space. It was neatly made and on the pillow was pinned a note, handwritten, from Melanie:

"Walt told me you'd be home this morning. I waited to hear from you. See you tonight."

Taylor read it twice, found it annoyed him for some reason he did not understand, and balled it up, went out to the kitchen and tossed it into the trash basket Melanie kept alongside the sink. For a moment, he thought about pouring himself a drink, then decided not to. He had come to a hell of a state, he thought, when even a simple note from his wife made him start drinking.

Instead, he headed for the bathroom, stripping off his clothes and dropping them on the floor as he went. He got a small petty satisfaction out of that because while Melanie was not much of a wife in any of the ways that counted, she was meticulously neat and the clothing on the floor would have made her furious.

He turned on the shower water as hot as he could stand it, then scrubbed himself hard until his skin was glowing red. Then he quickly switched off the hot water, turned on the cold and stood in it until he began to question his sanity. When he was done toweling himself off, he went to bed.

The alarm woke him a little past six in the evening. He went back to sleep and ten minutes later, the alarm woke him again. He walked to the television and turned on the news, in time to hear Dan Rather saying something about the Presidential address that would be broadcast later.

Taylor listened to the news without concentrating; his mind was on Melanie. Half the time, he really didn't care anymore whether he saw her again or not; the other half of the time, he could think of little but taking her to bed. He was sure he did not love her anymore but his lust for her had not faded a bit over the years.

Maybe it had never been love, only lust, right from the beginning. It had certainly been a mistake. Maybe he had just led too sheltered a life. He had seen his share of crummy bars while in the Marines, but had never developed a taste for cheap hookers like the rest of the men in his unit. Then, after the Marines, there had been the seven years at Carnegie-Mellon, getting his Ph.D. in systems analysis, and he might as well have spent that time in a monastery.

And when he did have any free time, there was always Lauren Carmody, the girl from back home, who was right in the neighborhood, getting her law degree at Duquesne. They had made great plans for the future. And then Taylor had met Melanie.

She was just out of high school and working as a waitress in a bar not far from Taylor's campus, one of those places with loud music and vomiting sophomores. Lauren Carmody had taken him there, insisting that he needed to get away from his computers. He saw Melanie, and two nights later went back by himself.

Melanie was blonde and tan, with a figure to shame a centerfold, laughing blue eyes, a perfect smile, and a laugh that sounded bell-like. High school was the extent of the nineteen year old's education but she seemed to have brains anyway.

At twenty-eight, he was nine years older than she was and it had taken him a long time to work up enough nerve to ask her out, lest she reject him as another dirty old man. She had accepted his offer immediately. They went to a movie and had a few drinks afterward and when he had taken her home she asked if he wanted to come in. He had stammered around for a few seconds and she had kissed him on the nose, called him sweet, and said good night. The next time they went out, she had insisted that they leave the movie halfway through and go back to her apartment. He spent the night and a couple of nights later, she called him up and asked him over for supper. They did not even get through the appetizer before they were making love on the floor next to the small dining table.

All that had been nine years before and if anything, Melanie's sexual appetite had grown, and now Taylor knew that Melanie was using other men to satisfy it. At first, it had been only while he was away on business but he suspected it was more than that now. He had no way to prove it—and no desire to—but there were too many dead-line phone calls that he picked up; too many people he didn't know—men and women—stopping at their table to speak when they went out for dinner; too many winks and nods from her to other people; too many whispered conversations when Taylor entered a room with her.

Not too much longer, he told himself. It couldn't go on too much longer.

When the CBS news ended, he switched to Peter Jennings on ABC. Jennings said that the President was going to make a major announcement about his ware on organized crime and

30

drug traffic in America. Outside, it had grown dark and Taylor was getting restless. He used the remote control to twang the set into silence, then picked up the phone to call Melanie's shop.

"Imaginating," the voice at the other end of the line said, "Eleanor speaking."

Taylor quickly formed her image in his mind. She was young—the same age Melanie had been when he had met her—and she looked enough like Melanie to have been a younger sister.

"Elly, this is Matt."

"Hi, Mister T. Did you just get back in town?"

"More or less," he half-lied. "Is Melanie there?"

The girl's voice changed from her chirpy cheeriness. "I'm sorry, Mister T, but Mel hasn't been in all day." There was a pause, then another change in the young woman's voice. "Is there anything I can do for you?"

"Thanks, Elly," Taylor said. "If she calls or stops in, let her know I'm home, will you?"

"Sure. Anything you want," Elly said, stressing the "anything" just a little harder than she had to.

"Thanks," Taylor said, feeling old and stodgy at his lack of interest in the girl. "I'll keep that in mind."

He went into the kitchen and found the refrigerator full—Melanie liked to cook for company if not for him—but holding nothing suitable for a sandwich. He telephoned for pizza to be delivered and thought he was turning into the junk food king of Washington, D.C., blamed it on his frequent traveling, and for the thousandth time in the last few months, decided he would quit his job and go become a millionaire computer genius.

Twenty minutes later, just before eight o'clock, when the doorbell rang, he rushed to the door, still in his pajamas. Pizza delivery boys in D.C. were notoriously impatient. Make them wait twenty seconds too long and they were gone. He often wondered what they did with the pizzas they failed to deliver.

31

Not the pizza boy but Melanie was standing outside the door. She was wearing an undersized too-tight sweater and a short leather mini-skirt with matching mid-calf boots that showed off her wonderful legs.

"Sorry, big boy. I forgot my keys," she said. She stepped inside and kissed him and immediately her tongue, and the taste of liquor, was inside his mouth.

"Did you get the note I left you?" she asked.

"Yes."

"Show me where you found it," she said.

"Why?"

She laughed, deep and throaty. She ran her hands from her thighs up along her torso to her breasts, cupping them underneath with four fingers and massaging the tips gently with her thumbs. The nipples were instantly erect.

"You never know, Gyrene. You might get lucky."

"The pizza's coming," Taylor said.

She dropped her hands and a look of incredulity passed over her face and Taylor thought again, perhaps for the millionth time, God, she's beautiful.

"What?" she demanded, her voice rising sharply.

"I called for pizza. The delivery boy should be here any minute."

"I don't believe it," Melanie said. "I simply don't believe it. You have your choice of me or a pizza and you want the fucking pizza. I don't believe it." She paused for a moment and Taylor realized she had been drinking more than he had first suspected. She had not been in her shop all day and she was liquored up. Just where had she been? Was it worth even asking?

"Come here, Matt," she said.

He hesitated.

"Come here. Come to momma."

Taylor stepped closer to her but not close enough. She reached out a hand, slipped it inside the fly of his pajama pants and pulled him close. His response was immediate. She looked

32

up at him, smiled, then slipped to her knees and lowered her face toward him.

Then the doorbell rang.

Taylor pulled back and quickly rearranged himself.

"It's the pizza. Have to answer the door."

He left her kneeling on the floor. When he returned, she was gone. He put the pizza on the living room coffee table and went to their bedroom door but it was locked. He knocked but there was no answer. He pounded on it, hard, until she yelled, "Go away. I don't want to talk to you."

"But, Mel . . ."

"Go away. Just go away."

"Hey, that's my bedroom, too, you know. I sleep there," he said, feeling ridiculous, negotiating like this with his wife.

"Not tonight, you don't. Sleep with your fucking pizza, hot rod."

Then there was silence from inside the room and then the sound of the shower. He stared at the door for a moment until he realized that he was acting like a fool, like a poor actor in a scene from a bad movie. Staring at the door didn't change anything. He could kick it down like John Wayne, or walk away understandingly like Alan Alda, or smear it with dog turds like Jack Nicholson.

He decided to be Alan Alda. He walked back to the television set, turned up the sound, got two mugs of Mickey's Malt Liquor from the refrigerator, and took them inside to wash down the pizza. His appetite was unmarred and he was chewing vigorously when the vaguely Russian-looking face of a newsman he detested appeared on the screen. He pressed the mute button on the remote control, and turned the sound back up only when the presidential seal appeared on the screen and Peter Jenning's voice pontificated, "And now, the President of the United States."

President Thomas Chesney was seated at his desk in the Oval Office when the camera switched to him.

He was a big man in his late fifties, craggily handsome in a

33

broken-nosed sort of way, and in his face and manner was still the star football player he had once been. His personal history had been entered whole into the lore of American political mythology, and probably not since Ronald Reagan's first term had there been a president so popular with the American people.

Chesney had grown up on a medium-sized wheat farm in the heart of the Great Plains. From there, he had gone on to Oregon State where he played middle linebacker on one Rose Bowl team and was twice named All-American. He turned pro and played for the Seattle Seahawks, being chosen for the Pro Bowl at the end of his third year. His fourth year had not gone so well. In an exhibition game the week before the season opened, his left leg was broken in four places. It never healed properly and so, the following year, Chesney quit pro football and went east to earn his Ph.D. in economics at the University of Chicago. Then he went back to Oregon State to work as the football team's defensive coach. He explained that this showed what a good economist he was, because football coaches' salaries were almost twice as high as economics professors'.

Two years later, he was promoted to head coach after the team had gone through a three-year losing spell. The fans expected a savior and he was it. The first season, his team broke even in wins and losses; the next season, they were back in the Rose Bowl. He was immediately hailed in the news media, especially in Oregon, as the greatest football genius since Knute Rockne and Vince Lombardi.

At the beginning of the next season, Chesney called a press conference. It was widely attended, because when he wanted to Chesney could put on a good show. That day's show was remarkable. He fired his starting offensive backfield and put half the rest of the team on probation. Drugs and gambling were the reasons he gave.

Chesney announced that he had discovered that the fired team members had been key figures in distributing cocaine among the rest of the team. He had also discovered, he said, that they had gotten most of the drugs free for agreeing not to

34

beat the point spread; they were dealing drugs as agents of gamblers.

And that was not the most sensational part of the press conference; that came when Chesney named some top-level officials in the university's administration and some very important alumni as being the channels through which the Las Vegas gambling mob had reached the players. Then he resigned as head coach.

Ten days later, Chesney's wife got into his car to drive their only daughter and a couple of neighbor kids to the story hour at the local library. The car exploded. Chesney's wife and the neighbor children were killed instantly. It took nearly six months and the pain of innumerable operations before his own daughter died. Some people said it was a blessing. After all, what life could a little girl have hoped to lead without arms or legs or sight?

For two years after his child's burial, Tom Chesney disappeared from public view. Only his closest friends knew that he had gone into retreat at a farm operated by an order of Catholic Brothers. Then in the middle of one summer, one of the TV networks announced that when college football started up again in the fall, Tom Chesney would be on camera as the network's color man. At first he worked the less important games, but the style that had served him so well at press conferences when he was a coach worked even better when he became a broadcaster and soon he was moved to the network's bigger games. Shortly after that, he married the young widow of a real estate tycoon.

No one had ever been prosecuted for the murders of Chesney's family and the others. Even his closest friends thought that he had worked hard to put the whole affair out of his mind, to somehow try to find peace through forgetfulness.

That was why no one was expecting much when he agreed to testify before a U.S. Senate subcommittee doing one of its periodic investigations into the state of big-time college sports.

And when Chesney asked the committee's permission to show some video tapes, no one was still expecting much ... and nobody expected to see pictures of the senior U.S. Senator from Oregon, a man previously known chiefly for his endlessly boring lectures on good government and helping the needy. Yet, here he was, on tape, ordering a gangland hit on a local civic reformer. No one was prepared for the mass of visual and documentary evidence detailing payoffs to state and federal officials to look the other way at drug-trafficking, loan-sharking, prostitution, and gambling. They were not prepared for the stack of statements from former college and professional athletes detailing how they had worked for and been paid by members of organized crime and their bought minions in government.

Most of all, the members of the Senate committee and those attending the hearing were not ready for the video tape of an Oregon state policeman explaining how he had wired the explosive charges in Chesney's car after being ordered to by one of the top men in his department.

A week after his appearance before the committee, Chesney announced that he was giving up his broadcasting job at the request of the network. He said that he was not sure what he was going to do. He had spent all his income and his insurance money and much of his second wife's money to come up with the evidence that he had presented to the committee. Now he just wanted to rest, he said.

But the public would not let him rest.

When he returned to Oregon, he was drafted by the opposition party to oppose the Senator whom he had exposed in his committee testimony. He won the election in the largest landslide in Oregon's history.

Nobody expected much of him in the U.S. Senate. Few knew or remembered that he had a doctorate in economics. Washington insiders expected a nice personable man with a knack for looking good on television, an attractive wife, and not much more. They were surprised because he worked hard and even more surprised when they found out how bright he was.

Chesney won a second term to the Senate and halfway through was persuaded to run for President. The only weakness anyone could spot in him was a lack of administrative experience at the top executive levels of government, and the party chiefs in the East counteracted this by naming as his running mate, Charles Garner Barkley, the blue-blooded ex-governor of Pennsylvania who had served as a cabinet officer and ambassador to Germany, and who was, by anyone's standards, thoroughly qualified for the White House.

The ticket of Chesney and Barkley won the general election by a handsome margin, if not quite a landslide, carrying forty states.

They breezed through their first term in office and their reelection was, this time, a true landslide. Now that second term was winding down and Barkley was planning his own campaign for President, but if anyone expected Chesney to serve his last eighteen months as a lame duck, they were mistaken.

Early on in his second term, the president had launched a major assault on the trafficking in drugs, and even the most cynical observers agreed that the traffic had been cut by at least half. Chesney had laid out the grand strategy and Vice President Barkley, obviously being groomed as the presidential successor, was put in charge of the campaign.

But the lingering weakness of the campaign was that although the amount of drugs in use had dropped, nothing had seemed to cut into the profits of the drug dealers. Fewer drugs were used but the prices were just raised to make up for the shortfall, and this meant that the dealers were making at least as much money as before.

That problem, according to the TV newsmen, was what the president planned to talk about this evening.

Matt Taylor watched and listened, chewing absent-mindedly now and again on pizza, while Chesney talked. The president was his usual self, talking easily and well, but his remarks seemed to be as much lecture as speech. He started out by sketching the history of organized crime in America; how it had come into its own during Prohibition and the halting attempts of government officials to curb its growth.

Finally, he recalled, during the Reagan presidency, federal prosecutors all over the country were turned loose to go after organized crime where it hurt most—in their wallets.

Mafia mobsters, their illegal businesses stripped from them, were pushed farther and farther into a corner where finally, almost all they had left was their narcotics empires.

He said that "the stranglehold of Organized Crime on American life has been broken," and commended the team headed by Vice President Barkley for what it had been able to accomplish. But now, he said, it was time to take the final step and to eliminate the presence of the Mafia in America.

"We have broken the back of the drug epidemic in the United States. But now it is time to do more." It was time, President Chesney said, to go after the Mafia's money, to find out how they hid it, how they laundered it, and how they used it. And then, to put a stop to it and take away their profits.

He paused for a moment, then reminded his audience that Al Capone was finally tripped up and jailed because he couldn't escape "the Tax Man," and despite all the killings and crime, and all the horrors Capone had inflicted on the United States, he was finally jailed on a charge of tax evasion.

"Ladies and gentlemen, I propose that we do this again. I propose a new war against these latter-day Al Capones, one that will strip them of their ill-gotten fortunes and send them to jail where they belong.

"Make no mistake, I'm talking about a war. But it's a war we're going to win, no matter what the cost, no matter how difficult the struggle. We shall win."

He announced he was setting up a new unit to battle Organized Crime. He had conferred with the Senate and he expected hearings to begin within the next two weeks on his plans to give this new unit broad sweeping powers to cut across state lines in his fight against crime.

He said that the unit would be staffed with "the best and the brightest from all throughout the federal government, and when we are done, we will have laid the Mafia and the scourge of narcotics to rest forever in America."

The men who would handle the job, the president said, would be Vice President Charles Garner Barkley and Anthony N. Plevris, director of the Internal Revenue Service.

"God bless you and good night," the President said.

Matt Taylor was stunned for a moment by the announcement. He remembered what Walt Fluory had told him earlier in the office and it became clear to him.

Fluory was close to Plevris, the head of the I.R.S., and he would have known about this special anti-crime unit. He had been hinting that Taylor was being considered for a spot in the new agency.

Matt Taylor, Crime Fighter. It had a ring to it, he thought, and he fell asleep on the couch later still testing the title in his mind.

CHAPTER FOUR

The telephone awakened him. There was a thick musky smell in the room. Melanie's sex perfume. She had already left. He remembered her grunting good-bye as she slammed the door closed behind her.

He lumbered up from the sofa. His back hurt from being twisted during the night on a couch too small for him. The phone was in the kitchen and kept ringing.

It was Larry Wu.

"Rise and shine, old buddy."

" Go fuck yourself and the rickshaw you rode in on," Taylor said.

"You coming to work today?" Wu asked.

"Naturally. Unless I won the lottery while I was sleeping."

"You didn't. I'll leave some stuff for you. Read it and then we'll talk."

"What stuff?"

"Read it first. Then we'll talk. Ta-ta, round eyes."

He hung up before Taylor could growl at him again.

While he made instant coffee from the hot water tap, Taylor thought again about Melanie. He thought that it was time to do something about her. Then he thought of Matt Taylor, Crime Fighter, and decided Melanie could wait.

When he got to the office, he looked into Larry Wu's cubicle but his friend was not there. The computer was turned off and both the display and the keyboard neatly covered as Larry always did when he left the equipment. A good carpenter takes care of his tools.

There was another new woman from the secretarial pool working in his outer office. She swiveled her chair around and smiled up at him. It was too warm a smile for anyone to offer at nine-thirty in the morning, but Taylor had gotten used to them. He had seen enough of them since coming to work in Washington.

It was not that he was inordinately handsome, although he had wavy brown hair and pleasant regular features with a strong jaw that more than one woman had said made him look like a solid citizen. No, the secretary's smile was less a comment on his personal appearance than it was on the total shortage of eligible men in Washington, D.C. The feminists might not like it, and he would never mention it to Melanie or anyone in her circle of trendies, but he thought that most of the women who worked in Washington still regarded themselves as young girls, waiting for a Prince Charming to haul them off to the junior prom in their brand new BMW. Scratch a yuppie career woman, he thought, and you'd find a woman not lucky enough yet to have found a husband.

"Hi, Mr. Taylor. I'm Tildie." She did everything, he thought, except say "Fly me."

"Morning. Have you seen Larry Wu?"

She pondered the question deeply, chewing on the eraser of her pencil very fetchingly while she did so. After about three seconds, she responded.

"No. I don't think so. But he might have come in when I went down to get coffee at the canteen. And a doughnut. I have a weakness for doughnuts. But I was only gone a few minutes. Maybe ten. More like five."

"Thanks," Taylor said. The girl was a ditz. "Do you think you could rustle me up some coffee and a doughnut?"

"Sure, Mr. Taylor." She stood up and stretched. She had a good body. "How would you like it?" she said.

Hanging upside down from a red velvet trapeze, he thought, but said, "Black, no sugar, please," and went inside to his office.

His desk top had been clear when he left the previous day. He remembered because it was so unusual; his desk was normally a clutter of letters, papers, computer printouts, and used plastic coffee cups. Now there were four neat stacks of paper on the desk.

He sat and started looking through the piles of paper.

The first stack contained computer printouts of the income tax returns that he had run across the previous day: Fred Kohler, Clyde Stallbarn, and Andrew McCabe. There were printout copies of four more returns, all using the same motel in Harker's Furnace as an address.

Each of the other three piles contained a half dozen more returns. All the names were different but each pile listed a different motel in Harker's Furnace as an address.

Something was hinky in Harker's Furnace, he thought. It did not surprise him that a small town like that should have four motels. It was in the middle of a big recreational area so no problem there. But it did seem exceeding strange that so many people should be claiming to live in motels there for purposes of filing their federal income tax returns. How the hell did twenty-four people live in motels in Harker's Furnace for an entire work year? He leafed through the returns again. Each man claimed to be self-employed.

Taylor looked up as Tildie, the secretary, came into the room with a plastic container of coffee and a doughnut on a napkin. She set it on the desk and stood there, seeming to await further instructions. Finally, he said "Thank you," and she smiled.

"I'll be outside if you need me," she said.

"Thank you," he said again.

When the young woman left, the obvious question jumped into his mind. Were all these tax returns like the three he had found yesterday, exact copies of the national averages on deductions and exemptions and contributions and all the other little flags that caught the eye of the I.R.S.'s audit system when they were out of whack?

He sipped his coffee and leaned back over the desk to glance through the figures again and as he did, he saw another piece of paper. It was an envelope under the fourth pile of paper. The envelope was sealed and had his name on it. Inside was a note from Larry Wu:

"Bingo, Matt. Every one of these returns exactly hits the national average for deductions. There's some real bad cheese being cut in Harker's Furnace." It was signed WUL which was the code name Wu used for computer transmissions.

Taylor whistled softly under his breath. Yesterday, those three returns he had found seemed like some kind of minor foulup. Today, twenty-four identical returns looked like a scam . . . a big scam.

He drank a big slug of coffee in one gulp, burned his mouth, then dialed Wu's extension. No one answered. He put on his jacket again and left carrying the stack of papers under his arm.

"I'm on my way up to see Walt Fluory," he told his secretary.

Fluory drummed his fingers on his desk and stared at the four piles of paper that Taylor had placed in front of him.

"So what do you think we have here?" he asked as he waved his hand over the papers.

"I'm not sure," Taylor said, "but it's sure worth looking into."

Fluory nodded and Taylor watched him, trying to figure out what he was thinking, but Taylor had never been good at that sort of thing and he just could not read anything from Fluory's expression.

"I think you're right. We could be on to something big

here," he said. "I'm going up to see Plevris in a few minutes and I'll talk to him about it. This may be something to get on right away." He stacked the four piles of returns into one high pile and asked, "Did you watch the president last night?"

Taylor nodded.

"What'd you think?"

"I thought I'd like to know what you meant yesterday when you said there might be a job opening up," Taylor said.

Fluory grinned. "Tell you what, Matt. What do you say we have dinner tonight, you and me, and we can talk it over?"

"Sounds good to me," Taylor said. He felt a small rush of anticipation. Fluory wasn't inviting him to dinner so he could tell Taylor to forget about it. There really was a chance to get on the new anti-crime unit. He got up from his seat.

Fluory said, "I'll call you with when and where." He looked down again at the pile of returns. "These things. If the director asks, you and Larry are the only two who know anything about them?"

"That's right."

"Okay. Talk to you later."

Taylor returned to his office and started working again on the file of the problems in the Philadelphia office. He had almost forgotten that he and Fluory were supposed to go there the following day, and he wanted to be familiar with the problems that might await them.

Unfortunately, they were the same old problems—bad equipment and bad personnel.

The time slipped by and his intercom rang.

"Mister Fluory's on the line," the secretary said.

Fluory was all apologies. "Matt, I'm afraid we'll have to scratch our dinner meeting tonight. Something else has come up."

"Oh. Well, sorry about that. We'll get a chance to talk in Philadelphia though."

There was a pause that lasted a beat too long.

Fluory said, "Yeah. Matt, I'm sorry about this time but it looks like you might have to spend a little more in Philly than I thought. Maybe a week, maybe two." He hesitated as if expecting a protest. When Taylor did not answer, Fluory said, "Afterwards, I'll arrange for you to get some time off that won't be counted against your vacation, okay?"

Taylor sighed. "Fine by me, Walt. Whatever you want."

"Okay. See you tomorrow."

"Wait, Walt," Taylor said.

"Yes?"

"Those returns from Harker's Furnace . . .?"

"What about them?"

"Did you have a chance to talk to the director about them?"

"No," Fluory said. "We got off onto other stuff and I didn't get the chance."

"Oh. Well, what should I do about them?"

Fluory answered immediately. "Don't do anything. I've got them and as soon as I get a chance, I'll talk to the director and then we'll put somebody on them. You and Larry have done a good job digging them out, but your job's done with them now. Just leave them to me."

"Okay," Taylor said but as he hung up the telephone, he felt vaguely dissatisfied.

At lunchtime, Taylor looked again in Larry Wu's cubicle but the man was not there. He walked over to the park, and went into the Mcdonald's, ordered a repeat of the previous day's lunch, and took it outside. The sky was turning gray and threatening rain.

Taylor ate his lunch slowly, waiting for his friend. Forty minutes later, he went back into the fast food restaurant to use the men's room and to order a container of coffee. When he came back outside, Wu still was not there. He drank his coffee slowly, waited another ten minutes and then went back to the office.

Larry Wu was not there either and he did not come in for the rest of the afternoon.

CHAPTER FIVE

The telephone was ringing as Taylor let himself into his apartment late that afternoon.

It was Elly, the young woman from Melanie's shop. Her voice was warm and almost purring, and Taylor wondered if that was the way she spoke to everyone.

"I hate to be the bearer of bad news," she said and waited.

Taylor responded a bit testily. "What is it, Elly?"

"Wellll," she said, drawing out the final "l" sound in a way that perhaps she thought was seductive. "Mel asked me to call and tell you that she won't be home for supper tonight." She paused again, obviously waiting for his reaction.

His only reaction was "Oh?" It was getting to be an old story with Melanie. Just like his alleged marriage. An old, tired story.

"She said she had to meet some buyers," the woman said, inflecting her voice to show that obviously she did not believe Melanie. "She said that I was to tell you she'd be very late and you needn't wait up for her."

"Thanks, Elly."

"It's a drag," she said.

"What's a drag?"

"Eating alone," she answered. "I know that, I eat alone most nights. Like you do and it's a real drag."

"I guess it is," Taylor said blandly. "Maybe a pretty girl like you should get a boyfriend."

"I'm trying, Mr. T. But there aren't many men around this city."

"Keep trying," Taylor said.

"I am, Mr. T. I am."

Taylor replaced the telephone on its cradle, looked around his empty apartment and decided the woman was right: it was a drag, always eating alone. He lifted the telephone and dialed a number from memory.

A young woman's voice answered.

"Katie, this is Matt. I was wondering if Larry's around. I missed him all day at the office and at lunch."

Katie Wu laughed softly. As she did, Taylor was able to visualize her. She was tall for a woman, especially an Oriental woman, tall and slim. Her hair was long, thick, and black, and her skin was smooth, peach-colored, and she moved with a sinuous grace that made it difficult, when he was around, for him to take his eyes off her.

It she had not been his best friend's sister, he would have made at the very least a major effort at seducing her, and if one could believe all the not-so-subtle hints Larry was always dropping, Taylor expected that such an effort might not go unrewarded. As things were though, Taylor thought of her—despite the physical distractions she caused him—as sort of a kid sister.

She said, "You won't believe this, Matt, but I was trying just now to call you at the office."

"Something's wrong with Larry?" he said.

"No, no. Unless you count an attack of computeritis. He went to the office early today, was back here by nine, and he's been locked in his study ever since, without eating or stopping for anything. Then, just a little while ago, he sticks his head out and yells, call Matt and let's all go to dinner."

"He didn't say who was buying, did he?"

"No, but when he's as happy as a clam like this, he always buys."

"Sounds serious," Taylor said.

"He had that look in his eye, Matt. Like Doctor Frankenstein must have looked when the grave robbers brought him the last part he needed."

"Well, I can't miss that," Taylor said. "Seven o'clock all right?"

"Sure. I've already made reservations. Szechuan tonight. You going to bring Melanie?"

"No," Taylor said.

"Good. See you at seven," Katie said, then hung up.

The Wu house was a red brick Georgian with white-painted wood trim, just a few blocks from Georgetown University. It had a small front yard and a large well-tended garden in back. The garden was one of Larry Wu's major hobbies.

The house itself had been bought and furnished with money Larry had succeeded in hiding from his creditors just before he had declared his computer firm bankrupt. Except for a trust fund for his aged parents who insisted upon living in San Francisco, the house had used up all his money. He shared it now with Katie who was making quite a name for herself as a graphic designer, doing posters and advertising layouts at home with computer printing equipment Larry had set up for her.

Taylor parked in the driveway alongside the house but before he could ring the bell, Katie Wu pulled the door open. She was dressed in a tight-fitting pink silk dress. It had been six months since Taylor had seen her and while he always remembered her as beautiful, he was never quite prepared, when he saw her, for exactly how beautiful she was. Her lips were full and slick as if she had just wiped them with some sort of oil. Her cheekbones were high and chiseled and her eyes were intelligent, with small laugh lines at the corners—lines she made no effort to hide. A man could get lost in those eyes: Matt knew what that meant now.

"The Master of the house awaits," she said as she smiled at Taylor.

She took his arm and led him to her brother's study. The house was far bigger and more complicated on the inside than it seemed from outdoors. Taylor felt slightly embarrassed as he felt Katie's breast against his arm, thought of unhooking his arm, but by the time he had decided to do it, they had arrived at the door leading into Larry Wu's work center.

"You'd better go in alone," she said, "and I'll try to make myself look good enough to go out with you two handsome fellows."

"Anything but a pillow case over the head will do," Taylor said. He rapped twice on the door and when Wu did not answer, he let himself in. Taylor had never been in the room before; it was large, almost twenty feet square, with a high ceiling. The look of the room brought a smile to Taylor because it was a wondrous mix of East and West. The back wall was all glass, opening with sliding doors to Larry's garden. The entrance wall and the wall to the right were covered floor to ceiling with shelves crammed full of books and magazines. On the other wall were only two things: a sofa stuffed with pillows and a simple, eight-by-ten, black and white ink drawing of a horse, set in a cheap black wooden frame.

A large U-shaped grouping of a walnut desk and several wooden tables backed onto the window, with a massive orthopedically correct executive-style swivel chair set into the slot of the U. The desk and tables were covered with the most impressive array of computer hardware and peripherals that Taylor had ever seen outside a major sales store.

Wu was seated in the chair. He was dressed in a black mandarin scholar's gown and hunched over one of the computer terminals sing-songing something to himself that it took Taylor several moments to recognize as Cole Porter.

50

"Sit down," Wu commanded without looking up. He waved an arm toward the sofa. "Don't bother me just now."

Taylor sat as Wu worked steadily at the terminal for a few long minutes, stopping his singing every now and then to curse loudly in Chinese.

He growled something that sounded to Matt like "Lu-dan," punched his desktop, and hunched further over the computer. Finally, minutes later, he clapped his hands, let out a whoop and twirled around in his chair, rapidly adjusting dials and tossing switches. At last it seemed he remembered that Taylor was in the room. He came around from the control center and clapped his friend on the shoulder.

"Getting there, old buddy. Getting there," He said.

"Getting where?" Taylor asked.

"Harker's Furnace. Remember yesterday, when—" Wu stopped as there was a knock on the door.

"I'll tell you about it later," he said. "I don't want Little Sister to worry."

"Worry about what?" Katie said as she entered the room. She was still wearing the same pink silk dress; she was as pretty and well made-up as she had been before, but whatever indiscernible change she had made to herself had seemed to pick her spirits up. Perhaps in her mind she was more beautiful than she had been; to Taylor, it seemed highly unlikely, if even possible.

Wu smiled broadly and kissed her on the forehead. "Nothing," he said. "Nothing at all."

It was loving and warm but a dismissal nevertheless and Katie reddened slightly. "Okay, wise and ancient master," she said with a bit of bite to her voice. "Now your humble servant has made reservations and we're going to be late."

"I'm ready. Let's go," Larry said.

"Not dressed like that. Not with me. This is a restaurant, not a masquerade ball. Get some real clothes on."

Wu winked at Taylor and left the office. Matt and Katie went to wait in the living room.

51

"And before you start pumping me," Taylor said, "I don't know what's going on either."

"Can't be all bad," Katie said. "I haven't seen Larry so up in a long time."

"I've got a question though," Taylor said. "What does "ludan" mean?"

Katie blushed and Taylor felt oddly embarrassed. "I'm sorry. It was what Larry yelled while he was working on the computer. At least I think that's what he yelled."

Katie said, "He was yelling at himself, I guess. It means, sort of, well, stupid person."

"Sort of?" Taylor said. He was amused at the flush of color still on her cheeks.

"Well, what the hell, you're family, almost," Katie said. "It literally means donkey's balls. Larry does a lot of old-fashioned mandarin swearing when he's working."

Before anything more could be said, Wu reappeared, dressed in slacks and sports jacket. They left Taylor's car in the driveway and walked quickly to the restaurant, arriving just as the maitre d' was about to give their reservations to someone else.

Larry Wu played the genial host at a long and leisurely dinner, leading the conversation through many subjects, none of which seemed even vaguely connected with what he had been working on: the techniques of Chinese painting, the short stories of Poe, the vagaries of tax systems around the world, the beauty of the Allegheny Mountains. Taylor listened halfheartedly, mostly wondering when Katie was going to have to go to the bathroom. The woman had bottomless kidneys. He kept filling her glass with plum wine and finally she succumbed and excused herself.

Even before she had left the room, Taylor said, "So what have you found out about Harker's Furnace?"

"I'd rather wait till I have the whole thing for you," Larry said. "You know how that is. You like to have the whole thing in hand first."

"Yeah, yeah, I know," Taylor said, "but what about the

returns you left on my desk? I thought you said they closed the door and nobody could get returns out of the computer."

As he expected, Larry grinned and said, "They weren't counting on Wu the Great, Wu the Wonderful, Wu the Genius Cyberneticist."

Taylor growled, "But what do you really think about yourself?" But the ploy had worked. No computer freak could ever resist bragging about how he had broken down a wall that some other computer freaks had put up to hide their work.

"Tell me, how'd you do it?" Taylor said.

Larry leaned closer over the table. "They did close down all the I.R.S. files on those names, but the mistake they made was in the copies."

"What copies?" Taylor asked.

"The computer copies that go everywhere. I went rooting around in the Social Security files, in the Labor Department's unemployment files. See, all those people—Fred Kohler and Stallbarn and McCabe and all the others—they pay the money to us, but it gets shipped around to other departments. And those departments kept the records of the names and the income, and that's where I found them . . . and all the others that I left for you."

"Pretty shrewd," Taylor said.

"Not a bad start," Larry agreed with mock modesty. "But, Matt, the I.R.S. records are still sealed; I haven't been able to break into *them* yet and we've got to figure out why."

"Why do you think?"

" 'Cause I think we found only the tip of the iceberg. I think there's more, a lot more, and I think it's bigger than just some flukey tax returns. I think this is maybe something big. Real big. Have you told anybody?"

"Just Fluory. He was going to tell Plevris but he didn't get the chance."

"What did Our Peerless Leader say?"

"Funny," Taylor said. "First he seemed hot on tracking it

53

all down. Then he called me back and said we'll worry about it later, after we get through the April 15th season."

Wu nodded. "I'm not going to wait for him. I think maybe one day more and I might have this."

"Why didn't you want Katie to hear about any of this?" Taylor asked.

"Because I don't know how big it really is. Shhh, she's coming."

Dinner ended but Larry clearly did not want the evening to be over. Taylor and Katie begged off. The young woman explained, "I'm supposed to go to this place tonight, maybe see some guy there."

"What kind of place?" Larry asked.

"Sort of a nightclub," she said.

"Good." We'll go with you to protect you. Is this the FBI guy you were telling me about?"

Katie nodded.

Wu said, "It's decided then. We'll go just to make sure the feds don't get fresh with my baby sister. All right, Matt?"

Taylor said, "I think I ought to get home."

"Nonsense," said Wu. "What's home?"

"Melanie, maybe."

"Exactly. You come with us."

Katie giggled and it was Taylor's turn to feel embarrassed. Did everyone detest his wife? Was his marriage such a joke that anyone, albeit best friends, felt free to mock it?

He said, "I'll have to call home first."

Wu said, "Go ahead. We'll wait."

Melanie answered the telephone on the first ring.

"I'm surprised you're home," Taylor said. "I thought you were taking some buyers out."

"I am," she answered. "Some of them are coming over here with some people from the shop. I'm just waiting for them now."

"A party?" Taylor groaned.

"Well, you know, Matt, actually you can skip it. Especially since you're not actually invited."

"Mel, that's my apartment. I'm your husband, remember?"

"Oh, I thought you were having a thing with the pizza boy," she said. There was ice in her voice.

"Forget it," Taylor said wearily. There was a pause before brightness returned to Melanie's voice.

"Where are you?"

"With Larry Wu," Taylor said.

"Why don't you stay at his place?" she suggested. "You know, you're not exactly the life of the party and you won't be able to sleep here anyway. There's going to be a big gang and buyers are loud, obnoxious people. Stay with Larry and we'll talk in the morning."

"Well . . ."

"Fine. Call me when you wake up, Matt," she said and the telephone went dead in his hand.

The three of them took a taxicab to the night club which barely deserved the name. It was a windowless, smoke-filled basement room in a run-down section of Washington, with undersized and overpriced drinks, and a three-piece jazz combo playing on a makeshift stage at one end of the room, its members apparently intent on seeing how much they could confuse each other.

Taylor felt very old. He remembered when jazz in clubs had both melody and rhythm and now this had neither. The trouble with trying to imitate geniuses like Wynton Marsalis and Charley Parker and Monk and Brubeck was that if you lacked their genius you wound up with only their excesses and not enough taste or vision to bring it back to the real world. No one seemed to care but him, though. Larry appeared to like the music and Katie was more interested in looking around the room to see if her date had come.

55

"You really like this crap?" Taylor leaned over to ask Wu over the din.

"I hate the music but I love what it means. It means America will always be a second-rate power," Wu said.

"Careful, China-boy. That second-rate power's paying your salary."

"Proof positive of my theory," Wu said.

Taylor felt Katie's hand squeeze his upper arm. "There he is," she said. "Don't look," she told Taylor as he began to turn toward the door. "I don't want him to think I was waiting for him."

"Naturally," Taylor said.

He had heard quite a bit about Dennis O'Leary since they had left the Chinese restaurant. He was an FBI agent; he was tall, good-looking, and smart. He had more of a sense of humor than FBI people were supposed to have. He was, altogether, in Katie's description, a man for the ages.

She had forgotten to tell him one thing. Dennis O'Leary was black. Taylor felt annoyed at his own surprise when he saw the tall black man walking across the floor of the music club. Why not? he had to ask himself. *Katie is all grown up and this isn't the Fifties anymore, so maybe you ought to grow up yourself, Matt. Or is it that you were a little jealous of all Katie's blabbering about the FBI man and now, because he's black, you don't regard him as so much of a threat anymore.*

A threat to what? He was married and Katie Wu was like a kid sister. *Grow up, Matt. Grow up.*

"Hello, Katie," O'Leary said. His voice was deep and seemed to carry, without any great effort, over the din in the barroom. "I hoped you might make it."

When she stood, he gave her a brotherly peck on the cheek. Taylor cleared his throat.

Katie introduced O'Leary to her brother and to Taylor, and as the FBI man sat down in the empty chair at the table, he told Matt, "So you're the guy she used to want to marry."

"Dennis!" Katie hissed.

Matt looked surprised. "You must have mistaken me for somebody else."

O'Leary shook his head. "No. Matt Taylor. Matt Taylor. I've heard enough about you to last a year."

"I never said any such thing," Katie said, and Matt saw she was blushing and said, "I'm just the big brother."

Katie nodded and O'Leary laughed. Taylor studied the FBI agent. He was not as tall as Matt but he was broad and looked bigger. In the dim lights of the club, his skin seemed to be a light coffee-with-double-cream color. He had a wide handsome face with a chiseled nose and faintly titled, slightly Oriental eyes. His handshake had been firm and strong when introduced to Taylor, but he had made no effort to crush Taylor's hand in his as so many men tried when introduced to someone as tall as Matt.

"Well, do I pass?" O'Leary asked.

"Beg pardon?" Taylor said.

"Do I pass? Inspection. You're staring at me."

"Oh. Actually I was thinking you didn't look much like an FBI agent."

"We're an equal opportunity employer now that J. Edgar's gone to the big racetrack in the sky," O'Leary said.

"I didn't mean that."

"What then?" O'Leary said.

"I don't know. I guess, well, maybe you don't look sneaky enough."

"Don't let appearances deceive you," O'Leary said. "I'm sneaky enough for all of us."

"I'll bet you are," Taylor said, and they all laughed.

O'Leary turned around and watched the three black musicians on the bandstand.

"Listening to this crap isn't some kind of rich Chinese cultural experience, is it?" he asked.

"Not that I know," Matt said quickly, answering for the table.

"Good," O'Leary said. "Let's get out of here."

57

He stood without waiting for other opinions. Obviously, Taylor thought, he was the kind of man used to having his own way.

O'Leary let Taylor pay the check and, holding Katie's arm with Matt and Larry trailing behind, led them on foot to a bar several blocks away, a small place with only a jukebox specializing in bluegrass music.

They drank beer and talked easily and O'Leary told them stories about the FBI academy.

"Damned near as bad as boot camp," he said.

"Boot camp?" Matt said. "Were you in the Navy?"

"Marines," O'Leary said.

"Hey, what do you know?" Larry said. "Matt was in the Marines too. A hero. They gave him a million medals, one for each of the wounds in his body."

"Ahhhh," Matt said in disgust.

"You were in Nam?" O'Leary asked.

Matt nodded.

"I didn't get there," O'Leary said.

"You didn't miss a thing."

"Damn it, a Marine. I knew there was something I liked about you. Even if you are one of Tony Plevris's flunkies," O'Leary said in good humor.

Larry went to the men's room and Taylor watched O'Leary dancing with Katie. They moved well together; he guessed before long they would move well together many times in many ways, if they hadn't already. They had just returned to the table when Wu came back from the men's room. He had stopped at the bar and was carrying four bottles of beer.

As he put the beer down, he leaned close to O'Leary and asked, "Have you noticed those two guys over there by the doorway?"

Without turning to look, O'Leary said, "You mean the big sandy-haired guy, about six two, one hundred eighty-five pounds, with the blue windbreaker, cords, and blue track shoes, and the other one, about five eight, one hundred fifty pounds, with a

58

brown and gray checked sports jacket and jeans, looks very Italian. Those the ones you're talking about?"

Trying to be casual, Taylor looked toward the door and saw that O'Leary's description of the two men was perfect. Katie started to turn and Taylor stopped her with a hand on her shoulder.

"Those are the ones," Larry said. "I think they started following us on our way here, a couple of blocks before we got here."

"No," O'Leary said, shaking his head.

Larry seemed surprised. "I was sure," he said.

O'Leary shook his head again. "They were sitting in a car outside the jazz joint where I met you. Then they followed us here on foot. They followed us all the way."

"I wonder why?" Katie said mildly.

"One way to find out," O'Leary said. As he rose, Larry and Matt started up, too, but he motioned them back down. "Just wait here and I'll handle this. If I need any help I'll give you the high sign."

They nodded and watched the FBI agent cross the room, pull up a chair, and sit with the two men they had been talking about. O'Leary seemed to be talking seriously with them and they smiled at him and all three stood up and shook hands.

O'Leary came back to the table, looking amused. "The great mystery's solved," he said. He took a lot of time then, pouring his bottle of beer into his glass, drumming with his fingers to the music, looking ceiling-ward, until Katie said, "Talk, dammit," and punched him on the shoulder with both tiny fists.

O'Leary laughed and said, "They're trainees."

"Trainees?" Larry said.

"From the bureau. They send them out to see if they can follow an experienced agent around town for a while without his making them. We made them so I told them to go home."

He nodded as if to say case closed and only minutes later, the two men left from the other table. Taylor watched them carefully. They seemed a little long in the tooth, a little old, to be FBI trainees. But who knew? It was equal opportunity now, as O'Leary had said. Maybe the FBI had a new quota for senior citizens.

After another round of beers, the four decided to leave and caught a cab back to the Wu home. But for a brief moment, as they were crossing an intersection, Taylor had the suspicion that he had just seen the two "trainees" sitting in a parked car, watching their taxicab go by.

There were three bedrooms in the Wu house, all on the second floor. Larry's was at one end of the corridor, Katie's on the other, with the smaller guest bedroom sandwiched in the middle.

They had all gathered in the living room for a nightcap and Wu, as he always did, asked Taylor if he wanted to sleep over and this time was surprised when Matt said yes.

A few minutes later, after finding that the taste of the brandy did not sit well on his stomach with the Scotch, plum wine, and beer he had sucked up all evening, Matt excused himself. Larry came up with him and waved good night to him in the hallway, nodded his head, and smiled.

"Tomorrow," he said. "I should have it figured out tomorrow."

As he was closing the door of the guest room behind himself, Matt heard Katie and Dennis O'Leary laughing downstairs in the living room, and for a moment, he felt very envious of the FBI man. It might be nice to laugh again with a woman. He had never had that with Melanie. It had started with sex; it had lived on sex; and it had died because it didn't have anything more substantial than a physical itch to keep it alive.

He quietly took off his jacket and shoes and lay on top of the bed covers, smoking, thinking that it was time for him to end his charade of a marriage. Tonight might be the worst—being ordered by his wife to keep out because he wouldn't like her friends. And he had acquiesced.

Again he heard the laughter of Katie and O'Leary rising from downstairs. The only woman he had ever laughed that way with was Lauren Carmody, but Lauren Carmody was a long time ago. What was the old line from the play: "but that was in another country and besides, the wench is dead."

Sleep would not come and he lay quietly in the darkness smoking. He heard soft footsteps outside his door and then he heard the door next to his open.

Katie had finally sent the FBI man home. Taylor wondered if he should wait a few minutes, then sneak over to her room, and talk to her. Tell her what he thought of her. If he could sort out what he really thought. If his thought were more than just a horny itch.

He had almost decided to do it. Then he heard a voice. And then another voice.

O'Leary was with Katie. They were whispering but in the deep stillness of the night, the sound was enough to carry through the wall into his room.

He could not make out the words, but they were soft too. He jabbed out his cigarette and tried to listen and tried to imagine what the two of them were doing, trying to imagine what Katie looked like, naked, with another man. Then he heard the sound of someone settling down on the bed and then another identical sound.

And then voices again.

And a giggle.

And then a voice moaning softly.

A male voice.

And then the soft rhythmic squeak of the bedsprings.

Feeling dirty, Matt Taylor got up softly, opened his door quietly and, carrying his jacket and shoes, went downstairs, dressed in the living room, let himself out, got into his car, and drove home. It was 3:00 A.M.

CHAPTER SIX

He parked his car in the private lot across the street from his apartment building, then sat in the car, smoking a cigarette, and looking up at the building.

He was home but he did not feel like being home and he did not feel like sleeping. Maybe some of his wide-awake tension came from all the liquor he had drunk that night, or maybe it came from just a jealous yen for Katie Wu's body, or maybe any woman's body. He could not remember the last time he and Melanie had made love, but it was measured now in weeks, not in days.

Other things nagged at his mind too. His growing dread of being with his wife. His nagging worry about the Harker's Furnace tax returns. An increasing weariness with his thankless job. And would being on a crime-fighting task force be any different? In the long run, wouldn't it just be more government work, more red tape, more bureaucratic bullshit?

He told himself that maybe the time truly had come for him and Larry Wu to quit the I.R.S., go into business for themselves, make a couple of million dollars each real quickly, and set up a string of ever-changing, ever-ingenious mistresses.

With that thought, he smiled a little, stubbed out his cigarette in the car's ashtray, went across the street, and rode the elevator up to his floor.

He started to put his key into the lock, but then noticed that the door was not closed fully. He swung it open and was immediately overwhelmed by the sounds and smells of a party.

He closed the door behind him; and no one seemed to notice his entrance. Perhaps people had been coming and going through the open door all night long.

There were thirty or forty people milling around in the living room. Only one lamp was on in the room and a pair of heavy bath towels had been draped over it, so the room was no brighter than if it had been illuminated only by a nightlight.

He could see the heads of more people outlined in the kitchen doorway at the far end of the room. He started to edge through the crowd, half-looking for Melanie, half-uncertain what he wanted to do. The crowd seemed unusually viscous; the more he pushed against any part of it, the more it seemed to cling to his body and gently but firmly to push back. There was a sort of undifferentiated sensuality to it. The crowd didn't seem to care who or what it rubbed up against, so long as it got its share of body contact.

And the party was unusually and strangely silent; there was a small undercurrent of conversation, occasionally a loud laugh, but there was no focus; there was no music; it seemed as if people had come merely to rub and to be rubbed.

He stopped near the kitchen door. He decided that what he wanted to do was to go into one of the bedrooms, but chances were that he would find an orgy in progress in either or both of them. The prospect held no appeal for him now. He turned toward the kitchen again and then slowly became aware of some female body parts moving slowly, caressingly against his side. For a moment, he considered not looking to see who it was and to merely enjoy the sensation but the temptation lasted only a moment; it might be Melanie.

He looked down and the owner of the body said "Hello, Mister T." It was Elly, the young clerk from Melanie's shop. He gulped slightly, straightened himself up, and leaned away from the pretty young blonde. He had seen her before and

63

known she was pretty, but in the dim light there was something different about her. Then he realized what it was: she was wearing heavy theatrical makeup with false eyelashes and dark tones to accentuate her cheekbones. Her dress, in front, was cut down almost to her waist. Her breasts rubbed against his upper arm. He tried to move back but it did no good; on his other side, he was being rubbed by a person more or less of the male gender. He leaned back toward Elly who seemed immensely pleased by that.

Taylor felt like one of those hapless husbands in a 1930s bedroom farce, sort of like Jimmy Stewart. The only problem with that was that his wife didn't have the character of Jean Arthur and he had strong doubts that this evening was going to have a happy ending.

He felt he had to say something. "I thought you were staying home tonight," he muttered softly to Elly.

"I planned to," she answered. "But then I got waylaid." She seemed to like the word so much that she repeated it, separating it into two clear syllables. "Way-laid."

"That's the way," Taylor said with a smile. "Err, you haven't seen Melanie around here anywhere, have you?"

Elly looked disappointed. "If she's not here in the living room, she's in one of the ... other rooms, I suppose. You're married to a very busy lady, Mister T."

She smiled again at him and moved closer to his arm. His hand brushed against the lower part of her belly. Her lips were parted and her head was tilted back, an invitation for him to kiss her.

"Excuse me," he said and pushed into the kitchen. That room was dark, too, lit only by a flickering votive candle on the butcherblock table, and filled, too, with bodies, buzzing, whispering to each other. Taylor saw liquor bottles on the side of the sink. A man was standing there, making a drink, and Taylor walked up to help himself and the man turned around. It was Walt Fluory. He handed Taylor the drink he had just made. "Here. You look like you need this more than I do."

Taylor wondered what the appropriate greeting was when you met your boss at 3:00 A.M. at a party in your kitchen. Before he could say anything, Fluory said, "I imagine you're wondering what I'm doing here."

He grinned. He spoke in a more-than-usually precise manner, carefully enunciating each syllable, the way a man does who has had too much to drink and is trying not to show it.

Taylor said nothing and Fluory moved closer and draped an arm around the bigger man's shoulders and moved his face close to confide in him.

"Well, I'll tell you what I'm doing here. I came home with your wife." He smiled a big Cheshire Cat grin. "I did. Really. I had a dinner meeting and then the people left and I was left there by myself, and Melanie and a whole bunch of these people"—he made a semi-coordinated wave of the hand at the door into the living room—"were all having dinner and they took pity on an old lonely bachelor and insisted I come back here to party with them. I was shanghaied. Carried off. I fought like hell. A veritable tiger, Matt, but it did me no good so here I am. I'll tell you something, Matt, my friend. That's one hell of a woman you've got for a wife. One hell of a woman."

Taylor did not want to talk to him. Just a sip of the raw Scotch that Fluory had given him had started his stomach churning. He realized he had drunk more than he thought and that he was no longer able to handle liquor as he once had.

"I've got to find Mel," he said, and before Fluory could respond, Taylor stumbled away and into the living room. The thickest cluster of people were gathered on the other side of the room, near the large windows, and Taylor worked his way toward there. He turned down an offer of a blast of cocaine and a hit on a joint. He stopped for a moment and slugged down the rest of the Scotch Fluory had given him. It hit him almost instantly.

Suddenly he felt tired and weak in every part of his body except his crotch. That felt like it was swelling into the most powerful muscle in the world, ready to explode and drown half

65

of the District of Columbia. His mind was fogged and his sight had narrowed down to tunnel vision, capable of seeing only what was in front of him. He wondered where Elly and her intrusive chest was. He would take her now. He scanned the room looking for her but in the dim light could not make out her face. Where was he? Oh. Looking for his wife. He thought he saw her brilliant blond hair in front of him. He lurched again in that direction, half-wondering if the other people in the room were as aware of the swelling in his groin as he was.

It was Melanie, and Taylor came up behind her as she was talking to three others: a young woman, a young man, and something else. She had on her flame-colored evening dress, the one that was cut low in back and high in front. As Taylor moved close to her, suddenly the lone light in the room went out and the room was plunged into darkness.

A voice called out: "Leave it out. Enough light. We have to conserve energy. Just don't get lost."

"Inside anybody else," somebody else called out, to laughter.

Taylor tried to put his empty glass down on an arm of the sofa but it missed and fell to the carpeted floor with a muffled tinkle. He pressed up close against the back of his wife who did not turn around but rubbed back against him. He focused his mind and in the dark, carefully undid the zipper at the back of her dress, running it all the way down past her waist. She still did not turn around. God, she is a slut, Taylor thought, and for that moment, he wanted that slut more than he wanted anything else in the world.

He ran his hands around under her arms and into the dress until his palms were cupping her breasts and his index fingers and thumbs manipulating her nipples. She squirmed and caught her breath but still did not turn. He turned, not removing his hands, and led her away, steering her through the crowd with one hand on each breast and his groin flush up against her backside. She moved willingly, although both had to shuffle along slowly. When they reached the bedroom door, she opened it and pushed inside.

There were no lights on in that room either and no one there that Taylor could see. She reached up to her breast and took his right hand. "Don't stumble, darling," she said. He bumped his shins against the bed and she stopped. In a few deft motions in the dark, he had his pants open and down around his knees. She pulled up her dress and then fell forward on the bed. She wore no undergarments.

"From behind," she said. "From behind."

Taylor rammed his body into hers, fast and hard, and came the same way.

Melanie groaned, let out a little hiss of air, and said, "Do me again. Please. Please."

Taylor did her again.

When he was done, he raised himself from her body. She continued to lay with her face buried in the satin comforter of their bed. Even though his eyes had grown accustomed to the darkness now, he could see nothing except her blond hair occasionally flashing a glint of random light. She had never looked up at him.

She mumbled into the bedspread. "I think I love you. What's your name?"

Taylor did not answer. He pulled up his pants and left the bedroom and the apartment. He felt as if he had just scrubbed his hands clean with strong soap.

CHAPTER SEVEN

Taylor awakened in a small dismal hotel room, walked leadenly from the bed to the bathroom and, using his finger as a toothbrush, tried to wash the taste of the previous night out of his mouth, but only partially succeeded.

Then he turned on the shower and stood under its stinging waters for ten minutes, constantly jiggling the controls from too hot to too cold and then back again, over and over.

He signed the bill at the hotel's front desk, then stopped at the hotel's coffee shop. He ordered orange juice, Danish and coffee, but when it came, its smell nauseated him and he left without eating any of it.

It was eight-thirty when he got home. The wreckage of the party was strewn everywhere. He looked in the bedroom for his wife but she was not there. The bed was mussed though, proof that it had been used by someone. He changed his clothes and packed enough to last for a week's trip to Philadelphia, thought about leaving a note for Melanie, decided against it, and drove to his office.

There was another new secretary in his outer office, this one middle-aged and frumpy. She gave him one disapproving disgusted look and said nothing, but her silence about his appearance was eloquent.

Taylor called Fluory's private line from inside his office. He wondered what time they would be leaving for Philadelphia. The phone did not answer and, after a while, Taylor hung up and called Fluory's secretary who told him that her boss had called in just a few minutes earlier and told her that he would be late. Taylor thought that wasn't like Fluory at all, but there wasn't anything to do about it but wait.

He asked his new secretary to fetch him some breakfast. She brought it in wordlessly—juice, Danish, and coffee—the same meal he had rejected at the restaurant, but this time he forced himself to eat. He had just finished when there was a knock on the door.

"Come in."

Fluory entered. He was dressed as dapperly as ever but he carried himself like a man with a bad hangover. He kept rubbing a hand across the top of his polished blond hair.

"No matter what you do," he said, "don't speak louder than a whisper."

"Okay," Taylor said in a normal tone of voice. Fluory cringed and Matt said again, in a mock whisper this time, "Okay."

"That's better."

Fluory settled himself gently into the chair in front of Taylor's desk and for a moment seemed to meditate on how well he had performed that difficult task.

"You might be able to tell, I've got one hell of a hangover."

"No one would ever guess," Taylor said blandly.

"You got any black coffee?"

Taylor nodded, hit the intercom, and asked the secretary to bring in more black coffee.

Fluory said, "You may already have guessed that we're not flying up to Philly today. Those screwheads up there aren't worth our agony. We'll go tomorrow."

He stopped talking as the secretary brought in a cup of coffee. Fluory rated a ceramic mug and while the secretary had studiously ignored Taylor, she seemed to dote on the higher-ranking man. When she left her bosom seemed to be pushed out a little further than before and her rear end swayed a little

69

more than was necessary. It was an effect Taylor had always been vaguely aware of that Fluory had on women; they all seemed to want to look their best for him.

"That was some party last night," Fluory said after she left. "What happened to you?"

"I don't know. I don't remember," Taylor lied. He was still annoyed at having found Fluory at the party, especially after Melanie had specifically disinvited her own husband because tax people were dull.

"When'd you get home?" Taylor asked.

"You got me," Fluory said. "But it was still nighttime, I remember that." He seemed proud of his achievement in leaving before daybreak.

"Did you see Melanie when you left?"

Fluory abruptly stood up. "It's all kind of a haze," he said, as if realizing he was being grilled and trying to cut off further conversation. He took a big swig from the coffee cup, left it on Taylor's desk, and walked to the door. "My girl will let you know about our new flight plans," he said. Then he went out and Taylor thought he could hear him talking to the secretary at her desk, and her laughing girlishly for a moment.

Taylor finished his coffee and Fluory's, too, as he thought about what he should do. It was all over with Melanie now; that much he knew. But now he would have to figure out how to tell her and when to tell her and what to say when she protested. One good thing: Melanie made more money than he did through her little art shop; alimony would not be a factor.

Nor, unfortunately, would child support. Melanie had seen to that. Several times, Taylor had raised the idea of having a family and Melanie had always sloughed it off. Plenty of time for that later, she had said. That was when she was sober. If she had been drinking, and lately she usually was, she thought she was W.C. Fields. "How would you like children, Melanie?" "On toast, Matt."

It was all too much to figure out. Taylor realized that what he had actually wanted most in life was simplicity: a simple

70

marriage, a simple fatherhood, a simple job where he made a simple good living. But nothing seemed to work out like that; everything seemed to be complicated and getting more complex.

But the business with Melanie was definite. That was over. Last night had proved it to him. The woman was a tramp and everyone had seemed to accept that fact but him, until it was brought home to him in a way beyond argument. No more rose-colored glasses; they were *finito*.

But it would all wait until he returned from Philadelphia.

Just before eleven o'clock, Larry Wu came into his office. the Chinese weren't supposed to be able to drink but Larry showed no signs of the night before.

Taylor started to apologize. "Sorry for sneaking out last night. I just couldn't sleep," he said.

Wu raised a hand to quiet him as if none of that mattered.

"I've just gotten a command performance request," he said.

"From who?"

"Whom. From Internal Security."

Taylor shook his head. Internal Security summonses were generally major ordeals within the I.R.S.; they were the tax department's CIA.

"What have you done?" he asked Wu.

"Damned if I know," Wu said and Taylor sensed that his friend was trying to paper over his apprehension at the call.

"Well, the good thing is it can't be important," Taylor said, "if they've got you scheduled for eleven o'clock. If it were a big deal, it'd be first thing in the morning or first thing after lunch so they could work you over for hours. Eleven o'clock means you'll be out by noon, no matter what happens."

"I suppose so," Wu said, but he did not sound fully convinced. "Anyway, I just wanted to let you know."

"I'll wait for you for lunch."

"Good. And here, hold my book. I bring it with me and they'll think I'm some kind of Communist fag," Wu said. He

71

handed Taylor the slim volume he had been carrying. Its title was *The Art of Chinese Painting*.

"You're allowed to read it," Wu said. "It may help you solve some of the puzzles in your life."

Taylor placed the book on his desk as Wu left. He left it there an hour later when Larry had not returned and Taylor went over to the McDonald's near the I.R.S. building and ordered lunch for himself.

It was almost 1:00 P.M. and Taylor was getting ready to leave when Larry Wu showed up. Without explanation, he started to pick at Taylor's leftover French fries.

"Well?" Taylor demanded.

"I think we may have really stumbled onto something," Wu said.

"Harker's Furnace?" Taylor said, and Wu nodded.

"That's all they wanted to talk about," he said.

"And?"

"And I told them what they wanted to know," Wu said.

"So now maybe it's time you told me," Taylor said.

Wu finished the last crumbs from the French fries.

"Okay. What I told them and what I think we've got here is maybe some kind of a scam. Those returns I left on your desk yesterday?"

"Yeah?"

"Remember, all those people were listed as self-employed. But I broke apart some files in the Labor Department and found their 1099's. They were all self-employed but they were all contractors or whatever for just one company—Harker's Furnace Incorporated. Now somehow, in this little town in Pennsylvania, this one little company is paying these guys a salary, and they're all living in motels and donating to charity and to political campaigns and paying house mortgages, although what the hell for I don't know if they all live in motels—and everything right at the national averages of all taxpayers."

Taylor shrugged. He still failed to see the pattern in what Wu had discovered.

"I think this is all some kind of a fraud. I would take odds right now that Harker's Furnace Incorporated doesn't exist, and that none of those people whose names are on the tax returns exist either."

"Did you tell that to Internal Security?" Taylor asked.

Wu nodded.

"And what did they say?"

"They seemed real interested in how I found out all the information I found out. Especially after I told them that all the records seem to be sealed somehow, outside the I.R.S.'s main computer network."

"They want to know how you got in?" Taylor asked.

"Naturally."

"And what'd you tell them?"

"Hey. I wasn't a boy wizard for nothing. I got in by knowing more about getting in than the guy who set up the program knew about keeping people out."

"I don't know," Taylor said. He looked in the French fries container for scraps but Wu had eaten them all. "Who'd try to keep us out of the computer? What's the point of the whole thing?"

"I don't know and I don't think they know. The only thing they knew is that I should stay the hell away from things that don't concern me. Naturally I promised I would," Wu said. "They were interested in you too. What exactly did you know? Naturally I told them you didn't know anything. That you were a committed federal employee and therefore knew nothing."

"Good. Let's leave it at that and leave it with them," Taylor said.

"Good, my ass," Wu snapped. "Matt, I didn't tell them everything."

"Uh-oh," Taylor said. "I'm not sure I like the sound of this."

"Matt. I've made contact with another computer. I don't know what it is or where it is, but it's outside of Washington and it's holding these Harker's Furnace records."

"What do you mean, it's outside of Washington?" Taylor asked.

"Just what I said. Physically, it's someplace else. And it's not part of the I.R.S. linkup. Matt, someplace in this country there's a private computer and it's got I.R.S. data in it."

Taylor paused a long while before speaking again. Finally, he said, "It's getting too deep for me, Larry. I think they gave you good advice. Let somebody else worry about it."

"Bullshit. I'm going to find out what's going on."

"Larry, I don't like it. You could get your butt in a sling."

"It doesn't have anything to do with you or with the office. I'm going to do it on my own time," Wu said.

"Why?"

"Because I don't like things that aren't tidy. I don't like puzzles that don't have a solution. And most of all, I don't like anybody telling me not to try to figure something out. Where's my book?"

"Oh. I left it on my desk."

"I want it back. I'm through casting pearls before swine," Wu said.

"Get it from my secretary. I'm going home," Taylor said.

Wu looked at him closely, then said, "Bad time with the wife last night."

Taylor nodded and Larry sighed. "Why didn't you marry Katie when I told you to?"

"When would that have been?" Taylor said.

"Anytime. Anytime before she met this O'Leary guy. She's much taken with him, you know."

"I figured that out," Taylor said.

"But he may not last. So next time, you be ready."

"Count on it," Taylor said.

The apartment was immaculately clean when Taylor let himself in an hour later, setting his suitcase just inside the door.

Other things were different too. There was a smell he could not place and a sound like humming.

He followed the sound to the kitchen. It was humming. Melanie was leaning over the stove, taking fresh baked bread from the oven. It was not the Melanie he had seen last night though, when she was evening-gowned, made up to the nines, and fucking strangers.

Now her hair was piled on top of her head and held in place with bobby pins. She was dressed in blue jeans and a man's shirt, and if the jeans were meant to be form-fitting, you could not tell from the way the shirt—his shirt—hung out over them. She wore no makeup, no jewelry and the air did not smell of her heavy expensive perfumes. When she turned to look at him, her face was puffy and her eyes reddened.

"Hello, Matt," she said. Her voice was soft and uncertain.

He nodded and she took a couple of tentative steps toward him.

"I was making a surprise for dinner. I thought we might eat in. Home, tonight."

She waited for him to respond but he said nothing. He was wondering what was going on. Was this some sort of joke, some extravagant charade? Was he supposed to forget last night's orgy in his happiness over a loaf of homemade bread?

"Thanks," he said finally and started from the room. She came after him, catching up with him in the living room. She reached out and touched his arm, gently. "Matt," she said. "I'm sorry."

He looked down at her. She seemed prettier than he could remember her being in years. Pretty in a real kind of way; not pretty out of a fashion salon and a cosmetics jar.

"I'm sorry, too," he said, mostly because he could not think of anything else to say. Where had this woman been during the last several years when the other Melanie kept reminding him of how dull he was; how boring his job was; how only her income enabled them to live like human beings; that the only people who counted in Washington were those with money and

75

power and that he, Matt Taylor, was too stupid ever to have real money and too weak ever to wield power? Where had this bread-baking, house-cleaning wife been all that time?

"I just hope that it isn't too late for us," she said, and then she was crying and her head was buried in his chest. He patted her back until she stopped and then they sat down on the sofa, not quite close enough to touch. It's a little late for all of this, he thought.

She cried. When she stopped, he said, "What's going on here, Melanie?" and she started crying all over again.

After a while, she started to talk between sobs.

"I woke up this morning and it was so awful. There were people here I didn't even know. Not very nice people either and you could tell that they'd been doing things that weren't nice and I saw it and I was feeling awful with my hangover and then I went into the bathroom and threw up all over everything. And then I went and kicked everybody out. All of them. Then I sat down and cried. I think I was just feeling sorry for myself and I wanted you to hold me, the way you used to, remember?"

Taylor said coldly, "I remember. I remember last night too. You didn't seem to find your friends so offensive then. Just jigging and fucking like all the rest of them."

She went on as if she had not heard him. "I couldn't stay around here so I went to the shop. And then I couldn't stay there either. I came back home to try to figure out what to do, and I saw you'd been here and you'd taken your clothes and you were gone."

She stopped talking long enough to search her jeans for a tissue, find one, wipe her eyes, and blow her nose.

"I didn't know what to do. I was losing it, really losing it. I could see all the things I'd done wrong, how I'd been such an awful wife. Then Walt Fluory called."

Melanie paused, as if for effect. Almost the same way that Fluory did, Taylor thought.

"And he told me your trip had been cancelled. It made me feel so much better, 'cause I knew you'd only taken your clothes

76

to go away on one of your damned trips and you weren't leaving me forever."

Melanie took her husband's left hand in both hers and played with his wedding band while she talked.

"Then I couldn't stand your coming home to the mess that was here and I cleaned up and then I called the office to try to talk to you but you'd gone." She seemed to fight to hold back her tears before she continued. "I was so scared that you wouldn't come home. I didn't know what to do. You believe me, don't you? Please. Say you believe me."

Taylor did not know what to say. He felt his resolve, his determination that this marriage was over, slipping away. He did not want to encourage her but he did not want to hurt her either. Instead of answering, he squeezed her to him, even as he thought himself a coward just postponing the inevitable. After a few moments, she kissed him, warmly but shyly, a young bride's kiss.

Taylor pulled away and they looked at each other. Melanie said, "I want you. I want you more than anything in the world. But I want us to wait. It'll be better later. Let's try being friends for a little while first."

Taylor felt himself being swept along on a wave he had never seen coming. "Anything you want," he said and Melanie kissed him hard on the lips and hurried from the room. "I'll finish getting dinner ready," she said.

Taylor showered and when he came out, dinner was served, with candles and wine. Following dinner, they did the dishes together and then made love on the sofa. After they had gone to bed and made love again, Melanie lay beside Taylor talking vaguely about plans for their future.

"What about the shop? Will you sell it?" Taylor asked.

She was silent for long seconds, then said, "I don't think that's wise. We're making a real go of it there now and I think it'll be a neat thing for you and me to have ... to share. We'll worry about that some other time. Tell me, what are you doing

77

at work? What's happening that's new and exciting? How's Larry?"

Taylor did not feel like telling her about Harker's Furnace. It was too complicated, too confusing.

He just said, "Nothing much new."

"You and Larry must be working on *something* though," she said. "For you to go out to dinner with him and all. Come on, you can tell me." She put her head on his bare chest. "Big spy stuff, right?"

"No. Nothing like that. Nothing at all," he said.

She sighed and said, "Well, I guess you'd tell me if you thought there was something to tell, wouldn't you?"

He grunted and Melanie said, "Make love to me again. Slow and easy and long. Until we fall asleep."

Taylor woke with a start. Melanie was not in bed nor in the bathroom, he could see through the open door. The clock on the table next to the telephone said 2:50 A.M.

He got up groggily and walked out into the living room. Melanie was on the phone. She smiled when she saw him and handed the receiver to him.

"Here. It's Walt. He just called. I didn't want to wake you."

Taylor shook his head to clear the cobwebs, took the phone and said, "Hello, Walt. Nice hour to be calling."

"Matt, things are going to hell in a handbasket up in Philadelphia. You've got to get there first thing in the morning before they open their doors."

"Okay. Should I meet you at the airport?"

After a moment's hesitation, Fluory said, "That's the problem, Matt. My secretary really screwed up and didn't book you. Now the plane's full and there's no way you can fly up there and still get there on time."

"Oh?" said Matt, half-sensing the request that was about to be made.

"Matt, I know this is a hell of a thing to ask . . ."

78

"Go ahead and ask."

"Could you drive up to Philly?"

Taylor sighed, then said, "I suppose. Yeah, I'll do it."

"Good. I knew I could count on you. Matt?"

"Still here."

"We're going to need some support help up there. Do you think Larry Wu could go with you?"

"Sure," Taylor said, "if you ask him. At least it'll be somebody to keep me company and stop me from falling asleep at the wheel."

"Good," Fluory said. "I'll call him right now and tell him you'll be by at about what ... four o'clock say?"

"Fine," Taylor said. "I'll see you in Philadelphia in the morning. This time, breakfast's on you."

Fluory chuckled and hung up.

Later, while shaving, Taylor wondered why he had not heard the telephone ring when Fluory called.

CHAPTER EIGHT

Looking sour, Larry Wu was both groggy and grumpy and only snarled when he climbed into Taylor's car. It was not until after they had gotten onto Interstate 95 out past the Beltway that he spoke.

"The next exit where there's something open, let's stop. I'm starting to get hungry."

Taylor looked at the digital clock above the mirror in the small Ford Escort. A few minutes after four o'clock. In the best of times it usually took him at least three hours to get to Philadelphia, and these were not the best of times.

Late March in the east is treacherous, and while the day had been sunny and warm, now the temperature had dropped, the wind had shifted around to the northeast and was staring to come in on them from off Chesapeake Bay. At this time of year that always meant foul weather: fog and probably rain, maybe sleet, and possibly even snow. And the further north they traveled, the closer they got to Philadelphia, the worse the weather was likely to become.

"Did you hear me?" Wu growled.

"Mmmm, you're pleasant today," Matt said.

"I've been up all night. Screw pleasant."

"Go to sleep," Taylor said. "Dream about food. I'll wake you when we get closer to Philly."

"Essene," Larry Wu said disgustedly.

"What?"

"Essene. Those were the guys who lived in the desert back before Jesus."

"I know who the Essenes were. Why me?"

"They were like you. They lived on prayers and air. They wouldn't stop either when their best friends were starving."

Taylor laughed. "Go to sleep or I won't stop at all." Wu hunched against the passenger door and in only a few minutes was snoring softly.

The miles droned by in the thump of the car as it moved from one slab of poured concrete pavement to the next. Taylor tried to count them but the best he could get was approximately one hundred twenty-five slabs to the mile. He was usually more precise with numbers than that but he blamed his inexactitude on the weather. The fog had begun to alternate with some mixture of rain and sleet and snow. The traffic was getting heavier, too, as it grew closer to dawn, most of it being overloaded semis. Each time one roared past Taylor's little compact, it seemed to bury the car under a deluge of the grime and water blowing off the truck's mudflaps, and to nearly shake the little car off the road with the air turbulence their passing had created.

The drive was also measured in its sporadic moments of blind terror. Taylor would let his mind wander off to the events of the past few days—the discovery of the Harker's Furnace returns; the party the night before; Larry's mysterious behavior; Melanie's sudden display of wifely affection—until it all became a jumble in his sleep-deprived brain, and he would nearly forget that he was driving along one of the most dangerous stretches of highway in the United States. And then another semi would come along, or two or three, and their passing would shake his car and cover his windshield with dirty, gritty water and Taylor would wage a white-knuckled battle to keep the car under control and on the road.

After what seemed an endless drive, Taylor was in and out of Baltimore. The traffic on the Interstate had exhausted him and he decided to switch over to the four-laned U.S. Route 40. It had the disadvantage of more closely hugging the edge of the bay and thus being more exposed to the bad weather, but it had the advantage of not having so many trucks on it at this hour, and he would rather deal with the weather than the trucks.

Beside him, Larry Wu snored peacefully, and around him the traffic had thinned out to an annoying trickle. Taylor decided to keep driving as long as Wu was asleep. By the time they had passed Aberdeen, the road had moved far enough inland that most of the fog had disappeared, but a few miles farther on, near Havre de Grace, the rain changed almost completely to sleet and snow. It was 5:28 by the over-mirror clock when Taylor crossed the Susquehanna river. The first hints of the coming dawn were appearing through the clouded sky and Taylor decided he would stop at the next roadside restaurant for some food and some cold water on his face.

He came around a long slow curve in the road and had to start quickly pumping his brakes. He must have been going faster than he had realized, he thought groggily, because the two lanes ahead of him were nearly blocked by a brownish station wagon and a red sedan creeping along side by side.

Taylor glanced up into his rearview mirror more as a precaution than anything else. There was a semitrailer coming up quickly but it was running bare and should have no trouble stopping in time. Just to be on the safe side, Taylor tapped lightly, twice, on his horn pad to alert the cars in front of him. They did not seem to respond but beside him Larry Wu was stirring slightly.

Taylor checked quickly in the rearview mirror again. The semi was still coming; perhaps it had slowed some, but as near as Taylor could tell, not enough. He could feel his palms start to sweat. The distances between his car and the cars in front and the truck behind were constantly growing tighter.

He stepped lightly on the gas, closing the distance more between him and the two cars that were blocking his way in front. Once more, he hit the horn, this time louder and longer than the last time. But it had no effect; the two cars still blocked the road in front of him and behind him the semi was quickly closing in. Taylor hit the horn again, longer, harder.

Wu awakened with a start. "What's happening?"

"Don't know," Taylor snapped. He nervously glanced back over his shoulder. The red semi had closed to within twenty yards.

There was still a bit of leeway in front of him and Taylor hit the gas, trying to close the gap between himself and the two cars ahead and at the same time, to give the truck driver more room in which to stop. Again Taylor pressed down on his horn and this time, he held it down. The car's horn took on a long mournful wail.

The two cars finally seemed to hear it. They jerked ahead, but still moved side by side, blocking any possibility of passing. Taylor accelerated too. And behind him, so did the red semi.

"This is your basic weird," Larry Wu said, as he glanced out the rear window of the car. "We're in a goddam vehicular sandwich."

Before Taylor could answer, the semi hit them. The sound struck them first, a sort of low crunching whoop of a sound, and then a split second later they felt the impact of the hit. Taylor and Larry were both shoved forward but their seatbelts clicked into action just a few inches before their faces would have collided with the windshield. Their bodies hung, seemingly poised in midflight for just an instant, and then they were flung back against their seats.

Without thinking, Taylor jammed on the brakes and almost immediately could feel the car start to slide, its rear end turning obliquely in the path of the truck.

Until now, Taylor thought, things had been happening much faster than he could even process the sensory input, much less react to it. But all of sudden, the world slowed down. Taylor could see clearly what was happening around him. Everything seemed to be in slow motion except himself.

Wu was yelling at him. Taylor could not at first understand

the words but then he realized Larry was telling him to take his foot off the brakes. Taylor thought about it for what seemed like a long time. Somehow it seemed to make sense. He took his foot off the pedal and the car seemed to jerk itself back into the forward direction it had been moving in before it had been hit. Taylor decided to help it. He grabbed the steering wheel tight and started pulling it hard toward the right. He was surprised to see another pair of hands doing the same thing. They belonged to Wu. Taylor glanced at the truck in the rearview mirrow again and was surprised to see that it had dropped back perhaps twenty yards. In front of them though, the station wagon and the sedan, while they had pulled ahead some, were still side by side blocking any escape on the roadway. Still, Taylor took a deep breath of relief.

"What the hell was that all about?" Wu asked.

"I don't know. Maybe the truck driver fell asleep."

"Maybe," Wu said. He turned halfway around in his seat. The semi seemed to be keeping its distance.

"You okay?" he asked Taylor.

"Yeah. You?"

"I'll survive," Wu said. "But remind me not to go anywhere with you any more. You're a pain in the ass, and if we had stopped to eat like I wanted, none of this would have happened."

"Well, we'll make up for that now," Taylor said.

While they were talking, he sensed some motion in the lane beside them. He looked out the window now, and in the lane to his left there was a dark-colored van with smoked windows.

"Glad they weren't there before," Taylor said. "It would have been good-bye for us."

"Oh, shit," Larry said.

"What?"

"Behind."

Taylor did not have time to look. The semi was boring down on them again, too fast to stop even if its driver had wanted to. Taylor reached for the brake, then remembered not to. Before he could get his foot off the pedal, though, the semi rammed into them knocking Taylor's car forward and into a slide. Taylor could feel his fender screeching against the van even before he became aware of the sound of tearing metal. He fought frantically with the wheel and somehow managed to straighten the car again. He looked ahead, quickly scanning the roadway. Ordinarily, he thought of this patch of highway as being mostly flat. He had forgotten all the small bridges over all the small side roads and streams. One such bridge over a stream was dead ahead of them.

The van on their left quickly dropped back half a car length and then turned, sharply and deliberately, into Taylor's car. The impact sent it sliding sideways toward the bridge abutment.

"Gas," Larry Wu shouted. "Gas, gas, gas. Step on the damn gas."

Taylor did, at the same time quickly twirling the wheel so that his car was headed first for the opposite, left-side bridge abutment, and then, split seconds before it would have crashed, right through the middle of the bridge. As he passed the bridge, from behind him came a tremendous screeching sound and a shattering clang.

"Good, you prick," Larry shouted. "That bastard in the van didn't make it. He hit the bridge."

There was no time to celebrate. Ahead, the two sedans had slowed down, blocking the way out, and again, the semi was back quickly closing in on them again. There seemed to be no escape. There was no shoulder to the road, only a long dangerous drop down toward God-knows-what.

Taylor thought a moment, then stepped on the gas, closing the distance to the two cars in front of him, even as the semi continued to close in on him. Taylor moved his car slightly toward the center of the road so that its right half was squarely aligned with the left half of the red sedan in the outside lane. There was still a foot or so of clear space between Taylor's left fender and the station wagon in the inside lane.

Wu saw what he was planning.

"Good. Let's hope it works."

The semi was accelerating; its driver seemed to sense a kill. It picked up speed and came barrelling into Taylor's car, but at the precise moment of impact, Taylor accelerated to, moving his front bumper up till it was touching that of the red sedan. The shock of the semi's impact was transmitted right through Taylor's car and into the sedan. Its driver was not prepared for it and he started to swerve. Almost immediately, the semi driver realized what was happening and slammed on his brakes.

Taylor stomped his accelerator to the floor and as the out-of-control red car drifted toward the side of the road, Taylor sped through the small space between it and the tan station wagon.

He was free. Wu had turned around in his seat to watch what was going on behind them. He did not describe it; only emitting a string of ejaculations that may or may not have been Chinese.

Taylor glanced back as he sped away. The driver of the red sedan had either panicked or badly calculated his moves. His car had turned clear around in the road, facing back the way it had come, and in the process had hit into the station wagon. Both seemed momentarily still in time, but only momentarily, for they were then spattered across the highway by the semi that had come plowing into them. Sparks flew; there was a faint flash of flame; then there was stillness.

"Should we stop?" Taylor asked.

"Maybe in Los Angeles," Larry Wu said. "Let's get out of here."

CHAPTER NINE

"Any theories?" Taylor asked.

"Somebody up there doesn't like us?" said Larry Wu.

They were sitting in a roadside restaurant, two miles down the road from the accident scene. Through the windows they could see row upon row of gas pumps. Inside the food service area, it was segregated into truckers-only and public sections.

Their waitress, a tall redheaded woman in her late twenties with a trim body but a tired-looking wary face, had brought them coffee without asking.

"Naaah. I think if God gets mad at us, he's going to send something more than four crazies from the demolition derby," Taylor said. He shook his head and Larry shrugged, and said, "Stop guessing. You know what it is."

Taylor stared at him for a moment, then suggested, "Harker's Furnace?"

"Naturally," Wu said.

"But why?"

"Because we found out something we weren't supposed to find out," Larry said. "Remember, I told you I was up all night?"

"Yeah."

"Well, I made contact with that other computer, the one that's got the Harker's Furnace files in it."

"Yeah? Where is it? Whose computer is it?"

"I don't know. I just got into their line but the other operator said he'd get in trouble if he talked to me. I thought I'd try again when I got somebody else working the machine. So that's what I did last night. And four hours later, somebody tries to kill us."

"I don't know," Taylor said. "It might just have been some crazy rednecks who thought you were going to move into their neighborhood or something. Some good old boys with a six-pack where their brains should have been."

"Believe that if you want," Wu said. "But not me."

"I guess we ought to call the police," Taylor said.

"Why?"

"Tell them what happened," Taylor said.

"Forget it. They know what happened," Wu said. "They got a road filled with wrecks back there." As if to underscore his point, a state police cruiser went flying by the front of the restaurant at high speed, its klaxon siren whooping. "Let them sort it out."

Taylor shook his head and rose from behind the table.

"No," he said stubbornly. "Got to let them know what happened. There might be somebody hurt back there, maybe dying."

As he walked away from the table, he heard Wu mumble: "It'd help if *we* knew what happened."

There were two of them: one tall, blond, and boyish-looking, wearing a natty trooper's uniform; the other of medium height, with ruddy complexion and worn blue eyes, in civilian clothes. They shook hands with Taylor and Wu and then dragged two chairs from a nearby table so they could sit at the end of the booth looking at the two other men. It was subtle but significant, Taylor thought; they were sitting at the end of the restaurant booth just as they would if they were expecting Taylor and Wu to try to flee.

The one in uniform was named Jensen; the other was Lieutenant Arthur Webster. The redheaded waitress brought them all more coffee.

The whole interview took perhaps half an hour with Webster asking the questions and Jensen watching them closely, never saying a word at first. After they had talked a while, Webster asked them if they would mind taping statements separately.

"Hold on," Larry said. "Now we've got a question."

"If I can," Webster said.

"What'd you find down the road?" Wu asked. "Is anybody hurt back there?"

Webster shook his head and said, "We found two wrecked cars. No drivers around, no sign of anybody being injured. And both cars had been stolen. That answer your questions?"

Wu nodded.

"Okay. Then let's get this finished," Webster said. Jensen took Wu and Taylor, one at a time, to another table and recorded their statements. Then the two policemen accompanied them outside to see the damage that had been done to Taylor's car.

By the time they were finished it was past six o'clock and nearly light. Webster said if anything came up, he would contact them.

"What now?" Larry Wu said after the policemen had walked off.

"On to Philadelphia, I guess," Taylor said.

They started to get back into Taylor's car but as he settled in the seat, Wu began patting his pockets frantically, almost as if he were trying to put out a fire.

"Damn. I bet I left it in the restaurant." He jerked open the car door and hurried back into the building. Taylor waited for him for a while and then got out of the car and went back into the truckstop. They met at the entrance door. Larry grinned and held up a paperback book.

"Couldn't leave this behind," he said. "I dropped it in the men's room.

Taylor glanced at the title; it was *The Art of Chinese Painting*, the same book Wu had left with him the previous day for safekeeping.

As they walked back across the parking lot, Taylor noticed that the two state policemen were still parked off in a corner of the lot, perhaps seventy-five yards away. It looked as if Webster were using the cruiser's radio.

Wu said in a low voice, "What kind of shape you in?"

"Best shape of all. I'm alive," Taylor said.

"Try to stay that way," Wu said. He handed Taylor his book on painting. "I don't like the looks of those guys over there."

Taylor stuck the book in his pocket and looked ahead. There were two men, big men, dressed like truckers, leaning against Taylor's now-battered car.

As the two men approached, one of the men at the car looked them over and said, "Taylor and Wu?"

Taylor nodded.

"Good," the other man said. "Wouldn't want to hit the wrong guys." He pulled a pistol from the outside pocket of his scuffed suede jacket. The other man did the same.

Wu moved before Taylor could even think. There was a blur and one of the gunmen was down, sitting on the pavement, from a spinning karate kick. But the other pointed his gun at Wu's midsection and pulled the trigger again and again and again. Larry's body jerked from the impact of the bullets but somehow they did not stop him and he lunged forward and wrapped his arms around his assailant's neck. Taylor looked on in horror for a moment, then screamed in rage and dove over the trunk of the car. He could see nothing now except a red haze in front of his eyes. It was Vietnam again. It was death and he had never wanted to feel it again.

The sound of the gunshots had a transforming effect on the truckstop parking lot. Voices called out. Doors slammed. People came running. Before Wu could drag him down, the gunman had fired three more rounds into his body and the young Chinese collapsed in a bullet-ridden, blood-spurting heap at the

90

man's feet. As the gunman pushed himself clear, Taylor was on him. His right forearm was wrapped around the man's neck; his left elbow pressed against the left side of the man's head; just pressure, hard, instinctive. There was a snapping sound and Taylor felt the man grow limp in his arms.

The second gunman had not been able to fire at Taylor for fear of hitting his own companion, but now as the body slumped and fell loose from Matt's arms, the man leveled his gun at Taylor. And then there was a shot from a different direction. Taylor felt a bullet hit the ground and rebound away. The gunman looked to his left, then turned and ran.

Taylor looked down at Larry Wu; he had seen enough death to recognize it; he imagined he could almost smell the aroma of blood in the air. Why? Was this the way life was supposed to end? Dead in a parking lot for some reason no one could understand? And then the two highway cops, Jensen and Webster, were standing there, guns drawn, and Taylor searched their faces for answers but they had no answers for him.

Taylor and the two highway policemen were back in the truck stop. Taylor was feeling sad and numb, both at the same time; the two cops were professionally tired.

"For the tenth time," Taylor said, "I can't figure out why anybody would want to kill either of us."

"That was easier for me to believe when you were telling me about some kind of mysterious highway accident that nobody but you saw," Webster said. "But now we got something else. We got somebody kills your friend. We got you breaking the bastard's neck and killing him. What we got is a lot of trouble and you're in the middle of it."

"I suppose so," Taylor answered wearily. "Can you guys leave me alone for a while? This is too much."

The policemen glanced at each other, and Jensen, the younger one in uniform, got up and walked out to the parking lot where an ambulance was getting ready to take away the bodies of Larry Wu and the dead gunman. The police had told Taylor that the second gunman had gotten clean away.

Now Webster stood and said, "Listen, I know this is hard on you. But I got to go to the john; don't go wandering off. Just sit here."

Taylor nodded numbly. Through the window of the restaurant, he watched the technicians load the body of his best friend into the ambulance and then drive off. No siren, he said to himself. He's dead. You don't need a siren. A siren made it too real. But the siren started blasting anyway as the vehicle left the parking lot.

Melanie. Maybe he should call her in case she heard something on the news, maybe tell her that he was all right. Would she care? Was today a day for being the loving wife, the way she had been the evening before, or would she be the hoydenish slut of the last year?

It was too tiring to think about. He folded his arms in front of him on the table and rested his head on them, his eyes closing slowly. He lost track of time. He drifted into a sort of shell-shocked stupor. First the incident with the semi; then the murder of Larry Wu. What could be next?

And then suddenly he was wide-awake and fully alert. Without moving his head, Taylor carefully studied the aisle next to his table. Someone was standing there and when Taylor looked up, he recognized the man. It was the other gunman, the one who had fled the parking lot when the police came on the scene. The man's eyes gleamed feverishly; his clothes were torn and muddy. There was dirt on his face and a gun in his hand.

Taylor pushed himself upright in the booth, knocking over the table as he did and startling the gunman at the same time. As the table fell, the gunman jumped backward and Taylor grabbed the heavy sugar container from the floor as he tried to scramble to his feet.

He threw the container but the man ducked and it went sailing past him, to hit the wall behind him. Suddenly, the diner was absolutely silent; Taylor knew people were watching; the gunman was smiling; he straightened up and aimed his gun at Taylor's stomach. Taylor saw the man's finger start to squeeze on the trigger.

And then Taylor watched the other man's face explode into dozens of bloody fragments.

CHAPTER TEN

"You know, you're not much help."

Matt Taylor squinted. The lights in the room hurt his tired eyes. It was mid-morning now and his body and mind were crying out for sleep.

"I'd help if I could," he said. "But I don't know anything."

Lt. Arthur Webster of the Maryland State Police sighed and shoved his chair away from the table across which he and Taylor faced each other. Both the table and the chairs were heavy institutional metal, painted a dead gray and covered with a darker-colored plastic. The room was bare and unadorned except for an insurance calendar on one wall and a list of instructions on what to do in case of fire beside the light switch next to the door. The floor was carpeted with some heavy duty fuzz that had long ago surrendered its color to too many spilled cups of coffee. The walls were covered with white tiles, decorated with soundproofing holes. The ceiling was a series of fluorescent lights hidden behind frosted plastic panes and which looked, at a glance, like a graveyard for dead flies because the little black dots of their sere bodies spotted the plastic panels.

Webster looked nearly as tired as the room and he acted as if Taylor were giving him a stomach ache.

"Let's try some names," he said with a weary sigh. "Roy Pingatelli?"

"I don't know anybody by that name. Who is he?"

Webster ignored the question. "Frank Maxey?" he said.

Taylor shook his head. "Him neither. Who's he?"

Webster half-smiled, studied Taylor for several seconds, then rubbed the back of his neck.

"What about Carlos Zorelli?"

"Zorelli?" Taylor repeated and Webster nodded.

"He's like some kind of big mob boss," Taylor said. "The President was talking about him on television the other night, even if he didn't use his name. He's from Philadelphia, I think."

"The city you were going to," Webster said ominously.

Suddenly Taylor was disgusted. "Yeah. Sure. Me and Larry and another hundred thousand people. What the hell's that got to do with Zorelli or whatever the hell his name is?"

There was a perfunctory knock on the door. Webster turned but before he could speak, the door opened and a young woman in a state police uniform entered. She was pretty but running to fat around the haunches the way a lot of police do, especially those whose jobs keep them sitting most of the day. She leaned over and whispered something into Webster's ear. The officer grunted and she left.

Webster swiveled back around on his chair to face Taylor; he ran his fingers through his hair several times. "You want more coffee?" he asked.

"No," Taylor said.

"I don't either but I'm going to get some." He walked to the door and Taylor leaned back in his chair and closed his eyes. Then he heard somebody calling his name. It was a struggle to open his eyes again and when he had it took him several seconds to remember where he was. He realized he had dozed off because Webster was sitting in front of him again. He had brought them each a styrofoam cup of coffee and a half full box of assembly-line doughnuts.

"Go ahead, eat," Webster said and pushed the doughnuts half across the table. "It's a hell of a way to start the day."

"Sure is," Taylor said. He took a doughnut; it was cold and

sodden with congealed grease. He washed it down with black coffee. "What happens now?"

"We checked you out," Webster said. "You're who you said you are and the big shots at the I.R.S. are saying to treat you nice. You never told me you had political clout."

Taylor was surprised. If he had clout, he had never known it before. Except for the Judge, but that was a long time ago. Who else gave him clout? Fluory? Plevris? Why did they even bother?

"Well, now that you know how powerful I am," Taylor said, "maybe you'll tell me, who were those guys you mentioned?"

"Pingatelli was the guy who shot your friend. And Frank Maxey was the one I blew away in the truck stop just before he could do the same to you."

"What about Zorelli? How does he tie in?"

Webster shrugged. "Those two thugs used to work for him, sometime ago."

"You think they were the guys in the accident before?"

"You think it was an accident now?" Webster said.

"Don't play word games with me, Lieutenant. I'm too goddam tired. No, it wasn't an accident. I mean the bastards on the highway who tried to kill us? You think these are the same guys?"

"I don't know. Probably. And I'm getting the distinct impression that somebody in the Mafia has a hard-on for you. And your dead friend."

Taylor shook his head. "Why us?"

"That's the big question, lad, and if you think of the answer, I wish you'd let us know."

Webster left the room and in a few minutes a clerk entered with forms for Taylor to sign. He read them as thoroughly as he could, although the words just blurred into and out of his mind. Basically, he guessed, they said that he had not been mistreated and that he would not sue the state of Maryland or the officers who had detained and questioned him. He briefly considered tearing them up but decided all he wanted to do was to get out of there. He signed where the clerk directed him to, then asked, "Is there anyway I can hitch a ride back to the truckstop to get my car?"

"You'll have to ask Lieutenant Webster," the clerk said in the I-just-work-here drone of clerks everywhere.

He found Webster inside a small office, staring with distaste at a six-inch-high pile of papers and reports.

"Worried about getting to Philadelphia?" the policeman said.

"Actually I was thinking more about getting my car," Taylor said.

"Sorry. Better forget that for a while," Webster said.

"How's that?"

"Remember, we had a gunfight that went over, through, and around your car. And that was after it was used for a game of dodge'm by a truck. It's evidence for a while."

"Oh," Taylor said. His brain was not working. The idea of somehow getting himself to Philadelphia seemed suddenly like an almost insurmountable task.

"Not to worry," Webster said. "For a man with as much political clout as you, the impossible is not only possible, it's ridiculously easy."

"Right," Taylor said. "I forgot my power."

"Right," said Webster. "I'll have one of our men drive you in to Philly. Right up to the door of your hotel."

"That's great. Except I don't know the name of my hotel."

"It's okay," Webster said. "We do."

Webster's man turned out to be a woman, the pretty one with the heavy hips. She seemed friendly enough, eager to talk to Taylor about the problems of being not just a woman cop, but a divorced mother to boot, and also about what had happened to him and Larry Wu. She was one of those talkers who did not require a lot of interaction to keep going, and Taylor dozed off and slept most of the way until they pulled up in front of the Peale House, his hotel, right in the middle of Philadelphia's downtown and, unarguably, one of the best hotels on the entire eastern seaboard.

Taylor checked in and was whisked up to his room. Once the bellhop had left, he stood in the middle of the living room wondering why he had been given a suite. Then he understood; it had been booked for both him and Larry Wu.

He wondered what to do next. There was the tax meeting that last night had seemed so earth-shatteringly important. There were the creature necessities; food, a shower, a change of clothing. Or two other things he looked forward to reluctantly—calls to Melanie and to Katie Wu. He flipped a coin in his mind and it came up Melanie.

He sat down at the escritoire, and dialed the familiar phone number. It seemed to ring a very long time before it was answered.

"Hello," the woman's voice said. It was Melanie's voice but it sounded somehow different, almost blurry.

"Melanie, it's Matt."

There was a pause at the other end and Matt thought he could hear bodies moving round. When his wife spoke again, she sounded different, more normal.

"Hi. What time is it there?"

"I don't know," Taylor said.

There was another pause and then she said, "Oh, balls. It's after ten. The damned alarm clock didn't go off again. I'm going to be late at the shop."

"There's been an accident," Taylor said. "And Larry Wu's been murdered."

"What?"

Taylor remembered the other times Melanie's voice had sounded the same as it had when she had answered the phone. It sounded that way when she had been happy and sated after a marathon session of lovemaking. Suddenly he was disgusted at speaking with her.

"I'm okay," Taylor said. "I'll call you later. Tonight or maybe tomorrow."

"Matt—"

"Good-bye," Taylor said. He thought he could still hear her calling his name as he hung up the receiver.

Taylor sat on the edge of the bed, feeling tired and dirty and disgusted. He stripped off his clothes and took a long shower, dressed and returned to the desk where he called Larry Wu's home. The voice that answered sounded half disgusted, half angry, half bone-weary.

"O'Leary?" Taylor said.

"Yeah?" the voice said suspiciously.

"This is Matt Taylor."

"Where are you, man? Katie's worried sick about you."

"I'm in Philadelphia. The Peale House. I just got here." He hesitated. "Katie knows?"

"She knows," O'Leary said. "The state cops in Maryland called a couple of hours ago. They weren't too clear on what happened or why."

"Where's she now? Maybe I should talk to her?" Taylor said. He didn't want to talk to her; her brother, his best friend, had been killed and Taylor could not help feeling some guilt for the death.

"No, don't bother," O'Leary said. "She's sleeping. She took it real hard and I got some stuff from a doctor friend of mine and knocked her out. Let her sleep. Tell me what happened."

Taylor told him about the wrecking effort on the highway and about the shootout in the parking lot and then the attempt on Taylor's life. He did not mention the fact that the police said the assassins were Philadelphia mob guys.

"Damn," O'Leary said. "Damn, damn. I told Larry about it. I told him to watch out. But he wouldn't listen."

Taylor was surprised. "Listen to what?"

"I told him yesterday afternoon that the word was out on the street that somebody was out to get him. Somebody real heavy."

"What do you mean?" Taylor demanded. "Who? Why?" A half-dozen more questions tumbled out.

"He didn't tell you?" O'Leary said.

"If he had told me something, I wouldn't be asking you," Taylor snapped.

There was a pause before O'Leary said, "It was just a rumor one of our guys picked up on the street. That Larry was in over his head on gambling and hadn't paid up and the bad guys were looking for him. The figure I heard was a quarter of a million."

Taylor let out a low whistle.

"He ever say anything about that to you?" O'Leary asked.

"Never," Taylor said. Taylor knew that Larry loved to gamble—he called it his Chinese genetic curse—but as far as Taylor knew, Larry never gambled much at any one time and he had always lived within his means. Was it a secret part of Wu's life that Taylor knew nothing about?

"Were there any names attached to the threats?" Taylor asked.

"No," O'Leary said.

"Do you think Larry got killed because of gambling?" he asked.

"I don't know," O'Leary said. "Gambling's not my field, but I don't know, I don't think big-time gamblers want your life; I think they want your money. And dead men don't pay. It doesn't scan for me."

"Maybe it'll come out in the wash," Taylor said sullenly. There was some more desultory talk and Taylor promised to call Katie in the early evening. Then he hung up. He was sitting at the desk deciding if he should call his office when the telephone rang, startling him.

"Matt," said the voice at the other end. "This is Walt Fluory."

"How are you doing, Walt?"

"Forget that. Are you okay? I heard what happened to you and Larry. Are you all right?"

"I'm okay," Taylor said.

"Listen, Matt. I'm downstairs. Come on down and let's have some coffee."

"Be right there." He picked up his jacket where he had tossed it onto the bed and headed for the door.

Fluory was waiting as Taylor stepped out of the elevator; his face looked worried and he stepped forward to greet Taylor and shook his hand, almost formally.

"This is a hell of a thing to have happen to two of my best men," he said. "A hell of a thing."

When they were sitting inside the restaurant over coffee, Taylor thanked Fluory for putting some heat on the police to get him released.

"Nothing," Fluory said with a hand flurry of dismissal. "What's the use of being a politician if you can't get anything done? You feel up to telling me what happened?"

Taylor nodded, then told Fluory the entire story. When he finished, Fluory was staring off into space as if meditating.

Finally, he said, "The Mafia? It doesn't make any sense, does it?"

"Not to me," Taylor said.

"And Larry said he thought it had something to do with those tax returns you guys dug out the other day? What was it, Harker Something?"

"Harker's Furnace," Taylor said.

"But he didn't tell you what he found out. Or suspected?" Fluory asked.

Taylor shook his head. "No." He hesitated. "The only other thing I can thing of . . . well, I don't even know if I should say this."

"Say it, man," Fluory said crisply.

"Maybe, I don't know, I don't have any first-hand knowledge of this, but maybe Larry was gambling and owed a lot of money.

Just a rumor." He searched Fluory's eyes. "You know anything about that?"

Fluory did not answer immediately. Instead, he searched the room for the waitress and signalled her to bring more coffee. After she had left, he lit a cigarette and said, "Okay, Matt. Cards on the table."

Taylor nodded.

"You know Larry was brought up before the Internal Security people yesterday?"

"He told me," Taylor said.

"You were going to be next," Fluory said. At Taylor's reaction, he grinned. "Nothing bad. You heard about the President's task force the other night. It looks like I'm going to go on it and I figured on bringing Larry and you with me."

Taylor just nodded.

"But before I can do that, I have to make sure that you are ... were ... both clean. That was Internal Security's job," he said. He looked at the end of his cigarette as if it were the most interesting object in the world. "The gambling rumor came up about Larry," Fluory said.

He leaned forward and lowered his voice. "Matt, I'm sorry. Larry denied it but that blew it for him on the task force anyway. We couldn't have somebody even rumored to be vulnerable working there."

"So that might be why Larry was killed," Taylor said. "It might have something to do with gambling."

Fluory leaned back. "Sure looks that way."

"It's all too heavy for me," Taylor said. He was tired and felt it. He wiped his hand across his eyes.

Fluory said, "I want you to take some time off, Matt."

"Well, as soon as we're done here in Philly."

"Forget Philadelphia," Fluory said. "It's not worth it and ... hell, I'll bring in somebody else. What do you think of Jenkins?"

Taylor shrugged. "Jenkins is good enough."

"Okay. Fine. I'm calling him up here. You go get lost. Go on vacation for a week. You need it. Get your head together."

"I don't think so, Walt," Taylor said.

"Why not?"

Taylor shrugged. "I don't know. I don't have anyplace to go, I guess."

"Well, think about it," Fluory said. The bill came and Fluory signed for it. They walked out to the lobby together.

Before Taylor walked away, Fluory sidled up to him as if sharing a confidence. "You know, I didn't get your answer."

"To what?" Taylor said.

"To the task force. You want to be on it?"

"Yeah," Taylor said. The thought flashed through his mind that this might be the best way to get whoever was behind Larry Wu's killing. Taylor wasn't some kind of masked avenger but dammit, if he found out who Larry owed money to, if he had any say at all, he would try to get the I.R.S. jumping all over that man with nailed boots. Maybe it wasn't the way Clint Eastwood or Sylvester Stallone might do it, but it was the best Taylor had.

"Good," Fluory said. "We'll talk about it when you get back to work." He shook Taylor's hand again, and walked briskly away.

Taylor got on the wrong elevator and had to ride down to the garage, before it worked its way to his upstairs room. It gave him a moment to think. Something hadn't quite rung true with the morning's events and revelations. It was possible that Larry Wu was deep in debt to some mob-affiliated gamblers, and maybe so deep that they would try to kill him as an object lesson. That was logical enough. But why, then, would they also try to kill Matt Taylor who owed no one anything? Were they just that uncaring about human life? Or was something more going on, something that neither he nor Fluory knew anything about?

He had no time to ponder the question because after he

walked down the corridor and unlocked his door, he saw that the room had been ransacked.

Somebody had very thoroughly searched it, turning over furniture, slashing mattresses, strewing the contents of his luggage all over the floor. Whoever it was had even gone so far as to cut open his tube of toothpaste and squeeze its contents onto the top of his writing desk.

CHAPTER ELEVEN

As Taylor looked around, he was startled to hear a sound coming from the bedroom of the small suite.

The sound was a thumping from inside the walk-in closet. The key was in the lock and when he turned it and opened the door, the maid, an overweight woman with a swarthy complexion and white-streaked hair, jumped out and into his arms, before she remembered herself and her position and pulled away from him. But her eyes were filled with relief. Pieces of sheeting had been used to tie her wrists and to gag her. Taylor removed them and then helped her sit down on the sofa.

"Thank you, sir," she said. Her voice had a faint accent and gave no hint of where she had been raised. Taylor got her a glass of water from the bathroom sink. She took the glass with a nod, sipped at it, then raised her eyes toward him.

"Maybe we should call the police?" she offered.

And then for a moment panic washed her features as the thought obviously hit her that perhaps Taylor was not the occupant of this room, but another robber.

"It's okay," Taylor said. "This is my room. You're all right now. Did you see who did this?"

The maid shook her head no.

"Did they say anything? What were they looking for?" Taylor asked.

"They didn't say a word to me. Except they told me to be quiet or they'd kill me. I tell you that made me be quiet. You'd be quiet too. For sure. But they sneaked up on me while I was cleaning the room and I didn't see them."

"Anything? Did you hear them? Their voices, what they sounded like. Did they say *anything?*"

"I remember something after they locked me in the closet," she said. She paused and drained the glass of water. Taylor took it back to the bathroom for another refill.

"What do you remember?" he asked as he gave her the glass.

"Something about tapes. They said they had to get tapes back from you."

"Tapes?"

The woman nodded, deepening Taylor's puzzlement. Tapes? He had no tapes. Except . . . He looked through the wreckage of the luggage on the floor. Usually, when he travelled he took a half-dozen cassette tapes of jazz albums with him. They appeared to be gone; at least he couldn't see them anywhere in the room.

But why would somebody take his jazz tapes? And commit burglary to do it?

"Shouldn't we be calling the police?" she said again, her voice wistful and plaintive.

Before Taylor could answer, the telephone rang. It was O'Leary. "I'll call you back in a minute," Taylor said and before O'Leary could answer, he hung up and turned back toward the maid.

"I'd really appreciate it," he said, "if you wouldn't tell anyone what happened here. I'm going to leave soon and the police might just make me miss my plane," he lied.

"Well, I should report it," she said, but seemed to waver.

Taylor took two twenty-dollar bills from his pocket and pressed them into the woman's hand.

"Please," he said. "As a favor to me. Let's just keep this unofficial."

"Okay," she said with a long sigh. "I won't tell anybody if you don't want me to." The money vanished into the pocket of her black uniform; she finished the water and then left the room, promising to come back in an hour and finish cleaning it up.

Taylor went back to the telephone and dialed Katie Wu's number to reach O'Leary. He let it ring a long time but there was no answer.

Ten minutes later, the telephone rang again and Taylor snatched up the receiver.

O'Leary told him the family needed a favor. "We need somebody to go back to Elkton and claim Larry's body," the FBI agent said. "I can't. I just can't get away and Katie's in no shape to do it. Can you?"

"When does it have to be done?"

"Sooner the better," O'Leary said.

Taylor ached all over from exhaustion. For a moment, he tried to think of an excuse for not going, then said, "Sure. I'll go. It won't be till this afternoon, though. Late."

"Fine," O'Leary said. "I'll pick up your expenses."

"Don't be an asshole," Taylor snapped.

"I'll try not to," O'Leary said.

After he hung up, Taylor leaned back in his chair, intending to rest for a moment. When he opened his eyes, he saw the maid entering the room. She looked at him as if they had never met before.

"I could come back later, sir," she said.

"No. I'm just on my way out." He had decided and he had something to do.

He took the elevator down two floors to where Fluory had said his room was. As the elevator door opened, he saw Fluory getting on the elevator across the hall. Two other men had just entered the elevator; one tall and solidly built; the other half a foot shorter and good-looking in an Italian sort of way. They both looked vaguely familiar.

Taylor called out, "Walt," and moved toward the other elevator. Fluory saw him, reached out his hand toward the elevator's control panel but the doors shut before Taylor could enter.

He waited for a moment watching the indicator arrow above Fluory's elevator door. It went all the way down to the lobby without stopping. When the next elevator came along, Taylor rode it to the lobby too.

Fluory was waiting for him.

"Sorry, Matt. Damned stupid of me. I always do that. I reach for the door-open and hit the door-close button instead."

Taylor shrugged. "Did you notice those two guys who got on with you?"

A strange look, perhaps puzzlement, crossed Fluory's face. "I don't think so," he said slowly. "What'd they look like?"

"Not important. I just thought I knew them from somewhere. Listen, I've been thinking. About that vacation?"

"Yeah."

"I've thought it over. I think I will take the couple of weeks off if the offer still stands."

"Sure does. You going to get away like I said?"

"I haven't decided yet," Taylor said.

But he had decided. There were things he wanted to look into, and the place he was going to start looking was Harker's Furnace, Pennsylvania.

CHAPTER TWELVE

Once, Larry Wu had asked Taylor if there was anything that really annoyed him. It had been a long boozy evening and Taylor and Wu had been talking about anything and everything that came to mind—the state of Matt's marriage, their growing dissatisfaction with working for the I.R.S.—and Wu had asked, "What does it take to get you upset? Matt, doesn't anything just plain tick you off?"

"Sure. A lot of things tick me off," Taylor said.

"Name one."

"I'll name a lot," Taylor said. "Sensitive, caring men tick me off. What rock 'n' roll sounds like today ticks me off. I get downright pissed at any beer made west of the Mississippi River. Television shows about women's friendships make me want to rip out my vertical control knob. Those all piss me off. And being lied to. That's the worst."

He thought of that conversation as he was driving back in a rental car to Elkton, Maryland, to claim his friend's dead body. Somebody was lying to him. He just didn't know who. But a lot of people seemed to have a stake in convincing him that Larry Wu had died because of a gambling debt, and Taylor just did not buy it. Not from Fluory, not from Dennis O'Leary, not from the Maryland state police, not from anybody. He did not believe that all those were intentionally lying to him themselves, but they were all spreading a lie that had come from someone, somewhere, and it was up to him to find out who.

The liars were doing a pretty good job, but something had happened that they did not know about, that they had not counted on.

Larry Wu's killers had screwed up. When they had been waiting for Larry and Taylor outside the truckstop, they had asked both of them their names. If they had been interested only in Larry, it would not have made any difference to them who his companion had been. They would just have shot both of them without checking on Taylor's identity. But they had checked. And they had made it plain that they were after *both* Larry and Taylor. That was where they had made their mistake, and the more Taylor thought about it, the only thing that he and Wu had had in common that anyone might find the least remote bit threatening was their stumbling over the Harker's Furnace file in the I.R.S. computer. And that was where Taylor was going to look.

When he got to Elkton, he decided to talk to Lieutenant Arthur Webster about making arrangements to claim Larry's body. There were two state police barracks in the town, one up on the JFK highway and the other out at the northeast edge of town, where Taylor finally found him. It was after five o-clock and Webster did not look happy. At first Taylor thought it might be because he was making the policeman late for dinner.

"I'll buy us both something to eat," Taylor offered.

Webster was looking more rumpled and his eyes were even more tired than they had been when they'd met before.

"No thanks." The words were civil enough, but the tone of his voice was cold and bitter. To hell with him, thought Taylor; there were just some people it was a waste of time trying to be nice to.

"What do you want?" Webster said.

"I was wondering if you people had finished with Larry Wu's

110

body yet," Taylor said. "His family would like to start making funeral arrangements."

Webster had been sitting behind his desk. He slowly got up and came around and sat down on its front edge so that he loomed over the seated Taylor.

"Finished? We haven't even started yet," Webster said. His voice contained a barely controlled anger.

Taylor shrugged. "Have any idea when you'll be done?"

Webster leaned down until his face was right in front of Taylor's. He started to speak but Taylor did not give him a chance.

This cop is going through some sort of happy horseshit game with me and I'm damned if he'll get away with it.

He stood up abruptly, almost banging into the trooper's nose as he did so. Webster rocked back and Taylor now loomed over him.

"You were saying," Taylor snapped.

Webster glared at him, then walked behind his desk and punched a couple of numbers on the telephone. He turned his back on Taylor.

"Sally," he said. "Listen, call up Wood's and tell them I'm sending a party named Taylor over to claim the body we sent them this morning. Yeah, that's right. I know it's peculiar. It makes me sick. Just do it."

He hung the phone down gently and sat at his desk, opened its center drawer and pulled out a sheaf of pink, white, and mint-green papers and rustled through them. He signed four of them and shoved them over in front of Taylor.

"Sign here and here and here," he said, pointing with a ballpoint pen that he tossed onto the papers. Taylor signed and tossed the pen back in front of Webster.

Webster separated the sheets after checking that they had been signed correctly. "The pink copy's yours. The green one goes to the funeral director." He looked up. "That's all," he said.

"Lieutenant, what are you pissed about?" Taylor asked.

111

"You don't know, do you?" Webster said.

"Stop talking in code," Taylor snapped. "Know what?"

Webster looked at him for long seconds before he said, "Sit down. Maybe I misjudged you."

Taylor sat, silently.

Webster said, "A murder's a murder and no cop likes to have people outside involved. First it's the I.R.S. butting in and then the FBI, and then when we were trying to get an autopsy done, the goddam governor's office calls and says don't do it and just release the body. Here's a murder that we've got the goddam Mafia involved in and we've got our hands tied."

Taylor shook his head. "I don't know anything about any of that. I'm just a guy who got shot at."

"And who killed somebody and I don't know why and I'm not allowed to find out why and that pisses me off," Webster said.

"No more than me," Taylor answered. "I wish you'd just find out what the fuck is going on so I don't have to worry about it anymore."

"You don't know what's behind this?" Webster said.

"No goddam idea," Taylor said.

"Let me tell you something, Taylor. You got yourself some bad enemies. Watch yourself."

Taylor sighed as he stood up. "I will. But I don't even know who they are or what they want with me."

"That's easy," Webster said.

Taylor raised an eyebrow in question and Webster said with a not-unpleasant smile: "They want you dead."

Taylor smiled back. "Then we're even," he said. "I want them dead too."

CHAPTER THIRTEEN

The funeral home had once been someone's mansion. It was huge, painted white, and built in some vaguely pre-Civil War style with great dollops of gingerbread added. It was a pleasant-looking monstrosity.

The man who greeted Taylor at the door was dressed neatly in a dark suit but spoke with a booming voice that seemed out of place in an undertaker's establishment. His name was Harold Sawicki.

He talked incessantly while he started to fill out the inevitable forms for the release of Larry Wu's body.

"We've had a lot of interest in your friend today," he said.

"The local cops, you mean?"

"Others too. The FBI just now."

"FBI? What did they want?"

"They wanted to look at the body and look through the personal effects. Of course I told them that all that stuff had been taken by the state police, but they wanted to look at the body anyway."

"You think that's odd?" Taylor asked.

Sawicki nodded. "Yes, actually. They seemed disappointed that the . . . dead man wasn't wearing clothes. I told them the police had the victim's clothes. It was like they had never seen a body before."

"You saw their ID's though," Taylor said.

Sawicki nodded. "I know, but I would think FBI men would know a little more about the real world than that." He snorted. "Expecting an accident victim to be still wearing his clothes. Really."

"Did you get their names?"

The undertaker shook his head. "I'm surprised really that you didn't see them. They left just before you arrived here."

Taylor signed some more papers and Sawicki said that he would hold the body until a hearse from a funeral home of Katie Wu's choosing came for the remains. Taylor left.

They were waiting for him in the parking lot and he recognized them. There were two of them. They were the two men he had seen on the elevator back at the Philadelphia hotel. And he remembered where he had seen them before. They were the same two men who had been following them the night he had gone out with Larry and Katie when they had met Dennis O'Leary in the Georgetown bar.

They were leaning against Taylor's rented Ford.

For just an instant, Taylor felt fear and considered running. Then he decided no more running. He worked some spit back into his dried-up mouth and walked toward the two men. It was only when he was a few paces away that he realized that they—or someone else—had opened the car's hood slightly.

The bigger of the two men walked forward a couple of steps to meet him and stood studying Taylor for a few seconds. The man was six feet tall and well built. He had thick, sandy-colored hair, a lightly freckled complexion, and frowning eyes that seemed to be no more than slits in his beefy face. He was older than Taylor had first thought—late thirties, maybe even early forties. He stood with his hands in the pockets of his well-tailored light gray suit.

"You're Matt Taylor. With the I.R.S." His tone of voice

made it plain that he was really asking a question, and Taylor nodded.

"That your car?"

"I rented it," Taylor said, and, realizing he was being grilled by some stranger, snapped, "And who the hell are you?"

"We saw somebody messing with your car. He got away before we could get him. We were just checking it out."

"Yeah? Who's we?"

The second man came up from the passenger side of the car. He was at least a head shorter than his companion and nearly as dark as the other man was fair. Taylor thought him Italian perhaps, or Greek. When he smiled at Taylor, his semi-ordinary face became extremely handsome. He had perfect gleaming white teeth and deep dimples in his cheeks.

He walked forward, extended a hand toward Taylor and Taylor, more in reflex than anything else, shook it.

"I'm Sal Gianetti," he said. "FBI special agent." He smiled again and released Taylor's hand. "This guy is my partner, John Polonowski. You've got to forgive him. He's been in the field too long and he keeps forgetting his manners when he talks to law-abiding citizens."

"So what do you want with me and what about the car?" Taylor asked.

As if to describe what he had been doing, Gianetti brushed imaginary dust from his dark blue suit.

"We've gone over it with a magnifying glass," he said. "Some guy was fooling with it but he didn't get a chance to plant anything. We must have scared him off in time."

"In time? In time for what? What would anybody be planting in my car?"

"A bomb," Polonowski said curtly.

"What for?" Taylor asked.

Polonowski shrugged. "To blow your balls off, I guess."

* * *

115

Ten minutes later, Taylor and the two men were seated in a small restaurant a half mile away from the funeral home. The only other customers were a couple of men in late middle-age who looked like the sort who would remain loyal to a restaurant they had been coming to all their lives, even when everyone else in town had started patronizing the plasticized, homogenized franchise jobs out on the edge of the highway.

On the other hand, looking at the sodden grayish excuse for a hamburger that the waitress had just put in front of him, Taylor wondered why the two old men were holdouts.

"Just off the top of my head, Matt—you don't mind me calling you Matt, do you?" Gianetti said, "I'd say you've got yourself a whole passel of trouble."

"It doesn't make any sense to me. Why would somebody put a bomb in my car? Why would somebody try to kill me? I don't know what the hell's going on."

"Oh, horseshit," Polonowski said and Taylor looked at him quizzically.

"You heard me. The stuff that comes out of the south end of a stallion going north. That's what you're handing us now," the burly sandy-haired agent said.

"Call it what you want," Taylor said, trying not to lose his temper. "I don't know what's going on here."

Gianetti put a hand soothingly on Taylor's arm. Taylor looked at him for a moment and Gianetti smiled, showing his dimples again. Taylor moved his arm away quickly.

"You know, John," Gianetti said, "he may be telling us the truth."

Polonowski let out a long, loud derisive snort, but he said nothing. He looked up as if counting the restaurant's ceiling tiles.

Gianetti smiled again at Taylor and Taylor found himself thinking that the FBI agent had beautiful eyelashes, but somehow they did not look real.

Gianetti said, "We're all colleagues in a manner of speaking, and I think we should all try to be friends." He touched Tay-

116

lor's arm again. Polonowski reached over, took Gianetti's hand and slapped it down onto the formica table top.

"Why don't you cut out that flaming faggot stuff and get on with it?" he snapped.

Suddenly, Taylor felt tired of being whipsawed by these two, tired of being a target of something he didn't understand, and he leaned forward toward Polonowski and said slowly, "Why *don't* we get on with it, pal? Maybe you can start by telling me what the hell you were doing trailing us around in Georgetown the other night. And follow it up with what the hell were you doing down at the hotel in Philadelphia? And what the hell the two of you were doing breaking into my room and tossing my crap around. Maybe that's a good place to start."

His eyes met Polonowski's. Neither man blinked. Gianetti broke the tension when he said, "Okay. Let's all fess up."

"It's about time," Taylor said.

"All right. Try this," Polonowski growled. "Your fucking friend was a fucking traitor."

He smirked but it vanished as Taylor said, "And you're a fucking liar."

"Boys, boys," Gianetti said in a soft oily voice. "We won't get anywhere this way. Let me tell it, John."

Polonowski shrugged and turned half away in his seat.

"We'll start at the beginning," Gianetti said. "John and I are on special assignment to the White House." He paused and Taylor said, "I'm impressed."

"We're kind of the house gumshoes," Gianetti said.

"More like the house niggers," Polonowski grumbled. "We get all the crap jobs. Like this one."

"Obviously a waste," Taylor said. "With your sparkling personality, you should be running visitors' tours around the building."

"You know, I don't like you," Polonowski said.

"But you don't scare me either, so why don't you just get off the snot and let your partner talk," Taylor said.

"Good idea," Gianetti said. "Anyway, we were advised last week that President Chesney was going to announce his new task force to go after the Mafia's money sources. They gave us the job of checking out people who might be assigned to work on the task force."

"And Larry Wu was one of them," Taylor said.

Gianetti nodded. "The name came from Fluory. He's your boss, right? And the preliminary check . . . well, I won't go into details, but it turned up that your friend owed a lot of money to gamblers. Gamblers with big mob connections."

Taylor shook his head. "That doesn't sound like Larry to me," he said.

"Anyway," Gianetti said, "that's what we were doing that night, trailing you people around the bars. We wanted to see who Wu's friends were."

"Hey, that little Chink girl's got a nice ass," Polonowski said. "You getting any of that?"

This time, Gianetti did not interrupt his partner; it was as if he also wanted to hear Taylor's answer.

Taylor said, "Polonowski, you've got a big dirty mouth to go with your little dirty brain. I'm just going to let that all pass."

"And if you didn't let it pass?" Polonowski said, leaning forward across the table and boring his eyes into Taylor's.

"Then I'd just kick your ass all over this diner," Taylor said.

The two men stared at each other until Gianetti rapped on the table with his knuckles.

"Let's stick to business," he said. "Anyway, we were following you and O'Leary made us in the bar, but we talked for a while and told him what we were doing, so he said he wouldn't blow our cover. He'd give you some kind of bullshit story."

"That he did," Taylor said.

"So we were still working on Wu when the two of you

118

went skipping off to Philadelphia. When we heard about the accident ..."

"The murder," Taylor said. "It wasn't any accident."

"Right. The murder. When we heard about it, we thought we'd get into your room and see if there was anything there tying Wu to organized crime."

"Why my room?" Taylor asked.

Gianetti shrugged. "Because you were Wu's friend; you were travelling together; maybe you were in it with him; who knows what the two of you might be cooking up together. Maybe we were wrong, but it seemed like a good idea at the time."

"You were wrong," Taylor said. "The maid you locked in the closet said she heard you talking about tapes. And some of my jazz tapes were swiped. What was that about?"

"A lot of times that's how people hide information," Gianetti said, "by recording it in the middle of a music tape. Yours were clean. You'll get them back."

"You've got lousy taste in music," Polonowski said.

"I left all my Frankie Yankovic music home," Taylor said. "I didn't want to take a chance of being mugged by some polka-crazed Polack and losing any of it."

Polonowski glared at him again and Taylor turned back to Gianetti. "What kind of information? What would Larry hide on a tape?"

"Look. We don't really know," Gianetti said. "We think he was in deep hock to the bad guys. Maybe he was monkeying around with I.R.S. stuff somehow to give them a break. We didn't know and we were just trying to find out. But we didn't find anything." He hesitated for a second. "If you were Larry Wu and you wanted to hide something, where would *you* put it?"

"I don't know. Some computer somewhere, I guess," Taylor said.

"That seems easy enough to figure out," Polonowski said.

"Either his computer at home or his computer at work. That shouldn't be hard."

"I'm afraid your knowledge of computers isn't as extensive as your knowledge of jazz music," Taylor said. "All you need is a telephone. Larry could have hidden stuff in almost any big computer in the United States. Maybe a dozen countries overseas too. A phone call gets you in; you put in what you want, and then you hang up, and your stuff stays hidden there until you call and access it by code."

Gianetti shook his head sorrowfully. "I was afraid you'd say something like that."

"Sorry but them's the facts," Taylor said.

"Everybody's always sorry," Polonowski said. "It makes me want to puke."

The two other men ignored him. Gianetti told Taylor, "When this started I would have sworn it was just gambling money involved. But somebody tried to kill you too. You're not a gambler, are you?"

"No. And neither was Larry."

Polonowski snorted again.

"Was there something you two were working on that might have somebody coming after you?" Gianetti asked.

Taylor did not hesitate before lying. "No," he said. "Nothing that I can think of."

"Well, you just better watch out for yourself," the dark-haired agent said. "That person we saw messing with your car. The guy who tried to shoot you. Something's going on and it concerns you and I don't want you killed on our watch."

"I'll try to cooperate," Taylor said drily.

"If anything comes up, I want you to get in touch with us right away," Gianetti said. He reached into his jacket pocket, then stopped and turned to Polonowski.

"Do you have one with our special number on it?" he asked.

Polonowski grumbled and jammed his hands into his pockets

and started searching, finally emerging with one badly bent business card with the seal of the United States on it.

Gianetti tried to smooth it out by running it over the edge of the table before handing it to Taylor.

"You can reach us through that number any hour of the day or night. Call us about anything."

Taylor glanced at the card and put it into his pocket. The two FBI men seemed to think the conversation was over, but not quite, not that easy.

"You said Larry was a traitor," he said to Polonowski. "Why?"

Before Polonowski could respond, Gianetti said, "Sorry. It's something Wu might have been involved in and we're not allowed to tell you."

"Did you guys question him when he went to the Internal Security people yesterday?"

"Yeah, we were there. He didn't spill anything," Polonowski said.

"He didn't have anything to spill," Taylor said.

"Time will tell," Polonowski said.

"Anyway," the other FBI man said. "Call us if you need us."

"I'd rather not," Taylor said. "I hope I never see you guys again as long as I live."

Gianetti laughed. "You will," he said. "Your name's on our list, too, for possible appointment to the crime squad. We'll be checking you out soon."

Polonowski stood up from the table. "If you live that long," he said.

Taylor watched from the window of the restaurant as the two men got into their late model Chevrolet and drove from the small unpaved parking lot. He dawdled over his coffee for an extra five minutes before paying the bill and going out to his own car.

He didn't know what was going on but things did not add up. Gianetti and Polonowski somehow did not ring true. Their questions weren't good enough and they did not probe hard enough. They had told him too much and had asked for too little in return. And they had not mentioned Harker's Furnace. Wu said that was all the Internal Security people had wanted to talk about. So these two did not bring it up, and instead gave him some crap about Wu being a traitor. Not in a month of Sundays.

He left Elkton, heading south toward Baltimore and then Washington. Five minutes down the road, there was a large service area on the right and he pulled in and quickly darted into a parking spot alongside a recreation vehicle and doused his lights and engine.

A few seconds later, several other cars pulled into the lot and he recognized Polonowski and Gianetti in one of them. They cruised slowly around the main area of the lot, obviously looking for his car. He waited until they were on the other side of the parking lot and then, without lights, he pulled out of the lot and got on the exit ramp leading north, back to Elkton. He took the first exit from the freeway onto a country road. He had driven for almost twenty minutes when the reaction to the day's events began to set in. He started to shake and the more he tried to stop, the more his body shuddered. He pulled over to the side of the road and tried taking deep breaths. Eventually, they worked. He started the car again and drove on for another twenty minutes until he came to a small mom-and-pop motel. He parked his car in the back, out of sight, and checked in, paying cash.

From his room, he called his home number but there was no answer. His watch told him it was after seven o'clock. Melanie should be home by now. For a moment, he had the husbandly worry that perhaps something had happened to her, but then he discounted the idea. He was out of town and Melanie was out partying. Why should today be any different from any other day?

He went into the small but clean bathroom and took a long shower.

When he stepped back outside, Dennis O'Leary was sitting at the small desktop in the room. What looked like a cutdown .45 caliber automatic was conspicuously resting on the desk in easy reach of the FBI man's right hand.

CHAPTER FOURTEEN

As he walked over to his clothing and began to dress, Taylor said, "I guess you just happened to find yourself in the neighborhood and dropped in."

The big black man laughed. "Something like that," he said.

"How much like that?" Taylor said.

"Not much. I've been following you since Philly."

"You called me in Philadelphia," Taylor said.

"That's right and I was down in the lobby," O'Leary said.

"You said you were in D.C.," Taylor said. He had his trousers on now and suddenly felt more secure, more in control of things. It was odd, he thought, but except in a locker room, a naked man always felt defenseless.

"When we talked early, I was in D.C. Then I hopped a helicopter and got up to Philly, and I called you back from there. I wanted you to think I was in D.C.," O'Leary said as Taylor rose from the bed and turned to face him.

"Why?"

"So I could see who was following you. Maybe figure out who was trying to hit you."

"Then I guess you saw your two comrades in arms from the FBI. What's their names? Polonowski and Gianetti."

O'Leary nodded. "The two guys I lied to you about in the bar in Georgetown. That *is* your next question, isn't it?"

"One among many," Taylor said.

"Yeah. Well, they told me they were checking on Larry, a background check. I couldn't blow their cover so I had to make up a lie about it."

"I get the feeling a lie is something you FBI guys make up real easily," Taylor said.

"Goes with the territory sometimes," O'Leary said.

"Did you follow me to the funeral home too?" Taylor asked. When O'Leary nodded, Taylor said, "Did you see somebody messing around with my car?"

"No."

"Those two gumshoes said *they* did. They were farting around under the hood when I got there."

O'Leary shrugged. "Maybe they've got better eyes than I do."

"And maybe they were lying too," Taylor said.

"I have to admit, that's a possibility," O'Leary said.

Taylor sat in a chair near the door. It forced O'Leary to turn around to talk to him and that meant turning his back toward his gun which was on the small desk table. Taylor was pleased to see that was what O'Leary did; anything that moved that gun farther from O'Leary's hand was a plus, Taylor thought.

"So. What do we do now? Send out for room service?"

"I don't like white people's food," O'Leary said. "You know what a strike force is?"

"I guess so. A group of federal cops and prosecutors that are supposed to go after big-time crooks," Taylor said.

"Close enough," O'Leary said. "But one of the main things about them is that they borrow guys from all branches of the government, the FBI, the Secret Service, the I.R.S., the whole schmear."

"Okay," Taylor said.

'Did you ever hear of Strike Force 73?"

"No."

"Good. If you had, it would mean we weren't doing our job right," O'Leary said.

"You're Strike Force 73?" Taylor asked.

"Part of it."

"And it concerns me? Larry Wu?"

"Yes."

"I'm all ears," Taylor said.

"That's an improvement," O'Leary said. "Anyway, Strike Force 73 has been working for two years now. We've been after Carlos Zorelli, the Philadelphia Mafia boss, and we're pretty damn close to shutting him down."

"How do you plan on doing that?"

"By getting to his money. By finding out where it's hidden and how it's laundered and then stopping it and confiscating it. It's really very simple."

"Right," Taylor said sarcastically. He did not even try to hide his amusement at what had been said. The job O'Leary described sounded reasonable in theory but would be next to impossible to actually do.

"Don't smirk," O'Leary said. "It's how Al Capone got sent away. It's how they've been banging mobsters all over the East Coast for the last ten years. Don't let them get to their money and then you ask them, 'You say you own two pinball machines and ten percent of a diner, then how come you can afford two yachts, four homes, and a chauffeur-driven Rolls-Royce?' And they can't answer so you send them to jail for tax evasion. Trust me, Taylor, it works. We're teaching bank employees how to spot laundered money; we've got customs agents smartened up; we've got guys in all the casinos to make sure nobody makes believe he won a million at the tables when he didn't bet a dime. We've got the bastards on the run. And Zorelli's the guy in our barrel right now."

"So how you guys gonna work with the new task force the President is setting up? Does that put you out of business?" Taylor asked.

"Maybe. We don't know yet. Probably." He had a disgusted look on his face.

"You don't seem happy," Taylor said.

126

"I work for a guy named Ari Cohen. He lives and breathes getting Zorelli. I don't know if some gang of politicians—named by a politician and headed by a politician—is going to be any improvement over what we're doing." He paused for a moment. "Your boss," he said with contempt. "Plevris. What the hell does the head of the I.R.S. know about organized crime and how to fight it?"

"Oh, I don't know. We're all quick learners over there," Taylor said casually, then added, "Did you know that Larry was being considered for the new task force?"

"I heard it. I don't know it for a fact," O'Leary said.

"You think Larry was in hock to the gamblers? That that was why he got killed?" Taylor asked.

He saw tension tighten O'Leary's face before the FBI man answered.

"No," he said. "I don't believe that."

"Then what do you believe?" Taylor asked.

"I believe that you and Larry found out something that somebody didn't want you to know, and that they tried to take you both out to silence you for good. I believe they got Larry and missed you and they're probably going to try again on you. That's why I followed you. To see if they showed up."

"The Zorelli gang?" Taylor asked.

"Yeah. And that's enough questions from you. Now my turn. Before he got it, Larry told me that he had a lead on some kind of big scam. Something, someplace, some fucking furnace or something in Pennsylvania. What was that all about?"

Taylor hesitated. Outside he could hear the chatter of night insects; it reminded him that he was alone in a room with a man with a gun and a man he didn't trust all that much. O'Leary knew something; how much was anybody's guess. But he probably knew more than he was letting on and Taylor decided that lying to him might be more dangerous than telling the truth.

"First of all, Larry didn't tell me what he might have found out," he said.

"Why not?" O'Leary said. The tone of his voice clearly expressed his disbelief.

"Because Larry and I are . . . *were* both computer people. You're a layman. He might tell you about something he was working on while he was working on it. But me, he'd wait until he solved the whole thing before he gave me any of it. Because if he gave it to me in pieces, he'd know I'd ask just the right questions to punch holes in his theories." Taylor shook his head. "With me, he'd wait until he had the whole thing."

"Katie tells me that her brother was a computer genius. You one too?" O'Leary asked.

"Yes," Taylor said honestly. "Larry and I are the best in the IRS. We're probably in the top ten in the country."

"I'm impressed," O'Leary said.

"Good. So, as I said, Larry didn't tell me what was going on, but I know what he was looking into."

And Taylor went on to tell O'Leary the entire story of the unusual tax returns from Harker's Furnace. When he was done, the black man shook his head. "I don't know what it all means," he said. "I was hoping for something simple, but I can't make head or tail out of that."

"All I know is that it looks like somebody was filing phoney returns. What it all means, I don't know."

"And Larry didn't tell you anything."

"No."

"He didn't give you his notes or tell you where they were or anything like that?"

"No," Taylor said. "But come to think of it, they'd be in his computer at home. Whatever he was working on, he probably kept on disc there."

"No," O'Leary said. "I had one of our guys go over his computer. There wasn't anything there that meant a damn thing, at least not in my line of work."

There was a long period of silence before Taylor said, "Well, that's that, I guess. We don't have anything."

"Too bad," O'Leary said, "for you."

"Why for me?" Taylor asked.

"Because I believe you. But I don't think the bad guys are going to, and I think they're going to come after you again."

"You think those two FBI guys are with the enemy?"

"No," O'Leary said. "J. Edgar would be spinning in his grave. I think they were just doing what I was doing."

"Which is?"

"Trying to find out who might be trying to kill you," O'Leary said.

"I've got another question," Taylor said.

"Shoot."

"Do you think Larry was involved in something . . . I don't know, treasonous?"

"He's your friend. You tell me," O'Leary said.

"I say no."

"Then why should I say anything different?" O'Leary asked.

"Because those two FBI goons hinted that he was dirty somehow."

"I don't know anything about that," O'Leary said, "and my guess is that it's a lot of bullshit and they're just trying to make themselves sound important."

"Okay. I appreciate the honest answer."

"You're welcome," O'Leary said.

"If it is an honest answer."

"It is," O'Leary said.

He shrugged his heavily muscled shoulders. "You know, I can't really hang around and play watchdog for you. What are you going to do?"

"I'm going on vacation for a while," Taylor said.

"Where to?" O'Leary said.

"I don't know," Taylor answered, then lied, "Someplace warm."

"Taking the wife?"

"I don't think so. We've got some problems," Taylor said.

"That's probably best," O'Leary said. "I don't think anybody's going to bother her. You're the only one who might know something. No point in two of you getting shot on the beach down in Puerto Rico. Your body alone ought to be enough."

"Jeez, you make a vacation sound real inviting," Taylor said.

"Just keep an eye over your shoulder, buddy," O'Leary said. "And trust no one."

Taylor grinned. "Not even you?"

"No one," O'Leary said. He started to his feet, then said,"You say Polonowski and Gianetti were fooling around under your hood?"

"The hood was unlocked. I think so."

"I'll be right back," O'Leary said. He left the .45 automatic on the desk as he left the room. Taylor thought for a moment of grabbing the gun before O'Leary came back. But for what? To defend himself? Against whom? If O'Leary had wanted to shoot him, he could have easily.

He turned on the television set. A Bonanza rerun had just come up onto the screen when there was a soft knock at the door.

O'Leary called through the door, "Taylor?"

"Yeah."

He opened the door and slipped quickly inside. He held out his hand to Taylor. "Here's a present for you," he said. He was holding a round black plastic case that looked like an old-fashioned typewriter ribbon.

"What is it?"

"It's a homing device. I guess our FBI friends planted it in your car so you don't get lost on them," O'Leary said with a grin.

Taylor looked at the unit for a moment, then asked, "Why are you doing this?"

'Damned if I know," O'Leary said. "Aaaah, maybe I'm just trying to screw them over a little bit because when that new task force is set up, I'll probably be working for them. Or be assigned to goddam Anchorage, Alaska. I don't know."

"Thanks anyway," Taylor said.

130

"Listen, I'm getting out of here. I want to be with Katie for a while. I'm leaving you that gun. It's loaded and it's clean. No one will trace it anywhere. You know how to use it?"

"Yeah."

"Oh, that's right. Larry said you were a big war hero. What did you do in the Marines anyway?"

"I killed people," Taylor said.

"That's right. You got one of the bastards, didn't you?"

"Yeah," Taylor said.

"Good for you," O'Leary said.

"And bad for them," Taylor said.

He watched from behind the drapes as O'Leary pulled his car from the motel's parking lot, then quickly grabbed his bag and ran out to his own car, got in and drove away.

Five minutes down the road to Philadelphia, he pulled onto the shoulder, got out of the car and tossed the FBI's homing device far out into the scrub brush that stretched as far back as the eye could see.

He drove another hour before finding another old motel on a side road and rented another room under the name of John Donne. He parked in the back, out of sight of the roadway, and double-locked the door to his room behind him.

After he settled into the dingy room, he lay on the bed, smoking. He wanted to talk to someone, and almost anyone would do. He dialed the number of his apartment but there was no answer. Melanie was out again, or at least not answering the telephone. And that, he decided, was that. The marriage was over and all that was left to be worked out now was the simplest, least messy divorce. He thought it should be clean and easy and so why, he wondered, did he feel so bad about it? It was probably just the stigma of failure, even in a marriage. His generation wasn't supposed to worry about things like that, but Matt Taylor did, and he couldn't escape the conclusion that if his marriage failed he was somehow, at least partly, to blame for it.

He thought of dialing Larry Wu's number and speaking to Katie but he decided that that would just be too painful right now. Maybe tomorrow.

The room had no television set and he looked around in the room's wastepaper basket, but there was no newspaper or magazine stashed away. He remembered Larry Wu's paperback book and retrieved it from inside his suitcase. Before lying down again on the bed, he propped a chair under the doorknob. Then he undressed, opened the cover of the book on Chinese painting, but fell asleep before he had read even one page.

CHAPTER FIFTEEN

The drive home across the state of Pennsylvania was long and wearing. When Taylor started out, fighting to get free of the metropolitan area traffic, he was too busy to do much thinking, but by the time he got to the Lionville exit of the Turnpike, his mind was churning away at the events of the last few days. That too passed away.

When he had crossed the Susquehanna River at Harrisburg, Taylor had stopped thinking about much of anything but the road and the music. He had made sure he rented a car with a cassette player and had been lucky enough to find a drugstore open on Sunday that sold tapes. He picked up a copy of the Modern Jazz Quartet's Last Concert album and played it over and over. The music had been a shared enthusiasm of his and Larry Wu's. It was as close as jazz came to Mozart—crisp and clean, full of melody and feeling and rhythm, and yet not overwhelmed by any of them. There was a precision to it, too, that once in a great while made it seem just a touch mechanical, but most of the time it soared. It was the kind of music that couldn't help but be loved by the same type of person who saw beauty in an elegant mathematical proof or a righteous computer program.

The miles slipped by with Taylor paying no more attention to the road than he absolutely had to in order to operate the car. Twice before he got to Pittsburgh, he moved off the toll road to eat. He was not really hungry either time, but he forced himself to take the break to combat road fatigue. The tension and turmoil of the last couple of days had taken their toll on him, he knew, and he was running on just his reserves of energy, and the brief food breaks gave him a chance to recharge his emotional batteries.

As he turned north off the Turnpike and onto I-79, Taylor noticed for the first time that the seasons had changed. Back in Washington, spring seemed to be well on its way, but here in the Allegheny Mountains of western Pennsylvania, it was still the last dragging days of a stubborn winter. Overhead, the skies were gray and long deep patches of snow still covered the ground in the lee of the winds and the sun. And every quarter-hour or so, his car would be assaulted by snow squalls.

He had almost forgotten how the weather was here, Taylor thought—how the cold and the chill lingered so long, and how glorious the spring was when it finally came. It had been a long time since he had been home . . . seven, almost eight years. And then he laughed at himself. After all that had happened and all the time away, he still thought of the hills of western Pennsylvania as home. He had never admitted that to himself before.

Taylor left the interstate at Jackson Center. From there, he picked up U.S. Route 62, for the hour's drive east to Iron City. But when he got close, he turned away from Iron City and drove west toward the town of Mercer. It took him a moment to realize why he had done it: It was because he was afraid of going home and he wanted to give himself a little more time to collect his thoughts. Who would he see, what would he say to them, what would they ask him, what would the answers be?

As he neared the courthouse square in Mercer, Taylor pulled the car into the parking area of an old-fashioned diner. He remembered stopping there often on his drives back and forth from Carnegie-Mellon University. In those days it had seemed as if he could never get enough to eat, and so he always stopped at the diner, even though his home was only an hour away down the road.

The interior of the diner looked as it had before: the shiny red vinyl booths; the slightly dulled chrome fixtures; the long counter; farmers and tradesmen talking quietly; kids squalling. Taylor took a seat at the counter. He and Lauren usually had sat at the counter, and so had Larry when he had come home on weekends with them.

Taylor ordered coffee and cherry pie and milk, the way he always had, and for a moment the waitress looked at him as if they might have known each other long ago, then seemed to decide that she didn't remember him.

Larry was dead now. They would never stop here again. Or anyplace else. And Lauren. That was history too. She had married and settled down and gone to work for the Judge. She had kept in touch with Larry and had been one of his personal lawyers when he owned the computer company. When he moved to Washington to work for the I.R.S., Larry and Lauren had kept in touch and through him, Taylor had learned second-hand about his old first love. Her husband was a cop but Taylor had forgotten his name. There had been a child and the child had died and so had the marriage. After Larry Wu had told him that, he had also told Taylor that Lauren always asked about him. Taylor finished his pie and coffee and milk, and left on the counter enough money to cover the bill and an oversized tip and walked out.

He went outside and drove home along the winding, up and down, forest and field-lined roads. And then he was going down the mile-long hill into Franklin, past the century-old grand houses of the first oil and steel millionaires, past the courthouse and up the winding four-lane highways crammed between the Allegheny River on the right side and the blasted-away wall of loose-lying sedimentary rocks on the left. He passed the old steel mills that gave his hometown its name, passed the newer string of pizza joints and discount stores and family restaurants, passed the half-mile-long, nearly deserted hulks of factories, and

135

then he was there. Above him on the hills stood the twin-bulbed St. Joe's Church. In front of him and to his right, French Creek poured into the Allegheny—both at near-flood levels as they usually were at this time of year, when the mountain snows had finally started to melt into runoff.

He stopped at a traffic light, wondering just what to do. All the time he had given himself to think about what he would do when he returned home, he understood he had intentionally spent *not* thinking about what he would do when he returned home. Someone behind him beeped a horn and he realized that he had sat halfway through the green light.

Taylor drove across the bridge and down into the small commercial district of the South Side. He would not go home again, he told himself. Not back to the house in which he had grown up. That was out of the question.

Taylor was reaching the end of the commercial area, coming to where the highway again snaked along the river—on the opposite bank now—and then on up over the hillsides and out to the wooded lands of the state parks and national forests half an hour beyond, out toward Harker's Furnace.

He turned back along the riverside drive into the center of town and across the other bridge and, without even thinking about it, he pulled into the parking lot of the big new motel that dominated this part of the downtown area. It rose eight stories high, the tallest building in the county. It took him nearly half an hour to get checked into a room. It was modern motel-decor, neither especially attractive or ugly, but it was functional, and it overlooked the river eighty feet below and the park that stretched from the motel down to the bridge and beyond. He took his time unloading his tired suitcase and packing things into drawers.

Everytime he passed it, he stared at the telephone and considered calling somebody—the Judge or Lauren or some old school pal—and telling them that he had come home, at least for a little while. And every time he was tempted to pick up the phone, he fought off the urge. When he was finished unpacking,

Taylor sat down on one of the two double beds and closed his eyes. Outside it was nearly dark. There didn't seem to be much more he could do this day. Better to wait and rest. But he could not fall off to sleep and a half hour later, he found himself downstairs in the motel's bar.

The room was dark and leather-seated and there were flickering votive candles on all the tables. Early Sunday evening did not seem to be a major rush hour among the town's drinkers, he thought, since there were fewer than a dozen people in the large room.

He sat at one end of the bar where somebody had left copies of the Erie and Pittsburgh Sunday papers. Taylor ordered a double Scotch without ice as he skimmed through the statewide news sections but found no story on Larry Wu's death and the attempt on his own life. His Scotch came and he nursed it as he perused the comic sections. It had been a long time since he had read the funny papers. Somehow they didn't seem to be very interested anymore in being funny. Every strip seemed to be about politics. Maybe nowadays, the comedy in newspapers was on the editorial pages, he thought, and then admitted ruefully to himself that there wasn't much of a change at all.

"Matt? Matt Taylor?"

He turned around. A man was standing near his elbow, smiling a self-conscious smile. He was near Taylor's age, of medium height, and built like one of those men who in their middle years give up their cigarette addiction and replace it with an addiction to running. He wore bifocals and had a receding hairline. His tweed suit was rumpled. The name that went with the man finally clicked into Matt's head.

"That's right," he said. "And you're John Smetts, aren't you?"

Smetts reached out a bony hand. "It's been a long time." They shook hands. Taylor had known Smetts all through their public school days and they had never especially liked each other. There was no reason for dislike, but it had been there all the same.

137

"Almost twenty years, I guess," Taylor said. "I'm surprised that you recognized me."

"Hey, you're one of the lucky ones. You've changed less than most of us have."

"I don't know if that makes me lucky," Taylor said and there was a long pause. Taylor did not have anything to add to that; what kind of small talk do you make with someone you have not seen in half a lifetime and someone you didn't like even back then. Especially when you're on a mission. Do you say, Hi, it's great to see you John; somebody's tried to kill me by truck, gun, and bomb in the last couple of days so I just decided to stop in and check out how the old gang's doing?

The silence was on the edge of being uncomfortable when another voice piped in.

"Are you the Matt Taylor that was involved in that shooting down near Maryland?" the voice said. It belonged to a young woman who had come up to stand alongside Smetts. She was blond, blue-eyed, and pretty in a fresh-faced cheerleader sort of way.

"That's a great ice-breaker," Smetts said with a chuckle. "Matt, this is Jenny Christopolous. Jenny, Matt Taylor, my old buddy from long ago."

Matt waited for her to extend a hand to shake but instead, the girl just stepped forward and said, "Are you?"

"Hold on," Smetts said. "How'd you know about a shooting that I don't know about?"

"Because I read the wire service and even if we didn't use the story, I thought it was interesting that an I.R.S. guy got killed and another one escaped at some truck stop in Maryland. I thought it might be a funny filler."

"Larry Wu who got killed was my best friend," Taylor snapped. "I don't think it was much of a funny filler." He turned back to his Scotch.

"Oh, Jesus, I'm sorry," the young woman said. She moved closer to Matt and touched his arm. "You stay in the newspaper business a long time and you get into the habit of not remem-

138

bering that dead people are real people; they're just stories to us after a while. Please. I'm really sorry."

Taylor turned back to the young woman and saw the distress in her face. After a moment, he shrugged. "I'm sorry for being testy too. You didn't know."

"Shake on it," Jenny said. She took Taylor's hand; her grip was firmer than John Smetts' had been. She smiled and Taylor could see the beginning of wrinkles at the corners of her eyes. She was older than he had first thought—probably around thirty or so.

"Jenny and I were just getting ready to have dinner," Smetts said. "Join us, Matt?"

Taylor was going to decline but Jenny had already said, "Of course he will," and was exerting pressure on his arm to steer him off the bar stool. He allowed himself to be led away to the back of the lounge where they sat in a quiet booth, Taylor facing the two of them across the table.

The waitress came with the menus and asked if they wanted a drink. Taylor ordered another Scotch; Smetts ordered the same. Jennie Christopolous just shook her head and when the waitress left, she explained to Taylor, "I don't drink anymore. I used to be an alcoholic. And a coke head. Until John here found me and saved me." She looked at Smetts with a smile that was half pixieish, half dogged devotion.

"Aaah, nonsense talk," Smetts said.

Taylor had not been prepared for that sort of confession. It was not the kind of thing he expected to hear in his hometown; it was more the type of instant familiarity that you got in California.

He could not think of a comment that would not sound sappy so he glanced at his menu then flapped it shut. Steak, potatoes, and a vegetable. Broccoli, if they had it. He knew it was trendy, but he had started eating it because everybody he knew and every restaurant he went into had started serving it, and now he found he even liked the damn stuff.

"I was working in L.A.," Jenny said when he looked up,

"when I hit bottom. I had known John a long time before and I called him up and told him I was going to kill myself. Well, he called the sheriff and they broke in and pumped my stomach and the next morning John himself was there. He checked me into this real fancy hospital—more like a resort, really—and then when I had dried out he flew out to get me again and he brought me back here and gave me a job."

Taylor looked at Smetts with a new sense of the man. He would never have thought him capable of something like that. And thus the nerds of our youth grow up to be real men, he thought. To his credit, Taylor thought, Smetts was blushing slightly and he said, "She makes it sound noble, Matt. I was just looking for cheap help."

"And I'm the cheapest broad you ever met, is that it? Answer carefully. Your life depends on it," Jenny said.

Smetts looked at Taylor and shrugged greatly, lifting his shoulders up to his ears. Taylor laughed, and Jenny said, "I keep proposing to him, you know, but he keeps turning me down. The only one he has eyes for is that Amazon Yuppie lawyer of his. You're from town, Matt. Have you ever met Lauren Carmody? The ice queen. I mean, my God, flaming red hair. And he's crazy about her and you know, I don't even think it's basically sexual. Can you imagine that? I mean, I think about it sometimes and I guess they must go to bed together—they can't sit around all the time and discuss the homeless, can they?—but I really think he's basically in love with her mind. Can you imagine that?"

Jenny looked at Taylor for an answer. The expression on his face caused her to turn to Smetts.

"Don't tell me, I know. I put my foot in my big Greek mouth again."

"Matt used to go out with Lauren," Smetts said mildly.

"Oh," Jenny said.

"Actually," Smetts said, "Jenny's closer to the truth than she thinks. Lauren and I talk about work. And the world. And the homeless too. And if my little Greek protégée isn't careful,

140

someday I'm going to give in to her nonsense and marry her and that'd serve you right, Jenny."

"Threats, threats. I'm tired of threats," Jenny said.

Taylor found the whole conversation growing awkward. He didn't know either of them, but if he ever saw two people who should love each other, it was Jenny Christopolous and John Smetts. And of course, he thought bitterly, he was a world-renowned expert on love, wasn't he? Didn't he marry Melanie in a great manifestation of love till death or a wife's itchy crotch, did them part?

He changed the subject.

"I gather the two of you work on a newspaper?" he said.

"The *Gusher*," Smetts said. "You remember our old home-town rag."

Taylor nodded and Jenny said, "John's the editor. He runs the whole shebang."

"With help," Smetts said. "Jenny's the city editor and a good one too."

"What a segue," she said. "So tell me about your friend's shooting," she said to Taylor.

"Are you asking as a newspaperman or as a friend from the old hometown?" Taylor asked.

"Let's try friend from the old hometown," she said.

"Okay," Taylor said. "Larry Wu was my best friend. We were on our way to Philadelphia to do some computer work there. I think somebody mistook us for two other guys. They shot Larry and tried to shoot me. They both got killed."

"You got one of them, right?" the young woman asked.

"I grabbed him. He hit his neck or something when he fell," Taylor said. "I didn't really have anything to do with it."

"Who were they?" Jenny asked.

"That's the point. The cops didn't know," Taylor lied. "Said maybe they were small-time hoodlums, but what the hell would they want with a couple of numbers crunchers for the I.R.S.? It's a mystery to me. Anyway, I just came up here for a couple of days to rest up before Larry's funeral, and so I really would

141

appreciate it if you didn't put anything in the paper. I'd rather be able to forget it for a while."

He looked at the two people across the table from him, pleading with his eyes. It was something he had totally forgotten; it never occurred to him that there might be stories in the newspapers or on television. It just made his job harder, he thought, if everybody knew who he was.

Smetts said, "You've got a deal, Matt. We don't really need the story and, besides, it's old news now."

"As long as you promise not to audit my tax returns," Jenny said.

"You can promise that one easily, Matt," Smetts said. "I don't pay her enough for her to cheat the feds."

The food came and they chatted lightly through the meal. Over coffee, Taylor said casually, "While I was driving up here, I passed a sign for Harker's Furnace. Wasn't there some big development going on there some years back?"

Smetts shook his head. "No. There was a lot of noise but nothing happened."

"What do you mean?"

"Some international corporation bought up a whole lot of property, remember the old military depot that used to be up there?"

"Yeah," Taylor said, although until that moment he had forgotten that Harker's Furnace had ever stored military equipment.

Smetts nodded. "Well, the environmentalists came out full-throat . . . you know, save the trees, screw the jobs, that kind of thing. But nothing ever happened. They patched the fence around the compound, but so far as anybody knows they never chopped down a tree, they never built a building, and pretty soon everybody forgot about it. I guess they pay their real estate taxes and that's that." He turned to the young woman on his left. "Check that tomorrow. Make sure that they do pay their taxes."

"Consider it done," Jenny said. "Maybe I'll even ask the great ice queen about it."

"Lauren?" Taylor said. "What's she got to do with it?"

"She was one of the save-the-tree lawyers who got involved in the whole thing. A lot of horseshit, if you'll pardon my French."

"Well, I wasn't really interested," Taylor said. "Like I said, it was just seeing that sign that jogged my memory."

"It'd give you a reason to talk to Lauren, if you needed one," Smetts said.

Taylor shrugged and tried to seem disinterested. "Maybe I will. If I get a chance."

Jenny said to no one in particular, "What makes me think this man is going to get a chance?"

CHAPTER SIXTEEN

The connection was bad.

"Melanie, it's Matt."

"Matt, where are you? I heard about it from Walt and then I read it in the paper. I was worried." There was a sharp accusatory edge in her voice and Taylor said, "Not so worried that you stayed home. I tried calling you last night."

"Well, where are you now? Are you all right?"

"I'm fine. I've just going to be gone for a few days. I want to sort things out. I just called to tell you ... well, be careful."

"What do you mean?" she asked, suddenly and totally alert. There was no better way, Taylor thought, to get her attention than to mention something that affected her personally. Calling her self-centered didn't do it justice. It was a total consuming concentration on herself and nothing else. How could he have ever thought he loved this woman?

"Just funny stuff going on, with Larry and me. I don't know what might happen next."

"You think I might be in some danger?" she said.

"I don't know. I don't think so, but watch out anyway."

"Fine," she said and the voice exuded sarcasm. "Somebody's probably going to try to kill me and you're off somewhere on vacation. Great. Don't you think your place is here with me, instead of out playing spy-hero? How many people have to die before you learn to butt out?"

"I think you're safer if I'm away from you," Taylor said. There was a moment's silence before he added, "I don't think my place is with you at all anymore."

"What do you mean by that?"

"Come on, Melanie. Nothing works for us. It's time for us to go our separate ways. Like you suggested. I'm butting out."

"Divorce? Are you saying divorce?" She was shrieking.

"Yeah. That's exactly what I'm saying."

"It's some other woman, isn't it? And that's where you are now. With some other woman. That's right, isn't it, you bastard?"

"Melanie—" he started but he heard a sound outside his hotel room door.

Melanie would not be silenced.

"Is it that Chinese cunt that's always had the hots for you? I always knew you were fucking her."

"Melanie, I've got to go," he said softly.

"You're not getting away to go with her," Melanie said. "I won't be made a laughingstock in front of my friends."

"Why not?" Taylor said. "I've been one for years."

He hung up the phone and rose softly from the bed. He took the automatic O'Leary had given him from the drawer of the nightstand and walked toward the door. As he reached it, there was a knock at the door.

He put his eye to the peephole and looked out into the corridor. A man stood there, his back to the door, carefully studying the opposite wall. He wore an overcoat of black Persian wool and a pearly gray homburg and carried a silver-handled walking stick. He was slightly above medium height and had broad shoulders and Taylor recognized him.

He opened the door and the man turned. He was, Taylor knew, seventy-seven years old, but his face was that of a man much younger; his van Dyke beard was neatly trimmed, and his eyes had the shrewd house-counting look of a poker player.

He studied Taylor from head to foot.

"Hello, Judge," Taylor said.

"I'd heard you came to town. I didn't want to miss you. May I come in? Or is the gun meant for me?" He nodded toward the automatic which Taylor was holding at his side. The younger man flushed and shook his head.

"Sorry, Judge. I . . . well, it's a long story. Come on in. I'm glad you came."

He stepped aside and the old man walked into the room slowly. From the way he moved, it was apparent that the walking stick was not just an affectation. He saw Taylor watching him move and grunted slightly.

"It's the damned arthritis," he said. "I guess it's not the worst thing that can happen to somebody my age."

"Guess not," Taylor said as he closed the door behind them. "So what's the gun for, Matt?"

Taylor tried a smile. "I thought you were the Jehovah's Witnesses, coming to welcome me to town. I like to be prepared for them."

He put the gun down on the dresser nearest the door. The old man was studying him again, then held out his hand. Taylor took it. And then the old man hugged him.

The Judge had never been a man to show his emotions; the last time Taylor could remember the old man holding him was in the bad days right after Taylor's parents had been killed. Taylor hesitated for a second, then put his own arms around the much shorter man and embraced him. They stood like that for long seconds before the Judge pulled loose, backed off, and sat down on the edge of the nubby, floral fabric-covered chair.

He took off his bowler and placed it on the small end table, he carefully ran his hands back across his silver hair to smooth it down. His nails were manicured, but the hands were big and strong, the way Matt had remembered them.

"Lot to catch up on, Matt," he said. "You all right, boy?"

"Yeah, Judge. I'm okay."

"And the gun?"

146

"Somebody tried to kill me. I guess I'm a little spooky."

"You here to hide out or are you looking for something?" the Judge asked.

"I didn't know I was that obvious," Taylor said.

"When you raise a boy like your own, you're going to remember everything about him. I read you like a book, boy."

"Yes, sir. You always did."

Matt sat on the bed, facing the old man. "How'd you know I was in town?"

"Do you have to ask?" the Judge said with a sly grin.

"I guess not. Actually, I guess I was wondering which one of your spies I ran into."

"All of them," the Judge said. "How's your wife?"

Taylor suppressed a smile; the Judge had never been able to bring himself to speak Melanie's name. Obviously that dislike hadn't changed.

"She's all right. I think we're going to get divorced."

The judge nodded; it was his turn to restrain a smile.

"And Lauren?" Taylor asked.

"She's fine. She's working with me, you know. Or I guess you'd say she's running the place. Damned arthritis kind of restricts my moving around."

"I didn't think it took much moving to pull strings," Taylor said amiably.

"After all these years, you finally figured me out?" the Judge asked.

"I always had you figured out," Taylor said.

The old man chuckled. "Anyway, Lauren's all right. She's still crazy about you, you know. Or I guess your friend, Larry, told you about that. I'm sorry about him by the way. He was a nice boy." Matt nodded.

"Anyway, maybe this time you'll do the right thing. You have a few more years to fool around, but Lauren doesn't. She's going to have to crank up her old baby machine pretty damn soon if she's ever going to use it again."

"Judge, don't play matchmaker," Taylor said. "That sent me out of here the last time. Seven years ago."

"Seven years, eight months and twenty-three days," the Judge said. "Give or take."

"Give or take," Taylor said.

"Don't get swell-headed, young man. I haven't been carrying those numbers around in my head. I just calculated it on the way driving over here."

"I didn't expect you carried them around."

After a long pause, the Judge said, "God, this is a dismal room. Get your coat on and let's get out of here."

"Where to?"

"We'll go over to the house. I left before dessert was served. You can sit and watch me fill my arteries with whipped cream."

Taylor hesitated for a moment and the Judge said, "You can bring your gun, if it'll make you feel more secure."

Taylor grinned and went to the closet for his jacket. He put it on and when he turned he saw the Judge dialing the telephone.

"Maggie," he said. "The boy's coming home with me. We'll be right there."

Strictly speaking, the Judge's house was not in Iron City. It was on a hillside southwest of town, overlooking the Allegheny River from almost a hundred feet up. It was an old, red-brick and gingerbread monstrosity that had been built by one of the tasteless, early oil barons a century before. If it had a few broken windows, assorted cobwebs, creaking shutters and doors, it could pass for a haunted house.

As it was it looked daunting as they drove through the high brick gates, and past the small sign that read

Frank M. Stevens,
Counselor at Law

and up a driveway that was steep and winding and would have scared off most people who had not been raised in the hills of western Pennsylvania.

148

Without ringing, they were met at the door by a handsome woman who seemed to be in her late forties. She had dark eyes and auburn hair that she piled atop her head. A dark green dress hinted at a fully ripened, mature figure without actually revealing anything. The Judge's wife had died in childbirth, ten years after their wedding. The baby had not survived either. The Judge had never married again. Soon after, Taylor, whose own parents had been killed in a car crash, had moved into the house as the judge's ward. He always remembered the Judge had employed similar-looking women to take care of him and his house. They usually lasted four or five years and then, apparently with great regrets on both sides, the Judge replaced them with others. He never talked about how he hired them or why he let them go.

"Maggie, this is my boy, Matt Taylor. He's in town for a while and don't ask me why. If we get along tonight, I'll probably ask him to stay, but he probably won't. Matt, this is Maggie Butterfield, who takes care of me and this place. She's the best housekeeper I've ever had. I even asked her to marry me but she turned me down."

"Wise woman," Matt said, smiling at Maggie who blushed slightly and shook his hand.

"I've heard a lot about you," she said.

"Only the good parts are true," Taylor said.

She shook her head with a pleasant smile. "There weren't any good parts."

Matt chuckled and Judge Stevens grabbed his arm to lead him down the hall.

"Judge, could I speak with you alone for a moment?"

"Sure," Stevens said. "Matt, go on ahead to the dining room."

Taylor wandered through the once-familiar rooms looking for changes, but not many had been made. In the past eight years, the house had not so much changed as it had grown even more personally a statement of the Judge's. The furniture was all

149

good, old, early American pieces; no Swedish Modern, no Louis Quinze. The only exceptions were the heavy Persian rugs that covered most of the floors and the delicate Chinese porcelains that decorated most of the rooms. Taylor saw that the Judge had apparently added American art to his enthusiasms. In just one room alone, Taylor could see a Hassam, an Eakins, and something early that looked like one of the Peale family's things. He had always regarded the Judge as rich—didn't children always regard adults as rich?—but the art collection bespoke a small fortune.

Taylor sat at the long oaken dinner table and a few seconds later, the Judge appeared. His face was flustered, as if he had been arguing.

He sat at the chair at Matt's left and slapped his napkin down onto his lap.

"It's damn foolishness, is what it is," he growled.

"What is?" Matt said casually.

"Lauren. She called and she was coming over. Then Maggie told her you'd be here, and she said she'd see me tomorrow instead."

"I guess she didn't want to see me," Taylor said.

"Why don't you two stop fooling with each other and do what you're supposed to do and stop making me old before my time?" the Judge said.

"Maybe we'd rather do what we think we're supposed to do," Matt said.

"That's a pretty good theory," Stevens said, "except the problem with it is that neither of you know what you want to do or ought to do or should do and you both need my guidance."

"Keep trying, Judge. Maybe one day you'll convince us," Taylor said lightly. But inside he was hurt; he wished Lauren had come running to the house when she'd heard he was in town. Maybe the books were right; maybe you couldn't go home again.

Maggie brought in a silver carafe of coffee and a platter laden with chocolate goodies and a silver bowl of whipped cream. Taylor drank coffee and watched as the Judge ate ravenously of the desserts. Then the old man stood and walked to a large cabinet and poured brandy for both of them in large snifters.

He brought them back to the table, set one in front of Matt, sat down, and took out a cigar.

"Can't smoke the damned things anymore," he said. "Just one a week I'm allowed. But I chew the hell out of five or six of them a day. A poor thing but 'tis my own. Now, boy. Tell me about this assassin who killed Larry. And about who's trying to kill you. And tell me what I can do to help."

CHAPTER SEVENTEEN

The Judge was sitting on his bench, high overhead, wearing formal black robes and the curled powdered wig of an English judge.

"There's one sure thing," he said, and his voice echoed even though the courtroom seemed to be endless and to have no walls. "Somebody's out to kill you."

Taylor stood on the ground in front of the bench, arguing against him. He had to tip his head far back to be able to see the Judge.

"There's *two* sure things," Taylor said. "You taught me that. Death and taxes." He paused and then added with what seemed to him a stroke of blinding genius, "Death and taxes. And I'm the tax man."

But the Judge seemed to pay him no mind. He rapped lightly with his gavel but the sound seemed to echo on down through eternity. "Another thing's sure, boy. You'll have to save yourself."

Taylor was at a loss for a moment.

He protested again. "The only sure things are death and taxes, not what you're saying. And I'm the dead man." He stopped speaking. What he had just said did not sound right, and yet he was not sure why.

The Judge leaned way over the bench so that it seemed he

was looking down on the top of Matt's head. He spoke in a low voice.

"Tell you another sure thing, boy," he said. "You're a poor pitiful pussy-whipped creature. That's sure. And you married the wrong one. Never should have married her. I could have told you that before. Damn . . . fact is, I did tell you. That's for sure."

"That was wrong what I said before," Taylor said. "I'm not the dead man. No. I'm the taxed dead man. No. I'm the dead tax man. No . . ." Sweat was pouring from his body as he stopped in confusion.

"There's *another* sure thing, for damned sure," the Judge said. He pounded with his gavel again and again and again. It felt to Taylor as if they were all inside a booming bass drum. "You'll need a new life. And a new wife. A new wife for life."

Taylor protested. But it didn't stop. It went on and on, and when he finally awoke, he was drenched with sweat. The sunlight was pouring through the window, the weak pale yellow sun of early spring. Taylor swung his feet out of the bed and onto the floor. There was a bad taste in his mouth. He had not drunk enough the night before to be hung over, but he had had enough to leave his morning mouth feeling thick and furry.

The dinner had adjourned into the Judge's study and the night had dragged on with Taylor retelling the events of the past few days over and over to the Judge. When the Judge finally seemed to have run out of questions, he had picked up the telephone on his desk, and punched in two digits.

"Billy," he said after a moment, "would you mind coming up to the main house for a couple of minutes?" The Judge chuckled slightly and then grew serious. "That might be a good idea," he said.

A few minutes later, there was a hard rap at the door and before the Judge could say enter or anything else, the door had swung open and a dark-eyed, dark-haired man of about fifty had walked in. He was tall and wiry and moved with the kind of grace and economy that nineteenth-century novelists had described Indians as having: something like a cross between the way mountain lions and wolves moved. The man looked around the room, stared at Taylor, but said nothing. There was something oddly familiar about his face but Taylor could not place it.

The Judge motioned the newcomer to a chair. "Drink, Billy?" he asked.

The man shook his head as he sat down. The Judge smiled. "Good," he said. "How long's it been?"

Billy ignored the question. "You needed me?"

The Judge's eyes narrowed. "How long's it been, Billy?"

"It would have been two months, but I was just starting to pour myself one when you called."

"Did you?" the Judge asked.

The man shook his head, slowly, almost mournfully. In the small wood-paneled room, he seemed to give off an odor that reminded Taylor of a pine forest.

"No," the man answered. "but I would have."

The Judge nodded knowingly. "Two months is still two months."

"It's a sin of intention, even if not of commission," Billy said.

"Believe that and we all fry in hell," the Judge said. "Coffee?"

The other man nodded; the Judge called Maggie on the phone and the three of them sat without speaking, watching the fire burn until the housekeeper returned with a tray full of coffee. Billy spoke his thanks quietly.

After Maggie had left, the Judge said, "Billy, this is my boy, Matt. Matt Taylor. You've heard me speak of him before."

Billy stood up and walked over to Taylor. He wiped his hand on his blue jeans before offering it to Taylor.

"Matt," the judge said. "This is Billy O'Baal. A direct descendant of Chief Cornplanter."

Taylor rose to shake the man's hand. He knew now where he had seen the face before. O'Baal looked like the painting of his famous ancestor that the Judge kept in the house's main parlor. Cornplanter had been a mixed breed, half white, half Seneca, who sometimes used his white name of John O'Baal. He had been one of the greatest war leaders of the Iroquois Confederation. During the Revolutionary War he had led some of the bloodiest raids against the Americans on behalf of the British. After the British surrendered at Yorktown, he had become an important peacemaker between the rest of the Iroquois and the Americans, who had not yet won the war on their western frontier.

"You might call Billy my guardian angel," the Judge said.

Taylor looked at him quizzically and the Judge said, "When I retired . . . seven years ago . . . after you left . . . well, some of the people I sent away were talking about getting even. Some of them even tried." He grinned. "Billy made sure they didn't succeed, and I want him to do the same for you."

Afterwards, Taylor tried to figure out why he had answered so quickly. Maybe it was from a sense of guilt that the Judge's life had come under attack, and Matt had not been there to help or to do anything about it, and the Judge had been forced to turn to a stranger for help and protection.

"No," he said.

The Judge bridled. "Why the hell not?" he snapped.

"I'm not sure," Taylor said. "I don't think I'm going to need anyone while I'm up here. Nobody knows where I am. And back in D.C., well . . ." He left the sentence unfinished.

Billy O'Baal had returned to his seat and continued to drink his coffee, as if what were being discussed had nothing to do with him.

"If you don't let me help you—" the Judge said, and then he stopped sharply in midsentence.

There was no argument and that surprised Taylor. The Judge didn't ever give in that easily. But he said simply, "Okay, have it your own way. But if there's trouble . . ."

"If there's trouble, trouble that I can't handle, then I'll call for help."

The Judge seemed to accept Taylor's decision with grudging good grace. They talked a while longer and the Judge seemed oddly concerned with how much Matt drank these days. He seemed satisfied when Taylor said, "Only a drop, and only once in a while." The conversation petered out and the Judge asked Billy O'Baal to drive Taylor back down the mountain into town. It was well past midnight when Taylor got back to the motel, his bed, and his dream of the Judge.

After a shower, Taylor descended to the motel's small restaurant. The first thing he saw when he walked through the door was Billy O'Baal, seated at a table near the door, watching the lobby and drinking black coffee. The Indian touched a finger to his forehead in a half salute as Taylor entered, but made no other sign. For a moment, Taylor considered ignoring him, but thought that was unnecessarily rude and joined him at his table.

"Mind if I join you?" he asked.

"Not so long as you don't block my view," O'Baal said.

"Watching for someone?" Taylor asked, and when O'Baal didn't bother to answer, Taylor pressed, "Who?"

O'Baal glanced at him, a look of mild amusement on his face. "Whoever's trying to kill you," he said.

Taylor thought about what he had said and asked, "How would you recognize them?"

"I will," O'Baal said.

"How long are you going to sit here?"

"As long as it takes," O'Baal said.

"And then what are you going to do?"

O'Baal brushed back his denim jeans jacket. Under his armpit was a shoulder holster with a pistol in it.

"Isn't that illegal?" Taylor asked.

"Not for me," O'Baal grunted. "Not around here."

The waitress came and Taylor ordered English muffins and coffee. After she had left, he said to the dark-haired man, "Didn't you understand last night, I said I didn't want your protection?"

O'Baal allowed himself a small smile.

156

"I understand fine," he said. "I understand what you said, and I understand what the Judge wants, and what the Judge wants is for me to keep you alive. When it comes down to what you want or what the Judge wants, the Judge wins every time."

"Just a natural born company man, aren't you?" Taylor snapped.

But the sarcasm seemed lost on O'Baal. Still staring at the door, he said softly, "Boy, ten years ago I was rotting in a jail cell, looking at life for a murder I didn't do. The Judge got me out and I owe him. Now if he says protect you, I protect you. And if he said kill you, I'd kill you without blinking an eye. I'm a company man, sure enough. But the Judge is the only company I work for. Are you going up to Harker's Furnace today?"

"I don't know. Probably," Taylor said.

"Don't go without me," O'Baal said.

Taylor nodded. His breakfast came and he ate silently, which did not seem to bother O'Baal at all, because the big Indian only kept staring at the entrance door to the motel.

CHAPTER EIGHTEEN

O'Baal was probably still sitting in the stupid motel, staring at the stupid door, Taylor thought smugly, as he drove carefully through the early spring snowstorm along U.S. 62, cutting across dense woodland skirting the Allegheny National Forest. He had left the Indian at the dining table and said he was going back to his room for a nap. Then he had sneaked out the back door of the motel and sped off in his car. He glanced at the rearview mirror. Even through the intensifying snowfall, he could tell nobody was following him.

So much for Big Chief Cornpone, the great Indian tracker. Screw him and screw the judge too. This was Taylor's problem and he was going to handle it himself.

At Tidioute, he turned east on State Route 47 toward Hearts' Content. Harker's Furnace lay along the road to Heart's Content, part of one of those little checkers of privately owned land surrounded on all sides by the national forest.

There was not much to the town: a crossroads with motels on three of its corners, a log cabin-style restaurant on the fourth, and alongside it a gas station, a general store, and a combination baitshop and souvenir stand. The trees—mostly beeches and maples—had been cleared back for about a hundred yards on all sides, partly to allow room for parking, and partly to provide a fire break in case the woods ever went up.

The motels seemed reasonably new and well kept but none of them was named White Pine Cabins, which was the address given for Fred Kohler and the other two names Taylor had pulled out of the I.R.S. computer files nearly a week before.

Taylor pulled into the gas station, parked his car in front of the free air hose, and walked inside. Nobody was in the office. Taylor went on into the service bay and saw someone leaning over the front fender of a Forest Service pickup truck, head and arms inside the engine compartment. There were some grunts and curses coming from whoever it was.

"Excuse me," Taylor called out. The voice under the hood yelled back, "Be with you in a minute, mister."

Taylor waited. The minute turned into five before the mechanic finally extricated himself from his work. He was in his late twenties, sturdily made, and wore his hair and beard like some lost flower child of the Sixties.

"Know anything about truck motors?" he asked.

"Add what I know to what you know and it's still what you know," Taylor said.

"Not my lucky day, I guess. What can I do for you, mister?"

"I'm looking for the White Pine Cabins," Taylor said. "I thought they were supposed to be here in Harker's Furnace."

"They are. Right across the street." He pointed toward the window with a wrench. "Right there."

The motel he pointed at was long, low slung, and finished in white aluminum siding. The sign in front said Dew Drop Inn.

"The Dew Drop Inn?" Taylor asked.

"That's it," the mechanic said. "Ain't that a hell of a name. We all tried to talk her out of it. It's too fucking corny, don't you think?"

"I guess so. But that's the White Pines Cabins?"

"Used to be before she picked that corny, fucking new name for it."

"Thanks" Taylor said. "I guess it could be worse."

"Could be. Old Mabel said we didn't get off her ass, she'd name it the Stick-It-Inn. She'd do it too."

"I guess we're all lucky then," Taylor said. He crossed the highway and entered the motel's tiny office, or at least the little piece of it that was not taken up by the office's occupant. The woman was old and Taylor thought he had never seen a fatter person in his life and yet, buried in all that flesh, there was a remarkably pretty girlish face. She spoke with a sweet, tremulous young girl's voice.

"Yes, sir. You've come at a good time. Slow season." She seemed to lurch forward as if to take the pen from the holder on the small desk.

"Thank you, but I'm not looking for a room," he said.

"Oh," The woman settled back again and Taylor wondered what kind of chair she was sitting on that could handle her weight. "Then what can I do you for?" she said and giggled at her own little joke.

Taylor took out his wallet and showed the woman his I.R.S. identity card. It said nothing about being with the I.R.S.'s investigative branch, but most people did not notice that anyway. Seeing the letters "IRS" were usually enough to impress most people. That was the good part; the bad part was that they generally went immediately into the defensive mode.

The old woman glanced at the card, then glared at him with one eye, half-shutting the other at the same time.

"So you're what my pappy used to call a damned revenooer?" she said.

Taylor decided to try the friendly approach.

"Well, sometimes we get that name. What was your father? Moonshiner? Rum-runner?"

"Worse," the old woman said.

"Worse?"

"Worse. Taught economics at Penn State. Hated those revenooers. Hated FDR. Hated anybody that had the right to collect and spend anybody else's money. Can't say I disagreed with him much either."

Taylor laughed. "Well, he was right. It's a rotten job, but

160

let's face it, somebody's got to do it. Why not a sweet, charming guy like me?"

"You're big anyway," the woman said. "I'll say that for you. Most tax people, I get the idea, they're nasty little twerps with faces like ferrets."

"Not a ferret in the family," Taylor said. "Maybe you can help me?"

The woman shrugged noncomittally.

"This was the White Pines Cabins?" Taylor asked.

"Still is technically. But it didn't make much sense calling her that any more."

"Why not?"

The old woman looked at him as if he were not too quick mentally.

"Look outside. See any cabins?"

Taylor glanced through the window. "No."

"Any white pines?" she demanded.

He shook his head.

"That's why. Haven't been any cabins here in four, five years; no pines in three. Pollution got them, I think."

"Sorry about that," Taylor said.

"Not your fault. But you'd think, you're coming here to talk to me, you'd look at some of those forms first that you people in Washington are always making us fill out, you'd know that these are still the White Pine Cabins *In*-corporated." She said the final word with decisive emphasis.

"Yes, ma'am," Taylor said. He felt like Sergeant Joe Friday. "But see, ma'am, I didn't really come to talk to you."

"Who then?"

"I'm trying to locate some men. They gave your motel as their address on their tax returns."

The old woman's expression visibly softened.

"That all?" she said. "Which ones you interested in?"

Taylor tried to mask his surprise. "How many have you got here?" he asked.

The old woman squinted her eyes and studied the ceiling for

a moment like some third-grader seeking inspiration during an arithmetic quiz.

"Six thousand, six hundred, and sixty-seven," she said slowly. "The same as Hanisek's Motel across the road there, and one more than Langston's out the other side."

"That's twenty thousand men," Taylor said.

"Men and women," she corrected.

"That's a lot of people," Taylor said. "It looks like you'd have a hard time fitting them all in."

The old woman laughed and sputtered, "They don't live here. Any damn fool could see that. They just use this place for a mailing address."

"Why?" Taylor asked.

"Hey. You're the government man. You ought to know that," she said.

"But I don't," Taylor said honestly.

"I guess these are all people who work down the road at the Installation." She pronounced the word as if it were spelled with a capital I.

Taylor gave her back the same pronunciation. "I don't know anything about the Installation," he said.

"Well, what do you know? Finally somebody's keeping a secret in this damn fool government."

"A secret installation?" Taylor said.

"What else could it be?" she said. "Must be secret government work going on there."

"And they've got twenty thousand people working there?" he asked.

The woman shrugged. "I never said that. I never saw them. Maybe they work in Timbuktu. I never saw any twenty thousand people, I know that for a fact."

"How many people are actually out there, do you suppose?"

The old woman shifted in her chair, carefully rearranging her mounds of fat.

"We keep trying to figure that out. The best any of us can figure is maybe two dozen or so. And mostly smurfs."

"Smurfs?" Taylor asked. He thought of little dolls with blue skin and long hair. "Smurfs?"

"You know. Tall skinny guys with glasses. And pens stuck in their shirt pockets."

"Ahh," Taylor said, starting to comprehend. "Maybe you mean nerds."

"Nerds, smurfs, what's the difference?"

"They're all like that?" Taylor said.

"Most I said. There's a couple drive by once in a while, they look like arm-breakers. You know the type, don't you?"

"Yes, ma'am."

"Now who were those people you wanted me to check for you?"

Taylor wrote down the names of Fred Kohler, Clyde Stallbarn, and Andrew McCabe and handed them to her. She slowly levered herself up out of the chair and disappeared into a closet-sized room behind the motel's reception desk. A few minutes later she was back.

"Yep," she said. "They're all on our books."

"When was the last time you saw them?" Taylor asked.

"Never saw them, at least not so's I'd know about it," she said.

"I'm confused," Taylor said.

"Naturally. You work for the government."

"How'd this all start? How'd you get involved in this?" Taylor asked.

"Just about a year ago. March, it was. This fella came to see me ..."

"What fellow?"

"Some lawyer fellow. I don't remember his name."

Taylor did not believe her but he nodded for her to continue.

"Anyway, he said that he represented people he wasn't 'at liberty'—that's what he said, 'at liberty,'—to tell me about, but that I could make some easy, honest money. All's I had to do was to let some people use this place as their mailing address for tax returns. I told him I didn't want to get into any trouble with the feds, I know how you people are, but he said that this *was* the feds and I didn't have to worry. And he'd pay me fifty cents for each person who used my address."

She stopped to cackle. "I never figured it was going to be some six thousand guys. That's three thousand dollars." She hesitated, looked at Taylor sharply, and said, "And I declare every penny of it on my tax return, sonny, so you can forget about that in case you're thinking about getting cute with me."

"So what do you exactly do for the money?" Taylor said.

"I get mail here addressed to a lot of people that aren't staying in the motel. It's all tax forms and things. I put all the mail in a box and every Friday somebody comes and collects it and that's that."

"Lot of refund checks too and stuff like that," Taylor suggested and the woman paused and reflected before answering.

"Actually, no refund checks. That's sort of odd, isn't it? Mostly just tax forms. Everything comes between January and April 15th, and then it's like nothing for the rest of the year. Oh, maybe a couple of stray letters now and again but nothing real much."

"And somebody always comes and picks stuff up on Friday," Taylor mused aloud. "Suppose you get a letter when you're not expecting it. Do you have a number to call? Somebody to tell about it?"

The woman shook her head. "No. Somebody comes by every Friday and I just wait. Most weeks, like I said, there isn't any mail to pick up. I don't have any complaints. It's three thousand easy dollars. No complaints in the other two motels either."

"Does the same person always come and pick up the mail?"

"No. Different people."

"You know any of their names?" Taylor asked.

"No. They just say they're from the Installation and I give them whatever I got. Sometimes a boxful, sometimes just one or two letters."

"So you think all these people are doing some kind of government work up at the Installation?" Taylor asked.

"Don't ask me. You're the government man. Don't you know?"

Taylor ignored the question and said, "So you don't know personally any of these three names?" He pointed to the names he had written down.

"Nope. Can't say as I do." She looked past Taylor toward the front window and said aloud, "Hey. Maybe I've got business."

Taylor turned and saw two men walking across the street toward the motel. He recognized them as the men he knew as FBI agents Sal Gianetti and John Polonowski.

CHAPTER NINETEEN

Taylor watched in a sort of disconnected fascination for a moment as Polonowski and Gianetti approached. His mind was too loaded down even to admit the questions that assailed him.

How did they know where he was? Dennis O'Leary had pulled their transmitter from his car. But here they were anyway. Was it possible that it was just a coincidence? That they weren't looking for him?

Not a chance, he thought as he snapped back to full alert. And somehow he had the real idea that their looking for him meant he was in danger.

He turned back to the fat woman. "Is there another way out of here?"

"No," she said, shaking her head and setting the folds of her neck to jiggling. "What's the matter with you? You look like you saw a ghost."

"I'm on a confidential mission," Taylor said quickly. "I'm not supposed to let anybody know I'm here. Can I hide in your back room until these guys go?" Without waiting for an answer, he moved around the desk.

"I guess so. And maybe you'll do me a favor sometime," she said."

"Don't tell them I'm here and you've got it." Taylor moved in the little storeroom and his heart sank when he saw that there was no window through which he could escape. He was trapped. He left the door open a crack so he could hear what was going on outside. Suddenly, he wished he had not been so damned sure of himself and that he had brought with him the pistol O'Leary had given him. He did not know if Polonowski and Gianetti were threats to him. Christ knew, they had had plenty of chances already to kill him if that was their plan, but he sure didn't think they had come all the way to western Pennsylvania to ask him if he liked to ski.

He looked around the room to see if there was anything he could use to defend himself, but the room, barely six by six feet in size, seemed to have been built only to store cardboard boxes. There was a folding card table in a corner with a ledger book opened on it and in a fleeting glance, Taylor noted that it seemed to contain lists of names.

Then he heard the bell over the front door tinkle and the woman's voice: "Afternoon, gentlemen. What can I do for you?"

He recognized Gianetti's oily voice. "We're with the FBI, ma'am." There was a moment's pause and Taylor guessed that they were showing the woman their identification. He was sunk, he knew. There was no way she was going to lie about his presence to two FBI men.

"We're looking for someone," Gianetti's voice sounded again. "His name is Matthew Taylor."

But before the woman could answer, the doorbell tinkled again as obviously someone else entered.

Then there was a voice that Taylor recognized but could not quite pin down. It sounded excited.

"Jesus, Mabel," the new male voice said. "What the hell did you do to that guy?"

A pause and the woman said, "What guy?"

"That big tall guy who was just in here. You try to take him to bed or something?" There was a chuckle. "I saw him hightailing it down the road in that rented Ford, going like ninety. You musta scared the pants off him."

Polonowski's gruff voice snapped. "What way did he go?"

167

"Down that way," the stranger's voice answered.

"Out of the way," Polonowski snarled. There was the sound of feet, another tinkling of the doorbell, harder this time, and then the door slamming. And then there was silence for a long moment before the woman's voice called out:

"Okay, young fella. You can come out now."

Taylor walked outside, just in time to see the two FBI men's car skidding off from its parking spot across the street. The fat woman still sat behind the desk. Leaning on the front of the desk was Billy O'Baal.

He looked at Taylor and said, "I guess they weren't no friends of yours, were they?"

"How'd you know I was here?" Taylor asked.

"Sonny, you couldn't get away from me if you was a small fish in a big ocean at midnight."

"I watched. I didn't see you following me," Taylor said.

O'Baal's face showed his obvious disdain for such a stupid remark. He merely said, "You done pestering my girlfriend?"

Taylor nodded.

"Then come on. You're so damned interested in this installation, I'll take you for a look."

O'Baal had sent the two FBI men off toward the south, back toward Iron City, so when Taylor got into his truck, the rangy Indian drove off toward the northeast. After about five miles, they came to a cyclone fence that paralleled the road, running ahead of them as far as the eye could see.

"This is the installation," O'Baal said.

Taylor nodded. "Ever been inside?" he asked.

The Indian seemed to consider his answer. "The old Army base closed down about ten years ago. I used to go in then. Good hunting. But then a couple of years ago they fixed up the fence. Haven't been back since."

That had been their total conversation since they had left the motel.

168

O'Baal drove on, keeping the fence on the right side of the truck. After a mile, they passed a gate in the fence. There were guardhouses on either side of the gate and a small Jeep parked next to one of the shacks, but there were no signs of any people around. O'Baal slowed down.

"Not much to see," Taylor said.

"The old army buildings are out of sight, down behind that rise," O'Baal said.

They kept driving. Another mile passed and the fence turned away from the road at a soft right angle, disappearing down a gully and into a stand of trees.

"Too late to go inside today," Taylor said. "I'll have to come back. After I talk to Lauren."

O'Baal did not answer.

The light had mostly faded from the sky. During the afternoon the snow had turned to sleet, then to rain, then had stopped. Now it was starting to snow again. They came around a curve in the road and down over the crest of a small hill.

"Up ahead," O'Baal suddenly said.

Taylor peered through the gathering gloom but could not see anything. The Indian started to slow and as he did, he took the gun from the holster under his denim jacket and laid it on the seat between them. Taylor looked at it, impressed by its size, and thought Buffalo Bill might have used a gun just like that one.

He glanced up again and then he saw it: a dark gray foreign car, probably a Maserati, pulled off to the side of the road, tilting to one side. Somebody was standing next to it.

Billy stopped as he drew alongside the car and Taylor lowered his window. The somebody was a young woman. She had on a gray wool dress that would have looked perfect at a cocktail party in either Georgetown or Manhattan. It covered her modestly and yet seemed to completely reveal the most beautiful body Taylor had ever seen on a live up-close woman: long and lean, narrow-waisted, with high, full breasts. She had thick black hair that fell below her shoulders, dark sparkling eyes, and a full mouth colored by deep red lipstick that, until that moment, Taylor had always thought looked trashy. The woman had a long thin nose and high cheekbones and was almost indescribably beautiful.

"Thank God you've come along," she said. "I was afraid I was going to freeze my bippy off."

Taylor grinned at her and said to O'Baal, "Pull over. Let's see what's going on."

O'Baal parked the truck ten yards from the Maserati, pulling off into the snow-covered brush to stop from blocking the narrow road.

Before getting out of the truck, the Indian slipped the gun into the waistband of his jeans and then zippered his jacket over it. The young woman was walking forward to meet them.

"Two knights in shining armor," she said. Her smile was perfect too.

O'Baal stared at her with a calm, deep penetrating look and then he flicked his eyes away to study the road in both directions. Taylor had trouble taking his eyes off the woman; she was even more beautiful than he had first thought.

She held out her hand to him. "I'm Angela Fox," she said.

Taylor wondered what she would do if he kissed her hand, but settled for shaking it, feeling vaguely foolish being so formal with a woman he met alongside a country road.

"Matt Taylor," he said and nodded toward the Indian who was leaning calmly against the back of the truck. "This is Billy O'Baal."

The young woman favored the Indian with another dazzling smile and Taylor thought he saw O'Baal's mouth move slightly in the direction of a smile for a fraction of a second.

"Don't you have a coat?" Matt asked her.

"In the car. I just got out when you fellows came along."

"What's the problem?" Taylor asked.

"A flat," the woman said. "And I feel like an idiot. I know how to change my own damn tires. But when I was packing for this trip, I remember taking the jack out to squeeze in one more bag and then I forgot to put the darn thing back in. It makes me so mad at myself I could just about spit."

Taylor could not imagine Angela Fox spitting, or eating, or coughing, or sneezing, or anything that was not just too, too elegant.

O'Baal walked off, circled the gray car, partly studying it, partly studying the woods that lined the road on either side.

"What do you think, Billy?" Taylor said. "Can we change the lady's tire?"

"I'll get my jack," the Indian said.

Taylor gave him a hand lifting the front seat of the pickup truck and extricating the jack. When they had it, O'Baal took his gun from his waistband and put it on the floor of the truck next to the accelerator pedal. As he did, the young woman got her coat from the Maserati. It was a silver fox, a fur coat naturally. Somehow Taylor had not expected her to have any other kind of coat, and she pulled it tight around her and stood next to Taylor while O'Baal swiftly and expertly went to work on the tire.

They were only inches apart but Taylor felt a little tongue-tied, as if afraid to speak to the woman for fear he might say something stupid.

She seemed to sense his discomfort.

"Matt Taylor, you said?"

He nodded.

"You a native of these here parts, pardner?"

"Where are you from?" Taylor asked.

"South. Near Philadelphia."

"Okay. To you I'm a native. To him, I'm not a native."

He thought it was clever; as soon as the words were out, they sounded flip and dumb. Why was he worried so much about not appearing dumb around this woman?

O'Baal had finished changing the tire. As he returned the jack under the truck's seat, the woman said to Taylor: "I suppose it would be tacky of me to offer to pay you two for your help."

"I suppose," Taylor said. Dumb, he thought. Dumb.

"I'm lucky all around then," she said with another dazzling smile. "You two could have been sex maniacs, rapists, or something. But instead you turn out to be decent guys and you work cheap. You made my day."

"You made ours too," Taylor said and finally felt satisfied with one of his remarks.

"Tell you what," she said. "If there's a place around here, suppose I buy you two a drink."

"Thanks, but my friend's on the wagon," Taylor said.

"You too?" she asked.

"No. But I'm not really familiar with what's around this neighborhood ... I ..."

"Trouble," O'Baal said. "Maybe."

The older man had come back to Taylor's side without making a sound. Taylor turned and looked down the road and saw a jeep wagon slowing down to pull up next to them. It was painted a vaguely official-looking, greenish gray and looked like the same one that had been parked at the main gate to the installation when they had driven by a few minutes before.

The Jeep stopped in the road and two men got out. They were dressed in what could either have been work clothes or uniforms of the same greenish gray color as their vehicle. They were thickset, clean-shaven men with weathered faces who looked as much like lumberjacks as anything else, Taylor thought. They wore identical caps of the same color as their clothes, with earflaps tied up on top, giving them a slightly military look. They were carrying what might have been rifles, except they looked too small, Taylor thought, for rifles.

"Damn," O'Baal said.

"Sawed-off shotguns," the young woman said softly.

The two men stood at the rear of the jeep and the one who had been driving said, "I don't suppose you folks know you're trespassing."

"No," Taylor said. "As a matter of fact, we didn't." He sensed O'Baal starting to move away from him back toward the open door of his own truck. But the other man in greenish gray came up closer and casually raised his sawed-off so that its barrel was pointed right at the middle of the Indian's belly. O'Baal stopped moving. The gunman was only five feet from him.

The driver tried a phony grin. "Now if it was up to me, I'd let you folks go. But you know how it is. Orders are orders."

"Why don't you just cut to the chase," Taylor snapped.

The phony smile vanished. "We're going to have to confiscate your cars and take you all back to the guardhouse."

"Why?" Taylor asked and the driver shrugged elaborately.

"Like I said. Orders are orders. Don't worry too much. The coffee's on, it's warm, and I guess we'll be letting you go as soon as we get the okay."

He gestured toward the jeep with his shotgun. "Now if you folks would just get in."

But O'Baal answered. "Horseshit," he said. "We're getting out of here." He turned his back on the guard and yanked open the door of the truck.

It happened so quickly that Taylor barely saw it, even from the corner of his eye. There was a blur of movement from where O'Baal was standing and then a sickening thud—the kind of noise made when metal smashes into flesh—followed by a deep moan and then momentary silence.

Taylor saw O'Baal collapsed on the ground, his face covered with rapidly spreading blood that was leaking onto the pure snow. Without thinking, Taylor lunged forward at the driver. But he was met by something ramming into his solar plexus. He stopped in mid-attack, feeling as if he had been impaled on some ancient warrior's spear. Then he fell heavily to the ground, collapsing onto the mud and snow of the roadway. For a moment, there was blackness and then he was awake again, the pain throbbing in his midsection, his body noisily gasping for air.

He felt someone pulling him roughly to his feet; his vision was still blurred but he could tell the driver was picking him up. Taylor looked into the man's face and expected to see some sort of bestial delight, the way all the bad guys looked after beating up on the hero in the movies. But it was not there. Instead the driver showed a sort of professional concern.

"Sorry about that, Mr. Taylor," he said, "but I couldn't let you jump me. You all right?"

Taylor pulled himself away from the other man, angry at himself for being ineffective again.

"Billy," he called out. "You okay?"

There was no answer and Taylor wiped his eyes clear and started for the Indian. As if in shock, Angela Fox still stood at the rear of the truck.

"Billy," Taylor called again and this time there was an answering groan. Taylor was at his side; at first the second guard in uniform tried to stop him, but the driver ordered him to leave them alone.

Taylor looked closely at O'Baal. It was hard to tell how badly he had been hurt. He had been smashed in the face by the guard's shotgun and it was apparent that his nose was broken. O'Baal's lips moved and Taylor leaned closer to hear him.

"I got it," O'Baal whispered. "In my belt."

Taylor crouched over the Indian and slipped the big pistol from O'Baal's waistband. Just then the guard who had struck O'Baal moved behind him and prodded Taylor with the barrel of his small shotgun.

"Okay, enough Florence Nightingale shit. On your feet."

Taylor rose slowly, then spun and slammed the barrel and housing of the gun against the side of the man's head. He dropped like raw dough, but even before he hit the ground, Taylor had spun in a crouch and had the pistol pointed at the driver.

But the driver had the shotgun aimed at Taylor.

"Mexican standoff," he said slowly. "You can shoot me but I'll get you. Nobody wins that way."

Damn it, he was right, and Taylor hesitated for a split second. With peripheral vision, he saw Angela Fox move away

174

from the rear of the truck and when the driver said again, "Like I said, a Mexican standoff," she snapped, "Not any more, asshole."

There was a shiny blue automatic in her hand, aimed at the driver's head, and as he glanced at her, she walked coolly toward him and put the barrel of the gun against his temple.

"Now drop the shotgun, Rambo," she said.

She jabbed him with the barrel of the gun and carefully he tried to turn his head toward her. Blood was roaring in Taylor's ears. He thought of shooting. Kill the bastard. Kill the other bastard. Kill all the bastards who had been coming after him day after day after day. But before he could act on the impulse, the driver dropped his sawed-off shotgun to the roadway.

He saw Angela kick the shotgun away, then order the driver: "On the ground. On your belly. Hurry up."

He did not know why, but he knew that she had things under control. He went back to O'Baal who was getting to his feet. The Indian's breathing was labored.

"Your nose is broken, I think," Taylor said.

"Won't be the first time," O'Baal grunted.

The guard whom Taylor had knocked to the ground groaned and Taylor picked up the man's shotgun. He had to restrain himself from driving the butt of it into the man's face. Instead he tossed the gun far off the road into the woods, then helped O'Baal into the passenger's side of the truck.

He came back to Angela who was crouched behind the driver's prone form, her pistol barrel expertly jammed against the base of his spine. If he moved, he was paralyzed; it was real simple and the man knew it; he did not move.

"Get the gun," she said and Taylor tossed it, too, far into the snow alongside the road.

The woman half-smiled at Taylor.

"Any ideas about what we do with these two?"

"Yeah. But we'd never get away with it."

"You're probably right," she said. She seemed almost sad about it.

The sun was down now but the sky still stubbornly held the last few traces of the day's light. The passing of the sun had taken with it all traces of the day's warmth. The wind had started to swirl snowflakes around them. Slowly, the other guard near the truck was getting to his feet. He was groggy, he looked around, then saw Taylor and his eyes narrowed in hatred. Blood oozed from a four-inch-long gash along the side of his cheek.

"Glad you came to join us," Angela said. "Now both of you, get your clothes off."

The men hesitated and the woman said, "What's the matter? You ashamed of something? Clothes off."

"You heard the lady," Taylor said. He waved his gun at the two men. "Undress."

The driver clambered to his feet and started to take off his clothing; the other guard followed suit. They stripped to their underwear.

"More," the woman said. "And shoes too."

The two men were soon naked, cold, embarrassed, standing there in the middle of the roadway, while Angela's laughing eyes taunted them.

"Put the clothes in your truck," she told Taylor. He did and then reached into their jeep and ripped out all the ignition wires under the dashboard. He threw the vehicle's keys out into the woods also, then returned to the woman's side.

"I think we can get out of here," he said.

"Why not?" She looked at the two guards. "There sure isn't much to see around here."

"Start walking," Taylor told them. He punctuated his order with a wave of the gun. "That way," he said, gesturing away from the entrance gate to the installation. The two men silently trudged off down the road.

Angela and Taylor watched them for a moment, then he opened her car door for her. She got inside and buckled her seatbelt.

"That's what I like. A girl who's safety conscious."

"Is that all you like?" she asked.

Suddenly he felt naked, too, and the words stuck in his throat.

"It's been fun, but next time let's do something a little less anti-social," she said.

"Next time?" he said.

"Of course," she answered, and then turned the Maserati into the roadway, made a rapid U-turn, and sped away.

CHAPTER TWENTY

Taylor hated hospitals, but most of all, he hated waiting in them. He remembered the last time. He had been just a boy then but he would never forget the endless sitting and pacing and crying while he waited for the news to come down.

Even then, as a child, he knew it was a bad omen when the doctor slowly entered the room and whispered something to the nurse. The doctor had tried to be kind but he did not seem to know what to say—or maybe just how to say it to a child. It would have been different, Taylor thought, if he had had one of his parents by his side to help cushion the blow. But they weren't there. That was the problem. They were both busy dying.

The doctor had come up to him and put an arm around his shoulder, sat down heavily on an uncomfortable chair, and told him that his father was dead but that his mother still had a chance. Taylor did his best to be brave, but it wasn't good enough. The doctor finally left and the nurse came; she was a middle-aged woman with a comfortable bosom that somehow smelled both sweet and antiseptic at the same time. Taylor remembered burying his face in her as he sobbed himself empty. An hour later, the doctor was back, telling young Taylor that his mother, too, was dead. There were no more tears for her just then. Instead, Taylor stared at the floor and chewed his lower lip and thought about his tenth birthday that was just a week away and the party that had been planned and how that would never be. He sobbed without tears and when he looked up, the Judge, who had just flown back from Washington, D.C., on a chartered plane, was there.

That was a quarter of a century ago.

Taylor had gotten Billy O'Baal to the Iron City hospital in a wild, stomach-churning ride over the hills and valleys, and when he had seen the old Indian into a doctor's care, had called the Judge. It seemed as if that had all happened hours before, but Taylor's watch said less than thirty minutes had elapsed.

Taylor looked up lackadaisically at a flurry of activity at the entrance to the emergency room, and saw the familiar, short, white-haired figure of the Judge striding toward him.

"Are you all right, boy?" he asked.

"I'm okay, Judge. Billy's the one."

"What happened? You weren't too clear on the phone."

Taylor gave him an abbreviated version of what had happened since Billy and he had decided to drive past the Installation at Harker's Furnace.

The Judge considered it for a moment, then harrumphed, "Sons of bitches, who in hell do they think they are?"

"Just what I've been trying to find out," Taylor said.

The Judge stood up and said, "Excuse me for a moment. I want to talk to the doctor if I can."

Without asking permission, he walked from the waiting room into the treatment center. When he returned, he was with a doctor and they were both laughing and talking softly. The doctor was a young woman, small and dark.

"Good news," the Judge told Taylor. He nodded at the doctor, whom Taylor thought looked too young for her position.

"Will Billy be all right?" Taylor asked her.

She answered in precise English with a middling amount of Filipino accent.

"Your friend looks like he was hit in the face with a baseball bat. Is that possible?"

179

"Something like that," Taylor said. "An accident."

The doctor seemed dissatisfied with the answer but let it go. Obviously she had learned the American lesson that important people are able to command more privacy than their less fortunate counterparts, and the Judge counted as a very important person in the local world.

"On television one night," the doctor said, "I was watching an old cowboy movie and somebody called John Wayne a tough old buzzard. It was a compliment, I think."

She smiled and Taylor thought it was a nice smile; it made her almost pretty.

"Your friend is a tough old buzzard too," she said. "Many things could have gone wrong, but it comes down to a broken nose and a slight concussion. But we will want to keep him overnight."

Taylor sank back in relief on one of the waiting room's hard wooden benches and the Judge went off with the doctor to arrange for O'Baal's treatment. When he came back, he said, "I saw Billy. He's okay. He's a grumpy bastard and didn't want to stay but I told him he had to. He blames himself for going to sleep on the job; he was worried you might be hurt."

"Hogwash," Taylor said. "If he hadn't gotten the gun I don't know what might have happened to us."

The Judge said, "I talked to Lauren just before she left Pittsburgh. She said she'd be back—" he took a pocket watch from his vest,"—just about now. I told her you wanted to talk to her but the young idiot was going to say that she couldn't talk to you." He smiled. "So I pulled rank. Anyway, she said she'll meet you at the Derrick Club for a few minutes on her way home."

He looked at his watch again. Elaborately. Unnecessarily.

"Way I figure it, you should head over there now."

"All right," Taylor said.

The Judge put a hand on his arm. "Matt, go easy on her. Losing the baby, her divorce, now her ex-husband being sick.

It's been a lot of tough times for her. You being married probably isn't going to make it a lot better."

"I'll remember, Judge," Taylor said.

The Derrick Club had been built nearly a hundred years earlier, in the waning days of the nineteenth century. Its original members had been the local titans of the oil and steel industry, their suppliers, and a few, a very few, of their out-of-town counterparts. Local legend had it that old John D. Rockefeller himself was not only turned down for admission to the club, but was allowed to enter as a guest only after a knock-down, drag-out special meeting of the hospitality committee; club members liked neither his personal style nor his buccaneering business practices.

Since the turn of the century, the Club had occupied the same premises: the top two floors of an old red-brick, Tuscan Revival, neo-Byzantine office building that took up one of the two best blocks in downtown Iron City. The first floor of the club was given over to the kitchen, billiards room, meeting rooms, offices, and small gym. The second floor was mostly sleeping and dining rooms, separated by an immense lounge.

The decor had originally run to heavy wood paneling, outdoor scenes by local artists, and sturdy brocaded chairs and sofas turned out by a local furniture maker. Had that been left alone, the club would have maintained a considerable Victorian period charm. But of course it had not been left alone. Every ten or fifteen years or so, some of the newer members of the club would start a movement to refurbish and update the club's appointments. They usually got a small start on the task before apathy or lack of money or nostalgia or some combination of the three would put an end to the effort. As a result, onto the original decorative base of the club was added bits and pieces of all the succeeding styles and fads of upper-class American interior design. It was an aesthetic mess but a comfortable one,

one that Taylor had come to like as a boy and young man and, now, was frankly glad to see again.

A telephone call from the Judge had arranged for his entry and he was in the lounge, working on his second Scotch, when he heard the sound of high heels clicking across the wooden parquet floor, approaching him from behind. Don't be too eager, he told himself; take it easy; be a little bit cool.

He waited for the heels to stop clicking, then counted to three, and looked up into the mirror over the bar. It was hard to tell. He turned around, not slowly but not too quickly either, and then stood up.

"Hello, Matt," she said.

"Hello, Lauren."

She looked different, he thought. Hell, she probably was different—a different person from the one he had grown up with and known to the point of love.

"Would you like a drink?" he asked.

"That would be nice."

"What shall it be?"

Instead of answering, she inclined her head toward the bartender across the room. He looked back, nodded, and smiled.

"Rick knows," she said. The bartender poured her a bourbon on the rocks.

"Should we stay here?" Taylor asked.

Lauren picked up her drink at the bar and started toward the door. She moved briskly, as if she were donating some precious *pro bono* time to a not very important client.

"There's a little sitting room down the hall here that I like," she said. Taylor followed her. She seemed very sure of herself, very much in control.

The room was small, probably only six by ten, but it had an oriel that projected out over the river. Lauren motioned him to a straight-backed chair while she took a rocker.

"How have you been, Matt? It's been a long time."

"I'm fine. And you?"

"Pretty well, thanks." She took a sip from her drink as Taylor watched her. Her features hadn't changed much—certainly not eight years worth—but her look had. There used to be something light and outdoorsy about her, a sort of natural unspoiled gaiety, but that had been replaced by something that looked . . . well, tough was the word that came to mind. He was not sure what made the biggest difference and then decided it was her hair. Bright red hair, lots of it, always slightly mussed, always blowing free was the way he remembered it. Now she wore it drawn back onto the top of her head in a tight bun. Her mouth was different, too; it seemed tight and prim, her lips thinner, as if she had found a way to keep them turned in, and it gave her face the look of someone who was always biting back pain. She had been a great beauty, but she seemed now to have found a way to obscure that fact.

"The Judge told me I might be able to help you with something," she said. "Something about Harker's Furnace."

"That's right," Taylor said.

"The Judge didn't exactly say, but I got the feeling that what we're talking about here is not an official I.R.S. matter, is that right?"

Taylor considered and decided he did not like the new Lauren much. It seemed as if she had read too many books on how to be a successful woman attorney and was following all the advice to the letter. It wasn't the physical parts of her that he did not like—as far as he could tell, she still had a good body and the tone and skin of her face were still fine—it was the person. Could he have been mistaken, he wondered? Was this the way she had always been? Was he wrong about every woman in the world?

"It's mostly personal business," Taylor said. "But it might eventually turn official. I don't know."

"I see," Lauren said. She leaned over to fetch a notebook from her purse. When she did, Taylor could see her breasts pushing against the navy blue fabric of her dress. He remembered how her breasts were covered with freckles and how they used to joke about his playing connect-the-dots with his tongue.

"What do you want to know about the installation?" she asked.

"Anything you can tell me. What's there? Who's there? Who's in charge? Who else can I talk to about it? Anything." He had decided that he would not tell her anymore than he had to. The old Lauren he would have told immediately, but this woman in front of him was a total stranger.

"Are you going to pay for this work?" she asked coolly.

Taylor stared at her, then responded, just as coolly. "Naturally."

"I'll talk to the Judge. Perhaps he'll waive the fee." She took a few more sips from her drink and then set it down.

"What do you know about the place?" she asked.

"Not much. It was an Army depot; it got sold. Environmentalists were worried about what might go on in there, but apparently nothing's gone in there and everybody seems reasonably satisfied with the state of things. Other than that, I draw a blank."

"I'll have to look in my files and see what I have there for you." She paused. "Is there anything else?"

"No. I guess not," Taylor said slowly.

She stood up. Taylor watched her and wondered at what precise moment in her life she had turned into a cold-blooded, self-important bitch.

"Would you like to have dinner?" he asked.

"I don't think so," she said.

"Why not?"

She stared at him hard but he could not read any expression on her face.

"It wouldn't be a good idea. You're a married man and I don't go out with married men unless it's strictly business."

That hurt.

"I'm sorry," Taylor said. "I thought we were old friends."

"We were a lot of things, Matt. And maybe friends was part of it. We were even more than that. We were going to be

184

married. And then you left me. And now we're nothing except lawyer and client."

She was right, Taylor thought. They had been more than friends but there was nothing he could do now to change the past and nothing he could say now that would save the present. He sat silently, meeting her eyes, and after a moment, Lauren picked up her purse and walked away.

CHAPTER TWENTY-ONE

It was after nine when Taylor got back to his motel and stopped at the desk to ask if there were any messages. The clerk at the desk—who looked like the high school's prettiest cheerleader ten years and two divorces later—gave Taylor a weary smile.

"You're popular," she said.

Taylor smiled back. "Only with bill collectors," he said as she handed him four message slips.

"You know," she said, "I remember you from school."

"Oh?" Taylor said, searching his memory but not finding the girl in it.

"We weren't in the same class or anything. There's no reason you should remember me. I was only in the eighth grade when you were a senior. But I remember going to all the football games to watch you play. I used to think you were the best-looking guy on the team."

Taylor laughed. "Me? The best-looking? You must have me confused with somebody else. Anybody else."

The girl laughed and admitted, "My friends all thought I was nuts too."

Taylor was deflated, but the girl said, "But I was right. I still like the way you look. Same nice blue eyes, same wavy hair."

Taylor almost felt like blushing and mumbled, "Thanks."

"If you're going to be here for a while," she said, "why don't you let me buy you a drink? Not here, of course. But there are lots of places nearby."

"I'm not sure," Taylor said. "I mean, how long I'm going to be here."

The clerk's smile turned slightly mechanical. For just a moment she looked very vulnerable, like someone who had lately started to receive more rejections than she had been used to getting.

"Fine," she said. "Maybe later." She looked up and down the desk as if she were trying to find some graceful way to end a conversation which had turned tedious.

"Oh," she said, leaned across the counter and tapped the first of the note messages in Taylor's hand. "This one called three times; said it was very important."

Taylor looked down at the message. It said, "Gianetti," and gave a number which had the same area code as Iron City but was still long distance.

"Thanks," Taylor said. He shuffled quickly through the other messages. One was no surprise; it was from the Judge. The other two were surprises. Katie Wu and Melanie. He wondered how they had known where to find him.

He must have been mumbling because the clerk said, "Excuse me?"

"Nothing. Just talking to myself."

"I do that too," the clerk said. "Got nobody better to talk to. Except my boy and he's only six so you can't really talk to him. You have any kids?"

"No," Taylor said. "My wife never wanted any." For the first time, he could feel a bit of bitterness surfacing over the prospects of a childless old age, a feeling that he had never known he had.

"Same with my second husband," the clerk said. "As a matter of fact, I think that's why we're split. Hell of a world, isn't it?"

"I'll drink to that," Taylor said. For some reason, that little

187

comment seemed to cheer the clerk who turned out to be named Joanie—"Not Joan, I never liked Joan"—Anders, and had lived in Iron City all her life.

Taylor excused himself finally, got back to his room, and called his home phone in Washington. He let it ring a dozen times before he hung up disgustedly. How long ago had it been that he had decided things were all finished between Melanie and himself. Two hours? Two days? He could not remember, but why the hell did he bother calling? Still, it might have been important. Like it or not, Melanie was still his wife, and that was an obligation. Maybe something came up that she needed him for. Taylor sat on the soft motel chair. That was ridiculous, he thought. There was nothing that he and Melanie needed each other for anymore.

Still he dialed the number of her shop.

"Imaginating," the voice at the other end of the line said. "This is Eleanor."

"Elly, this is Matt Taylor. I'm looking for Melanie. Is she in?"

The tone of her voice was like a child's trying hard to hide something, but half-hoping that she would be found out.

"Sorry, Mister T. I haven't seen her in a while."

That invited questions. How long had it been, exactly, since she had seen Melanie was the obvious question. Taylor ignored it. "If you see her before I do, just tell her I called."

Elly sounded irked. "Of course. Anything else I can do for you? I'm sorry we didn't get more of a chance to talk at that party the other night."

"Me too," Taylor said, hung up, and shook his head. Why were women falling all over him the last few days? He sure hadn't gotten any better-looking. Maybe he was rich now. Maybe he had won a lottery and everybody knew it but him. It was the damnedest thing.

Katie Wu answered her telephone on the second ring.

"Katie. This is Matt."

"Matt? Matt Who?" she said.

"Matt Taylor. You know. The only round-eyes you said you could ever love despite the color of his skin."

"Let me see. Matt Taylor. It seems to me that I vaguely remember hearing that name once or twice in the past—the distant, distant past."

"I'm sorry, Katie. I should have called earlier. This has just been awful with poor Larry. I'm sorry I couldn't prevent it."

"Matt, I'm just glad you got the bastard."

"Yeah," he said numbly. He had succeeded in putting Larry's death out of his mind, but now talking to his sister, it all came back. He could see again the body of his dead friend lying on the cold wet pavement of the parking lot. "Any idea who the guys were? Did you hear anything from the police?"

"The police said nothing," Katie said. "Dennis checked and said they were just some goons, but whether they were working for somebody or not, nobody knows."

Taylor remembered that two nights earlier, O'Leary had told him that the two gunmen were probably involved with Zorelli, the gang boss from Philadelphia. It was Matt's guess that O'Leary had just not wanted to burden Katie Wu with such speculation. It was how he, himself, would have handled it.

"Well, maybe we'll find out," Taylor said. "How are you holding up?"

"Fine," she said, "except for being abandoned by my lover."

"O'Leary? What'd he do?"

"What did he do? I'll tell you what he did. I wake up and he's gone. Didn't even say goodbye. Just gone. Christ, I hate him. And I hate you too. And I hate Larry. I hate all of you damned men, going off and leaving me. Damn you all."

She started to cry and Taylor just held the phone helplessly. What can you do when someone is crying on the other end of the phone? You can't put an arm around them to comfort them. All you can do is wait.

After a little while, she stopped crying.

"Damn it, I'm so fucking sick of crying it makes me sick."

"Tell me what happened," Taylor said.

"Dennis said he was taking some time off from the job, just to help me get through the funeral. Then the bastard takes off on Saturday and goes God knows where. He gets back and last night he's here and this morning he's gone. Aaah, the hell with it. The hell with him. The hell with you. And that goes for your wife too."

"My wife?" Taylor said.

"Yes. Sweet Melanie came to see me. I thought, isn't that nice, she's come to express her condolences. So instead, she said she just couldn't understand why you were fooling around with me. Are you leaving her?"

"Yes."

"Good. That's what I guessed. She wanted to know where she could reach you. I told her I didn't know."

"How did you reach me?" Taylor asked. "How did you know?"

"I tried to reach Dennis by phone and I wound up talking to his boss, some guy named Ari Cohen. He told me where you were. I wanted to let you know about the funeral."

"When is it?" Taylor asked.

"It's Thursday," she said. "You don't know anything about this, do you?"

"No," Taylor said, totally mystified.

"Matt, what's going on? What *the hell* is going on?"

"I don't know," he answered. "What are you talking about?"

"I talked to Cohen and he told me to tell you there would be a ticket for you Wednesday night at the Continental counter at Pittsburgh Airport. Nine o'clock flight."

"Nice of him but I was planning on driving back," Taylor said.

"That's what I mean, Matt. He said to tell you to fly."

"Why?"

"Because he said if you try driving, you'll probably be killed."

"By anybody in particular?" Taylor asked.

"All he said was the bad guys," Katie said softly.

"I'll try not to let them see me coming," Taylor said.

"Matt, are you involved in something? Are you risking your life because of what happened to Larry?"

"Don't worry, Katie. I'm all right and you've got enough things to worry about."

"Matt, I don't want anything to happen to you. Not now especially."

"Don't worry, Katie. Nothing will."

Polonowski answered the phone with a long growling, "Yo-o-o?"

"This is Matt Taylor. You were trying to reach me?"

"I'll be damned. Hold on."

The line went blank for a fraction of a second, then some music came up. It was a sweetened-up version of an already-syrupy Beatles tune. A moment or so later, the music stopped and there was a series of electronic clickings and hisses. Then a human voice, one that sounded as if it were echoing down the entire length of the trans-Alaskan pipeline.

"Matt. This is Sal. Sal Gianetti. I'm so glad to hear from you. How are you doing?"

"Fine. What do you want?" Taylor said abruptly.

"Matt, we really must get together and talk. There are so many things to be discussed. How about lunch tomorrow?"

Taylor thought about the nerves of these two men harrassing him and snapped, "Let's stop the friendly bullshit and tell me what you want."

"Not on this line," Gianetti said. "We should meet. You must have questions."

"Yeah. Like how'd you find me?"

"We have our ways," Gianetti said.

"And what the hell do you want with me? Why are you following me around?"

"Would you believe that we're on your side?" Gianetti said.

191

"No," Taylor said. "I wouldn't believe that for a freaking minute."

"Well, we are. And we're just trying to make sure that nothing happens to you."

"Because of my association with Larry Wu, that well-known international traitor?" Taylor said.

"That's closer than you think," Ginaetti said.

"You know," Taylor said, "I'm getting tired of you and your bullshit. People are trying to kill me and everytime they do, you two Laurel and Hardys are around."

"Tomorrow. We could talk tomorrow," Gianetti said. "You could still make your plane. Nine o'clock from Pittsburgh, isn't it?"

"How do you know about that?"

"I know a lot about you. Almost everything." When Taylor did not respond, Gianetti said, "And a piece of advice. I really wouldn't trust that darkie friend of yours, if I were you."

"O'Leary?"

"Naturally," Gianetti said.

"You act like you know a lot but you don't tell me anything," Taylor said.

"I'll tell you about it when we meet. If you're still ..." He paused significantly.

"Alive?" Taylor asked.

"No, no. I was going to say if you were still interested. As a gesture of good faith, I could give you the number where your wife could be reached right this minute, if you're interested."

That was totally unexpected. Taylor was silent for a moment as he realized someone was spending a lot of time and money to keep track of Matt Taylor and the people around him.

"That won't be necessary," he said, fighting to keep his voice steady.

Gianetti chuckled. "So it's come to that. I figured it would eventually."

Matt did not rise to the bait of the other man's insinuations. Instead, he said, "I can't make lunch tomorrow. I've already got an appointment. How about three o'clock here? At the hotel."

"That will be fine," Gianetti said. "In the meantime, Matt, stay away from Harker's Furnace."

Before Taylor could respond, the telephone went dead in his hand.

CHAPTER TWENTY-TWO

In the time-honored tradition of hospital personnel everywhere, the information clerk at Iron City General would tell him only that Billy O'Baal was in stable condition, then refused to tell him what "stable" meant, so Taylor telephoned the Judge, but he was out and not expected back before midnight.

Taylor dozed on the bed for a few minutes, then awoke with a start. He thought he heard a sound at the door.

He rummaged through the end table for the gun O'Leary had given him. As he held it in his hand, he had a sudden sharp thought. Supposed Gianetti were right and he shouldn't trust O'Leary. Maybe the gun was empty. Or worse yet, filled with shells that would explode in Taylor's face if he fired it. He hefted it in his hand. Screw it. He would use it as a club if he had to.

He tiptoed across the room and stood back behind the door. He heard the sound of a key and then saw the doorknob turning. He jumped over in front of the door and swung it open, his pistol aimed at the midsection of whoever was standing on the other side.

The maid screamed. Taylor waved his free hand as if to say, "No, No," but it did no good. The maid's eyes opened wide; she held her hands high in the air like somebody in an old cowboy movie.

A door opened down the hall and an elderly man stuck his head out. Taylor hid the gun alongside his leg and said to the maid, "Come in. I'm sorry. I thought you were a burglar."

He looked down the hallway at the old man and smiled at him in what he hoped was a friendly manner.

When he came back into his room, the maid followed him. She was pretty in a faded, fighting-forty sort of way and reminded Taylor of what a motorcycle groupie might look like when she had finally passed her peak years.

"It's okay," she said. "I'm used to guns. I used to have a husband who ... well, actually, we weren't married, but ..." She rambled on for a full sixty seconds and Taylor did not try to stop her. Finally she took a deep breath and said, "Actually, I was coming in to turn your bed down. It's getting late." She looked at a watch that was pinned upside-down to the breast pocket of her black and white uniform.

"I'm sorry," Taylor said again. "Really, really sorry." And he was. He was in fine spooky shape, almost plugging a motel maid, afraid of telephones, luncheon meetings, cars on the road, and his own shadow. What the hell was he involved in and how the hell did he get out of it?

He tucked the gun into his waistband, out of sight of the maid, then took a couple of bills from his pocket and pressed them into her hand. "Really, I'm sorry."

She looked at the money and said, "Are you sure? I mean there wasn't anything to it. Not really."

Taylor just smiled at her. "Fine," he said. "But I'd appreciate your not mentioning it. They'd likely throw me out into the street."

She raised a finger to her lips. "Mum's the word," she said.

There was an awkward moment of silence before Taylor said, "Do you know if the restaurant's still open?"

She glanced again at her upside-down watch. "It closed at 9:30, but you can still get a sandwich in the cocktail lounge."

"Okay. Thanks a lot," Taylor said, and left the maid turning down the bed in his room.

The cheerleader clerk smiled at him and he nodded back as he went down a side hallway to the dark cocktail lounge. He was not really hungry—that had just been an excuse to get out of the room without any more embarrassment—so he went to the end of the empty bar and ordered a Scotch on the rocks.

He was sipping it when a woman's voice at his shoulder spoke, deep and slightly blurry.

"Drink up," she said. "It's one of the two best ways to finish a long day."

He turned to see Angela Fox standing behind the stool next to him. He pushed his own stool back and stood up, surprising himself slightly. Nowadays men—at least in Washington, D.C.—didn't practice old-fashioned manners when it came to women, and he thought he had forgotten how.

"Hello," he said. When she smiled at him, he said "Am I supposed to ask what's the other best way to finish a long day?"

"Only if you don't know what it is," she said. "Mind if I sit down?"

"No, please," he said, thinking how beautiful she was, and how she was certainly a refreshing change from his earlier encounter with Lauren Carmody, the Ice Princess.

"You're staring," she said.

"You're right," he said. "With good cause."

She laughed. Like her speaking voice, it was a deep throaty sound that Taylor found very sexy.

"Can I get you a drink? Or coffee?" Taylor asked.

"It better be a drink," she said. "If I have coffee after ten, I stay awake all night."

Taylor started to apologize and she smiled again. "Of course there are some times you like to stay awake all night."

Was she teasing him? Was this a come-on? He couldn't tell from her expression and he waved to the bartender to come down the bar. He ordered another Scotch for himself; Angela wanted a Dry Sack on the rocks.

After the drinks came, she said, "If this were a singles bar, I could ask you if you come here often." She took his hand

196

and fingered his wedding band. "But, of course, you're not single."

"No," Taylor said. "How about you?"

"Am I single? Or do I come here often? First time here, actually. And single. In my line of work, it's almost an occupational hazard."

"Great segue," Taylor said. "What's your line of work? Besides rescuing guys who are being held up alongside the road."

"You won't laugh?" she said.

"There are a lot of things I might think of doing with you, but laughing isn't one of them."

"Keep the rest on a list. Keep it handy," she said. "Jobwise, I'm a private eye."

He laughed and she pouted. "You said you wouldn't."

"Sorry," he said. "I just would have expected somebody with a face like a footprint, in a trenchcoat that didn't fit."

"All my clothes fit," she said.

"I noticed."

"Gallant," she said. She pronounced it "goll-ANT." "Christ, I love gallant. Keep talking that way and you could do anything you wanted to me."

She looked down and sipped her drink.

"I'll keep that in mind," he said.

They were both silent for a second, both sipping their drinks. Their eyes met in the mirror behind the bar.

"An awful thought just struck me," Taylor said. "Am I part of your job? Did you come here to pump me?"

"Pump or be pumped. Isn't that one of the rules of life?" she asked. "No, unfortunately, you're not part of my mission."

"And your mission, if you choose to accept it, is . . . ?"

"Divorce case," she said. "Very dull. In fact, the only exciting thing that's happened to me since I got here was meeting you." She looked at him and ran her tongue across her teeth in a burlesque of seductiveness.

"Now I have a question for you," she said softly in his ear.

"What's that?" he said.

"What color underwear am I wearing?"

"How could I be expected to know that?" he said, startled, despite himself, by the girl's boldness.

She took his left hand, placed it between her legs, under cover of the bar, and slid it up between her thighs.

"I figured it out," he whispered in her ear. "You're not wearing any underwear."

She whispered back. "And you also figured out I'm ready. So can we go up to your room now, or do I have to beg?"

"If I make you beg, will I get anything I want?" Taylor asked.

"Yes. And if you don't make me beg, you'll get anything you want too."

Matt hesitated for a moment. The truth was that in all the dismal years of their marriage, he had never cheated on Melanie. He had thought about it a lot; many times he had considered taking a run at Katie Wu; but always some old rule in his head—probably stuck there by the Judge—said that husbands shouldn't cheat on their wives. But that was then and this was now and in his mind and in his heart, he was no longer married to Melanie. The divorce, still to come, was just a formality; the real fact was, that from here on in, he was single.

"Let's go," he said. He tossed ten dollars onto the bar and left, without waiting for change, holding Angela's hand. They took the first elevator up to his floor and before he had locked the door of his room behind them, she had unzipped his trousers and put her hand inside.

"Are you carrying a gun," she whispered in his ear from behind in an imitation of Mae West, "or are you just glad to see me?"

"Actually, both," he said. As he turned, he opened his jacket and showed her the gun jammed into his belt.

Before he could react, she yanked it from his waistband and stuck the barrel against his belly.

"Now get your clothes off. Or else."

For an instant, he was startled and his expression must have

198

showed it, because she handed him the gun back. He took it and she dropped to her knees in front of him in mock fright.

"Don't shoot, don't shoot," she said. "I'll do anything you want."

"Talk is cheap," he said. "Let's see some evidence." He put the gun on the dresser inside the door, and with a strong arm lifted her to her feet. His hands reached the zipper behind her dress and slid it down. She wriggled out of the dress and let it fall at her feet.

She was wearing high-heeled shoes, nylons with a garter belt and nothing else and Taylor thought she was the sexiest woman he had ever seen. She stepped forward into his arms, pulled his head down to kiss her and then instead began to lick his face, while her hands busied themselves with his buttons and his clothing.

His clothes were on the floor alongside hers and she took his penis in her hand and pulled him toward the bed. She let go as she slid in under the cover. For a moment he hesitated and looked toward the light switch.

"Leave the lights on. I want to see your face when I do you," she said throatily.

She pushed him over her, straddling her, and pulled his body to her. And then she stopped and she laughed aloud and said, "I love that. I love it all. And I want it all. All ... all night long ... all of it ... get in me. Please. Get in me."

She wrapped her legs around him. He could feel the smoothness of her nylons against his waist and the coldness of her shoes against his buttocks and he pressed his body into hers. She was warm, wet, and as he buried his body deep into hers, she gasped and began to writhe under him.

"More, more," she said. "Deeper. Dammit, as hard as you can."

He began to slam into her. With some women, it had seemed to cause pain, but with this woman, it only intensified her need.

She cried again. "More, Matt. Give it to me. Give me everything you've got. I want all you have."

She tightened her legs around him and used her feet to pull him even closer to her. Her tongue toyed with his nipples and then began sucking them as hard as she could. It was a pain but a sweet pain, and then he could contain himself no longer, and with a gasp he exploded into her at just the moment she let out a shout which she muffled by pressing her mouth into his chest. "I'm coming," she moaned.

He had come but he kept thrusting into her, feeling himself sliding through the mixture of their juices and then she shivered as a spasm gripped her body. She stiffened and then arched her back violently, lifting both of them up, away from the bed, and then she slowly subsided and Taylor slowly lowered himself onto her, then reached under and grasped her buttocks and turned both of them on their side, facing each other. There he rested, breathing fast, hard. He closed his eyes as she snuggled up against his chest. He rested but after only a few seconds, she pulled away from him and he opened his eyes to see her kneeling alongside him on the bed.

She smiled at him as she lowered her face to his body. "Don't fall asleep," she said. "The night's only just started."

She was as good as her word. Matt had thought that Melanie was sex-driven, but he decided that hers was only a healthy active interest, compared to Angela who seemed obsessed. They made love everywhere in the room; in the chair in front of the television; standing up as Angela leaned forward to look out the window over Iron City; in the shower where they soaked for long minutes, washing the perspiration and the juices from their bodies. Time had lost all meaning for him. It might be midnight; it might be four o'clock. Finally they were back in bed. Angela lay in the crook of his arm; the lights were still on in the room, as they had been through all their lovemaking. For a while, Matt thought that she was asleep but then Angela purred and said, "It hasn't been like that in a long time."

"Look me up again in another year," Taylor said. "When I'm ready to take you on again."

"You mean you're calling it quits?" she said.

"My body called it quits for me."

"I may just have to test that theory," she said.

"Did you save my life today so you could take it tonight?" he asked. His left arm was asleep and he extricated it from under her head and reached for a cigarette on the end table.

"Well, if that's the way you're going to be, I guess it's time to get down to business," she said.

She sat up in bed, letting the sheet fall from her body with an utter lack of self-consciousness. She stretched over to her purse and took out a pair of reading glasses, a ballpoint pen, and a notebook.

"You don't think I just came here for sport, do you?" she asked.

He lit a cigarette and growled, in mock seriousness, "Okay, get it over with. I'm tired of you women just using my body to get your way."

"Well, I'm sure not vacationing in this armpit," she said. "I told you I was a private investigator and this is work. I'm looking for a guy at this thing that everybody around here calls The Installation, but when I went there today they wouldn't let me in. I had just left when I got that flat."

"They're not very friendly," he said casually.

"What do you know about them?" she asked. In a parody of secretarial efficiency, she touched the tip of her tongue to the end of the ballpoint pen, poised it over her notebook, and gave him a simpering smile.

"Not much," Taylor said. "It used to be an Army base until about ten years ago. Then the government closed it down and the place was vacant for about seven or eight years. Finally, some investors bought it. The locals got up in arms, I'm told— you know, environment, don't build a factory on our beautiful useless land, that kind of thing—but whoever bought it apparently didn't build anything, and so the whole issue just went to sleep. Some people work up there now, but nobody knows what they do."

"You seem to know a lot about it," she said. "Are you a private detective too?"

"I'm the only thing worse. I'm a tax man with the I.R.S.," he said.

"Oh, balls. You mean you're going to audit me if I write you off as a business expense?"

"With pleasure," he said. "I'm going to come right to your house and lie in your bed until you pay up. You said you're looking for somebody. Who's that? Maybe I know him."

"God. Would that be a lifesaver? I'm working on a divorce case. It's messy and involves lots of money. I'm after a guy named Bill Galligan. Does that name mean anything to you?"

He started to answer, "I'm not familiar with—" but was interrupted by a light knocking on the door.

Angela pulled the covers up instinctively.

"Expecting someone?" she said. "An irate wife, maybe?"

Taylor shook his head.

"No," he said. He looked at the clock on the TV across the room. It was just after midnight.

There was more knocking. He got up and put on his trousers which still lay on the floor. He went to the door, stopping with his hand on the gun which rested on the dresser.

He opened the door and looked out. The woman there had long flowing red hair and a sensuous, almost wanton attitude in her stance. She did not look like the woman he had been talking to earlier in the evening. But she was.

He unfastened the door's chain, and said, "Hello, Lauren."

"Don't look so surprised, Matt," she said. "You really didn't expect me to come back?"

"Not after this evening," he said. "I got the impression you'd be happy if you never saw me again."

"Well, you were wrong. Now don't just stand there. Get out of my way and invite me in."

Without waiting for the invitation, she pushed the door open and brushed by him. But then she stopped inside the entryway as she saw the male and female clothing tossed on the floor.

"Oh," she said and there was real pain in her voice.

"Lauren," he said. "I'm sorry."

He reached out a hand to touch her shoulder, but she pulled away from it, as if it were electrically charged.

"No, I'm sorry Matt. I shouldn't have come. I should've known better. I was a fool."

When she turned, there were tears in her eyes. She tried not to look at him as she said briskly. "The Judge asked me to tell you that he'd like to meet you for breakfast. We'll meet downstairs at seven." She lifted her eyes to his. "Will you be up by then?" she said, unable to hide the hint of sarcasm in her voice and suddenly she was the cold, sour, old-before-her-time woman he had spent an hour with earlier.

"I'll be up," he said.

"Fine. Good night," she said and brushed by him and hurried away.

CHAPTER TWENTY-THREE

Angela insisted on riding down in the elevator with Taylor in the morning. When the door opened, the Judge was waiting for him but when Angela saw him, she moved quickly and gracefully into Taylor's arms and kissed him with considerable panache. Taylor felt his ears redden with embarrassment but she would not stop until an elderly couple getting off the elevator behind them went through a round of throat-clearing and excuse-mes, trying to open a path to the restaurant.

"Dinner tonight?" Angela asked Taylor. "If we're both still in town?"

"I don't know yet. My schedule's pretty loose. I'll call you. Where are you staying?"

"Outside town. I'll call you."

She looped her arm in his and walked across the lobby to where the Judge was waiting.

"I'll be in touch," she said to Taylor and then kissed him lightly on the nose. She looked at the Judge and said, "He's all yours. I've hardly abused him at all." Then she did the unheard of—she reached out and tweaked the Judge on the cheek.

"Judge," Taylor said. "This is my friend Angela Fox, Angela, Judge Stevens."

The Judge smiled broadly. "Young lady, we used to have an expression for girls like you."

"Oh really. What was it?"

The judge smiled benignly, magisterially. "You're much too young to hear it," he said, "and I'm much too much of a gentleman ever to say it."

Angela looked at him for several seconds, then laughed her usual deep, full-throated laugh, tweaked him on the cheek again, and strode away.

The Judge watched her appreciatively.

Taylor said, "What was the word you used to have for girls like her?"

"Cunt," the Judge said. "Some words never go out of fashion. That is if her performance upstairs was the equal of her performance down here."

"Even better," Taylor said.

"Well, good for you. Come on. Let's get some breakfast."

Taylor looked around the lobby. "Where's Lauren? Wasn't she supposed to meet us here?"

"She'll be along directly. I wanted a chance to speak to you alone first."

The hostess was ready to dance attention on them and the Judge let her. She showed them to the largest, best table in a corner of the room, next to the picture window. A moment later, a cute and giggly teenage waitress took their order and then came back with their coffee. The Judge talked to her for several minutes about her father and her older brother and then hustled her off.

"You can tell," he told Taylor, "that I've been around a long, long time. I'm now a beloved old character. It wasn't all that long ago, though, that I was a double-dyed son of a bitch and the subject of some really brutal gossip, most of it true."

"You're feeling pretty philosophical this morning," Taylor said.

"I suppose you could say that," the Judge said. He turned and waved at people at a table in the corner.

"You'll have to excuse me, boy. I've got to work the crowd for a couple of minutes. If I don't, there'll be talk. Or worse yet, they'll all be stopping by here."

Matt watched him go and was impressed at how expert the Judge was, stopping to talk to everyone he knew for a moment or two, exchanging small talk and making dates as he went. But then the Judge, he thought sourly, was expert at everything, including trying to live Matt's life for him.

As his guardian, the Judge had tried to schedule everything in Matt's life and as he grew older, Taylor had begun to chafe under the pressure. His rebellion had started in small ways. The Judge had said no football in high school; football was too dangerous, so Matt had tried out for and wound up starring for the team as a running back. The Judge was unhappy but had said nothing, and for Matt each act of defiance made the next one easier. The Judge had always assumed that Matt would go to law school, so the youth became interested in computers instead. The Judge wanted him to get a student deferment to avoid service in Vietnam, so Matt had enlisted in the Marines and volunteered for service in Nam. The Judge clearly had wanted him to marry Lauren, so when Melanie came bimboing along, Matt was ready to jump at—and on—an alternative.

It was not—it had never been—that he wanted to hurt the Judge, because the affection between the two of them had always been honest and strong. He loved the Judge, and if he was sure of anything in the world, it was that the Judge loved him as a son. Nor did he ascribe the Judge's behavior to some dictatorial impulse in the older man. No, it was simply overprotection. The Judge plainly wanted Matt always to be in places and situations where the Judge could come to his rescue if need be, and Taylor had decided, without even thinking it through, that if he was ever going to grow up, he had to grow up as his own man.

And while the Judge had never given him orders on what to do, his wishes were clear, and when Matt constantly defied them, a rift had sprung up between the two men—a rift that was still there and still deep enough that neither of them had talked about it since Taylor had come back to Iron City.

Taylor looked up. The Judge's timing was impeccable as always. Just as he was finishing up the last table full of friends, breakfast was being delivered to their own table.

They ate quickly. Neither spoke while they ate; the Judge out of long-standing habit; Taylor because he remembered the Judge's habit.

"There," the Judge said, pushing away his plate and pulling his coffee cup in front of him. "I can fight forty tigers today."

Taylor canted his head. There was a reference there but he could not quite place it.

"You don't remember," the Judge said. "Do you?"

Taylor shook his head slowly from side to side.

"That's okay," the Judge said. "I really wouldn't expect you to. It was a long time ago."

"What was?"

"It was from a book I used to read to you. Even before your mother and father died. I must have read it to you three hundred times. And then, after the accident, after the first bad part was over, the first time I knew you were going to be able to get along, that's what you told me. 'I can fight forty tigers today.' I've never forgotten."

The two men looked at each other for a long time without speaking.

"You've been gone a long time, son," Stevens said, then looked down. "Damn, I've got to stop calling you that."

"It's the best thing I've ever been called,"Taylor said. "I don't mind."

The Judge smiled and said. "You're growing up," Then he harrumphed once or twice before speaking again. "Listen, Matt, I've got to talk to you man to man and I don't want to lose you again. Understand? So don't get mad and walk out on me. Just listen, and trust me that I'm not trying to do anything to hurt you or belittle you or any of that sort of crap. Okay?"

"Okay."

207

The Judge looked uncomfortable, sipped again at his coffee, and said, "I don't know what this is that you're involved in. The only thing I can think of is that it's some secret government stuff that you shouldn't be involved in and that's dangerous to you. I think you ought to forget about it."

Taylor started to speak but Stevens raised a hand to quiet him.

"Let me finish," he said. "I think you ought to forget about it. And I think you ought to forget about the I.R.S., and I think you ought to come home. You belong back here. With me. With all of us. Now you can say your piece."

"You think I should just turn and run away, after these goons put Billy in the hospital yesterday?" Taylor asked.

"Yes," the Judge said. "And if you were to ask Billy, he'd tell you the same thing probably. No great harm done. Watch and wait your turn. Some day the same bear will be old and weak and that's when you put a spear in his heart."

"Judge, I'm sorry. But it's not just Billy. They killed Larry ... they ..."

"You don't know that," Stevens said. "Maybe somebody *did* kill Larry over gambling debts. You don't know."

"I don't know but I do know it wasn't gambling debts. And they killed Larry and they tried to kill me and for all I know, they're going to try again, and I don't know what it's all about, but I'm going to, by God, find out. Somebody's got to pay for Larry."

"I just don't want it to be you," the Judge said.

"I'll be careful. I'm always careful," Taylor said.

"Like you were in Vietnam?"

"I got home alive, didn't I? A lot didn't."

"Getting home with four wounds and six decorations is a little more risky than you make it sound," Stevens said.

"Bottom line, Judge. You taught me that. I got home in one piece. And I'm staying on this thing until I figure it out. I owe that to Larry. Now, about the rest of it ... maybe you're right. I'm sick and tired of Washington. I told you that the marriage

208

is over and I'm getting tired of holding the I.R.S. together with tape and rubber bands, so I think it might be time to pack that all in.''

"Good.''

"*When* this is done," Taylor said. "Sorry, Judge. That's the way I feel.''

"Well, I tried," Stevens said. He hesitated as the teenage waitress brought them more coffee.

When she left, he said, "Now about Lauren. She stopped by the house late last night. She just left you at your room and she was crying. I hadn't ever seen that before. Take it back. The day after the baby died, she cried. Last night, she was hurt. Real bad.''

"I hadn't planned it, and certainly not to hurt her.''

"Of course, you didn't," Stevens said. "But there's some things you ought to know. For instance, Lauren's in love with you. She always has been. She never stopped, even when you flaunted that little blonde chippie of yours in her face. She loves you now.''

"You couldn't prove it last night. Not by the reception she gave me at the club.''

"Hell, boy, what do you expect from a woman? They're all crazy as hell. You ought to know that. Even the smartest of them. They just see things different from us men and that's the way it is. Anyway, Lauren still wants you and you could do a lot worse.''

"I think I'd better get *her* to say that to me," Taylor said.

"Don't hold your breath. These are bad times for her and I don't know how talkative she'll be.''

"Bad? How are they bad?" Taylor asked.

"She'll have to tell you that herself. Hush now. Here she is.''

They rose as the young woman approached their table; her eyes were badly bloodshot and tried to avoid Taylor's as he helped her with her chair. The Judge had signalled the waitress; obviously he knew Lauren's habits because he ordered her a light breakfast without asking.

"I'm sorry I'm late. I stopped at the hospital."

"And?" the Judge prodded.

"Billy is raising hell. He wants out.

"What do the doctors say?" Stevens asked.

"Just about what you'd expect. They'll let him go, but they advise against it and they'll take no responsibility for what happens to him if he leaves."

The Judge pushed his chair back. "Then I'd better go and spring the prisoner," he said. "I don't want any damn Iroquois warrior on a rampage over there."

Lauren started to object to his leaving but the Judge brushed it aside.

"You know more about this stuff than I do. As far as I'm concerned, use all our resources. I'll take care of the billing." He looked at Taylor. "Dinner? Eight o'clock, my house." He looked at Lauren and said, "You, too, young lady."

Again she started to object; again she was shushed.

"It's firm's business. Matt's my client and I want you there." He turned and left without waiting for an answer. Matt watched and, as he expected, the Judge spoke to the restaurant hostess on the way out, making sure the check was put on his account.

Lauren hoisted a big briefcase onto the chair next to her and began burrowing through it. In a few minutes, she had most of the breakfast table covered with piles of papers. She gave Taylor a quick noncommittal smile.

"In just a second," she said.

Taylor watched her and could feel the gloom spread over his spirits. His mood was beginning to match the weather outside through the window; cold, gray, dismal. Lauren looked different yet again. No more tightly controlled lady lawyer like yesterday afternoon, but no semi-vixen like last night either. Her red hair hung loose but somehow looked presentable enough for court. Her dress was a warm pearl gray that was businesslike, yet at the same time left no doubt of her essential womanliness. It was a good package.

And to top it off there was the perfume. It smelled vaguely familiar to Taylor, and that was something because he seldom noticed perfumes, much less able to tell them apart. But this one was different; light and slightly spicy at the same time. It took him a moment to remember that it was the kind he always used to buy Lauren; he couldn't remember its name but he could remember the times she used to wear it for him—just the perfume and nothing else.

"I was saying . . ." Lauren said. There was just the hint of the old-fashioned schoolmarm in her tone.

"I'm sorry," Taylor said. "I had something else on my mind."

Her voice softened a trifle.

"Would you rather do this later?"

Taylor shook his head. "No. Now's as good a time as any's likely to be. Why don't you show me what you brought?"

"Where to begin?" she said, then answered herself. "John Smetts told you that a few years ago I was the attorney for an environmental group that was interested in stopping construction up at Harker's Furnace?"

"That's right," Taylor said.

"I stopped at the office this morning before I came over, to dig out and Xerox some of the stuff I had from back then." She gestured at the stacks of papers on the tabletop.

"You must be an early riser," Taylor said.

"Not especially," she said. "I didn't sleep well."

Taylor said, "I'm sorry," and started to say more but she did not let him.

"You can look though these files yourself," she said, "but in general I know what's here."

"Which is?"

"Let me start at the beginning, Matt. I don't know what you're looking into, or what this is all about, but as far as I'm concerned the Installation is a blessing."

211

"How's that?" Taylor asked.

"After they closed down the army base there, there were a lot of rumors about it being reopened as a nuclear waste dump or depot or whatever rotten use Washington might want to make of the land. That always had people worried. Finally, the General Services Administration said it was going to sell off the land, and the scare stories started again. Some guy wanted to build a garbage processing plant that would make fuel out of dog doo, or something. Somebody else wanted to build some kind of low-cost housing instant slum. Then they were talking about theme-style amusement parks, with traffic and hot dog wrappers and Coke cans all over the landscape."

"Sounds grim," Taylor said.

"It *was* grim. It seemed like every day there was another lunatic idea in the paper, and that's when I wound up representing the environmentalist group. We went to Harrisburg to protest to the governor, and we went to Washington to talk to the Interior Department."

She must have noticed the look on his face because she said, "What's wrong?"

"Nothing," Taylor said. "Generally, I think environmentalists are a lot of busybodies who are trying to stop other people from making a living."

"A lot of them are," Lauren snapped. "But we weren't. We just kept trying to get guarantees that whatever was put there would preserve the landscape. Remember, we're talking about something that's right on the fringe of a national park. Anyway, I didn't think we were getting anywhere, and then the sale day came and there was only one bidder, and they guaranteed in writing that before anything was built there, it would have to be approved in a vote by the people of the county. They also said they planned, for the indefinite future, to keep the land in its present condition, and had no construction plans at all. And as far as I can tell, that's what they've done, and that's why I've got no argument with them."

"Granted. Just who are these paragons of virtue who bought this property?" Taylor asked.

"To begin with, you're dealing with big money," she said. "They bought five square miles up there. What's that? More than three thousand acres. The asking price by the General Services Administration, when it sold the land for the government, was $2,500 an acre. So we're dealing here with seven-and-a-half million dollars."

"That's impressive," Taylor said.

"This is impressive too," she said. "It's all mortgage free. At least as far as state and county records are concerned. There may be private loans, but there's no way of knowing about that."

"And the owner?" Taylor pressed.

"It's just about what you'd expect. It's a consortium of companies, based all over the United States. The companies are things like Jack's Hollow Land Company, Lencers Incorporated, Gravel Lick Associates, the Tom's Run Corporation, Vixen Enterprises, and so on."

"Those names mean anything?"

"Apparently not. They mostly take their names from roads or landmarks up in that area."

"And no clue who's behind them. Nothing on the incorporation papers or anything?"

"I don't know."

"You don't know?"

"Look, we were fighting our battle on a shoestring. What little we had was going for bus trips to Harrisburg and Washington and a Xerox machine. We couldn't afford to dig too deep. And then we won. We got the concessions we wanted, so there wasn't any point in digging deeper."

She paused.

"And maybe something else," she said. "I was pretty green. I knew *in general* what we should do, but that's a hell of a long shot from knowing how to do it."

Taylor tried to be conciliatory. "No sense worrying now about what's past. What about now? Who pays their tax bills? Who gets their mail? That kind of thing."

She smiled; and it was a welcome relief from her red-ringed eyes. "You're pretty knowledgeable about this stuff," she said.

"Hey, you're talking to the tax man. Nobody can hide from us," he said lightly.

Lauren picked up another pile of papers and glanced through them.

"Just about what you'd expect on a deal like this. A bunch of blue chip law firms. Most of them top-drawer."

"Anybody I would recognize?" he asked.

"I'd have to go through them, but for a project like this, most likely," she said. "Big money means big firms and big firms mean big names. High-priced law is like incest. Everybody winds up sleeping with everybody else."

She looked down at her coffee cup.

"So what do you think's out there at the Installation?" he asked. "Any ideas? From what I gather, it's pretty much of a mystery."

"Maybe yes and maybe no," she said.

"What do you mean?" he asked.

"Look. Nobody spends seven million dollars plus for land they don't plan to sell or use. Not in the real world. So what does that tell you?"

"That the land's being used. But for what?" he asked.

"Think about it. They haven't built any buildings. They haven't built any roads. The only thing they've built is a fence around their property to keep out trespassers. From what I'm told, maybe a couple of dozen people work there on those five square miles. What does that sound like to you?"

"Like something secret is going on," Taylor said.

"Exactly my idea," she said. "I think our government bought this land from itself through a phony corporation, and is using it for something secret that they don't want anybody to know about."

"And your environmentalists aren't worried about that?" he said.

"No," she said with a sharp edge in her voice. "You might not understand, but there are people—and I happen to be one of them—who care about the land, but don't jump on every save-the-snail-darter bandwagon that comes along just because it's trendy. I don't think they're making zombies up there, or creating nerve gas to wipe out Pittsburgh, or creating an android army to march into Moscow. I think it's probably something prosaic . . . secret but ordinary."

"I'd like to know more," he said.

"Even if it is government?" she said. "You work for the government. You're not afraid, maybe, to step on some big boy's toes?"

"I've been stepping all over somebody's toes for the last week," he said. "I might as well find out whose."

"All right," she said. "I'll dig into those corporations; I'll try to get hold of the lawyers who handle all the business for these people; I'll give it the good try and see what I can come up with. Should I call you if I get something? Or will you call me?"

Taylor looked at her. There was still a barrier between them, invisible but palpable. Her eyes were moisting up and she tried to wipe them with the back of her hand.

"I'm sorry, Matt. I seem to be getting into the habit of making a fool of myself."

"That's okay," he said. He could think of nothing better.

"I'm sorry for last night. The way I acted both times. At the club and then upstairs in your room. I had no right."

"Don't worry about it," he said.

"I *am* worried. Really worried. Yesterday was just about the worst day ever. Next to the day, maybe, when you told me you didn't love me anymore."

"I was stupid," Taylor said.

Lauren pushed her seat back from the table.

"I've got to get out of here," she said, "before I start blubbering like a baby and completely disgrace myself."

"All right. Would you like some company?"

She surprised him by reaching over and squeezing his hand. "Yes," she said, "I would."

Matt could not remember if Judge Stevens was a good tipper or not, so he left an extra five dollars for the waitress, then followed Lauren out through the door into the parking lot and down into the small part that ran along the river.

"I'm just going to blurt it all out," she said. "That's the only way I'll ever tell you. So don't try and say anything, please, until I'm done, okay?"

"Go ahead."

The morning was chill and damp and the hills that ended in sheer walls of stone at the edge of the business district effectively blocked any warmth from the early sun. Lauren's coat had been made to look good and not to keep her warm. As they walked they had come up to the small, green band shelter. Taylor led the way up its few steps and over to one side. Its back was to the river and so it did a reasonable job of blocking out the cold wind.

"To begin with," she said, "I didn't go to Pittsburgh on a case yesterday. I went with Mike. You've never met him, but he's probably the finest, nicest, most gentle man I have ever known. Most ways, he's a lot nicer than you, though you'd never know it to look at him. If you can imagine Clint Eastwood about thirty pounds heavier, that's the way he looks. And that's the way he acts. Tough as nails."

Taylor didn't say anything but he could feel a coldness inside him that did not come from the weather.

"That's why I married him," Lauren said. "Because he was big and tough and gentle to me. Always. All ways. I don't mean to hurt your feelings, Matt, but that's the truth, and I have to tell you it, so you'll understand. I was so grateful when he asked me to marry him. I almost thought that no one would ever want me again, except, maybe, for a couple of nights roll in the hay.

216

"But being grateful wasn't enough. We both had it figured out pretty quickly, before we'd been married a year. We talked about it. I told him that I would learn to love him eventually. But he knew. He knew I still loved you, even if it didn't make any sense. So I got pregnant. I wanted to show him that I loved him, even if I didn't, and the baby seemed the best way to prove it. Little Mickey was the best little baby ever. I know every mother thinks so, and maybe I'm prejudiced, but he was really a great little kid."

Lauren stopped talking. For a moment, she fought a battle for self-control and seemed to win it.

"It was working," she said. "I wanted so much to love Mike. And the baby was so wonderful. And I think Mike loved me. I know he did."

She gestured with her hand.

"In the summertime they have concerts here," she said. "The music isn't always great. But it's the thought. We used to come a lot. We'd bring the baby."

Tears came to her eyes now and she did not try to stop them. Taylor moved closer, but she put out a hand and rested it on his chest, keeping him from any contact.

"I was talking to someone," Lauren said. "I thought Mickey was with his dad. He thought the kid was with me. It wasn't anybody's fault, really. He was such an active boy. Not even two, but he could walk and run anywhere. That's what happened."

She pointed toward the river.

"It was dusk. It took hours to find him. By then it was too late, of course. He must have slipped on a rock and hit his head and just gone under without a sound."

She coughed a couple of times and took out a handkerchief and blew her nose.

"That was two years ago this coming summer," she said. "I tried to be a good wife to Mike after that. I really did. And he tried too. But I wasn't. I don't mean I was unfaithful, or anything like that. I didn't shut him out of my bed. I talked to him

217

every day. We went places. I made his meals for him. But there was nothing left and one night he just told me he was leaving. There were no fights. It was all very civilized, but it was all very over."

She smiled a sad smile and stared for a long time at the river before talking again.

When she spoke, she did not look at him.

"There were some bad times after that. Nothing dramatic though. I'm not a very dramatic person. I did a little bit of drinking. I planned on sleeping around, but when it came right down to it I backed away. I spent all my time at work . . . an automaton . . . except for the Judge and his housekeeper . . . They kept me human.

"I kept meaning to go see you. Larry told me that he thought your marriage was pretty rocky, but that you didn't know it yet. But I didn't, and time passed, and I thought I'd gotten over you. I went out with John from the newspaper for a while, but we both knew there was nothing to it, especially when he met that little chickie girl reporter of his." She barked out a harsh little laugh. "Face it, I'm a washout with men.

"Then two days ago, Mike called me up. We hadn't talked in months. He tells me he's scared. He's in the University Hospital in Pittsburgh, and could I please come down and see him Monday morning. He wouldn't tell me what was wrong, so I agreed to go. Then I went to see the Judge and Maggie and we get the call that you're back. It was like the world was doing flip-flops.

"Let's walk some more," she said. "I'm getting numb from the cold standing here."

They went back through the parking lot and crossed the street to a McDonald's and ordered more coffee.

"Mike's dying," Lauren said. "It's some brain tumor, and there isn't a damn thing they can do. First, it'll blind him. And then it'll kill him, if it doesn't drive him crazy first.

"Mike doesn't deserve this. He deserves better. First, his kid.

Then, his wife. Now this. And what did he ever do to deserve it?"

She stopped talking for a moment, but when Taylor tried to speak, she shushed him.

"You know what I was worried about when I was driving down to Pittsburgh yesterday?" she asked. He shook his head.

"I was wondering whether or not you and I could make love last night. I was trying to figure out some way to let you know how I felt about you, and how much I wanted you, but it kept getting in my way that you were a married man. I guess that's silly stuff, but that's what happens when you're all Catholic and twelve inches thick. I don't know who I felt sorrier for coming home, Mike or myself. Myself, I think. It's so horrible for him. You know, I think he's going to go on as long as he can, pretending . . . no, not pretending . . . acting as if nothing serious is wrong. And then when he can't do that any longer, I think he's going to put his gun in his mouth and blow his brains out. I think that's what he's going to do. I really do.

"But then I got to the Club and saw you . . . I don't know . . . nothing clicked. There you were. You had left me and caused all my misery. And now did you think I was going to be the instrument for you to betray Melanie, by spreading my legs for you? God, how I hated you at that minute. So I was a bitch, and I'm sorry, and I went home and had a good cry and a couple of drinks and thought, what the hell, Melanie's not my concern, and the Judge's Maggie had told me I needed a man and I decided that if you could use me, I could use you. That's what I wanted last night, just your body. At least that's what I told myself. So I tarted myself up and went to your room. I tell you, I'm a washout with men."

She finished her coffee in an angry gulp.

"So that's all of that," she said. "What's been happening to you lately? Anything interesting?"

Taylor told her everything.

CHAPTER TWENTY-FOUR

Matt walked Lauren back to her office and then returned to his motel room. It was almost 11:00 A.M.; his bed had been made and he sprawled across the covers and thought.

He was supposed to meet Gianetti and Polonowski in a little more than four hours, but the more he thought about it, the less he wanted to. And yet he wondered what they wanted, and just who they really were.

He lit a cigarette, coughed once—the motel cigarette machine only had high-tar brands—and considered his options. The cigarette seemed to make things clearer. That's what they were good for: thinking and killing you.

He reached for the telephone, took a worn-looking business card from his wallet, and dialed the number written on it. The phone rang seven times before it was answered. That was unusual for a government phone, Taylor thought.

"Hello," said a voice at the other end. It sounded tired and angry and, come to think of it, "hello" was not your normal government-issue telephone response either.

"I'm calling for Dennis O'Leary," Matt said. "He told me I could reach him at this number."

There were a few loud pops and hisses on the line before the voice spoke again.

"Who's calling?"

"Is O'Leary there?" Matt persisted.

"I'm not sure. Who's calling?"

"Thanks," Matt said. "I'll try some other time."

He hung up, although he was not quite sure why. He had wanted to tell O'Leary that Laurel and Hardy—Gianetti and Polonowski—had run him to ground, despite O'Leary's having yanked their tracking device from his car. He wanted to know how they had done that. He wanted to know why Gianetti had told him not to trust O'Leary, and just what O'Leary thought about that. He wanted O'Leary to tell him whether or not he should go through with the three o'clock meeting with the two FBI men.

He dialed Walt Fluory's private office number back in Washington and was surprised when Fluory answered the phone personally. Fluory's secretary was one of those nine-armed models of efficiency who seemed to regard every telephone call that got through to her boss as a blot upon her character.

"Walt, this is Matt Taylor."

"Matt. How the hell are you? Is everything all right? Where are you?"

"I'm fine, Walt. Listen, I've run into a couple of FBI guys who say they were checking out Larry for the anti-mob unit. They've kind of been dogging me around. Gianetti and Polonowski. You know them?"

"No. I don't think so," Floury said slowly.

"They were the same guys I asked you about before. They were on the elevator with you at the hotel in Philly."

"Sorry, Matt. I come up blank. Did they mention me?"

"No. But they said they were working for the White House and checking out people who might go in the new bureau. They mentioned Larry, and then they said they'd probably be looking into me too. I just wanted to know if they were on the level."

"Probably are," Floury said. "I mean there aren't a lot of people who'd have any knowledge of how we'd do background checks on personnel in their new unit. But I'm just surprised I

221

don't know anything about them." He paused. "What do you think?"

"I think there's something smelly about them," Matt said. "Thanks, Walt."

"Hold on, hold on. Where the hell are you? What are you doing anyway? You are getting some rest, aren't you?"

"Nothing but rest," Matt said. "I'll call you in a day or two." He hung up before Fluory could ask any more questions, or squeeze out answers to the ones he had already asked but which Matt had ignored. Like, mainly, where he was.

Taylor changed from his suit into old chinos and a heavy sweater, replaced his wing tips with his leather sneakers, grabbed a ratty old jacket from his closet, and left the room. Downstairs in the lobby he looked around, but as best as he could tell, no one was watching him.

Only a block from the motel, Taylor found a gun shop and bought the U.S. Geodetic Survey's topographic maps for the area occupied by Harker's Furnace and the Installation. At the same store, he ordered a bag of sandwiches to go and, after some negotiations, rented a large thermos and filled it with hot black coffee. Outside, he scanned the sidewalks and storefronts, but as far as he could tell, he was still alone.

He walked back to the motel's parking lot to pick up his rental car. He rang for the elevator to the second parking level, but when it did not come quickly enough to suit his edgy nerves, he began climbing the gray metal utility stairs. He was only halfway up when he heard voices above him coming down. For a split second he kept going up, paying no attention. And then a warning signal inside his brain sounded. Matt stopped moving. There was no mistaking the voices he had heard. It was Gianetti and Polonowski, carrying on their apparently never-ending argument.

Matt spun and hopped down the half flight of stairs to the ground level. He landed lightly and pushed through the fire door.

There was no one else in the ground-level parking area and

Taylor ducked behind a car and waited for the two FBI men to come out and exit to the street. They passed ten feet from him, close enough for him to hear a piece of their conversation.

Polonowski said, "I'm tired of this bastard. I'd like to be rid of him once and for all."

And Gianetti answered, "All things in due time, John. All things in due time."

Who were these bastards? And why were they after him?

After they left, Taylor ran up the stairs, got his car, and sped out of town. This time, he did not retrace his route of the day before to Harker's Furnace. Instead, he followed the narrow winding river road to a spot a bit north of the crossroads settlement and a little south of the Installation's outermost boundary.

The riverbank was lined with small houses and cottages, most of them still with the winter-abandoned look of their species.

Behind one cottage, he saw canoes half-hidden on racks in what could pass for a small barn. Matt pulled into the home's driveway, out of sight of the road, but within full and easy view of both the house and the barn.

No dog barked. No one came to meet him. All was still.

He got out of the car and shouted, "Hello. Hello. Anybody home?" There was no answer, nor did anyone respond to his knocks on the front door.

Inside the barn, he found four aluminum canoes. He spread out his topographical map atop one of the boats and studied it. The river wound right along the edge of the Installation, and there were old lumber or fire roads leading up in the general direction of the place's front gate, as well as a road just inside the fence that circled the place.

Until now, he had made no decision on what he was going to do, but when he saw that the canoes were not chained down and that the paddles were neatly stacked in a special bin along the wall, he decided to enter the Installation from the river side.

He hefted one of the paddles. It was a finely worked piece

of wood, wide across the blade and thin through its edges, well balanced, and of the perfect length to suit his stroke.

He lifted a canoe onto his shoulders and carried it the forty yards down to the riverbank. Then he came back and pulled his car up close behind the barn, gathered up his thermos and sandwiches, and picked up the paddle he had chosen.

As he launched the canoe, he realized it had been a long time since he had been in one—probably more than ten years—and it showed. The launching was sloppy and Matt's pants legs were soaked, but a few moments later he was in the middle of the river, paddling laboriously upstream.

Once there had been a beauty and a serenity, even an elegance to canoeing, he remembered. But it had precious little today with pushing an aged, leaking hulk of a canoe two miles upstream though a river in early, bone-chilling spring flood.

How did the old song go?
Dip, dip, and swing them back
Flashing like silver.
It was true as far as it went, but it left out the important parts. Like the effect of all that dip, dip, and swinging them back on muscles that had not swung a paddle in a decade. After the first twenty minutes, each stroke of the paddle had become sheer agony. And there was no stopping. Each time he tried to rest, the river shoved him back downstream. A minute's rest wiped out five minutes of paddling. It was a hopeless equation and there were only two choices: give up or keep going without stopping.

A heavy mist hung over the river, making it impossible to see either shoreline. He did not know if it was possible to walk the shore to get to the installation.

He kept paddling. The muscles across the back of his shoulders knotted and burned, his upper arms turned to napalm jelly and caught fire, his forearms went numb.

It all made no difference to the river.

And he knew that what was happening to his arms and shoulders was only the beginning. Canoeing was like riding a bike: once you learned how, you never completely forgot. But there was canoeing and there was canoeing. Once upon a time, Matt could have paddled for hours and never splashed more than a cupful of water into his canoe, so effortless and deft was his paddling technique. But no more. Now it seemed that each time he lifted his paddle on the forestroke, he dashed a gallon of water into the canoe. Part of it sprayed across him, soaking his clothes and chilling him through and through. The rest of it just settled into the bottom of the canoe and formed a sloshing pond that was beginning to cause him some concern. The canoe could only take on so much water before it would sink, and besides, it was coming damn close to soaking his bag of sandwiches.

The weather was worsening. A fine, hard-driven mist—made up of equal parts of rain, sleet, and snow—had settled over the water, and the visibility, which had been low, was now zero.

He had not been able to see the river banks. Now he could not see what was in front of him either and was navigating by sound and by touch. He knew that even in the water's spring surge, in many places there were rocks just barely below the surface, waiting to reach up and snag the bottom of the aluminum canoe. Twice, so far, he had run aground on them and had to battle his way off, poking and pushing with his paddle and hoping that he would not break the fragile piece of wood in the struggle. Each time, he had escaped from the rocks, only to be turned sideways in the stream and nearly swamped. And each time, the canoe had been turned back downstream by the force of the water, and Matt had found himself being swept along, back in the direction from which he had come. Getting headed back upstream again had required a tricky and exhausting battle to make a U-turn in the middle of the river, again exposing his canoe to the danger of being tipped broadside.

He grew more worried as he glanced again at the bottom of

the canoe. He was kneeling in three inches of water and his gunwales were riding precariously low.

If I had time to worry, I would start worrying right about now, he thought. If he capsized, there would be no rescuer and he would be completely on his own in water, cold enough to numb him in only a few minutes, and a current just as likely to whirl him down into a deep pit as it was to dash him on the big rocks that lined the banks.

And the bottom of the canoe was still filling with water.

He leaned forward, straining to listen to the river. There was something ahead, something big. He could tell from the change in the river's sound. It could be almost anything. A half-sunken car. Shallows. Rapids. A big rock. Lots of little rocks. An island.

The water was filling the bottom of the canoe faster, he decided his only choice was to put in to shore and take his chances with what he might find there. Matt turned the bow of his canoe for the left bank. The boat had shipped too much water and its steering was sluggish. He would just have to paddle harder, work harder. He concentrated on pushing the river back. He strained to see where he was going, but the mist had grown even thicker, now a dense fog. It was ridiculous, he thought, but he was lost on a river that was not even a hundred feet wide.

Disaster struck in two blows. The first came with a thudding jolt. The canoe has hit something, Matt thought, almost dispassionately. There was a sound as he was thinking, a screeching, tearing sound, the scream of aluminum being ripped open by a dull rock. He glanced forward and saw a gaping hole torn in the side of the canoe. That wasn't supposed to happen to these kind of canoes, he thought. Never in a million years. They were just too strong. And yet it had happened.

The second blow came a second or two after the first. It struck him across the face and nearly dumped him from the boat. It was hard and wet and later on, he would realize that it was the branch of a small tree reaching out over the water from the small island where he had run aground.

He fell backward into the canoe and then somehow rocked forward. The world was a red and yellow haze now, with purple and black splotches around the edges. *I must save the ham sandwiches. And the thermos. The manager of the gun shop will never forgive me if I lose the thermos.*

The back end of the canoe where he had been kneeling was now nearly underwater and Matt scrambled forward, slightly uphill toward a massive overhanging rock. The bow of the canoe had somehow been impelled into one of its crannies. He reached down to grab the bag of sandwiches and the thermos in one hand, and used the other to pull himself upward. The scramble seemed to go on forever, when he finally came to a stop, he found himself on a small table of rock and dirt perhaps a dozen feet above the surge of the river.

There were trees there, too, and Matt walked to one of them and sat down with his back against it. He could still see flashes of bright colors before his eyes from when the tree limb had slugged him across the face. Eventually, the flashes turned to balls and the balls to stars and then the colors faded. The left sleeve of his worn leather jacket was ripped and he could see blood oozing from the tear. He sighed, poured himself a cup of coffee, and ate one of the ham sandwiches from the bag. It was waterlogged but it did not matter. He drank another cup of coffee and ate another sandwich and then stood up. The fog over the river was the same, but the fog in his brain started to clear.

He looked around himself at the island. It was perhaps twenty yards long and ten wide. He took the topographical map from his pocket, opened it up on the ground and perused it, but he could not find the island he was on. He swore softly to himself and put the map away.

He was cold and wet and there was no cover. That was an invitation to a disaster of another order. It would be sheer stupidity, he thought, to escape death by drowning, only to die from exposure to the cold.

A fire. He needed a fire. He patted his shirt pocket but his

227

cigarette lighter was not there. Then he had an idea. The gun. He had brought it with him. He could use the muzzle flash to start a fire. Then he would be warm and, eventually, dry. Now where the hell was the gun? The canoe.

He went back to the canoe. Half of it was under water and the gun was not in the part above water. He would have to climb back down to the canoe and somehow work his way along its sides, searching the sunken part for the weapon. It would be gingerish work.

Matt stood atop the rock, considering how to get down to the canoe, and finally detected a couple of indentations in the rock that might serve as hand and toe holds.

He started carefully, making sure that his toe was firmly wedged into the stone and that he had good handholds before he lowered himself over the side. The second toehold was easier to get to than the first, but when he reached out with a foot for the third, he fell, a short fall, not even seven feet, but he hit the freezing water with an impact that took his breath away.

He immediately sank beneath the water and when he came back up the world was black. He was lost in total blackness and for just an instant, he could feel panic clawing at him. It was a physical feeling, a cold hard ball in the pit of his stomach, it reached up through his windpipe and grabbed the back of his throat. He fought it and willed it away and then he knew where he was. Somehow, someway, his fall had twisted the canoe upside down and he was under it, his head in an airpocket formed by its shallow hull.

He reached his hands up over his head, exploring the space above him. To his surprise, he touched something heavy and metallic. He remembered he had stuck the gun under one of the metal canoe's cross struts and now he yanked it out, shoved it down into his belt, and then forced himself to lower his head once more into the cold, onrushing river.

He went down and thought for a moment that maybe he should stay there. There would be no more killings that way.

Everybody would be safe. Lauren would be happy without him. Melanie would get his insurance.

And the bastards who killed Larry Wu would get away with it. That last thought changed his mind, and he forced himself back up to the surface.

In the open again, he found himself in the shallows. He tried to stand, and when he was almost to his feet, the river whished him away. He fought to keep his head above water but every time he took a gulp of air, his body would slam against the rocks that formed the river bed and he would lose the air once more. It happened over and over again and Matt was growing very tired. He wanted to stop fighting, to just rest.

But not quite yet. One more gulp of air. Ohhh, one more rock. One more gulp of air. It has to end. Somehow. Sometime. Soon. It has to end.

And then it was over.

He lay on a tiny spit of gravel, free of the river. He lay there a long time and them pulled himself to his feet. He could see the river bank. He was separated from it by a few small, almost placid, tongues of water, rivulets that he could easily cross in one determined leap.

He moved forward, stumbling and leaping and crawling until he was on shore, lying on a deep bed of pine needles.

And he closed his eyes.

CHAPTER TWENTY-FIVE

He never wanted to get up again. Time to sleep, he told himself. He had worked hard, fought the river, and won. Now his reward was to sleep.

He began to shiver. His teeth chattered. Funny, he thought, his teeth had never chattered before. In fact, he never had known anyone whose teeth really did, except maybe little Amy Cochran's. But she was just a skinny little kid and she would turn blue even if she just went in swimming too long on a cool summer's day. He wondered what had ever happened to her. Maybe she would be swimming today in the river. Maybe she would find him. They could go swimming together. It was a grand day for a swim.

Matt shivered some more and curled himself into a fetal position. *Go to sleep and then you'll be warm. No more shivering, no more teeth chattering. Just a nice warm long sleep and everything will be all right. Nothing to worry about. Nothing.*

He could feel his eyelids drooping and warmth beginning to spread over his body. *Funny about that. I'm warm and it's still snowing. Or sleeting. Or something.*

"Get up, you lazy worthless hunk of excrement," a voice said. "Get up. What do you want to do? Die? Then die doing something useful. Not like this. Get up."

"Huh?" Matt said. He stirred softly and slightly raised his head. He looked and moved like a baby being gently roused from its afternoon nap.

"You heard me," the voice said. "Get up or die."

Matt sat upright. The voice was familiar. From far, far in the past. He patiently searched his memory for the name of its owner. The name was right there on the tip of his tongue, but somehow he could not say it.

"Go away," Matt said. "I don't know you. Don't bother me. I'm tired. I need my sleep."

"Horse-puckey," the voice said. "And double horse-puckey." The voice's owner was obviously fighting to keep back the obscenities he really wanted to speak.

"Semple," Matt shouted out. "That's who you are. Gunnery Sergeant Semple. I remember you. You were our drill instructor at boot camp. Parris Island."

"Very clever," the voice said. "Very, very clever. Now just get the heck up and start moving. Or else you'll die. Right here. Today. And nobody will find you until the porcupines have chewed your eyeballs out."

"Start moving where?" Matt said.

"Wherever you have to go," the voice said.

Matt stood up and looked all around. There was no one there. He was entirely alone.

"Who are you?" he demanded.

The voice laughed. "You don't know?" it asked.

"No. I don't know."

The voice laughed again; it laughed long and hard and then it faded away.

Matt felt very alone and very cold. He began shivering again but this time, he knew, he would find no refuge in the deadly embrace of sleep.

He needed to get warm. He saw his gun lying on the ground and thought of his plan from before, the plan to start a fire with the muzzle flash. He laughed aloud, bitterly. It was stupid, stupid and useless. The gun produced no muzzle flash to speak

231

of. He had damned near drowned for a scheme that was worse than witless.

He looked away from the river and saw a small cave created by an overhang on the riverbank fifteen yards away. In there, at least, he could be out of the wind and sleet while he collected himself and figured out his next actions. The wind was from behind him and he was instantly warmer once he took a sitting position inside the small cavelike formation.

His lighter. Where the hell was it? He remembered smoking in the rented car and using his own lighter. But it wasn't in his top shirt pocket. He raised himself to a crouch and began searching and found the disposable Butane lighter in his right front pants pocket. He tried to rub the lighter dry between his cold hands and then depressed the button on top. It lit on the first try. He stifled a cry of victory, stashed the lighter in the back of the cave out of the weather, and crawled out to find some kindling. With the butt of his gun, he broke loose a lot of dead wood chips from the underside of a fallen tree, stuffed them into his pockets and carried them back to the cave.

He made three more trips before he had a respectable-looking pile of wood inside the cave. His wallet was soaked from his encounter with the river but there were two pictures of Melanie inside plastic sleeves and when he took them out, they were still dry. He tore them into long strips, crumpled them up, and stacked slivers of wood around and over them. He torched the small pile with the lighter; the flames caught and in only a few minutes he had a fire going. He began peeling off his clothing. It was cold, naked in the woods, but it was colder with the wet clothes on. He started to wring out the garments one at a time and when he was done, he repeated the process. And then once more. By the third wringing the condition of his clothing was improved to damp and slowly, laboriously, one at a time, he dried them over the smoky flames of the fire. He took the occasion to examine his injured left arm and saw a vicious-looking two-inch-long gash in the upper part of his bicep. It hurt like hell, he thought, but no big deal.

As the fire burned down, he struggled back into his clothes. It wasn't laundromat-quality drying, but it would do; the heat of his body should get rid of any residual dampness.

The question now was: which way to go. He might be near the Installation, but he did not know. If he followed the river, he would eventually come to some cottages or some other sign of civilization. If he turned inland, he might find the secret camp at Harker's Furnace. He stepped outside into the weather, stuck the gun into the belt of his pants, and started inland.

Within twenty yards, he was in to the tree line—beeches, maples, and oaks on the fringes, with pine and hemlock a bit farther back. It was still too early in the year for any leaves to appear on the deciduous trees, but the conifers behind them were already starting to heavy up with needles.

For the first five minutes, the land sloped gently upwards and the going was easy. Once back from the fringe of the forest, the trees opened up. In here the trees were old, at least a hundred years old, and so they lifted high into the sky carrying most of their needled branches with them, making a dense overhead canopy but leaving the floor of the forest relatively open. The only impediments to progress at this time of year were the tangle of tree roots, a litter of boulders, and frequent, dense clumps of rhododendron called slicks. The boulders had been deposited fifteen thousand years ago, back when the last glaciers had covered the area. Some were relatively small, a few yards across and three or four feet high, but others were huge, the size of a large frame house. Most of the time Matt could go around them, but once in a while he had to climb over them.

The rhododendron slicks were something else. Early in the summer they would be beautiful—covered with fat, sensuous pink and purple and white flowers, some as large as a man's head—but now, before the flowers came, their branches grew in clumps, not quite bushes and not yet trees, in patches that could ramble on for twenty or thirty yards in any direction, all tangled together, winding about one another like copulating snakes. They tended to keep their leaves even in winter: big,

233

green-brown reptilian-looking things that felt disgustingly slimy to the touch. Sometimes the leaves formed a crown ten feet high, but other times they were at knee level. At its best, walking through a rhododendron patch was like moving through a convention of beginner pickpockets. At its worst, it was like trying to swim through a school of angry squid.

Matt stopped to catch his breath. The ground had grown steeper. He looked upwards and ahead, but could not see the top of the ridge line. The fog was settling in heavier, ahead and behind him was all a gray blur. He looked up, trying to catch some hint of light in the sky from the sun, trying to guess the time, but there was no brightness to be seen. It must be mid-afternoon at least, he thought, and that was bad news because darkness came early here at this time of year, and once it had arrived, his chances of making it back to the river were zero, unless he waited till morning.

If he kept going much longer, Matt thought, he would have committed himself to spending the night on the mountain. It was not a pleasant thought. Even though he could probably build another fire, trying to survive by its side at night would be an entirely different story. Perhaps, he thought, it was time to retreat; go back to the riverbank and walk along it until he found someone's house. Perhaps he should just call O'Leary, tell him what he knew and what he suspected, and let him handle things from there.

He looked back over his shoulder, back toward the river and relative safety. Then he thought of Larry Wu's body, lying lifeless in a parking lot, and he growled aloud, "Fuck it," and started forward again, trudging through the trees and slicks following the rise of the ground before him.

Matt had just scaled a house-high rock face when he came upon a fence. He had not been able to see it from below in the gathering gloom and fog. The poles supporting it had been set in holes drilled right into the bare rock, as close to the edge as it was possible to get. The steel mesh part of the fence rose ten feet high and above that the support poles bent outward, carrying four strands of wire. The two lower strands were barbed; the two upper wires rested on little white ceramic insulators. Electrified, he thought.

He hung onto the fence by his fingertips, surveying the situation. There was no way to continue upward. He looked back over his shoulder. It was probably only twenty-five feet to the ground, but it was still enough to make him uneasy. He had never been good at heights.

He cursed himself for not going around the rock when he had the chance, instead of climbing straight forward, up and over the top. He knew though why he had done it, even if he felt foolish admitting it. He was afraid of heights; so this day he felt he must challenge them.

He started back down, groping for each step. He made the first toehold and the second, but not the third. For an instant, he scrabbled at the rock face, desperately clawing for a hold. After he had found it and caught his breath, he noticed the bloody finger streaks he had left on the rock. He started to shiver again. He could fall, he told himself, and probably not be killed. He was not that high up. Still, he would probably wind up with something broken and the thought was unsettling. Immobilized, he would freeze to death and be food for predators. He felt his knees weaken and he shivered. His injured left arm ached.

He tried to see a way out of his predicament, but there were no toeholds below him, and there did not seem to be anything to either side. That meant dropping backwards and hoping for the best—or going back up. He started climbing again.

When he reached the fence again, he grabbed it and leaned forward, taking advantage of the two inches of leeway which the construction permitted on the edge of the rock.

Off to his right, the rock face receded, leaving an overhang that he would probably not be able to get across. To his left, he could see little except that the rock seemed to curve away in a gentle arc. A poor choice, but no other presented itself.

He began moving to his left, sideways, an arm's length at a

time. It was hard, slow going. Most of the time, he was hanging in space, moving along with his belly pressed tight into the wire mesh, supporting himself with the strength of his shoulders and arms and bleeding fingers. He lost track of time. His arms burst into flames of pain, but after a long time they burned themselves out and he felt numb. He kept moving, trying not to think that he had probably moved no more than thirty or forty yards along the fence.

And then the fence made a ninety-degree turn away from him. Square edges are virtually unheard of in nature, yet here was one as the fence followed a sharp corner of the stone it was imbedded into. Getting around the corner would be tricky.

Matt hung on desperately and craned his neck around the edge. What he saw was either the solution to his problem or his biggest obstacle yet.

Just where the fence made its turn, there had been a minor landfall. For the space of nearly three support posts, the fence hung in mid-air. The rock that had anchored the posts had fallen away beneath then and there was a gaping space wide enough for Taylor to somehow jam his way through and up the other side, if he could maneuver properly. Once that was done, he would be past the fence and, he hoped, free of any other obstacles.

He looked behind him, then glanced down, and had to fight off a wave of nausea. While he had been worming his way along the fence line, he had paid no attention to what had been happening to the ground below him. Now he saw that the ground had fallen away. No longer was he dangling a relatively safe twenty or thirty feet above the ground. He was now at treetop level and for white pines—which was what the trees were—that could mean anywhere from eighty to over a hundred feet high.

He felt trapped.

He closed his eyes until the nausea passed and tried to think his heart back to a normal pace. It almost worked. He had to go back, he told himself. Back to where he was not all that far above the ground, and then take his chances sliding or jumping back off the rock.

He opened his eyes and looked back along the way he had come. It looked different somehow and at first he could not figure out how. And then it came to him. Most of the rock had disappeared from view in the gathering darkness. He could not go back because he would not be able to see where to go. And he could not stay where he was much longer, not with the dusk rapidly closing around him.

He stretched out his hand and grabbed the wire mesh to his left. He pulled on it slightly, checking its unsupported strength. It gave slightly, then held. He shifted more weight and it gave some more, but not as much as the first time. Then he said to himself, "To hell with it," kicked his feet back, and began a fast, frantic, hand-over-hand scrambling along the fence until he was approximately halfway along the unsupported section.

He hung there by his arms, half out of fear of what he had to do next, half resting, building up his strength to do it. Above him, he could see the fence sagging more. He did not bother looking again at the darkness gaping away at his feet.

Then came the hardest part. He had hold of the fence about halfway up its side. Very slowly, he let himself down until his fingers were grasping the second-lowest links. If the fence gave way, or if he let go now, he told himself, there would be no second chance, no safety factor, nothing to make a last desperate grab at. He tried to put the thought out of his mind.

He let go of the fence with one hand and twisted his body so that he could reach his free hand underneath and grab the fence from the other side. It was an easier maneuver than he had thought it would be. He was now hanging from the underside of the unsupported fence, like some maniacal gibbon.

He let go with his other hand and maneuvered it also to the inside of the fence, and was now hanging, looking outwards, his back toward the rock face.

All he had to do now, he told himself, was pull himself upwards, hand over hand, to the top of the mesh fence and then sidle along six or seven feet to where the fence again was solidly imbedded in the top the rock he had been crawling along. Once that was done, he would be safe.

Sweat ran down his forehead and into his eyes and it burned as if someone had blown pepper into his face.

He began his climb. His hands were sweaty, too, and beginning to cramp, the pain in his arms had come back, growing sharper and sharper. He could feel spasms in the thin muscles across the front of his chest. He reached out one more time to pull himself to the topmost part of the fence, but his fingers could not close on the steel mesh and suddenly he felt himself falling.

Falling.

He let out an involuntary shout and grabbed desperately for the fence. He caught it and his body was jerked to a stop.

The impact from his body was too great for the steel mesh.

Slowly, slowly, it began sagging under Taylor's weight. He held on desperately. He was going to die, he thought. This time for sure. He watched the fence above him bend and seem to tear.

And then from somewhere inside him came a tremendous surge of energy. Everything grew clear. It was easy. One hand over the other to the top—two, three times faster than before. Then a sideways swing and a jump and Matt was safe on top of the rock.

Somewhere inside the Installation.

CHAPTER TWENTY-SIX

He was cold and wet, but he was more tired than either of the other things so he slept, a deep shivering sleep that lasted longer than he expected, for when he awoke, the fog was deeper than it had been, and the hint of moon through the haze came from far across the sky.

He rose and tried to shudder some warmth into his body, but what nagged at him was the realization that he had probably gotten into the Installation but, now here, he did not know what he was looking for. He felt like an idiot: tipping the canoe, risking his life with stupid heroics on the rock face; and now facing some sort of reconnaissance mission with no idea of its purpose.

Then he heard a noise.

At first, he was not even aware that he had heard it. It was not so much a noise as it was a change in the night sounds all around him. He felt his ears listening even before his brain told him what was going on. Finally, it all registered. Some kind of vehicle was coming. But he could not tell from where, because the thick trees seemed to muffle the sound and spread it equally all around him. He sat to wait, and, after a few seconds, lights appeared. They came from Taylor's left and below him, and he was relieved to see that they were moving fairly smoothly. That meant there was a road down below.

The vehicle rolled up, following the cones of its headlights through the moisture-laden fog, and then seemed to stop right below him. The motor stopped. For a moment, he could hear the soft sounds of radio music, and then he heard two doors slamming.

He heard a muffled voice and then another, louder, saying, "That's roger. We'll check the hole in the fence and then had back in. Ten four."

Matt slipped away from the lip of the rock and tried to remember the layout of his position. A few seconds later, he heard the sound of two sets of footsteps gingerly working their way up to the broad, flat top of the rock on which he was perched.

The voice he had just heard broadcasting over the radio said, "Shit. I hate this job."

A second voice said, "I kind of like it." It was a woman's voice. And it was too close.

Matt lowered himself down the back edge of the rock, hung there by his fingertips, and prayed that they would just flash a searchlight around, see nothing, and get the hell out of there before his fingers tired and he fell-who knew how far—to the hostile ground below. Already his arms and shoulders ached. His toes scuffed against the rock face and finally found an indent where he could perch the tips of his feet and take some of his body weight off his arms.

He sensed, rather than saw, a light flashing in his direction. Then he heard the footsteps moving away from him, along the top of the rock. He heard the man's voice.

"There. You see the break?"

"I see," the woman said.

"Probably a deer," the man said. "They go over the side sometimes. The dogs chase them. Come back tomorrow and I bet you find a dead deer down there. It's one hell of a drop. Close to a hundred feet, I guess. Hey, keep your hands to your-self."

"I was just trying to get them warm," the woman's voice said.

"If you want to get them warm, put them in your own pockets," the man's voice said.

"They told me you didn't like women," the woman's voice said accusatorily.

"Oh, yeah? Well, I like women fine, but I don't like them out here, where you drop your drawers and you take the chance of getting bit on the ass by a rattlesnake. But I like them fine. Just fine."

"Let's go back," the woman's voice said, not even attempting to hide her disgust. Her feet were already moving back toward Matt, back toward the pathway down the hillside.

"Sure. We'll go back," the man said. "And forget that stuff that I don't like women, huh? I told you, I like you all fine, but not out here. Some place else."

"Sure," she said, sarcastically. "Always someplace else."

And then there were two sets of footsteps moving past Matt, and he heard them skidding down the face of the rock. His arm muscles could not take the strain anymore and he slowly pulled himself back up onto the shelf and lay there, trying not to pant from the exertion and the fear.

Below him, he heard the two doors slam again and the motor start. The vehicle ground noisily into gear and then coughed off down the road, and Matt crouched and watched its taillights vanish over a hill.

Matt waited a minute longer until the sound of the vehicle had faded, and then slid down the hillside to the road.

The road was rougher than he had thought it would be, really not much more than a fire road, and it seemed to spend most of its time skidding up and down hills.

He walked until he could walk no further, than sat and rested, then got up and walked again. Overhead, the skies were starting to clear and occasionally a star twinkled through. Around him the fog was wisping away and he could now see the road in front of him. It seemed to drag on forever, endlessly, never reaching a destination.

Then he came around a curve and down a long hill and there it was. The Installation.

It was a cluster of a dozen Army-type barracks buildings set down into a bowl-like depression in the earth. Matt guessed that only the three buildings in the center were being used, because they were ringed by a string of mercury vapor lights mounted atop poles, and the area seemed as bright as a baseball stadium infield during a night game.

Matt moved quickly off the road to his left, into the woods and up a small rise. He kept going until he came to a clear patch overlooking the Installation and stopped there.

A few feet over the crest on the Installation's side, a large tree had toppled, landing in such a way as to provide a bench for anyone wanting to watch what was going on down below. Matt climbed up on the squishy, rotted trunk, and slipped and slid his way along it until he came to a place where he had both a big branch for a backrest and good sightlines into the Installation.

There seemed to be only night lights on in the biggest of the three buildings within the circle of floodlights. Another building was totally dark and Matt guessed that it might contain personnel sleeping quarters. In the third, smallest building, there were a few lights on in one end of the structure and Matt waited to see if he could spot any movement inside.

But after fifteen minutes, the lights went out, and just then four people came out of the building. They were laughing, and to Matt's surprise, their voices carried on the cold night air and he had no trouble making out what they were saying.

"The best part was that scaffolding all around the Statue," a young male voice said.

"You're wrong," a woman answered. "The best part was that cute little Chinaman."

"Wrong," another male voice said. "Wrong as usual. He's Japanese."

"Korean," another female voice said.

"Actually," the first male voice said, "he's from Cleveland."

There was laughter as they walked in the direction of the other darkened building. They were arguing about a movie and Matt could remember going to see it and walking out halfway through. He couldn't remember why, though.

Maybe the movie was the last social event of the night. Matt decided to wait, and fifteen minutes later, the large ring of floodlights was turned off and the Installation vanished into darkness.

Matt stood and stretched his sore muscles and tried to ignore the aching in his left shoulder. Then, crouching, darting, his muscles trying to remember the movements of the days in Vietnam, Matt came down the hillside toward the largest of the three buildings and darted under a bush along a side wall. He waited a few minutes to make sure that he had set off no alarms, and then slowly worked his way around all four sides of the building before coming back to his starting point.

The big barracks, Matt discovered, was divided in half on the inside. The back half was all one big room and from some faint security lights that had been left on, Matt had been able to look through the windows and see that the room was given over entirely to a Chrin 210-D computer, probably the best constructed and most expensive machine being made anywhere in the world.

The front half of the barracks was divided in half again. Part of it was used for cubicles—not big enough to qualify as real offices, but probably serving that purpose for the Chrin's operators and programmers. The rest of the front half of the cabin was given over to a lounge with a sofa, two overstuffed chairs, a few card tables, a kitchenette, and a television set that was still playing. It was showing an old western and he found that he was able to hear the dialogue, filtering through the vent of an in-the-wall air conditioner alongside him.

He had almost decided that he would go to the back of the

building and try to break a window to enter the computer lab when he thought he saw a flicker of movement from the sofa on the far side of the lounge.

He peered inside but everything was still again. But then, suddenly, a door leading into the lounge opened and a small wall lamp came on.

Standing in the doorway was a tall, unkempt figure.

Matt could hear his words clearly through the air conditioner vent.

"Barf. Barf. Barf," the figure exclaimed.

Matt stared at him from the corner of the window and as the man moved farther into the room, Matt could see his features more clearly. He looked like everybody's idea of the typical computer super-nerd—from the pencil pal in his white shirt pocket to the taped black horn-rims, the stained ill-fastened tie, and the lank unruly red hair topped off with an Alfalfa-style cowlick at the back.

"Barf," the figure said again.

As Matt watched, two heads gradually rose above the back of one of the sofas.

"Talk English, Ralphie," a young woman's voice said. Her voice was slow and drawly and did not sound any too bright to Matt. Then she stood up from the sofa, straightening her blouse and buttoning her jeans. She was tall and freckle-faced with sandy hair and a face that looked as if it should be on some 4-H Club recruiting poster. But the body, at least what Matt could see of it, was strictly from *Penthouse*.

"I *am* speaking English," Ralphie said. "It's just that you chomping civilians don't understand it."

That said, Ralphie pointed his hand at them, fingers and thumb pointing stiffly straight ahead, and moved the top two fingers and thumb up and down in unison in a chomping motion while the two bottom fingers stayed still.

The second head spoke. It belonged to a young man who at first glance might have been Ralphie's clone.

"Any luck yet?" he asked.

244

"Nil," Ralphie said. "I was over before and I've tried commmode everybody I could think of till I was damn near fried. I don't know what to make of it. It's just like Nuj has dropped off the world and into another dimension."

"He hasn't been gone that long," the girl said.

"I agree," Ralphie said. "He hasn't been gone that long. But it's not like Nujinsky to be gone at all. This is an absolute pessimal situation."

"Have you thought about going to security?" the girl asked.

"Nuj said not to," Ralphie said. "He said they were the last people he wanted to know. He was getting strange about them."

"What strange?" the girl said. "We do people's tax returns. We're like H. and R. Block. It's not like it's secret work. Nujinsky's missing. Tell Security."

"Nuj said not to," Ralphie insisted.

"What about this other guy that Nuj was talking to last week. What was his log-in?"

"WUL," Ralphie said. "W . . . U . . . L."

Ralphie plopped down into one of the big chairs and rubbed his eyes savagely. "This WUL seems to be nowhere around either. I couldn't raise him on the network before. I'm worried about Nuj."

"You ought to crash for the night," the girl said. "See how you feel in the morning."

"I think I will. I think I will," Ralphie said. He got up and started for the door.

"The bag-biting front door is down again," he said. "I've put some tape over the thing so it won't slam shut and lock us all out."

"That's good," the girl said as she sank back onto the sofa. Her boyfriend slid down beside her.

Ralphie come out of the building onto the front porch. Matt tried to burrow into the shadows but Ralphie turned and walked in the other direction toward the sleeping quarters. Matt tried to catch his breath as he figured out what it all meant.

Obviously, one of the Installation's computer men was missing after having made contact on one of the computer nets with someone named WUL.

And WUL was the log-in name that Larry Wu had always used.

CHAPTER TWENTY-SEVEN

When had it all begun?

Seven days ago? Eight?

He had found those strange tax returns on a Tuesday. On Friday, Larry Wu had been killed. Now another Tuesday had come and gone. It was Wednesday and tomorrow Larry would be buried.

Taylor wondered if he would be there for the burial. Or maybe he would be needing one himself.

So many things he had learned in such a short time, Matt thought. He had learned about Melanie. And about himself. He was learning that the world was a lot more dangerous place than he had ever thought outside of war; that whether you saw them or not, there were often huge sinkholes of depravity and corruption and evil just under your feet, and some time or another they were liable to open up and suck down the poor, innocent good people walking along on the surface of life. Like Larry Wu. That was a lesson he had learned; those were the metaphysics of the last week.

And he had learned just how fluid time was. It did not always flow the same way. Sometimes, like in the duel with the truck on the highway or in fighting the river, seconds seemed to stretch on and on, moving like a great muddy viscuous river. But other times, it jumped in spurts, days and nights moving past so quickly that they were all a jumbled blur. The whole past week had been some weird combination of the two, and try as hard as he could, Matt could not remember any part of it in which time had seemed to move in its normal, stately cadenced way.

All of life was a learning experience, he told himself. *And maybe the greatest learning experience in life is dying, asshole, so you'd better pay attention to what's going on.*

He glanced through the window again toward the couple on the couch, the farmer's daughter and the nerd clone, waiting for them to finish their coital coupling. The couch was vibrating but it still seemed to take a small eternity and the girl seemed to die a thousand noisy small deaths before ending it all with a soul-rending scream. For a few moments, they were so still that Matt wondered if in fact he had misinterpreted what was going on and the girl actually had died.

But then she was sitting up, shoving the young man off her and pulling her shirt back onto her magnificent torso.

"Not bad for a nerd," Matt heard her say.

He too was getting dressed, half-standing, half-crouched, hopping around on one foot while he struggled with his pants.

"Thanks," he said. "And on a scale of one to a hundred, you're a good solid three."

The girl whooped, knocked him over, and pounced on top of him. For a moment, Matt was afraid that he would have to wait through another coupling but then the two pulled themselves apart.

"Time to go," the young man said.

"I like time to come better," the young woman said.

"Is that all you ever think of?"

"No," she said. "During work hours, I think about computers. They *really* turn me on."

They both laughed, finished dressing, and left. Matt waited until five minutes after their footsteps had faded away before letting himself into the building through the front door.

His first stop was the computer lab in the rear of the building. It took his eyes a few moments to adjust to the dim light thrown by the illuminated clock on the wall. Like most such labs, this one was a hybrid—a hygienically clean, total mess. There was no dirt to be seen anywhere, but on the other hand, every available surface was covered with stacks of neatly aligned papers, some of the stacks only an inch or two high, other stacks knee-deep.

Against the wall that divided the lab from the rest of the building was a row of metal cabinets. Most of them held row upon row of ten and twenty gigabyte metal discs. One of them was filled with what looked like the Chrin 210-D's operating manuals.

Matt opened the first manual on the top left, to skim it, but could not. The light was too dim to read by.

He walked to a floor lamp, started to turn the switch, and then stopped. If anyone outside were to see just one lamp on in the lab, it might attract attention by its very peculiarity. He left the lamp alone, walked back to the door and turned on the main light switch. The lights came on with a cold fluorescent sheen and Matt hoped that by being so blatant, he would not attract any unwanted attention.

He went back to the manual, skipping and skimming it quickly. It held no surprises, all factory-issue stuff. The next manual too. He looked out the windows, resting his burning eyes. The sky was no longer black; it had turned a dark gun-metal gray. He probably had a half hour left at best. After that, he would have to expect to be interrupted by the early risers on the morning crew, sneaking in to log some unauthorized computer time.

On the next shelf were row upon row of three-ring binders. Taylor pulled out the first of them and flipped it open.

Bingo.

It was a book of names, addresses, what appeared to be annual salaries and tax deductions, and what were undoubtedly Social Security numbers. The first name in the binder was Aaron, Bradley B.; the last name was Dziewicki, Michael A. The binder next to it contained last names beginning E through J inclusive. The third binder in the row held names starting with K through Q and the fourth binder held last names beginning with the letter R through Z.

He went back to the third book and skimmed through to the page where he would expect to find Fred Kohler's name. It was there.

It took him a moment to remember the other names he had pulled out of the I.R.S. computer a week before. Finally, they came to him. Clyde Stallbarn and Andrew McCabe. They too were in the right places in the books.

For the next few minutes, he spot-checked all four of the ring-leaf binders and when he was done, he sat back with a sigh and a self-congratulatory grin. All the names carried Harker's Furnace addresses, and according to his quick calculations, there were about twenty thousand of them. That squared with what the fat lady at the motel had told him—that each of the three motel owners served as mail drop for about six thousand seven hundred names.

There was no doubt in Matt's mind that he had found the source of whatever it was. The only question was: what the hell was it?

He put the binders back on the shelf and started pulling out other volumes. At first they were harder to decipher. They seemed to be fairly standard spread sheets reporting the updated financial condition of hundreds upon hundreds of small to medium-sized businesses, arranged alphabetically by location. Matt got down the volume that covered the Washington, D.C., area and flipped through it. He recognized at least a dozen of the businesses. They—apparently unlike the Harkers Furnace names—were real.

He stared at the lists and then at the sky outside. It was growing lighter by the moment. He would need more time with these books if they were going to mean anything to him, but he could see no chance of getting to study them. They were too bulky to carry and besides, if he stole them, he would tip his hand to whoever was running the operation.

From the looks of the printouts, it was obvious that the information contained on them had come from the computer. What he really had to do, Matt knew, was somehow to break into the machine and drain its brain.

And right now that was easier said than done.

To begin with, Matt knew, he would have to have the passwords that let him in. He got up and started pacing up and down. Computer operators were notorious for their lax security habits. He was willing to bet a dollar to a doughnut that somewhere in one of the offices, one of the people who worked there had Scotch-taped his passwords either to his computer terminal or to the pull-out tray on his desk. Or else left them in a notebook neatly labelled "Passwords."

It would be risky trying a search this late, he knew, but he had to do it now; he might never again get another chance.

He turned off the lights in the main computer lab, went back out into the corridor, and from there moved down the smaller hallway to his left where the offices were. The doors to the first four offices were closed and locked, but the door to the fifth office pushed open at a touch. There was a small piece of notepaper taped to the pull-out tray of the desk, covered totally with Scotch tape to prevent it from tearing and from coffee spills. A small sign on the desk read "Andrew Nujinsky."

Matt turned on the office light and looked at the note eagerly. At first, it made no sense. Not that it was written in gibberish or even in some foreign language. Instead, it was written in some peculiar hand, with letters that did not quite look normal.

He looked at the strangely shaped letters and swore. He stared at them and they seemed dimly recognizable. *Where have I seen these before?* It took him another twenty seconds or so before the answer came and then it was simple. He had not seen them since he had been a student at Carnegie-Mellon and some of his classmates had prided themselves on their

251

mastery of Tolkien's books about the hobbits and Middle Earth.

The letters were from something Tolkien called the Feanorian alphabet. His memory was flooding back. The alphabet, according to Tolkien, had been in common use during the Third Age of Middle Earth throughout the Westlands. It was nonsense, but the kind of nonsense that computer nerds swallowed whole and memorized in toto, probably just to prove that they could do it.

From a top drawer he took a pen and paper and began to copy the elvish list.

Enough for one night, he told himself when he was done; he replaced the pen, closed the desk, turned off the light, and hurried down the hallway toward the front door.

Just as he neared the front door, it was pulled open from the outside. And in the first flash of surprise, Taylor realized that he did not feel fear. All he felt was anger. Anger that he had come this far and was discovered at the last moment.

And he also experienced a feeling that he had not known since the days in Vietnam: the knowledge that if he had to, he would kill. And ask no questions of himself afterward.

Taylor saw the man before he himself was seen. It was not one of the uniformed guards, come to investigate the lights in the computer headquarters but obviously one of the computer specialists, a young man dressed in trousers that were too short, a jacket that was too long, and a shirt that was incorrectly buttoned at the collar.

There was no turning back and as the young man looked up and saw him, with surprise on his face, Matt growled: "I wish you guys would remember to turn off the lights at night. This getting shipped over here every night to clean up after you turkeys is getting old."

He brushed by the young man. As he reached the door, he remembered something else and spun around.

"And tell everybody else no more with this tape on the front door. What the hell we got security for if you guys tape all the doors open?"

Behind him, the young man grumbled, "Meeting you is one helluva rotten way to start a day, pal," But Matt pretended not to hear him, ripped the piece of adhesive tape from the front door lock, then closed the door behind himself.

Slow. Casual, he told himself, as he strolled off away from the computer lab and toward the road that led up out of the complex. When he was up on top of the hill, able to look down at the old military barracks buildings he turned left, toward the river, hoping for a quicker way back outside the boundary fence than the twisted, tortuous route he had followed the night before.

He moved across a wide hillside meadow and then reached the treeline and kept on walking in the direction of the river, travelling faster now that he was out of sight.

The sun was coming up and the sky was a clear French blue. It was hard to remind himself that only twelve hours earlier he had been in danger of freezing to death in these same woods.

He reached the electrified fence. Beyond it, down a long steep slope, was the river. To the left, the fence ran downhill to where a wide loop in the river seemed to come up to meet it. Matt turned in that direction, walking quickly, keeping his senses alert for any sign of danger.

He had not gone far when he came across what seemed to be a heaven-sent gift. A large, fairly young pine rose up next to the fence and spread a long thick branch out over it onto the other side. The ground on the Installation side, where the pine grew, was higher than that on the other side, so that anyone trying to enter the Installation from outside faced a formidable task. Leaving the Installation, though, would be fairly easy. In a few minutes, Taylor had climbed the tree, inched his way out on the branch, and dropped over the fence onto the ground on the other side.

Safe. Safe.

He had not realized how tense he had been and how much his heart was pounding. He sat down on a tree trunk to rest. And then he heard the sound rushing through the underbrush.

There was no time for anything. No time for thinking. No time for preparation. No time for fear. Matt heard the sound and then before he could react to it, he was sprawling, falling backwards head over heels off his seat, tumbling and rolling, down, down, down a long hill. His back ached—a dull heavy thudding pain—and the arm he had injured yesterday was hit with a sharp, surging tingling pain that raced up and down the limb, seeking out new nerve cells to attack—finding them.

For a split second he lay on his back, wondering what had happened and if it were all over and done with. The sky above him was still the same rich, deep French blue it had been just moments before. The mud beneath him was soft and oddly comforting. An accident of some sort? What had happened?

Then there were more sounds behind him. He tried to twist his head in that direction but before he could, his brain was overwhelmed by new sensations, sensations of a hot putrid stench.

Fucking fool. He must have closed his eyes a moment before while he was sitting on that log because now he knew where the stench and the attack had come from. A huge, drooling dog face was rushing toward him, its jaws wide agape and strange strangled sounds coming from its throat.

Instinctively, he twisted his neck aside. The effort cost him in sharp pangs of pain that surged all through his body, and then worsened as he threw up his wounded left arm to protect himself. The dog's jaws missed his throat but they clamped down instead on the arm. They clamped and they held, as the dark beast shook its whole body, trying through main force to rip the arm loose from Taylor's body. Matt yelled out in agony.

The sound must have surprised the animal because for just a fraction of a second it loosened its grip on his arm and when it did, Matt was able to pull free. The freedom lasted but an instant, then the animal was back on the attack, trying again for his throat. There was no other choice—Taylor thrust the already mangled arm between the creature's jaws and endured in as much silence as possible the biting of his flesh through the thin sleeves of his jacket.

The pain turned his world purple and black and in some strange way, cleared his mind. Afterward he would remember the moment as a sort of catharsis. *No more,* he thought. *No more! No more! No more!* And yet, it was not a thought; it was more like a scream, a scream in his mind, but it was not just in his mind—it was in all of him, all through him, in every single cell of his body.

He used his bleeding arm as a lever, took his other hand and pushed it backwards until the creature was bent in a reverse half-circle and then, Matt buried his teeth in the animal's throat.

It did no good. Through centuries, through the millenia of civilization, man's teeth had degenerated from being powerful offensive weapons into something suitable only for courtship and quiche. But the counterattack surprised the dog which fought back, writhing and turning and spinning, now letting go of Matt's arm, now biting it again with ever-increasing fury. The animal fought not just with its teeth. It used its claws as well, raking and tearing Matt's body with its razor-nailed feet.

Man and animal rolled and twisted in the mud of the previous night's snow, Matt losing blood and strength, the animal gaining everything. They rolled out of the mud and onto the rocks and Matt had no chance to think. There was only instinct left.

He grabbed and groped and came up with a fist-sized rock in his hand. He brought the stone up and smashed the animal in the face with it, in the spot just above its muzzle and right between the eyes. He smashed it a second time, then a third and a fourth. The creature stopped its attack, moving to disengage in a stunned, stupefied manner. Matt did not stop his attack. He smashed the animal in the face again, and this time it did not try to move, neither to attack nor to retreat. Matt smashed it again, and the animal looked at him plaintively and then began to convulse in its hindquarters. Matt hammered it again and again, and the creature went down.

Matt backed away. Somewhere, far away, he thought he could hear someone calling the dog. If it was true, he had no intention of staying around to greet him.

He looked down on the animal with a mixture of respect and hate. The animal was whimpering now, its flanks heaving, blood trickling from its mouth and nose.

Matt got up and started walking slowly down the hill toward the river. He felt weak, dizzy, disoriented. Blood oozed from his mangled arm but he was too weak to care about it. Every thought was an effort, every step an agony. It took him far too long to move, Matt knew. He was bound to be found out and captured and then ... and then what? Killed? Like Larry Wu had been killed? Imprisoned? He did not know and he was too tired to care very much. He kept moving toward the river.

The first time the dog attacked him, it had come at him silently; the second time it was all noise and fury.

Matt had almost reached the final downslope to the riverbank. Above him on the hillside, he could hear at least two men's voices calling to one another, sounding worried, sounding angry.

Matt ran; he had come to one of those bare patches amid the trees and skirted it to the left in order to try to stay hidden. Near the treeline, next to the bare patch of ground, was a large laurel slip, thirty yards wide and half that across. He could see that it was an old slip, its individual trunks closely packed, their branches forming a densely tangled and low-hanging mass.

Just as he was coming parallel to the slip, he heard the unmistakable deep-throated growl of a dog about to attack. He glanced back over his shoulder. It couldn't be. The animal was too big. It was thigh-high, thick, and long. Its coat was a sleek and shiny mosaic of browns and blacks and white hairs that undulated smoothly over its powerful muscles.

He looked at the animal as it growled again deep in its throat and he thought, *This animal can do nothing to hurt me.* The thought surprised him but then he thought, *I've been through so much so far and there's no way he can hurt me.* Then the shock came. Could it be the same animal? *I killed it. I killed it with a rock back up on the hill.* And yet it was the same dog. Of that, he was certain.

The animal had stopped; blood ran from its nose and mouth, but it seemed to grin, seemed to know what he had been thinking. Matt's confidence wavered and then sank.

His arm brushed up against his belt and then he remembered the pistol. He had had it with him all along. The dog growled again and lowered itself into a pouncing position unusual for a dog, more like some large cat. Matt took the gun from his waistband and flicked the safety off.

He was ready, Matt thought. He just hoped that the gun had not been damaged by all that it and he had been through in the past eighteen hours; he hoped that the ammunition hadn't been ruined by its immersion in the river.

He was ready to fire. And then he heard two more men's voices, closer than the first two.

He could not fire. He was still too far from the river, a hundred yards away, and could not get there if the guards up on the hill knew where to find him. He was too weak and too tired and too injured to move quickly enough to escape. That meant no gun. That meant he would have to move quietly, without disturbing the sounds of the woods. That meant he would have to face the dog again with his hands.

He began backing away from the dog, moving into the laurel slip. The animal took a couple of small steps forward, changing

257

the sound in its throat as it went, as if to tell Matt that whatever game he wanted to play, in the end the dog was the superior creature and would win.

Matt stepped back again and again, his gun always carefully held out in front of him, ready for use if it finally came down to that. There was one dog and four guards. He had enough bullets for all of them if it came to that.

The dog kept following him.

Matt had reached the farthest point into the slip that he could go and still stay on his feet. The dog had followed, never allowing the distance between them to grow by more than an inch or two.

This was where it would end, Matt told himself. Here in the laurel slip, away from the eyes of any men. *Just a boy and his dog.*

He bent over and picked up a handful of earth and dead, rotting rhododendron leaves and threw them in the dog's face. The dog growled more and showed more teeth. Matt did it again, a second time and a third. The fourth time, the dog came at him.

He had steeled himself for the dog's attack but he had underestimated its strength and its leap sent him sprawling onto his back. He felt the gun fly from his hand.

The fight was a near-repeat of the first one, but this time both animal and man had less room in which to maneuver. Somehow though, Matt ended up briefly on top of the dog, his legs pinning the animal to the ground and his arms stretching the creature's neck and spine back—back almost to the snapping point. It was no use. He was not strong enough. His burst of adrenalin-induced energy had long since passed and he was tiring quickly.

It was then that he saw the lost gun. It was his last chance. But it was a dozen feet away, and to get it he would have to set the dog free and once he had done that ... well, once he had done that he had better be damn sure that he got the gun quickly and used it.

He rolled the dog over onto the side so that he was as close as he could get to the weapon. He held on and held on, willing his arms to let go of the beast, but his body would not obey his mind.

Let go, he told himself one last time, and this time he let go. The dog thrashed around and pulled itself free and stood still for a moment, bewildered by its sudden freedom.

Matt scrambled on elbows and knees, clawing desperately toward the gun. The laurel slip seemed to conspire against him, its trunks springing up suddenly, unexpectedly, blocking his path. The branches pulled and tore at his back and his clothes. And then there was the dog again.

It came at him with a renewed fury, but the same branches and trunks and tendrils that had impeded Matt's progress did the same to the dog. It attacked, but could not quite get to the man, and Matt kept kicking it away as he struggled toward the gun.

Finally, he had the cold hard steel in his hand. Now he had to will himself to turn over on his back and let the dog come up over him. He had to do it that way. He had to get the dog right on top of him so that he could fire the bullet and use the dog's own body to muffle the sound of the shot.

He started to turn over but could not. He could feel the dog tearing again at his legs and the thought of what lay in store for him when he turned to face the creature almost paralyzed him. He counted slowly to five, then shoved himself over on his back, baring his throat to the kill-crazy animal.

The dog was on him. Its open jaws reached for his throat and Matt carefully moved the gun up under the dog's throat and pulled the trigger. The dog stopped for an instant—as though surprised by the muffled sound—and then renewed the attack. Matt pulled the trigger again.

Finally, the animal let go of Taylor. It let go its bladder and bowels in practically the same moment. Then it died on top of him, oozing blood and gore and waste products all over him.

Matt did not care. He was alive. He lay there for a moment rejoicing in that fact, trying to rebuild enough energy to pull himself out from under the dead animal.

He could hear the voices of the four men coming nearer. He pulled himself out from under the dog and deeper into the laurel slip. Then, as an afterthought, he grabbed one of the dog's paws and pulled the animal in after him, out of sight.

He waited. After awhile, the men's voices went away, cursing the dog. Taylor waited till he could hear them no longer.

Slowly, Matt worked his way out of the laurel patch and quickly covered the distance down to the river. He stood on the bank for a while, trying to figure out where he was. His best guess was that he was a half mile farther upstream from where he had come ashore the day before.

He headed downstream, staying on the riverbank. To his disgust, he saw that it was not a difficult walk at all and all the heroics of yesterday with the canoe were unnecessary. He could just have walked to the Installation's fence.

He saw his car up ahead. He took the keys out from under the floor mat and started the engine. After a few minutes, he turned on the heater to warm himself.

From the glove compartment, he took a pencil and an old credit card receipt and wrote a note to the owner of the canoe, telling him to contact Judge Stevens for reimbursement. He planned to put the note under the cottage's front door.

But the weariness overtook him.

First, he would sleep for a few minutes. Just close his eyes.

He was awakened by a knocking on the window.

His hand flew to the gun in his belt and aimed it at the window, even as he was turning, even as he saw O'Leary standing there, a big smile creasing his black face.

Matt sighed, dropped the gun on the seat, and rolled down the window.

"Nice to see you, Taylor," O'Leary said with a grin. "The woods are beautiful this time of year, aren't they?"

He stopped talking for a moment and wrinkled his nose.

Then he said, "By the way, you really ought to do something about your personal hygiene."

CHAPTER TWENTY-EIGHT

"I'd like to see you explain this one to the rent-a-car company," O'Leary said.

"What?" said Matt.

"You're messing all over their nice new car."

Matt looked down. A tiny rivulet of blood was seeping through his jacket sleeve, oozing down onto the car's seat, and there spreading out into an ever-widening stain.

"I'm bleeding," Matt said. It seemed to come as a complete surprise to him.

"You're right," O'Leary said blandly. He slowed the car. "You want to stop for a minute? Get out and walk around a bit? Fresh air might help."

Matt nodded. He tried to speak but couldn't. He could feel his throat clogging up with vomit. O'Leary hurriedly pulled the car to the side of the road and Taylor jerked open the door. He was almost fast enough. He could feel it coming, taste its rancidness in his mouth. He tried to hold it in, fighting back the indignity of it, but did not succeed, and sprayed the half-open car door and the front of himself with the egesis.

"I'm sorry," he said. "Really sorry."

And then the world went dark on him.

For a long while, he was faintly aware of movement of curves being whooshed around, hills and dips being taken at too-high speeds, at hands pulling and tugging at him.

He woke slowly, consciousness coming back before sight. He could feel more hands on him, cool hands, strong hands, feminine hands. He tried to sit up and new waves of nausea swept over him and he went down into the blackness again. He woke one more time and thought, *This has to stop happening, this coming back to consciousness in places I don't recognize.*

"Where am I? Who's there?"

"It's okay, sweetcakes," O'Leary's voice said. "You just sissied up on me and I had to take you somewhere to get patched up."

Matt smiled a little; O'Leary's voice was oddly reassuring. This time he was able to keep his eyes open and to sit up. He was back in his old room, the room he had grown up in at the Judge's house.

"What time is it?" he asked.

O'Leary glanced at his watch. "A little after one. Take it easy. Plenty of time before we have to get going."

There was a soft knock on the door and when O'Leary went to answer it, Matt closed his eyes for a few moments. He opened them when he felt a woman's hand touching his.

"We were worried about you," Lauren said.

"We?" He looked around. O'Leary had left the room.

"All of us. Me, the Judge, Billy. Mike, my husband." She paused. "My ex-husband. He was the one responsible for finding you."

"How's that?"

"When no one saw you last night, we got worried. So I called Mike. The hospital just released him. He called some friends of his at the state police barracks and had them start an unofficial search for the car. Out near the Installation."

Matt nodded. He got out of bed, shakily, and noticed for the first time that he was naked except for a too-short hospital gown. Lauren did not seem to notice.

"And O'Leary? How does he fit in?" Matt asked.

"Katie Wu called yesterday. She was looking for you. She said a friend of hers would be coming in last night. And then O'Leary arrived. Anyway, a friend of Mike's spotted the car this morning." She stopped talking and bit her lower lip. "Don't do that again. Please. Don't come back into my life and then just disappear like that. I was afraid you were dead."

Matt squeezed her hand and waited. After a moment, she cleared her throat, sat up a little straighter, and removed her hand from his.

"So this morning, O'Leary went out to the cottage on the river and waited for you to come back. We had decided that if we hadn't heard from you by noon, that Mike and Billy and O'Leary would go in after you."

Taylor was surprised. It had been years since he had felt that anyone, except Larry, had cared enough about him to put themselves at risk over him.

For the first time since he had awakened, Matt looked down at his arm and saw it was neatly bandaged.

"Good job," he said, smiling at Lauren.

"A friend did it. And pumped you full of antibiotics and painkillers and that sort of thing."

"Doctor?"

"A pediatrician. He was worried about what look like bites and claw marks. He asked me if it was a rabid animal."

"No," Matt said. "A guard dog. I'm safe."

They ate lunch with the Judge and O'Leary in the main dining room. Everyone seemed reluctant to ask him what he had found out at the Installation, and for his part, Matt was just as happy about that. He needed time to sort things out and to figure it out for himself.

But as Maggie, the Judge's housekeeper, was serving coffee, Matt called the Judge aside.

"Judge, that motel up at Harker's Furnace. The woman up there had a notebook filed with names of people she got mail for at the Installation. Do you think Billy O'Baal can go up and try to get it from her?"

"Don't see why not," the Judge said. He went to a telephone in the hall while Matt went back into the dining room.

Later, after they had finished their coffee, O'Leary looked at him and said, "Well, it's up to you."

"What's up to me?"

"Going back," O'Leary said. "The funeral's tomorrow."

Matt had forgotten.

"I'll be ready in a half hour," he said.

Lauren dropped her napkin and hurried from the room.

"What's the matter with her?" Matt asked.

"Can't you see, you ignorant young pup?" the Judge said.

Matt felt himself bristling, but let it go when the Judge added, "She's worried about you. She doesn't want you to go."

"I've got to," Matt said.

"We all know that. But it doesn't make it any easier," Stevens said.

They had gotten his suitcase from the hotel, and up in his bedroom he dressed in fresh clothes and then repacked the bag slowly. He saw Larry Wu's paperback book on Chinese painting and stuck it into his jacket pocket. Someday, he would read it, he told himself. It was an obligation now.

Lauren came in and stood just inside the doorway.

"Don't be upset," he said, walking toward her.

She came forward into his arms.

"I was going to go back with you, Matt. But I can't. It's Mike. He spent all night and most of the morning on the road looking for you, and it took more out of him than he thought it would. He's in pretty bad shape today, and I should be here."

"I understand," Matt said. "He must be some kind of man."

"He is. The perfect man for just about any woman. Except me."

* * *

Maggie met him on the stairway, yanked the suitcase from his hand, and insisted on lugging it down and loading it into O'Leary's car herself. Matt watched as she walked away, tall, tight, trim, and he felt good for the Judge. When you were in your seventies, Maggie was probably the perfect person to have around to share your house. And your bed.

He found the Judge in his small study just hanging up the telephone.

"That was Billy. Bad news," the Judge said.

"Oh?"

"Those records out at the Dew Drop ... they were stolen night before last. And the other two motels hadn't kept any records. Sorry, Matt."

"Somehow I expected it. Listen, thank Billy for me, will you, Judge? I appreciate everything he's done for me."

The Judge smiled. "You've got a fan there, Matt. Somehow he's got this idea that you saved his life the other day when that guy cold-cocked him with the rifle."

"Well, that's not so. But I'll see him when I get back."

For a moment, the two men faced each other awkwardly across the room. Then the Judge rose, came and put his arms around the taller Matt.

"Come back, Matt. Come back for good. We want you here."

Matt hugged him back.

"When I'm done, Judge. I've got to go."

Later, driving in the car, O'Leary said, "That Lauren? She used to be your main squeeze?"

"How is it you law enforcement types have this absolute genius for trivializing everything?" Matt asked.

"That means yes?"

"Yeah."

"What kind of moron gives up a lady like that for a two-bit chippie like your wife?"

Matt seemed to think about his answer very carefully.

266

"A two-bit moron?" he finally said.

O'Leary grunted his agreement.

"Here's I-79 up ahead," Matt said. It had grown dark, and again a light powdery snow had started to fall, making driving difficult. They would have to turn south on the Interstate to get to Pittsburgh and their guaranteed safe flight.

"We're not going that way," O'Leary said.

Matt suddenly came alert. He shifted back to the far corner of the passenger's seat, reached for his pocket, then remembered he had not seen his gun since he had passed out in the car after escaping from the Installation.

"Nervous?" O'Leary said.

"Why should I be?"

"Maybe even scared, just a little. Like maybe I'm not what I say I am. And maybe you're in deep trouble being here with me?"

Matt looked at him, then nodded. "Maybe a little," he admitted, and O'Leary laughed.

"Don't worry, my friend. I'm your buddy and I'm going to see that you come out of this whole thing all right, or I'll die trying."

"Then why'd you pass up I-79?" Matt asked.

"Because we're going to Cleveland," O'Leary said.

"Cleveland?"

"Do I hear an echo in this car?" O'Leary said. "Yes. To Cleveland. The Best Location in the Nation. Alias, the Mistake on the Lake. We're going to fly from there."

"Why?"

"Come on, son. Even a tax man ought to be able to figure that one out."

"Yeah," Matt said. He knew what it meant. Too many people knew about his travel plans and he was still in danger. And he still didn't know why.

It was easier in Vietnam. There he had known who the enemy was and who his friends were. Action was easy, he thought, when those elements were in place. Now he could not understand the cast of characters at all. Did he have a friend in all this? Was there anyone he could trust?

He looked again at O'Leary, hunched forward over the wall, pushing the car at too fast a speed through the misty snow.

And he decided to tell him everything.

It all spilled from him. The sudden appearance of Gianetti and Polonowski in Iron City. Their following him. The assault on Billy O'Baal near the Installation and the intervention of the mysterious Angela Fox. How the two FBI men knew about his flight plans, and how he had overheard them talking about something that just might be the killing of Matt Taylor. His trip to the Installation and what he had found there. Billy O'Baal's finding out a few hours before that the motel owner's records had been stolen.

Then he stopped and O'Leary said, "We could have used those records. I wonder who nipped them?"

"Do you have to ask?" Matt said. "Obviously your two friends from the FBI. How the hell did they know I was up here when you ripped their tracker out of my car?"

O'Leary shrugged. "Got to be a leak some place," he said.

"That's reassuring. I think the bastards want to kill me, and you're telling me they've got a line into my movements."

"I don't think so," the black man said. "I think maybe they shoot off their mouth a lot, but I don't think they're the bad guys."

"They're doing a pretty good job of convincing me that they are," Matt said. "And don't forget, they gave me that crap about Larry Wu being a traitor. These bastards aren't on the level."

"Time will tell," O'Leary said.

"Yeah. Time and my murder."

"I'm hoping it won't come to that. It'd look bad on my record," O'Leary said. "I'm pissed about those names at the motel though. I could have used them."

"Maybe I can still get them," Matt said.

"How do you do that?" O'Leary asked.

"If I can get into the computer at the Installation. Maybe they're there. And they might still be in the computers at the I.R.S."

"Better forget that one," O'Leary said.

"What do you mean?"

"Last Monday, my boss sent me over to the I.R.S. to dredge out all those Harker's Furnace returns?"

"Yeah?"

"They all disappeared. There's not a single return in the whole I.R.S. system with a Harker's Furnace address. Just plumb disappeared."

CHAPTER TWENTY-NINE

The flight from Cleveland was delayed by the bad weather, and O'Leary and Taylor spent the time sitting in the airport's dismal cocktail lounge knocking down Scotches, for Matt, and beer for O'Leary.

"You drink too much, boy," O'Leary told Matt after he had ordered his fourth Scotch.

"Runs in the family," Matt said. "My father was a well-known boozer in Iron City. I always figured that was the reason for the accident that killed my folks."

"How old were you then?"

"Ten," Matt said.

"It's tough at that age, losing your family."

"Tough at any age," Matt said.

"Yeah, but not as tough as ten," O'Leary insisted. "When you're younger, you're too young to remember much and it's easy to forget. And when you're older, you're almost grown, so you're going to be on your own soon anyway. But ten years old, you're right in the middle. The Judge raise you?"

Matt nodded.

"There's some bad wood between you two," O'Leary said. "What is it?"

"I don't know," Matt said. "He raised me and I think when I was a kid I figured if he didn't take me in, I would have gone to a real family with a mother and father and everything. And then when I got older, I decided the Judge was trying too hard to be like my father. He wanted me to do this, to do that, study this, go there, marry here ... I don't know, I guess I'm too much like my father so I did everything the opposite way. When I got married, the Judge and I drifted apart. I guess he's disappointed in me."

"He's a lot like you," O'Leary said.

"I don't see it," Matt said.

"Stubborn, wants his own way, bossy ... sound like anybody you know?" O'Leary asked.

"I don't recognize myself in that description at all," Matt said and O'Leary laughed.

Since deciding to take O'Leary into his confidence, Matt had found a lot to commend in the FBI man. He was smart and he had a sense of humor. And why shouldn't he, Matt thought. If the black man had been a dummy, a dullard, Katie Wu wouldn't have had anything to do with him.

At forty-three, O'Leary was six years older than Matt. His mother had been black, his father white: and both his parents had skipped when he was only a few years old. He had been raised by Italian neighbors. Before joining the FBI, he had been a Philadelphia policeman but, he said, it was a racist city, and there was no way a black man was going to rise in the police ranks.

When he was assigned to the anti-crime Strike Force 73, he drew Philadelphia because of his past association with the city.

"It must be frustrating work," Matt said while they were on the plane.

"Why do you say that?"

Matt shrugged. "It seems like the mob is eternal in America," he said. "So you put a couple of guys away and a dozen more jump up to take their places. They're like weeds, aren't they?"

"When you weed a garden, you've got to pull them all out," O'Leary said. "We've put a hurting on them in Chicago, in

New York. Mob's in trouble. But that damned Zorelli in Philly just somehow hangs on like a toothache. That's why our interest in you, boy. If Zorelli wants you dead, we want you alive, until we find out why he's after you."

"And after that?" Matt asked with a sour grin.

"We'll buy you a putty nose and eyeglasses and a plastic mustache and tell you to move to Canada and open a candy store," O'Leary said.

"Thrilling prospect."

"What's the matter? You want to live forever?"

"No. But I thought I'd try a few more years anyway," Matt said.

"We'll see what we can do."

A warm, gentle spring rain was falling when their flight set down at Dulles after midnight. Katie Wu met them at the gate and hugged each of them, O'Leary with noticeably more fervor.

The events of the last week had left their marks on her face, Matt thought. There were tension lines alongside her eyes that he had never seen before, and she seemed to have a sort of tightly sprung nervous energy that did not match her normal soft, laid-back personality.

"I'm sorry about it all, Katie," Matt told her. "How are you holding up?"

They were walking from the terminal. Katie said, "You know, Matt, once I got annoyed at you because I asked you how you liked working in the I.R.S., and you said the place was like a Chinese fire drill. Just another racist round-eye."

"I remember," he said.

"Hold on," O'Leary said. "If I knew he was a racist, I wouldn't waste my time trying to keep him alive."

Katie ignored him. "Anyway," she told Matt, "now I know what you mean. Our *house* is a Chinese fire drill. The family is in from San Francisco and they wander around the place all day long, screaming at each other in Mandarin. One puts

272

something down, the other one picks it up, then they yell at each other. It's a zoo." She flicked an imaginary cigar in a W.C. Fields impersonation: "By and large, I'd rather be in Philadelphia."

Matt shook his head. "No, you wouldn't," he said. "Not Philadelphia."

As he looked down and spoke to Katie, he noticed that O'Leary's eyes were surreptitiously scanning the passenger terminal and he thought, *Great welcome home. With an FBI bodyguard who's worried about my getting murdered.*

O'Leary stashed them in the coffee shop while he went to use the telephone across the terminal. Softly, he told Matt, "Stay awake, old buddy."

He sat facing Katie across the scarred formica-topped table and took her hands in his.

"I'm really sorry, Katie. I would have given anything for it not to happen. You know that."

"I know, Matt. You did all you could."

He shook his head. He could see O'Leary watching them from an open telephone booth in the middle of the terminal floor. "Not until I get the bastards responsible, Katie. Not until then." And then there didn't seem to be much more to say.

O'Leary came back before their coffee arrived.

"Come on," he told Matt. "My boss wants to see you now," and he took Katie's arm and led them toward the terminal exit.

The ride into town in Katie's big Lincoln Continental was surprisingly slow, and the conversation was desultory until Katie, following O'Leary's directions, let them off at the entrance to the VIP area attached to the Executive Office building near the White House.

As Matt got out of the car, Katie said, "You'll come to the funeral tomorrow?"

Matt nodded and realized he had not even thought about where he would spend the night.

"I'll be at your house in the morning," he said.

"Okay," she said. "I need you there, Matt."

"I know." He squeezed her hand and, carrying his suitcase, walked off after O'Leary.

To get into the building, they had to pass through two separate checkpoints, at the second of which Matt was photographed and a special temporary pass prepared for his use.

Walking away, he let out a low whistle.

"Damn, you think with all this rigamarole, we were going to have a midnight snack with the President," he said.

"Why not?" O'Leary said. "It's not every day he gets a chance to meet a real American hero who's laid his life on the line in the never-ending war against crime."

"Stuff it, O'Leary," Matt said.

They took a self-service elevator to the top floor and O'Leary led the way into a surprisingly barren-looking suite of offices. A young man was waiting for them at the receptionist's desk. He looked like a pro football linebacker; there was an automatic pistol on the desktop next to his right hand.

"The man's waiting for you," he told O'Leary, who nodded and let Matt into an inner office.

The office was a mess. It stank of stale cigar and cigarette smoke. Stacks of paper were piled high on every flat surface, including most of the uncarpeted floor. The furniture looked like World War II surplus.

A man was sitting behind the large desk at the end of the room, working in the glow of a single desk-mounted banker's lamp. At first, Matt thought he looked like a gnome. He was short and round and he did not have to stand up for Matt to tell there was an unhealthy load of fat around his middle. His hair was black, curly, mussed-up and thinning on top, both front and back. His face was little better: the eyes were squinting and watery; there was little chin; and his nose looked as if it should be fronting some gigantic, malevolent bird of prey.

He looked up as they entered, grunted, and looked back down at the papers before him.

Matt put down his suitcase and followed O'Leary to the desk. The FBI man said, "Matt, this paragon of politeness is my boss,

Ari Cohen. I can already tell he likes you. If he didn't like you, he would have turned the desk light off."

Cohen looked up, then rose, and Matt extended his hand. For just a brief moment, Cohen studied him, almost as if trying to decide whether or not to shake hands. Finally, he extended his hand. Matt noticed that there were Band-aids on two of his fingers. He was surprised at the strength of Cohen's handshake.

As O'Leary looked around and found two folding metal chairs in a corner, Cohen picked up two cardboard bakery boxes from a table behind him and shoved them across the desk.

"Danish on the left, doughnuts on the right," he said. "Help yourself. There's coffee, too, but no cream. I'm trying to cut down on the calories, keep my weight under control. I was starting to get a little chunky there for a while, isn't that so, Mr. O'Leary?"

Matt sat down in front of the desk as O'Leary answered, "I've always regarded you as a striking figure of a man, Ari."

The FBI man walked across the room and poured two cups of coffee from an oversized urn.

As he reached for a piece of Danish, Matt looked at Cohen's desk clock. Next to it was a picture of two of the most beautiful women he had ever seen. One looked to be in her late thirties; the younger one looked the way the other must have looked when she was in high school.

Matt leaned back; he had not realized he was so hungry. Cohen leaned across the desk and said, "I'm going to tell you a story, Taylor. I tell it to everybody I want on our team.

"You may know that I hold this job by special request of the President, and you know about his wife and kid being blown up by the druggies. It's all part of the background."

He picked up the picture of the two women on his desk.

"This was taken five years ago," he said. His voice seemed to lose all its animation. "A year after it was taken, my wife was dead. Cancer. A hell of a way to go. But you can't blame anybody for that. Six months after that, my daughter was worse than dead and there's lots of people to blame for that."

275

He put the picture down and stared at it for a moment, then seemed to make a determined effort to look away.

"I kind of cut myself off from her when my wife died," he said. "I was selfish and stupid and self-pitying, and my daughter was only seventeen. She needed somebody to help with her pain and I wasn't there. Drugs were."

He looked across the desk at Matt and seemed slightly embarrassed.

"Look," he said. "This whole damn story is maudlin and melodramatic and all the rest of that crap. But it doesn't matter. Life is maudlin and melodramatic and often crap."

He stopped talking and took a long time to light a cigarette.

"Anyway, I'll make a long story short. She ran away, she got hooked on heroin. She became the worst sort of sleazy whore you can imagine. It took me almost two years to find her and get her back. She's still not well, but she's improving all the time. At least that's what I tell myself. That's how I got into this job."

"Who did it?" Matt asked. "Who was responsible?"

"Besides me?" Cohen asked as he stubbed out the cigarette. When Matt did not respond, he said, "I was a federal prosecutor in south Jersey, just across from Philadelphia. That's Carlos Zorelli's turf and I was stepping on his toes. When he found out my girl was into drugs, he turned her into a personal project. I'm going to get that man if it's the last thing I do. So help me God. And that's where you come in, young fellow."

"I was wondering," Matt said.

He heard a soft sound from alongside him and glanced at O'Leary. The FBI man was asleep and snoring softly.

Cohen said, "Let him sleep. He's heard my lecture before, and I think you've kept him on the go for a couple of days. Our problem with Zorelli is that he's the smartest of the guinea goons. We've put them away in New York, in Chicago, in Boston. But we've drawn a blank on Zorelli. He's just as active, just as dirty as he ever was, but we can't find his money. He's been too smart, and we don't know how he's laundering his profits. Now you and your friend ... what was his name ... ?"

"Larry Wu," Matt said.

"You and he stumbled onto some strange tax returns and right after that, Zorelli's men try to kill both of you. That makes you my number one priority. You know those returns have vanished from the I.R.S. computers?"

Matt nodded toward O'Leary. "He told me. How could that have happened?"

"We were hoping you could tell us. You're the big I.R.S. computer expert," Cohen said.

"Do you think someone at the Service deep-sixed them?"

"Well, it's a working hypothesis," Cohen admitted, "but I don't like to think somebody at the I.R.S. is involved in something rotten. Christ, it's bad enough you people rob us blind on taxes, without being criminals too. Anyway, are you going to help us?"

"If it helps nail Larry's killers, you got it."

"Good. Now start at the beginning. And leave nothing out."

Matt was getting tired of telling the story, but he did it again. The telling and retelling and questioning went on for almost two hours, during which time O'Leary drifted in and out of sleep. Finally Matt was done. He got up and poured himself another cup of coffee.

"What do you think is going on in Harker's Furnace?" he asked Cohen.

"I hoped you could tell me," the federal attorney said.

"Something dirty. I'm sure of it," Matt said. "Why don't you just get a subpoena and bust into the place?"

"We don't have enough possible cause yet to get a subpoena. And if we did, with their security up there, they might just shit-can everything before we ever got inside the gate. Maybe, with you sneaking around up there, they've hidden everything all ready."

"I don't think so," Matt said.

"Why not?"

277

"First of all, I don't know if anyone knew I was there."

"What about the dead dog?"

"That happened outside the security fence. They may think it was just killed by a hunter passing by. And that's if they find it. I hid the body pretty well."

"Okay. So the records are still there," Cohen said.

"Larry got into that Installation computer somehow," Matt said. "I think I can too."

"And what do you think you could find?" Cohen asked.

Matt felt a tinge of annoyance at what he thought was the man's denseness.

"Dammit, I think you can find the names of twenty thousand or so people who *may* be taxpayers, but don't seem to exist. Who the hell are they? What are they doing? I think you can find a list of a lot of businesses and maybe, just maybe, they all belong to Zorelli. And maybe I can find out what the fuck is going on that's worth my friend getting killed."

"Good," Cohen said blandly. "I just wanted to hear you say it. Just so you know what you're looking for. Welcome aboard."

"You know I was being considered for that new anti-crime task force that's being set up?" Matt said. "How is your work going to coincide with theirs?"

"First of all, Matt, I'm not your usual bureaucrat. I'm not interested in building an empire, cutting out my own little piece of government turf that no one but me can step on. No, I want to tear down an empire. Zorelli's. And anything that'll help do that, well, I'm in favor of. Technically, our Strike Force is going to be absorbed into the new agency—if it gets by the Senate hearings next week and gets created. We won't have any trouble, at least not from this end. I just want Zorelli away."

He paused as O'Leary woke up again with a start, shook his head, and stared around the room as if wondering where he was.

"Welcome back," Cohen said.

"Did I miss anything?"

"Nothing you haven't heard before," Cohen said.

Matt said, "I've got to ask you about these two FBI guys. Gianetti and Polonowski. Is there a chance that they're on the wrong side?"

"Back to them, I see," O'Leary said.

"You slough them off, but I can't. From that horseshit story about Larry being involved with spies, and then following me around, and keeping tabs on my wife, and talking like they planned to kill me ... if I had to pick a leak in this place, it'd be them."

Cohen sighed and looked at O'Leary. "What are these guys up to?" he asked.

"I don't know," O'Leary said. "I just think they're blowhards."

"Well, I'll check them out," Cohen said.

"What do you want me to do?" Matt asked.

"Find yourself a nice quiet computer somewhere and see if you can find out what's going on." He laughed sharply. "We're asking you a lot for a civilian. Your ass may be on the line. But you're the only game in town; the only guy who knows anything about computers that I trust."

"You must have your own computer people with the Strike Force," Matt said.

"Sure. And maybe in twenty years, they can figure out how the I.R.S. system works. Sorry, Matt, you're the guy on the inside. I've got to use you. If you want to sign on."

"I already did," Matt said.

The intercom on Cohen's desk buzzed and he picked up the telephone. He listened for a few moments and then spoke:

"Now's as good a time as any, sir," he said.

He hung up the phone and said to O'Leary and Taylor, "We've got lots of work to do. Matt, I'm glad to have you with us. I'll arrange for a leave of absence from the I.R.S., pay and bullshit we'll straighten out later."

He walked them both to the door. Just as they reached it, there was a peremptory knock and it swung open. The man who entered was every inch the aristocrat: tall and lean, with a full head of wavy white hair, and piercing blue eyes. It was a face Matt knew well.

"Ah, Ari," the newcomer said. "I seemed to have rushed things a bit. Sorry to be so rude."

"No problem, Charlie," Cohen said. "I've just finished recruiting the newest member of our Zorelli project."

"Oh?"

"Sorry. Forgetting my manners. Charlie, this is Matt Taylor, the new man. You remember O'Leary, of course."

"Of course," the other man said.

"Matt, I assume you recognize my favorite vice president of the United States, Charles Garner Barkley," Cohen said.

"Mr. Vice President," Matt said.

Barkley extended his hand. "Good to meet you. Welcome aboard."

"Thank you," Matt said.

"Do you know anything about government?" the vice president asked.

"A little," Matt answered.

"Well, here's all the rest you need to know," Barkley said. "Most people in government are full of wind and dishwater and you can't trust them out of your sight. This guy's the exception." He clapped a hand on Ari Cohen's shoulder. "The one man I know whose word you can put in the bank and watch it draw interest. You'll have fun here ... Taylor, is it?"

"Yes, Sir. Matt Taylor."

"Nice to have you with us."

O'Leary took one of the staff cars when they left the Executive Office building parking lot. Matt had to turn in his identification pass to the guard at the gate.

"The funeral's only a few hours from now," O'Leary said. "You want to stay at my place or you want to go home?"

"No to both. I'd just as soon get a hotel room until I figure out what I'm going to do, and how I'm going to do it."

"Any place special?"

"Just any place nearby," Matt said. "By the way, I didn't know you were such a big operator. Vice President, all of that."

O'Leary held up one hand with his middle and index finger overlapped. "Me and Charlie are just like that," he said. "The day I didn't marry his virgin blond daughter was just one of the saddest days of his life."

He looked at Taylor. "And if you believe that, there's always the Brooklyn Bridge for sale."

He dropped Taylor at a modest-looking hotel—perhaps three years away from being considered seedy—only a dozen blocks from Ari Cohen's office. He waited outside while Matt talked to the desk clerk to make sure there was a vacancy. When Matt came back outside, O'Leary said, "Should I pick you up in the morning to go to Katie's?"

"No, I'll cab it," Matt said.

"Okay. You still got that gun I gave you?" O'Leary asked.

"No. I left it back in Iron City."

O'Leary grinned. "I know. Here it is, dummy." He handed it through the open window to Matt who stuck it into his waistband.

"Thanks."

"Be careful. I don't like double funerals," O'Leary said as he drove away.

Matt stood under the shower in the clean bathroom of his small but neat room, and for the first time in almost two weeks felt as if things made some sense.

He knew now that he was on the right side with Ari Cohen's Strike Force, and that he had been correct to trust O'Leary.

Mysteries remained, but they were mysteries he could help solve. What was going on at the Installation? And what did the Harker's Furnace tax returns mean?

But the lines were drawn. On one side was Carlos Zorelli, the Mafia boss of Philadelphia, and all that he stood for. And on the other side was Matt Taylor with O'Leary and Cohen and even the President and Vice President of the United States. The good guys.

He had not felt so good in a long time. He would do his job; he would help nail the bastards who had killed Larry Wu. And he would do it with a computer, and with his talent and training. The jungles of Vietnam were far behind him; his days of living on the edge of death were over. There were people who were paid to do that kind of work, and his life was no longer about killing. And when that job was done, then, and only then, would he decide if he was going to stay with the government or go back to his old home in Iron City.

That thought reminded him that there were still problems to be solved in his life. A divorce from Melanie. And Lauren was waiting for him back home. He knew now that he had never stopped loving her, and even though they had lost some time, they could make it up when they were together. And it did not have to be in Iron City. If he wanted to stay with the government, there was no reason that Lauren could not come to Washington to be with him. There were a lot of jobs open in Washington for bright women attorneys, especially one with as well-connected a sponsor as the Judge.

It would work. Everything would work.

He turned off the shower, dried himself, and stepped into the hotel room.

Gianetti and Polonowski were there. Gianetti sat on the edge of the bed; his partner was sprawled in the room's overstuffed chair.

Gianetti smiled at him and Polonowski got briskly to his feet.

"Come on. Get some clothes on. You've got to come with us."

CHAPTER THIRTY

He felt numb.

He had tried to get the gun O'Leary had given him, but he had stashed it in the drawer of the end table, and the two FBI men were watching him too closely for him to make a grab for it.

He pulled on his clothes slowly.

"What's this all about?"

"In a few minutes, Matt, all your questions will be answered," Gianetti said in a voice dripping understanding and vaseline.

"I just want to know—" Matt started, but Polonowski interrupted him.

"In a few minutes, he said. Now get dressed. And if you're thinking of making a try for the gun in that drawer, forget it."

He walked out with Gianetti at his side and Polonowski following them. Matt knew that the FBI man had a gun trained on his back. He would have to play out this hand and see what happened.

The two men herded him into a car parked a half block from the front door of the hotel. Polonowski sat in the rear next to Matt.

"Where are we going?" Taylor asked.

"Just wait," Gianetti said.

Their destination was a public parking garage only a half-dozen blocks away. They took a ticket from the dispensing machine, drove up to the top level, and pulled in close to a long black limousine that was parked in a far corner of the garage.

"You get out here," Polonowski said.

Matt wondered if he should run for it. Then the rear door of the limousine opened and a figure leaned forward and beckoned to him. Matt recognized the face of Vice President Barkley, who gestured for him to come into the car.

Matt stumbled from the FBI men's car and got into the backseat with Barkley who said crisply to his driver:

"Go wait with the other two. We want to talk alone."

When the driver had left and gotten into the car with the two FBI men, the vice president looked at Matt and said, "Sorry for all this secrecy. But it is necessary as you'll see. Matt Taylor. You're Frank Stevens' boy, aren't you?"

"He's my foster father," Matt said.

"Good man," Barkley said. "We handled a lot of cases together. A lot of people think that he should have run for Congress instead of me. If he had, he might have been sitting here instead of me."

"I didn't know he was active in politics at all," Matt said.

"Oh, yes. He was planning to run and, truth, I would have supported him. Then there was some kind of automobile accident or something—I don't remember, maybe some relatives of his were killed—and he decided he didn't have the time for politics."

"That's when my folks were killed. I never knew that," Matt said.

"Well, Frank's pretty tight-lipped about things," Barkley said. "Anyway, when you see him, please give him my best."

"I will, sir."

"And be sure to tell him nothing of what I'm about to tell you," the vice president said. Matt could see a smile on the man's handsome features.

"No, sir."

"I know you're wondering what this is all about," Barkley said, "and to tell you the truth I shouldn't even be telling you about it. But I think sometimes in this world we have to trust somebody, and if you're a fraction of the man your foster father is, well, I'll take my chances with you, young fellow."

"Thank you, Mister Vice President."

The white-haired man held a thumb and index finger up before his face.

"Matt, we're only this far from a national catastrophe that maybe you can help prevent." He paused for a moment. "I won't go back over all the background. You know it better than I do. But I want to tell you what the Installation at Harker's Furnace is all about."

Matt nodded.

"You know who owns Harker's Furnace?" the Vice President asked, and when Matt shook his head, Barkley said, "We do. The United States government. It's the most secret installation we have in the world."

Matt coughed.

"Up there, Matt is kept the identity and the payroll of every agent who works for any branch of the government. I'm not talking about FBI or tax men, people who work pretty much out in the open. I'm talking undercover ... well, I mean, spies is the best word. Informants for police agencies. Undercover operatives in foreign countries. CIA agents under deep cover. They're all in the computers at Harker's Furnace." He paused for a moment as if to let Matt digest that news.

"Somehow, a few months ago, some of the files up there got caught up in the I.R.S. computers. Don't ask me how it happened; I don't understand those damned things. All I know is it happened and nobody knew about it until you and your friend ran across them. Since then, we've been trying to get them back. Matt, I don't have to tell you what these records would do if they got into the wrong hands. There'd be a bloodletting all over the world of people who have been working secretly for our side.

285

"We've got to get those records back without anyone knowing that they even exist. I need your help, son."

In the darkness of the car, Barkley reached over and put a hand on Matt's shoulder.

"What can I do?" Matt asked.

"I'm sure Ari's told you to try to find out where the missing tax returns are; to find out what's going on in Harker's Furnace. To find out what your friend knew and where he might have hidden his information. Is that right?"

"Pretty much, sir," Matt said.

"Okay. Well, I want you do do the same thing. With one big exception. I want you to report back to me. Tell me anything you find, anything you don't find."

"And Mr. Cohen?" Matt asked.

The vice president's answer was immediate. "Tell him nothing. Just tell him you're still looking and you haven't found it yet."

"If you don't mind, sir ..."

"No, go ahead, Matt. What is it?"

"Why don't you just tell Cohen what's going on? Why all the subterfuge?"

"Matt, what I told you back in Ari's office before was the truth. He's one of the few men I would trust with my life. But Strike Force 73 is a leaky sieve, and if I told Ari something like this, before noon tomorrow, half of Washington would know about it. You find us that information; get it to me. Let us get those files back in Harker's Furnace where they belong. And then, when it's all over, I'll tell Ari just enough to get him off of it. And no one will be hurt." He turned away from Matt and looked out the automobile's smoked rear window. "There are tens of thousands of lives involved, Matt, and they're all in your hands. I have to ask you again. Will you help?"

"Of course, sir. You know, don't you, that Larry Wu was no spy."

"Of course he wasn't. Whoever said that?"

"Those two FBI men." Matt pointed to the car in which

286

Gianetti and Polonowski were sitting with the Vice President's chauffeur.

"They've got too much of a flair for the dramatic," the Vice President said with a voice edged with disgust. "Good men, but they like playing cops and robbers too much. Someday, they're going to wear my patience thin."

"Sir, there's still one question."

'Yes?"

"Why did Zorelli have Larry Wu killed? Why did they try to kill me?"

"Matt, I wish there were an easy answer for that. I don't have one. Let me tell you what I know. Strike Force 73 isn't the only government agency working on that damned mobster's case. We've got other people ... well, let me say that we've got people inside his crime family, high up. The men who killed your friend, and tried to kill you, used to work for Zorelli, that's true. But from what we've learned, they were ... what do they call it? ... on the lam from Zorelli. Bizarre as it sounds, it looks as if you just ran into these men when they were drunk or high on drugs or something, and ... well, with tragic results. From all we can find out, it doesn't appear Zorelli had anything to do with it at all. I'm sorry, Matt, but I think your friend died for nothing, and that no one, except a couple of crazies acting on their own, was to blame." He paused. "I know what you're thinking. Two of them are dead, but whoever the rest are, they ought to pay for Larry's death. Well, I agree, and I promise you, they will. Our agencies will run them down and they'll pay for their crime. That's a promise. And the Judge will tell you, I don't make promises lightly."

He sighed. "Now my political future's in your hands. If you breathe a word of this to anybody, if it leaks out, it'll bring me down, it'll bring this administration down, and with the harm it does to our national interest all over the world, it might even bring our country down. That's a lot of responsibility for such a young man, and I'm sorry to put it on you, but I just don't have much choice. Nobody else can do it, Matt. I want you to know, Matt, I don't forget the people who stand on my side, who stand on the side of our country. If I am ever elected President, you're the kind of man I'll want on our team. You might not know this, but Tony Plevris talks about you often. He says if it weren't for you, the I.R.S. would fall apart in six weeks. I think that kind of talent should be acknowledged and if I'm elected, it will be. Tony will be coming to the White House with me; maybe it's time we had a non-political type running the I.R.S."

"That's not necessary, sir, even to talk about a thing like that. I'll see what I can find out."

The vice president clapped him on the shoulder. "That's the kind of spirit I like," he said. "Anything you find out, report to me, and no one else. You can get me through Gianetti and Polonowski. They can always reach me, twenty-four hours a day. But talk only to me. The fewer who know the details of what we're doing, the better off we'll be."

"I understand," Matt said.

Barkley reached across him and opened the rear door of his limousine. The interview was over.

As Matt got out of the car, Barkley said, "Please give my best to the Judge. But I count on you not to tell him anything we've discussed tonight."

Matt nodded and switched places in the other car with the vice president's chauffeur. Gianetti did not start his car's engine until the Vice President had been gone for a full three minutes.

The two FBI men drove him back to his hotel. No one spoke, although when they stopped at the hotel, Gianetti said, "Want me to come up and tuck you in?"

But Matt did not even bother to answer him. He moved stolidly out of the car, went inside the hotel, and walked up the stairs to his room.

CHAPTER THIRTY-ONE

Larry Wu was buried later that morning in a small, tree-lined cemetery in the Virginia countryside, a short half hour's drive from the funeral home.

When Matt arrived, a Methodist minister was droning his way through some laudatory words before a room filled with mourners. Matt noticed that most of those who had come to pay their last respects were co-workers from the I.R.S.'s main office.

Katie Wu, dressed in black with a hat and black veil sat in the front, sobbing softly. Wu's parents were to her left; on her right side was the husky figure of Dennis O'Leary.

As Matt waited in the back, Walt Fluory entered the room, still wearing a light topcoat, and came to stand alongside him.

Matt nodded to him and Fluory whispered, "Helluva thing, isn't it?"

Matt nodded again.

"How you doing anyway?" Fluory asked. "You feeling any better?"

"I'm okay," Matt whispered back. He wished that Fluory would shut up; Matt always felt awkward at such occasions when he wound up standing next to someone who insisted on holding a conversation.

"I just want you to know there's no hurry about getting back to work. Take all the time you need," Fluory said. He looked up at the taller man and grinned. "Hell, we don't even need you. Everything's running like clockwork."

"On April 15th, I'll remind you that you said that," Matt said.

"Are you staying in town?" Fluory asked.

"I went home for a few days but now I'm back in town," Matt said, and then wondered why Fluory should think he was staying anywhere except at his Washington apartment. He was not able to ask him that question though, because the people in the room rose to their feet as the minister intoned a benediction.

Then, in the pattern made smooth and almost painless by the skill of the funeral director, people began filing past the casket. Matt did not join them; from the back of the room, he could see Larry Wu's profile and he knew, without closer examination, that the body in that box did not look anything like his friend of so many years. Larry was dead and that mass of chemicalized tissue and bone in the casket had no relationship to him. To remember what he had been in life, Matt did not have to see him dead. And besides, Matt had already seen him dead once—lying, bleeding, in a snowy asphalt parking lot. Once was enough.

As the crowd started to move toward the doors of the chapel, Matt saw his wife, Melanie, walking into the room. She was wearing a dark knee-length coat, but it was unbuttoned and he could see that beneath it she was wearing an orange plaid miniskirt and some kind of sheer material blouse. Her makeup was heavy, but of daytime shades, and it served only to accentuate her great healthy-model beauty.

She saw Matt and Fluory and came over to stand by them.

"Oh shit, Matt," she said. "I'm sorry I'm late."

"It was nice of you to come anyway," Matt said.

"I thought it was my only chance to talk to you," she said. Matt saw Fluory walk away to greet somebody else from the I.R.S. office.

"Are you coming home with me now?" Melanie asked. "I miss you."

"No," Matt said. He wished she were not here; he did not want to have to get into this now, but if she pressed him, he would.

"What do you mean, no?" Melanie said sharply.

"Look, Mel. We're done. Over. Finished. As soon as I clean up a couple of things, we'll see the lawyers and do the thing neat and clean. Let's not fantasize that we had one of the great marriages in history, and if only we talked to each other, we could work it out. We've got nothing to say to each other. Not now, not ever. Now if you'll excuse me ..."

He started to walk away but she grabbed his arm and yanked him around to face her. Her sky blue eyes were narrowed with anger. "Not that easy," she said. "Not that easy."

"Don't make it into a fight, Mel, he said. "You can't win." He turned again and saw Fluory coming toward them. His wife released her grip on her sleeve, brushed past him, and said, "Walt, will you drop me off home?"

Fluory looked over her shoulder at Matt, with a quizzical expression on his face. Matt nodded and Fluory said, "Sure. I'm leaving now."

"Fine," Melanie said, took the man's arm, and walked toward one of the chapel doors. Matt let her get well away from him before he went outside and got into his rental car for the processional drove to the cemetery.

Few of the people who were at the funeral home made the drive and there were only a handful of mourners at the graveside as Larry was lowered into the ground.

Afterwards, Matt went back to Larry's home where there was a big gathering that ran well into the afternoon. Gradually, as the day darkened and a chill rain began to fall, most of the people left. Finally, only Matt and O'Leary and the elder Wus were still there, and then the old people went upstairs to the room Katie had prepared for them.

Katie was going through the motions of cleaning up after

her departed guests when she started crying. It was the first time during the whole day that she had wept openly. O'Leary went over to her after a few moments and folded his arms around her; to Matt it looked like a small child being enveloped by a bear.

He felt like a voyeur watching them, so he went into the kitchen, poured himself a cup of black coffee and took it into Larry's office.

Katie had told him to treat the office as if it were his own, explaining that she knew less than nothing about Larry's computers and eventually the task would fall to Matt to dismantle the whole operation and probably try to sell it all.

"In the meantime, Matt, use it if you want to," she had said. "And besides, it'll give you a place to hide out from these crazy screaming Chinese relatives."

Idly, he turned on the machine's power, then turned back to the desk and saw a pile of hard discs stacked neatly next to an out basket. The first one was labeled in ink: "CONFIDENTIAL" and he inserted it into the viewing screen.

The computer whirred for a moment and then a message appeared on the screen:

"ENTER SOCIAL SECURITY NUMBER FOR ACCESS."

Matt thought that odd. It certainly wasn't much in the way of security, because anybody could dig out Larry Wu's Social Security number and enter it into the machine and access the contents of the computer's memory. So the command to enter the Social Security number wasn't going to deter anyone from getting into the computer. And it wasn't necessary for Larry to have put that reminder on the screen. He would certainly remember that he was using his own Social Security number as the access code.

No. Something didn't make sense. If Larry had wanted to keep this file secret, he would have just coded it: "ENTER PASSWORD FOR ACCESS." He would know that the password was his Social Security number; and the people he wanted to keep out of the file would not know. It was not Larry to be illogical.

Unless ...

Matt looked at the command on the screen for a long while, then slowly tapped in his own Social Security number.

The machine gave a faint whistle, the computer equivalent of a nod, and then the command faded from the screen and was replaced by another message. It read:

"Dear Matt,

If things have come to this ... that you are purloining my letter ... then I guess the worst has happened. I'm going to give you a book. I think we bit off a big chunk but the answers you need are in there. Just be careful. And let me impose on our friendship one more time. Take care of Katie for me.

> Adios, kemo sabe,
> WUL."

Matt read the message and then reread it again. Finally, he removed the disk from the computer, stood up, and hid it between some books in the bookshelves along the far wall. Then he turned off the computer.

The book. Larry had given him that book on Chinese brush painting. It was now back in Matt's hotel room; he had remembered putting it in the end table next to the gun as he was unpacking.

Larry had found out something and whatever it was, the code to it was in the book on painting. Matt had planned to spend the night back at his room anyway, so he would get a chance to look at the book then.

He sat back down at the desk, sipped his coffee, and finally called Lauren's number back in Iron City. Her telephone did not answer, but he found her at the Judge's house.

"Are you all right, Matt?" she asked.

"Yes, Lauren. I'm fine. I'm going to have to stay in Washington for a day or two," he said.

"Is it safe for you there?"

"Yes," Matt said. "Everything's under control. Don't worry. How's—" He started to say "your husband," but then corrected himself. "How's Mike?"

"Some days are better than others," she said sadly. "It just doesn't look good."

"I know. I'm sorry," he said. He went on to tell her about Larry's funeral.

"I wish I could have been there," she said. "Tell Katie how sorry I am."

"I already did," Matt said.

"By the way," she said, "I'm plugging away on the Installation ownership. It's a whole interlocking set of corporations, foreign *and* domestic, but I'll figure it through."

He wanted to tell her that she need not do that anymore. From the vice president, he had learned the ownership of Harker's Furnace. The federal government itself owned it. But, who knew? Maybe she needed the task to keep her busy, to keep her mind off Mike and his problems, so he said only, "Keep on it. I know you'll figure it out. And I'll see you real soon."

"Can't be too soon for me," she said. "I love you, Matt."

"I know. I love you too."

"Hold on. The Judge wants to talk to you," she said.

Then Stevens was on the line.

"Just wanted to let you know, boy. They found a body near the Installation."

"Whose? Who's they?" Matt said.

"Some kids. They were up there, getting the family cabin ready for spring, and they find a body stuck in some sunken tree branches. The body looked like it had been burned or mutilated somehow because the fingerprints were pretty chopped up and the State Police don't have much to work on. So it's just an unidentified body."

"They have a cause of death?"

294

"Drowning," the judge said. "But no name."

Matt knew the name. There was a sinking sensation in the pit of his stomach as he remembered the computer people at the Installation talking about their missing co-worker. What was his name? They called him "Nudge," and he seen a desk nameplate for an Andrew Nujinsky. He thought about mentioning it to the Judge. But that might get people stomping all around the Installation, and that might just blow the whole secret operation up there, by taking it public. And that had been the vice president's worst fear. Matt said nothing and finally the Judge asked, "Boy, you there? You all right?"

"Sorry, Judge. Sure. I was just thinking. Listen, I've got to go now. I'll see you in a couple of days."

"Be careful."

"Always," Matt said.

"Never," the Judge responded, and the two men hung up simultaneously.

Matt finished his coffee and put the cup back in the kitchen. He found Katie and O'Leary sitting together on the sofa, watching an old movie on television.

Just as he said, "Katie, I'm going to go back to the hotel," the front door bell rang.

Matt waved a hand. "Don't get up. I'll get it."

When he opened the front door, Angela Fox was standing there.

"Hello, Matt."

"Angela. What are you doing here?" he said.

"I've got business in Washington and when I drove up, I saw your friend's death notice in the newspaper. It had the address and I thought you might be here. Did I come at a bad time?"

"No, no, I'm sorry. I was just surprised to see you. I'm just getting ready to leave, but come on in."

He escorted Angela into the spacious living room. Katie and O'Leary rose to their feet when they saw Angela. Matt stifled a smile at the almost-theatrical doubletake O'Leary did when he saw her. Angela had the kind of beauty that produced that response in men.

"Katie," he said, "this is my friend, Angela Fox. Angela, this is Katie Wu and Dennis O'Leary."

Angela stepped forward and shook the big FBI man's hand. "Mister O'Leary," she said and turned to Katie. "I'm very sorry about your brother. I hope I'm not intruding."

"No," Katie said. "The worst is over."

"I was just in town and I thought I'd look Matt up," Angela said. The two women, as women always did, were sizing each other up. Matt looked at both of them and decided it was a dead draw in the beauty department.

There was a moment's silence and Matt said quickly, "Anyway, I was just getting ready to leave so we'll be moving along. I'll be back to see you tomorrow, Katie. I'll take up your offer to use Larry's computer, if you don't mind."

"Of course not," Katie said. She came forward and hugged Matt. "You're like my only brother now."

Matt patted her back, then nodded to O'Leary and left with Angela.

Angela insisted upon driving him back to his hotel in her Maserati. At first, he protested.

"I need my car. I have to drive back here in the morning," he said.

"Any reason I can't drive you back?" she asked. He hesitated a moment and she said, "Or didn't you think we were going to spend the night together?"

'I hadn't thought of it at all," Matt said. He hoped that was a gracious response.

Angela laughed softly and pushed him into her car.

"How quickly they forget," she said. She closed the door behind him, smiled, and added, "And how thoroughly I will remind you."

On the way back to his hotel, Angela told him that she had

"a small corporate thing" that she had to check out in Washington, and she had hoped she would run into him.

"But why are you staying in a hotel?" she asked. "Don't you live here?"

"My wife and I just separated," Matt said.

"Good."

"Why good?"

"Because a separated man is a single man," she said. "You won't have any guilt about giving me what I need."

Matt thought for a fleeting instant of Lauren, back in Iron City, and then consciously forced her from his mind.

"No guilt at all," he said.

If he had thought Angela had exhausted all her sexual inventiveness back in Iron City, he was quickly disabused of that notion. She had said he could give her what she needed and he realized that "need" was the correct word. She had her mouth on him, almost before the hotel room door closed behind them. She was over him, under him, around him, her smooth body glistening with perspiration, her want almost a palpable thing with a life of its own. They made love for hours, and each time Matt thought they were done, that she was sated, she smiled and purred and was at him again, tantalizing with tongue and hand and breast and buttock. Unlike most women he had known, she had no need to be told that he loved her, that this was an important thing, that it was more than just two well-oiled ships slipping by each other at night.

"If they ever make screwing an Olympic event, I'm signing up," she said.

"Let me handle the television rights," he said. "I'll make us both rich."

"Not a chance. You're going to be my partner."

"Oh, how we suffer for art," he said.

And finally they were done. He lay next to her atop the bedcovers smoking a cigarette, and when she seemed at ease, he asked her: "What ever happened to the divorce case you were working on in Harker's Furnace? You ever find your missing man?"

"No," she said casually. "I asked at the gate and there's no Galligan working there. So I don't know what to make of it."

"I didn't think you private eyes gave up that easily," he said.

"I haven't given up at all," she said. "I'm just going at it a different way. Find people who knew him; track down his parents, the rest of his family. Sooner or later, I'll find him." She took his free hand and placed it on her bare breast, then closed his thumb and index finger over her nipple, which instantly became erect.

"I always get my way, tax man," she said. "You said you were interested in that place up there too. You find out anything?"

"No. But I had the brains to give up," Matt said.

They chatted on, inconsequential small talk, but Angela's answers grew softer and less frequent and finally, she was asleep. Matt got up and sat on the edge of the bed, making sure that he had not awakened her. Satisfied by her deep, regular breathing, he pulled open the door to the end table. The pistol was where he had left it, and underneath it was the book on Chinese painting that Larry Wu had given him. He opened the book ad skimmed through it quickly.

The book was an elaborate, dull dissertation on the various types of brush stroke used in Chinese painting, illustrated with full-page Chinese ideographs. Matt did not know what to expect. Perhaps some notes in the margin, perhaps a piece of paper secreted in the middle of the book. There were neither of those things.

But at the back of the book there was an index that listed, with their names in English, the different brush strokes used in Chinese painting. And four of the names had been underlined with pen.

Matt read the names carefully, but they meant nothing to him. He looked through the book again, just to satisfy himself that there was not any other clue that he had overlooked. But the four underlined phrases were all that there was. He closed the book, put it on top of the night stand, lit a cigarette, turned off the lamp, and smoked in the dark, thinking.

Before the cigarette was finished, he was satisfied that he knew what Larry Wu had done. He jabbed the cigarette out in the ashtray and fell instantly, contentedly asleep.

CHAPTER THIRTY-TWO

"See you tonight?"

"I don't know," Matt said. "I'm afraid I might have an appointment." He glanced over at Angela, who appeared disappointed.

"Well, if you change your mind, I'm registered at the Biltmore. Give me a call." She took her right hand from the steering wheel and placed it on Matt's thigh. "And thank you for last night," she said.

Angela smiled, then playfully shoved him toward the door of her car.

His rented Ford was still in the driveway of the Wu home. The doorbell was answered by O'Leary who looked over Matt's shoulder at the Maserati speeding away from the curb, and said, "Taylor, you're a man of surprising tastes. Was she as good as she looked?"

Matt did not feel like discussing his sex life with O'Leary, so he merely grunted noncommittally and asked, "Where's Katie?"

"She went with her parents to the airport. She'll be back later." He walked away from the door, leaving it open, Matt followed him into the kitchen and poured himself a cup of coffee.

"You'll be working on Wu's computer?" O'Leary said.

"Yeah."

"Let us get started."

"Us?" Matt said."

"Naturally. I want to be around when you find those missing returns from Harker's Furnace."

Matt shook his head. "Sorry, O'Leary, but that's not the way it works."

"What isn't?"

"First of all, I don't know if I'm going to find anything. Second, if I do, it may take me two days, a week, longer, I don't know. Third, I can't work with somebody looking over my shoulder. It makes me nervous."

None of it was true, but it was the best that Matt could think of. He had instructions from the vice president to tell no one but the vice president if he found the missing spy roster. He could not take a chance of O'Leary watching him work and jumping to a correct conclusion.

"Christ, I hate you prima donnas," O'Leary growled, then shrugged. "Do whatever the hell you have to do."

When Matt entered Larry Wu's office, he locked the door behind him, turned on the large computer, and using the telephone modem and his personal identification number, entered the I.R.S.'s main computers.

At one time, doing that had given him almost a physical thrill, knowing that spread out at his fingertips were the records of more than a hundred million Americans. Now, however, he had done it so often that to him it was not any more special than picking up a telephone and being able to dial a number on the other side of the country.

From his inside jacket pocket, he took the book of Chinese painting and opened it to the index where the four foreign phrases had been underlined by Larry.

He worked without actually thinking of what he was doing. His mind was busy recalling the computer note that Larry had left for him, with its awkward reference to a "purloined letter."

That had been the key. Wu had been a student of the work of Edgar Allan Poe and "The Purloined Letter" was one of

Poe's most famous stories. In the tale, people were unsuccessfully trying to find a compromising letter. Then Poe's detective, Dupin showed up and found the letter almost instantly. He was the only one smart enough to realize that the villain had simply put the letter in an old envelope and left it out in plain sight, and all of the searchers overlooked it just because it was too obvious.

Matt was betting that Larry Wu had done the same thing. That he had broken down the wall someone had built, and managed to find the Harker's Furnace files in the I.R.S. computers. To hide them, he had simply put "new envelopes" on them—in other words, new labels and then hid them back in the same I.R.S. computers.

And Matt believed that the new "Labels" were the four Chinese brushstrokes underlined in Larry's book.

He looked at the book carefully. Larry had given it to him only ten days ago, just minutes before he was shot, but already it seemed like half a lifetime had passed since then.

Slowly, he started to type the names of the brushstrokes onto the computer monitor. Without realizing it, he was talking softly to himself.

"*P'i ma ts'un*. Brushwork like spread-out hemp fibers. And *Kuei p'i ts'un*. Brushwork like the wrinkles on the devil's face." He started to hum as he placed the other two Chinese phrases into the computer.

The whole process took less than an hour.

He could find no record of the Harker's Furnace returns in the main I.R.S. computers, so he switched over to the agency's regional computer hookups. First Philadelphia ... and using the Chinese phrases as an access code, he was rewarded by a long list of names, addresses, and numbers flashing on the TV screen.

Quickly he inserted a large storage disc into the computer and put the list of names into permanent memory. Now that the names were safely stored, he began to scroll them on the monitor screen, rolling the names up from bottom to top. He stifled a small cry when he saw the name of Fred Kohler finally appear. This was it. He had found the missing list, or at least part of it.

He found more of the names in the Holtsville, New York, computer, and the final batch hidden in Los Angeles. He recorded all of them on the memory disc, then exited from the I.R.S. computer network and turned off Larry Wu's machine.

"Good boy, Larry," he said under his breath, and he could not resist feeling a little proud at how quickly he had decoded Larry's secret message to him.

He heard somebody at the door and called out "Yes?", even as he took the memory disc from Larry's computer and slid it under the blotter atop the desk.

"Matt, it's Katie. Do you want some lunch?"

"Sure. Coming right out."

He waited until she walked away from the door, then picked up the computer disc and carried it to the bookshelves. He glanced at the titles, then with a small smile, placed the disc inside the front cover of *The Collected Works of Edgar Allan Poe.* Larry, he thought, would have been pleased by the touch.

He found Katie sitting at the old oaken table in the kitchen, walked over, and kissed her on the cheek.

"Where's O'Leary?" he said.

"He said he was going to the office, but if you had anything to tell him, to call him right away." As Matt sat down, she got up and began to get plates and silverware from one of the large cupboards in the room.

"How do you feel, Katie? he asked.

"It's starting to sink in. I'm all right. Matt?"

"Yes."

"Dennis told me that you're working on something secret and that I shouldn't ask you any questions about it." She waited until Matt nodded, then added, "So I won't. But I've got to know one thing. Will this help us find out why Larry was killed?"

For a split second, he did not know how to answer her.

O'Leary and Cohen believed that the missing tax returns were somehow connected to Zorelli in Philadelphia and his organization had ordered Larry's death. And Matt Taylor's too. But the truth, from the vice president, was that Larry's death had been a tragic random act of violence and that the missing Harker's Furnace tax returns had nothing to do with it. There was no good answer to give Katie. He did not want her to think that he had given up on bringing Larry's killers to justice, but he did not want to fill her with false hope either.

He answered in his mildest voice, "I don't know, Katie. I hope so."

"Okay," she said. "I just couldn't live with the idea that nobody will pay for Larry's death."

"Somebody will," he said, even though there was no payment due. Maybe someday he would be able to tell her the broad outlines of the truth. Maybe someday when she was not hurting the way she was now. Maybe someday. But not today.

They ate platters of cold salad and sandwich meat that had been left over from the previous day's gathering at the Wu home, and slowly Katie seemed to rise out of her despondency.

She insisted upon telling him about her love life, which was good and getting better. Even her family liked O'Leary, she said, and were willing to overlook the fact that he was black.

"They must be mellowing," Matt said.

"In a way," she said. "You know, Chinese in this country, well, they've had so much prejudice thrown at them over the years, that I guess they think twice before they dump it on somebody else. Maybe that's what growing up is all about."

"Maybe."

"Enough about that. Are you going to make me plead?"

"Plead for what?"

"For what?" she said with a large smile. "For the lowdown on who that raving beauty was who came to collect you last night. Boy, talk about a man's world. Split up with your wife just a couple of days, and the beauties are coming out of the woodwork after you."

"I'll have you know that woman and I have a very serious business relationship," Matt said with mock stuffiness. "I'll have you know that she is a private detective."

"With the emphasis on private?" Katie asked, and when Matt's face flushed, she laughed aloud.

"Don't get flustered, big brother," she said. "I'm not expecting you to kiss and tell. It's not serious, is it?"

Matt shook his head. "Just two Vaseline jars sharing one shelf."

"Bragging sexist swine," she said. "I caught a glimpse of Melanie at the funeral home yesterday. It was nice of her to come."

"No, it wasn't," Matt said. "She came to order me to come home."

"And?"

"I told her to get lost."

"Good. You should have done it years ago."

"Everybody seems to have known that but me," Matt said. "Does that mean I'm stupid?"

"No, Matt. It just means that you're the last of the romantics. You believe in marriage and fidelity and one-man one-woman and all the stuff you read on the Hallmark cards. And it just takes you a long time to figure out that you're being jobbed. Because you want so much to have happy endings. That's why women are always crazy about you, big brother. Present company included."

"Well, thank you. That's nicer then telling me I'm stupid."

Katie Wu grinned. "Amounts to the same thing though," she said.

Later that afternoon when Katie went out to buy groceries, Matt called the telephone number on the business card that Gianetti had given him.

"I've got to talk to our friend from the parking garage," Matt said. "You know who I mean."

"Do you have something for him?" Gianetti asked.

"Yes," Matt said.

"I'll get back to you. You're at Wu's house?"

"I'm leaving. So I'll call you back."

"All right. You haven't mentioned this to anyone, have you?"

"Stick it, Gianetti," Matt said. "I'll call back at five o'clock."

He left Katie a note that he would be in touch later, and drove his rental car back to his hotel. He had two Scotches in the run-down cocktail lounge, before calling Gianetti back.

"Meeting's all set," the FBI man said. "You at your hotel?"

"Yes."

"I'll be by for you at eight o'clock."

Matt hung up and went back to the bar for another drink. This would soon be over and he looked forward to putting it behind him, so he could get on with his life. But not even the Scotch could help him figure out exactly what direction his life was going to move in.

CHAPTER THIRTY-THREE

It was 9:00 P.M. when Gianetti drove his nondescript bureau car into the garage of a private row home in the Georgetown section of Washington, D.C., and led Taylor up a back stairway into a softly lit, booklined study that overlooked a small flood-lighted garden.

Vice President Barkley was sitting behind a large mahogany desk. He rose when Gianetti entered the room and said, "Sir, Taylor is here." The FBI agent stood aside, let Matt enter, and then left the room, closing the door behind him.

As Matt walked across the thick carpet toward the Vice President, he saw another man leaning against a conference table at the side of the room.

"Hello, Matt," the vice president said, shaking his hand firmly. "Of course you know your boss, Tony Plevris."

"Of course," Matt said and turned to Plevris. "Evening, sir."

Plevris nodded but made no effort to come forward to shake hands. In the dim light from the lamp on the desk, Matt could recognize the tax director's saturnine features, the sharply hooked nose that was mirrored in the pointed widow's peak hairline. His heavy-lidded eyes seemed to be closed in the shadowed light, and he appeared to Matt as he always had appeared: as a hard-fisted hatchetman whose loyalty was to politicians and not to political systems. They came into Washington with every administration, and the best ones seemed to hang around long after the departure of the politicians whose coattails they had rode in on, because they developed a reputation for being able to get things done. Plevris, now the unofficial head of Vice President Barkley's campaign for the presidency, had gotten that kind of critique for his work at the I.R.S. Even Matt, who liked to grumble about the impossibility of running the federal tax system, would admit that Plevris had gotten the agency running efficiently, when only eight years before it had been in danger of breaking down completely. But he could not help wondering what he was doing here, when this matter concerned spies and informers and had nothing to do with taxes or the I.R.S.

"Sit down, Matt," Barkley said, waving him to a chair in front of the desk. "I appreciate your getting back to me so fast. You've got something for us?"

Matt reached into his pocket and put the book of Chinese painting on the desk in front of the vice president and said, "I found the Harker's Furnace files." As he looked up, he saw Plevris come forward out of the shadows to sit alongside the desk near Barkley.

"That's wonderful," Barkley said with a large smile.

Plevris said, "Where'd you find them, Taylor?"

"They were in the I.R.S. computer system," Matt said. He didn't like Plevris's almost-rude manner with him and decided that he would make Plevris ask him what he had learned, rather than volunteer all the facts.

"Impossible," Plevris said. "We scoured that system totally. They weren't in there."

"There's scouring and then there's scouring, Mr. Plevris," Matt said. He tried to keep the edge out of his voice but apparently failed, because the vice president moved into the tension between the two men.

"Suppose, Matt, you tell us about it your own way. Tony, wait until he's done before you ask any questions."

308

Plevris hesitated, then nodded. "Yes, sir."

"Go ahead, son," Barkley told Matt. He picked up the Chinese book. "What's this all about?"

"Larry Wu dug out the Harker's Furnace returns and then, for some reason, decided to hide them. I don't know why. So he stashed them in different regional computers around the country. You couldn't find them, Mr. Plevris, because your people didn't know what to look for."

"And you did?" Plevris said.

"Please, Tony. Please. Let Matt talk," Barkley said.

"I didn't know what to look for until I found this book." Matt leaned forward and opened the book to its index. "These four underlined Chinese phrases. Larry used them to code the Harker's returns. Without knowing the code, no one could retrieve them. I was lucky enough to run across this book and figure out the code."

"And the files are still in the system?" Barkley asked.

"Yes sir. They're safe there unless somebody else has the code."

"And no one does," Plevris said, as he picked up the book and looked at the Chinese language phrases.

"That's right."

"I take it you did this work on Mr. Wu's computer," the vice president said.

"Yes, sir, that's right."

"Did you find anything else there that I might be interested in? About the Installation at Harker's Furnace, for instance?"

"No, sir," Matt said. "Larry might have been in contact with the computers up there, but I think that was a personal thing between two computer hackers."

"Hackers?" the vice president said.

"Sorry. That's just a nickname for computer buffs. As I say, I think Larry might have been talking to somebody up there, but I think it was personal, and I didn't find anything in Larry's computer files about it."

309

"Thank God," Barkley said. "You know, Matt, how dangerous a leak could have been. You told no one else?"

"No, sir."

Matt noticed Plevris pick up the painting book and stick it into his side pocket.

The vice president rose and Matt did too.

"There's one thing, Mister Vice President."

"What's that, Matt?"

"I've been dodging Ari Cohen and O'Leary, but they're going to be able to track me down. Is it okay if I tell them that they should talk to you?"

"Naturally," Barkley said. "And first thing in the morning, I'll get hold of Ari and fill him in on just enough to keep him happy. But don't you worry about it. They won't be pestering you anymore."

"Okay, sir. Thank you."

"Taylor, are you still interested in going onto a new strike force?" Plevris asked abruptly.

"I hadn't been giving it much thought, Mr. Plevris, but I think so."

"Okay. I'll arrange it. I understand you're on vacation?"

"That's right."

"You coming back Monday?" Plevris asked and when Matt nodded, the I.R.S. director said, "Come on up to my office then. We'll get the paperwork moving."

"Okay, sir," Matt said.

The vice president came around the desk and shook Matt's hand again and walked him toward the door. "Gianetti will drop you back off," he said. He opened the door; the FBI agent was standing outside in the hall.

As Matt left the room, the vice president called his name.

"Matt?" Taylor turned and Barkley said, "You've done America a great service. We won't forget you. Count on that."

CHAPTER THIRTY-FOUR

Matt went into the hotel bar for a nightcap to settle his nerves before going up to his room. Something about Gianetti, something besides the obvious feeling that the FBI agent was a swish who wanted to get his hands on Matt, unnerved him and made him uncomfortable.

He remembered a movie poster he had seen once when he was young, for some Humphrey Bogart movie. It read: "Most dangerous when he was smiling. And smiling all the time." That might have been it. Gianetti, unlike his dour, sour-faced partner, seemed always to have a smile on his face. And there just weren't that many funny things going on in the world.

As he sipped his Scotch, he thought, *Well, it's over. With luck, I'll never have to see Gianetti again. And never have to think about Harker's Furnace again. Time to get on with your life, boy.*

He realized that he did not know what direction that life was going to take. Plevris had promised him a job with the new anti-crime strike force. That was the immediate future. And then there was Lauren. She was in his future too. He thought about it for a while, and then realized that he had not thought about Larry Wu, and he tried to rationalize the guilt away. Larry had been his friend, but his death was a tragic chance occurrence, not part of any larger scheme that Matt could track down to earth to find some guilty mastermind under it all. No. It was a tragedy, but it was a random tragedy, and Matt had killed one of the men and the police had gotten the other. There was nothing left to do about it. Matt had done all he could and it was over and someday he—or Dennis O'Leary— would be able to explain it all to Katie.

He was just finishing his drink, ready to order another, when the bartender came to him and said, "Your name Taylor?"

Matt nodded.

"Phone call for you. You can take it down there." He pointed to the end of the bar where the receiver lay on its side. Matt had been so deep in his own thoughts he had not even heard the telephone ring.

"Hello."

"Matt, it's Walt. I'm over at your apartment. You'd better get here right away." Fluory's voice seemed strained with tension.

"Why? What's the matter?"

"It's Melanie, Matt. I can't talk. Just hurry."

The telephone went dead in his hand and Matt fumbled in his pocket for money, dropped a five-dollar bill on the bar and went out to the street to grab a taxicab.

Melanie. What has she done now?

The apartment door was unlocked and Taylor rushed inside. Fluory was in the living room, with a drink in his hand. The man was barefooted. He was wearing slacks and an unbuttoned shirt open to the waist. He had no undershirt on. He looked up as Matt entered the room.

"Walt. What's wrong? Where's Melanie?"

"In the bedroom," Fluory said.

Matt ran by him into the bedroom. The odor of Melanie's musk perfume saturated the air. His wife was lying naked on the bed, her blond hair splashed out on the pillow behind her, her face a vision of absolute repose. He ran to her side to feel her pulse but it was not necessary. He could tell by the rhythmic rise and fall of her satiny breasts that she was alive. Behind him, he heard Fluory come into the room and Matt leaned over and held Melanie's hand.

Without turning, he asked, "What's the matter with her, Walt?"

"Nothing, Matt. She's just been well-fucked and well-drugged. So why don't we let the little twat sleep it off, shall we?"

There was a hard edge to Fluory's voice that snapped Matt's head around. His boss was standing in the doorway, holding a gun in his hand, aimed at Matt.

Taylor stood up from the bed.

"Walt. What the hell is this?"

Fluory stepped into the room and gestured at Matt with the gun. "Just get outside."

At a safe distance, he followed Matt into the living room, then pushed him into a soft chair.

"Just sit there."

"Come on, Walt," Matt said. "Let's stop fooling around." He started to rise from his chair, but Fluory pulled back the hammer of the gun and cocked it.

"I'll use it, Matt. Now sit down."

Matt sat back down and Fluory, with the gun still trained on Matt backed away to the small table that held the telephone, squatted down so he could look at the dial and Taylor at at the same time, and punched out a phone number.

"He's here," was all he said into the phone and then hung up.

Matt was perched on the front edge of the soft chair. He tried a smile. "Well, Walt, before you murder me, maybe you'll tell me what this is all about?" Maybe Fluory had found out that Matt had gotten into the I.R.S. computer system to find the Harker's Furnace returns. Maybe he thought Matt had done something wrong. Maybe he didn't know that Matt was working on the direct orders of the vice president. Maybe he was calling the police or somebody to take Matt into custody. Matt could explain it all, if he just had the chance.

"What it's all about, Matt, is that you stuck your nose where it didn't belong and now you're going to pay for it."

"I don't know what you're talking about, Walt. And Melanie. You said she's drugged?"

"Fucked and drugged," Fluory said, snapping out his vile words with a sort of brisk pleasure. "I thought I'd slip one into her for old time's sake. Sort of a good-bye hump."

It was all going too fast for him. There were a thousand questions he wanted to ask, but they were buzzing around in his head like a swarm of angry bees, and he could not pluck one out of the air.

"Mel? You?" was all he could manage.

"For three years, you dumb sap. Every time your back was turned. The night I sent you and Wu to Philadelphia, I was in this apartment five minutes after you left and five minutes after that, I was in Melanie. Tell me, how does it feel to be married to the biggest tramp in Washington, D.C.?"

"You're not going to shoot me because you've been sleeping with my wife. Who'd you call?"

"The people who *are* going to shoot you," Fluory said coldly. There is was, that goddamned grin again. The man's eyes glistened like an animal's

Matt's brain was racing. "Mind telling me why I'm going to get shot?" he asked, even as he was thinking: *If someone's coming up here to shoot me, I've got to get the gun away from this drugged-up bastard.* His own gun was back in his hotel room; it had never occurred to him that he might need it.

"Sure," Fluory said. He began to recite as if reading from a newspaper clipping. " 'Matthew Taylor, Internal Revenue computer expert, and his beautiful wife, Melanie, were found today shot to death in their apartment. Police said the couple, who had separated several weeks ago, had obviously quarreled and shot each other to death.' How's that for openers?"

"This is stupid, Walt. Melanie and I broke up. I don't care if you sleep with her twenty-four hours a day."

"It doesn't have anything to do with Mel, you idiot. If somebody screwing her was going to get you shot, half the men in this city would be packing guns after you. Do you know she used to blow salesmen in the back room of her shop? Do you know I'd send you out of town, come up here and screw her brains out, and two hours later she'd go out to pick up some trick in a bar. You should have put a meter on her, Matt. You'd be rich instead of dead."

As he reached down to pick up his drink from the table, Matt saw movement behind him and Melanie, still naked, came out of the bedroom into the living room, rubbing her eyes with the backs of her knuckles in a childlike gesture. Her mouth dropped open when she saw Matt on the chair."

"Matt. This isn't what it looks like," she said. Fluory wheeled toward her when he heard her voice, then turned back to aim the gun at Taylor again. Melanie obviously had not noticed the weapon because she came across the room toward Matt and stood before him.

"I was so lonely without you here," she said, looking down at him. "And Walt was available. And I needed a man real bad. But nothing happened. He couldn't get it up." Even as she spoke to him, Matt could see her nipples springing erect.

"That's not what he said," Matt answered.

"Oh. He told you. Well, he could get it up. And up. And up. God, could he ever." She laughed and turned to Fluory and then, for the first time, seemed to notice the deadly-looking dark blue revolver in his hand.

"Walt. What are you doing with that gun?"

"Didn't you know, Mel?" Matt asked from behind her. "Your little bedmate is going to have the two of us killed."

"What?" she said.

"Sit down, Melanie," Fluory snapped. "We're waiting for someone."

He waved her toward the sofa with his gun. From behind, Matt could see her shoulders shrug.

"What are you talking about?" she said, but Fluory reached forward and tried to shove her down onto the couch. Instinctively, she clutched his arm and when she fell, she pulled him off balance. It was the chance Matt had been waiting for. He sprang from the chair as Melanie and Fluory thrashed about in a tangle of arms and legs for an instant. Then there was a deep-throated explosion that echoed and re-echoed in the room. There was a moment's silence and then a second explosion.

Melanie fell to the floor in a sitting position and looked up at the two men with an expression of total surprise, total horror, on her face. Matt could see her out of the corner of his eye: two huge holes now existed where her left breast had been.

Then Matt was on Fluory. In the background he heard Melanie cough once. Then he heard the sound of the intercom doorbell from the lobby. He ignored both sounds as he grabbed Fluory's wrist and twisted the weapon back around so that it was pointed at its owner. Fluory seemed to stare at the gun in frozen fascination as Matt kept twisting. Later, he would not be sure exactly how it happened: it seemed to him that Fluory's hand began to convulse somehow, involuntarily, and then pulled the trigger. The bullet seemed to explode his face instantly and the gun flew from Fluory's hand and clattered off across the floor.

The man slumped to the floor and Matt slowly stood up. He was not sure that it wasn't he himself who had been shot, but he felt no blood on his face. On the floor, Fluory was staring sightlessly at the ceiling. Matt turned from him and saw Melanie in a heap. Her eyes, too, were open and there was no need for him to feel for a pulse. He had seen enough corpses to know that his wife was dead.

The intercom. The doorbell had rung and someone who wanted Taylor dead might be on his way upstairs right now.

He looked frantically around the floor for Fluory's gun, but it was not in sight. He looked down at Fluory and his anger overwhelmed him and he kicked his shoe viciously into the dead man's face. Then he ran to the hallway door. A few feet away was the elevator and the arrow indicator over the doors showed that it was on its way to his floor.

He ran in the other direction to the stairway. He entered the stairwell and waited there for a split second until the elevator doors opened.

As Gianetti and Polonowski came out of the elevator, Matt turned and ran down the stairs.

CHAPTER THIRTY-FIVE

At the apartment building's first-floor level, there were two fire doors. One led out into the building's lobby; the other—all bedecked in warning signs—opened into the gardens surrounding the building.

Matt first opened the doorway to the gardens and immediately the air was filled with the ringing of bells and the deep-throated warning whoop of the burglar alarm. It kept ringing even as Matt closed the door and went through the other door into the lobby.

He was met by the two night time security men.

"Mr. Taylor," one of them started to say, but Matt gasped, "My wife. Shot. She's been shot. Call the police." Then he pushed his way between the two bewildered guards and dashed through the ornate lobby and out the front door.

A slow warm drizzle had begun. The street was empty with no taxicab in sight. He glanced behind him, saw some activity in the lobby, and ran across the wet slick roadway toward the entrance to the Metro. At this time of night, trains had stopped running, but the station itself was kept open.

A long, steep escalator dropped down to the train level but it had been turned off. Matt tried to run down but it was hard to maneuver on the small flat metal steps.

At the bottom of the escalator the barricades were open and

out on the platform, a few men were moving around, slowly sweeping away a day's worth of debris. Matt dashed past them and out to the end of the platform, where he stopped.

He looked back. Gianetti and Polonowski had both just reached the bottom of the escalator. They were holding guns. For a moment, Matt thought he was trapped, then looked down over the side of the platform. The idea of starting off into the dark subway tunnel with two gunmen chasing him was one of the least appealing he had ever come up with, but the alternative was worse: being caught and killed.

He looked down at the tracks again, moved back a few feet, and took a running jump. He landed on all fours between the two lines of shiny metal track and scrambled to his feet. Behind him, he saw the two FBI men approaching the platform's edge. Then he turned back into the tunnel and ran into the swallowing black.

Behind him, he heard shouts. Then he turned around a curve in the tunnel and the darkness grew deeper.

He heard Gianetti's voice calling out to his partner: "Take it easy, John. He's not going anywhere."

And then Polonowski's gruff voice, much nearer, responding: "Fuck take it easy. This bastard's history."

Matt kept running. Behind him there were more sounds, but this deep in, the tunnel muffled them, distorted them, echoed and re-echoed them, till at last they made no sense.

His breath came in pants, his legs felt leaden, and the arm he had injured at the Installation began to throb again. He ran until he could run no more, then ran some more.

Finally, he stopped running just for a moment to catch his breath. An instant later something big and strong and very powerful knocked him over, pummeling him to the ground. For a moment, he was too tired to fight. If he just quit now, he told himself, it would all be over, no more questions, no more problems. And then he kicked that thought out of his mind.

He heard Polonowski growl, "Finally, you bastard, you get yours." The man's voice gave Matt a new strength and he pulled his knees up to his chest, rolled over on his back and let his opponent's full weight climb up on top of him. Then he kicked out as hard as he could and Polonowski grunted and fell to the side.

As the attacker fell away, Matt grabbed his arm and started twirling him around. A small, detached spectator part of Matt's mind watched and laughed. It was like the game of Dizzy they had played as kids. One kid, the biggest one usually, would grab another one by the arm and twirl him round and round in a circle and then suddenly let him go and everybody would watch while the twirlee—was that what the kid was called?—would stumble and stagger around while trying to stand upright.

Matt let go. There was a tripping sound, a crash, and Polonowski swearing. "A bullet for you, you prick," and then another stumbling sound. Matt prepared himself for another onrush, but then there was a scream.

There were crackling sounds and hissing. Little blue sparks flew up from the ground, followed instantly by the smell of badly burned meat. Then silence.

Behind him another voice, "John, John. Where are you? You okay?"

No, Matt thought, John wasn't okay. And the dumb Polack would never be okay again because he had grabbed hold of the third rail and been fried, as he deserved to be, like a thug in an electric chair. Matt wanted his gun but was afraid to go near the man's body.

"John, John." Gianetti's voice was frantic now and Matt started running away from it.

Finally, ahead of him, he could see the lights of another station. He ran faster. The station was not as well lit as the one he had entered and there seemed to be no workers around. He hoped that he could get back out to street level.

He carefully stepped over the tracks, put his hands on the platform, and pulled. He was halfway up when a shot rang out. Matt could hear it whistle past his ear. He dropped back down into the tunnel, ran ahead another twenty feet, then lunged up with a rolling dive onto the platform.

"You're dead meat, Taylor," Gianetti's voice came. "Dead meat."

Matt rolled across the platform, sure that by staying low he was not in Gianetti's line of sight. He pushed open an exit gate, ran up the out-of-service escalator and kicked open the door to the street. A cab was cruising by slowly and Matt jumped into the back of it and snarled at the driver:

"Move it."

When he was a half block away, he looked back and saw Gianetti standing in the middle of the street.

CHAPTER THIRTY-SIX

He rode in the cab for about fifteen blocks until he saw the lights of a business district ahead, then got out, walked two blocks and caught another cab, this time one of the radio-free gypsies that cruised D.C.'s streets late at night, looking for non-English-speaking tourists to gouge.

He told the driver to cruise around the business district, not to talk, to expect a large tip, and then—ignoring the no-smoking sign—lit a cigarette and leaned in the corner of the back seat to think.

They had lied to him. Fluory had not said it in so many words, but it was obvious that Vice President Barkley and Plevris, the head of the I.R.S., had decided he was expendable.

Had they also lied about what was at the Installation?

Perhaps it did *not* contain the personnel files of America's spy forces? It was more likely, he thought, that what he knew about Harker's was so important that they could not take the chance that he might tell anyone. Once he had found out what Larry Wu had done with the tax files, he had become expendable.

That made sense to him in a rough Tennessee windage kind of way. But did that mean they had also arranged the murder of Larry and the earlier attempt on Taylor's life?

He shook his head and angrily tossed the cigarette out the

window. There were too many questions, not enough answers, and no one he could get the answers from. Could he trust O'Leary? Could he trust Ari Cohen?

The answer was no and the rest of the answer was clear. He would have to find out himself what was going on in Harker's Furnace, and then use that knowledge to buy his life. And if anyone had ordered Larry's killing . . . if it had been more than just a tragic accident . . . then he would use that knowledge, too, to bring them down. It wasn't just Larry. Poor Melanie lay dead in their apartment, and while she was a tramp and a poor excuse for a wife, she hadn't deserved to die that way. She was another due bill, and someone would have to pay it. That thug whose neck he had broken when Larry was killed and Polonowski, sizzling on a subway track, weren't enough. They were just pawns in this chess game, but somebody was pushing those pieces around the board and that was the person who must die.

"Still keep driving?" the cabbie asked.

Matt thought for a moment. He could not go back to his hotel. It was only in police shows on television that the cops never thought about using a telephone. His hotel would already be staked out, and if he went there to try to get his gun, he would surely be picked up.

But a gun wasn't the thing he needed most to stay alive. What he needed was for the enemy to know that he was not expendable, that they could not afford to try to kill him again. He needed control of the Harker's Furnace tax records. That meant Larry Wu's house, and they might not have thought of it yet. It still might not be under guard.

"Stop at that phone up there," he said. He called the Wu's house from the telephone on the nearest street corner, but there was no answer, so he got back into the cab and gave the driver Wu's address.

When the driver reached the block, Matt had him drive around twice, while he anxiously scanned the streets, looking to see if anyone had the house under surveillance. When he was convinced that it was safe, he had the driver park around the corner, a quarter of a block away.

"What's my bill so far?" Matt asked.

"Nineteen-fifty," the driver said. "Plus tip, remember."

Matt dug into his pocket and rifled through the wad of bills he was carrying until he found a fifty.

He tore it in half and gave one half to the driver.

"I want you to wait here for me with your lights out. I'll be about fifteen minutes or so. Then I'll give you the other half of the bill."

"Hey, I don't like this. What good's a half a half a hundred?" the driver asked.

"No more use to me than to you," Matt said, "so don't argue, just wait."

Larry's house was dark. Matt slipped into the narrow alleyway that separated it from its identical neighboring building. The side door key was where Larry always left it, under a fiberglass rock in a concrete flower pot at the side of the door.

He let himself in, walked quickly with easy familiarity through the kitchen to the hallway that led to Larry's office, went inside, locked the door, drew the heavy drapes, and then turned on the light.

Quickly he turned on Larry's computer, hooked it up to the telephone modem, and let himself into the I.R.S.'s main computer network. Fortunately his memory was good, and he was able to accurately type the names of the four different Chinese brush strokes that were the access code to the Harker's Furnace files.

But this time, the computer did not respond to his entry request. The machine waited, then flashed on the screen:

"NO SUCH FILES IN COMPUTER MEMORY. PLEASE CHECK ACCESS CODE AGAIN."

The bastards. They had already removed the files, or at least re-labeled them so that Matt could not get at them. He slammed his fist on the desk in frustration.

And then he remembered the memory disc he had put in the

library's bookshelf earlier in the day. He ran around the desk and found the disc in the book of Edgar Allan Poe's works, and quickly booted it into the machine.

It instantly flashed up the long rows of numbers and addresses and salaries and taxes paid. No one had tampered with it.

For a moment, he thought of just sticking the disc under his arm and running off with it, but then he realized that might not be good insurance at all. If he were caught, and the memory disc taken from him, it might indicate that all he had was on that disk, and he was again expendable.

It wouldn't do.

Where to hide the information?

Then it came to him. If it had worked once, it would work again. So he let himself back into the I.R.S. computer network and transferred all the Harker's Furnace data back into the Philadelphia regional network.

For a long moment, he wondered how to label the file to keep it safe from anyone else's eyes. Then he remembered something the Judge had told him years ago when they were talking about an unpopular court case the Judge was handling.

"Fiat iustitia ruat caelum."

Though the heavens fall, let justice be done.

It seemed appropriate somehow and Matt labelled the new file with the Latin Phrase, then disconnected the phone connection and turned off Larry's computer.

He stuck the disc in his pocket, then paused, took a pen and a note paper from Larry's desk and wrote a note to Katie.

"Dear Katie,
Melanie is dead but no matter what you hear, I didn't do it. I'll be all right. Love, Matt."

He turned off the lights, dropped the note on the kitchen table, and then went back outside. Before stepping onto the sidewalk, he crouched down alongside the entry gate and glanced up and down the street. When he saw no one, he quickly walked away toward the spot where he had left the cab.

Just as he reached the corner, he saw the headlights of a car speeding down the street from the far corner and paused to watch. The car slid to a stop in front of the Wu house and two men jumped out.

Matt turned the corner, got into the cab, and told the driver, "Let's get out of here."

The driver pulled away, then said, "Where to?"

It was a question Matt could not answer. They would be looking for him everywhere, and he had no close friends, except Katie, that he could rely on, and already her house was off-limits.

For a moment, he thought of Elly, the young blonde from Melanie's *Imagining* shop. But she would not hide him. As soon as she learned Melanie was dead and that he was suspected, she would hand him to the police. She might have an itch for him, but it wasn't that big an itch that she would risk arrest.

His car was back at the hotel and by now they would have found it, too, and at this hour, the car rental places were closed for the night. If there was a manhunt underway for him, bus, train, and air terminals would all be watched.

Where? Where? Where would he be safe?

Angela Fox.

She was his only hope. He forced himself to think where she was staying, and then told the driver: "Take me to the Biltmore."

A block from the hotel, he stopped the cab, gave the driver the other half of the torn fifty and twenty more dollars besides, then called the Biltmore from a pay phone on the corner.

He was connected to Angela's room. Her voice was sleepy as she answered the telephone.

"Angela, it's Matt Taylor."

"Looking for a good time, sailor?"

"Something like that."

"Get on up here," she said.

326

CHAPTER THIRTY-SEVEN

"I must be slipping," Angela said. "I figured after last night, you'd be out of action for at least a week."

When she let him into her lavish hotel room, she was wearing only a long diaphanous silk negligee that somehow made mysterious again a body he already knew very well. She spoke after kissing him in greeting and pressing her soft body against his.

"You're not slipping," Matt said. "I'm sort of here on business."

"Oh," Angela said, stepped back and smiled. He noticed that she still had makeup on. Did she sleep in it? Or had she put it on quickly after he called? "If this is business, should I get a note pad or something?"

But apparently, from the look on her face, she knew he was not joking, and she led him across the room to the chair and sat him down.

"What is it, Matt? What's wrong?" she asked as she walked across the Oriental carpet and perched on the edge of the bed.

"My wife's been killed. I think the police will be after me for it," he said. He glanced up and at the look of shock in her eyes, said quickly, "I didn't do it. It's a frame-up. There are a couple of other people dead too."

"If it's a frame-up, who's behind it?" she asked.

"Angela, I can't tell you that," he said.

"Then why are you here?"

"I needed a place to stay the night, where they won't get at me."

"And I should trust you, but you can't even trust me enough to tell me what it's about?" she said. There was a brisk businesslike air to her voice that Matt had not expected.

Matt sighed. "Look, Angela. I've stumbled across something that affects national security. I can't tell you, but it's something to do with spies. I turned the information over to the right people in government. I think they're the ones who killed my wife and tried to kill me."

"Why? If you did the right thing and turned over this whatever-it-is?" she asked.

"Because I don't think they want anyone alive who knows the secret," he said.

"Who's involved?" she asked.

"Everybody," Matt said leadenly. "Everybody. The freaking government, the tax people, the goddam FBI."

Angela got up and walked to her suitcase, which was lying unzipped on a rack on the far side of the room. "Then you don't have a chance," she said. "They'll kill you."

"Maybe not," he said and Angela stopped fumbling in the bag and turned to face him.

"How's that?" she said.

"The information I gave them? Well, I stole it back. If I'm killed, it'll get public."

He was holding the computer disc in his hands and Angela said, "Is that it? Is the information on there?"

"Yeah," Matt said. "But not just there. I stashed it somewhere else too." He thought for a moment and said, "Can I use your phone?"

She nodded her head toward the instrument on the headboard of the bed.

He dug around in his pocket for the worn business card that Gianetti had given him, then dialed the number.

The telephone was answered with "Yes?"

"Let me talk to Gianetti," Matt said.

"Who's calling, please?"

"Matt Taylor. Hurry up. I'll hold on fifteen seconds and no more."

He was up to thirteen when Gianetti's voice came onto the line.

"Matt. Where are you?"

"Forget that, Gianetti."

"Hey, why'd you run?"

"Because you bastards tried to kill me," Matt snapped.

"We didn't even know it was you," Gianetti said. "We found those two bodies and we were just chasing what we thought was the killer."

Matt sighed. "Gianetti, you can stick all that bullshit up your ass. I want you to get hold of Plevris."

"Now how would I do that?" Gianetti said.

"I really don't care. But I'm calling back in exactly fifteen minutes and I want to talk to him. Make sure you can switch this call there."

He hung up without saying goodbye.

He looked up at Angela who shrugged and said, "Who are those people?"

"An FBI man. He and his partner tried to kill me tonight. His partner got killed in an accident while he was chasing me. The other guy I want to talk to is the head of the I.R.S."

"He's involved in this ... this thing you stumbled over?" she asked.

"I don't know," he said. "Angela, I don't think it's good that you ask me any questions. It might just make you a target too. Maybe I ought to just get out of here. This was a mistake, involving you."

"No, wait," she said. "At least make your phone call in fifteen minutes. You're better off here."

She walked across the room and turned on the television set. "The news should be coming on," she said. "We'll see if you're as famous as you think you are."

329

He was. The shootings in his apartment was the lead story on the local news. A black newscaster with horn-rimmed glasses solemnly intoned:

"Three people—one of them an FBI agent—are dead tonight in a bizarre incident that may have grown out of a love triangle."

Matt stared at the screen in numb fascination as the newscaster read off the names of the dead. He looked up and nodded his thanks as Angela pushed a water glass of brandy into his hand.

The newscaster said that Fluory and Melanie had been killed in their apartment and that Matt had been seen running from the building moments later. Two FBI men, who were in the building on other business, gave chase into a subway tunnel. Apparently one of the FBI men collared the suspect, but in the scuffle, Polonowski was electrocuted by contact with the third rail. The suspect escaped, the newsman said, and police were seeking to question the dead woman's husband, Matthew Taylor, 38, in the shootings.

"We'll be following this story tonight and will have further information as it becomes available," the newsman said.

Angela turned off the television. "So you're a fugitive. I've got to be more careful who I let into my room," she said. Matt sipped the brandy and she asked, "Is that the way it was? Was this guy, Fluory or whatever, sleeping with your wife?"

"Yes," Matt said, sighing slowly. "That's what he told me but that wasn't what it was about. He had a gun on me. He called those FBI guys who were going to come up and kill me and Melanie. Before they got there, there was a scuffle and he shot Mel and then himself while we were fighting for the gun."

"Maybe you should turn yourself in and tell them that," she said.

"Yeah. And who'd believe me? Secret plots. Spies. FBI killers. I can hardly believe any of it myself. And I wouldn't last long enough to tell anybody anyway. I'd be dead before I reached the holding cell. Listen, this was wrong. I'm getting out of here."

He put down the glass and started to rise but Angela pushed him back down onto the bed.

"Make your telephone call," she said.

He dialed the number, asked for Gianetti and when he identified himself, the FBI man said, "Here's Mr. Plevris."

Plevris came on talking. "Matt," he said, "You've got to get in here and straighten this all out. Fluory dead, you wife, I don't know what's going on. I think for your own safety, you'd better get in here quickly."

"Sorry, Mr. Plevris, but I think you know very well what's going on, and that's why I'm not coming in. I just called to tell you that I've got the Harker's Furnace files."

"Oh, come on, Matt. I already stripped them from the regional computers, right after our earlier meeting."

"I know, but I had a copy I didn't tell you about and now I've stashed it, and you tell your bully boys, if anything happens to me it goes right to the *Washington Post.*"

"Easy, Matt, easy. I know you must be upset. Why don't you come in and let's talk things over?"

"We talked earlier. Then your guys tried to kill me. Forget it. Once is enough."

"You're making a mistake, Matt, and I think our mutual friend, Charlie, would tell you that too."

"No thanks. Just remember. Anything happens to me and the tapes go to the *Washington Post.*"

He hung up the phone.

He looked up as Angela sat on the bed next to him.

"Is that right?" she said. "You've arranged for this all to get public if you get killed?"

"It will," Matt said.

"Where'd you stash them then?" she asked casually.

"I don't think you want to know that," he said.

"No," she said slowly. "I guess you're right. So where do we go from here?"

"I don't know," he said.

"I'm a licensed private investigator. If I don't want trouble with my license, I should turn you over to the police," she said.

"I'll leave now," he said.

She touched his leg.

"Except," she said. "Except that I don't know that there's a warrant out for your arrest, just that the police want to question you. So that's a different thing. Especially . . . listen, Matt, are you asking me to work for you?"

"No. Yes. I don't know," he said.

"Yes, you are. Now you're my client," she said. "I don't ever have to hand up a client."

"Good. Then I'm your client."

"I insist on getting paid in advance," she said, and grabbed Matt and pulled him back playfully onto the bed with her.

But when Matt did not respond, she let him go and said, "I'm sorry. That was thoughtless. Your wife's dead and I'm fooling around."

"It's okay," he said, then sat up and took the telephone again. This time, he called the Judge's number in Iron City. The old man answered the telephone himself and Matt said, "Judge, there's been some trouble. Melanie's dead."

"What? How'd it happen?"

"Judge, I can't talk now. Listen, no matter what you hear, I didn't do it. The cops are after me, but I'm okay."

"I can be on a plane in an hour, son," Stevens said.

"No. Don't do that. I'll call you tomorrow. Please tell Lauren so she's not shocked if she hears something on the news."

"All right, boy. Anything else you need? Money? A lawyer in Washington?"

"Not now. Talk to you tomorrow."

"I'll be waiting by the phone," the Judge said.

* * *

Sleep did not come easily. Matt drifted in and out of the consciousness, his restless mind a jumble of visions of Melanie with bullet holes in her breast, Larry Wu lying dead in a parking lot, Fluory with his face partly blown off, and Polonowski sizzling against a railroad track. And those were just the deaths he knew of. There was probably that computer man, Nujinsky, from the Installation. There were the two dead gunmen. And how many others?

And for what? For what? He wrestled with that problem in his mind over and over during the night, and finally fell deeply asleep knowing that he could only find the answers at the Installation. He was going back to Harker's Furnace.

When he awoke, he saw Angela fully dressed, sitting at the room's small dining table, sipping a cup of coffee. A pile of Sunday newspapers lay on the chair alongside her. She smiled at him.

"Rise and shine, sleepyhead." She waved at the newspapers. "I've just been reading your press notices. You're quite the dangerous man."

He struggled out of bed and took the other seat at the table. She had a container of black coffee for him; it was still hot, and the first taste of the strong bitter liquid seemed to shake some of the cobwebs from his brain.

He moved the pile of newspapers to the table in front of him and groaned. The story of the three deaths had made Page One on all three newspapers and his picture was splashed all over the front pages. He recognized the picture. It was almost nine years old, cropped from his and Melanie's wedding picture. It had stood on the dresser in the bedroom of their apartment.

The headlines about multiple killings, jealous husband sought, told enough, and he put the papers back onto the chair.

"Not interested?" Angela said.

"Maybe later. I can't stand looking at them now."

"So we're off to Harker's Furnace?" she said.

He looked at her, puzzled. "I was planning to go. How'd you know?"

"I haven't known you a long time, Matt, but I think I know what's in your head. You're going back there to find out what's going on."

He nodded. "But you said 'we're' off?"

A smile rippled across her beautiful face. "You're my client. Whither thou goest, I go," she said.

"I don't want you getting involved," he said. "You've done too much already."

"Don't worry. You'll get my bill." She turned suddenly serious. "Chances are you couldn't get out of town without me anyway. So take your shower or whatever it is you do, I'm going down to check us out of this dump."

She did not stay so that he could argue with her. When he came out of the shower, she was back in the room, taking her gun from the open suitcase, and putting it into the purse. She pointed to a plastic bag on the bed.

"You're in luck. The store downstairs was open and I got you some new underwear and socks."

He emptied the bag onto the bed and said, "What's this?"

"Your picture's all over the place. The sunglasses and the baseball cap will make you harder to recognize. Just until we get out of town."

"Don't you have a job in town . . . a case? Can you just drop it and go with me?" Matt asked.

"Stay here and miss the action? Don't be a fool," Angela said. "Now get dressed."

A half hour later, they were on the Beltway, Washington, D.C., receding behind them, pushing west at high speed in Angela's smoke-gray Maserati.

"Lighten up on that pedal," Matt said. "If we run by a radar Smokey, we'll both be in the can."

"Don't worry about it. I just flash my tin at them and off we go."

"As long as that's all you flash," Matt said with a small smile. It seemed as if he had not smiled in years.

"One man at a time," Angela said.

After another forty-five minutes, Angela pulled into a road-side truckstop for gas, and suggested that he get some coffee for them. He put on his sunglasses, pulled his baseball cap down over his face, and entered the restaurant.

Inside he stopped at a bank of telephones, fished in his pocket for change, and dialed the Judge's home number.

The Judge answered on the first ring.

"Judge, it's Matt."

"Are you all right, son?"

"As well as can be expected. Listen, do you know your neighbor's phone number?"

"The Waldrons? Sure."

"Then here's what I want you to do. Give me the number, then scoot over there right away. I'll call you there in exactly five minutes."

Judge Stevens did not argue. "Okay," he said. He gave Matt the phone number, had Matt repeat it, then hung up.

Matt checked his watch, went into the restaurant and got two containers of black coffee and a handful of chocolate bars. When exactly five minutes had passed, he re-entered the phone booth and dialed the neighbor's number the Judge had given him.

Stevens answered.

"Yes, Matt."

"Sorry for the runaround, Judge," Matt said.

"You think my phone is tapped?" the Judge asked shrewdly.

"I don't know, but you have to assume it is. And you'll have to assume that you'll be under surveillance. So we've just got to be careful."

"Are you all right? The out-of-town papers all had the story today. What is this about murder?"

"It's a frame-up, Judge. I'll tell you about it when I get there."

"You coming here? Isn't this the first place they'll look for you?"

"Yeah, but I don't have any choice. It's the FBI after me,"

335

Matt said. "They can run me down anywhere. Anyway, here's what I need you to do. Do you have a pen?"

"Go ahead," the Judge said.

"I need a place to stay. Someplace secluded, with a telephone, and decent electricity."

"Keep going," the Judge said. "I'll stop you if I have any trouble."

"And I need some supplies. They're probably going to be tough to get on a Sunday."

"Let me worry about that," the Judge said.

Matt started to rattle off a string of technical names of computers and software.

"Did you get all that?" he asked.

"Got it. What else?"

"And I can use a handgun."

"Okay."

"That's it, I think," Matt said. "Judge, I can't come to your house, and I can't telephone you there. As I said, we've got to assume you've got a phone tap and surveillance on you, so just be careful."

"Son, I was being careful before you were born," Stevens said.

"Do you have the telephone number of another neighbor?"

"Sure. Will Palmer."

"I'll call you there at six o'clock tonight. You can give me the location of the house then."

"All right," the Judge said. He gave Matt the Palmers' telephone number, hesitated, then said, "Be careful, son. We need you. And we'll work things out; remember what I used to tell you."

"What was that?" Matt asked.

"*Fiat iustitia ruat caelum.* Though the heavens fall, let justice be done."

"Hold that thought," Matt said. "Thanks, Judge. Six o'clock," Matt said and hung up.

336

He brought the coffee out to the car, got in, and Angela sped off.

"That must be the slowest restaurant in the world," she grumbled.

"I stopped to make a couple of phone calls," Matt said. "I had to find a place for me to stay."

"Correction," she said. "For 'us' to stay."

CHAPTER THIRTY-EIGHT

It was easier to sleep than to explain, so Matt let Angela do all the driving—although, in truth, she had not even offered to let him behind the wheel of her Maserati—and dozed on and off all the way across Pennsylvania.

When she realized he was not going to be a conversational partner, Angela had loaded up the cassette deck and played recordings of operas at high volume—with which she sang along in the very, very earnest style of the naturally tone-deaf.

Once in a while, Matt shook himself from sleep, and the woman immediately turned down the volume and tried to engage him in chitchat, but gradually, over the miles, it turned into a monologue as Angela told him her background. Born in America, wealthy parents, raised in Switzerland and Spain, parents died while she was in a convent ... Matt remembered laughing about that and Angela smiled, reached over and squeezed his crotch, and said, "So I've been making up for lost time."

She had come back to America, liked Philadelphia best of all the American cities she had seen, and settled there. Angela started going out with a private detective, had been brought into the firm by him, and when he died, just took over the operation of the business.

"So that's my life story. What's yours?"

Matt snored a response.

Up went the opera volume.

They stopped to eat later and managed to be approaching Iron City just about six o'clock. While Angela gassed up, Matt telephoned the number the Judge had given him.

Stevens was obviously relieved to hear from him. He told Matt he had gotten the use of a cabin in the woods, located on an unpaved dirt road about twelve miles from the city.

"It's only a cottage, but it's got electricity, a backup generator, and a pair of telephones," Stevens said. "And I was able to get your equipment in there and hooked up today."

"On a Sunday? Somebody must owe you a big favor," Matt said.

"Hell, that would have made it easy, son," the Judge said. "The hard part was getting it done and not letting anybody know I was involved in it."

Naturally he had been careful, Matt thought. The Judge had always been careful. Matt said, "Good work," and the Judge answered, "you get out there. Door's open. I'll see you there later," and before Matt could protest, added, "Don't worry about it. I'm not exactly a moose stomping through the woods, you know."

"Who'd you call?" Angela asked when he returned to the Maserati.

"A friend," Matt said. "Let's get moving."

They found the cabin with no trouble. Apparently, only the one unpaved road led to it, bumping and curving its way through a half mile of forest, making it pretty hard for anyone in a vehicle to sneak up unnoticed. And the structure itself, a typical vacation-style A-frame, was set back from the roadway, surrounded on all sides by several hundred feet of clearing, chopped from the heavy dense woods.

With the air of assumption practiced by someone used to behaving that way, Angela let Matt lug their bags into the small building as she searched for the light switch. The lights came on as he fought the luggage into the room. Against the far wall was an obviously brand new desk and table, holding the computer equipment he had asked the Judge to provide. The cabin itself was neat and warm, for which Matt was thankful. Computers tended to get spooky when they were allowed to get too cold.

Angela stood in the middle of the room, her arms outstretched like Loretta Young playing a TV hostess, and said, "Our first little love nest, Matt."

"My work hovel," he said.

Angela smiled. "Don't worry. The urge will return."

Matt shook his head. "You got me here safely and for that, thanks. But I don't think you ought to stay here. It might get dangerous."

Angela hooked her thumbs into the broad leather belt that encircled her tiny waist, thrust out her pelvis, and ambled back and forth in a passable imitation of a movie cowboy. "Shucks, partner," she said, "I reckon my job here ain't done 'til I've rid this valley of owl-hoots."

She smiled at him, but Matt said, "I can't tell you what I'm doing but they ... whoever they are ... they're not going to know that. It's dangerous, Angela."

"Are you afraid I'm going to try to squeeze information out of you?" When he did not answer right away, she said, "Well, forget it. I can smell national security stuff a mile away and I'm not interested in getting involved. I'm just hanging out with you 'cause you're my client. And you're a good lay."

"Well, on that note, I'd like to welcome you to Iron City with semi-open arms," a familiar voice said from the open doorway behind Matt. He turned and saw Judge Stevens there, grinning broadly.

Without missing a beat, Angela responded to him, "I'll put you on my dance card, Judge, in case he gets stubborn."

"Oh, to be seventy again," the Judge said.

"Do you two stand-up comics mind if I get a word in?" Matt said. He stepped toward the Judge who came forward and threw his arms around Matt.

"You okay, son?" he asked.

"Hanging tough, Judge. How'd you come down the road without us hearing you?"

"You're just not as smart as I thought you were," the Judge said, as he released him from his bear hug. "I didn't come down the road. I was already here. Watching the house from out in the woods."

"Should have known you'd be cautious," Matt said.

"Have you checked out that stuff?" the Judge asked, waving toward the computer apparatus. "Is it what you want?"

"Haven't looked at it yet, but I know it's okay," Matt said. "As long as it works."

"It'll work," the Judge said. And then there was an awkward silence during which Stevens nodded slightly in Angela's direction. The gesture was meant for Matt but Angela obviously noticed it because she said, " 'I'm going out to walk around. Let you two talk for a while."

She pulled on a suede leather jacket and went toward the front door.

"Don't step in any bear traps," the Judge said, as she closed the door behind her.

"Sorry, son, I don't know how much she knows, and I didn't want to talk around her."

"She knows as little as I could get away with telling her," Matt said.

"You're all over the news," the Judge said. "Even the *Gusher*. I couldn't get them to keep it out. How'd it all happen?"

"Come on in the kitchen. We'll talk while I try to find some coffee," Matt said. He told the story to the Judge as he prepared an old percolator pot of coffee on the electric range.

His meeting with Ari Cohen and then later with Vice President Barkley. Barkley's revelation that the Installation was the central headquarters for some kind of Joint Intelligence Group and a clearinghouse for the country's spies, informers, and secret agents. He told how he had broken through Larry Wu's code and found the missing Harker's Furnace tax returns. And right after turning them over to the Vice President, the attempts were made to kill him. And Fluory and Melanie and Polonowski, the FBI man, were killed instead.

"And here I am, and it's one helluva mess," Matt said.

"What about Barkley? You think he was behind it? You think he was lying?"

"I've kicked that one around in my head for the last twenty-four hours," Matt said. "I don't know. He must have put out the order to kill me. But I don't know if he was lying about what's up at the Installation or if that spy stuff is all true and he just thought I knew to much to be allowed to live. I just don't know. Only thing I know is that somebody's after me and if they haven't figured it out already, they will soon. And this is the place they'll be looking."

"Then why'd you come here?" the Judge asked.

"Look, Judge, let's face it. I'm a dead man. There's no way I can stand up against the Feds and all their power if they want me dead. But just maybe I can change their minds if I get something to bargain with."

"The computers?" the Judge said.

"Right. I'm going to get into the Installation's computers and find out what the hell is going on in there."

"You think that'll keep you alive?"

"I don't have any other ideas right now," Matt said.

"Well, I've got a few. You're not going to die that easily, son." Stevens shook his head.

"I'll go down fighting anyway," Matt said.

"Don't talk about going down. It's not going to happen. You know, don't you, that Barkley and I were once pretty close. Anything to be gained by my talking to him?"

"I don't think so, Judge. Not yet, anyway. That just ties you in with me, and puts everybody in danger. I need you to be able to move around a little bit for me, do the things I can't do. And I imagine Barkley will be calling you one day on his own. Let him make the first move." He paused. "Why are you smiling?"

"You said you needed me. In all these years, that's the first time you've ever said that."

"Maybe it's the first time I ever *did* need you," Matt said.

"No." The Judge shook his head. "It's just the first time you ever realized it."

The moment was getting too sentimental, and Matt turned to pour coffee for them and said casually, "I'll pay you back naturally for all the computer stuff."

"Don't be a damn fool, boy. I'll just take it out of your inheritance. Something else. I don't like to ask you about it, but I guess I'd better."

"Go ahead," Matt said.

"Melanie's funeral. Should I get somebody in Washington to take care of it?"

Matt sighed. "You know, my wife was killed in front of my eyes last night, and I haven't thought about her for a total of two minutes since then. What's wrong with me?

"You've been busy staying alive. That does exert a powerful claim on one's attention."

Matt thought quickly. "Melanie's got family back in Ohio. Let them deal with the funeral," he said. "At least for a little while, until we see what happens here."

"Whatever you want, Matt. One more thing. Lauren'll be coming up here soon. She's got some of those books and stuff you wanted." He squinted in puzzlement. "What do you do with the other young lady?" he asked, nodding his head toward the kitchen wall as if pointing outside toward Angela.

"Is it wise for Lauren to come here?" Matt said. "The more people know about this place, the riskier it is."

"I couldn't keep Lauren out of it," Stevens answered. "She loves you, remember? And give me some credit, Matt. No one's coming up here that we don't want here. I've seen to that."

"Well, I can't have her here and Angela too. But I don't think Angela will go willingly."

"Naturally. Not since you're so great in bed," the Judge said drily.

"That's just the way she talks," Matt said, trying to hide some of the embarrassment he felt discussing sex with the older man.

"*And* the way she acts," the Judge said. "Don't worry, I'll get her out of here."

"Now you know why I need you," Matt said. "To handle my dance card."

"What's a father for?" the Judge said, then put his head down and sipped at his hot black coffee.

Before they had any further chance to talk, they heard a sound at the front door and ran out into the living room.

Angela was standing just inside the door, her hands held behind her by a slim young man with coal black hair and eyes like midnight. Angela was struggling to free herself and the Judge barked, "Timmy. It's okay." He nodded and the young man released her. She rubbed her wrists and the man said, "She had this." He extended his hand and showed them Angela's small automatic pistol.

"It's mine," Angela snapped. "Who is this cretin?"

The young man ignored her. "I was watching her, she was walking around, but then she took the gun out."

"It's all right, Timmy. You did the right thing. But Miss Fox is a friend of ours."

"Oh. Sorry ma'am," the young man said.

He handed the gun back to Angela, who looked for a long second as if she were going to use it on him.

But the man paid her no attention and went back outside.

"Who was that?" Matt asked.

"Billy O'Baal has a large family around these parts," the Judge said. "I think he's got most of them out in the woods, watching this house and the road. They know you and me; they didn't know Miss Fox."

"Hell of a reception," she said as she slipped the gun back into her purse.

"I told you these woods can be dangerous at night," the Judge said. He reached behind him and, out of view of Angela, pushed Matt toward the kitchen. Matt complied and went back to finish his coffee.

A minute later, Angela stepped inside and said, "I'll be going with the Judge now. We'll talk tomorrow."

She came forward and kissed him, then walked away without further explanation. Matt went into the living room in time to see the two of them walking outside with her luggage. When the Judge returned, Matt asked, "How'd you do that?"

"I just told her if she thought you were good in the sack, I taught you everything you knew."

"Liar."

"I know, but don't tell her that. Let her find out for herself," the Judge said. He reached inside his coat pocket and handed Matt a .22 automatic and a box of ammunition. "I almost forgot this," he said. "It's loaded. And it's clean. No records. If you have to use it, don't miss."

Then he, too, was gone and a moment later, Matt heard the roar of Angela's Maserati as it pulled away from the house. The Judge never stopped surprising him.

CHAPTER THIRTY-NINE

It might have been an hour or three hours later when Lauren arrived. Matt had been at the keyboard, getting user-friendly with the computer equipment the Judge had secured for him, when he was interrupted by a kiss on the neck, turned, and saw Lauren standing behind him. A large plastic shopping bag, filled with books, stood on the floor beside her.

This was yet another Lauren Carmody. When he had first seen her on his last trip to Iron City, she had been playing the part of the old iron-assed, leather-haired schoolmarm. Hours later, she came at him all tarted up. Neither guise fit her. But tonight, she looked like the Lauren Carmody he had grown up with, had loved, and—he realized, seeing her—he still loved. Her flame red hair was loose and soft around her face; she wore only the lightest makeup, but it was just enough to make her rather remarkable complexion look even more creamily transparent. Her eyes, large and intelligent, were brushed with laugh lines, and her mouth was full and lush, made that way by nature and not cosmetics. All in all, it was the face of a woman that a man could laugh with and love with and live with.

Unless the man made some stupid choices along the way and wound up rotting in a faithless, loveless marriage to someone else.

346

"Nothing to say?" she asked him, smiling.

"Just that I'm damned glad I've got bodyguards," Matt said. "You could have been anybody and I didn't even know you were here."

"Not much chance of just anybody getting in here," she said. "Billy's got a whole damned tribe of Sioux warriors or something out there patrolling the woods." She paused for a moment, then blurted out, "Oh, fuck all that," and came forward and into his arms. "Oh, Matt. I was so worried about you. So worried." And then she wept softly as Matt stroked her back, comforting her.

"We're going to be all right now, aren't we?" she asked him. "You and me. Forever. Tell me, Matt."

"You and me, forever Lauren. Like it always should have been." *Unless, as is very likely, I get my brains blown out sometime in the next twenty-four hours.*

She pulled his head down to kiss her. They stayed like that, embracing for a long time, then went to sit on the sofa with their feet up, drinking coffee, Lauren laughing at Matt's moronic attempts to start a fire in the fireplace, finally rescuing him and getting a blaze underway in just a few minutes. And then talking, old friends, talking warm and intimate as in the old days.

He had dreaded telling her the story of the last few days. Not just because he was tired of telling it—which he was—but because it had always been Matt's practice, when dealing with something complicated, to keep it to himself until he had it worked out. He usually found that the act of telling someone else about a problem often had the unwanted effect of pushing him toward a specific position or policy, when in fact he should have kept all his options open.

But as the fire roared on and an hour passed, then two, he was surprised to find that he had told Lauren the entire story; that, without seeming to squeeze him, she had pulled out the whole sequence of events. Before she had arrived, he had made up his mind to tell her nothing, because the less

347

she knew, the safer she was. He was firm on that; he would not change his mind about it; and yet here she had the whole tale, and he was not even aware of having told her. It just all came out in old friend's talk, and he was annoyed with himself.

And Lauren knew *that* too.

"Come on," she said. "You thought you were going to keep me in the dark?"

"Something like that," he admitted sourly.

She laughed and lay her head on his shoulder again. "You could never keep a secret from me, Matt."

"Stop making me feel inadequate. Here, maybe I'm battling the entire spy apparatus of the United States, and you twist me around your finger like licorice."

"Lack of character," she said. "It was always your fatal flaw."

"Nice choice of words," he said, but when he felt her flinch, he pulled her closer to him and kissed her again, this time the kiss of lovers, not friends, and she responded, pulling him down onto the sofa alongside her, pushing her body insistently against his. And then, as abruptly as she had begun, she stopped and primly began adjusting her clothing.

"Not like this," she said. "Not here, not now. Not yet. There's too much to clear up first."

"Sure," he said. "I understand."

"No, you don't" she said. "Matt, I think I've got some of the answers you need."

"I'm all ears," he said.

She dropped her hand onto his lap.

"Well, maybe not all ears," he admitted.

"You said you didn't know whether Barkley was telling you the truth or not about the Installation," she began.

"Yeah?"

"I don't think he is." She turned on the sofa to look more directly into his face. "Matt, I've been working almost every

348

waking hour on the ownership of the Installation. You never saw anything like it."

"How so?"

"Well, the way ownership was hidden wasn't unusual. It's pretty standard technique actually. I guess you tax men must know about it. Dummy companies owning dummy companies. And partnerships. And investment firms. And so on and so on. What was unusual here was the level of duplicity. The Judge tells me that in this kind of thing you generally find one company owning a second company, but when you find out who owns the first company, you've got it. Usually, there are only three layers. But here, in some cases, there were thirty and forty layers. I tracked them all, hundreds of companies, some of them legitimate, some of them with no noticeable business life. And I found what put them all together."

"Which was?" Matt asked.

"The law firm which handled it. Weiskopf, Sapir and Durand."

"That mean something to me?" Matt asked.

"It used to be Weiskopf, Sapir, Durand and Barkley."

"As in Charles Garner Barkley, Vice President?" Matt asked.

"The same," she said. She paused. "No comment? What do you think?"

"I think it shows that Barkley's involved with the Installation," Matt admitted. "But I don't think it shows that it's not what he says it is. A secret government installation. If I were the President and I were starting one up, I think I might very well use the vice president's old law firm to handle the work. Keep it in the family in a way."

He felt sorry about his comments. Lauren had worked hard and he hated to shoot her theory full of holes so easily. But she was just shaking her head.

"You don't get it, do you?" she said.

"I guess not," he said truthfully.

"I keep forgetting you're not a lawyer," she said.

349

"Don't forget that," Matt said. "It's one of my finer points."

"If you were the government, and you wanted to set up some kind of secret ownership of the Installation, you sure would *not* use the vice president's old law firm. Because if I can track it back thirty, forty layers with just my reading glasses and a telephone, anybody with a staff could break it in three hours. The President'd be opening the door to a big internal scandal. No. What you'd do, what the President would do, would be to go overseas, what they call off-shore. You'd do your ownership in the Bahamas. Or even Luxembourg. That's better because it's part of the European Common Market. You can transfer all the money you want and no questions are asked anywhere. Criminals use it all the time. I've read that the KGB, even the CIA, uses Luxembourg. Using domestic companies and a domestic law firm with all the potential for leaks and publicity . . . no, Matt, it just doesn't scan."

"Maybe you're right," Matt said.

"I know I'm right," Lauren snapped.

"Well, we're going to find out soon enough," Matt said. He rose and went back to the computer station. "Come on over."

Lauren pushed a rolling chair next to Matt's place at the computer. "Take those phone books," he said, "and look in the Yellow Pages for clubs and associations."

As Matt worked with the computer, Lauren moved quickly through the large stack of out-of-town directories, tearing out pages. She was bent over the pages, reading glasses perched on the edge of her nose, her lips pursed, her brow knit in concentration. She had her legs crossed at the knees and she was leaning forward from the waist and, for the first time, Matt noticed that she was wearing no bra. He stared at her for a moment and then he scooted his rolling chair closer to hers, put his index finger under her chin and lifted her lips to meet his. At first she seemed surprised and then she returned the kiss warmly. The kiss lingered on and Matt lifted his hands to cup her breasts; she moved slightly so that his hands filled with her. The kiss grew in intensity; and finally Matt moved back and looked at her. Lauren's eyelids were fluttering, her breath was coming in little-baby sighs and the base of her throat was flushed.

"So now a lesson in computer security," he said.

"After that?" she said. She shook her head. "In high school, we used to have a word for guys like you."

"Keep it in mind. I'll ask questions later," he said.

"Go ahead, computer man," she growled.

"First though, remember, I told you I put those Harker's Furnace tax returns back in the I.R.S. computer?"

"Yes?"

"I just want to make sure that it worked and they're still there," Matt said. "They're my insurance policy. See, that's what I was getting at. There are two major problems if you want to find out what's in a computer. First, you have to have the door opened for you. And second, you have to have the address of what it is that you're looking for."

"Any problem with either of those?" Lauren asked.

"I hope not. The door should be easy. The I.R.S. system and I are buddies. I'm one of the half-dozen people in the country who can get into any of their machines, anytime, anyway."

"And the address of what you're looking for?"

"When Larry first put the files into the computer, he tagged them with Chinese painting names. I gave those to the vice president and Plevris, and even before the first bullet was winging at my head, they got the returns out of the files. So I put them back in but with a different label this time."

As he was talking, Matt was hooking up the computer with the telephone modem connection. A minute later, he dialed a number, then tapped a personal code onto the computer's keyboard.

"Dammit, good," Matt exclaimed.

"What's 'dammit good'?" Lauren asked.

"They figured me for dead. Nobody thought to change the entry codes for the service's computers."

351

"That would have been a boot in the butt," she said, "if after all this, you couldn't get inside them."

Matt shrugged. "I know everybody's access codes. I'd enter somehow." The computer monitor began to flash a sequence of numbers.

"I'm in now," he said. "Now I've got to get into the Philadelphia bank of computers."

"How do you do that?" she asked.

"There's a separate access code for each regional computer. I know them all."

"Golly, you're smart," Lauren said, and when he looked at her, she was fluttering her eyelids as if about to swoon.

"Smartass," he said. "There. Now we're in Philly. Now let's see if the Installation returns are where I left them."

As Lauren moved close and looked over his shoulder, Matt typed onto the computer screen:

"Fiat iustitia ruat caelum."

"Very nice," Lauren said. "You should have been a lawyer. 'Let justice be done, though the heavens fall.'"

"The Judge has been talking to you, too, I see. Anyway, it's the way I've been thinking these days," he said. After only a second or two, the computer screen filled with words and began scrolling its way through a long list of names, salaries, and tax payments.

"That's it," Matt said excitedly. "Still there." He typed some instructions rapidly into the computer, the screen went dark, and he turned off the telephone connection.

"What'd you do?" she said.

"I got out of there, before anybody noticed I was in. I just wanted to make sure the material was still there." He looked at her. "Lauren, you're the only one now who knows where that's hidden and how to access it. If anything happens to me . . ." He left the words unspoken.

"Nothing's going to happen to you, Matt," she said and squeezed his upper arm.

"All right. That was the easy one," Matt said. "Getting

into the Installation's computers might not be such a piece of cake."

"The password a problem?" she asked.

"I don't know. When I was out there, I saw a bunch of words in strange letter on a slip of paper that was taped to a desk. The letters were elvish."

"Elvish?" she repeated.

"As in Tolkien's *Lord of the Rings*."

"That's why you had me find this?" she said, reaching into the bag and bringing out a copy of Tolkien's *The Return of the King*.

He took the book from her and began leafing through it, talking absently as he did. "Right. I have to transpose that elvish writing into the English alphabet. It's been years, but I remember this book shows how. Here it is. This is the dull part. Why don't you go make some coffee?"

When Lauren returned, Matt gave her a big grin. "Done," he said. He showed her a piece of paper with strange non-English words written on it.

She shook her head. "It's Greek to me," she said.

"Elvish," he corrected, "and let's hope it's not Greek to the computer."

"There are five words." he said. "I suspect that in order to get into their system, you have to enter all five in the correct sequence within a certain amount of time."

"And if you don't what happens?"

Matt shrugged. "Damned if I know," he said.

Lauren sipped her coffee, staring at the computer screen.

"There's blank spots in all this," she said.

"Such as?"

"For one, what are we trying to get out of the Installation? What are we going to know when we know it? And another thing, where do we store it? Or keep it?" She pointed at the personal computer before Matt. "Surely we can't store it all in there." She waved at the ripped pages from the telephone books. "And what about these? Where do they fit in?"

"Last question first," Matt said. "The phone book pages are to get phone numbers from. It's like this: most computers, as part of their security system, are able to backcheck on calls coming into the system and show the phone number they've originated from. Once they've got that, it's a simple matter usually to identify the caller."

"Hold on. Couldn't that happen with the call you just made into the I.R.S. computer? You made it right from this phone," Lauren said.

"Good point and good observation," Matt said. "Except, the I.R.S. computers don't have a phone checkback system. They were always telling me it cost too much, but someday some hacker is going to get in there and make chaos out of the United States tax records. I might just do it myself before this is all over."

"Don't. You go back to work for them and you'll just have to undo your own mess," she said.

"Somehow I've got the feeling that I'm never working for the I.R.S. again," Matt said. "Anyway, I'm guessing that the Installation's computer has the phone security system and we don't want them suddenly appearing here in the middle of the night. So what we do is run a little delay pattern. See, I can use this computer and call up a phone number, let it ring a while and then, if nobody answers, I can cut into their circuit and place an outgoing call so that it seems to be coming from the number I originally called. Got that?"

"Yes," she said. "But can't they tell that you're doing that?"

Matt smiled. "Sometimes yes, sometimes no. But I'm not going to make it easy for them. What I do is call up my first number and do the switcharound . . ."

"Right. You said that."

"But then, from the first number, I call a second number. And from that one a third. And then from there, a fourth. And so on. What I'm counting on is that their security equipment isn't good enough to trace the signal back very far."

"Okay," she said. "But what about the Yellow Pages here? Clubs and associations?"

"That's my safety factor. See, the people we're up against play rough. If I used just any phone numbers, there'd be a good chance that the bad guys would come down pretty hard on whoever's number it was."

Lauren nodded. "I understand. You could be putting some innocent person in danger."

"Right. Instead of me being the only innocent person in danger," he said. "So I'm not taking a chance on using anybody's number. Instead we'll use, say, the Girl Scout Council in the San Fernando Valley and the Humane Society office in Boston and the Bar Association in New York City. See? Even the dumbest bad guys would be able to figure out that those phones were just being used by somebody else. So, no danger to innocent bystanders."

"My hero," she said, only half-joking.

"Now your other question. Where do we store whatever we get out of the Installation? I don't know. I want to see what's in there and what it means. Maybe I only have to store some of it. I'm not sure. But it's time to find out."

Matt laid the Yellow Pages out in front of him and started circling, then calling different numbers printed on those pages. Between each call, he drove into the computer a string of telephone company codes that enabled him to cut into the unanswered lines.

"Here's a good one," Matt said. "The Wa-Wa Club in North Bergen, New Jersey. That should give them pause if they start trying to track this all down. And the St. Patrick's Day Parade Committee in Jersey City." He started to whistle softly to himself as he worked. Lauren thumbed idly through the pages of the Tolkien book which she had persuaded a friend who worked at the Iron City Library to get for her, even though it was Sunday afternoon.

Matt hunched over the keyboard of the small Furioso computer. After a few seconds he stopped, listened to the telephone, and punched in a new number on the phone case. Almost immediately the phone began ringing at the New Orleans headquarters of the American Society for Philately. Again, he typed at the keyboard and waited. He repeated the process again and again until he was certain that not even the Chrin computer at the Installation could backtrack the trail along the nation's telephone lines.

He punched in the computer's number at the Harker's Furnace Installation, waited, and in a few moments, a response appeared on his video terminal. Matt smiled to himself. This was it, he thought. This was the big one. And then the Installation's computer demanded that he identify himself.

Damn, Matt thought. A totally stupid mistake. He'd spent so much time finding the passwords into the heart of the machine that he had forgotten the basics, the user-identification he would need. The Installation's computer was becoming more insistent and threatening him with all sorts of electronic mayhem. He thought quickly. What was the name of that programer out there who had disappeared? Nujinsky and they called him Nuj. He didn't know how to spell it but he would have to make a guess. Computer people liked short ID's. Quickly, he tapped onto the keyboard: "NUJ."

The computer seemed to digest that for a moment, then the screen went blank, and then the word: INSTRUCTIONS? appeared on the screen.

The computer at the Installation was open.

Now came the tricky part, Matt told himself. Getting into the machine's main programming. He typed in the request and was instantly challenged for the passwords. He looked down at the piece of paper he had been working on, then typed in "Eldamar," his own transliteration of the first word he had found stuck to the terminal out there, written in Tolkien's elvish alphabet. He considered waiting before typing in the second password from Middle Earth, then decided to just plunge ahead. He typed in "Lefnui," "Nwalme," "Yavie," and "Primula,"

356

and when he was done, the machine burped electronically a couple of times and began displaying the Installation computer's main programming.

He watched it roll over his display terminal for several moments, then let out a soft groan that made Lauren look up from the sofa to which she had retreated with a book.

"What's the matter?" she said.

"I don't recognize the language," he said.

"Bad, huh?"

"Worse than bad," he mumbled and hunched himself over the terminal in a way that signalled the end of all conversation for a while.

There was no way around it, no easy way out: he would have to teach himself the language as quickly as possible and hope that the bad guys didn't catch on that they were being raided. He hoped there was a real good movie being shown this night at The Installation, and that all the computer people were in there watching it and loving it and demanding that it be shown twice.

A computer language was just that: a formal set of shorthand instructions to allow man and machine to communicate with each other. Ninety percent of the world's computers were outfitted with one of the three major electronic languages—Basic, Cobol, and Fortran— and Matt was familiar with all those and another half-dozen besides. But this damned computer did not respond to any of them.

It turned into an elaborate, intellectual cat-and-mouse game. Matt began poking and prodding at the computer's program, first trying out a few simple commands, making mistakes, trying again. For all its awesome speed, a computer was actually nothing more than a superfast calculator. All the magic that a computer seemed able to perform was based upon its simple-minded ability to add one and one and get two, but to do it tens of millions of times a minute.

A computer might be capable of building a giant mountain of logic, but basically it did it in caveman style, by piling a

357

little handful of dirt on top of another handful of dirt, but doing it all at almost the speed of light, so that, by sheer perserverance, what had started out as a little handful of dirt had grown into a mountain of handfuls.

Breaking into its language meant, first of all, learning how to get the machine to add one and one. From that all else could be built.

It took him almost an hour to recreate the language to get the machine to do that simple task.

And then it came onto the monitor. It was couched in computer symbols and flow diagrams and a string of digits that would frighten off a college math professor, but what it said to Matt was "one plus one equals two."

The breakthrough.

He had gotten inside the machine's brain and now he could look through it into the brain of the program's developer.

Time to get down to serious work.

First, he stretched and yawned. The time spent scrunched over his keyboard had taken its toll in sore arms and shoulders: the glowing light of the monitor, too, had brought on a headache. But there was no stopping, no turning back, not now.

He glanced over at the sofa. Lauren had pulled her feet up and was sleeping. He could hear her soft sibilant breathing across the room.

Matt swiveled his chair back around to face the monitor once again. Whoever had built the language had been a genius. Matt almost wished he had had a chance to meet and know and work with the guy. There was a fascinating, simple elegance to the way the damned thing worked. If most computer languages played to a thumping rock 'n' roll beat, this one was a bossa nova—half funny inventive jazz, and half supple intoxicating rhumba. A masterpiece created by a genius and it was just a damned shame that the bad guys had it.

He wondered if the Installation's computer genius was the man called Nuj—the one who had made the mistake of talking over the machine to Larry Wu and who, for his indiscretion,

358

had wound up as a murdered body, floating face down in a cold winter river.

He hoped not. He hoped the man who had put this machine together lived to be an old man with many grandchildren, many smart children who would recount tales later on of how wise the old man had been.

Or was that what he wished for himself?

Back and forth he pushed the machine. Building on his small arithmetical breakthrough, he invaded the machine, violating it, forcing it to give up first one, then another, then a flood of its secrets. And then, an hour, maybe two hours later, the machine's brain stood before him, naked, vulnerable, surrendering. In that moment he understood the crime of rape as one involving power, not sex.

He demanded that the computer produce its files.

But the machine instantly responded:

"CANNOT COMPLY. DATA NOT LOADED."

Matt swore in a scream of anguish. He pounded his fists on the desk and Lauren, startled by the noise, rose to her feet and walked quickly toward him, frightened by the look of pure rage on his face.

"What's wrong?" she asked.

"I'm inside the Installation's computer but there's nothing there. Just coded running instructions. All their files are on discs and they're physically separated from the computer except when it's being run."

"So you're saying you can't get hold of their back records?"

He sighed. "Not this way. Goddamit, though, I'm going to give them something to think about."

"What's that?"

"I'm going to plant a virus in the damned machine," he snapped.

"What's a virus got to do with a computer?" Lauren asked. She leaned over his back, looking with him at the computer display screen and rubbing her thumbs into his tension-locked neck muscles.

"A lot," Matt said with a scowl. "It's just what it sounds like. It's a set of instructions that I get into the computer's main running program. Leave it there and like a cancer, it gradually expands and squeezes out all the legitimate instructions. Given enough time, it'll kill the system without the operators being able to do a damned thing."

She sat at the edge of the desk and looked at him shrewdly. "Matt, are you doing that just because you're angry and you're blowing off steam, or is there a valid reason for it?"

"No. Fair question, lawyer lady, but there's a reason. If I gum up their operating procedures, it might keep them all busy enough so that they don't have a chance to transmit the records anywhere. It buys us time." He realized he had been snapping his answers at her and he shook his head and smiled gently. "This is going to be a long evening," he said. "If I were you, I'd get back on that couch."

The stubbornness in his voice must have convinced her, because she smiled, nodded, and said, "Call if I can help."

"Sure thing," he said, but before she had even gotten back across the room, he was hammering at the computer's keyboard, everything else in the world already out of his mind.

If breaking the computer's code had been hard work, this was mind-bending. Creating a virus by itself was not terribly complicated. Any computer whiz could do it in a dozen lines of programming or less—if *all* he wanted to do was to gut the system he was entering it into.

But Matt had another consideration. He wanted to immobilize the Installation's computer, but he did not know the extent of its contact with the I.R.S. computers. He could not risk putting any virus into the Installation that might spread into the I.R.S. system and destroy the entire computer tax capability of the United States.

He worked slowly and cautiously.

He had tried once to explain a computer virus to a layman, but he had not gotten very far. The problem was that if it translated into words at all, they were the nonsense words of

Lewis Carroll—not the mild Lewis Carroll who wrote *Alice in Wonderland* and told stories for children, but the cold, insidious mathematic puzzle-maker whose riddles could bend your brain with their backwards logic.

He played with the keyboard like a master musician trying to pull a melody from the air. Mozart ... Gershwin ... Tchaikovsky might have felt like this in the middle of creation, he thought. Maybe even God felt like this.

His mind worked and yet another piece of his mind—a small fragment—stood back and watched, and later that piece of his mind could tell him what he had done.

It was in the nature of telling the computer: If one and one is two, proceed with your regular program. But if anything in your program tells you to add five more, the answer is not seven but six. And proceed with step six. Except if proceeding with step six leads you next to step seven: in that case, proceed with step nine.

Except if one and one is still two, then proceed with step twelve.

But add four to it to get step sixteen.

But if 16 is an even number, go back to step one, but in that case one and one equals three.

Only a madman could have accepted the instructions he was giving the computer, and that, Matt understood, was the way it should have been because he was making the computer insane. That was the nature of planting the virus.

But here—at each separate step of the way—he put in another uncoded message that if the machine should be linked with another computer, it should simply close down.

Do not transmit data. Do not receive data.

Just close down.

And when reopened, follow my new instructions. One and one is three.

* * *

It took more than two hours. When he was finished his shirt was soaked with sweat.

But he had done it. If anybody ... anybody asked the Harker's Furnace computer to do anything more complicated than add one plus one, the machine was going to roll on endlessly, sending orders, contradicting its own orders, moving around at random through the program, eating up data and sending back nonsense.

And no one would be able to stop it.

He knew at that moment that Larry Wu would have been very proud of him.

He broke down the telephone links that he had set up, and then shut off his own Furioso computer.

He stared at the blank monitor and said, "Chew on that, you sons of bitches. Chew on that."

And then he felt Lauren standing behind him. He looked up at her, too excited to feel sheepish and she said, "You did it, huh?"

"I did it," he answered in soft exultation. "I did it. Now they can't transmit those damned records anywhere before I have a chance to get them."

"I thought you said you couldn't get them," she said.

"I can't get them over the telephone. But I've been there and I've seen the big giga-discs their stuff is stored on."

"You mean you're going to go back into the Installation? And physically steal their computer records?"

"Yes," Matt said. "There's no other way. It has to be done."

His eyes made it clear that there was no room for protest, so she said simply, "But not tonight," and took his arm and led him to the stairway that went upstairs to the bedroom lofts.

Lauren preceded Matt into the room, fumbled for the light switch, and then closed the door behind them after Matt entered.

For a moment, they stood there, awkwardly, side by side, like two strangers who had just picked each other up in a bar, gone to a motel room, and now were wondering if this was really the right thing to do. Matt knew how Lauren must feel, because he felt the same way himself. He turned to take her in his arms but she had moved away to the far end of the room where she was pulling tightly closed the curtains on the pair of windows over the bed. As she turned on the small lamp on the night table, she said softly, "I don't mind having Billy's men watch the house, but I'll be damned if I'll have them peeking into our bedroom."

The small lamp came on and Matt smiled as he saw Lauren remove the silk scarf from around her neck and drape it over the top of the lampshade. She had always liked soft lights. Matt turned off the overhead light and they looked at each other across the room for a moment until Lauren smiled, reached her hand to the top button of her blouse, and said, "I guess I have to do everything myself."

"Not that, you don't," Matt said thickly. He came to her side, pulled back the covers and pushed her back gently onto the sparkling white sheet of the bed. Then he knelt on the floor and slowly began to undress her, trailing his fingers up and down her body. As her breasts came free of her clothes, Matt lowered his mouth to them and said softly, "I would have been disappointed if you'd outgrown your freckles."

Lauren's eyes were closed. "Connect the dots, Matt," she said. "Connect the dots with your tongue."

"My favorite game," he said as he slid up onto the bed alongside her, his mouth not leaving the fullness of her breast. He felt Lauren's hands fumbling with his belt and his zipper and the buttons of his shirt, and then—almost without his realizing how it had happened—they were naked, facing each other on the bed, and Lauren was sucking and chewing on his lower lip. Matt's arms were around her. He lowered his hands to her smooth, muscular buttocks and pulled her closer. She lifted her left leg up over his hip and then he felt her hands on him and she was rubbing him against the warm moist valley between her legs.

"Don't say anything, Matt. Don't do anything. Let me do it," she whispered as she circled his ear with the wet tip of her tongue.

"I hate pushy women," Matt said.

"You've just got to learn to push back," Lauren whispered again, and Matt felt himself slide inside her. Her smooth belly pushed against his; then she lowered her left leg and Matt felt himself locked inside her, being alternately squeezed and released by her sexual muscles. He joined her rhythm, stroking and withdrawing in time with her contractions, and then her body began to spasm under him and she said, "Oh, Matt, now. Now." And as he rolled her onto her back, she curled her legs behind his buttocks and used her heels to pull him deeper into her and then their mouths met in a kiss, which stifled both their cries, as they spent with each other.

For long minutes, they licked the insides of each other's mouth, and then Matt thought that his weight might be uncomfortable for her to bear, but as he started to lift himself off her on his hands, she shook her head and pulled him down to her again.

"You don't get off that easy," she whispered, and then he felt her muscles tightening around him again, squeezing, releasing, milking him into her. He needed sleep, he was too tired, and his body would not obey his mind, but despite knowing all that, his body came alive again, and when he was throbbing inside her, Lauren rolled them both onto their sides and kissed his eyes closed and said, "Now sleep, darling."

And Matt said, "I love you."

"I know," she said.

"I've always loved you."

"I know."

He opened his eyes to search her face and saw her in front of him, smiling, almost glowing, and she leaned forward and licked his eyes closed again. "I always will love you," he said.

"I know," she said.

And Matt fell asleep in her arms.

CHAPTER FORTY

He slept dreamlessly, like a man in a coma, but awoke aroused and reached across the bed for Lauren, but she was gone. He groaned when he looked at his watch and saw it was almost noon. Overhead, he could hear heavy rain splattering on the roof. The day outside was dark, dreary.

Fresh clothes had been laid out for him on the bed, and after showering and brushing his teeth, he dressed and walked downstairs.

It would have to be tonight, he was thinking. If he waited any longer to get into the Installation, they would have too much time to prepare a reception for unwelcome visitors. The rain would make the going sloppier, but if it kept up, it might provide a welcome cover.

He heard voices in the kitchen and paused on the steps for a split second. He expected Lauren, but who else would there be?

He found Lauren seated at the table there with the Judge and Angela Fox and a big hulking-shouldered man wearing a down-filled hunting jacket.

"Welcome to the world," Lauren said as he entered the room, and all the faces turned toward him. Matt thought that if the Judge and Angela had spent the night in bed sports, both of them looked pretty good nevertheless. The thought almost brought a smile to his face, but was interrupted by Lauren saying, "Matt, this is Mike Wojno."

The big man stood up and reached out a strong, hairy hand. Matt took it and their eyes met. There was pain and hurt in Wojno's eyes, but the expression on his face was amazingly serene.

"Pleasure," Matt said.

Wojno nodded and said, "Lauren's told me about you," and it was Matt's turn to nod.

He turned away and nodded his greetings to Angela and the Judge. As usual, Stevens was right on target. He said, "Matt, in case you're wondering what we're all doing here, let's get one thing straight. First of all, it's safe. A fly couldn't get near this house without us knowing about it."

He looked sharply at Matt's face as the younger man sat down and a cup of coffee was placed before him by Lauren.

"And Lauren's told us about your plan to go into the Installation, and we've been figuring the best way to do it."

"Hold on, Judge," Matt said, coffee cup poised on its way to his lips. "This is my problem and I don't think anybody else should be involved." Mike Wojno, he noticed, was just staring at him calmly, as if the outcome of the discussion was the least important thing in the world to him.

"Now, for a moment, you listen, Matt," the Judge said. "The last time you went in there, you nearly got caught, *and* you nearly got killed by some damned mutt. We all want to keep you alive. This time, we've decided you're not going in alone."

"Oh, great," Matt said sarcastically. "What do we do? Drive up to the front gate and march in? Maybe we should hire a band?"

"Maybe you should just listen to the Judge," Wojno said, in a voice as big and steady as the man himself appeared to be. It did not seem possible to Matt that here was a man who was dying of a malignancy.

Matt nodded and sipped his coffee.

"Mike is going in with you," the Judge said. "And Billy

O'Baal. Billy's out now figuring out the best way in, considering this crap weather.''

Matt looked again at Wojno. "Mike, how do you feel about that? You're a cop and I'm a fugitive. Why are you buying into my problems?"

"I don't know anything about your problems or why you want to get into the Installation," Wojno said slowly. "I'm on leave of absence from the state police, and the Judge told me you didn't do anything wrong. That's good enough for me." He stared at Matt for a second, then looked away with finality, as if that portion of the conversation was ended forever.

"You're all running a risk," Matt said.

"Hell, nobody lives forever," Angela said. It was the first time she had spoken since Matt entered the room and he wondered how the Judge had introduced her to Lauren. "This is Angela Fox, Matt's bimbo and bodyguard." Or maybe Angela had made just such an introduction of herself. He wouldn't have put it past her.

He looked around the room at the faces again and decided that there was no point in arguing. Their minds were all made up.

It was agreed that Wojno and Billy O'Baal would meet Matt at the cabin at seven o'clock and leave from there. His part in the meeting apparently over, Mike Wojno stood and said, "I guess I'll be going then. Some things to do."

Without self-consciousness, Lauren kissed his cheek and Wojno started out of the kitchen. Matt followed him outdoors and they stood on the roofed porch, out of the driving rain, and Matt said "I appreciate what you're doing, Mike."

"I'm not doing it for you," the husky man said. "It's for Lauren. She's yours now. If you want her."

"You mean if she'll have me," Matt said.

"I said what I meant," Mike said, his face still placid and calm. "She lent herself to me for a while, but she's always known that she belongs to you. That's not self-pity. That's just the way it is."

"Why are you telling me this?" Matt asked.

"You ought to know," Wojno said. "I don't have much time left. I mean time when I'll be any good to myself or anybody else. The doctors want me to start treatment right away, but I don't think I will. It'll just prolong things."

He started to open the door of his four-wheel drive Jeep. "You know," he said, turning around, "I was the one responsible for the kid's death. I was supposed to be watching him, but I didn't."

"I didn't know," Matt said. "Lauren didn't tell me."

The burly man smiled slightly. "She wouldn't because that's Lauren, and that's why I'm going with you." Matt must have looked perplexed because Wojno said, "It's not for you. Or your crusade. Or whatever. It's for Lauren, like I said. I took the last thing from her that she really loved. I let the baby drown. Ever since, I've been looking for some way to make it up to her. You're the way. I'm going with you, and I'm going to do my damnedest to keep you alive and well."

Matt said "I'm glad you're coming with me. And that's no lie."

Wojno shook his head. "Wouldn't matter anyway," he said. "I'm coming." And then he swung his body into the Jeep, and drove away in a spray of mud and gravel.

As he started back inside, Matt was met by the Judge and Angela Fox.

"We'll be on our way soon."

"Should I call you when we're done tonight?" Matt asked.

"I don't think so," the Judge said. "If you're right, my phone's already being bugged. But Billy has orders to report to me as soon as you're all back. We'll see what you get tonight, we'll talk tomorrow and figure out what we're going to do next." He sprinted out into the rain to start his car, an old green Chevrolet that Matt had never seen before. Obviously the Judge had borrowed it.

Matt turned to Angela. "Is everything okay here with you?" he asked.

"You mean, am I sleeping with the Judge?" she said with a smile, and he regretted being so transparent that anyone could see through him. She answered her own question. "No. He's been a perfect gentleman. Of course, if I stay at that house another night ..."

"Watch out for Maggie, the housekeeper. I think she's got dibs on the Judge," Matt said with a grin.

"I've noticed," she said.

"I feel better that you're not around here anyway. You've done enough."

"I wanted to be here, but you've got the Ten Little Indians running around through the trees protecting you, and you've got Lauren inside to take care of your other needs. So I guess I'll just hang out and smell the flowers until something comes up and you need me. Or someone does." She smiled and winked at him, then said, suddenly serious, "Do you expect trouble tonight?"

"I don't know," he said.

"Well, be careful. I don't pretend to know a lot about what's going on, but it sounds like bad people ... *big* bad people ... are on the other side, so you watch yourself."

The Judge's car pulled in front of the porch and Angela darted out and slithered inside. As the car pulled away, Matt noticed that she had slid across the front seat and was already sitting almost shoulder to shoulder with the silver-haired old man.

"Better watch yourself, Judge," Matt mumbled under his breath as he went back inside. As he came into the kitchen, Lauren threw her arms around him and kissed him, warm and wet, and then the two began to rinse the coffee cups and saucers from the table.

"So, that's your friend, Angela," Lauren said in an offhand manner. She had her back to him and he couldn't see her face.

"My private detective," Matt said, trying to be just as offhand.

370

"Yes, of course," Lauren said. "You've known her a long time?"

"Not really. You know she helped me get out of Washington in one piece."

"I'm sure that's the way she likes you best," Lauren said. "In one piece."

"Now, I don't think ..." Matt started and then he saw Lauren's shoulders moving up and down as she stood at the sink. He turned her around and saw her face convulsed with silent laughter.

"Sneaky bitch," he said.

"I love it when you're being sanctimonious, Matt," she said, trying to stop laughing. She mocked him. " 'My private detective.' Oh, yes, Very busy detecting my privates. 'Got me out in one piece.' Oh, yes. One long piece. Oh, Matt, I don't care that you slept with her. Just look at her. How could you resist?"

"It wasn't planned. It just kind of happened."

"I know," she said. "And if it just ever kind of happens again, I'll cut your balls off."

"But how do you really feel?" he said and they both laughed. "Anyway," he added, "I think she's done with me. I think she's got her eyes on the Judge."

"You noticed that too?" she said and when Matt nodded, she said, "Seems a little old for her."

"She told me she's rich, but maybe she was lying. Maybe she's a gold digger and is going to con the Judge out of his money."

"If she can con Frank out of anything, she's welcome to it," Lauren said. She shrugged. "Maybe she just likes older men. She took up with you, didn't she?"

He imitated a scolding look. "Wash the dishes, woman. The man has work to do. I'll be back in a little while."

She turned quickly. "Where are you going?"

"I want to get to a pay phone and call Katie Wu, just to let her know I'm alive," Matt said. "I owe her that."

371

"Of course you do," she said. "Why don't you call her from here?"

"Her phone's probably tapped," Matt said. "They can trace any call I make from here, and it's too hard to set up a turn-a-round phone call in the daytime, 'cause most all those numbers I used last night would be in operation during the day."

Lauren nodded and said, "Well, just be careful."

He went outside to Lauren's car. The keys were inside but as he started the motor, the driver's door opened. A young Indian man, not more than twenty one or twenty two years old, stood there and said "Where are you going?" He was wearing a wide-brimmed leather hat and the rain dripped off onto his black rubber slicker.

"To find a pay phone," Matt said.

"Move over. I'll drive you," the young man said.

"I can drive myself."

The young man smiled, mirthlessly, showing large, perfect, white teeth. "Billy says no. He says I take you where you're going."

Matt thought about arguing the point for a moment, then slid over on the seat. "Okay," he said. "Let's do it."

The young man got behind the wheel and drove off down the unpaved roadway. Before he got to the blacktop county road, he stopped the car, stepped outside and turned in a circle. Then he got back inside and continued driving.

"What was that for?" Matt asked.

"Just to let our friends know it was me, and that everything else was all right," the young man said.

"Our friends?"

"Billy's friends. They're keeping an eye on things."

"How many of these friends are there?" Matt asked. He had the sudden sinking feeling that somehow Billy's relatives had peeping-tommed him and Lauren last night as they were making love. Hell, there might be one hidden under the bed for all he knew.

"Enough to keep an eye on everything," the young man said without a glimmer of humor.

"You related to Billy?" Matt asked, after they had driven down the county road for about two miles.

"Around here, all us redskins are related," the young man said, hunching over the wheel, peering through the heavy downpour.

Matt shrugged and looked out the window. In the sideview mirror of the small Pontiac, he saw the parking lights of what appeared to be a pickup truck following them. For a brief instant, he had a flashback of that last night with Larry Wu, of the trucks that had tried to run them off the road, and without really understanding why, he said, "There's a truck behind us."

The young man glanced up into the mirror and nodded. "There's supposed to be," he said.

Another two miles down the road, he turned off the blacktop onto a rutted old road that looked like a testing ground for defective asphalt. Matt noticed, in the mirror, that the pickup truck turned off after them.

A mile later, the young man drove into a single-pump gas station that would have looked at home in Lil Abner's Dogpatch. An old hound dog lay on the front porch, out of the rain; the gas pump was made of glass and metal, had no dials, but instead had a hand crank on the side. The Indian drove past the tank to the side of the building where there was an old glass-doored phone booth.

"That phone works," he said.

"Thank you." As Matt stepped inside the booth, he noticed that the pickup truck had pulled off the road, too, and was waiting near the gas pump.

Matt fished around in his wallet for a few moments and found a federal government telephone credit card. No one would expect him to use that, and there were thousands of them in use by federal employees. It would be weeks before the billing would drift back into the I.R.S. office, and by then he would have won or been killed. Either way, it wouldn't matter anymore. He used a quarter to rouse the operator, gave her Katie Wu's number and the credit card billing. As usual, the operator was polite and efficient. Traveling around the country, Matt had found that the bigger the city, the dumber and surlier the phone operators. If that was true, out here the operator should be a gem.

He heard the telephone ringing. Once, twice, three times, and then Katie Wu's voice breathless.

"Hello?"

"Katie, it's Matt."

"Matt." She was unable to keep the excitement from her voice. "Where are you? No, never mind. Don't answer that. Are you all right?"

"I'm fine, Katie. I don't have much time. Did you get my note?"

"Yes. You didn't have to leave it. I know you didn't do anything like that." She sighed. "I'm so happy you called. Five minutes later and ..."

"And what?"

"I'm on my way out of town, Matt. I'm going out to San Francisco to stay with the family for a while."

"Why? Are you okay?"

"We had a little fire here, Matt. Larry's workroom was destroyed."

"When was that?"

"You were here Saturday night. I found your note when I got home. I went to bed, not even knowing what was going on, and then while I was sleeping, I heard fire engines. Larry's whole damned studio went up. Firemen came in and got me out."

The bastards, Matt thought. They had torched Larry's office without even caring that Katie was asleep upstairs. They could have killed her and they didn't even care.

"You weren't hurt?"

"No. I'm okay. But then the next morning, I found out what happened to you, and I figured maybe it's time to get out of here for a while. The house isn't liveable anyway until it's fixed, so I've already got workmen here putting it back together. Matt, you think somebody set that fire?"

"Yeah. I do. What does O'Leary say?"

"He told me to go to San Francisco for a while. And he told me yesterday that if I heard from you, I should tell you to call him. Will you?"

"I don't know, Matt said. "I'm laying low for a while."

"Good, Matt, that's probably best. Oh-oh, my cab's honking."

"Katie. Go. Have some fun. Enjoy yourself. We'll be talking soon."

"You know the number on the coast?"

"Yes."

"Okay. I have to run. Matt, take care of yourself. I love you, big brother."

"I love you too, Katie."

"Are you going to be all right?"

"Better than all right. I'm going to win and these bastards are going to pay."

He heard a small sob in her voice and then, weakly, she said, "Kill them all, Matt. Kill them all."

And then she hung up.

He was silent, sunk into his own thoughts, as he drove back to the cabin with the young Indian man. He had no doubt that Larry's office had been put to the torch. They were afraid that maybe somewhere there, Larry had hidden something, some files, some clues to the Installation's operation, so they were taking no chances and they set it afire. And if Katie Wu had been burned to death in the process, well, what was one slope more or less? He gritted his teeth and let the hate simmer inside him. Someone was going to pay, sooner or later.

CHAPTER FORTY-ONE

They left at seven o'clock sharp. When Billy O'Baal came into the house, Matt realized it was the first time he had seen the big Indian since he had taken him to the Iron City hospital with a broken nose.

"They did a pretty good job on you," Matt said, pointing a finger toward Billy's nose which was only slightly swollen. "You're as beautiful as I remember you."

Billy grinned and looked at Lauren. "You think it's safe for me to go with him, or is he going to try to kiss me?"

"I think it's safe enough," Lauren said, winked at Matt, then came forward to kiss Billy warmly.

The rain was still cascading down when Billy O'Baal brought them black rubber slickers and black hats. As they drove off, Matt crammed between Billy and Mike Wojno in the front of Billy's pickup truck. The wiry Indian warned, "Temperature's dropping. We're going to see snow yet."

They drove far to the west of the river, west even of the Installation's boundaries, then north, hooking through the Seneca Indian reservation, and then south again on some Forest Service fire roads. They came to a stop on the side of a hill, near an old, abandoned, natural gas pumping station.

"I looked at the maps," Billy said without prologue. "We will go that way." He pointed south across a stream and over a heavily wooded hill. "We make tracks, we'll get some of the hard part done while there's still some light in the sky."

They started walking. It took longer than Matt expected, because Billy seemed to want a rest break every fifteen minutes or so. Matt thought this was curious; he would have expected Billy to be able to track through these woods at top speed for hours on end.

Only during the fourth rest stop—when he looked at Mike Wojno and saw how hard and labored his breathing was—did Matt realize that Billy was calling the rest breaks for Mike's benefit and only pretending to be tired himself.

It might have been two hours; it might have been three when they came to the high chain-link fence which ringed all the Installation's property. Matt looked up at the threatening barbed wire strands which topped the fence, but before he could speak, Billy O'Baal had dropped to his knees in the mud and was methodically cutting through the bottom links with a small fence cutter he had slipped from the pack on his back.

He ripped out a dozen links, then folded the fencing back, and nodded the other two men to move through.

Matt shook his head. "I don't want to be a killjoy," he said, "but how the hell do we find this place on the way back?"

"I'll be able to smell the fresh cut wire," O'Baal said.

"What?" Matt said. Wojno chuckled. Billy shook his head and pulled a small black device, about the size of a pack of cigarettes, from his trousers pocket. He pressed a switch atop it, then hung it high up near the top of the fence. "Transmitter," he said. "I'll get us back within a couple of hundred yards. This'll do the rest of the job. Now get a move on, will you?"

After they had gotten about five hundred yards from the fence, O'Baal stopped and checked the small radio receiver in his back. A small red light pulsed regularly and Billy said to Matt, "See, don't worry. Transmitter's working fine. I'm not going to let you get lost out here."

It was almost eleven o'clock when they reached the road that

Matt had followed the last time he had been inside the Installation, so he took the lead. They stopped at the top of the same hill he had stopped at before. Below them, most of the Installation's three working buildings were still lit. Occasionally somebody would dart through the rain from one building to another. It was too early for bedtime.

They hunkered down behind the hill and settled down to wait for the hour to grow late. Billy broke out their rations from the pack on his back: thermoses of coffee and hot soup, thick ham and roast beef sandwiches.

"Lauren really knows how to provision a gang of burglars," Wojno mumbled, and Matt chuckled. They ate the rest of their meal in silence, then settled back beneath a small rock outcropping, trying to stay warm. After a few minutes of sitting still, Billy O'Baal moved off wordlessly into the night.

It was almost 1:00 A.M. when he returned.

"Find anything?" Matt asked.

"Nothing I could see," Billy said. "But it's just not right. I had the feeling I was being watched all the time. Like they were waiting for us, daring us to come."

"Maybe they are," Wojno said. He reached under his slicker, opened his jacket, drew his revolver from its holster, and checked the ammunition before replacing it. They were all wearing sidearms—something Matt had not done since Vietnam, and which he had sworn to himself never to do again.

Maybe Billy was right. They probably were waiting. But somehow or other, he had to get into the computer lab and get the giga-discs that contained the Installation's records.

He peered out over the rock formation. Below him, the Installation seemed to have settled in for the night. Lights were out and the computer center was totally in darkness.

"I'm going in," he said. "I want you two to wait out here for me. If something happens to me, maybe you can help."

"Good plan," Wojno said drily.

"I'll take a better one," Matt said.

"Not from me," Mike said. Matt looked at Billy who said,

"Don't ask me. Me only trusty scout, loveable sidekick, kemo sabe."

"Go screw yourself, Cochise, and the horse what brung you." Matt paused. "Half hour with a break. An hour outside. See you."

"Hope so," Mike said.

Matt got to the computer center quicker this time than last. He made a hurried circuit of it and then came back to the front door. The overhead security lights around the encampment were off for the night but he was taking no chances. Under cover of some bushes, he reached out his hand to the front door, tried the knob, but found it locked.

He went back alongside the building and found the window that led to the small lounge of the building. He picked up a small rock from the ground, then hesitated for a moment. If he broke a window, it might set off an alarm. What then?

What then, he decided, was that he'd jump in through the window, run to the lab, grab the giga-discs if he could, then dive out another window and run like hell and hope to escape.

"Who needs this shit?" he mumbled to himself. There probably wouldn't be any alarm, he decided. Even though the front door was locked now, he had seen no alarms when he had been here before. An alarm system might just be impractical, because the computer people like to work with the machine at all odd hours, and they were notoriously lackadaisical about calling security first to let them know they were entering the building. In this place, if there were an alarm, it'd be ringing with the frequency of telephones in a tax office on April 14th.

It was all very logical, and while he did not know if he really believed it or not, it made him feel better to think he was acting with some kind of planned sense.

Matt stood up, tried to muffle the sound as best he could with his body, and broke the top of the window leading into the lounge. He fished his hand carefully through the hole, unlocked the window, lifted it and climbed inside, then closed the window behind him.

He walked down the corridor and directly into the comp lab at the end of the hallway. He stood in the lab's semi-darkness for a long time, adjusting his eyes to the dim glow from the wall-mounted electric clock.

Suddenly, the light switch behind him snapped on with a ferocity that seemed impossible. Light switches did not get angry, he told himself. He turned around slowly, even as he was fishing inside his coat to put his hand around the grip of his gun.

Standing inside the door was a young man, tall, thin, red-haired, and bedraggled from the rain. Matt had seen him before. He paused just a second, then said, "So, you're Ralphie," and reached out his hand and walked toward the nervous-looking young man.

"My brother told me all about you," Matt said. "Nuj says you're one of his best friends."

Ralphie looked at Matt for a moment, then said, "And you're a fucking liar, mister."

CHAPTER FORTY-TWO

Matt stopped, his hand still outstretched. In the racks of supplies over Ralphie's shoulder, he could see the row of giga-discs.

He could cold cock Ralphie now, grab the discs, and be gone. And maybe he would hit him too hard and kill the young man. Or maybe he wouldn't hit him hard enough, and ten seconds after he left, Ralphie would have the dogs and the security guards after him.

Matt let his hand fall casually to his side.

"You're right," he said. "I'm a liar."

Ralphie threw his hair back up out of his eyes with a quick jerk of his head.

"Fucking-A, I'm right," he said. "Fucking-A."

"You know Nuj is dead, don't you?" Matt asked. That was the best way, he thought: bang Ralphie over the head with it right away, before he had time to figure out what was going on, or what he should be doing. Such as calling Security.

Ralphie inclined his head forward half an inch or so, just enough so that Matt could not see his eyes.

"I didn't know," he said. "But maybe I suspected. What happened?"

"They found his body in the river a few miles downstream,"

Matt said. "Beaten, mutilated. Apparently he got some of your friends pissed at him."

"Not my friends," Ralphie said. He paused. "Damn. Damn. Damn. I knew that's what happened to him. I just knew it."

Matt said nothing for a few moments. He tried to remember how the heroes in the movies handled this sort of situation, but it didn't work. His mind went blank.

Finally, he just said, "I'm sorry."

Ralphie looked up. His eyes were moist, Matt noted without surprise.

"You were pretty good friends, huh?" he said.

"Better than that," Ralphie said. "He was my guru. We shared everything. All our thoughts, all our ideas."

Matt said softly, "What were his thoughts about this place?"

Ralphie looked up at him and his eyes narrowed, as if in recognition.

"You're the one, aren't you?" he said softly. Then more firmly. "You're the one. I know it."

"Which one is that?" Matt asked.

"Don't play dumb," Ralphie said. "You're the one who broke in here last week. And you're the one who planted that damned virus in my machine."

Matt said nothing but his silence seemed to confirm Ralphie's suspicions.

"They're looking for you," Ralphie said. "They're out all over the place tonight. Most of them are waiting down by the river for you to come like you did the last time. They were told you were coming." He grinned like a junior high school show-off.

"I was right, wasn't I?" he demanded. "Wasn't I?"

"You were right," Matt admitted.

"Fucking-A, I was right. Fucking-A. I just knew it. Now tell me your name."

Matt told him the truth. Ralphie considered it for a minute, his brow knitting and purling as he pondered.

"Matt Taylor. Matthew Taylor," he said, then snapped his fingers.

"I've got it. You were on the news. The TV news. You went around killing a whole lot of I.R.S. people or something." He looked at Matt, and seemed suddenly to understand that he was in a room alone with a crazed mass murderer, because he began to back, ever so slightly, toward the door.

"Hold on, Ralphie," Matt said. "I didn't kill anybody, and that's the truth. The people who killed them in Washington were the same ones who killed your friend, Nuj. The same ones who killed my friend, Larry Wu. Remember WUL?"

Ralphie looked at him a long time, as if he were trying to decide something important.

"Something bad is going on here, isn't it?"

"I think so," Matt said.

"What?"

"I'm not sure. That's why I'm here. I'm trying to find out. And that's why they've been killing my wife, my friends. Your friend, Nuj."

"Who are you?" Ralphie snapped sharply. "Not your name, but who are you, really?"

Matt looked at the clock on the wall. He had been there almost twenty minutes already. Wojno and Billy would be getting worried if he wasn't back soon.

"I'm sorry," he started to say. "I don't have time to—"

"Tell me," Ralphie said. "Tell me. Or I call for help."

Matt took out his pistol. Ralphie was scared, really scared; Matt could tell. But the young man didn't back down.

"You don't want to fire a shot," he said. "So tell me, or else."

There was something childishly defiant in the "or else." Matt pursed his lips, then said quickly, "Matt Taylor. I'm the head computer honcho for the Internal Revenue Service. My friend Larry Wu and I ran across some returns that used this address. We thought they were phonies. When we tried to check them out, someone killed Larry; tried to kill me. They're still trying

383

to kill me. I think this place is hooked up with organized crime, somehow."

He watched Ralphie's face. The young man seemed catatonic. Matt said, "Where do you stand?" but Ralphie cut him off.

"Don't interrupt," he said. "I'm processing input."

After fifteen seconds, Ralphie spoke again.

"I'm on your side," he said. "What do you want?"

"Those." Matt pointed to the giga-discs on the shelf. "I want to take them back and go through them and see what I can find out."

"No way, Jose," said Ralphie.

"Why not?"

'Because they're all blanks, that's why not. I told you, they must have heard you were coming and they came in and made substitutions. That little fag, Gianetti, you know him?"

"Yeah, I know him."

"He came in today. We were all working, trying to find out what the hell was wrong with the computer. It was your damned virus screwing everything up, but it took me a while to figure that out. Anyway, Gianetti said, 'Close it down, we're taking the discs.' "

"Any idea where they put them?"

"Probably in the safe over in the security shack. Forget it, Taylor. That's definitely a dynamite job to get in there. Anyway, they moved the discs, and then took most of the people down by the river to watch for you. They even have us standing shifts in here. I was out for coffee when you got in, but I guess you were lucky I was the one you ran into. 'Cause I listened, 'cause Nuj was my friend. I think anybody else was here, they would have called the security on you."

"I need those discs. I've got to find out what's going on here," Matt said.

"You really think it's organized crime?" Ralphie said.

"What do you think it is? What is it you do here?"

"We were told never to tell."

"That was before they murdered your friend," Matt reminded him.

Ralphie hesitated a moment. "We keep track of payrolls. We figure out people's salaries; we figure out the right average amount of deductions they ought to take. We do lists of when they ought to make their quarterly tax payments and how much. We're like fucking H. and R. Block, except we do it every day. I know, this is too much computer for that little amount of work, but we have all these companies that the paychecks are drawn on, and we have to make sure that everybody winds up paying their taxes."

"The people on the payrolls?" Matt said. "The ones you figure taxes on, who do you think they are?"

"What do you mean?"

"Well, their returns all give their address as Harker's Furnace. But they don't live here and they don't work here. Who the hell are those people?"

"I don't know. I don't think they exist," Ralphie said.

"Why's that?" Matt asked.

"Because once in a while, the I.R.S. sends a notice and says so-and-so owes some money, or so-and-so is going to be audited. Well, whenever that happens, we just prepare a memo that so-and-so died last month, and we pay whatever is the disputed amount and let the I.R.S. close the file. Now look, if these were real people, we wouldn't be so quick to just say, 'Oh, too bad, I.R.S., he died and you can't talk to him.' That's why I think they're fakes."

"Who actually writes the paychecks to these people and sends the tax money to the government?" Matt asked.

"Some law firm in Philadelphia handles all that kind of stuff. I've seen their name but I don't remember it," Ralphie said.

Matt pressed his memory, then said, "Does Weiskopf, Sapir and Durand sound like it?"

"No. That's not the one," Ralphie said. "Does this all mean something?"

"It's starting to make some sense," Matt said. "I have to

get my hands on those discs." He glanced at the clock again. Time had run out.

Ralphie took a piece of paper off a nearby desk and wrote something on it, then handed it to Matt. It was a telephone number.

"What's that?" Matt asked.

"It's Dial-a-Sad-Animal-Story," Ralphie said. "It's in Akron, Ohio."

"What?"

Ralphie repeated what he had said.

"Why?" Matt asked.

"Around here," Ralphie said, "we like to call it. All of us do. Almost every day. Sometimes more often than that."

"So?"

"You know how to rig a turnaround circuit on a phone, don't you?" Ralphie asked.

"Yes."

"Good. At ten o'clock tonight, have one set up on that number. And have your computer tied in."

"Why?" Matt asked.

"I'll be sending you a present," Ralphie said. "About six discs full."

Matt went back out through the side window. The rain had finally stopped and a brisk wind had sprung up, chasing the clouds away. Overhead the moon was shining brightly, and off to one side of it, Orion—the only constellation he had ever been able to identify except for the Big Dipper—twinkled and glowed.

But the compound's floodlights had been turned back on. He would stand out like a sore thumb if he tried to go directly up the hillside, and he realized that he would have to follow the service road out of the camp. Here and there around the settlement, he could see dark silhouettes moving from one building to another. He started walking from the compound, trying to look casual and unhurried. Careful, he told himself. You've done this once before; you can do it again.

Somewhere in the brush on the hillside straight ahead, Billy O'Baal and Mike Wojno should be waiting for him. If nothing has happened, he thought.

He walked without watching where he was going. He walked watching the stars in his best computer nerd fashion. And so he bumped into and almost knocked down a young man who came out from behind a building and cut across his path. The man wore the khakis of one of the compound's uniformed guards.

The impact almost knocked the man down toward a large puddle of near-frozen mud. Matt reached out, grabbed the man's jacket, and hauled him back to the comparative safety of the roadway.

"Thanks," the guard said.

"Sure thing," Matt said, trying hard to keep his voice calm and undistinctive. He started to walk on.

"Excuse me?" the guard said.

"Yes," Matt said. He turned slightly to face the other man, and as he did, he felt the cold chill again. It ran all the way up and down his back and on out to his fingertips, leaving them tingling.

"Sorry, but we've got instructions tonight to ask everybody for ID."

"Sure," Matt said. He patted his breast pocket. He started groping in his back trousers pocket, as if for his wallet.

"Damn," he said. "I left it back in the cabin. What do we do now?" He glanced upward, then back at the guard, and tried to put a note of panic in his voice. "Orion's in confluence with the Big Dipper with spiral nebulonic involvement. It won't last more than another five minutes. I can't miss it."

He looked at the guard, pleadingly, hoping he would tell him to get on with his spiral nebulonic involvement. Instead, the guard said, "You won't have to miss it. I'll just call this in on the radio."

387

Matt nodded as the young man unhitched his walkie-talkie and moved it toward his mouth. Matt took a couple of steps forward and slipped the gun from his pocket.

"I think you should forget about using your radio," he said. "And let's just keep walking down this path."

The guard saw the gun; it was his turn to nod. He started to put the walkie-talkie back in its sling on his hip. While he was doing that, the sounds coming from the instrument changed slightly. For just an instant, the normal crackle of background static was interrupted by three little beeps.

"What's that?" Matt demanded.

"What's what?"

"The three beeps."

"Nothing special. Just a time check. Every half hour they beep us."

Matt hesitated. He wondered how he would set up a time check system for security guards. "How are you supposed to answer it?" he asked.

The guard hesitated.

"How?" Matt snapped.

"With our names."

"Go ahead."

"It's too late. Ten seconds and then they send help," the guard said. His voice sounded like he was gloating, but it only lasted a second, because Matt slugged him alongside the head with the side of the gun and the young man dropped like a wet towel. Matt quickly dragged him off the pathway, out of the reach of the lights, then turned to run up the roadway away from the compound.

"Hold it right there, buddy," a voice from behind him said.

He turned to face the voice. A flashlight beam shot out of the darkness and caught him full in the eyes, blinding him. Then, as suddenly as it had appeared, the light was gone. There was the sound of a brief scuffle and then Mike Wojno's voice.

"Let's get out of here, Matt."

He and Billy moved alongside him, and the three set off up

the roadway, then back through the fields across which they had entered the Installation.

"Get what you wanted?" Wojno asked him.

"Close enough," Matt said.

"Good," said Wojno.

About five hundred yards ahead of them, Matt saw, against the starlit night sky, the outline of a stand of trees. *Once we get there, into cover, we'll be all right,* he thought.

Then the sky vanished overhead as they moved into the thick forest. Billy O'Baal led the way through the dense growth, as surefootedly as if the path had been illuminated by floodlights.

There was a lot of ground yet to cover before they were free of the Installation's property, Matt knew, but every step took them farther away from the compound's main guard force that Ralphie had said was assembled down near the river.

It had taken them almost three hours to walk into the compound. Now, ninety minutes into their escape, Matt's biggest worry was whether Mike Wojno could make it. His breath came heavy and labored as he struggled to keep up with the other two men, and O'Baal called more frequent rest periods.

To Matt, the trek back toward Billy's truck was all mud: mud in infinite varieties. Sticky mud, black mud, brown mud, mud so thick you could almost walk on it, and mud so cold it would freeze your skin on first contact. Everything but warm mud.

They made another rest stop and Matt noticed that the sky ahead seemed to be growing lighter. Another two hours and it would be dawn.

And then, far behind them, they heard a sound that ran a chill down Matt's back.

"It's the dogs," Billy said. "They've got the goddam dogs after us."

"Can we get out before they get us?" Matt asked.

"Be shaving it pretty close," Billy said.

"Then we better get moving," Mike said, lumbered to his feet, and started off.

The sky kept growing lighter; the three men kept plunging

389

forward. Billy let Matt catch up to him and said, "Something's funny here."

"What's that?"

"Hear those dogs? They're not getting any closer. They're still just as far away as they were before."

"Maybe they lost our scent," Matt said hopefully.

Billy shook his head. "Not in weather like this, not just after a rain. Everything's fresh and pretty, and the only thing on God's earth that's got a stink is us."

"What does it mean then?" Matt asked, watching Mike Wojno moving leadenly ahead of them. The man was clearly beyond exhaustion now, obviously just driving himself forward on his reserves of sheer will.

"I don't know," Billy said. "But I think we'll find out soon."

The radio receiver brought them back unerringly to the hole Billy had ripped in the fence. O'Baal picked up the small transmitter unit and slipped it back into his pocket, then led the way under the wire and out into an open field.

They walked on till it was nearly dawn, and just as the sky was turning a reddish gray in the east, they reached the hill overlooking the road where Billy's pickup had been parked.

One of the Installation's green utility wagons was parked forty yards behind it. And down, around a bend in the road perhaps four hundred yards away, was parked another of the wagons.

"Now you know why they weren't catching up," Billy said. "They were driving us here. They got us penned in now."

Billy and Matt slumped onto the ground to rest and Wojno knelt next to them.

"Listen," he said. "When I give you guys the signal, you race like a bastard for that truck and follow me."

"What are you going to do?" Billy said.

"Thin out the odds some," Mike said.

Matt shook his head. "We all go. Too damned dangerous for just one man."

"More than one can't sneak in," Mike said. "No point ar-

390

guing, just do what I say." He hesitated, then reached a hand out and shook Matt's.

"Been fun, Matt," he said. "See you later, Billy."

Then he was gone off into the brush.

Matt hissed to Billy, "This might be a suicide mission."

"He knows that," Billy said calmly. "But when you're dying anyway, maybe getting a chance to pick when and where you die ain't the worst thing."

He moved away and Matt followed him to the top of the rise where they could look down and see the pickup and the two security vehicles which had it penned in. From the high vantage point, they could also see Mike as he worked his way slowly across the side of the hill, to a point behind the nearest Jeep. Then he started down the hillside. They lost him as he came out on the road, just behind the Installation vehicle.

"Get ready to run like a big-ass bird," Billy said.

Suddenly, across the cold mountain air, Matt heard the sound of a scuffle. He looked toward the Jeep and saw Mike struggling with two men from the vehicle. Then there was a thud, and another thud, as Wojno slugged each of them with the butt end of his gun. He jumped into the Jeep, started the motor, and waved an arm toward Billy and Matt. They ran down the hillside toward the truck, but before they got there, Mike had driven by their pickup and moved down the road in the direction of the other Installation truck. He stopped in the roadway until Billy and Matt were inside the pickup; then Matt saw his arm reach out of the Jeep and fire his gun into the air, once, twice, three times.

Mike seemed to wait a moment. Then up ahead, coming around the curve of the road, Matt saw the headlights of the other security vehicle, its driver obviously attracted by the shots. Wojno took off toward that Jeep. Billy and Matt followed but could not catch up. Wojno must have been going at least sixty when he plowed headfirst into the oncoming vehicle. There was a terrific crunch of metal, some screams, and both vehicles slid off the side of the road. Billy stopped and Matt, gun in hand, jumped out to see if he could help Wojno.

But the man was dead, crushed beneath the steering wheel, his eyes staring forward sightlessly.

CHAPTER FORTY-THREE

A funeral gloom hung over the house in the woods when Matt and Billy O'Baal returned. The day was a dark oppressive gray, the sky looking so leaden that Matt almost felt the need to hunch down so as not to bump his head on it.

The Judge and Lauren were waiting inside for them. Matt walked up to the woman, put his arms around her, and said, "I'm sorry. They were waiting for us and Mike didn't make it."

The Judge thumped his fist on the kitchen table in anger and Matt felt Lauren shudder in his arms.

Then, almost as quickly as it had started, the sobbing ended and Lauren pulled back from him.

"I won't cry," she said. "I think that's what Mike was hoping for. Was it quick?" "Yes," Matt said. "And he picked the time and place."

Lauren nodded, as if Matt were only confirming what she already knew, then brushed by him wordlessly, and left the room.

Succinctly, because the fatigue was starting to wash over his body in a great flooding wave, Matt told the Judge what had happened at the Installation.

The Judge listened quietly, nodding occasionally, and when

Matt was done, he asked, "Have you figured out what's going on?"

"I think so," Matt said. "But I'm going to wait until I get copies of those tapes from the Installation."

"*If* you get them," the Judge said. "A lot of things might happen."

Matt nodded. He knew what the Judge meant. A simple false step, a careless mistake, and Ralphie at the computer lab, instead of sending tapes to Matt, might just become another corpse floating in the river.

"They had extra guards on," Matt said. "They expected us."

Stevens said, "That might not mean anything too much, son. It was probably a pretty logical assumption that you'd be going back there." The Judge looked over where Billy O'Baal was sitting at the kitchen table. He had not said a word since entering the house along with Matt. "Billy," the Judge said, "I want you to put more security around this house. Take no chances. I don't want them to get lucky if they try to kill Matt again."

O'Baal nodded, then stood to leave with the Judge.

"I want to think this through, Matt. There's got to be a way to deflect these people from you." He paused. "Get some sleep, son, and call me when you get the tapes.

After the two other men had left, Matt went upstairs to his bedroom in the sleeping loft.

He found Lauren lying in the bed, and when he sat alongside her, she pulled down the covers to expose her naked body.

"Matt, I want you to make love to me right now."

"Are you sure?" Matt asked.

"Please. Now."

And she pulled Matt down on top of her body.

The last time they had made love, Lauren had chosen the way, the pace, but now she just opened herself up to Matt, in a wordless demand that he bury himself deep in her body. And the last time had been good, fed by their desire for each other, but this time was even better for Matt, because he felt he was being driven by Lauren's engulfing need for him. She pushed herself up to him, as if trying to bring him deeper inside her than was humanly possible, and when Matt responded, she stifled a small cry of pain and said, "More, Matt. More. Just like that," and as Matt burst into her, he understood her need and her wish.

When they were done, she lay still a long time, then said, "That was important. Do you know why?"

"Because you want me to make you pregnant," he said.

She pulled back from him, looking surprised.

"How did you know?"

"I knew," he said.

"I succeeded," she said. "I'll have your baby in me, Matt. I know it."

"In the middle of death, there's always life," Matt said.

She raised herself up on one elbow and looked down at him.

"I really love you," she said. "I really do."

"And I love you too," Matt said, and Lauren began to laugh. And then she cried. And then she laughed again.

It was after nine. Outside it was snowing. Matt had dialed the sad-animal-story number in Akron several times, just to assure himself that something so patently ridiculous was real. It was, and Matt watched the wall clock as the hands creeped around until a quarter to ten and then he picked up the telephone, set the receiver on his computer's modem, and began building his turnaround sequence of calls.

Ten o'clock came and went. Five minutes after. Ten. A quarter after. Almost ten-thirty. Matt was ready to give up when a series of green letters began inscribing themselves across his computer's screen.

"Ready to receive?" they spelled out.

"Ready," Matt typed back.

Matt flicked the switches activating his disc recorder and waited, listening to the telltale whine and whistle coming over his phone line. Three minutes later another message appeared on his screen.

"Prepare second disc," it said.

He did the necessary things and typed back: "Prepared."

He filled ten discs, and when he was done, the screen went blank. There was no signoff, no farewell message, just a pale green, empty screen.

For two more hours, Matt scrolled the contents of the discs back and forth across his video display screen. Two discs contained the names and tax records of more than one thousand businesses. The other eight discs bore the names and personal tax records of twenty thousand different people, both men and women, who were employed in those businesses.

"I've got it," Matt finally said, and turned to look at Lauren, who had been sitting on the couch, watching him. But she had fallen asleep, and Matt got up and covered her with a blanket before going back to the telephone.

There was one piece left to complete the puzzle and the man who could fill in that piece was Ari Cohen, head of the anti-Zorelli strike force.

This time, Matt did not bother to run the telephone call through any false numbers. Instead, he dialed directly to Cohen's office in Washington, D.C.

"Hello," a man's voice answered.

"Let me speak to Ari Cohen, please."

"Who's calling?"

"My name's Taylor. He'll speak with me."

"I'm afraid that's impossible, Mr. Taylor," the voice said coldly. "Mr. Cohen is dead."

"Dead? How?"

"Last night. Killed by a hit-and-run driver near here."

The news hit Matt with the force of an electric shock. "Is O'Leary there?" he asked after a moment.

"No. We haven't seen him in three or four days." The man hesitated and asked, "Can anyone else help you?"

"No," Matt said despairingly. "Nobody can help me now."

He replaced the telephone and sank his head into his hands. Cohen dead. And probably O'Leary too. They had been all he had and now it was Matt Taylor, alone, against the world.

CHAPTER FORTY-FOUR

Matt stepped out onto the front porch of the house in the woods and lit a cigarette. Before even taking his first puff, he sensed someone close to him, and when he looked toward his left, one of Billy O'Baal's Indian guards—this one a swarthy-looking man of about thirty—stepped up onto the porch. He held a handgun casually at his side.

"Evening," he said. "Everything all right?"

"Fine," Matt said. "How many of you people are around here anyway?"

"Enough," the man said. "You need something?"

"I want to go into town to see the Judge, but I want somebody near the house here to keep an eye on Miss Carmody."

"Easy enough," the man said. He stepped off the porch and disappeared into the darkness. A moment later, Matt heard the sound of an owl calling close by. It was followed by the sound of another owl, farther away. Then there was silence, but before Matt had finished his cigarette, the Indian was back on the porch. Another, younger, man was with him.

"This is Paulie," the swarthy man said. "He'll take you to the Judge. I'll stay here."

"Good," Matt said. He went back inside the house, called the Judge to tell him he was on his way, and then left a note on the table next to Lauren, telling her where he had gone. He kissed her lightly on the lips before he left.

As they drove through the gates of the Judge's mansion, Matt felt that they were being watched. He looked carefully all around the property but did not see anyone, until he saw the faint glow from a cigarette back under a stand of trees. So Billy O'Baal had this place under guard too.

The young Indian drove his ramshackle old Plymouth directly into the Judge's ground-level garage, and when Matt got out, the Judge was waiting for him. He opened the door and led Matt up to his study where there was a carafe of steaming coffee on the table.

"So?" the Judge said without preamble.

"The stew is getting thicker," Matt said, as the Judge poured coffee for both of them.

"Did you get the tapes from the Installation? Did you learn anything from them?"

Matt nodded. "The tapes came in on time. Judge, I think they tie the vice president in with Carlos Zorelli."

"The place doesn't have anything to do with spies then?" the Judge asked.

Matt shook his head. "No, not that I can see. What I got on the tapes was a list of businesses all over the country, and the names of some twenty thousand people on the payrolls of those businesses. But, Judge, the names are phoneys. I'm sure of it."

"How are you sure?"

"Something one of those computer guys told me when I was up at the Installation. He said that they kept tax records on all these people. But if any of them were ever audited or owed money, they would just pay the bill and tell the I.R.S. that the man had died. Well, you don't just say a guy is dead, when the guy is still alive. What happens when he wants to file next year's tax return and the fed computers show that he's dead?

I'm sure these are just made-up names of people who don't exist."

"I'm not sure I understand," the Judge said. "Why? And what would it have to do with Zorelli? And Barkley?"

"The last few years," Matt said, "the feds have been cutting sharply into the mob. The old Al Capone way. They haven't been able to break their businesses—the drugs, the prostitution, the gambling—but what they've done is to get the big guys and nail them on tax evasion. If you live like you're making ten million dollars a year, but you don't have any reported source of income, you're evading taxes somehow. And they've been putting the hoods in jail for that. The only one they haven't been able to put a dent in is Zorelli in Philadelphia."

"Okay. I follow that. But what about Harker's Furnace?"

"Bear with me," Matt said as he finished his coffee and poured another cup. "I think Zorelli's been the smartest. What I think he's done is he's bought up, over the years, a lot of small businesses."

"That list of businesses you got from the computer?"

"Right," Matt said. "Now suppose you've got a legitimate business that takes in, say, a thousand dollars a week. Maybe a small Chinese laundry or something. Now you've got a chunk of money from an illegal drug sale or something. You can't get your hands on it because the government is watching. But what stops you from dumping some of that money every week into your Chinese laundry? So that instead of taking in a thousand dollars a week, it takes in five thousand dollars a week. Over the course of a year, that's two hundred thousand dollars extra you moved through that company. Multiply it by a thousand businesses and all of a sudden, you're talking hundreds of millions of dollars ... maybe a billion dollars or more ... that the feds can't say came from gambling or narcotics or shakedowns or whatever."

"I understand that part," the Judge said. "But how does that help Zorelli?"

"Okay. Stay with the idea about the laundry that used to

make a thousand dollars a week, and now it makes five tho
sand a week. What you do is you put ten people on their pay
roll. Ten people who don't exist. You pay them each, say, twent
thousand dollars. They file their tax returns, they pay thei
taxes, which only amount to a couple of thousand dollars
person. What's left over is clean. You can do anything you wan
with it."

The Judge whistled softly. "You're telling me that Zorell
has found a way to use the Internal Revenue Service itself t
launder his dirty money," he said.

"Exactly," Matt said.

"That's astonishing."

"I know," Matt said. "And when Larry and I stumbled ove
it, that made us very dangerous to them. And they killed Larry
and tried to kill me. They're still trying."

The Judge stood up and went to a cabinet across the room
and took out a large cigar. As he lit it, he said, "There's stil
a lot of loose ends, Matt. How do you tie this in with the vice
president?"

"A couple of ways. First of all, he and Plevris lied to me
about this being an intelligence operation, a clearinghouse for
spies. That's horseshit. Second, Vice President Barkley's old
law firm is the one that wound up buying Harker's Furnace.
Third, as soon as I turned over to him the information on where
Larry had hidden the Harker's Furnace returns, his guys—those
two FBI men—tried to kill me. That's a pretty good start at
jumping to a conclusion. There's just one thing more I need to
nail it down."

"What's that?" the Judge asked.

"I want to be able to tie Barkley's old law firm to Zorelli
and to these businesses. If I can do that, the chain's complete."

"How do you think to do that?"

"I don't know," Matt said. "Tonight, I called Ari Cohen. I
mentioned him to you; he's the head of the Zorelli strike force."

"And?"

"And he's dead. Hit-and-run accident, and that sounds like

a phoney to me. I wonder if he was getting too close. If he was stepping on too many toes. But he was my hope. I was going to give him what I had and let him run with it while I laid low for a while. Now? I don't know." Matt shook his head.

"You're just going to stay a target and they'll pick you off whenever they get a chance," the Judge said.

"That's the way it looks," Matt agreed. "Worst thing is, I don't see any way out. I can't go battling the FBI, the vice president. Hell, there's a warrant out for my arrest for killing Polonowski, Melanie. I get picked up and you can bet on it that I'm going to get a bullet in the brain, and somebody will have some bullshit story about me being armed and dangerous and trying to escape so they had to shoot me."

The Judge blew a leisurely smoke ring, then rose and walked over to the bag that held the computer discs. He lifted one and looked at it, as if he expected it to tell him something. "There's a way to fight back," he said. "And keep yourself alive."

"You've definitely got my attention." Matt said.

"I've given this a lot of thought." The Judge replaced the disc in the bag and sat down in the heavy armchair facing Matt. "You've got to go public."

"Public? What do you mean? How?"

"What we've been doing, Matt, is playing their game with their ball and their rules. They kill Larry and they try to kill you and we don't respond. Then they decide they've got to keep you alive for a while because you're the only man who might be able to find out what Larry did with their files. So we go that way for a while. Then you tell them, and they try to kill you again, and they kill a lot of people in the process, and I'm getting tired of all of it."

"I'd rather be playing golf myself," Matt said. "So how do we go public?"

"We get the press involved. Blast your story all over the media. You've been otherwise occupied so you probably haven't noticed, but on Friday, the Senate is going to open hearings on the new super agency the President wants to fight organized crime. Barkley's going to be the first witness. I think you ought to be a witness, too, son. But I think it ought to be done with all the drumbeats of publicity. I think you ought to be in every newspaper, on every television station in the country. We've got to make it impossible for them to try to kill you because too many people will be watching. And then we'll let the pieces fall where they may."

Matt chewed his lower lip. Something about the idea made him uncomfortable. Was it just his natural reticence? His chronic desire to stay out of spotlights? Worrying about things like that was kind of stupid, he thought, when the alternative might be his just simply getting killed.

"Suppose I'm wrong, Judge," Matt said. "Suppose the Installation really is a clearinghouse for intelligence activities?"

"You're not wrong," the Judge said. "But even if you are, the Installation's outlived its usefulness. The government can just close it down, put its files somewhere else, and maybe it'll have a few months of bad press, but no real harm will be done. Too many people know about the Installation now for it to be of any more service. And it's not worth your life."

"How do we go public?" Matt asked. "I don't know anything about this."

"I do," the Judge said. He picked up the telephone on the small table next to him and pressed one number. Then he said, "Billy. Go get him." And he hung up.

"Go get who?" Matt asked.

"John Smetts from the *Gusher*. I've had him standing by," the Judge said. "But I haven't told him anything. He doesn't even know you're in town."

Matt poured more coffee for himself. Without looking up, he said, "You know, Judge, there you go again. Making my decisions for me. Trying to run my life. Why do you do that?"

"Doesn't it go without saying, Matt? I care about you."

"Caring's one thing. Bossing's another thing. You treat me like your little boy. And I'm not a boy, I'm a man. And I'm not your son."

The Judge relit his cigar.

"But you are, Matt. I'm your father. Not Jesse Taylor. Me. Your mother even named you after me. Frank Matthew Stevens."

"You? I don't understand." He fell back into a chair.

"Matt, your mother and I were lovers for ten years. Jesse was the town drunk; he was impotent. Your mother never loved him; it was just a kid thing."

Matt shrugged. 'Divorce. Why didn't she divorce him?"

"I asked her that question a thousand times, Matt. The Church. She couldn't bring herself to do it. And she had this idea that somehow if she left him, he would wind up killing himself, and she couldn't take that responsibility. Do you know how it hurt, Matt, to know you were my boy and to watch you grow up, and know I couldn't ever tell you? So your mother stayed with Jesse to save his life, she thought, and then he got drunk one night and insisted on driving and killed the two of them. And I got you."

"Why didn't you ever tell me?" Matt asked.

The Judge shrugged elaborately. "The time was never right. When you were young, I thought it would make you think badly of your mother. Later on, you were rebelling against me and ... well, I don't know, maybe I guess I didn't know if you'd believe me. And then you left and there just wasn't a chance. You know, Matt, there's a painting by an artist named Albright. It shows a hand reaching toward a doorknob and on the door is a funeral wreath. And the title of the painting is 'That which I should have done, I did not do.' My whole life's been like that painting, Matt. I should have but I didn't. And all I can tell you is, as much as I'm hurting you now, I've been hurt more than that every day for the last thirty-eight years. I didn't insist that your mother leave Jesse, and maybe that makes me responsible for her death. So I'm bossy with you, I apologize, but I won't change, Matt. I don't want anything to happen to you. At least not if I can do anything about it. I lost your mother. I won't lose you."

It was the longest speech Matt could ever remember the Judge making. When the old man was done, they sat looking at each other for long seconds without speaking. Then Matt said, "Father, huh?"

"Afraid so, son."

"Does Lauren know?"

"No. No one knows. Except now you," the Judge said.

"It's good to know," Matt said.

"It's good to tell somebody. And it doesn't have to leave this room, Matt."

"The hell with that," Matt said. "When this is over, I'm going to put an ad in the paper and tell the world."

"When this is over," the Judge said and smiled.

CHAPTER FORTY-FIVE

"You!"

John Smetts had been led into the Judge's study by Billy O'Baal, who nodded to Matt, then left the room.

Smetts had stepped inside, then stopped abruptly when he saw Matt standing in front of the bookcase against the far wall. The Judge was sitting in his easy chair.

Smetts, his eyes owlish behind his thick glasses, stared at Matt for a moment, then looked at Stevens.

"I shouldn't be here. I should be calling the police." He glanced back at Matt. "You're wanted all over for murder," he said.

"And you call the police and maybe you'll get a reward," the Judge said. "But if you listen to Matt, maybe you'll win a Pulitzer Prize. What's worth more to you?"

Smetts hesitated and Matt stepped into the center of the room.

"John," he said, "hear us out. Then if you want to call the police, you can."

Smetts looked hard at him for a moment, then nodded his head, and sat on the sofa. Matt poured him a cup of coffee.

Before he could talk, the Judge said, "Since it's my house and I'm the oldest, maybe I'll preside over this meeting."

Matt suppressed a smile. Somehow the Judge's take-charge

nature seemed less offensive now that Matt knew the man was his natural father. Maybe we always turn the other cheek to family, he thought.

"First of all, John," the Judge said. "Matt hasn't murdered anybody. Not his wife, not his boss, not that FBI man. Nobody."

"That'd be easier to believe if I didn't see the wire services every day, talking about a nationwide manhunt for you," Smetts said.

The Judge said drily, "Do you believe everything you read in the newspapers?" But when Smetts did not smile in response, Stevens said, "A lot of people have been trying to kill Matt. And it all has to do with the Installation out in Harker's Furnace. Somehow, Matt's friend and he found some curious income tax returns from the people who are supposed to be working out there. The only problem is that there's about a thousand times more returns than there seem to be people. That's curious because ghosts don't pay taxes in this country."

The Judge picked up the plastic shopping bag that contained the computer discs. "In here, John, is the record of what's going on at the Installation."

Smetts took the bag, glanced at the discs, replaced them, and looked up at Matt.

"I'm going to take some notes," he said, with a slight air of belligerence in his voice.

"Go ahead," Matt said, and the newsman fished a pen and spiral bound notebook from an inside jacket pocket.

"Matt," the Judge said. "Why don't you walk John through this right from the beginning? Step by step. I'm liable to leave something out."

"Okay," Matt said and began to talk.

Smetts was good. He asked the right questions at the right time, but without busting into Matt's train of thought or slowing down his narrative.

The simple re-telling took more than an hour. Matt left nothing out, and when he was done, Smetts placed his pen on the table.

"If this place is a mob front," he said, "the implications are astonishing. The Vice President of the United States is neck-deep in narcotics dealing. That's a Pulitzer for sure." He looked up with a smile. "Who says exciting things don't happen in the boonies?"

Matt laughed and the Judge nodded.

"Do you believe him?" Stevens asked.

Smetts said, "It's too bizarre not to believe him. Why the hell would you roust me out of bed to bring me here if you were going to give me some cock-and-bull story? Of course I believe him. So now what? Why me?"

Stevens said, "Because the only way we can keep Matt alive is to take this story public. And I know politics and law some, but nothing about the press. I thought you were the man to help us."

"There's one hole in the story," Smetts said. "All you have connecting the vice president's old law firm with the operation at the Installation is the ownership Lauren traced. But that computer guy . . . what was it, Ralphie? He said the law firm didn't handle the payroll checks and the tax checks, so that's not good enough to go with. You go with a story like this, you have to have it all nailed. Otherwise they pick you apart on the discrepancy, and use that to make the whole story look wrong."

"I know it," Matt said. "That was what I was counting on Ari Cohen to pin down. And then he got killed. So what do I do?"

"You do nothing and you talk to nobody else. You can keep busy by making me copies of these discs. We're lucky one way. Jenny Christopolous is down in Philly on a political story. I'm going to have her check the news files down there, and maybe some courthouse records, to see if there's some way to tie the law firm to the Installation's day-to-day operation. If we get that, bingo."

"What about timing?" the Judge asked. "When do you run a story?"

"It's already Wednesday morning. It'll take Jenny some time to dig around. Meantime, I'll be working on the rest of it. Matt, are you going to testify on Friday?"

"I'd like to be there," Matt said.

"Then I'd go with the story in my early Friday editions. Don't worry about it. I'd put it on the wire services, too, and give it to the networks. It'll be going all over the world when you set foot in that hearing room."

"Good," Stevens said. "You know, John, you're Matt's only defense. Only you can keep him alive."

Smetts got to his feet and stretched his tall gangly body into a yawn. "I'll do a better job of it if I can get a little sleep tonight," he said.

"I'll have Billy take you home. But you take care of yourself."

"You betcha. I'm a lover, not a fighter, Judge."

Smetts stepped forward and shook Matt's hand. "This is an important thing you're doing," he said. "It took a lot of balls to take on the world."

"I didn't do it by choice," Matt said.

"'And some have greatness thrust upon them,'" Smetts quoted. "I need you, I'll reach you through the Judge."

After he left, Matt said, "Calling him was a good idea, Judge. I sort of feel now that I'm not alone."

"You were never alone, son," Stevens said. "We'll see how Smett's girl—what's her name, Jenny—does. If they draw a blank, well, there are other ways to play this game. Now I suppose you want to get out of here."

Matt nodded, stood up, and shook hands with the old man.

"We'll talk tomorrow," Matt said. He walked to the door, then stopped. "By the way, I forgot to ask. Where's Angela?"

"She left," the Judge said. "Night before last. As I remember it, she said something about this town being dull and me being dull and you being all booked up. Let's see. Her exact words as I recall were, 'I'm going someplace where I can get some nookie.' "

Matt grinned. "Too bad, Judge. You missed a good thing."

He was almost out the door before he heard the Judge say, "And who said I missed it, young Mister Smartass?"

CHAPTER FORTY-SIX

Lauren Carmody awoke to the smell of bacon burning in the kitchen. She had still been asleep when the young Indian drove Matt back to the A-frame cabin in the woods, and to surprise her, Matt had decided to cook her breakfast.

But once he had the bacon in the frying pan, he went back inside the living room and began to copy the data on his computer discs onto another set of discs.

As usual, he became engrossed in his work and only noticed something wrong when Lauren jumped off the couch and yelled to him, "The house is on fire."

He looked at her sheepishly.

"I'm cooking breakfast," he said.

"Good plan," she said and ran into the kitchen.

Later, after she had aired out the house and disposed of the charred bacon and cooked a real breakfast, she sat with Matt at the table, and he told her what had happened at the Judge's the night before.

He told her all of it.

"Did you ever suspect the Judge was my father?" he asked.

"I always suspected," she said. "But I never knew."

"How come you saw it and I didn't?"

"Because you were so busy being macho and worrying about

growing up and not letting anybody push you around, that you never noticed that the Judge loved you," she said.

Matt thought that over as he ate. "Your bacon's better than mine," he said.

"Fried wood is better than your bacon."

"Do you think it's because you're such a good cook that the Judge wanted me to marry you?" Matt said.

"No. I think it was because he thought I'd keep you out of trouble," she answered. She reached across the table and wiped a spot of egg yolk from Matt's mouth.

"Well, I guess I can't disappoint my father," he said.

"Matt, is that a proposal?"

"Great bacon and a great ass too. How could it be anything but a proposal?"

"I'll accept if you help me with the dishes," she said.

"And if I don't help you with the dishes?"

"I'll accept anyway, but then make your life miserable."

"Take me to your sink," Matt said.

He could not help thinking, as he was making a halfhearted attempt do dry the dishes with a ratty old hand towel, that maybe the chaos, the tragedies of the past ten days, were behind him. The Judge had been right. Using Smetts, the editor, to take Matt's case public would make Matt unattackable. It might be a hard story to sell, but the truth was on Matt's side, and he had always regarded himself as naive enough to believe that in the long run the truth would win out. And after all these years, even though it took the awful reality of the deaths of Melanie and Mike Wojno, he and Lauren would be together as they always should have been. Maybe finally some light showed at the end of the tunnel. He did not feel that he was abandoning Larry Wu's memory. If he could bring down the whole scheme, It would be the best way to avenge Larry.

Lauren mumbled something.

"What?"

"Maybe you'd better re-think your proposal," she said. "I don't think dear sweet Angela would have you drying dishes."

"She's gone. Out of sight, out of mind," Matt said.

"In sight and in your pants," Lauren said.

"She was never any competition for you anyway," said Matt.

"If you say so," Lauren said and turned a smiling face to him. "Say so, dammit. Say so."

"I say so." And Matt put his arms around her and kissed her and Lauren said, "I wasn't really jealous anyway. I kind of liked Angela."

"Good," Matt said. "Maybe I'll invite her over to keep me company on those long nights when you're in court waiting for a jury to come in with a verdict."

She hit him with the towel. "And maybe you'll die," she said.

Matt napped until mid-afternoon when the Judge called him from a safe phone.

"How are you doing with the copies of those tapes?" he asked.

"Fine," Matt said. "Almost done."

"Good. I talked to Smetts. He said that his girl reporter has found something in Philadelphia."

"What?"

"We don't know. John said she was a little nervous about talking about it on the phone. She thought maybe somebody was following her, but she was sending it all up by messenger."

"If she can tie Barkley's law firm to those companies, then we're in business," Matt said.

"Let's hope," said the Judge.

The copying was finished; the new set of tapes were in an envelope with Smetts's name on them, when Billy O'Baal came to the house in his pickup truck, and told Matt, "Better hurry. Judge wants to see you now."

The raw-boned Indian was quiet on the way into town. To

Matt's questions, he simply replied, "I don't know. Judge said come and get you. I got you."

He parked behind the editorial offices of the *Gusher* on Iron City's main street and then, hand on the butt of his gun, walked Matt in through a back door and up to Smetts's office. A tired-looking old man—wearing an eye shade and sitting at the kidney-shaped desk—and three young women in blue jeans seemed to be the entire editorial staff on duty.

When he entered Smetts's office, Matt was shocked at the expression on the thin, balding editor's face. He looked like a man who had marched into hell and had to fight his way back out; his eyes were red-rimmed, and his mouth set in a thin hard line.

The Judge sat on an old tan fabric-covered couch on the far side of the room. He rose as Matt entered and said, "Jenny's been hurt."

"How? What happened?"

Smetts answered, his soft voice overriding the Judge's. "Somebody beat her up in Philly. Left her in an alley," he said. His voice was dull as if it were inadequate to express his pain. He looked at Matt and tears glistened in his eyes. "Damn you, Taylor. Damn your eyes."

"I'm sorry, John. How is she?"

"She's going to be all right. I'm having her flown here."

"Naturally, no idea who did it," Matt said.

"Naturally," Smetts said.

"John, all deals are off. I didn't want you people to buy into my trouble. Let's just let it go. I'll figure something else out," Matt said.

Smetts wiped his face on a damp-looking gray handkerchief. "Not a chance, Taylor. The bastards who did this are going to pay. Nobody walks from this one. And maybe when it's all over, I'm just going to punch you in the face for involving us in this."

"I'm sorry, John. I truly am."

414

There was a long awkward silence, finally broken by the Judge who said, "Sit down, Matt. We're waiting for the package that Jenny sent. Billy's gone over to meet the bus that's bringing it in."

At that moment, there was a soft knock on the door and O'Baal let himself in. He had a manila envelope in his hand, which he gave to the Judge, but Stevens glanced at it and handed it across the desk to Smetts.

Billy said, "I'll be outside," and the Judge nodded.

With nervous hands, Smetts ripped open the envelope and pulled out a sheaf of papers, Xerox copies, which he glanced through with a quick, practiced eye.

There was a handwritten note, penned on the back of a greeting card, and Smetts read it with the intensity of a man trying to memorize the words. Then he looked across the room at Matt.

"All those companies you find in the Installation's files? The vice president's law firm doesn't handle any of them."

Matt felt his heart sinking in his chest, but before he could respond, Smetts said, "But this is just as good. The lawyers for those companies are Resnicow and Holzer."

Matt looked puzzled and Smetts said, "Jenny's note says they used to be Resnicow, Holzer and Plevris. That's *your* Plevris, from the I.R.S. And the firm's got a reputation, Jenny says, for doing some of Zorelli's work. There's your linkup, Matt."

"Of course," the Judge said. "They couldn't afford to have Barkley's old firm involved in the day-to-day operations up there. But they couldn't afford to take it too far away either. Plevris's old partners were the obvious answer. To give them their due, they probably don't even know what it is they're involved in."

Smetts was looking down again at the papers. From across the desk, Matt could see that some were photocopies of newspaper clippings.

415

"Just a lot of personal crap on Zorelli," Smetts said, as he tossed the clippings away from himself impatiently and saw them scatter onto the floor. "If that guinea bastard was behind the attack on Jenny, we'll see him fry."

"Who else?" Matt said. "Zorelli or his friends in government, it's all the same thing." He leaned forward to pick up several clippings which had fallen on the floor. He glanced at the top one and felt his body turn cold.

Stevens obviously noticed the look on his face because he said, "What is it, Matt?"

Silently, Matt handed forward the topmost clipping and the Judge looked at it, then read it aloud. "Reputed Philadelphia crime figure Carlos Zorelli is pictured in a Rome restaurant with an unidentified young beauty. Some say the young woman is Zorelli's daughter, being educated in Europe, but there is no official record of the Zorellis ever having had children."

The Judge looked up from the clipping. "It's Angela."

"Zorelli's daughter," Smetts said and rose to take the clipping from the Judge's hand.

"No wonder," Matt said. "No wonder she found me the last time I was here. And then she looked me up when I went back to Washington. And then she insisted on coming back up here with me. She's one of them."

The Judge had a distracted look in his eye. "Zorelli, Zorelli," he mumbled to himself.

"What?" Matt asked.

"Zorelli. In Italian, doesn't that mean 'little fox'?"

"Pidgin Spanish," Matt said. "But close enough. She went to school in Spain."

"Angela Fox. Zorelli's daughter," the Judge said.

"And she's the one who tipped them off the other night that we were going into the Installation. And she left because she thought we were all going to wind up dead and there wasn't any point in hanging around," Matt said. He looked at the Judge and then at Smetts as if for an answer. "She's had a

416

hundred chances to kill me in the last week or so. Why didn't she?"

Both men were silent before Smetts said, "Maybe her job was to keep you alive until they found out what you knew."

Matt nodded. It made sense to him. It was the only answer that did make any sense.

Smetts said, "Don't worry about it. This picture will reproduce just fine, and she's just another link in the chain. Now will you two get out of here? I've got a lot of work to get started on. And leave those discs for me."

He turned away from them, turned on the monitor of his deskside word processor and spoke aloud:

"By Jenny Christopolous and John Smetts. I think she'll like that."

The Judge and Matt stood, and Matt said, "Mind if I use your phone? I promised Lauren I'd call."

"Help yourself," Smetts said, waving toward the phone at the end of the desk.

Matt dialed the number. When it didn't answer, he let it ring a long time. He felt a growing taste of fear in his throat as he told the Judge, "There's no answer."

The Judge walked quickly into the hallway outside Smett's office. Matt heard him say, "Billy. Radio in to your men at the cottage. Have them check and see that Miss Carmody's all right."

Matt heard Billy's feet running down the hallway from the Judge. He turned to say goodnight to Smetts, but the newsman was already hunched over his word processor, brow furrowed in concentration, and Matt left the office quietly.

He walked downstairs with the Judge, and when they got to the truck parked at the loading dock behind the newspaper, Billy was just turning off his truck radio.

"It's okay," he told the Judge. "That woman Angela came by and Miss Carmody went with her. Said they were going to get a bite to eat."

"Oh, my God," the Judge said.

"They've got Lauren," Matt said.

They drove back to the Judge's house, three across the front seat of Billy O'Baal's truck.

"Wait for me, Billy," Matt said, and walked inside with the Judge.

While the Judge went to find out from his housekeeper if there had been any calls, Matt went upstairs to the old room that had been his all through his youth, and through college, and which he had left only after deciding to marry Melanie.

He opened up the closet and found a worn leather bag. Rooting around in the bottom of it, he found what he was looking for—a long, thick-bladed knife in a leather scabbard with buckle straps. Matt pulled up his right trouser leg and as he strapped the knife to his calf, heard the Judge say, "What are you doing?"

"Never mind that. Have there been any calls?"

"No," the Judge said.

"Well, they don't want Lauren, they want me. So they'll call me. You stay here and man the phone. I'll go back to the place in the woods, in case they call there."

"What's the commando knife for?" the Judge said again.

"They'll want to deal. I'll give them a deal," Matt said in a lifeless voice. "Do you have a small gun in the house?"

"Just my Magnum," the Judge said.

"Too big."

"Wait. I think Maggie has some kind of ladies' gun in her room."

"Get it," Matt said briskly.

The Judge was back a few moments later with a small, five-shot, .22 caliber automatic.

"That's just right," Matt said. He took the weapon, checked to see that it was loaded, and stuck it into his trousers pocket.

"Matt, maybe we should call the police," the Judge said.

"You don't have to be involved. And Lauren was married to a cop. They'd help."

Matt shook his head. "They'd mean well, but they'd bluster around with sirens and flashing lights and get her killed. This is my job."

"Matt ..."

"Judge ... Dad ... this is something I know about and you don't. I'll get her back."

He walked to the door but as he brushed past the judge in the hallway, the old man threw his arms around him and hugged him. "Be careful," he said.

"I will. But if anything happens, tell Smetts I said to go ahead with the story. No matter what happens to me they can't get away with this."

And then Matt turned and walked away quickly before the Judge saw the tears that suddenly welled up in his eyes.

CHAPTER FORTY-SEVEN

The telephone in the cabin rang at midnight.

"Hello, Matt. This is Angela."

"Hello, Angela. Or should I say Miss Zorelli?"

"Oh. So you've figured that out?"

'Where's Lauren?"

"Miss Carmody is taking a nap," Angela said. "Don't worry. She's all right. I think we have to discuss a trade."

"What kind of a trade?" Matt asked.

"You've got something we want, and I've got something you want."

"Where should I meet you?"

"I'll send somebody for you," Angela said. "But I don't want those goddam Apache warriors on your trail. Anybody follows you, and your girl friend dies. Is that clear?"

"Very."

"You know, Matt, I never could understand why you preferred her to me," Angela said.

"Simple. She's a human being. And you're a piece of garbage."

There was a pause for a couple of seconds. Then Angela said, "Lighten up. It's not as bad as all that. I've figured out a way for everybody to be satisfied, and nobody else to get hurt."

"A little late to be worried about people's lives, isn't it?"

"Better late than never," Angela said lightly. "Somebody will be there for you soon. Bring those computer tapes. *Ciao*, darling."

Matt depressed the receiver button, then called the Judge to tell him Lauren's abductors had made the contact.

"What should we do, son?" the Judge asked.

"Stay out. It's my game now," Matt said. He hung up, went outside, and whistled up one of Billy O'Baal's Indian guards.

"A car's coming for me. Go down the road and tell them to let it through without any trouble," Matt said.

The young dark-haired man nodded and trotted off down the unpaved roadway.

Back inside the house, Matt found the first gun the Judge had given him, a .38 Police Special revolver with a holster. He hooked it onto his belt, placing the holster and gun at the small of his back. Then he put on a long jacket to cover it.

The smaller gun—the automatic that the Judge had gotten from Maggie—Matt reached under his belt and slid down inside his underwear, below his testicles. He put the giga-discs that contained the Installation's records in a plastic bag, then perched on the edge of the couch to wait.

It was only fifteen minutes until he heard the front door open behind him. Matt stood up and turned slowly. In the doorway, a large smile creasing his too-pretty features, was Gianetti, the FBI man. There was a gun in his hand.

"I told you we'd meet again," Gianetti said.

"Let's can the chatter, Queenie, and get out of here," Matt said.

"I love it when you talk mean to me," Gianetti said with a nervous little giggle. "But not so quick." He waved the gun. "Lean against that wall over there."

Matt complied and the FBI man came up behind him and ran his fingers down Matt's sides, then down his back. His hands touched the gun at the back of Matt's belt, reached under his jacket, and extracted it from the holster.

"Well, well, well, what have we here?" Gianetti said.

"Okay," Matt said. "You finished?"

"Not so quick," Gianetti said. He tossed Matt's gun onto the sofa behind him, then patted down both sides of Matt's legs. He found the knife strapped to Matt's right calf, then released Matt, and backed away.

"Okay, turn around," he said. "Now, lift up your right pants leg slowly. Slowly."

Matt did, exposing the knife.

"Take it out very carefully. By the handle," Gianetti said. "Now put it on the floor and move over there."

Matt moved away and Gianetti picked up the knife by its handle, then hefted it in his hand.

"And what's this for? You planning on camping out?" he said.

"Actually," Matt said, "I was planning on cutting off your useless balls and making paperweights out of them."

Gianetti smiled, without humor. "I've heard worse ideas," he said. "Maybe we'll just take this along with us. It might come in handy." He gestured to the plastic bag on the sofa. "These the computer discs?"

Matt nodded and Gianetti dropped the knife inside the bag and said, "Let's go, tough guy. Angela's waiting."

"And we mustn't keep our Mafia friends waiting, must we?" Matt said sarcastically.

"No, we mustn't," Gianetti agreed. "Angela gets mad easily. You know how nymphomaniacs are. Or at least you ought to."

Keeping his gun on Matt, he opened the trunk of his compact car and dropped the bag holding the discs and the combat knife into the trunk.

"You drive," he said. "I'll be sitting in back. And naturally, there's a gun on you, so don't do anything childish," he said.

"Naturally," Matt said. He drove away from the house, feeling the small automatic resting hard and cold against his genitals.

Down the road, he saw Billy standing next to his pickup truck which was parked sideways across the roadway.

"Now what the hell is going on?" Gianetti growled. He leaned forward over the back seat and jabbed the point of the gun into Matt's neck. "No funny moves," he said. "Just tell Cochise to let us through and no jerking around."

Matt rolled down his window as Billy strolled over to the car. Suddenly, from under the trees that bordered the roadway behind him, six ... no, eight Indian men stepped forward and bordered the road. Most of them cradled rifles across their arms.

"Evening, Matt," Billy said. He leaned his forearms on the window opening of the car.

"Evening, Billy," Matt said. "Move the truck, will you? My friend and I here are just going out for a ride."

Billy leaned a little into the car, craning his neck as if to see Gianetti in the rear seat. "Everything's all right then?" he said to Matt.

"Everything's fine," Matt said. "So you can make sure that all your men stay here and nobody follows us. Understand?"

"Sure do. Well, have a nice night." He waved toward the back seat. "You, too, sir," he called out, then got into his truck and pulled it off the roadway to let Matt pass.

As Matt drove away, the young Indians stared sullenly at him passing by.

Matt heard Gianetti chuckle as they reached the main road. "You've got some weird friends, Matt," the FBI man said.

"I collect Indians. You collect criminals," Matt said. "I like mine better."

"No accounting for taste. Turn right up there," Gianetti said.

Matt harbored no delusions that Angela and her cohorts had any plan to keep him alive. As far as they were concerned, he was meat to be processed, and while Gianetti had obviously been prepped and kept telling him that, "Everybody's going to come out of this all right," Matt knew the Gianetti's actions in directing Matt right to Angela's hideout spoke louder than his words. There was no need for deception on the drive, no need for Matt to make left turns and counteracting right turns to get

423

to someplace actually nearby—because Matt wasn't coming back. It didn't matter whether or not he knew where their hideout was. Dead men didn't talk.

"You've made things a lot tougher than they had to be," Gianetti said. "If you had just gone along, everything would have been simple."

"Sorry for complicating your life," Matt said.

"Turn right here. It doesn't matter. Angela's got a way for everybody to come up smelling like a rose."

"And I'm the tooth fairy and I promise to leave a quarter under your pillow if you're a good boy."

Gianetti laughed. "I'm always a good boy," he said. "Ask any of my friends. Slow down now. It's up here on the left."

It was another house in the woods, barely ten miles from where Matt had been hiding out. Angela Fox was in the living room, dressed in what seemed to be lounging pajamas. She sprang to her feet as the two men entered, but gave Matt hardly a glance.

"Were you followed, Gianetti?"

The FBI man shook his head. "No. I was watching the whole way. Not a car in sight."

"Good. You've got the discs?"

Gianetti held up the plastic bag. "Here. And a souvenir." He fished the knife from the bag and showed it to her. "He was wearing this. A gun too."

As Gianetti tossed the knife onto a large chest near the door, Angela said to Matt tauntingly, "Quite the warrior, aren't you?"

"Love, not war," Matt said. "Where's Lauren?"

"She's upstairs and she's perfectly well," Angela said. "I gave her a couple of pills to put her to sleep. Why don't you sit down, make yourself comfortable?"

"I want to see Lauren."

"There's plenty of time for that. Anyway, there's not much

to see. One sleeping woman's pretty much like another. Or hadn't you noticed?"

She waved Matt to a seat on the couch, then sat across the room at a cheap, formica-topped desk. For the first time, Matt noticed that there was a small handgun on the desk. She said to Gianetti, "I'll take those." When he handed her the bag of tapes, she said, "Go outside and keep an eye on things."

"You'll be all right here with him?" Gianetti said.

Angela smiled, a dazzling show of teeth and mirth and self-confidence. "Perfectly all right. Outside."

When Gianetti left, she said, "Something about that man puts me on edge."

"Probably because he doesn't want to go to bed with you," Matt said. "That must be a new experience."

She shrugged. "It happens though. Even your friend, the Judge, turned me down."

"He always had good taste," Matt said.

"Come on, Matt, now. Let's end the animosity and the cheap shots. We're here to talk business. And, truth is, you're not doing anybody any good by getting me angry. Right at this minute, I'm the best friend you have in the world."

"Why? Because you're going to keep me alive?"

"Yes."

"How are you going to do that?"

"It wasn't easy convincing anybody, but you're going to have to recant. Let your friends know you were wrong, that the Installation really is a spy center."

"And then what?" Matt said.

"You get lost."

"I'm wanted for murder. How do I get lost?"

"You go to Europe. We've got friends. A new identity, and no one will be the wiser. You'll live to see your grandchildren."

"And Lauren?"

"She goes with you."

"And the Judge?"

"He'll believe whatever you tell him," Angela said.

"Billy O'Baal," Matt said.

"The big Indian? He doesn't give a damn about what's going on. If the Judge told him to be quiet, he wouldn't say a word for the next fifty years." She paused and smiled. "See. It takes care of everybody. Your Chinese friend, Katie, she's young and she'll forget it, and she didn't know anything to start with."

"You seem to have it all worked out pretty well," Matt said casually, but his mind was racing. She didn't know. Was it possible that she did not know about John Smetts and Jenny Christopolous and the story they were working on? Was it possible that she did not know that Matt had put copies of the Harker's Furnace tapes in Smetts's hands?

"Not a loose end in sight," she said. "So what do you say?"

"Okay. I recant. Can we go now?"

Angela laughed. "Well, not quite so quick. There's a little unfinished business. Like, where did you hide the tapes you and your friend found in the I.R.S. computers? You told me you locked it up with another code and I'd need to have that before we could make a deal."

"I don't have any problem with that," Matt said. "You can have it. I'm tired of fighting all you people."

"Fatigue is the beginning of wisdom," she said. "You didn't stand a chance against us, you know. Even though you do live a charmed life."

"If you can tell me how this life of mine has been charmed, I'd like to hear it."

"Right from the beginning," she said. "When you and Wu found those computer records, the plan was simply to punch your tickets. But you managed to get out of it. And then we found out that Wu had hidden the records and we had to keep you alive to find out where they were. That's when I got on your case. To stay close to you, to see if you found anything out."

"And here I thought you were just in love with my body," Matt said.

"That too," Angela snapped back. "So you found the files

and gave them to the Vice President, but you escaped before they could kill you. Remember the other night when you came to my hotel room? I couldn't believe my good luck. I was standing there at my suitcase with my back to you; I had my gun in my hand, I was ready to turn around and shoot you, and then you said you had hidden Larry's files again. So you were off the hook one more time. I couldn't kill you. I had to hang on with you. Then I was overruled."

"Who by?" Matt said. "The Vice President?"

"That numbskull?" she said, with a short bitter laugh. "Forget it. He never overruled anybody or anything in his life. My father. I told him you were going into the Installation and he wanted you captured—tortured until you talked and then disposed of. That's when I left."

"Didn't want to be in on the kill, huh?" Matt said.

She shook her head. "Actually, no. But then you got out and I had to come back. When we found out that you got the records from the computers at the Installation, we had to snatch your girlfriend to get you to listen to reason."

"How'd you know I got those records?"

"Your computer nerd friend, Ralphie, wasn't as tough as you. He talked right away, as soon as he was asked."

"You people don't have any regard for life, do you? And for what? A bundle of money?"

"Matt, you don't know the size of the bundle," Angela said. Her long, painted fingernails drummed on the grip of the small gun on the desk alongside her. "The Installation's just a pilot program. We've had that going for only about a year and we've been able to launder more than a half a billion dollars." She laughed hard and loud. "Can you believe it? The I.R.S., your fucking I.R.S., is our partner in laundering drug money. And that's just the start. We're planning two more operations just like it. We'll be washing a billion dollars a year. You know what that means. For openers, we're going to buy the election for Barkley. We're going to own the President of the United States. And that means we own the country. Do you really think we were going to let you or your friends or a couple of lives stand in our way?"

"You killed Ari Cohen, didn't you?"

"We did. I didn't do it personally, but we did. He was getting too close, and he wouldn't back off. So the poor man had a tragic accident."

Her eyes were glistening as she stared at Matt, and in that moment, he hated her more than he had ever hated anything in his life. Nothing mattered to her except money, except power. In a world run by people like her, there would be no room for good. Only the evil would endure. It took him an act of will not to jump across the room at her and try to tear out her throat before she got her hands on the gun.

"One thing I don't understand though," he said, surprised at how calm his voice was.

"What's that?"

"After you wash all this money through different companies with different imaginary employes, how does the money get to your father? It is his, right?"

"Yes, it's his. That's the easiest part," she said. "You can put it anywhere. Overseas accounts. Tax-exempt bonds. All in phoney names of phoney employees. It's always there for you. And if you want to donate money to a Presidential campaign, you just write a check. And the money is clean and fresh, all taxes paid."

"Your father's a very smart man," Matt said.

"Don't kid yourself. He's my father and I love him, but he's like the rest of the Mustache Petes. They don't understand that this is a new age, and it's better to pay your small tax and have the use of the rest of the money than to insist on keeping every dollar, right up till the minute the feds come beating on the door. That's why the organization is all down the toilet."

"Your idea, then?" Matt said.

"Right, and a damned good one too."

"And here I thought you were just another bimbo with hot pants."

428

"Appearances can be deceiving," she said. "So. Now we need to know where you hid the tax files."

"Are you all finished now with your song and dance?" Matt asked abruptly.

"What do you mean?"

"Save that bullshit for somebody who believes it. First of all, I know I'm never walking out of here alive. Fair enough. It was me against you people and you won. Recant and run away? Horseshit. As soon as I tell you what you want to know, you're going to have that fag out there put a bullet between my eyes. Okay. But you get nothing until Lauren is out of here and safe."

"Matt, I—"

He extended his hands in front of him, palms up, in a gesture that clearly said "knock off the nonsense."

Angela hesitated, then said simply, "Okay." She picked up the gun from the desk and held it in the palm of her hand and spoke without looking at him. "I should have known I couldn't get over on you." And then she did look at him. "Why the hell did you have to be such a stubborn bastard?"

"Good genes, I guess," Matt said. "No more talk."

"What's your proposal?"

"You give Lauren the keys to that car and she drives off. Then I go with you and Gianetti. I'll tell you whatever you want. I'll sign any kind of confession you want. And then you kill me, and make believe it was suicide, or an accident, or whatever it is you guinea thugs are big on these days. And that's that."

"I don't think you're the kind of man to 'go gentle into that good night.' "

"I'm just tired of fighting you people," Matt said. "I know I can't win, and I'm tired of running and getting other people killed. So let's get it over with."

Angela smiled. "You've got a deal, tax man."

CHAPTER FORTY-EIGHT

The drug had not yet worn off and Lauren moved like a hospital patient as Gianetti helped her down from the upstairs bedroom. She was fully dressed and Matt was glad that she did not appear to have been hurt.

Her eyes were heavy-lidded, disoriented, but when she saw Matt, they opened wide, and she pulled away from Gianetti and ran across the room to him.

"Matt, I ..."

"Are you all right?" Matt asked, as he held her.

"Yes. They gave me something."

"It's okay now. You're going home."

"What about you?"

"I'll be along in a little while," Matt said. "What I want you to do is to take the car, go to the Judge's house, and wait there for me. You understand? Can you drive all right?"

"I'm okay," Lauren said. "What's going on here?"

"Don't worry," Matt told her. "I've got everything all worked out. Now, hurry up and go."

Gently, but firmly, he pushed her away from him and started to lead her to the door.

"That's far enough, Matt," Angela's voice snapped out in the room. "Gianetti will get her on her way."

Lauren held onto his hands, but Matt pulled himself free and nodded again. "It's all right," he said. "Go now."

As she followed Gianetti outside, Matt sat on the couch and looked across the room at Angela who still sat at the small desk.

"Okay," she said. "Let's have it."

"Not so fast," Matt said. "When she's on her way."

They waited a moment; a car's motor started outside; then the vehicle pulled away from the house. A few moments later, Gianetti came back inside and took up his position inside the front door.

"All right," Angela said. "She's gone. Now talk."

Matt nodded. "I put the files in the Philadelphia I.R.S. computer. They're coded with a Latin phrase. 'Fiat iustitia ruat caelum.' Should I spell it?"

Angela looked up from the desk where she was taking notes on a small pad. "You forget," she said with a smile. "My daddy sent me to the best schools, and Latin was my best subject."

"It must be a great comfort to know the right thing to say when all your thugs are shooting each other in the street," Matt said.

"Don't be crude," Angela said, as she reached for the telephone.

She dialed a long distance string of numbers, waited and then without identifying herself, repeated into the telephone what Matt had just told her. She spelled the Latin phrase—correctly, Matt noticed—and then said, "Let me know right away."

Then she hung up.

"What do we do now?" Matt asked.

"We wait to see if you were telling me the truth," she said.

"I was," he said. "That was Plevris you called?"

Angela hesitated a moment, then shrugged. "Why not? Yes, your old boss and *our* partner. If you're going to subvert the tax system, it helps if you have the boss of Internal Revenue on your side."

"It works for me," Matt said.

The telephone rang, a harsh jangle in the softly lit room. As Angela picked it up, Matt glanced behind him at Gianetti who was leaning casually against the door, his automatic in his hand, his eyes fixed on Matt. When he saw Matt looking at him, he smiled, but without humor.

Matt looked back at Angela, who said simply, "Okay," and hung up the phone. She smiled at Matt, then looked past him at Gianetti and said, "We're done here. Take him out in the woods and kill him."

"My pleasure," Gianetti said. "Let's go, Taylor."

Matt stood and grinned at Angela. "Not even a kiss good-bye? For old time's sake?"

"It wasn't that memorable," she said coldly. "And besides, we have to be moving. We've got things to do." She walked toward the stairs. "When you get him out there," she told Gianetti, "tell him what we have to do. I'm sure he'd like to know."

As she walked up the stairs, Gianetti came toward Matt and waved the gun toward him. "Get moving, Taylor. Payback time."

It would be soon now. They were seventy-five yards away from the house, moving through the heavy trees of the surrounding woods. The forest was filled with insect noises. Gianetti was following him, five feet behind, and Matt reached down, unzipped his fly, reached inside, and took out the small automatic pistol.

It felt warm and comfortable in his hand.

Gianetti's voice barked. "This is far enough, I guess. Stop."

Matt halted and turned halfway back toward the FBI man. He held the gun at his side, away from Gianetti, out of the man's view.

"What was it Angela wanted you to tell me?" he said.

"Oh," Gianetti leaned his back against a tree. "You think your girlfriend's all right?"

Matt did not answer.

"Well, she's wallpaper. And so's your Judge. And the little Chink girl. And all your friends that you got involved in this. We're going to punch all their tickets."

"Why?" Matt said. "I told you everything you wanted to know."

"Because this is too big an operation to take chances with. We're talking about taking over a country. What's a couple of lives when you're talking about that?" He paused. "See, Taylor, you're not as smart as you thought you were. I finish you and then we go and finish the rest of them."

"I can't let you do that," Matt said.

"How are you going to stop us?" Gianetti said. His grin was almost incandescent in the bright overhead moonlight.

"This, for openers," Matt said, turned, and shot him in the face.

The shot echoed throughout the woods. Gianetti slid down the side of the tree onto the soft floor of the forest. His gun was still in his hand. Matt stood alongside him, looked into the man's dead eyes, started to walk away, then hesitated. Angela would probably be expecting a second shot. He fired another shot into the ground, extricated the gun from Gianetti's hand and stuck it into his belt, then ran back toward the house. It was only as he was running that he realized that he had just killed a man—without feeling, without hesitation, without remorse. He pushed the thought out of his mind. There were more to kill.

"Un bel di . . ."

Angela's singing resounded through the house, light and happy. She might have been dressing for her first date, Matt thought, as he walked softly up the steps to the bedroom level.

He pushed the bedroom door; it squeaked as it opened. Angela stood with her back to him, pushing down the lid on a well-worn leather suitcase. Without turning, she stopped in mid-aria and said, "Take this down to the car and let's be on our way."

Matt did not move as Angela walked to a dresser, picked up a small atomizer of perfume from amidst a stretch of cosmetic supplies, sprayed it on her wrists, then dropped the perfume bottle into her purse.

She began to sing again, but her mouth froze open as she turned and saw Matt in the doorway.

"Oh."

"Surprise," Matt said.

Angela lunged for her purse, but Matt was quicker than she was.

"Don't," he barked as he grabbed her wrist and yanked away the small gun she had in her hand and tossed it across the room onto the floor.

Her chest heaved. Then she turned to him and looked up into his eyes.

"I'm sort of glad you made it," she said.

"I bet you are."

She pressed her body against his. "Matt, it doesn't have to be this way, you know?"

"No? What way could it be?"

"You and me. We could go. We could go to Europe. I'm rich, Matt. The two of us, we'd never work again."

He still held her right wrist in his left hand. She pushed her pelvis against him and pressed her face against his throat. As she murmured, "Let's do it, Matt, let's do it," she began to lick his neck with the tip of her tongue.

He felt her body tense and pushed her away, just as her left hand swung at him. She held a pair of scissors, and it missed his throat only by a fraction of an inch. Matt backed away and Angela jumped toward him, holding the scissors over her head, screaming, "You bastard, you bastard," and then she was on him and Matt pressed the gun against her stomach, even as he ducked his head to avoid the blades of the scissor, and squeezed the trigger.

Muffled by her body, the gunshot made only a faint coughing sound in the room. Angela slumped, then fell backward onto the floor. The blood from her stomach wound spread garishly across the gray woolen dress she wore.

Matt knelt alongside her.

"I'll send help," he said.

Her eyes rolled in her head, as if she were scanning the room to search him out. Then her gaze fixed on him and her mouth contorted and she spat out, "Die, you son of a bitch. Die."

And then her head lolled off to the side. Matt felt for a pulse in her throat, but he knew the gesture was unnecessary. Angela was dead.

He turned away from her and ran down the steps to the telephone in the living room.

Gianetti had said they were going to kill everybody, Lauren, the Judge, everybody. For all Matt knew, there might be goons right now on their way to the Judge's house ready to murder anything that moved. He had to warn them.

As he started to dial the Judge's number, he heard a sound behind him.

He turned around as a voice said, "Put the phone down, Taylor. Or your girlfriend gets it."

Matt looked to the door. Lauren stood inside. Behind her, holding the muzzle of a pistol to her temple, a grin creasing his chocolate face, was Dennis O'Leary.

CHAPTER FORTY-NINE

"I thought you were dead," Matt said.

"Nope," O'Leary said. "Just on vacation. Accrued time. You could look it up. Keep moving."

He was herding Matt and Lauren through the woods away from the house where Angela Zorelli's body lay. Lauren clung to Matt's arm; he could feel her body shivering, both with cold and fear.

It was deepest night now in the woods. He had been there less than an hour before with Gianetti, but this time there was something different. Matt sensed it, rather than knew it, and then he realized what the difference was. The woods now were silent; a tomblike quiet hung over them. There were no cricket sounds, no birds, no rustling of small animals through the brush. It was as if all the wildlife of the forest had stopped to wait and to watch the final act in Matt and Lauren's life.

The only sound apart from their own struggle through the low-hanging tree branches was O'Leary grunting behind them, only about five feet away, as he also moved through the heavy undergrowth. Soon, Matt knew, he would make a move. O'Leary was too smart to turn these killings into a performance. He would not stop and tell Matt, "Well, this is it." And then jaw with him for a few minutes before pulling the trigger. No. Without warning, he would squeeze off a shot into the back of Matt's skull and then when Matt dropped, he would kill Lauren at his side, and walk away without looking back.

"And now what?" Matt asked.

"You know the answer to that, Taylor," O'Leary grunted. "You two can't live. Or anyone else who knows. This is too big to take chances on."

"You were with them all the time, on *their* side?" Matt said.

"You don't read enough detective books," O'Leary said. "Of course, I was with them. Those two clowns, Polonowski and Gianetti, and I were playing good-guy bad-guy with you, trying to find out what you knew. But we were always working together."

"How long?" Matt asked. He spoke without turning around; if he turned to look at O'Leary, the FBI man might take it as a signal that they had walked far enough into the woods. Softly, he squeezed Lauren's arm in reassurance.

"The tax scam was only a couple of years," O'Leary said. "But I was with Zorelli since before I got into the Bureau. He helped me out back in Philly, and I stick with my friends."

"Like Ari Cohen?" Matt said.

"Ari just wouldn't stop looking," O'Leary said. "He had to go down, or else he would have ruined everything."

"So you didn't object when they killed him?"

"Object? I drove the car that did it," O'Leary said.

There was still not a sound in the woods around them. And then Matt heard one loud owl's voice. And a split second later, another on the other side of them.

And then O'Leary said, "Goodbye, Matt."

O'Leary took the telephone and listened as it rang on the other end of the line.

When it was answered, he said, "It's finished. They're all taken care of." He listened for a few moments and said, "Everybody's all right. We're just going to get lost and lay low for a couple of days."

Then he handed the telephone receiver back.

CHAPTER FIFTY

They sat in the front parlor of the farmhouse in the rolling hills of Virginia, only a few helicopter minutes from Washington, D.C.

The home belonged to Wilbur Strunk, who had been a law school classmate of Judge Frank Stevens, then had gone on to a career of government service for the United States. He had held three cabinet positions, had been the U.S. Ambassador to the United Nations, had chaired more presidential fact-finding commissions than anyone could remember, and had counseled presidents, both Democratic and Republican, for more than a quarter century.

Strunk was a huge, hulking man with bushy eyebrows that grew wild, and when he blinked, they seemed to hide his eyes from view. He sat with his hands hidden somewhere in the folds of his bulbous lap, chewing stolidly on an unlit pipe.

For forty-five minutes, without an interruption, the Judge had been telling the story. Finally, he was done. He stopped and looked across the coffee table at Strunk, who said slowly, "You don't call me in fifteen years, Frank. But when you do, you've sure got a helluva story to tell. Anybody else know about this?"

Judge Stevens glanced at his watch. "In three hours, the *Gusher*—that's the paper back in Iron City—is going to run the story and give it to the wire services too. That's why I thought it was important the president know about it first."

"Any chance of stopping this ... *Gusher* from running the story?" Strunk asked.

"I wouldn't ask them," the Judge said.

"I wouldn't either," Strunk said.

The room was filled with silence for perhaps seconds. Then the Judge said, "You believe me?"

"Of course, I believe you. And I believe the story too. There are too many bodies lying around for it to be a fake. And besides, there was never such a thing as a central spy registry in Harker's Furnace."

"You know that for a fact?" the Judge said.

"Yes."

"If you don't mind my asking, how do you know?" Stevens said.

"Because I told him." The answer came from another man who had just entered from an adjoining room. Everybody rose to their feet.

"Mister President," Strunk said.

"I wanted to hear it all with my own ears," President Chesney said. "I hope you don't mind, but that's why I was eavesdropping in the other room."

He came across the floor, a big man—still husky with the football muscle of his youth—he brushed past the Judge and extended his hand to Matt and Lauren.

"I'm glad you both made it," he said. "You've done a very great service for our country." He looked back at the Judge. "You did a good job, sir."

"I'd like to take credit for it," the Judge said, "but it wasn't my doing. That crazy Indian who works for me ... it was his idea to drop the transmitter into the car when Matt was driving off with Gianetti. And it was just luck that he and his whole tribe picked up the signal and arrived in time to save Matt and Lauren when they were out in the woods with O'Leary."

The president sighed. "Well, three cheers for luck then. And what about O'Leary?"

"He's safe under lock and key," the Judge said. "I didn't know what else to do with him. He's an FBI man; I couldn't just turn him over to the police. Not until I spoke to Mr. Strunk first."

The president nodded and turned toward Strunk. "What do you think, Wilbur?"

"Perhaps I should call Senator Palmer and ask him to postpone this morning's hearing?" Strunk said.

The president thought for a moment, then shook his head.

"I don't think so," he said softly. "I don't think so."

The hearing was set to begin in five minutes. The room where it was to be held was one of the bigger ones in the Capitol, expensively and beautifully lined with heavy oak paneling. It was the room usually chosen when a hearing might be important enough to draw national television coverage, because it looked so full of the dignity of the American state.

The eight members of the Senate Select Committee on Crime—gathered in open session to consider President Thomas Chesney's proposal for a new anti-crime agency to be headed by Vice President Charles Garner Barkley—were seated in a semi-circle at the head of the room, on sort of a raised platform.

Barkley, immaculately dressed in a blue pinstripe suit with his trademark red patterned tie, stood in the center of the room at a witness table, with Anthony Plevris, head of the Internal Revenue Service. Midway between the witness table and the committee's stand was a small penned-in area crammed with little writing benches that had been reserved for the press. Only a handful of reporters were present and they looked bored. Most of the forty people in the spectator's seats were Senate employees, there to watch their bosses perform.

The room buzzed with chatter as technicians moved around, checking microphone sound levels. The two men who manned the television cameras had already placed them in position at the side of the room and were sipping coffee from styrofoam containers and arguing about professional basketball. The senators at the desks checked through the papers before them and awaited the arrival of Senator William Palmer, senior senator from New York, chairman of the committee.

He was noted for his punctuality, but it was five minutes after ten before Palmer entered the hearing room from a door leading to one of the anterooms. He was a tall slope-shouldered man with the innocent angelic expression of someone who has just entered a room by accident. But his acid tongue had made him a favorite of reporters, and his shambling figure was well known on the nation's television screens.

The room came to some kind of informal order as Palmer walked behind the other senators to his seat in the middle of the long dais. Vice President Barkley sat down at the witness table with Plevris at his side. Palmer struck his gavel on the marble pad in front of him.

"Mister Vice President, ladies and gentlemen, my colleagues, I apologize for my tardy arrival. It could not be helped. I know we were expecting to begin today with testimony from Vice President Barkley, regarding the need for a new agency to fight organized crime in the United States. However, something has arisen that I'm sure you will agree warrants a change in our plans. Ladies and gentlemen, the President of the United States."

As Senator Palmer rose to his feet, people around the room got to their feet and looked at each other in surprise. Since the time of Lyndon Johnson, it had been almost unheard-of for a president to pop into a committee hearing virtually unannounced. The main door in the rear of the committee room opened and President Chesney, flanked by a half-dozen Secret Service men, entered. Two of the Secret Service men stayed with him; the other four peeled off to take positions at the corners of the room.

Barkley stepped away from the witness table and walked forward to meet the president. But Chesney ignored his outstretched hand, brushed by him, and went to stand in the middle of the floor between the witness table and the senators' seats. One of the television cameramen was frantically swivelling the big floor-mounted camera about, to try to get the President in the frame. The reporters leaned forward in their seats.

The nine senators sank back into their seats to wait for Chesney to begin. The president stood before them, and when he spoke, his voice was muted, and some would say later, almost sorrowful.

"I appreciate your kindness, gentlemen, in affording me this opportunity to speak to you. I would give my life that it had not been necessary."

At the witness table, Vice President Barkley sat back down in the traditional vice presidential posture when presidents were speaking—hands folded in front of him on the table, staring attentively at his superior.

Chesney did not turn to look at him. He continued to speak in his soft dispassionate voice.

"I have presented you with a proposal for a new agency to counteract the lingering power of organized crime in our nation. I knew this was a necessary proposal. But only several hours ago, it was brought to my attention exactly how necessary it was, because I was brought evidence of a scheme by which organized crime planned to buy ... yes, gentlemen, to *buy* the government of the United States."

There were a few gasps of surprise from the audience. The reporters scribbled furiously at their desks.

"It was a scheme, Senators, that has resulted in many lives being lost. It was a scheme that reached even into the inner chambers of the White House itself.

"Senators, this nefarious scheme was prevented by the actions of one brave and honest man, who stood up to threats, to bribery, to attempts upon his life, to prove that there is one sure thing in this world—that the government of the United

States of America is not, cannot, and will not ever be, for sale to the highest bidder.

"I have brought this brave man here to tell you all that he has learned. I have also taken the liberty of calling in the federal marshals to preserve his safety . . . and yours. I ask your indulgence, gentlemen, in listening to the testimony of Mister Matthew Taylor."

The president turned to the entry doors again as three marshals led Matt inside and down the long aisle to the front of the room. Following behind him were Lauren Carmody, Judge Frank Stevens, and Wilbur Strunk.

President Chesney met Matt alongside the witness table, shook his hand, and put his arm around Matt's shoulders. "Don't worry," he said. "Just tell it to them the way you told it to me."

And then Matt saw him turn to the witness table where Vice President Barkley sat, his face frozen in a horrific realization of what was about to happen, and the president said softly to his vice president, "And may God have mercy on your rotten soul."